$19⁵⁰

V6/—

1952   4ᵗ Ed.

MANUAL OF
FOREIGN LANGUAGES

MANUAL OF

FOREIGN LANGUAGES

*For the Use of Librarians, Bibliographers, Research Workers,
Editors, Translators, and Printers*

FOURTH EDITION, REVISED AND ENLARGED

By
GEORG F. VON OSTERMANN, PH.D.
Foreign Language Editor (Retired), U. S. Government Printing Office

New York
CENTRAL BOOK COMPANY, INC.
1952

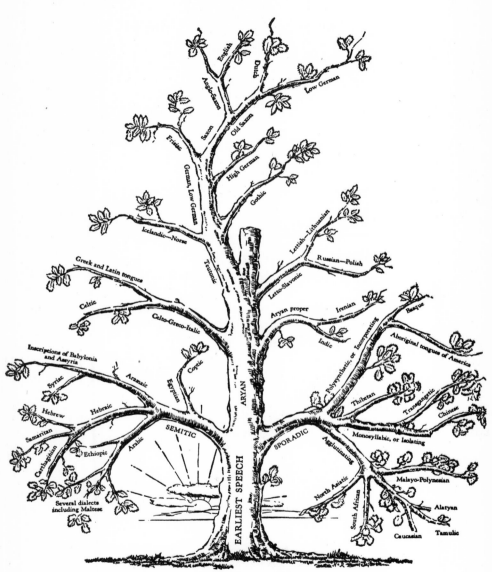

A SUGGESTED LINGUISTIC TREE.

PUBLISHER'S PREFACE TO THE FOURTH EDITION

Sixteen years have passed since the publication of the third edition of the Manual of Foreign Languages.

The unusual demand for this most important of reference tools occasions this revised and enlarged fourth edition. Long out-of-print and practically unobtainable, it is our pleasure to make the Manual available once more to librarians, cataloguers, bibliographers, editors, printers, students in the field of foreign language, and to the vastly increased number of scientific workers whose research involves them in the use of such languages.

As in the third edition, the chief grammatical features of the more important modern languages have either been corrected or augmented. In particular, the following languages have undergone extensive revision: Afrikaans, Bohemian, Esperanto, German, Modern Greek, Norwegian, Portuguese, Roumanian, Spanish, Swedish, and Turkish.

An additional language, namely Estonian, now makes its appearance, and a new feature, the tabular charts of the Languages and Monies of the World, will we hope be found of interest and value.

Special acknowledgment is made to Fr. Berard Haile, O.F.M., in charge of the Indian Schools on the Navaho Indian Reservation, for his article on New Navaho.

Resetting the Manual anew was impossible since no one typographer in the United States, and probably in the world, with the exception of the Government Printing Office, had available for our use even a small portion of the many unusual type faces to be found therein. We wish to indicate, therefore, that all portions of the third edition not requiring change have been reproduced in this new edition by the photographic process. Corrections and minor additions have been "stripped" in, and all new material, set in type for the first time, is presented in a format approximating as closely as possible that used in the third and prior edition.

Comments and suggestions bringing to our attention, errors, either philological or typographical, will be welcomed. If warranted, an errata sheet will be prepared and distributed to all users of this work.

PREFACE TO THIRD EDITION

The growing appreciation of the Manual of Foreign Languages made necessary this third edition, which called for much revision and the addition of a group of languages that were not contemplated in previous editions. The chief grammatical features of the more important modern languages have been amplified with a view to affording editors, cataloguers, and bibliographers, as well as printers, a broader, more adequate basis of information for their respective tasks. The features presented, however, were not intended to comprise a comprehensive treatise, but rather a suggestive skeleton outline that would give an adequate view of the structure of each language. The manual is purposely condensed for ready reference, and is intended merely as a guide, not a textbook. In general, only elementary rules and examples are given, and owing to limits of space there has been no attempt to deal exhaustively with any one subject. Minor exceptions exist to some of the rules given, especially in the Romance languages, and changes are being made in many of the languages, but a close adherence to the usage indicated will be sufficient for most foreign-language work.

Special acknowledgment is due the Honorable Augustus E. Giegengack, United States Public Printer, for his interest and enthusiastic support of this work. It was largely through his advice and cooperation that additions were made to the list of languages contained in this edition, especially the tongues and dialects used on the African continent. Recent developments in that portion of the world have caused renewed interest in the languages of its inhabitants. This, coupled with the unusual demand for the first two editions of the Manual of Foreign Languages encouraged the author to renewed effort, and it is hoped that this revised and enlarged manual will be of value to students and workers in the field of foreign languages and to scientific workers in research involving the use of such languages.

In former editions detailed acknowledgment was made of invaluable assistance rendered by members of the staffs of the Library of Congress, the American Bureau of Ethnology of the Smithsonian Institution, leading universities, and by other scholars recognized as authorities in language study. The author also wishes to acknowledge the many helpful suggestions that have enabled him to correct errors, both philological and typographical, that have appeared in previous editions.

CONTENTS

CONTENTS

CONTENTS

MANUAL OF
FOREIGN LANGUAGES

FOREIGN LANGUAGES

THE ALPHABET

The modern alphabet is derived from the Phoenician, through the Greek and Latin. The Phoenician, in turn, probably was patterned originally from the Egyptian hieroglyphics, which were given Semitic values.

The first man who desired to convey an idea other than by motions or speech drew a picture that would be understood by his fellow tribesmen. This can be illustrated by a drawing taken from an American Indian's message (fig. I, *a*), by which he wished to convey the information that he had gone by canoe for many sleeps to an island. This was drawn probably on the tanned hide of his tepee.

There was always a tendency, under stress of time and material, after writing began to be used, to conventionalize an earlier picture. This may be illustrated by the Chinese ideogram for mountain in its earlier pictographic and its later conventionalized form (fig. I, *b*). The Assyrian bull's head (fig. I, *c*) illustrates, in the primitive form, a greater advance from the pictographic; and, in the latter, what happened when the scribes began impressing cuneiform characters on wet clay with a wedge-shaped awl.

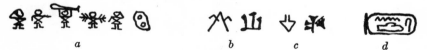

| *a* | *b* | *c* | *d* |

FIGURE I.—*Development of writing: a, American Indian; b, Chinese; c, Assyrian; d, Egyptian.*

The Egyptian writing dates from at least 4000 B.C. The cartouch (fig. I, *d*) contains the name of Send, a Pharaoh of the second dynasty, and is regarded as the earliest bit of writing extant. The Egyptian characters were of two kinds, the hieroglyphic that was cut on the wood or stone work of the temples, and the hieratic, written or painted on wood or papyrus, usually with a pointed reed. The hieratic forms were cursive and more rapidly written than the hieroglyphics, but their derivation from the older characters can be seen. (See fig. II, column 2.) The characters also began to lose their identity as pictures of objects and began to represent sounds, becoming true letters. For example, in the Pharaoh's name above referred to, the reading is not "bandage, water, hand," the original significance of the characters, but S N D (the vowels omitted, as usual with early writing).

The early Semites came into contact with the Egyptians on numerous occasions, one of which is narrated in the books of Genesis and Exodus in the Hebrew Bible. They learned the art of writing, and put it to use in their commercial ventures. Moses is thought to have been inducted into the Egyptian priestly class and to have learned to write, as the art of writing was confined to the priestly class at that time.

A connection between the Egyptian characters and the Phoenician characters, the oldest of which date from about 1850 B.C., is found in the Sinai inscription, discovered recently, which dates from about 1500 B.C. (See fig. II, columns 3 and 4.)

1

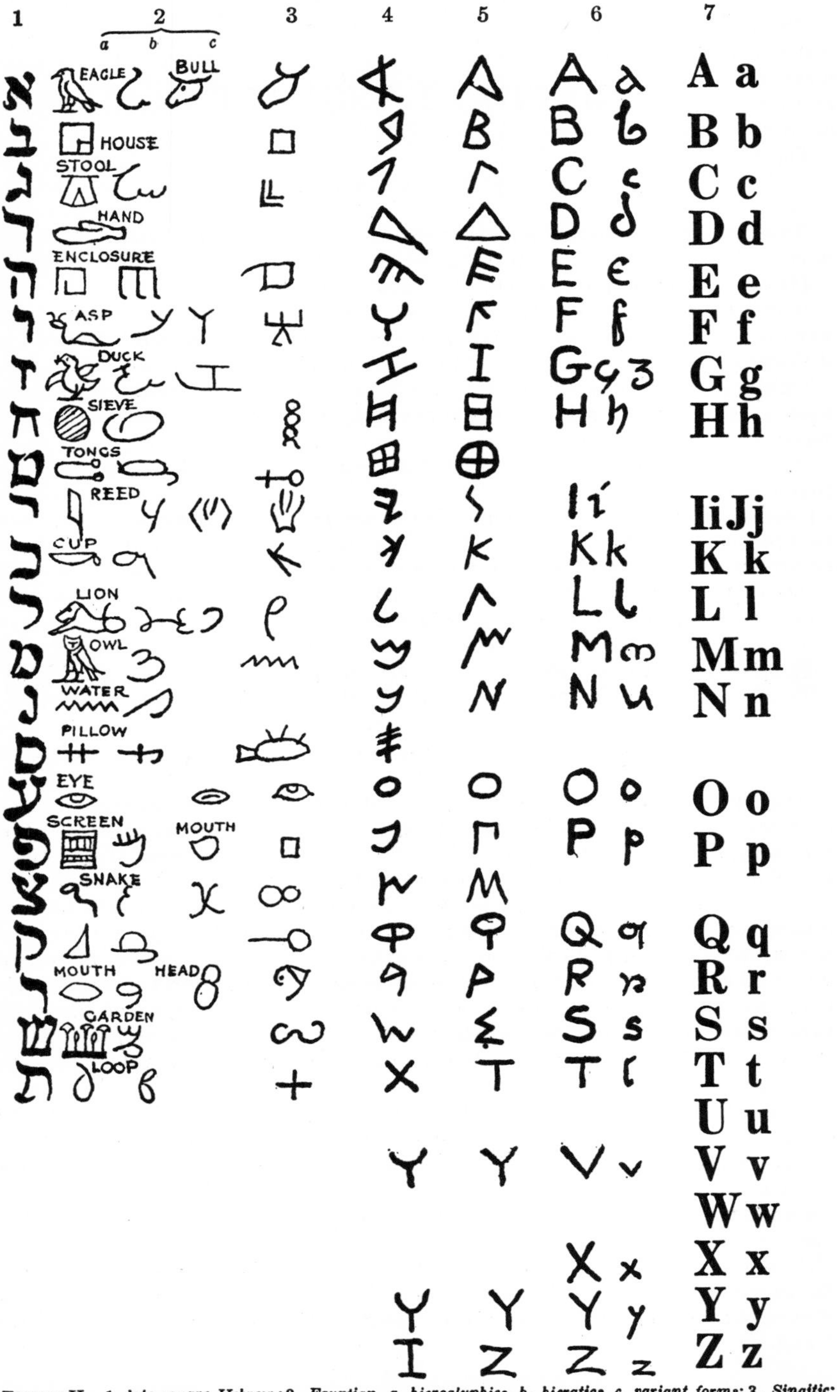

FIGURE II.—1, *late square Hebrew;* 2, *Egyptian, a, hieroglyphics, b, hieratics, c, variant forms;* 3, *Sinaitic;* 4, *Phoenician (Moabite stone);* 5, *early Greek;* 6, *Latin capitals and uncials or cursives;* 7, *Modern roman capitals and lower-case.*

The Phoenicians were great traders, and carried on an extensive commerce by sea, reaching as far, in their small vessels, as the British Isles. They communicated the art of writing to the Greeks, and the earliest forms of Greek writing are dated from the seventh to the fourth centuries, B.C. The earliest Latin inscriptions date from about the year 200 B.C.

The modern majuscule or capital letters owe their forms to the characters that were cut in stone on monuments, etc., and that required great care and time to produce. There finally grew up a more hastily produced flowing character, written first on papyrus and later on vellum with brushes, reed pens, and feather pens. This became the minuscule, or lower-case letter.

The earliest printed books were attempts to reproduce manuscripts by the use of movable type. The similarity between the Gutenberg Bible and contemporary manuscripts can be seen by comparing them, as may be done at the Library of Congress.

These manuscripts were written with a broad-nibbed pen that made heavy down strokes. From this originated the black-letter type, in which works on theology, law, etc., were customarily written and at first printed. The three German text types, the Fraktur, the Gotisch, and the Schwabacher, originated from the black-letter.

Lesser works, known as the humanities, were written in a simpler hand than the black-letter, which was reserved for the graver subjects. Printing followed the scribes in this respect, but the humanistic letters proved to be so much more legible that they were, after a while, used almost exclusively as a letter text in western Europe. It is from these that we have obtained the ordinary roman letter, called by the Germans "Antiqua". Finally Aldus invented the italic, so as to get more matter on a page.

In figure II, column 1 are given the square Hebrew characters, of a late form, but significant for comparison, and forming the best key letters available. In column 2 are the Egyptian (a) hieroglyphic, (b) hieratic, and (c) variant forms of the letters concerned. Column 3 gives the Sinaitic characters, column 4 the Phoenician (Moabite stone) alphabet, column 5 the early transitional Greek characters, and column 6 Latin capitals and uncials or cursives, some of them quite late, to illustrate the origin of upper- and lower-case roman. Column 7 gives the modern roman alphabets for comparison.

An attempt has been made to present in the text also some of the nonroman alphabets. The Far Eastern languages have alphabets all their own. The near eastern languages—e.g., Arabic and Coptic—have pursued a different course. The Cyrillic and Glagolithic were developed from the Greek, with the aid of some of the ancient runes for peculiar Slavic sounds. Modern Russian and the other Slavic alphabets have been romanized as nearly as circumstances will permit.

SELECTED LIBRARY AND BIBLIOGRAPHICAL TERMS

	Volume	Page	Edition	Part	Number (Issue)	Revised	Enlarged
Afrikaans	boekdeel	bladsy, pagina	uitgave, ediesie	deel	nommer	verbeterde	vergrooterde
Albanian	vëllim	fáqë	botim	pjësë	numêr	revizue, përsëre	përshtuem
Bohemian	svazek, kniha	strana	vydánf, náklad	část	čislo	znovuvydano	zvëličenf
Bulgarian	томъ	страница, страна	издание	частъ	номеръ	ревизирано	разширено
Catalonian	volum, tomo	plana	edicio	part	número	revisió	aumentada
Croatian	svezak	strana, stranica	izdanje	deo	broj	ispravljeno	rašireno
Danish	bind	Side	Udgave, Oplag	Del	Nummer, Hefte	gennemset, revideret	revidet, forøget
Dutch	Boekdeel	bladzijde, pagina	editie, uitgave	deel, afdeeling	nummer, aflevering	herziene	vermeerderde
Esperanto	volumo	paĝo	eldono	parto	numero	rewiderida	
Esthonian	köide	külg	wäljaanne	osa	number	järel waadata	laajennettu
Finnish	teos	sivu	painos	osa	numero	korjattu	augmenté
French	volume, tome	page	édition	part, fascicule	numéro	revisé	augmenté
Gaelic	cuiṁṫse	teaċanać	cuṫo	ctoò	uiṁir	aiṫceaṫsum	meaṫouiṫim
German	Band	Seite	Auflage, Ausgabe	Teil	Nummer, Heft	revidiert, bearbeitete	erweitert, vermehrte
Greek	τόμος	σελìς	ἔκδοσις	μέρος	ἀριθμός	ἀναθεώρησις	ἐπέκτασις
Hebrew	כרך	דף	הוצאה, מהדורה	חלק	מספר	מתוקן	הרחב
Hungarian	kötet	lap	kiadás	rész	szám	kijavitot	megnagyobbitot
Italian	volume	pagina	edizione	parte	numero	riveduto	aumentato
Latin	volumen	pagina	editio	pars	numerus	recognito	amplificato
Latvian	sējums	lappuse	izdevums	daļa	numurs		

Language	volume	page	edition	part	number	revised	enlarged
Lithuanian	tomas, knyga	puslapis	laida, leidinys, išleidimas	dalis	numeris	perziureti	padidinti
Norwegian	bind	side	utgave, oplag	del	nummer, hefte	gjennemset	udvidet
Polish	książka, tom	stronica	wydanie, edycya	część	numer	przejrzenie	rozszerzać, powiększzał
Portuguese	volume, tomo, livro	pagina	edição	parte	numero	revisado	aumentado, alargado
Rumanian	tom	paginǎ	edițiune	parte	numero	revizuire	lărgi
Russian	томъ	страница	изданiе	часть	номеръ	исправленное, пересмотренное	дополненное
Serbian	книга, свезак	страна, страница	издање	део	број	поправљено, прегледано	допуњено, повећано, рашпрено
Slovak	svazok	strana	vydanie	čast', del	число	znovuvydano	зведичен
Slovenian	zvezek	stran, stranica	izdaja, natis	del	številka	pregledano	повечано
Spanish	volumen, tomo	página	edición	parte	número	revisado	ampliando, aumentado
Swedish	volym, band	sida, page	upplaga	del	häfte, nummer, numro	genomsedd, reviderad	tillökad, förökat
Turkish (new)	cilt	sahife	tabi, neşr	cüz	sayı	tetkikedilmiş	tezyit edilmiş
Ukrainian	том	сторінк	видання	частина	число, випуск	перероблене, виправлене	розширене, розповнене
Welsh	cyfrol	dalen	argraffiad	rhan	rhif	adolygiad	ychwanegiad
Wendish	kniha	strona	wydanie	źel	numer	nowywydanie	
Yiddish	בוך, באַנד	זײַט	אויסגאַבע, אויפֿלאַגע	טייל	נומער	רעװידירטע	פֿאַרגרעסערטע

ALPHABETS OF CYRILLIC ORIGIN

Modified Cyrillic	Transliteration	Russian	Ukrainian	White Russian	Bulgarian	Serbian
А а	a	А а	А а	А а	А а	А а
Б б	b	Б б	Б б	Б б	Б б	Б б
В в	v	В в	В в	В в	В в	В в
Г г	g	Г г	Г г	Г г	Г г	Г г
Ґ (Ѓ) ґ	ġ	—	Ґ ґ	Ґ ґ	—	—
Д д	d	Д д	Д д	Д д	Д д	Д д
Ђ (Ћ) ђ	đ	—	—	—	—	Ђ ђ
Е е	e	Е е	Е е	Е е	Е е	Е е
Є є	ē	—	Є є	—	—	—
Ё ё	ë	Ё ё	—	Ё ё	—	—
Ж ж	zh	Ж ж	Ж ж	Ж ж	Ж ж	Ж ж
З з	z	З з	З з	З з	З з	З з
И и	ī	И и	И и	—	И и	И и
І і	i	І і	І і	І і	—	—
Ї ï	ï	—	Ї ï	—	—	—
Й й	ĭ	Й й	Й й	Й й	Й й	—
Ј ј	j	—	—	—	—	Ј ј
К к	k	К к	К к	К к	К к	К к
Л л	ļ	Л л	Л л	Л л	Л л	Л л
Љ љ	l̦	—	—	—	—	Љ љ
М м	m	М м	М м	М м	М м	М м
Н н	n	Н н	Н н	Н н	Н н	Н н
Њ њ	ń	—	—	—	—	Њ њ
О о	o	О о	О о	О о	О о	О о
П п	p	П п	П п	П п	П п	П п
Р р	r	Р р	Р р	Р р	Р р	Р р
С с	s	С с	С с	С с	С с	С с
Т т	t	Т т	Т т	Т т	Т т	Т т
Ћ (Ђ) ћ	ć	—	—	—	—	Ћ ћ
У у	u	У у	У у	У у	У у	У у
Ў ў	ŭ	—	—	Ў ў	—	—
Ф ф	f	Ф ф	Ф ф	Ф ф	Ф ф	Ф ф
Х х	kh	Х х	Х х	Х х	Х х	Х х
Ц ц	t͡s [1]	Ц ц	Ц ц	Ц ц	Ц ц	Ц ц
Ч ч	ch	Ч ч	Ч ч	Ч ч	Ч ч	Ч ч
Џ џ	dzh	—	—	—	—	Џ џ
Ш ш	sh	Ш ш	Ш ш	Ш ш	Ш ш	Ш ш
Щ щ	shch	Щ щ	Щ щ	—	Щ щ	—
Ъ ъ	″ [2]	Ъ ъ	—	—	Ъ ъ	Ъ [3] ъ
Ы ы	y	Ы ы	—	Ы ы	—	—
Ь ь	ʼ	Ь ь	Ь ь	·Ь ь	Ь ь	Ь [3] ь
Ѣ ѣ	i͡e [1]	Ѣ ѣ	—	—	Ѣ ѣ	—
Э э	ė	Э э	—	Э э	—	—
Ю ю	i͡u [1]	Ю ю	Ю ю	Ю ю	Ю ю	—
Я я	i͡a [1]	Я я	Я я	Я я	Я я	—
Ѳ ѳ	f	Ѳ ѳ	—	—	—	—
Ѵ ѵ	ẏ	Ѵ ѵ	—	—	—	—
ж	ü	—	—	—	ж	—

[1] As initials in proper names, first word of a sentence, etc.: I͡A, I͡E, I͡U, T͡S.
[2] Final disregarded.
[3] Obsolete.

SLAVONIC LANGUAGES

The Slavonic languages may be divided into three groups:

(a) The Western, which includes the Polabian, Polish, Sorb or Wendish, and Czechoslovak; the first of these is now dead. It was spoken in parts of Holstein and Hanover, in Mecklenburg, on the island of Rügen, in Brandenburg, and Pomerania. Closely connected with it is the Polish, which possesses an ancient literature. Sorb or Wendish is spoken along the river Spree in both Upper and Lower Lusatia; it formerly occupied a much larger area and formed a natural transition to the other languages of this group. Czech and Slovak are really two separate, though closely related, literary languages which are spoken in Bohemia and Slovakia, respectively.

(b) The Eastern group comprises Great Russian, commonly known simply as Russian; Little Russian, now generally known as Ukrainian, and also formerly known as Ruthenian in those parts of former Austro-Hungary where it was spoken; and White Russian, only recently elevated to the dignity of a literary language.

(c) The Southern group includes Slovene, Serbo-Croatian, and Bulgarian. Serb and Croatian are identical languages, but the former uses the Cyrillic while the latter uses the Latin characters. The so-called Kaj dialect, which is spoken near Zagreb, is a link between the Slovene and the Serbo-Croatian. The Macedonian dialects occupy a midway station between Serb and Bulgarian. The language used by the first Slavonic translators was an old form of Macedonian Bulgarian which has influenced all of the orthodox Slavs to a greater or lesser degree.

Originally all of these groups employed the Cyrillic alphabet, but a movement started in those countries under the influence of the Roman church has resulted in the adoption of the Latin alphabet in all of these Slavic countries except Russia and Bulgaria, and among the true Serbs in Yugoslavia.

Á	Albanian, Bohemian, Hawaiian, Hungarian, Icelandic, Portuguese, Samoan, Slovak, Spanish, Tagalog	Č	Bohemian, Latvian, Lithuanian, Serbo-Croatian, Slovak, Slovenian, Wendish
á̧	Gaelic	ʻc	Fox
À	Catalonian, French, Italian, Latvian, Portuguese (reformed), Rumanian, Tagalog	Cʻ	Dakota
		Ç	Albanian, Catalonian, Eskimo (no. 2), French, Iroquoian, Polish, Portuguese
Â	Albanian, Chinook, Fox, French, Iroquoian, Maidu, Malay, New Turkish, Pima, Portuguese, Rumanian, Tagalog, Tsimshian	ç	Dakota, Osage
		ċ	Gaelic
		5	Cherokee
		ꝺ	Cherokee
Ä	Chinook, Eskimo (no. 2), Finnish, Fox, German, Iroquoian, Kwakiutl, Maidu, Malay, Pima, Swedish, Tsimshian, Zuñi	5ⁿ	Cherokee
		Ď d' ď	Bohemian, Slovak
		ḋ	Gaelic
		Ð ẟ	Anglo-Saxon
Å	Finnish, Norwegian, Swedish	Ð ẟ	Icelandic
Ā	Anglo-Saxon, Cherokee, Chinook, Cree, Dutch, Eskimo, Fox, Iroquoian, Kwakiutl, Latin, Latvian, Maidu, Malay, Persian, Samoan, Takelma, Tsimshian	Ð đ	Serbo-Croatian
		DŹ	Polish
		DŹ	Polish
		DŽ	Latvian, Serbo-Croatian, Wendish
		d'	Pima
Ă	Dutch, Iroquoian, Malay, Pima, Samoan	É	Bohemian, French, Hawaiian, Hungarian, Icelandic, Portuguese, Samoan, Slovak, Spanish, Tagalog
Ã	Rumanian		
Ã	Portuguese	È	Catalonian, French, Italian, Latvian, Portuguese (reformed), Tagalog, Takelma
Ą	Dakota, Lithuanian, Polish		
ą	Cherokee, Navaho	ė	Gaelic
ȼ	Cherokee	Ê	Albanian, French, Kwakiutl, Lithuanian
ȧ	Eskimo (no. 2)		
Ą	Choctaw	Ě	Bohemian, Slovak, Wendish
Aⁿ	Choctaw	Ê	Chinook, Esperanto, French, Kwakiutl, Portuguese, Slovenian, Tagalog, Tsimshian
ǟ	Iroquoian		
ᴬʻ	Fox	Ę	Anglo-Saxon, Latvian, Lithuanian, Polish
ᵃʻ	Fox		
ā̇	Takelma	ę	Navaho, Polish
a·	Navaho	Ē	Anglo-Saxon, Chinook, Dutch, Eskimo, Fox, Hupa, Kwakiutl, Latin, Latvian, Lithuanian, Maidu, Malay, Persian, Tsimshian
aˇ	Navaho		
ą̣	Caddoan		
á̧	Caddoan		
ạ̈	Caddoan	Ĕ	Dutch, Iroquoian, Latin, Malay, Pima
ā̧·	Caddoan		
ā̧·	Caddoan	Ė	Lithuanian
â·	Caddoan	e·	Navaho
æ·	Navaho	ȩ	Cherokee
æˇ	Navaho	ʻ	Chinook, Kwakiutl, Tsimshian
Æ	Anglo-Saxon		
Ḃ b'	Wendish		
ḃ	Gaelic		
Ć	Polish, Serbo-Croatian, Wendish		

8

əᶜ	Fox
eᵉ	Takelma
e·	Navaho
eˇ	Navaho
ţ	Gaelic
Ğ	New Turkish
ğ	Navaho
Ġ	Dakota
ŝ	Gaelic
Ģ ģ	Latvian
g	Chinook, Eskimo (no. 2), Tsimshian
g·	Chinook, Kwakiutl, Tsimshian
gᵏ	Fox
ĝ	Tsimshian
H ħ	Dakota
Ḥ	Persian
Í	Bohemian, Catalonian, Hawaiian, Hungarian, Icelandic, Portuguese, Samoan, Slovak, Spanish, Tagalog
ì	Italian, Latvian, Portuguese (reformed), Rumanian, Tagalog
î	Chinook, French, Kwakiutl, Latvian, New Turkish, Rumanian, Tagalog, Tsimshian
ï	Catalonian, French, Malay, Portuguese (reformed)
ī	Anglo-Saxon, Chinook, Cree, Dutch, Eskimo, Fox, Hupa, Iroquoian, Kwakiutl, Latin, Latvian, Maidu, Persian, Takelma, Tsimshian
ĭ	Dutch, Iroquoian, Latin, Pima
i	Gaelic
į	Lithuanian
i·	Navaho
iˇ	Navaho
ḷ	Dakota
'I	Osage
ɩᶜ	Fox
ɩⁱ	Takelma
Iⁿ	Choctaw, Osage
'Iⁿ	Osage
ʃ	Esperanto
Kᶜ	Dakota, Pima
Ķ	Cherokee, Dakota, Osage
Ķ	Latvian
Ǩ	New Turkish
k'	Navaho
kᶜ	Cherokee, Takelma
k·	Chinook, Kwakiutl, Tsimshian
k!	Chinook, Kwakiutl, Maidu, Takelma
k·!	Chinook, Kwakiutl, Tsimshian
'k	Fox
ķ	Zuñi
ḵ	Zuñi
k̲	Zuñi
ļ	Chinook, Kwakiutl
ļ!	Chinook, Kwakiutl
l!	Tsimshian
Ļ	Latvian
Ĺ	Slovak
Ĺ l'	Slovak, Wendish
ṁ	Gaelic
Ḿ	Wendish
mᵐ	Fox
m!	Tsimshian
Ñ	Hupa, Iroquoian, Maidu, Pima, Spanish
Ņ	Latvian
Ń	Polish, Wendish
ÑG	Tagalog
nⁿ	Fox
n!	Tsimshian
ñg	Pima
Ň	Bohemian, Slovak
ń	Navaho
ɴ	Dakota, Iroquoian
Ó	Bohemian, Catalonian, Hawaiian, Hungarian, Icelandic, Polish, Portuguese, Slovak, Spanish, Wendish
Ò	Catalonian, Italian, Latvian, Portuguese (reformed), Wendish
Ö	Finnish, German, Hungarian, Icelandic, Maidu, New Turkish, Swedish
Ô	Chinook, French, Kwakiutl, Portuguese, (reformed) Slovenian, Tagalog, Tsimshian
ǫ	Cherokee
Õ	Portuguese
Ő	Hungarian
Ō	Anglo-Saxon, Chinook, Dutch, Eskimo, Fox, Hupa, Latin, Maidu, Persian, Takelma, Tsimshian
Ŏ	Dutch, Latin, Pima
Ǫ	Anglo-Saxon
ǫ	Navaho
o·	Navaho
oˇ	Navaho
Oⁿ	Choctaw, Osage
ó	Gaelic

'O	Osage
ŏ^u	Takelma
ŌŌ	Eskimo
o^c	Fox
ṕ	Wendish
P̣	Dakota, Osage
P'	Dakota
p!	Chinook, Kwakiutl, Maidu, Takelma, Tsimshian
'p	Fox
p'	Pima
p̣	Zuñi
ṗ	Gaelic
q!	Chinook, Kwakiutl, Tsimshian
q̇	Eskimo (no. 2)
ŗ	Tsimshian
Ŗ	Latvian
Ř	Bohemian, Slovak
Ŕ	Wendish
R'	Eskimo
Ṣ	Polish, Wendish
Š	Bohemian, Latvian, Lithuanian, Serbo-Croatian, Slovak, Slovenian, Wendish
's	Fox
s·	Takelma
ś	Gaelic
Ṣ	Persian, Rumanian
Ṡ	Dakota
Ş	New Turkish
ŠĊ	Polish
Ť ť ł	Bohemian, Slovak
Ţ	Rumanian
Ṭ	Dakota, Osage
ṫ	Gaelic
t'	Cherokee, Pima
tc!	Chinook
ts!	Chinook, Kwakiutl, Takelma, Tsimshian
't	Fox
'tc	Fox
^d tc	Fox
t!	Kwakiutl, Maidu, Takelma, Tsimshian
ts·!	Takelma
ŧ	Zuñi
ŧc	Zuñi
ŧs	Zuñi
ł	Navaho
Ů	Bohemian, Catalonian, Hawaiian, Hungarian, Icelandic, Portuguese, Samoan, Slovak, Spanish, Tagalog
U̇	French, Italian, Latvian, Portuguese (reformed), Rumanian, Tagalog
Û	French, Hupa, New Turkish, Pima, Tagalog
Ṳ	Catalonian, Eskimo (no. 2), French, German, Hungarian, Maidu, New Turkish, Portuguese (reformed), Spanish, Takelma
Ū	Anglo-Saxon, Chinook, Hupa, Latin, Latvian, Lithuanian, Maidu, Persian, Takelma
Ŭ	Esperanto, Iroquoian, Latin, Pima
ū^u	Takelma
ü^u	Takelma
Ụ	Dakota
Ű	Hungarian
Ů	Bohemian, Lithuanian, Slovak
θ	Gaelic
Ų	Lithuanian
u·	Navaho
u˘	Navaho
U^n	Choctaw
'U	Osage
Ŵ	Welsh
w^w	Fox
'w	Takelma
w!	Tsimshian
x̣	Cherokee
x̧	Chinook
x·	Chinook, Kwakiutl
x^u	Kwakiutl
Ẏ	Dutch
Ŷ	Bohemian, Icelandic, Slovak
Ỹ	Welsh
y^	Fox
y!	Tsimshian
Ż	Dakota, Lithuanian, Polish
Ź	Polish, Wendish
Ẓ	Persian
Ẕ	Persian
Ž	Bohemian, Latvian, Lithuanian, Serbo-Croatian, Slovak, Slovenian, Wendish
'	Dakota, Fox, Iroquoian, Maidu, Malay, Persian, Pima, Samoan
'	Cree, Dakota, Fox, Hupa, Iroquoian, Persian, Pima, Samoan
'	Hupa, Malay, Navaho, Persian, Samoan
'	Iroquoian, Kwakiutl
˘	Malay

LANGUAGES USING CERTAIN DIACRITICAL MARKS

Albanian: Á Â Ç É Ë Ê Í Ó Ú

Anglo-Saxon: Ā Æ Ę Ē Ī Ō Ǫ Ð ð Ū

Bohemian: Á Č Ď d' ď É Ě Í Ň Ó Ř Š Ť
ť ŧ Ů Ů Ý Ž

Caddoan: ą á ȧ ā· ᵃ· ᵃ·

Catalonian: Á Ç É Ě Ï Í Ó Ò Ú Ü

Cherokee: ã ą ɋ ʞ ʞ k' ö· ɔ ɔ· ɔⁿ t' ú x̣
x̣

Chinook: ā â ä ē ê g g· ī î k· k! k·! ʟ
ʟ! ō ô p! q! tc! ts! ū x̣ x· ᶜ

Choctaw: Ą Aⁿ Iⁿ Oⁿ Uⁿ

Cree: Ā Ī ᶜ

Dakota: Ą C' Ç G Ĥ ħ Į Ķ Ķ' ⁿ Ṗ P' Ś
Ṭ Ų Ż ' ᶜ

Dutch: Ā Ä Ē Ě Ï Ï Ō Ŏ Ÿ

Eskimo: Ā Ē Ī Ō O͞O R'

Eskimo: (no. 2): à ä ç g q̌ ü

Esperanto: Ĉ Ĝ Ĥ Ĵ Ŝ Ŭ

Finnish: Ä Å Ö

Fox: ā ä å ᶜc ē gᵏ ī ᶦk mᵐ nⁿ ō ᵖp ᶰs ᶜt
ᶜtc ᵈtc wʷ yʸ ᶜᵎ Aᶜ aᶜ eᶜ iᶜ oᶜ

French: Á Â Ç É Ë Ě Ï Ï Ô Ô Ü Û

Gaelic: ʌ ƀ ċ ʋ ɇ ḟ ṡ 1 ṁ ʘ ṗ ṡ ṫ ú

German: Ä Ö Ü

Greek, see p. 69.

Hawaiian: Á É Í Ó Ú

Hungarian: Á É Í Ó Ö Ő Ú Ü Ű

Hupa: ē ī ñ ō ū ú̓ ᶜ

Icelandic: Á Ð ð É Í Ó Ö Ú Ý

Iroquoian: ā ä ä Ą ç è ï ĩ ñ ŭ ⁿ ' ' '

Italian: Á É Ì Ò Ù

Kwakiutl: ā ä å ē ë ê g· ī î k· k! k·!
ʟ ʟ! ô p! q! t! ts! x· x̣ᵘ ᶜ '

Latin: Ā Ă Ē Ĕ Ï Ĭ Ō Ŏ Ū Ŭ

Latvian: Ā Ā Č DŽ Ē Ē Ę G ġ Ì Ī Ī Ķ
Ļ Ņ Ò Ŗ Š Ü Ū Ž

Lithuanian: Ą Č Ę Ė Ē Į Š Ů Ū Ų
Ž Ż

Maidu: ā ä å ē ī k! ñ ō ö p! t! ū ü '

Malay transliteration: Ā Â Ä Ā Ē Ë Ï ' ᵛ ᶜ

Navaho: a· a ᵛ ą ą· ą ᵛ æ æ· œ ᵛ e· e ᵛ ę
i· i ᵛ k' ñ o· o ᵛ ǫ· u· u ᵛ ų š ʇ ž ǧ ᶜ

Osage: ⁿ Ç ' E Í ' I Iⁿ 'Iⁿ Ķ 'O Oⁿ 'U P
Ţ

Persian transliteration: Ā Ē Ḥ Ī Ō Ṣ
Ū Z Z̧ ' ' ᶜ

Pima: å ä ä ē ī ñ ð ŭ ü ŭ ñ g t' d' k' p' ᶜ ᶜ '

Polish: Ą Ć DŻ DŹ Ę Ń Ó Ś ŚĆ Ż Ż

Portuguese: Â Á Ã Ç É Ê Í Ô Ó

Portuguese (reformed): À Á Â Ã Ç È
É Ê Í Ï Ó Ò Ô Õ Ú Ü

Rumanian: Â Ă Ă Î Î Ş Ţ Ŭ

Samoan: Ā Ā Á É Í Ó Ú ' '

Serbo-Croatian: Č Ć Đ đ DŽ Š Ž

Slovak: Á Č Ď d' ď É Ě Í Ĺ Ľ Í Ň Ó Ř
Š Ť ť ŧ Ů Ů Ý Ž

Slovenian: Č É Ô Š Ž

Spanish: Á É Í Ñ Ó Ú Ü

Swedish: Å Ä Ö

Tagalog: Á Â Ã É Ê Ë Í Í Ï NG Ó Ô
Ô Ú Û

Takelma: ā ā ᵉ e ᵉ è ïⁱ ī k ᶜ k! ōᵘ ō p! s· t!
ts! ts·! ūᵘ ū üᵘ ü ᶜw

Tsimshian: ā ä å ē ê g g· ĝ ī î k· k·!
l! m! n! ō ô p! q! t! ɍ ts! w! y! ᶜ

Turkish (New): Â Ç Ğ Î Ķ Ö Ş Û Ü

Welsh: Ŷ Ŵ

Wendish: Ḃ b' Ć Č DŽ Ĕ Ĺ Í Ł Ḿ Ń
Ó Ṗ Ŕ Š Ŝ Ẃ Ż Ż

Zuñi: ä ḳ ʞ ʞ p ŧ tc ts

ALBANIAN

A	a	*a* in father	NJ	nj	*ni* in opinion
B	b	*b*	O	o	*o* in only
C	c	*ts* in nets	P	p	*p*
Ç	ç	*ch* in church	Q	q	*ky* sound in cute
D	d	*d*			(always)
DH	dh	*th* in father	R	r	*r*, weak
E	e	*e* in end	RR	rr	*r* strongly trilled
Ë	ë	*e* in term	S	s	*s*
F	f	*f*	SH	sh	*sh* in shut
G	g	*g* in garden	T	t	*t*
GJ	gj	*gy* sound in exiguous	TH	th	*th* in thin
H	h	*h;* almost *kh*	U	u	*oo* in ooze
I	i	*ee* in greet	V	v	*v*
J	j	*y* in young	X	x	*dz* in adze
K	k	*k*	XH	xh	*dj* in adjective
L	l	*gl* in Italian egli	Y	y	*u*, French (lieu)
LL	ll	*ll* in wall	Z	z	*z*
M	m	*m*	ZH	zh	*s* in pleasure
N	n	*n*			

The Albanian was formerly written in Turkish, Greek, and Latin characters in the different parts of the country, but Latin is now the official script for the two principal dialects, Gheg and Tosk, and there is evidence of a strong Latin influence in the root words, as also in capitalization.

Syllabication
Division is on the vowel, with a consonant going with the next syllable; if there be two consonants they may be divided, unless it be the indivisible *dh, gj, ll, nj, rr, xh,* or *zh.*

Accent
The stress generally, though not always, falls on the next to the last syllable, e.g., *Pipilo;* but also *Vasíl* (Basil), and *kúngulli* (pumpkin); the accent is seldom written, however, but when the circumflex is used it indicates that the vowel is strongly nasalized.

Articles
The indefinite article (*nji*) precedes the noun and is variable for both masculine and feminine.

The definite article is *i* for masculine singular, *a* for feminine singular, and *t* for both masculine and feminine plural. It is never a separate word, but always a suffix, e.g., *mal,* mountain, and *mali,* the mountain; *are,* field, and *ara,* the field; *male,* mountains, and *malet,* the mountains; *ara,* fields, and *arat,* the fields.

The attributive article is always a separate word and is found before every attributive genitive, most adjectives, and all possessive pronouns. It agrees with its antecedent noun in number, gender, and case.

Cardinal numbers

nji	one	dh(j)et	ten
dy	two	njimëdhétë	eleven
tre, tri	three	dymbëdhétë	twelve
kátër	four	trimbëdhétë ⎫	
pêsë	five	trimdhétë ⎭	thirteen
gjáshtë	six	njizét	twenty
shtatë	seven	nji qind	hundred
tétë	eight	mijë	thousand
nånd	nine		

Ordinal numbers

pari	first	dh(j)étët	tenth
dyti	second	njëmëdjéti	eleventh
treti, treta	third	dymbëdhétët	twelfth
kátërt	fourth	trimbëdhétë⎫	
pésët(i)	fifth	trimdhéti ⎭	thirteenth
gjáshtët	sixth	njizétet	twentieth
shtátét	seventh	qindët	hundredth
teti	eighth	mijtë	thousandth
nándë(t)	ninth		

Months

janár	January	shtatúer⎫	
frúer, shkurt	February	shtator ⎭	September
mars	March	tetúer⎫	
prill, -i	April	tetor ⎭	October
maj	May	nandúer⎫	
qërshor	June	nentor ⎭	November
qorriq	July	dhetúer⎫	
gusht, -i	August	djetor ⎭	December

Days

diélë	Sunday	ënjte	Thursday
hánë	Monday	prémtë	Friday
marte	Tuesday	shtúnë	Saturday
merkúrë	Wednesday		

Seasons

prendvérë, -a	spring	vjéshtë	autumn
vérë	summer	dímën	winter

Time

órë	hour	múaj	month
dítë	day	vjet	year
jávë	week		

ANGLO-SAXON

A	a	*a* in German Mann	N	n	*n*	
Ā	ā	Preceding sound length-ened	O	o	*o* in German Gott	
			Ō	ō	*o* in low	
Æ	æ	*a* in at	Q	ǫ	*o* in not	
Ǣ	ǣ	Preceding sound length-ened	Đ	ð } Þ	þ }	(⁵)
B	b	*b*	P	p	*p*	
C	c	*k*¹	R	r	*r*, trilled	
D	d	*d*	S	s	Voiceless sound, except *s* between vowels has *z* sound	
E	e } Ę	ę }	*e* in let, men				
Ē	ē	*e* in they	T	t	*t*	
F	f	(²)	U	u	*u* in full	
G	g	(³)	Ū	ū	*u* in rule	
H	h	(⁴)	W	w	*w*	
I	i	*i* in hit	X	x	*x*	
Ī	ī	*i* in machine	Y	y	*u* in German hübsch	
L	l	*l*	Œ	œ	*o* in German schön	
M	m	*m*				

¹ The *kw* or *qu* sound is represented by *cw; cs* has value of *x*.
² This letter has two values. In the initial and final positions, in the combinations *ff, fs, ft*, and in the medial position it has the usual (voiceless) sound; between vowels and voiced consonants it has the sound of *v*.
³ Almost always like *g* in German sagen or like *y* in you, according to its pronunciation with guttural or palatal vowels; when doubled it is pronounced like *g* in go; *cg* sounds like *dg* in ridge.
⁴ Like *h* in German ach when guttural, otherwise as *h* in German ich.
⁵ These two characters are used without distinction to give the *th* sound as in thin, except between vowels and voiced consonants where the voiced spirant is employed, as in thine. The second is called "thorn."

The Anglo-Saxon is of Teutonic origin; introduced into England about the fifth century, the West Saxon dialect became dominant for literary purposes during the reign of Alfred the Great (871–901), and maintained its supremacy until the close of the Anglo-Saxon period.

The following is a sample of one of the Anglo-Saxon faces of type used in the classical period:

Capitals: ᚪBℂDЄFᵷ ᛈIKLᚳNOPRSTUᛈXYZÐᛈ3

Lower case: a b c ᛒ e ᚠ ᚷ h ı ᛈ k l m n o p ᛈ·ᚾ ᚱ ᚳ u p x ẏ z ð

Diphthongs

The diphthongs are *ie, īe, ea, ēa, eo, ēo, io, īo*, and these (both long and short) receive the stress on the first element, the second, being unaccented, is very much obscured in pronunciation; *ea, ēa* is equivalent to *ae + a* (perhaps more nearly *ae + uh*); otherwise the component parts will be pronounced as shown in the table.

Accent

Simple words are accented on the first syllable, while substantive compounds receive the stress on the first and the accent of the second component is usually retained as a secondary stress. A verbal compound is accented on the radicle syllable of the verb, the prefix being unaccented.

Cardinal numbers

ān	one	tīen	ten
twēgen, tū, twā	two	ęndlefan, -lefan, -lufan	eleven
ðrie, ðrīo (ðrēo)	three	twęlf	twelve
fīower (fēower)	four	ðrēotīene, -tene, -tyne	thirteen
fīf	five	twēntig	twenty
siex	six	ān ǫnd twēntig	twenty-one
siofon (seofon)	seven	hundtēoutig, hund, hundred }	hundred
eahta	eight		
nigon	nine	ðūsend	thousand

Ordinal numbers

forma, formesta, fyrmest, fyrest, fyrst; āerest }	first	eahtoða, -eða, -eoða	eighth
		nigoða, -eða, -eoða	ninth
		teoða	tenth
ðder, æfterra	second	ęndlefta, ęllefta	eleventh
ðridda	third	twęlfta	twelfth
fēowerða, fēorða	fourth	ðrēotēoða	thirteenth
fīfta	fifth	twēntigoða, -tiga	twentieth
siexta	sixth	ān ǫnd twēntigoða	twenty-first
seofoða, -eða	seventh	hundtēoutigoða	hundredth

ARABIC

Name	Isolated	Final	Median	Initial	Transliteration tone value	Remarks
Alif	‏ا‏	‏ا‏			—, ’	Spiritus lenis
Bē	‏ب‏	‏ب‏	:	!	*b*	
Tē	‏ت‏	‏ت‏	:	;	*t·*	
Sē	‏ث‏	‏ث‏	:	;	*t*	English *th*, mute
Jīm	‏ج‏	‏ج‏	‏ـج‏	‏جـ‏	*ǵ*	Varies in different dialects, hard *g* in gay to the French *j*
Hē	‏ح‏	‏ح‏	‏ـح‏	‏حـ‏	*ḥ*	Strongly aspirated
Khē	‏خ‏	‏خ‏	‏ـخ‏	‏خـ‏	*ḫ*	As in Scotch loch, **guttural**
Dāl	‏د‏	‏د‏			*d*	
Ẓāl	‏ذ‏	‏ذ‏			*ḍ*	Weak glottal
Rē	‏ر‏	‏ر‏			*r*	
Zē	‏ز‏	‏ز‏			*z*	Voiced, as *s* in sat
Sīn	‏س‏	‏س‏	‏ـسـ‏	‏سـ‏	*s*	Voiceless, as *s* in German grüszen
Shīn	‏ش‏	‏ش‏	‏ـشـ‏	‏شـ‏	*š*	*sh*
Ṣād	‏ص‏	‏ص‏	‏ـصـ‏	‏صـ‏	*ṣ*	*sz*, glottal
Dād	‏ض‏	‏ض‏	‏ـضـ‏	‏ضـ‏	*ḍ*	*d*, hard, glottal
Tā	‏ط‏	‏ط‏	‏ـطـ‏	‏طـ‏	*ṭ*	*t*, hard, glottal
Zā	‏ظ‏	‏ظ‏	‏ـظـ‏	‏ظـ‏	*ẓ*	*ts*, usually
Ain	‏ع‏	‏ع‏	‏ـعـ‏	‏عـ‏	‘	Semitic guttural
Ghain	‏غ‏	‏غ‏	‏ـغـ‏	‏غـ‏	*kh*	Like German *ch*.
Fē	‏ف‏	‏ف‏	‏ـفـ‏	‏فـ‏	*f*	
Qāf [1]	‏ق‏	‏ق‏	‏ـقـ‏	‏قـ‏	*q*	Guttural, hard
Kēf	‏ك‏	‏ك‏	‏ـكـ‏	‏كـ‏	*k*	Soft
Lām	‏ل‏	‏ل‏	‏ـلـ‏	‏لـ‏	*l*	
Mīm	‏م‏	‏م‏	‏ـمـ‏	‏مـ‏	*m*	
Nūn	‏ن‏	‏ن‏	‏ـنـ‏	‏نـ‏	*n*	
He	‏ة ه‏	‏ـة ه‏	‏ـهـ‏	‏هـ‏	*h*	
Wāw [2]	‏و‏	‏و‏			*w*	English bilabial *w*
Yē	‏ى‏	‏ى‏	‏ـيـ‏	‏يـ‏	*y*	

[1] Also Kāf.   [2] Also Vāv.

The expansion of Islam during the 7th and 8th centuries spread the Arabic language over many countries where it is spoken in one form or another and sometimes in connection with a local language. Its influence is manifest even in modern Spanish. There are dialectic differences even in Arabia, but the written language has almost invariably conformed to that type which is called "classical Arabic".

Most pure Arabic words can be traced back to a triliteral root, and some of two consonants only. For instance, from the root *ktb* (write), we get *katabnā* (we wrote), *naktuba* (we will write), *katib*^{un} (writing, a writer), etc.

The Arabic verb has but two tenses: Perfect and imperfect. The meaning of the simple verb may be modified by the addition of one or more letters to the root, in which manner about 14 conjugations may be formed.

There are two articles: Definite, *al* (the) preceding the noun, and the indefinite, *un* (a, an) attached to the end of a noun, etc., *al maliki* (the king); *malikun* (a king).

There are two declensions of nouns in the singular and only two genders, masculine and feminine.

With the exception of the first two, which are adjectives, the cardinal numbers are all substantives and are followed, from 3 to 10, by the genitive of the broken plural whenever possible, taking the feminine form when the objects numbered are masculine, and vice versa; from 11 to 99 by the accusative singular, and from 100 to 1,000 by the genitive singular.

There is no record of any written Arabic literature prior to the Koran, and the poems and proverbs of the northern Arabs really form the beginning of Arabic literature.

NOTE.—The characters Ain and Ghain appear to be hard gutturals; Ghain is always *g*, but from a grammatical standpoint Ain cannot be well defined in any of the three Near Eastern languages. While at best it has only a very short sound, it cannot be omitted from the alphabet because of the effect it has on the proper pronunciation of the words.

It is also considered a vowel, especially at the beginning of words, taking the place of *a*, *ā*, *i*, *ī*, *u*, *ū*. In a median position it generally takes the place of *i* or *ii*, depending mainly on the proper relation of the words and its nearest transcription and pronunciation into the Latin alphabet.

ARABIC LIGATURES

Lām-Alif	Ain-Jīm	Kēf-Lām	Lām-Mīm
Bē-Lām-Alif	Ghain-Jīm	Kaf-Lām-Dāl	Lām-Bē-Mīm
Bē-Alif	Fē-Jīm	Lām-Dāl	Lām-Tā-Mīm
Tā-Alif	Qāf-Jīm	Lām-Ẕāl	Mīm-Mīm
Sē-Alif	Fē-Hē	Lām-Rē	Mīm-Jīm-Mīm
Nūn-Alif	Qāf-Hē	Lām-Zē	Mīm-Hē-Mīm
Yē-Alif	Fē-Sē	Lām-He	Mīm-Khē-Mīm
Jīm-Alif	Kēf-Jīm	Lām-Wāw	He-Mīm
Hē-Alif	Kēf-Hē	Bē-Lām-He	Bē-Nūn
Khē-Alif	Kēf-Khē	Lām-Lām	Bē-He
Ain-Alif	Lām-Jīm	Lām-Lām-He	Kēf-He
Ghain-Alif	Lām-Hē	Jīm-Lām	Kaf-Lām-He
Fē-Alif	Lām-Khē	Hē-Lām	Bē-Yē
Qāf-Alif	Lām-Mīm-Jīm	Khe-Lām	Tā-Yē
Mīm-Alif	Lām-Mīm-Hē	Be-Mīm	Sē-Yē
Bē-Mīm-Alif	Lām-Mīm-Khē	Be-Be-Mīm	Nūn-Yē
Tā-Mīm-Alif	Mīm-Jīm	Be-Tā-Mīm	Yē-Yē
Sē-Mīm-Alif	Mīm-Hē	Be-Sē-Mīm	Jīm-Yē
Nūn-Mīm-Alif	Mīm-Khē	Be-Nūn-Mīm	Hē-Yē
Yē-Mīm-Alif	He-Jīm	Bā-Yē-Mīm	Khē-Yē
Hē-Mīm-Alif	Bē-Rē	Jīm-Mīm	Šin-Yē
Kēf-Alif	Tē-Rē	Hē-Mīm	Shīn-Yē
Kēf-Mīm-Alif	Sē-Rē	Khē-Mīm	Tā-Yē
Kēf-Lām-Alif	Nūn-Rē	Lām-Jīm-Mīm	Zā-Yē
Bē-Bē	Yē-Rē	Lām-Hē-Mīm	Ain-Yē
Bē-Bē	Ain-Rē	Lām-Khē-Mīm	Ghain-Yē
Bē-Jīm	Ain-Sā	Ain-Mīm	Fē-Yē
Bē-Hē	Ghain-Rā	Ghain-Mīm	Qāf-Yē
Bē-Khē	Ghain-Sā	Fā-Mīm	Kēf-Yē
Ṣād-Jīm	Mīm-Rē	Qāf-Mīm	Kēf-Lām-Yē
Dād-Jīm	Mīm-Sā	Kef-Mīm	Lām-Yē
Ṣād-Hē	He-Rē	Kef-Lām-Mīm	Mīm-Yē
Dād-Hē			He-Yē

ARMENIAN

Ա	ա	Ա	ա	a	Ծ	ծ	Ծ	ծ	dz	Ջ	ջ	Ջ	ջ	dsh(tch)

Ա ա Ա ա a	Ծ ծ Ծ ծ dz	Ջ ջ Ջ ջ dsh(tch)
Բ բ Բ բ b(p)	Կ կ Կ կ k(g)	Ռ ռ Ռ ռ rh(ṙ)
Գ գ Գ գ g(k)	Հ հ Հ հ h	Ս ս Ս ս s
Դ դ Դ դ d(t)	Ձ ձ Ձ ձ ds	Վ վ Վ վ v
Ե ե Ե ե ¹e(ye)	Ղ ղ Ղ ղ l(gh)	Տ տ Տ տ t(d)
Զ զ Զ զ z	Ճ ճ Ճ ճ dj(j)	Ր ր Ր ր r
Է է Է է ē	Մ մ Մ մ m	Ց ց Ց ց ts(tz)
Ը ը Ը ը ĕ	Յ յ Յ յ y(h)	ㅣ ㅣ ㅣ ㅣ u(v̇)
Թ թ Թ թ th(ṭ)	Ն ն Ն ն n	Փ փ Փ փ ph(p)
Ժ ժ Ժ ժ zh	Շ շ Շ շ sh	Ք ք Ք ք q(kh)
Ի ի Ի ի i	Ո ո Ո ո o(wo)	Օ օ Օ օ ō(o)
Լ լ Լ լ l	Չ չ Չ չ ch	Ֆ ֆ Ֆ ֆ f
Խ խ Խ խ kh	Պ պ Պ պ p(b)	

¹ ե = i instead of e in the ending *եան* or *եանկ* in family names, e.g., Dash*i*an *not* Dashean.

This table shows the vertical and slant letters of Armenian with their English equivalents. In the roman transliteration columns, the first letter represents "classical" Armenian; the second letter (in parentheses) modern Armenian usage, when it differs. In case the latter mode is followed, letters enclosed in parentheses must be used to avoid confusion.

Vowels are: *ա* (a), *ե* (e or ye), *է* (ē), *ը* (ĕ), *ի* (i), *ո* (o or wo), * լ* (u or v), *o* (ō). Compound vowels: *աւ*, *այ*, *եա*, *եո*, *եւ*, *իւ*, *ու* and *ոյ*. Diphthongs: *իա*, *իէ*, *իո*, *իօ*, *իու*, *ուի*, *ուէ*, *ուա*, *ուո*, *էո*, *էու* and *էի*. Contractions: *և* for *եւ*, and *ﬆ* for *ստ*. Capitalization is the same as in English Accents are not used in Armenian.

Syllabication
In the division of Armenian words, a syllable is usually an articulate sound, as—*առ* ar, *նա* na, *տար* tar, *աղտ* aghd, *որմ* worm, *բարդ* part, *քարն* karn. A syllable may also be composed of six letters, as—*սիամբք* siampk, *չիւրբք* chiurpk. Two or three consonants are sometimes formed before or after a vowel. Double consonants often mark the end of a syllable, as *տարր* darr, *քաղաքք* caghack, but a syllable may end with a vowel or diphthong if it is preceded by one or more consonants. Separated syllables usually begin with a consonant. Compound vowels or diphthongs are never separated in the division of words.

Articles
Indefinite article *մը* (a or an) follows the noun to which it belongs. The *մը* becomes *մըն* when it is followed by a word which begins with a vowel, as *այ*, *իմ*, *ինք*, *էր*, etc.
Definite article *ը* (the) is added to the end of nouns terminating in a consonant, and *ն* to nouns ending in a vowel.

Figures

Figures (1, 2, 3, etc.), are used as in English.

The letters of the Armenian alphabet are also used as numbers. [In classic literature a line is generally placed over the letters when used as numbers]:

ա	1	*ժ*	10	*ճ*	100	*ռ*	1000
բ	2	*ի*	20	*մ*	200	*ս*	2000
գ	3	*լ*	30	*յ*	800	*վ*	3000
դ	4	*խ*	40	*ն*	400	*տ*	4000
ե	5	*ծ*	50	*շ*	500	*ր*	5000
զ	6	*կ*	60	*ո*	600	*ց*	6000
է	7	*հ*	70	*չ*	700	*ւ*	7000
ը	8	*ձ*	80	*պ*	800	*փ*	8000
թ	9	*ղ*	90	*ջ*	900	*ք*	9000

The new letters *o* and *ֆ* have no numerical value.

Cardinal numbers

զրօ, ոչինչ	zero	*տասնեւեօթը*	seventeen
մէկ, մի	one	*տասնեւութը*	eighteen
երկու	two	*տասնեւինը*	nineteen
երեք	three	*քսան*	twenty
չորս	four	*քսանեւմէկ*	twenty-one
հինգ	five	*երեսուն*	thirty
վեց	six	*քառասուն*	forty
եօթը	seven	*յիսուն*	fifty
ութը	eight	*վաթսուն*	sixty
ինը	nine	*եօթանասուն*	seventy
տասը	ten	*ութսուն*	eighty
տասնեւմէկ	eleven	*իննսուն*	ninety
տասներկու	twelve	*հարիւր*	hundred
տասներեք	thirteen	*երկուհարիւր*	two hundred
տասնեւչորս	fourteen	*երեքհարիւր*	three hundred
տասնեւհինգ	fifteen	*հազար*	thousand
տասնեւվեց	sixteen	*միլիոն*	million

Ordinal numbers

առաջին	first	*քսաներորդ*	twentieth
երկրորդ	second	*երեսուներորդ*	thirtieth
երրորդ	third	*քառասուներորդ*	fortieth
չորրորդ	fourth	*յիսուներորդ*	fiftieth
հինգերորդ	fifth	*վաթսուներորդ*	sixtieth
վեցերորդ	sixth	*եօթանասուներորդ*	seventieth
եօթներորդ	seventh	*ութսուներորդ*	eightieth
ութերորդ	eighth	*իննսուներորդ*	ninetieth
իններորդ	ninth	*հարիւրերորդ*	hundredth
տասներորդ	tenth	*հազարերորդ*	thousandth

Months

Յունուար	January	*Յուլիս*	July
Փետրուար	February	*Օգոստոս*	August
Մարտ	March	*Սեպտեմբեր*	September
Ապրիլ	April	*Հոկտեմբեր*	October
Մայիս	May	*Նոյեմբեր*	November
Յունիս	June	*Դեկտեմբեր*	December

Days

Կիրակի	Sunday	*Հինգշաբթի*	Thursday
Երկուշաբթի	Monday	*Ուրբաթ*	Friday
Երեքշաբթի	Tuesday	*Շաբաթ*	Saturday
Չորեքշաբթի	Wednesday		

Seasons

գարուն	spring	*աշուն*	autumn
ամառ	summer	*ձմեռ*	winter

Time

ժամ	hour	*կէսօր*	noon
օր	day	*երիկուն*	evening
եօթնեակ	week	*Զատիկ*	Easter
ամիս	month	*Ծնունդ*	Christmas
տարի	year	*Կաղանդ Նոր Տարի*	New Year's Day
առաւօտ	morning		

Abbreviations

[In classic literature a line is placed over the abbreviated letters]

ամ. *ամենայն* (all, whole)
Ած. *Աստուած* (Deity)
բզմ. *բազում* (many, several)
եւ (and)
ը. *ընդ* (in, on)
թն. *թոյն* (poison)
պս. *պէս* (as, same as)
վս. *վասն* (for)
Սր. *Սուրբ* (Saint)
Պատ. *Պատուելի* (Rev.)
Բժ. *Բժիշկ* (Dr.)
Պ. *Պարոն* (Mr.)

Տիկ. *Տիկին* (Mrs.)
Օր. *Օրիորդ* (Miss)
ձեռ. *ձեռագիր* (manuscript)
թե. *թերթ* (folio)
թ. *թիւ* (number)
շր. *շարք* (series)
դէմ. *ընդդէմ* (versus, against)
եւայ. *եւայլն* (et cetera)
այս. *այսինքն* (that is)
Մ.Ն. *Միացեալ Նահանգներ* (United States)
Ամ. *Ամերիկա* (America)

Conjunctions most frequently used

եւ, *եւ*, or *ու* = and
եւս = still, more
կամ, *թէ* = or, either
բայց, *այլ* = but
չըլլայ թէ = lest
այ'ս է = it is, to-wit
ինչպէս, *որպէս* = as
մինչդեռ = whereas, wherefore
որ = that
քանթէ = than
եթէ, *թէ* = if
նաեւ = also
ալ = too
թէ' ... *թէ'* = both ... and
կա'մ ... *կա'մ* = either ... or
ոչ ալ = nor

ո'չ ... *ո'չ* = neither ... nor
վասն = for
իսկ = even
այլ եւ = but also
այսպէս = so
այնպէս որ = so that
երբ, *երբոր* = when, as
թէեւ = though
ուստի = therefore
արդ = then
մինչեւ որ = until
քանի որ = since
մինչ = while
եթէ ոչ = otherwise
թէ ինչու = why
հետեւաբար = consequently

BOHEMIAN (Czech)

A	a	Final *a* in America	N	n	*n* [4]
Á	á	*a* in arm	Ň	ň	*ny* in canyon [5]
B	b	*b*	O	o	*o* in opinion
C	c	*ts*	Ó	ó	*o* in lord
Č	č	*ch* in child	P	p	*p*
D	d	*d* [1]	Q	q	*q* in question [3]
Ď	d' ď	*d* in French diable	R	r	*r* in rest
E	e	*e* in end	Ř	ř	*rsh* [6]
É	é	*e* in ere	S	s	*s* in sink
Ě	ě	*ea* in beatitude [2]	Š	š	*sh*
F	f	*f*	T	t	*t* in test
G	g	*g* in great [3]	Ť	t' ť	*t* in French tien
H	h	*h* in ham	U	u	*u* in push
I,Y	i, y	*i* in lick	Ů,Ú	ů, ú	*u* in rude
Í,Ý	í, ý	*i* in pique	V	v	*v*
J	j	*y* in yes	X	x	*x* in expect [3]
K	k	*ck* in stick	Z	z	*z* in zeal
L	l	*l*	Ž	ž	*z* in azure
M	m	*m*			

[1] Takes sound of *d'* when followed by *ě* or *i*.
[2] When it follows *d, n, t*, these letters take soft sound of *d', ň, t'*, and *ě* then sounds like *e*.
[3] Occurs only in foreign words.
[4] Sound of *ny* when followed by *ě* or *i*.
[5] *Ň* is used quite frequently for *ň* in modern publications.
[6] Peculiar to Bohemian.

g, q, and *x* appear only in foreign words.

As in many of the other continental countries, the Latin alphabet has replaced the German in the Bohemian language.

Stress is always on the first syllable.

Vowels with the acute accent are sounded long.

Punctuation is according to the general rules of the English language.

Syllabication

Division occurs after a vowel, as *stra-ka, ba-vl-na*. In the second syllable of the latter it will be observed that *l* (as also is true of *r* and *v*) frequently has the characteristics of a vowel.

The consonants *šk, sk, št, st,* and *sd* must not be divided, and they form the beginning of a syllable.

Division also occurs between two vowels or two consonants.

When *l, r,* or *ř* occur before a vowel, they also take along the preceding consonant (with the exception of *n*), and also the indivisible consonants *sk, šk, st, št,* and *sd.*

Phonetics

Some words contain no vowels and the consonants *l* and *r* take the place of a vowel, though softer. They are pronounced as though there were a slight *e* before *l* or *r*: *vlk* (velk); *prst* (perst).

The following will be of interest and serve as a guide with similar words:

lehky (light) is pronounced lechky	bez práce is pronounced bes práce
nehty (nails) is pronounced nechty	*v* final is pronounced *f*
kde (where) is pronounced gde	*h* final is pronounced *ch*
kdo (who) is pronounced gdo	*z* final is pronounced *s*
v Praze is pronounced f Praze	*ž* final is pronounced *š*

ď final is pronounced *ť*

Since the hard *i* cannot follow a hard consonant, the latter must be softened:

h changes to *z*	druh (comrade)	druzi (comrades)
ch changes to *š*	hoch (boy)	hoši (boys)
k changes to *c*	voják (soldier)	vojáci (soldiers)
r changes to *ř*	bratr (brother)	bratři (brothers)

Accent
Stress is always on the first syllable, but in the case of polysyllabic words a secondary stress falls on the odd syllables (on the third or fifth). Stress is not indicated by diacritical marks.

Adjectives
The adjectives agree with the noun in gender, number and case. The following illustrates that agreement for the nominative case of the masculine and feminine forms:

Prepositional prefixes
pod movement underneath: podepsati (to sign a document).
pro action carried through: proniknouti (to pierce).
pře carrying over or across: přeskočiti (to leap over); also a repetition: přešiti (to sew over).
před before: předplatiti (to pay in advance).
při motion towards: přiblížiti (to approach).
roz expansion or separation: rozbiti (to break); also intensity of action: rozpáliti (to heat).
s, se a gathering together: spřateliti (to make friends); also descendent: shořeti (to burn down).
sou union: souhlasiti (to agree).
u ability: unésti (able to carry); also thoroughness: umořiti (to wear until death).
v, ve inward motion: vzbuditi (to wake).
vy outward motion: vyhoditi (throw out); also upward motion: vyrůsti (grow up).
vz upward motion: vzlétnouti (to fly up).
z thoroughness in the verb: zyhnouti (to perish).
za going beyond: zablouditi (to go astray).

	Singular		Plural	
Masculine:				
Animate	velký voják	big soldier	velcí vojáci	big soldiers
Inanimate	nový kabát	new coat	nové kabáty	new coats
Feminine	dobrá škola	good school	dobré školy	good schools

The endings are as follows: Nominative singular, masculine, -ý, and feminine, -á; nominative plural of masculine animate, -í, and for the inanimate, -é; the latter is also the ending for the nominative plural, feminine.

Comparison
There are three forms in the comparison of objects: *silný* (strong); *silnější* (stronger); *nejsilnější* (strongest). Normally, the comparative is formed by suffixing -*ější* to the positive, and, for the superlative, prefixing *nej-* (most) to the comparative.

Pronouns
Personal pronouns are unnecessary to indicate person and number since the verbal endings indicate these very clearly. The following are used only in emphatic statements.

Ja	I	my	we
ty	thou (you)	vy	you
on	he	oni	they
ona	she	ony	they
ono	it	ona	they

Possessive pronouns are declined as follows:

	Masculine		Feminine	Neuter
Singular	můj	my, mine	mé, moje	má, moje
	tvůj	thy, thine	tvé, tvoje	tvá, tvoje
Plural	mojí	(animate)	—	—
	mé, moje	(inanimate)	má, moje	mé, moje
	tvoji	(animate)	tvá, tvoje	tvé, tvoji
	tvé, tvoje	(inanimate)	—	—
Singular	náš	our, ours	naše	naše
	všá	your, yours	vaše	vaše
Plural	naši		naše	naše
	vaši		vaše	vaše

Gender

All nouns ending in *h, ch,* or *k* are masculine and those of living beings take *a* in the genetive, while those of not living beings take *u* (*vrah, raroh, drak, kmotr, bratr, soh, strach, mech, krok, kopr*).

All nouns ending in a consonant, which have *a* or *u* in the genitive, are masculine.

Nouns ending the nominative singular in *a* are feminine and take *y* in the genitive singular (*matka, žena, sestra,* etc.), but some masculine proper names are exceptions to this rule (*Franta, Hanka,* etc.).

Nouns ending in *o* are neuter (*slovo, olovo, proso, bahno, oko*), but exceptions are masculine proper names (*Otto, Matějko, Volko,* etc.).

Nouns ending in *st'* (*ast', est', ist' ost'*) are feminine, but the following are exceptions to this rule: *břest, chřest, křest, mest, šelest, chrást, plást, host, (Radhost, výhost), most, rost (rúst, zrúst, odrost, výrost,* etc.), *list, pist, prst, púst, šúst, masopust.*

Nouns ending in *e* (*ě*), with genitive ending in *ete* (*ěte*) or *ene* are neuter: *pachole, hádě.*

Nouns

Nouns of the first declension end with a consonant in the nominative singular, and *a* in the accusative, the latter being replaced by *y* in the plural: *syn* (son), *syna, syny.* The nominative plural ends in *i.*

The possessive case of this declension ends in *a* in the singular and *u* in the plural:

Nominative	pán	gentleman	páni	gentlemen
Objective	pána	the gentleman	pány	the gentlemen
Possessive	pána	of the gentleman	pánu	of the gentlemen

All nouns of this declension are masculine, being divided into two classes, the first denoting animate and the second inanimate things.

The indirect object is indicated by the dative case, answering the question of "to whom?"; *Dám knihu hochovi* (I gave a book to the boy). The singular and plural forms are as follows:

Masculine animate	pánu *or* pánovi	pánům
Masculine inanimate	stromu	stromům
Feminine	škole	školám

The vocative case is used in direct address: *Pane! dej mi chleb* (Sir, give me bread).

The past tense in the first two persons is formed from the participle and the auxiliary *býti,* while the third person is the participle alone:

byl jsem	I was (masculine)	bylo jsem	I was (feminine)
byli jsme	we were	byly jsme	we were
myl jsi	you were	byla jsi	you were
byli jste	you were	byly jste	you were
on byl	he was	ona byla	she was

The instrumental case expresses an instrument or the cause of an action: *piši pérem* (I write with a pen); it is used after a passive verb to denote the actor: *bylo to učiněno vojákem* (it was done by the soldier); it is used to express passage through: *jdu lesem* (I will walk through the forest); and, finally, it is used with the preposition *s* to denote association: *mluvim s matkou* (I talk with mother).

The following are the case endings of *holub* (pigeon), an animate masculine noun:

	Singular	Plural
Nominative	holub	holub*i*
Objective	-a	-y
Possessive	-a	-ů, -ův
Dative	-u, -ovi	-ům
Locative	-u, -ovi	-ech, -ích
Instrumental	-em	-y
Vocative	-e	-i!

Case endings of *strom* (tree), inanimate masculine, are as follows:

Nominative	strom	strom*y*
Objective	strom	strom*y*
Possessive	-u	-ů, ův
Dative	-u	-ům
Locative	-ě, -u	-ech, -ich
Instrumental	-em	-y
Vocative	-e!	-y!

Case endings of *ryba* (fish), feminine, are as follows:

Nominative	ryba	ryby
Objective	-u	ryby
Possessive	-y	ryb
Dative	-ě	-ám
Locative	-ě	-ách
Instrumental	-ou	-ami
Vocative	-o!	-y!

Case endings for *město* (city), neuter noun ending in *o*, are:

Nominative	město	města
Objective	město	města
Possessive	-a	měst
Dative	-u	-ům
Locative	-ě, -u	-tch
Instrumental	-em	-y
Vocative	-o!	-a!

Verb

The negative si formed by adding -*ne* to the verb: *znam* (I know); *neznam* (I don't know). The single exception is *jest* (je), is; *neni*, is not.

There is no progressive form of the verb, and thus *slyšim* (I hear), may also be used for "I am hearing",

Almost all verbs have the suffix -*ti* in the infinitive, while the masculine participle is often formed by using -*l* instead of -*ti*. The past participle adds -*i* in the masculine plural, -*a* in the feminine singular, and *y* in the feminine plural: *žák mluvil* (the pupil spoke); *žáci mluvili* (the pupils spoke); *sestra mluvil* (the sister spoke); *sestry mluvily* (the sisters spoke).

IRREGULAR VERBS

First person		Infinitive		Past participle	
jsem	I am	býti	to be	byl	was
mám	I have	míti	to have	měl	had
jdu	I go	jíti	to go	šel	gone, went
čtu	I read	čísti	to read	četl	read
vidím	I see	viděti	to see	viděl	seen, saw
slyšim	I hear	slyšeti	to hear	slyšel	heard

The last two are not irregular, but belong to a special class.

Questions are formed by transposing the pronoun and verb, but, since the former is usually omitted, the sign of interrogation indicates the question: *čtete knihu?* (do you read a book?) When the subject is a noun, the verb precedes the noun in a question, except when an adverb *proč?* (why?), *kdy?* (when?), *kde? kam?* (where?), is used to introduce the question.

The present indicative of *slyšeti* (to hear), is as follows:

slyším	I hear	slyšíme	we hear
slyšíš	you hear	slyšíte	you hear
slyší .	he hears	slyší	they hear

The future tense of *budou* (to be) is as follows:

budu	I shall be	budeme	we shall be
budeš	you will be	budete	you shall be
on, ona, ono	he, she, it	oni, ony, ona	they will be
bude	will be	budou	

Conjugation of verbs having *ě* or *e* as a root vowel differ from that of *slyšeti* only in the third person plural: *uměji* (they know), but *slyši* (they hear).

COMPOUND VERBS

Many verbs are formed by the addition of prefixes, which yield a great variety of meanings. These verbs denote an action which was or will be completed. Thus they have no present tense, but the present form is that of the future.

jiti	to go	{ jdu	I go
přijíti	to come (go to)	{ půjdu	I shall come
přišel jsem	I have come	přijdu	I shall come
přinésti	to bring	—	
najíti	to find	odjíti	to leave (go away)
		udělati	to make and finish

There may be two or three prefixes for the purpose of further modification:

sledovati	to follow	*ná*sledovati	to follow closely
*pro/ná*sledovati	to pursue	*na/pro/ná*sledovati	to pursue when one is weary of it

Verbs are divided into four groups, with subdivisions, according to the endings of the present indicative. Those whose present indicative or participle is formed by root changes are classed as irregular: *jiti* (to go); *jdu* (I go); *šel jsem* (I went).

I. (a) *nés-ti*, to carry, to bear.   (b) *vinou-ti*, to wind.
     Infinitive, *nésti*.   Infinitive, *vinouti*.
     Imperative, *nes!*   Imperative, *vin!*

	Singular	Plural	Singular	Plural
Present indicative	nesu	neseme	vinu	vineme
	neseš	nesete	vineš	vinete
	nese	nesou	vine	vinou
Past participle	nesl	nesli	vinul	vinuli
	nesla	nesly	vinula	vinuly
	neslo	nesla	vinulo	vinula
Passive participle	nesen	nesni	vinut	
	nesna	nesny		
	nesno	nesna		

(c) *tisknou-ti*, to print, to press.   (d) *věs-ti*, to lead
     Infinitive, *tisknouti*
               { *tiskni!*   Infinitive, *věsti*.
     Imperative { *tiskněme!*
               { *tiskněte!*   Imperative, *veď!*

	Singular	Plural	Singular	Plural
Present indicative	tisknu	tiskneme	vedu	vedeme
	tiskneš	tisknete	vedeš	vedete
	tiskne	tisknou	vede	vedou
Past participle	tiskl (tisknul)	tiskli	vedl	vedli
	tiskla	tiskly	vedlo	vedly
	tisklo	tiskla	veden	vedla
Passive participle	tištěn (tisknut)		vedla	

NOTE.—Forms in parentheses are new.

II. *vola-ti*, to call.   III. (a) *Prosi-ti*, to ask for, to beg.
     Infinitive, *volati*.   Infinitive, *prositi*.
     Imperative, *volej!*   Imperative, *pros!*

	Singular	Plural	Singular	Plural
Present indicative	volám	voláme	prosím	prosíme
	voláš	voláte	prosíš	prosíte
	volá	volají	prosí	prosí
Past participle	volal	voláli	prosil	prosili
	volála	volály	prosila	prosily
	volálo	volála	prosilo	prosila
Passive participle	volán	—	prošen	—

(b) *drže-ti*, to hold.
Infinitive, *drželi*.
Imperative, *drž!*

(c) *umě-ti*, to know.
Infinitive, *uměti*.
Imperative, *uměj!*

	Singular	Plural	Singular	Plural
Present indicative	držím	držíme	umím	umíme
	držíš	držíte	umíš	umíte
	drží	drží	umí	umějí
Past participle	držel	drželi	uměl	uměli
	držela	držely	uměla	umělly
	drželo	držela	umělo	umělla
Passive participle	držen	—	umĕn	—

IV. (a) *milova-ti*, to love.
Infinitive, *milovati*.
Imperative, *miluj!*

(b) *bi-ti*, to strike, to hit.
Infinitive, *biti*.
Imperative, *bij!*

	Singular	Plural	Singular	Plural
Present indicative	miluji	milujeme	biji	bijeme
	miluješ	milujete	bijes	bijete
	miluje	milují	bije	bijí
Past participle	miloval	milovaly	bil	bili
	milovala	milovaly	bila	bily
	vilovalo	milovala	bilo	bila
Passive participle	milován	—	bit	—

Cardinal numbers

jeden } jedna } jedno }	one	osm	eight
		devět	nine
		deset	ten
dva } dvě }	two	jedenáct	eleven
		dvanáct	twelve
tři	three	třináct	thirteen
čtyři	four	dvacet	twenty
pět	five	dvadcet jeden	twenty-one
šest	six	stov	hundred
sed(u)m	seven	tisíc	thousand

Ordinal numbers

prvý } první }	first	devátý	ninth
		desátý	tenth
druhý	second	jedenáctý	eleventh
třetí	third	dvanáctý	twelfth
čtvrtý	fourth	třináctý	thirteenth
pátý	fifth	dvacátý	twentieth
šestý	sixth	stý	hundredth
sedmý	seventh	tisící	thousandth
osmý	eighth		

Months

leden (led.)	January	červenec (červec.)	July
únor (ún.)	February	srpen (srp.)	August
březen (břez.)	March	září	September
duben (dub.)	April	říjen (říj.)	October
květen } máj } (květ.)	May	listopad (list.)	November
		prosinec (pros.)	December
červen (červ.)	June		

Days

neděle	Sunday	čtvrtek	Thursday
pondělí	Monday	pátek	Friday
úterý	Tuesday	sobota	Saturday
středa	Wednesday		

Seasons

jaro, *n.* ⟩ vesna, *f.* ⟩	spring	podzim ⟩ jeseň ⟩	autumn
leto, balvan, ⟩ hlavní, trám ⟩	summer	zima	winter

Time

hodina	hour	měsíc	month
den	day	rok	year
týden	week		

BULGARIAN

А	а	*a* in father	С	с	*s*	
Б	б	*b*	Т	т	*t*	
В	в	*v*	У	у	*oo* in book	
Г	г	*g* in good	Ф	ф	*f*	
Д	д	*d*	Х	х	*ch* in Scotch loch	
Е	е	*e* in very	Ц	ц	*ts* in hoots	
Ж	ж	*s* in pleasure	Ч	ч	*ch* in church	
З	з	*z*	Ш	ш	*sh* in shawl	
И	и	*i* in ink	Щ	щ	*sht* or *st* in German Stein	
Й	й	*y* in boy	Ъ	ъ }	*u* as in but; at the end	
К	к	*k*	Ь	ь }	of a word mute.[1]	
Л	л	*l*	Ѣ	ѣ	*ìe* or *ye*[2]	
М	м	*m*	Ю	ю	*u* in union	
Н	н	*n*	Я	я	*ya* in yard	
О	о	*o* in not	—	ж[3]	*u* in but	
П	п	*p*	—	іж[4]	*iu*	
Р	р	*r*				

[1] When ъ is mute it is for the purpose of rendering the preceding consonant hard; when ь is mute, it renders the preceding consonant soft.
[2] In an accented syllable often pronounced like the я (ya).
[3] This letter originally occurred in Old Slavonic and had a nasal pronunciation. Now, however, nasals are found only in some of the Bulgarian dialects.
[4] This letter seems to be going out of use, being sometimes supplanted by я, pronounced very short.

Bulgarian, which belongs to the south-eastern Slavic language group, is spoken by people of Ugo-Finnish origin who migrated from northern Russia and conquered the Slavic tribes whom they found in what is now known as Bulgaria, adopting their language as well. The principal characteristic of this language is the use of the definite article at the end of the nouns: *car-at*, *zemja-ta*, *nebe-to*.

This language has many similarities to other Slavonic languages, especially in syntax and grammatical structure. A thorough knowledge of it will thus enable the student to translate the others quite accurately. The first four lines of the Lord's Prayer, given below, will illustrate this similarity:

Bulgarian.—Tatko ny kojto si v nebe-to, neka da se svjati ime-to tvoje, da dojde carstvo-to tvoje; da bude volja-ta tvoja kakto na nebe-to, taka i na zemja-ta.

Russian.—Otěc naš kotorj jesi na něbesach; da svjatiťsja imja tvojo, da pri-d'ot cárstvo tvojo, da buděť volja tvoja kak na něbesach i na zemli.

Ukrainian.—Otče naš ščo na nebi! Nechaj svjatitsja imja tvoje. Nechaj priide cartsvo tvoje. Nechaj bude volja tvoja jak na nebi, tak i na zemlj.

Polish.—Ojcze nasz, który jest w niebie, święć się imię twoje, przyjdź króle-stwo twoje, bądź wola twoja jako w niebie tak i na ziemi.

Slovenian.—Oče naš, ki si v nebesih, posvečeno bodi ime tvoje. Pridi kraljev-stvo tvoje. Zgodi se volja tvoja, kakor v nebesih, tako na zemlji.

Serbo-Croatian.—Oče naš koji' je si na nebesima, da se sveti ime tvoje; da dodje carstvo tvoja, da bude volja tvoja i na zemlji kao na nebu.

Bohemian.—Otče náš, kterýž jsi v nebesich, posvěť se jméno tvé. Přijd' krá-lovství tvé; bud' vůle tvá, jako v nebi tak i na zemi.

Punctuation is very similar to that in the English language.
Initial capital letters are used for all proper names, including proper adjectives; also names of months and days of the week.

Syllabication

Division of words is the same as in the Russian (pp. 225, 231)

Cardinal numbers

единъ, една, едно	one	деветь	nine
два, двѣ	two	десеть	ten
три	three	единайсеть	eleven
чет(е)ри	four	дванайсеть	twelve
петь	five	тринайсеть	thirteen
шесть	six	двайесеть	twenty
седемь	seven	сто	hundred
осемь	eight	хиляда	thousand

Ordinal numbers

първий, първа, първо	first	седмий	seventh
		осмий	eighth
вторий, втора, второ	second	деветий	ninth
		десетий	tenth
третий, трета, трето	third	единайсетий	eleventh
		дванайсетий	twelfth
		тринайсетий	thirteenth
		двайсетий	twentieth
четвъртий[1]	fourth	стотий, стотний	hundredth
петий	fifth	хилядний	thousandth
шестий	sixth		

Months

Януари	January	Юли	July
Февруари	February	Августъ	August
Мартъ	March	Септември	September
Априлъ	April	Октомври	October
Май	May	Ноември	November
Юни	June	Декември	December

Days

Недѣля	Sunday	Четвъртъкъ	Thursday
Понедѣлникъ	Monday	Петъкъ	Friday
Вторникъ	Tuesday	Сжбота	Saturday
Срѣда	Wednesday		

Seasons

пролѣть	spring	есень	autumn
лѣто	summer	зима	winter

Time

часъ, саатъ	hour	мѣсецъ	month
день	day	година	year
седмица, недѣля	week		

Articles to be disregarded in filing

тъ, та, то; *pl.* тѣ
единъ, една, едно

---

[1] Beginning with this number only the masculine forms of the ordinals are given. The feminine and neuter may be formed, as in the preceding three cases, by changing ий to a and o, respectively.

BURMESE

Character	Transliteration	Character	Transliteration	Character	Transliteration
အ	*a*	ဂ	*ga*	ဒ	*da*
အာ	*â*	ဃ	*gha*	ဓ	*dhà*
ဣ	*i*	င	*nga*	န	*na*
ဤ	*ī*	စ	*ca*	ပ	*pa*
ဥ, ဥ	*u*	ဆ	*ch'a*	ဖ	*pha*
ဦ	*ŭ*	ဇ	*ja*	ဗ	*ba*
ဧ	*ē*	ဈ	*jha*	ဘ	*bha*
အဲ	*ă*	ည	*ña*	မ	*ma*
ဩ	*o*	ဋ	*ṭa*	ယ	*ya*
ဩော		ဌ	*ṭha*	ရ ၇	*ra*
ဩော်	*au*	ဍ	*ḍa*	လ	*la*
ံ	*an*	ဎ	*ḍha*	ဝ	*wa*
က	*ka*	ဏ	*ṇa*	သ	*sa*
ခ	*kha*	တ	*ta*	ဟ	*ha*
		ထ	*tha*	အ	*a*
				ဠ	*ḷa*

NOTE.—Continental sounds are used in transliteration.

Vowel signs

ā	i	ī	u	ū	e	ă	o	au

This alphabet is borrowed from the old rock-cut Pali of India, and thus, together with a number of its words, is of Indian origin.

The language is monosyllabic and agglutinative, and is more nearly like the Chinese than the Indian. A single syllable may have a great many meanings, depending on the tone used or the manner in which the syllable is stressed. In writing, these syllables are differentiated by accents (points) which are placed under or after the characters. A point under the character indicates the soft or acute accent, while two, one above the other, after the character indicate the grave accent.

With English, Burmese is the official language of Burma, although Hindostani is widely spoken.

Numerals

၁	1	၅	5	၉	9
၂	2	၆	6	၀	0
၃	3	၇	7		
၄	4	၈	8		

CATALONIAN

Character	Tone value
a	*a* in Spanish; *a* in French Paris; *a* in French âme; *e* in German Gabe
b	*b, p*
c	*k; kk* after accent; *g* before voiced tone; mute in *nc; s* before *e*
ç	*s* before *a, o, u; z,* voiced, before *m*
ch	*k;* occurs only in chor, choral, chorista
d	*d* as initial and before or after consonants; *th* between vowels and voiced consonants; *t* before unvoiced tone and as final; *g* in combination *dj;* mute after *n* and between *r* and *s*
e	*e,* open, in French mère; *e,* closed, in French é; as in German Gabe
f	*f*
g	*g,* hard, as initial and before *a, o, u,* and a consonant in the initial syllable; *gg* in the combination *gl,* but only when it occurs after the stressed syllable; *k,* when before final mute *s; g,* medium soft, between a vowel and mute consonant; *g,* soft, when initial before *e* or *i; gg,* soft, in the combination *tg* or *ig; ch* in the combination (final) *ig;* French *j* when initial before *e* or *i; ng* as in ring before *n*
gu	*g,* hard, before *e* or *i; g,* medium soft, after a vowel and before *e* or *i; gu* before *a; gu,* medium soft, after a vowel and before *a*
gü	*gw* in Gwendolyn, before *e* or *i*
h	Always mute
i	*e* in we
j	*j* in Jew when initial; otherwise French *j*
k	*k;* occurs only in foreign words
l	*l,* when initial and elsewhere when between vowels; *l* in milk when at close of a word or syllable; *lj* in combination *tl*
l.l	*ll,* generally pronounced as a single *l*
ll	*ll,* like *ll* in Spanish gallo
m	*m*
n	*n; ng* before *c* or *g;* sometimes *nj* before *ll* or *x; m* before a labial
ny	*ñ,* as in Spanish
o	*o,* open, as in French mort; *o,* closed, as in German so; *u* in unstressed syllables
p	*p,* before and between consonants; like Italian *p* before vowels; *pp* in the combination *ple,* when after the stress; *b* when final and the following word begins with a voiced tone; mute after *m*
qu	*k,* before *e* or *i; qu* as in English before *a* or *o*
qü	*qw,* same sound as in question
r	*r,* weak lingual between and after vowels and after all consonants, except *l, m, n;* rolled lingual when final, after *l, m, n,* or when doubled; mute when final in *-er, -ar, -or,* or in carnselada
s	*s,* voiceless, sharp, when initial of word or syllable after a consonant, as well as before a mute consonant or at the end of a word, and in *ss; z,* between vowels, before vowels and *h,* and after *n;* mute in the combination *igs*
t	*t,* before and between consonants; Spanish *t* before a vowel; *d,* before a voiced sound; *g,* in the combinations *tg, tj; ce, ci* in *tx;* mute when final after *n, l;* before *ll;* in the verbal ending *-itzar=iza;* before *m,* and between *r* or *s*

CATALONIAN—Continued

Char-acter	Tone value
u	*u*, closed, as in German Uhr; mute when the preceding word ends in a vowel; *ü*, which occurs in the combinations *gü* or *qü* before *e*, has the *gw* or *qw* sound
v	*b*, when initial and after a consonant; *v*, bilabial between vowels
x	*ks*, in the prefix *ex-* before a mute consonant; *gz* between vowels; *š, ts* sound, when initial, when initial after a consonant, when final, and in the combinations *ix; ce, ci* (Italian) in combination *tx; z* in combination *ix* between vowels in syntactic combinations; *ǧǧ* in combination *tx* between vowels, as also before voiced consonants in syntactic combinations
z	*s* in German Rose, when initial or toward end of word; unvoiced, sharp *s* after *t*

NOTE.—*y* occurs only in the combination *ny*.

Catalonian is the language of 4,500,000 people living in a long and rather broad district extending along the eastern border of Spain, the island of Sardinia, and in the French Département des Pyrénées Orientales. There is an extremely wide divergence in the dialects spoken in the different districts, but Central Catalonian, which is used in Barcelona, is the literary language of the present. Catalonian is one of the so-called Romance languages.

Accents and signs

The grave and acute accents are used to indicate not only stress but also the quality of the vowel bearing the accent. The grave denotes the open and the acute the closed vowel. The *a* takes only the former, *i* and *u* only the latter.

The cedilla *ç* is used for the unvoiced *s* sound before *a, o,* or *u*.

The apostrophe indicates the elision of a vowel, as *l'home,* the man.

The hyphen is used to divide syllables, in compounding, and to connect the verb and the personal pronoun: *pa-re,* father; *compta-gotes,* drop counter; *vestir-se,* he dresses.

The dieresis is used on the *ï* to denote that it does not form a diphthong with the vowel preceding, and on the *ü* to show that the *u* is to be sounded in the combinations *güe, güi, qüe, qüi.*

The stress is either on the last syllable, or, most often, on the penult or the antepenult. In view of the uncertainty of locating the proper stress, it is suggested that a sign be used only in case the stress is on the antepenultimate or on the last syllable, and thus all words not bearing a written accent would be stressed on the penult.

Syllabication

A single consonant goes with the following syllable: *ne-bo-da,* niece; the same is true of the semiconsonants *i* and *u* when between vowels: *es-gla-iar,* frighten; *pe-ua-da,* footprint; also the second of a double consonant: *im-mò-bil,* immovable. The combinations *bl, br, cl, cr, dr, fl, gl, gr, gu, ll, ny, pl, pr, qu,* and *tr* also go with the following syllable. The first of a double consonant does not go over, and the prefixes *des, en,* and *trans* always remain intact.

The articles

	Singular	Plural
Definite:		
Masculine	el, l'	els
Feminine	la, l'	les
Indefinite:		
Masculine	un	uns
Feminine	una	unes
Personal:		
Masculine	en	
Feminine	na, n'	

Cardinal numbers

un, u, una	one	dèu	ten
dos, dugues (f)	two	onze	eleven
tres	three	dotze	twelve
quatre	four	tretze	thirteen
cinc	five	vint	twenty
sis	six	vintiun, vintiú	twenty-one
set	seven	cent, -es (f)	hundred
vuit	eight	doscent, -centes (f)	two hundred
nou	nine	mil	thousand

Ordinal numbers

primer	first	desè, dècim	tenth
segón	second	onzè	eleventh
terç, tercer	third	dotzè	twelfth
quart	fourth	tretzè	thirteenth
cinquè, quint	fifth	vintè	twentieth
sisè, sext	sixth	ventiunè	twenty-first
setè, sèptim	seventh	centè	hundredth
vuitè, octau	eighth	milè, milèsim	thousandth
novè	ninth		

The ordinals also have a feminine which is formed as follows: Those ending in a consonant take an *a* (primera), while *na* is added to those ending in *è*, and the accent is dropped.

Months

janer, jener	January	juliol	July
febrer	February	agost	August
març	March	setembre	September
abril	April	octubre	October
matj	May	novembre	November
juny	June	desembre	December

Days

diumenge	Sunday	dijous	Thursday
dilluns	Monday	divendres	Friday
dimars	Tuesday	dissabte	Saturday
dimecrez	Wednesday		

Seasons

primovera	spring	tardor	autumn
estiu	summer	ivern, hivern	winter

Time

hora	hour	mes	month
dia	day	any	year
setmana	week	segle	century

CHINESE

No.	Character	Sound	Definition	No.	Character	Sound	Definition
1†	一	i¹	one	30†	口	k'ou³	a mouth
2	丨	kun³	a downstroke	31	口	wei²	an enclosure
3	丶	chu³	a dot	32†	土	t'u²	earth
4	丿	p'ieh³	a left stroke	33†	士	shih⁴	a scholar
5	乙	i⁴	a curve	34	夂	chih⁴	a step
6	亅	chüeh²	a crook	35	夊	ts'ui¹	to walk slowly
7†	二	êrh⁴	two	36	夕	hsi¹	evening
8	亠	t'ou²	a cover	37†	大	ta⁴	great
9a†	人	} jên²	a man	38†	女	nü³	a woman
b*	亻			39†	子	tzŭ³	a son
10	儿	jên²	a man's legs	40*	宀	mien²	a roof
11†	入	ju⁴	enter	41†	寸	ts'un⁴	an inch
12†	八	pa¹	eight	42†	小	hsiao³	small
13*	冂	chiung³	a limit	43	尢	wang¹	lame
14*	冖	mi⁴	to cover	44†	尸	shih¹	a corpse
15*	冫	ping¹	ice	45	屮	ch'ê⁴	a sprout
16†	几	chi¹	a stand	46†	山	shan¹	a hill
17*	凵	k'an³	receptacle	47a†	巛	} ch'uan¹	a stream
18a†	刀	} tao¹	a knife	b*	川		
b*	刂			48†	工	kung¹	work
19†	力	li⁴	strength	49†	己	chi³	self
20*	勹	pao¹	to wrap	50†	巾	chin¹	a napkin
21*	匕	pi³	a spoon	51†	干	kan¹	a shield
22	匚	fang ¹	a basket	52	幺	yao¹	small
23	匸	hsi³	a box	53†	广	yen³	a shelter
24†	十	shih²	ten	54	廴	yin³	to move on
25†	卜	pu³	to divine	55*	廾	kung³	folded hands
26	卩	chieh²	a seal; knot	56	弋	i⁴	a dart
27	厂	han⁴	a cliff	57†	弓	kung¹	a bow
28*	厶	szŭ¹	private	58	彐	ch'i⁴	pointed
29†	又	yu⁴	and also	59	彡	shan¹	plumage
				60*	彳	ch'ih⁴	a left step

CHINESE—Continued

No.	Character	Sound	Definition	No.	Character	Sound	Definition
61a† b* c*	心 忄 小	hsin¹	the heart	86a† b*	火 灬	huo³	fire
62†	戈	ko¹	a spear	87a† b*	爪 爫	chao³	claws
63†	戶	hu⁴	the family	88†	父	fu⁴	father
64a† b*	手 扌	shou³	a hand	89	爻	yao²	intertwine
				90*	爿	ch'iang²	a bed
65†	支	chih¹	a branch	91†	片	p'ien⁴	a strip
66a b*	攴 攵	p'u¹	to rap	92†	牙	ya²	a tooth
				93a† b	牛 牜	niu²	an ox
67†	文	wên²	literature				
68†	斗	tou³	a peck	94a* b*	犬 犭	ch'üan³	a dog
69†	斤	chin¹	a catty				
70†	方	fang¹	square	95	玄	yüan²	dark
71	无	wu²	without	96a* b*	玉 王	yü⁴	jade
72†	日	jih⁴	the sun				
73†	曰	yüeh¹	to speak	97	瓜	kua¹	a melon
74†	月	yüeh⁴	the moon	98†	瓦	wa³	a tile
75†	木	mu⁴	wood	99†	甘	kan¹	sweet
76†	欠	ch'ien⁴	to owe	100†	生	shêng¹	to beget
77†	止	chih³	to stop	101†	用	yung⁴	to use
78†	歹	tai³	bad	102†	田	t'ien²	a field
79	殳	shu¹	to kill; staff	103†	疋	p'i³	a roll of cloth
80†	毋	wu²	do not	104*	疒	ni⁴	disease
81†	比	pi³	to compare	105*	癶	po⁴	back to back
82†	毛	mao²	hair	106†	白	pai²	white
83†	氏	shih⁴	a clan	107†	皮	p'i²	skin
84	气	ch'i⁴	air				
85a† b*	水 氵	shui³	water				

CHINESE—Continued

No.	Character	Sound	Definition	No.	Character	Sound	Definition
108	皿	min³	a dish	128†	耳	êrh³	an ear
109†	目	mu⁴	an eye	129	聿	yü⁴	a pen
110	矛	mou²	a lance	130a†	肉	jou⁴	flesh
111†	矢	shih⁴	an arrow	b*	月		
112†	石	shih² ᵃ	a stone	131†	臣	ch'ên²	a statesman
113a†	示	shih⁴	to reveal	132†	自	tzu⁴	self
b*	礻			133†	至	chih⁴	to reach
114	禸	jou	a track	134†	臼	chiu⁴	a mortar
115†	禾	hê²	grain	135†	舌	shê²	the tongue
116a†	穴	hsüeh⁴	a cave	136	舛	ch'uan³	to oppose
b	穴			137†	舟	chou¹	a boat
117†	立	li⁴	to stand	138†	艮	kên⁴	a limit
118a†	竹	chu²	bamboo	139	色	sê⁴	color
b	竹			140a	艸	ts'ao³	grass
119†	米	mi³	rice	b*	艹		
120a	糸	mi⁴	raw silk	141*	虍	hu³	a tiger
b*	糹			142†	虫	ch'ung²	an insect
121	缶	fou³	earthenware	143	血	hsüeh⁴	blood
122a	网	wang³	a net	144†	行	hsing²	to go
b	四			145a†	衣	i¹	clothes
c	罒			b*	衤		
d	罓			146a	西	ya⁴	to cover; *hsi* (west) is often used for this radical.
123†	羊	yang²	a sheep	b	西		
124	羽	yü³	a wing	147†	見	chien⁴	to see
125†	老	lao³	old	148†	角	chiao³	horn; an angle
126†	而	êrh²	and; yet	149†	言	yen²	words
127	耒	lei³	a plow	150†	谷	ku³	a gully
				151†	豆	tou⁴	beans

ᵃ It takes the second tone when used as a verb.

CHINESE—Continued

No.	Character	Sound	Definition
152†	豕	shih^{4}	swine
153	豸	chai^{4}	a reptile
154†	貝	pei^{4}	a shell; valuable
155	赤	ch'ih^{4}	bare
156†	走	tsou^{3}	to walk
157a†	足	tsu^{2}	the foot; enough
b	𧾷		
158†	身	shên^{1}	the body
159†	車	ch'ê^{1}	a cart
160†	辛	hsin^{1}	pungent
161†	辰	ch'ên^{2}	time
162a	辵	cho^{1}	to go
b*	辶		
163a	邑	i^{4}	a city
b*	阝		
164†	酉	yu^{3}	wine; harvest
165	釆	pien^{4}	to separate
166†	里	li^{3}	a Chinese mile
167†	金	chin^{1}	metal; gold
168†	長	ch'ang^{2}	long
169†	門	mên^{2}	a door; gate
170a	阜	fou^{4}	a mound
b*	阝		
171	隶	tai^{4}	to reach to
172*	隹	chui^{1}	birds
173a†	雨	yü^{3}	rain
b	⻗		

No.	Character	Sound	Definition
174†	青	ch'ing^{1}	green; azure
175†	非	fei^{1}	no
176†	面	mien^{4}	the face
177†	革	kê^{2}	hide; to strip
178*	韋	wei^{2}	dressed leather
179	韭	chiu^{3}	leeks
180†	音	yin^{1}	sound
181†	頁	yeh^{4}	a page
182†	風	fêng^{1}	the wind
183	飛	fei^{1}	to fly
184†	食	shih^{2}	to eat
185†	首	shou^{3}	the head; first
186†	香	hsiang^{1}	incense
187†	馬	ma^{3}	a horse
188†	骨	ku^{3}	a bone
189†	高	kao^{1}	high
190	髟	piao^{1}	bushy hair
191	鬥	tou^{4}	to fight
192	鬯	ch'ang^{1}	herbs
193	鬲	li^{4}	a cauldron
194†	鬼	kuei^{3}	a demon
195†	魚	yü^{2}	a fish
196†	鳥	niao^{3}	a bird
197*	鹵	lu^{3}	rock salt
198	鹿	lu^{4}	a deer
199	麥	mai^{4}	wheat
200†	麻	ma^{2}	hemp
201†	黃	huang^{2}	yellow
202	黍	shu^{3}	millet

CHINESE—Continued

No.	Character	Sound	Definition	No.	Character	Sound	Definition
203†	黑	hei¹	black	209	鼻	pi²	the nose
204	黹	chih³	embroidery	210†	齊	ch'i²	uniform; regular
205*	黽	min³	a frog	211	齒	ch'ih ³	front teeth
206	鼎	ting³	a tripod	212†	龍	lung²	a dragon
207	鼓	ku³	a drum	213	龜	kuei¹	a tortoise
208	鼠	shu³	a rat	214	龠	yüeh⁴	a flute

* Indicates the more important of the radicals.
† Indicates complete characters as well as radicals.

NOTE.—The superior figures in the "sound column" indicate the number of the tone used.

A large percentage of the Chinese characters are a combination of two parts, the radical and the phonetic. The radical is a key indicating the group to which a given character belongs. This is the most important function of the radical. In many cases, however, it gives a hint as to the meaning of the character. At present there are 214 radicals, which, for convenience, are grouped according to the number of strokes they contain, i.e., the number of lines required to write them. Not all of the 214 radicals represent, in and by themselves, complete words, many serving only as mere roots from which full-meaning characters are constructed. The radical may be written at the top, bottom, left, or right of the character of which it is a component part, but its usual position is at the left. Many radicals change their form when written as parts of other characters. (See table.)

Romanization

Among English-speaking peoples, Sir Thomas Wade's system of writing the sounds for Chinese characters has been adopted as standard. The romanized sounds for all the characters number about 400 and are derived from combinations of 27 "initials" and 40 "finals." In some "sound groups" as many as 26 characters, all written differently with different meanings, have the same romanized spelling. The initials are: *a, ch, ch', ê, f, h, hs, i, j, k, k', l, m, n, o, p, p', s, sh, t, t', ts, ts', tz, tz', w,* and *y.* The finals are: *a, ai, an, ang, ao, ê, eh, ei, ên, êng, i, ia, iang, iao, ieh, ien, ih, in, ing, iu, iung, n, ng, o, ou, rh, u, ua, uai, uan, uang, ui, un, ung. uo. ŭ, ü, üan, üeh, ün.*

Tone

The tones are regular vocal modulations which result in different inflections of the same sound, so that a Chinese sentence spoken slowly with the tones clearly brought out has a sing-song effect on the foreign ear. The tone is as essential to the word as the sound itself, and, like the latter, it is not fixed, but is in a constant state of evolution, as illustrated in the differences of intonation in the various dialects spoken in different parts of China. Four tones—the even upper, even lower, rising, and falling—have been distinguished, and in the Cantonese dialect each of these is again divided into an upper and a lower series and a ninth tone has also been added. In speaking, it is not necessary to give each word its full tonic force, since quite a number of words, such as the enclitics, have no intonation whatever, while in others the degree of emphasis depends on the tone itself as also, at times, on the position of the word in the sentence.

Digits

	Transliteration	Common form	Commercial form [1]	Special form [2]
1	i	一	丨	弌 or 壹
2	erh	二	丨丨	貳 or 弍
3	san	三	丨丨丨	叁 or 弎
4	szu	四	ㄨ	肆
5	wu	五	ㄆ	伍
6	liu	六	亠	陸
7	chi	七	二	柒
8	pa	八	三	捌
9	chiu	九	夊	玖
0	ling	零	〇	

[1] These are supposed to be of Graeco-Bactrian origin but are known by the Chinese as Soochow or business characters. When 1, 2, and 3 come together, they are written alternately vertically and horizontally.

[2] These are used on drafts, pawn tickets, etc., as being less liable to fraudulent alteration.

Fractions

	Character and sound	Contracted form
One tenth	錢 ch'ien[2]	朩 or 才
One hundredth	分 fên[1]	丨 or 卜
One thousandth	釐 li[2]	厘 or 兀
One ten-thousandth	毫 hao[2]	毛
One hundred-thousandth	絲 ssŭ[1]	糸
One millionth	忽 hu[1*]	
One ten-millionth	微 wei[2]	
One hundred-millionth	纖 hsien[1]	僉
One billionth	沙 sha[1]	
One ten-billionth	塵 ch'ên[2]	

Cardinal numbers

	Characters and sound	Remarks
One	一 i[4]	
Ten	十 shih[2]	Lengthened form 拾
Hundred	百 pai[3]	Lengthened form 佰
Thousand	千 ch'ien[1]	Lengthened form 仟
Ten thousand	萬 wan[4]	Contracted form 万
Hundred thousand	億 yi[4]	
Million	兆 chao[4]	
Ten million	經 or 京 ching[1]	
Hundred million	垓 or 姟 kai[1]	} 垓 and 秭 sometimes change places.
Billion	補 pu[3] or 秭 tzŭ[2]	
Ten billion	壤 jang[3]	
Hundred billion	溝 kou[1]	Also written 冓
Trillion	澗 chien[4]	
Ten trillion	正 chêng[4]	
Hundred trillion	載 tsai[4]	

Ordinal numbers

The cardinals are used but preceded by the character *ti*.

First	ti[4]-i[1]	第一	Seventh	ti[4]-ch'i[1]	第七
Second	ti[4]-êrh[4]	第二	Eighth	ti[4]-pa[1]	第八
Third	ti[4]-san[1]	第三	Ninth	ti[4]-chiu[3]	第九
Fourth	ti[4]-ssŭ[4]	第四	Tenth	ti[4]-shih[2]	第十
Fifth	ti[4]-wu[3]	第五	Eleventh	ti[4]-shih[2]-i[1]	第十一
Sixth	ti[4]-liu[4]	第六	Twelfth	ti[4]-shih[2]-êrh[4]	第十二

Dates

In China two methods are used to record a date; first, the method of the cycle; the year 1864, for example, is called the *chia tzŭ* year. This system is unsatisfactory; the combination *chia tzŭ* occurs every 60 years, and so an indication is usually given pointing to the particular cycle, e.g., *T'ung Chih chia tzŭ* year.

T'ung Chih is the reign-title or *nien-hao* of the Manchu emperor who ascended the throne in 1862. The *chia tzŭ* year of his reign was 1864. The other method is by the reign-title or *nien-hao* of the emperor, together with a number which indicates the year of his reign: *T'ung Chih* 3d year is equivalent to our 1864. The year 1934 is recorded as the 23d year of the Republic of China: *Chung hua min kuo erh shih san nien.*

Days

The days of the week are indicated by the use of the term for Sunday, followed by a figure. For example, Monday is *hsing-ch'i-i*, first day of the week; Thursday is *hsing-ch'i-ssŭ*, the fourth day of the week, etc. Two terms are in general use, *hsing-ch'i* and *li³-pai⁴*, which, standing alone, also mean week.

Sunday	li³-pai⁴-jih⁴	禮拜日	Thursday	li³-pai⁴-ssŭ⁴	禮拜四
Monday	li³-pai⁴-i¹	禮拜一	Friday	li³-pai⁴-wu³	禮拜五
Tuesday	li³-pai⁴-êrh⁴	禮拜二	Saturday	li³-pai⁴-liu⁴	禮拜六
Wednesday	li³-pai⁴-san¹	禮拜三			

Months

January	chêng⁴ yüeh⁴	正月	July	ch'i¹ yüeh⁴	七月
February	êrh⁴ yüeh⁴	二月	August	pa¹ yüeh⁴	八月
March	san¹ yüeh⁴	三月	September	chiu³ yüeh⁴	九月
April	ssŭ⁴ yüeh⁴	四月	October	shih² yüeh⁴	十月
May	wu³ yüeh⁴	五月	November	shih²-i¹ yüeh⁴	十一月
June	liu⁴ yüeh⁴	六月	December	shih²-êrh⁴ yüeh⁴	十二月

Time

chung¹-tien³	hour	yüeh⁴	month
jih⁴	day	nien²	year
hsing¹-ch'i¹ } li³-pai⁴	week		

Surnames

Chinese surnames are usually written first, followed by the personal name, thus in the name *K'ang Yu-wei*, *K'ang* is the surname, not *wei*. Personal names can usually be distinguished by the hyphen.

DANISH

A	a	*a* in rather; also *a* in cat	P	p	*p* in pay
B	b	*b*	Q	q	*k;* always followed by *v* or *u; kv* is usually substituted
C	c	*k* before *a, o, u; s* before other vowels			
D	d	*d,* initial; *th,* soft, between vowels	R	r	*r*
			S	s	*s,* sharp
E	e	*a* in care; also *e* in met	T	t	*t*
F	f	*f*	U	u	*u* in full; also *u* in true
G	g	*g,* hard initial, soft final; mute between vowels	V	v	*v*
			W	w	*v*
H	h	*h,* mute before *j* and *v*	X	x	*ks,* which is usually substituted for *x*
I	i	*i* in flit; also *ee* in flee			
J	j	*y* in yet	Y	y	*ü* in German über
K	k	*k*	Z	z	*s*
L	l	*l*	Æ	æ	*ä* in German Fähre
M	m	*m*	Ø	ø	*ö* in German Götter
N	n	*n*	AA	aa	*aw* in law; sometimes represented by *å*
O	o	*o* in rot; also *o* in globe			

The Latin alphabet is universally used in Denmark, with the addition of *æ, ø,* and *aa.*

The *c, q, w, x,* and *z* are used only in words of foreign origin and in proper names; *aa* is not a double *a,* but a single letter; it is sometimes placed first in the alphabet. The sound of *av* is like *au* in the German word lau, *aj, eg,* and *ej* like *i* in pie, and *oj* like *oy* in boy.

When final, the *d* is not sounded after *l, n, r,* or *t*—*Haand* (hăwn), hand—or before *t* and *s.*

The *g* loses its distinctive sound in monsyllables after a vowel: *mig* (mei) me.

The combinations *sk* and *st* have the same sounds as in English.

Capitalization

In the official Danish language all nouns are capitalized; however, some modern authors tend to follow the English usage.

Syllabication

A consonant between two vowels usually goes with the following vowel (*ta-le*); when two or more consonants occur between two vowels, the last consonant generally goes with the following vowel (*brænd-te*); *sk, sp, st,* and *str* are usually not separated, but added to the following vowel (*hvi-ske, læ-spe, bed-ste, ven-stre*). Compound words are divided according to their component parts (*Kirke-gaard, ind-til*).

Punctuation

The punctuation in the official Danish language rigidly follows the clausal construction of the sentence, especially in regard to the use of the comma; however, many modern writers tend to follow the English usage.

Accentuation

Ordinarily accents are used only in foreign loan words and in certain proper names.

Stress is very important in Danish, but there are so many rules governing it that it requires actual personal contact with a native in order to acquire the various modifications.

Where the word is of genuine Norse origin, the stress rests on the radical syllable, as *ren'lig* (*ren*, clean); *uren'lig* (unclean).

In compound words the stress is usually on the syllable which marks the leading component, *Frederiksborg'*.

Articles

There are three distinct articles, which must agree in gender and number with the noun to which they refer: The indefinite and two forms of the definite, the latter two known as the "postpositive" or "noun article" and the "prepositive" or "adjective article", respectively.

	Singular		Plural	
	Common gender	Neuter gender	Common and neuter	English
Indefinite	en	et	—	a, an
Definite:				
Postpositive [1]	-en, -n	-et, -t	-ene, -ne	the
Prepositive [2]	den	det	de	the

The definite article is generally employed as in English, but, contrary to English, is required by abstract nouns (Liv*et* er langt, life is long), and in places where possession is understood (Drengen satte Hatt*en* paa Hoved*et*, the boy placed *his* hat upon *his* head).

Gender

There are but two genders, common and neuter: *en Seng*, a bed; *et Bord*, a table. Formerly there was a feminine gender for inanimate objects, which still persists in the dialects of some districts.

Although, in general, the common gender includes all words designating living beings (*en Person*, a person), exceptions are words which indicate a special class of beings without reference to sex, as *et Barn*, a child. It also includes names of trees, flowers, and of special vegetable products, as *Vin*, wine; also words ending in *e*, *de*, *hed*, *skab*, and *dom*, when they imply conditions and properties: *Varme*, heat; *Højde*, height; *Dumhed*, stupidity; *Ondskab*, wickedness; *Manddom*, manhood; also those ending in *ning*, *else*, *sel*, *st*, and *en*, when they indicate action or active principle: *Læsning*, reading; *Styrelse*, direction; *Færdsel*, traffic; *Fangst*, capture; *Løben*, running.

The neuter gender includes names of places and metals, as also words ending in *eri*, *at*, and *ium*: *Krammeri*, trumpery; *Krat*, thicket; *Kollegium*, college; also words for distinct kinds or parts of plants, as *Træ*, tree; also *Mandfolk*, a male; *Fruentimmer*, a female.

Some words are of uncertain gender (*en* or *et Blyant*).

Many nouns vary in meaning in accordance with the difference of gender:

en Ark, an ark	et Ark, a sheet of paper
en Lem, a drap-door, shutter	et Lem, a member, limb
en Øre, a coin	et Øre, an ear
en Søm, a seam	et Søm, a nail

Compound nouns have the gender of the last word of the combination.

Nouns

The plural is formed in various ways:

1. By effecting no change at all from the singular: *et Dyr*, an animal; *flere Dyr*, various animals.

2. By adding *-e*: *Dreng*, boy; *Drenge*, boys.

3. By adding *-er*: *Træ*, tree; *Træer*, trees.

4. By changing the radical vowel: *Mand*, man; *Mænd*, men; *Gaas*, goose; *Gæs*, geese; *Barn*, child; *Børn*, children. In some cases this results in a transposition of the terminal letters: *Fader*, father; *Fædre*, fathers; *Moder*, mother; *Mødre*, mothers.

---

[1] Employed as suffix to noun, when not modified by adjective.
[2] Precedes the adjective modifying the noun.

5. Nouns ending in *el*, *en*, or *er* often drop the last *e*: *Engel*, angel; *Engle*, angels; *Lagen*, sheet; *Lagner*, sheets; *Ager*, field; *Agre*, fields.

6. Words having double consonants drop one of them in the plural: *Himmel*, heaven; *Himle*, heavens; *Middel*, method; *Midler*, methods; *Datter*, daughter; *Døtre* daughters. However, those with one or more unaccented syllables ending in a consonant double the latter in the plural: *Bal*, ball; *Baller*, balls.

Cases.—There are three cases: Nominative and objective (which are always the same in form), and genitive, or possessive, formed by the addition of *s* (by *es* if ending in *s*, *x*, or *z*), or by *'s* if the noun is a proper name terminating in *s*.

Adjectives

Adjectives must agree in number and gender with the noun which they qualify as well as with that to which they stand in the relation of predicates:

et lidet Hus, a little house
Vejen var hende for lang, the way was too long for her

The plural adjectives *faa* (few), *mange* (many), and *alle* (all), may be used with a singular verb and without the adjective article:

der kommer faa Mand, a few men are coming
Klokken er mange, it is late (the clock is many)
alle gang, every (all) time

Adjectives may be used in the place of nouns, the latter being understood:

hun elskede den Gode, she loved the good (man, person)
de Stolte, the proud (people)

Some adjectives, expressing worth or obligation, follow the objective noun:

Præsten er den Ære værdig, the clergyman is of the honor worthy.

In titular distinctions, the adjective follows the noun: *Knud den Store*, Canute the Great.

When preceded by a definite article, they always end in *e*, both singular and plural.

When preceded by the indefinite article, or used predicatively, they end in *t* in the neuter singular, and in *e* for both genders in the plural.

Adjectives are compared by adding *ere* (or *re*) for the comparative, and *est* (or *st*) for the superlative. Many adjectives are compared by preplacing *mere* (more) and *mest* (most). Some, also, have irregular comparison: *god* (good), *bedre* (better), *bedst* (best), etc.

The following table illustrates the employment of articles, nouns, and adjectives in their various forms and relations:

English	Danish	
	Singular	Plural
a man	en Mand	Mænd
a man's	en Mands	Mænds
a good man	en god Mand	gode Mænd
the man	Manden	Mændene
the man's	Mandens	Mændenes
the good man	den gode Mand	de gode Mænd
a tower	et Taarn	Taarne
of a tower	et Taarns	Taarnes
a good tower	et godt Taarn	gode Taarne
the tower	Taarnet	Taarne
of the tower	Taarnets	Taarnenes
the good tower	det gode Taarn	de gode Taarne

Pronouns

Pronouns inflect as to number and case, but the genitives of the personal pronouns inflect also as to gender, as these are merely forms of the possessive adjective.

The following table gives the declension of the personal and interrogative pronouns; most of the others decline analogously.

	Singular			Plural		
	Nomina-tive	Genitive [1]	Object-tive	Nomina-tive	Genitive	Objective
I	jeg	min / mit } mig	vi	vor / vort } os		
thou (familiar)	du	din / dit } dig	I [2]	jeres(ederes) / jert } jer(eder)[3]		
you (polite)	De	Deres	Dem	De	Deres	Dem
he	han	hans	ham			
she	hun	hendes	hende			
it { common / neuter	den / det	dens / dets	den / det	} de	deres	dem
who	hvem		hvem	hvem		hvem
what	hvad	} hvis	hvad	hvad	} hvis	hvad
which	hvilket		hvilket	hvilke		hvilke

[1] Where two forms are given, the upper is for the common gender, the lower for the neuter.
[2] This form is capitalized to distinguish it from the preposition *i* (in).
[3] Variant forms.

Verbs

The following table gives in paradigm the auxiliary verbs *have* (to have), *være* (to be), the strong (or irregular) verb *give* (to give), and the weak (or regular) verb *elske* (to love) The verb forms are the same for all persons.

Tense and mood	To have	To be	To give	To love
Present infinitive	at have	at være	at give	at elske
Perfect infinitive	at have haft	at have været	at have givet	at have elsket
Future infinitive	at skulle have	at skulle være	at skulle give	at skulle elske
Present participle	havende	værende	givende	elskende
Past participle [1]	haft	været	givet	elsket
Present indicative	har	er	giver	elsker
Past indicative	havde	var	gav	elskede
Perfect indicative	har haft	har været	har givet	har elsket
Pluperfect indicative	havde haft	havde været	havde givet	havde elsket
Future indicative	skal have	skal være	skal give	skal elske
Future perfect in-dicative	skal have haft	skal have været	skal have givet	skal have elsket
Present subjunctive	have	være	give	elske
Present conditional	vilde have	vilde være	vilde give	vilde elske
Past conditional	vilde have haft	vilde have været	vilde have givet	vilde have elsket
Imperative	hav	vær	giv	elsk

[1] The past participle when used as an adjective inflects in gender and number.

The passive voice is formed with the aid of the auxiliary *blive* (to become) and the past participle: *jeg bliver elsket* (I am loved) or by adding *s* to the present infinitive of the verb: *jeg elske* (I am loved).

Cardinal numbers

en (een)	one	nitten	nineteen
to	two	tyve	twenty
tre	three	en og tyve	twenty-one
fire	four	tredive	thirty
fem	five	fyrretyve (fyrre)	forty
seks	six	halvtredsindstyve	fifty
syv	seven	(halvtreds)	
otte	eight	tresindstyve (tres)	sixty
ni	nine	halvfjerdsindstyve	seventy
ti	ten	(halvfjerds)	
elleve	eleven	firsindstyve (firs)	eighty
tolv	twelve	halvfemsindstyve	ninety
tretten	thirteen	(halvfems)	
fjorten	fourteen	hundrede	hundred
femten	fifteen	hundrede og en	one hundred
seksten	sixteen		and one
sytten	seventeen	to hundrede	two hundred
atten	eighteen	tusind(e)	thousand

Ordinal numbers

første	first	sekstende	sixteenth
anden	second	syttende	seventeenth
tredje	third	attende	eighteenth
fjerde	fourth	nittende	nineteenth
femte	fifth	tyvende	twentieth
sjette	sixth	enogtyvende	twenty-first
syvende	seventh	tredivte	thirtieth
ottende	eighth	fyrretyvende	fortieth
niende	ninth	halvtredsindstyvende	fiftieth
tiende	tenth	tresindstyvende	sixtieth
ellevte (elvte)	eleventh	halvfjerdsindstyvende	seventieth
tolvte	twelfth	firsindstyvende	eightieth
trettende	thirteenth	halvfemsindstyvende	ninetieth
fjortende	fourteenth	hundrede og første	h u n d r e d
femtende	fifteenth		and first

Note.—Hundred(e) (100) and tusind(e) (1,000) have no corresponding ordinals.

Months

Januar (Jan.)	January	Juli	July
Februar (Feb.)	February	August (Aug.)	August
Marts	March	September (Sept.)	September
April (Apr.)	April	Oktober (Okt.)	October
Maj	May	November (Nov.)	November
Juni	June	December (Dec.)	December

Days

Søndag	Sunday	Torsdag	Thursday
Mandag	Monday	Fredag	Friday
Tirsdag	Tuesday	Lørdag	Saturday
Onsdag	Wednesday		

Seasons

Foraar	spring	Efteraar	autumn
Sommer	summer	Vinter	winter

Time

Time	hour	Maaned	month
Dag	day	Aar	year
Uge	week		

Abbreviations

Adrs	Adresse, address, c/o	Hds.M.	Hendes Majestæt,Her Majesty
Afs.	Afsender, sender	Hr.	Herr, sir, Mr.
ang.	angaaende, concerning	if.	ifølge, according to
Anm.	Anmærkning, remark, observation	jf., jfr.	jævnfør, compare
A/S	Aktieselskab, joint-stock company	Kap.	Kapitel, chapter
		kgl.	kongelig, royal
B., Bd.	Bind, volume, volumes	Kl.	Klokken, o'clock; Klasse, class
bl.a.	blandt andet, blandt andre, among other things, or others	Kpt.	Kaptajn, captain
		Kr.	Krone, crown; Kroner, crowns (coin)
d.	død, dead		
d.A.	dette Aar, this year	m.a.O.	med andre Ord, in other words
D.D.	Dags Dato, the date of the day, this day	m.fl.	med flere, with others, and others
d.M.	denne Maaned, this month		
d.v.s.	det vil sige, that is, that is to say	m.H.t.	med Hensyn til, with regard to
Dr.	Doktor, doctor	m.m.	med mere, et cetera, and more, and so forth
etc.	et cetera, et cetera		
Eks.	Eksempel, example (illustration), e.g.	N.B.	nota bene, mark (notice) well
Em.	Eftermiddag, afternoon, p.m.	N.N.	nomen nescio, Mr. * * *, Mr. such a one
f.	født, born	Nr.	Nummer, number
f.A.	forrige Aar, last year	o.s.v.	og saa videre, and so forth, etc.
f.Eks.	for Eksempel, for instance		
ff.	følgende, the following	obs.	observer, observe
fhv.	forhenværende, former, late	P.s.	Postskriptum, postscript
		R.	Ridder, knight
Fig.	Figur, figure	Red.	Redaktør, editor
Fm.	Formiddag, forenoon, a.m.	S.	Side, page; Sider, pages
Forf.	Forfatter, author	s.D.	samme Dato, same date
Frk.	Frøken, Miss	S.u.	Svar udbedes, an answer is requested
gl.	gammel, old		
H.M., Hs.M.	Hans Majestæt, His Majesty	sml.	sammenlign, compare
		vedr.	vedrørende, concerning

DEVANĀGARĪ

Character	Transliteration	Character	Transliteration	Character	Transliteration	Character	Transliteration	Character	Transliteration
Vowels		**Diphthongs**		**Palatals**		**Dentals**		**Semivowels**	
अ	a	ए	e	च	ca	त	ta	य	ya
आ	ā	ऐ	ai	छ	cha	थ	tha	र	ra
इ	i	ओ	o	ज.	ja	द	da	ल	la
ई	ī	औ	au	झ	jha	ध	dha	व	va
उ	u	**Gutturals**		ञ	ña	न	na	**Sibilants and Aspirates**	
ऊ	ū	क	ka	**Cerebrals**		**Labials**		ग्म म	śa
ऋ	ṛ	ख	kha	ट	ṭa	प	pa	ष	ṣa
ॠ	r̄	ग	ga	ठ	ṭha	फ	pha	स	sa
ऌ	ḷ	घ	gha	ड	ḍa	ब	ba	ह	h
ॡ	ḹ	ङ	ṅa	ढ	ḍha	भ	bha	**Rare lingual**	
				ण	ṇa	म	ma	ऴ	ḻa

Ligatures

Character	Transliteration	Character	Transliteration	Character	Transliteration	Character	Transliteration	Character	Transliteration
क्व	} ka	क्व्य	kvya	ग्य	gya	ङ्क्र	ṅkra	च्च	cca
ʻ		च	} kṣa	य	gra	ङ्क्ष	ṅkṣa	च्छ	ccha
क	k	ঌ		ग्र्य	grya	ङ्क्ष्व	ṅkṣva	च्छ्र	cchra
छ	kṛ	द्	kṣ	ग्ल	gla	ङ्ख	ṅkha	च्छ्व	cchva
क्क	kka	क्ष्म	kṣma	म्व	gva	ङ्ख्य	ṅkhya	ञ	cña
क्त	kta	च्य	kṣya	घ	} gha	ङ्ग	ṅga	च्म	cma
क्त्य	ktya	क्त्व	kṣva	ʽ		ङ्ग्य	ṅgya	च्य	cya
क्त्व	ktva	क्स	ksa	घ्र	ghna	ङ्ग्र	ṅgra	छ	cha
क्न	kna	ख	} kha	घ्म	ghma	ङ्घ	ṅgha	छ्र	chra
क्म	kma	ঌ		घ्य	ghya	ङ्घ्य	ṅghya	छ्य	chrya
क्म्य	kmya	ह	kh	घ्र	ghra	·ṅghra	ṅghra	ज	} ja
क्य	kya	ख्य	khya	ङ	ṅa	ङ्ण	ṅṇa	ʼ	
क्र	kra	ग	} ga	ङ्क	ṅka	ङ्म	ṅma	३	j
क्र्य	krya	ʽ		ङ्क्त	ṅkta	ङ्स	ṅsa	ज्ज	jja
क्ल	kla	ই	g	ङ्क्त्य	ṅktya	च	ca	ज्ज	jj
क्ल्य	klya	ग्ध	gdha	ङ्क्त्व	ṅktva	च्	} c	ज्ज्व	jjva
क्व	kva	प	gna	ङ्क्य	ṅkya	ॄ		ज्म	jma

DEVANĀGARĪ—Continued

Character	Transliteration	Character	Transliteration	Character	Transliteration	Character	Transliteration	Character	Transliteration
ज्य	jya	ण्ठ	nṭha	दू	dū	ङ्घ्य	nghya	ब्ज	bja
ज्र	jra	ण्ड	ṇḍa	अरू	arū	न्त	nta	ब्द	bda
ज्व	jva	ण्ड्र	ṇḍra	दृ	dṛ	न्त्य	ntya	ब्ध	bdha
ज्ञ	jña	ण्ड्र्य	ṇḍrya	द्ग	dga	न्त्र	ntra	ब्ब	bba
ज्ञ्	jñ	ण्ढ	ṇḍha	द्ग्र	dgra	न्थ	ntha	ब्भ	bbha
झ	jha	ण्ण	ṇṇa	द्घ	dgha	न्द	nda	ब्य	bya
ज्झ	jjha	ण्य	ṇya	द्द	dda	न्द्र	ndra	ब्र	bra
ञ	ña	ण्व	ṇva	द्द्ब्र	ddbra	न्ध	ndha	भ	bha
ञ्	ñ	त	ta	द्द्य	ddya	न्ध्य	ndhya	भ्	bh
ञ्च	ñca	त्	t	द्द्र	ddra	न्ध्र	ndhra	भ्ब	bhba
ञ्च्म	ñcma	त्	t	द्द्व	ddva	न्न	nna	भ्य	bhya
ञ्च्य	ñcya	त्क	tka	द्ध	ddha	न्न्य	nnya	भ्र	bhra
ञ्छ	ñcha	त्त	tta	द्ध्य	ddhya	न्प्र	npra	भ्व	bhva
ञ्छ्र	ñchra	त्त्य	ttya	द्ध्व	ddhva	न्फ	npha	म	ma
ञ्ज	ñja	त्त्र	ttra	द्न	dna	न्म	nma	म्	m
ञ्ज्म	ñjma	त्त्व	ttva	द्ब	dba	न्य	nya	म्	m
ञ्ज्य	ñjya	त्थ	ttha	द्ब्र	dbra	न्व	nva	म्न	mna
ट	ṭa	त्न	tna	द्भ	dbha	न्स	nsa	म्प	mpa
ट्क	ṭka	त्प	tpa	द्भ्य	dbhya	प	pa	म्प्र	mpra
ट्ट	ṭṭa	त्प्र	tpra	द्म	dma	प्	p	म्ब	mba
ट्ट्य	ṭṭya	त्फ	tpha	द्य	dya	प्त	pta	म्भ	mbha
ट्य	ṭya	त्म	tma	द्र	dra	प्त्य	ptya	म्भ्र	mbhra
ट्स	ṭsa	त्म्य	tmya	द्र्य	drya	प्त्र्य	ptrya	म्म	mma
ठ	ṭha	त्य	tya	द्व	dva	प्न	pna	म्य	mya
ठ्य	ṭhya	त्र	tra	द्व्य	dvya	प्प	ppa	म्र	mra
ठ्र	ṭhra	त्र	tra	द्व्र	dvra	प्म	pma	म्ल	mla
ड	ḍa	त्र्य	trya	ध	dha	प्य	pya	म्व	mva
ड्ग	ḍga	त्व	tva	ध्	dh	प्र	pra	म्स	msa
ड्घ	ḍgha	त्स	tsa	ध्न	dhna	प्ल	pla	य	ya
ड्ड	ḍḍa	त्स्न	tsna	ध्म	dhma	प्व	pva	य्	y
ड्य	ḍya	त्स्य	tsya	ध्य	dhya	प्स	psa	्य	-ya
ढ	ḍha	थ	tha	ध्र	dhra	फ	pha	य्य	yya
ढ्य	ḍhya	थ्	th	ध्व	dhva	प्ल्य	plya	य्र	yra
ढ्र	ḍhra	थ्य	thya	न	na	न	na	य्व	yva
ण	ṇa	द	da	न	na	ब	ba	र	ra
ण्	ṇ	दु	du	न्	n	ब्	b	रु	ru
ण्ट	ṇṭa	द्रु	dru	न्	n	ब्घ	bgha	रू	rū

52 FOREIGN LANGUAGES

DEVANĀGARĪ—Continued

Character	Transliteration	Character	Transliteration
ल	la	थ्य	sthya
ऌ	l	थ्र	sthrya
ल्क	lka	ष्ण	ṣṇa
ल्ग	lga	ष्प	ṣpa
ल्प	lpa	ष्प्र	ṣpra
ल्म	lma	ष्म	ṣma
ल्य	lya	ष्य	ṣya
ल्ल	lla	ष्व	ṣva
ल्व	lva	स	sa
व ⎫ va		स् ⎫ s	
⎬		⎬	
ठ	v	स्क	ska
व्य	vya	स्ख	skha
व्र	vra	स्त	sta
व्व	vva	स्त्र	stra
श ⎫ śa		स्थ	stha
⎬		स्न	sna
श् ⎫ ś		स्प	spa
⎬		स्फ	spha
श्च	śca	स्म	sma
श्च्य	ścya	स्म्य	smya
श्न	śna	स्य	sya
श्य	śya	स्र	sra
श्र	śra	स्व	sva
श्ल	śla	स्स	ssa
श्व	śva	ह	ha
श्श	śśa	हु	hu
ष	ṣa	हू	hū
ठ	ṣ	हृ	hṛ
ष्क	ṣka	ह्न	hna
ष्ट	ṣṭa	ह्न	hna
ष्ट्य	ṣṭya	ह्म	hma
ष्ट्र	ṣṭra	ह्य	hya
ष्ट्र्य	ṣṭrya	ह्र	hra
ष्ट्व	ṣṭva	ह्ल	hla
ष्ठ	ṣṭha	ह्व	hva
		ळ	_la_

The Sanskrit, Hindī (Hindustani), Marathi, Guajarātī, as well as quite a number of modern Indian languages use the Devanāgarī alphabet, which has been in process of development from more ancient languages ever since the 7th century of the Christian era. There are neither lower case nor italics and the text reads from left to right.

Consonants always end with short a sound, and are classified as gutturals, palatals, cerebrals, dentals, labials, sibilants, and aspirates.

The vowels can each be expressed by two different characters. Those shown in the first column of the table occur only when they form an independent syllable at the beginning of a word. Besides these we also have the following vowel signs which are placed above, below, before, or after the consonants:

ा	ā after	ृ	ṛ below
ि	i before	ॢ	l below
ी	ī after	ॣ	ḷ below
ु	u below	े	e above
ू	ū below	ै	ai above
ृ	ṛ below	ो	o above and ा after
		ौ	au above and ा after

• Anusvāra ⎫ Show nasalization of vowels and
ँ Anunāsika ⎭ are placed above the characters

: Visarga ⎫ Aspirate signs, of which the
+ Jihvāmūlīya ⎬ first is most commonly used
ᵥ Upadhmānīya ⎭

‐ under the letter indicates lack of stress or the primary stress of the syllable

over the syllable indicates the secondary stress

Virāma (below) indicates absence of vowels
| At the end of a phrase
‖ At the end of a sentence
ऽ Used in dividing words and also indicates the elision of an a after e or o, or the union of aa

र Over a consonant indicates that an r sound precedes the consonant
Under a consonant indicates that an r sound follows the consonant

Numerals

१ २ ३ ४ ५ ६ ७ ८ ९ ०
1 2 3 4 5 6 7 8 9 0

In Devanāgarī the words are spelled exactly as they sound, so that if a person knows how to speak Hindi he will have no difficulty in learning to read it, it being merely necessary to learn the alphabet.

Continental sounds are used in the transliteration.

DUTCH

Ā	ā	a in French art	M	m	m
Ă	ă	a in father, but much shorter	N	n	n; final, often silent
B	b	b in bay	Ō	ō	o in low
C	c	s before e, i, ij, y; otherwise k	Ŏ	ŏ	o in not
			P	p	p
			Q	q	k in key
D	d	d; t when final	R	r	r trilled
Ē	ē	a in pale	S	s	s in sister
Ĕ	ĕ	e in met	T	t	t
F	f	f	U	u	Long, u in du; short, oo in book
G	g	g in go; fiinal, ch in loch			
H	h	hā	V	v	v in vanish
Ī	ī	ee	W	w	w
Ĭ	ĭ	i in thin	X	x	ks⎫ in foreign words and
J	j	y in year; French j in loan words	Y	y	i ⎭ proper names only
K	k	k	Z	z	z in zeal before vowels and w, otherwise s in sister
L	l	l			

The Dutch use 26 Latin letters; but of these, q, x, and y are used only in foreign words. They have a unique ligature, ij, which in manuscripts is very often changed to ÿ. When this ligature is the initial letter of a word at the beginning of a sentence, both are capitalized: IJs, ice; IJverig, zealous.

As in the German, the principal part of some compounds is written but once: Taal-, lees-, en schrijfboeken, grammar-, reading-, and copybooks.

Dutch is the language of some 10 millions of people living in the kingdom of the Netherlands, northern Belgium, and a small portion of northern France. It is also spoken in the colonial possessions of the Dutch East Indies, Dutch Guiana, and the Antilles. In South Africa a new language (Afrikaans), similar to "High Dutch" has been developed, the grammar of which has been much simplified. The United States has also about a quarter of a million people whose mother tongue is Dutch. In Ceylon it was used as the official language of both church and State in the eighteenth century, but it is now extinct there, which may eventually be the fate of the Negro-Dutch of the former Dutch Antilles.

Originally the language occupied an independent position among the Low German dialects used along the North Sea coasts and the Baltic from Dunkirk to Poland.

As the Dutch are a maritime nation and at various periods have been under the domination of other countries, the tongues of many peoples have left their imprint. There still exists considerable difference between the colloquial and the written languages. The more dignified formal terms were originally southern Dutch, while colloquial speech has preserved the original linguistic forms. The original language of the Belgian provinces, West and East Flanders, Antwerp, Brabant, and Limburg, as well as French Flanders, still has a wealth of dialects, as in the middle ages, which are generally grouped under the name "Flemish." These are generally spoken, though the Dutch language is the one taught in the schools.

Capitalization

Capitalization is very much the same as in English. The following exceptions should be noted:

When the first word of a sentence is represented by one letter only, the second word has the initial capital: 's Avonds is het koud, in the evening it is cold.

The article or preposition between Christian and family names is not capitalized: Jan ten Brink, Mathias van der Velde.

Personal and possessive pronouns referring to the Deity are capitalized.

While ik, I, is lower-cased, the personal and possessive pronouns of the second person are capitalized: Gisteren heb ik Uw brief ontvangen, Yesterday i received Your letter.

Phonetics

Double vowels are merely lengthened sounds of the respective single vowels: Thus *oo* is sounded like a long *o*, not like *oo* in the English word "book".

There are a few combinations that have special sounds, as shown in the following table:

Dutch	Sound	Dutch	Sound	Dutch	Sound
aai	*aye*, meaning "yea"	ie	*ü*, German	sch	Initially, *s+ch;* medially and terminally, *s; sh* in foreign loan words only
au	*ou* in house	ieu	*eeu*		
ch	*ch* in Scotch loch; in foreign words, like the foreign sound	ij	like Dutch *ei*	ui	*eu* in French deuil
eeu	*öw* in German Löwe	lj	*li* in million	uu	*ü*, German, long
ei	*ay* in French payer	oa	Same as long *o*	uy	Same as Dutch *ui*
eu	*ö*, German	oe	*oo* in book		
gn	*ny* in canyon	oei	*ooy*		
		ou	*ou* in house		

Accents

The circumflex indicates that two syllables are contracted into one: *Daân*, deeds; *Goôn*, gods; *liên*, people.

The dieresis is used to indicate that two vowels are to be pronounced separately: *Zeeën*, seas; *met drieën*, with three; *oliën*, to oil. However, if two vowels cannot represent a regular sound, the dieresis is omitted: *Israeliet, modeartikelen.*

The acute and grave accents are used for stress on a vowel: *één gulden*, one florin; but *een gulden*, a florin; *dáár is het*, there it is; *daar is hij eindelijk*, there he ís finally; *èn de een èn de ander*, the one as well as the other; *óf dit óf dat*, either this or that.

Syllabication

Avoid dividing short words as much as possible, but where necessary observe the following rules:·

In compound words the component' parts of each word must remain intact: *Eer-ambt*, post of honor; *door-een*, together; *elk-ander*, each other.

Words with prefixes *be-, ge-, her-*, etc., or with suffixes, *-aard, -achtig*, musť be treated the same as compound words in dividing.

A single consonant between vowels is added to the following syllable, as *dee-len*, to divide; *ne-men*, to take; *la-chen*, to laugh; *li-chaam*, body; note that the *ch* is inseparable.

Where two consonants occur together, they are split: *ber-gen*, mountains; *gan-zen*, geese.

In the case of three or more consonants division is phonetical: *vor-sten*, monarchs; *ven-ster*, window; but *amb-ten*, offices; *erw-ten*, peas; *art-sen*, doctors; *koort-sen*, fevers.

Foreign words, or those of foreign origin, are divided according to pronunciation: *le-proos*, leprous; *A-driaan*, Adrian.

Articles

The definite and indefinite articles each have two forms, that for the definite being *de* for masculine and feminine, and *het* for neuter. The declension is as follows:

	Singular			Plural	English
	Masculine	Feminine	Neuter	for all genders	
Nominative	de	de	het, 't	de	the
Genitive	des	der	des	der	of the
Dative	den	der, de	het	den	to the
Accusative	den	de	het, 't	de	the

Aan het is used for the dative singular, neuter gender, since *den* is no longer in use, though still found in some old expressions.

In the dative singular *ten* and *ter* are often substituted for *te den* and *te der*.
The indefinite articles are *een*, masculine and neuter, and *eene*, feminine. The declension follows:

	Masculine	Feminine	Neuter	English
Nominative	een	eene	een·	a (an)
Genitive	eens	eener	eens	of a (an)
Dative	eenen, een	eener, eene	eenen, een	to a (an)
Accusative	eenen, een	eene	een	a (an)

The article is often used before common nouns as well as before proper names, and is also used in practically all places where it would be used in English.

The definite article is used before concrete ideas which represent a class, genus, or species; it is omitted after the words *allé* and *beide*, and where the possessive pronoun is used in English: *Hij redde mij het leven*, he saved my life.

The indefinite article is used after *ooit* or *nooit*, if followed by the subject of the sentence; before the word *gedeelte* in the phrase *een gedeelte van*; it is omitted after *menig* followed by a singular noun; and also in many adverbial phrases: *Menig maal, eetlust hebben*.

Adjectives

Adjectives (including past participles) are used in three ways:

(*a*) Attributively (i.e., preceding the noun), in which case they are declinable, taking endings as follows:[1]

Case	Singular			Plural all genders
	Masculine	Feminine	Neuter	
Nominative	goede (goed)		goede (goed)	goede
Genitive	} goeden	} goede	} goeden	
Dative				goeden
Accusative	goeden (goed)		goede	goede

(*b*) Predicatively, in which case they take no endings.

(*c*) Substantively, in which they are declined like nouns.

Adjectives are compared regularly by the addition of *er* and *st* to form the comparative and superlative, respectively.

Gender

There are three genders: Masculine, feminine, and neuter.

The masculine includes males of all kinds, most trees, stones, most coins, mountains, months, and most primary nouns corresponding with the root of a strong verb; also all dissyllabic nouns ending in *-aar, -aard, -erd, -el, -em, -sem, -lm, -rm, -er*, and most words ending in *-en;* also all words ending in *-ing* (unless derivaties of verbs), and *-ling*, and words ending in *-dom*, which express state or condition.

The feminine words include females [2] of all kinds, some names of materials, most flowers, grains, fruits, vegetables, and foreign produce, names of vessels,[3] letters of the alphabet, numerals, notes and intervals of music, as also the foreign names of musical instruments; all dissyllabic substantives ending in *-e* and most of those ending in *-de, -te*, which denote inanimate objects; all derivative nouns with suffixes *-heid, -nis, -teit*, and all nouns ending in *-iek, -age, -ij, -ei*, and *-uw;* most words ending in *-ing, -st,* or *-t,* formed from verbal roots; also words ending in *-schap* and denoting an organization.

Words of the neuter gender include names that express an entire class of animals, as also the names of young animals; collective nouns, and the names of most materials; the infinitive mood of verbs and all other parts of speech used as nouns; names of geographical subdivisions; all diminutives ending in *-je;* words

---

[1] Under certain conditions, attributive adjectives take no endings: (1) When not preceded by another word; (2) when preceded by a possessive adjective or indefinite article; (3) when quality refers to profession and is preceded by *een: een goed jager* (a good hunter), but *een goede jager* (a kind hunter).

[2] Except *het wijf*, a low, vulgar woman.

[3] Except those ending in *-er*, which are masculine.

ending in -*dom*, except those expressing a state or condition; words ending in -*schap*, which express a dignity, an occupation, or a territory; all words ending in -*sel*, and most nouns formed from the root of a verb with the prefixes *be-*, *ge-*, *onder-*, *ont-*, or *ver-*.

Compound nouns have the gender of the principal word.

Number

All nouns take *en* or *s* to form the plural, though a few neuter substantives take *er* before the plural ending -*en: ei, eieren;* while a few take -*er-en* as well as -*er-s: blad, bladen* or *bladers; hoen, hoenderen* or *hoenderes.*

Nouns

There are two declensions: Strong and weak. The former form their genitive singular with the ending *s*, the latter with (*e*)*n*. The weak nouns are few in number. The following table presents the various declensional endings:

Case	Strong		Weak	
	Singular	Plural	Singular	Plural
Nominative Genitive Dative Accusative	— s [1] (e) —	} s (en) [2]	{ en (e)	} en [2]

[1] Feminine nouns take this ending only in proper names or nouns showing blood relationship: *Maries hoed* (Mary's hat); *moeders verjaardag* (mother's birthday).
[2] See "Number".

In conversational style the possessive is generally expressed by the preposition *van* (of), rather than by the genitive case.

Pronouns

The following table shows the declension of the personal pronouns followed by that of the possessive pronominal adjectives, which agree with the noun in gender, number, and case:

English	Singular				Plural			
	Nomin-ative	Genitive	Dative	Accusa-tive	Nomina-tive	Genitive	Dative	Accusa-tive
I	ik ('k)	mijns (-er)	mij (me)	mij (me)	wij (we)	ons (onzer)	ons	ons
you	du [1]	—	—	—	gij (jij)	uws (uwer)	jou (u, je)	jou (u, je)
he	hij	zijns (-er)	hem	hem	zij (ze)	{ huns (-ner)	} hun	{ hen (ze)
it	het	—	het	het				
she	zij	haars (-er)	haar (er)	haar (er, ze)	zij (ze)	haar	haar (er)	haar (er, ze)
my[2] { Masc. Neut. Fem.	} mijn mijne	mijns mijner	mijnen mijne(r)	{ mijnen mijn mijne	} mijne	mijner	mijnen	mijne

[1] This form is no longer used, being replaced by the plural. In polite conversation *U* is used for both singular and plural, with the verb in the third person singular or second person plural.
[2] The other possessive pronouns are declined analogously.

Verbs

The following table shows the conjugation of the auxiliary verbs *zijn* (to be), *hebben* (to have), the strong, (irregularly formed) verb *geven* (to give), and the weak (regular) verb *wenschen* (to wish). The persons shown are those of the first and third singular, and first, second, and third plural, in the order given. The forms in parentheses are the variations for the subjunctive mood.

	zijn	hebben	geven	wenschen
Present participle	zijnde	hebbende	gevende	wenschende
Past participle	geweest	gehad	gegeven	gewenscht
Present	ben (zij)	heb (hebbe)	geef (geve)	wensch (-e)
	is (zij)	heeft (hebbe)	geeft (geve)	wenscht (-e)
	zijn	hebben	geven	wenschen
	zijt	hebt (hebbet)	geeft (gevet)	wenscht (-et)
	zijn	hebben	geven	wenschen
Past	was (ware)	had (hadde)	gaf (gave)	wenschte
	was (ware)	had (hadde)	gaf (gave)	wenschte
	waren	hadden	gaven	wenschten
	waart (waret)	hadt (haddet)	gaaft	wenschtet
	waren	hadden	gaven	wenschten
Future [1]	zal			
	zal			
	zullen			
	zult			
	zullen			
Conditional	zou (-de) ⎱zijn	hebben	geven	wenschen
	zou (-de) ⎰			
	zouden			
	zoudt			
	(-det)			
	zouden			
Present perfect	ben geweest, etc.	heb gehad	heb gegeven	heb gewenscht
Past perfect	was geweest, etc.	had gehad	had gegeven	had gewenscht
Future perfect [1]	zal geweest zijn, etc.	zal ⎱gehad hebben zou ⎰	zal ⎱gegeven hebben zou ⎰	zal ⎱gewenscht hebben zou ⎰
Past conditional	zou geweest zijn, etc.			
Imperative	wees (singular)	heb	geef	wensch
	weest (plural)	hebt	geeft	wenscht

[1] The future tenses have no subjunctive.

The passive is formed by means of the auxiliary *worden* (become): *hij wordt gestraft* (he is punished).

In dependent clauses the finite verb is always placed at the end: *Ik geloof dat hij hier geweest is* (I believe he has been here).

Cardinal numbers

een, één	one	tien	ten
twee	two	elf	eleven
drie	three	twaalf	twelve
vier	four	dertien	thirteen
vijf	five	twintig	twenty
zes	six	een en twintig	twenty-one
zeven	seven	honderd	hundred
acht	eight	duizend	thousand
negen	nine		

Ordinal numbers

eerste	first	tiende	tenth
tweede	second	elfde	eleventh
derde	third	twaalfde	twelfth
vierde	fourth	dertiende	thirteenth
vijfde	fifth	twintigste	twentieth
zesde	sixth	een en twintigste	twenty-first
zevende	seventh	honderdste	hundredth
achtste	eighth	duizendste	thousandth
negende	ninth		

Months

Januari (Jan.)	January	Juli	July
Februari (Feb.)	February	Augustus (Aug.)	August
Maart	March	September (Sept.)	September
April (Apr.)	April	October (Oct.)	October
Mei	May	November (Nov.)	November
Juni	June	December (Dec.)	December

Days

Zondag	Sunday	Donderdag	Thursday
Maandag	Monday	Vrijdag	Friday
Dinsdag	Tuesday	Zaterdag	Saturday
Woensdag	Wednesday		

Seasons

lente, voorjaar	spring	herfst, najaar	autumn
zomer	summer	winter	winter

Time

uur, ure. stond, stonde	hour	week	week
		maand	month
dag	day	jaar, jaartal	year

Articles to be disregarded in filing

de	het, 't	een	eene

ESPERANTO

A	a	*a* as in pa	K	k	*k*
B	b	*b*	L	l	*l*
C	c	*ts* in wits	M	m	*m*
Ĉ	ĉ	*ch* in church	N	n	*n*
D	d	*d*	O	o	*o* in go
E	e	*a* in air	P	p	*p*
F	f	*f*	R	r	*r* trilled
G	g	*g* in go (always hard)	S	s	*s* in so
Ĝ	ĝ	*g* in gem (soft)	Ŝ	ŝ	*sh* in show
H	h	*h*, aspirated	T	t	*t*
Ĥ	ĥ	*h*, guttural, *ch* in loch	U	u	*oo* in soon
I	i	*e* in we	Ŭ[2]	ŭ	*u* in bull
J[1]	j	*y* in yet	V	v	*v*
Ĵ	ĵ	*s* in pleasure	Z	z	*z*

[1] *J* is like the English semivowel *y*, and therefore at the end of words forms the diphthongs *aj, ej, oj,* and *uj*.
[2] *Ŭ* forms with *a* and *e* the diphthongs *aŭ* (pronounced like *ou* in house), and *eŭ* (pronounced like the words *eh* and *who*, quickly uttered, without any aspirate, *eh-hoo*).

GRAMMATICAL RULES

1. There is only a definite article, *la*, alike for all sexes, cases, and numbers; it may be dispensed with.
2. Substantives terminate in *o*, and *j* is added for the plural. There are two cases: Nominative and accusative; the latter being obtained by the addition of *n* to the nominative. Other cases are expressed by means of a preposition (*de* for genitive, *al* for dative, and *per* or other prepositions according to sense for the ablative).
3. The adjective ends in *a*, and cases and numbers are as with the substantive. The word *pli* indicates the comparative, and *plej* the superlative.
4. The cardinal numbers are not declined.
5. Personal pronouns are *mi, vi, ĝi, ĝi* (referring to thing or animal), *si, ni, vi, ili, oni*; possessive pronouns are formed by adding the adjective termination, and declension is as with substantives.
6. There is no change in person or number with the verb; *as* is the termination for the present tense, *is* the past tense, and *os* the future tense. For the conditional mood the termination is *us*, and for the infinitive, *i*. Participles with an adjectival or adverbial sense end in *ant;* active past, *int;* active future, *ont;* passive present, *at;* passive past, *it;* passive future *ot*. All forms of the passive are formed by using a corresponding form of the verb *esti* and a passive participle of the required verb. *De* is the preposition with the passive.
7. Adverbs end in *e*, and degrees of comparison are as with adjectives.
8. All prepositions require the nominative case.
9. All letters are pronounced.
10. Accent is always on the penultimate syllable.
11. In compound words the principal word comes last.
12. Omit the word *ne* where there is another negative word.
13. Words take the termination of the accusative to indicate direction.
14. Every preposition has a definite and constant meaning, but if in doubt use the preposition *je*, which has no independent meaning, although the accusative may be used without a preposition.
15. Foreign words are used without change, receiving only the spelling of the Esperanto.
16. The final vowel of the substantive and the article may be replaced by the apostrophe.

Esperanto is a "made" language intended by its inventor, Dr. Zamenhoff, to become a ready medium of world communication. Radicles are taken from various languages to which a system of suffixes is added to provide a grammatical structure.

Syllabication

A syllable is necessary for every vowel regardless of how many come together; there are no double vowels: *tra-i-re, bo-a-o, me-ti-ist-o, zo-o-lo-gi-o.*

Punctuation

The present custom is for each writer to follow the rules of his own language since it is impossible to change the meaning of a sentence by punctuation, as is often the case in English.

Capitalization

Considerable latitude is permitted in the use of capital letters, but certain seemingly international styles have been adopted. Names of countries are capitalized, but the names of races, with the correlative adjectives and adverbs, are not: *Francujo,* France; *franco,* a Frenchman; *franca,* French; *france,* in French. The same rule applies to churches, orders, and political parties. The names of the days of the week are not capitalized.

Diphthongs

Aŭ	*ow* in how	Eŭ	*eh-oo* as in *they who*
Aj	*i* in high	Ej	*ay* in saying
Oj	*oy* in boy	Uj	*ui* in ruin

Interrogation is denoted by *ĉu*: *Ĉu li legas?* Does he read? Double negatives are not used: *Mi nenion trovis,* I have found nothing.

Parts of speech

The indefinite article is a part of the noun, if used: *Rozo estas floro,* a rose is a flower, but *patro kaj frato,* father and brother. The definite article *la,* the, is invariable: *la patro,* the father; *la patrino,* the mother. It is never used before proper names: *Unuigitaj Statoj Amerikaj,* (the) United States of America. It is used, however, before nouns denoting classes of persons or things: *La homo estas mortema,* man is mortal.

The nouns invariably end in *o*: *patro,* father; *patrino,* mother; *arbo,* tree. The plural is indicated by the letter *j*. The objective case takes *n* in both numbers: *Mi havas floron, birdon kaj libron,* I have a flower, a bird and a book; *mi havas florojn, birdojn kaj librojn,* I have flowers, birds and books. Possession is denoted by *de* and *de la*: *La ĉapelo de Johano,* John's hat; *la domo de la patro,* the father's house. The feminine is formed by adding *-in*-before the termination *o* or *oj*: *patro, patrino; edzo* (husband), *edzino* (wife).

All adjectives as well as participles used as adjectives end in *a*: *forta,* strong; *riĉa,* rich; *brava,* brave. If it qualifies or refers to a noun in the objective case it must take the sign of that case (*n*): *Mi trovis junan birdon en la ĝardeno,* I found a young bird in the garden. The adjective may be either before or after the noun it modifies. Adjectives must not be used as adverbs, nor adverbs as adjectives. Comparison is as follows: *Vi estas tiel forta kiel li,* you are as strong as he; *vi estas pli forta ol li,* you are stronger than he; *li estas la plej kuraĝa homo en la mondo,* he is the most courageous man in the world.

The personal pronouns *mi* (I), *vi* (thou, you), *li* (he), *si* (she), *ĝi* (it), *ni* (we), *ili* (they) form the objective case by adding *n*, as in the case of nouns. The possessive pronouns, which are essentially adjectives, are formed by adding *a* to the corresponding personal pronouns: *mia,* my, etc.; these also use the *n* to form the objective case, and *j* to form the plural.

Verbs

All verbs are regular and belong to a single conjugation. The final *i* denotes the infinitive mood:

am*i,* to love.

mi am*as,* I love; li am*as,* he loves, etc.

vi am*is,* you loved; ili am*is,* they loved, etc.

si am*os,* she will love; ĝi am*os,* it will love, etc.

mi am*us,* I should or would love, etc.

am*u,* love!

The active voice has three participles which help to form the perfect tenses:

anta (final), present active = English *ing*;

inta (final), past active = English *ed*;

onta (final), future active = no English equivalent: *mi estas amonta,* I am about to love.

The passive voice also has three forms:

ata (final), present passive: *amata,* loved (now);

ita (final), past passive: *amita,* been loved;

ota (final), future passive: *amota,* about to be loved.

Prepositions

The preposition "by" which precedes the complement of the passive voice is *de*: *li estas amata de ĉiuj,* he is (being) loved by all.

Prepositions govern the nominative case: *li kuris al ni*, he ran to us. Every preposition has a fixed, definite meaning and care should be exercised in choosing the proper one. Use *je* when the choice is not definite, or omit the preposition altogether and use the objective case: *li ĝojas je tio* or *li ĝojas tion*, he rejoices at (over) that.

Adverbs

There are two classes of adverbs: those derived from adjectives, nouns, etc., which always end in *e*: bon*e*, well; and those which are by nature adverbs and have no distinctive ending. The first class are compared in the same way as adjectives. Adverbs usually immediately precede or else follow the word qualified.

It will be noted that the words in the last four columns are formed by prefixing certain letters to those in the second column. Each of these prefixes has a definite signification as shown in the box headings.

LIST OF CORRELATIVE WORDS

	Indefinite **I**	Interrogative Relative **K**	Demonstrative **T**	Distributive **C**	Negative **Nen**
Quality	Îa Some (kind of) Any (kind of)	K̂ia What (sort of)?	T̂ia That (sort of) Such (a)	Ĉia Each kind of Every (kind of)	N̂enia No (kind of)
Reason	Îal For some reason For any reason	K̂ial For what reason? Why?	T̂ial For that reason There- fore	Ĉial For every reason On every account	N̂enial For no rea- son On no ac- count
Time	Îam At some time Sometimes, ever	K̂iam At what time? When?	T̂iam At that time Then	Ĉiam At all times Always, each time	N̂eniam At no time Never
Place	Îe At any place Somewhere	K̂ie At what place? Where?	T̂ie In that place There	Ĉie At each place Every- where	N̂enie At no place Nowhere
Manner	Îel In some way Anyhow	K̂iel In what way? How? Like, as	T̂iel In that way So, thus, as	Ĉiel In every way In each way	N̂eniel In no way Nohow
Possession	Îes Some- body's Anybody's	K̂ies Whose? What per- son's?	T̂ies That one's That per- son's	Ĉies Everyone's Each one's	N̂enies Nobody's No one's
Thing	Îo Something Anything	K̂io What (thing)?	T̂io That (thing)	Ĉio All Everything	N̂enio Nothing Naught
Quantity	Îom Some A little	K̂iom How much? What quan- tity?	T̂iom So much That quan- tity	Ĉiom All The whole quantity	N̂eniom None
Individuality	Îu Someone Anyone	K̂iu What per- son? Who, which, what?	T̂iu That one That (thing)	Ĉiu Everyone, every Each (per- son)	N̂eniu Nobody No one No, None

It will be noted that the words in the last four columns are formed by prefixing certain letters to those in the second column. Each of these prefixed has a definite signification as shown in the box headings.

Cardinal numbers

unu	one	naŭ	nine
du	two	dek	ten
tri	three	dekunu	eleven
kvar	four	dekdu	twelve
kvin	five	dektri	thirteen
ses	six	dudek	twenty
sep	seven	cent, cento	hundred
ok	eight	mil	thousand

Ordinal numbers

unua	first	naŭa	ninth
dua	second	deka	tenth
tria	third	dekunua	eleventh
kvara	fourth	dekdua	twelfth
kvina	fifth	dektria	thirteenth
sesa	sixth	dudeka	twentieth
septa	seventh	centa	hundredth
oka	eighth	mila	thousandth

Months

Januaro	January	Julio	July
Februaro	February	Aŭgusto	August
Marto	March	Septembro	September
Aprilo	April	Oktobro	October
Majo	May	Novembro	November
Junio	June	Decembro	December

Days

dimanĉo	Sunday	ĵaŭdo	Thursday
lundo	Monday	vendredo	Friday
mardo	Tuesday	sabato	Saturday
merkredo	Wednesday		

Seasons

printempo	spring	aŭtuno	autumn
somero	summer	vintro	winter

Time

horo	hour	monato	month
tago	day	jaro	year
samajno, septago	week		

Article to be disregarded in filing

The definite article is *la*.

ESTHONIAN

Estonia is located on the eastern shore of the Baltic Sea and is bounded by the Gulf of Finland on the north, Russia on the east, and Latvia on the south. It was formerly a part of the Russian Empire, but was declared independent on February 24, 1918, and its independence was recognized by Soviet Russia by the treaty of February 2, 1920. At this writing it is impossible to forecast the future of the republic, which was overrun by Nazi hordes early in World War II, as the Soviets are determined to do away with the belt of small, independent countries on their western frontier, all of which were founded during World War I.

The Estonian language belongs to the Fino-Ugrian language family, which includes seven west Finnish languages, including also, Finnish, Livian, and others like Mordvinian, Vogulian, and Hungarian. In its development, the Estonian has been influenced by the Lithuanian, Gothic, and Slavic, as well as by the Swedish, German, and Russian languages. There are two dialects, that in the north, which is known as the Reval dialect, and, in the south, the Werre dialect. The former is the literary language.

A	a	*a* as in sof*a*	P	p	*p* as in *p*ut
B	b	*b* as in *b*ird	R	r	*r* as in *r*ace
D	d	*d* as in *d*ark	S	s	*s* as in *s*ilent
E	e	*e* as in y*e*t	T	t	*t* as in *t*alk
G	g	*g* as in *g*on*g*	U	u	*u* as in p*u*t
H	h	*h* as in *h*orse	W,V	v	*v* as in *v*ote
I	i	*i* as in p*i*ll	Ä	ä	*a* as in *a*t
J	j	*y* as in *y*en	Ö	ö	*i* as in b*i*rd
K	k	*k* as in *k*ing			*u* as in German *über*,
L	l	*l* as in *l*i*l*y	Ü	ü	nearest English, p*u*pil
M	m	*m* as in *m*an	Õ	õ	as in Russian Mы, *we*,
N	n	*n* as in ma*n*			nearest English,
O	o	*e* as in d*o*g			*wo*men

The diphthongs are *ae, oe, oi, öi, õe, õu*, and *iu*.

Long vowels are written doubled: *saba*, tail; *sabaas*, boot. However, *päiw*, day, is used because it is actually pronounced *päiw*; also *käed*, hands, because it is derived from *käsi*, genitive, *käe*.

Even the long *õ* and *ü* are doubled: *põõsas*, wreath, (pronounced *põesas*); *nüüd*, now, (pronounced *nuid*).

There are but three words that use *õe*: *õel*, bad; *nõel*, needle; *sõel*, sieve.

No true Estonian word begins with *b, d*, or *g*: *Pibel*, Bible; *krihwel*, griffel, etc. However, in modern loan words, they are used: *baromeeter*, barometer; *detsember*, December; *grammatik*, grammar.

In modern borrowed words the *c, f, q, v, x, y*, and *z* are also used.

Capital letters are used at the beginning of a sentence and in proper names of people and places, as well as in address: *Jumal*, God; *Lutherus*, Luther, etc. Names of months, days of the week, etc., are not capitalized.

Syllabication

A single consonant between vowels begins the next syllable: *ne-mad*. When there are two or more consonants, only the last belongs to the following syllable: *kõr-gõs, pähk-lad*. Double vowels must not be divided, but, where there are three vowels, the last begins the next syllable: *prou-a, öu-es*.

Stress

The principal stress is almost always on the first syllable: *pea'-lik, kau'-nis*; exceptions are *maa-ilm'*, world, and several interjections and foreign words: *to-ho', ma-ni-fe'at*, etc. A secondary stress also occurs on the third, fifth, etc., syllables: *kõ-ne-la-ma;* to speak. In compound words each part retains its own stress: *hõ'be-ra'ha*.

Tone length or range is the time given to sound a letter. There are four gradations, that for *a* being as follows:

1. *sada*, hundred;
2. *saada*, send the letter;
3. *saata*, infinitive "to send";
4. tahan *saada*, I will receive.

Tone length depends on the individual sounds of the tonal sylable; of these there are three:

1. *kabi*;
2. *kapi* uks;
3. *kappi* panema.

The same word may range from one tone length to another: Nominative, *käsi*, the hand (first range); genitive plural, *käte* peal kandma, carry in the hands (second range); anna *kätte*, give it to me (third range). In inflection this is very important.

Parts of Speech

1. The subject (noun) or substantive: *asi-sõna*;
2. The adjective: *omandus-sõna*;
3. The numeral (singular or plural): *arw-sõna*;
4. The pronoun: *ase-sõna*;
5. The verb: *aeg-sõna*;
6. The adverb: *määrsõna*;
7. The preposition and postposition: *ees-ja taga-sõna*;
8. The conjunction: *side-sna*;
9. The interjection: *hüüd-sõna*.

There are no articles, nor is there any distinction as to gender. There are three inflections: Declination changes, comparison, and conjugation. Every noun and adjective has a stem and an ending: linna*s*, in the city.

Comparison

Positive: *suur*, large; *wanna*, old. Comparative: *suurem*, *wanem*. The superlative has no distinctive ending, but is formed by placing *kõige* before the comparative: *kõige suurem*, the greatest; *kõige wanem*, the oldest.

A simple rule for forming the comparative is to add *m* to the genitive singular:

Singular	Genitive	Comparative
suur	suure	suurem
kuulus	kuulsa	kuulsam
libe (smooth)	libeda	libedam
waga (holy)	waga	wagam

The following are exceptions:

hea (good)	param (better)
palju (much)	enam (more)

The substantives used adjectively also have a comparative: *koer poiss*, rascal (*koer* is literally dog); *koeram poiss*, a greater rascal.

Pronouns

The personal pronouns are *mina*, I; *sina*, you; *lema*, he, (she, it); *meis*, we; *teis*, you; *nemad*, they.

The reflexive pronouns are *enese* and *oma* for all three persons. In the nominative *ise*, self, is used for emphasis: *mina pesen ise-ennast*, I wash myself.

Demonstrative pronouns are *see*, this; *sama*, the same; *säärane*, such a one; *too*, that (you); and the compounds, *sesinane*, *seesame*, even the same; *seesugune*, such a one; *samasugune*, even such a one.

Nouns

In order to decline a noun properly it is necessary to know the nominative, genitive, and partitive in the singular number.

From the genitive singular are derived the nominative plural and the singular of all other cases, except the illative and essive singular of several classes of nouns.

The partitive plural and essive singular declinable nouns are always strong.

	Singular (this)	Plural (those)	Singular (that)	Plural (these)
Nominative ..	see	need	too	nood
Genitive	selle	nende	tolle	nonde
Partitive	seda	neid	toda	noid
Illative	selle*sse*, se*sse*	nende*sse*, nei*sse*	tolle*sse*, to*sse*	nende*sse*, nei*sse*
Inessive	selle*s*, ses	nende*s*, nei*s*	tolle*s*, tos	nene*s*, nei*s*
Ellative	selle*st*, sest	nede*st*, nei*st*	tolle*st*, to*st*	nende*st*, nei*st*
Allative	selle*le*, selle	nende*le*, neile	tolle*le*, tolle	nende*le*, neils
Adessive	selle*l*, se*l*	nende*l*, neil	tolle*l*, tol	nene*l*, neil
Ablative	selle*lt*, se*lt*	nende*lt*, neilt	tolle*lt*, tolt	nende*lt*, neilt
Abessive	selle*ta*	nende*ta*	tolle*ta*, toota	nende*ta*
Comitative ..	selle*ga*, seega	nende*ga*	tolle*ga*, tooga	nende*ga*
Terminative .	selle*ni*, seni	nende*ni*	tolle*ni*, tooni	nende*ni*
Essive	selle*na*	nende*na*	tolle*na*	nende*na*
Translative ..	selle*ks*, seks	nende*ks*, nei*ks*	tolleks	nende*ks*, nei*ks*

Pronouns

The interrogative pronouns are *kes mis*, who, what; *kumb*, which one (or two), and *missugune*, what sort of.

The relative pronouns are *kis*, *mes*, and *missugune*.

Simple indefinite pronouns are as follows:

	Genitive	Partitive	Substantive
iga	iga	iga (igat), each	igaüke
üke	ühe	üht, someone	
muu	muu	muud, another, some other	
mitu	mitme	mitut, many	
mõni	mõne	mõnda, many a one	
kõik	kõige	kõike, all; plural, kõik, kõikide, kõiki	
koku (inde-clinable), entire, all			
mõlemad	mõlemate	mõlemaid, both	

The compound pronouns are:

keegi (keski)	kellegi	kedagi
miski	millegi (mingi)	midagi
ei keegi	ei üksi, no one	
ei miski, nothing		
ei kumbki, neither of of the two		
igaüks	igaühe	igaüht, each
mõni*ngas*	mõninga	mõningat, many a one
mingisugune, anyone		

There are two numbers, singular and plural, and 15 cases, the most important of which are the nominative, genitive, partitive, and accusative. All the other cases are derived from the genitive and partitive singular. The accusative is like the genetive in the singular, and the nominative in the plural. There are three declensions: the weak, the strong, and the mixed.

There are two classes of words in the first declension: (*a*) Those which have the same terminal vowel in the partitive singular as in the genitive, and (*b*) those that end in -*d* in he partitive singular. The former are divided into three classes: 1, Those having a single long syllable; 2, those with two syllables and a terminal vowel, and 3, those multisyllabic words with terminal consonant and secondary stress on the second syllable:

Singular

	I	II	III
Nominative	laew, ship	müür, wall	suwi, summer
Genitive	laewa	müüri	suwe
Partitive	laewa	müüri	suwe

Plural

	I	II	III
Nominative	laewa*d*	müüri*d*	suwe*d*
Genitive	laewa*de*	müüri*de*	suwe*de*
Partitive	laewu	müüri*sid*	suwe*sid*
		müüre	

Those ending in -*d* have (*a*) unisyllabic words with terminal vowels, and, if polysyllabic, foreign words with stress on the last syllable; and (*b*) bisyllabic words ending in -*i*, with a short initial syllable:

Singular

	I. land	II. work	III. individual	IV. goose	V. sea
Nom.	maa	töö	partei	hani	meri
Gen.	maa	töö	partei	hane	mere
Part.	maa*d*	töö*d*	partei*d*	han*d*	merd

Plural

	I. land	II. work	III. individual	IV. goose	V. sea
Nom.	,maa*d*	too*d*	partei*d*	hane*d*	mere*d*
Gen.	'maa*de*	too*de*	pastei*de*	hane*de*	mere*de*
Part.	mai*d*	too*id* (too*sid*)	partei*sid*	hane*sid*	mere*sid*

In the first declension there are also a number of bisyllabic words ending in -*e*, -*a*, and -*i* that form their partitive singular with *i*:

Singular

	servant	master	George	Estonia
Nominative	pere	herra	Jüri	Eesti
Genitive	pere	herra	Jüri	Eesti
Partitive	pere*t*	herra*t* (herra*d*)	Jüri*t* (Jüri*d*)	Eesti*t* (Eesti*d*)

Plural

	servant	master	George	Estonia
Nominative	pere*d*	herra*d*,	Jüri*d*	
Genitive	pere*de*	herra*de*	Jüri*de*	
Partitive	pere*sid*	herra*sid*	Jüri*sid*	

The second or strong declension includes (*a*) bisyllabic adjectives and subjectives with two or more syllables ending in -*e*; (*b*) some terminals in a vowel other than -*e*, and (*c*) some ending in a consonant:

Singular

	yoke	clotn, dress	countenance
Nominative	ike	riie	pale
Genitive	ikke	riide	palge
Partitive	ike*t*	riie*t*	pale*t*

Plural

	yoke	clotn, dress	countenance
Nominative	ikke*d*	riide*d*	palge*d*
Genitive	ikete	riie*tc*	pale*te*
Partitive	ikke*id*	riide*id*	palge*id*

Those ending in vowels other than -*e* include *lõuna, õhtu, neitsi, weski,* as well as all "verbal nouns" ending in -*ja*: *armastaja,* sweetheart; *andja,* giver, etc.

The third or mixed declension includes (*a*) monosyllabics ending in *l, m, n, r, s,* with a long vowel: *keel, kõrs, uus,* etc.; (*b*) bisyllabics ending in -*si*: *käsi.* hand; *mesi,* honey; *wesi,* water; *süsi,* coal; *tõsi,* truth, etc.; (*c*) those ending in -*lane, -line, -mene,* etc., having secondary stress on the penultimate syllable: *eestlane, armuline, päikcne,* etc.

Singular

Nominative	inim*enc*	eest*lane*
Genitive	inim*ese*	eest*lase*
Partitive	inim*est*	eest*last*

Plural

Nominative	ini-*mesc-d*	eest-*lase-i*
Genitive	ini-*meste*	eest-*las-te*
Partitive	ini-*mesi*	eest-*lasi*

There are also the abstracts ending in -*us* and -*is*: *kogardus*, *lopetis*:

	Singular	Plural
Nominative	kogard*us*	kogu-*duse-d*
Genitive	kogu*duse*	kogu-*dus-te*
Partitive	kogu-*dus-t*	kogo*dusi*

Of the bisyllabic words ending in -*us* only those belong to this declension that have the principal stress on the first syllable; the others belong to the second declension.

The most commonly used irregular nouns are the following:

juus, hair	laps, child	pisut, few
kaas, lid	mees,|man	rohi, grass, medicine
kohus, duty, court	õlu, beer	rehi,|threshing floor
küüs, claw, nail	paas, flake, stone plate	soe, warm
laas, desert	paras, appropriate	uks, door

Illustrations of the more important cases are given below for *jalg*, foot (first declension); *saabas*, boot (second declension), and *keel*, tongue, language (third declension):

	Singular			Plural		
	Nomi-native	Geni-tive	Parti-tive	Nomi-native	Geni-tive	Parti-tive
1. Weak	jalg	jala	jalga	jala*d*	jalga*de*	jalgu
2. Strong	saabas	saapa	saabas*t*	saapad	saabas*te*	saapa*id*
3. Mixed	keel	keele	keel*t*	keele*d*	keel*te*	keel*i*

	Illative	Allative	Essive	Illative	Allative	Essive
1. Weak	jalga (jala*sse*)	jala*le*	jalga*na*	jalga-*de-sse* (jalgu)	jalga-*de-le*	jalga-*de--na*
2. Strong	saapa*sse*	saapa*le*	saapa*na*	saabas-*te--sse*	saabas-*te--le*	saabas-*te--na*
3. Mixed	keele keelde (keele*sse*)	keele*lc*	keele*na*	keel-*te-sse*	keel-*te-le*	keel-*te-na*

Adjectives

The adjective attached to the noun is completely declined, except in the abessive case (-*ta*), comitative (-*ga*), and terminative (-*ni*), where it retains the genitive form:

	Singular The large book	Plural The large books
Nominative	suur raamat	suured raamatu*d*
Genitive	suure raamatu	suurte raamatu*te*
Partitive	suurt raamatu*t*	suuri raamatu*id*
Illative	suurde raamatu*sse* (suure*sse*)	suurtesse raamatute*sse*
Allative	suur*le* raamatu*le*	suurt*ele* raamatutu*le*
But—		
Abessive	suure raamatuta [without]	suurte raamatute*ta*
Comitative	suure raamatu*ga* [with]	suurte raamatute*ga*
	suure raamatu*ni* [until]	suurte raamatute*ni*

TABLE OF CASES

Case	Singular		
	Ending	Question	Example
Nominative ...		who, what	maja, the house
Genitive		whom	maja, the house's
Partitive		who, what	maja, a (the) house
Accusative ...	Like genitive[1]	whom, what	maja, a (the) house
Illative	-see	in where	majasse, in the house
Inessive	-s	into what	majas, into the house
Elative	-st	out of what	majast, out of the house
Allative	-le	to what	majale, to the house
Adessive	-l	by, to what (whom)	majal, at the house
Ablative	-lt	from|where (whom)	majalt, from the house
Abessive	-ta	from what (who)	majata, without house
Comitative ...	-ga	with what(whom)	majaga, with the house
Terminative ..	-ni	to where, until when	majani, (up) to the house
Translative ...	-ks	where to , to what purpose	majaks, to a house
Essive	-na	like what	majana, like a house

[1] Like the genitive.

Case	Plural			
	Ending [2]		Examples	
Nominative		-d	majad	kärawad, door
Genitive	-de	-te	majade	wärawate
Partitive	-sid	-id	majasid	wärawaid
Accusative	([3])		majad	wärawad
Illative	-desse	-tesse	majadesse	wäsawatesse
Inessive	-des	-tes	majades	wäsawates
Elative	-dest	-test	majadest	wärawatest
Allative	-dele	-tele	majadele	wärawatele
Adessive	-del	-tel	majadel	wärawatel'
Ablative	-delt	-telt	majadelt	wärawatelt
Abessive	-deta	-teta	majadeta	wärawateta
Comitative	-dega	-tega	majadega	wärawatega
Terminative	-deni	-teni	majadeni	wärawateni
Translative	-deks	-teks	majadeks	wärawateks
Essive	-dena	-tena	majadena	wärawatena

[2] The first is ending for the weak and the second for the strong declension (first and second declensions).
[3] Like nominative (or a vowel).

Verbs

A verb is either transitive or intransitive, and there are but two tenses: present and preterit. It has two infinitives and also an affirmative and a negative; the present is also used for the future. There are two numbers and three persons; except in the third person, the passive is impersonal. It has three moods: indicative, conditional, and imperative.

> ma palun, I request; ma palusin, I requested;
> ma paluksin, I would ask; palu, request.

In order to conjugate a verb properly it is necessary to know both infinitives, the indicative present and the preterit passive participle.

From the first (always strong) infinitive, with -ma are formed (1) the preterit active; (2) the participle with -w; and (3) both verbal nouns, with -ja and -mine: wiskama, to throw: wiskasin, wiskaw, wiskaja, wiskamine.

From the second infinitive, with -da (or -a) are formed (1) the active imperative (except the second person singular); (2) the adverbial infinitive, with -es, and (3) the preterit participle witn -nüd; wisata; wisakü, wisates, wisanud.

From the indicative present are formed (1) the second person singular of the active imperative, and (2) the conditional: *wiskan, wiska, wiskasin*.

The weak stem in the preterit passive participle always takes the ending *-tud* (or *-dud*), and thus forms the basis for the entire passive voice: *wisatud, wisatakse, wisati wisataks*, etc.

The following table illustrates all verbal forms. There are, however, other compound verbal forms which are formed with the aid of the auxiliaries *olema* and *saama*.

CONJUGATION OF THE AFFIRMATIVE OF REQUEST

Number and person	Active	Passive
Indicative present		
Singular		
1st person	ma palu*n*	
2d person	sa palu*d*	
3d person	ta palu*b*	
		palu-*ta-kse*
Plural		
1st person	me(ie) palu*me*	
2d person	te(ie) palu*te*	
3d person	nad palu*wad*	
Preterit		
Singular		
1st person	*ma . palu-si-n*	
2d person	sa palu-*si-d*	
3d person	ta polu*s*	
		palu-*t-i*
Plural		
1st person	me(ie) palu-*si-me*	
2d person	te(ie) palu-*si-te*	
3d person	nad palu-*si-d*	
	nad palu-*si-wad*	
Conditional		
Singular		
1st person	ma palu-*ksi-n*	
2d person	sa palu-*ksi-d*	
3d person	ta palu*ks*	
		palu-*ta-ks*
Plural		
1st person	me(ie) palu-*ksi-me*	
2d person	te(ie) palu-*ksi-te*	
3d person	nad palu-*ksi-d*	
	nad palu-*ksi-wad*	
Imperative		
Singular		
1st person	——	
2d person	palu	
3d person	palu*gu*	
		palu-*ta-gu*
Plural		
1st person	palu*gem*	
2d person	palu*ge*	
3d person	palu*gu*	
Participle		
Present	palu*w*	*p*al-*u-ta-w*
Preterit	palu*nud*	pal-*u-t-ud*
Infinitive		
I. local	palu*ma*	
III. adverbial	pàlu*da*	paluta-*ma*
Verbal inessive ...	palu*des*	
Verbal nouns		
1	palu*ja*, the one who asks	palu-*t-us*, that one
2	palu*mine*, the asking	who was asked

NEGATIVE CONJUGATION

Indicative present	ma sa ei palu et'c. ta etc.	ei palu*ta*, etc.
Preterit	ma sa ei palu*nud* etc. ta eti.	ei palu*tud*, etc.

Number and person	Active	Passive
Conditional	ma sa ei pal*uks* ta etc.	ei palu-*ta-ks*, etc.
Imperative Singular 2d person ...... 3d per son	ära palu ärgu palü*gu*	ärgu palu-*ta-gu*
Plural 1st person ...... 2d person ...... 3d person	ärge*m* palu*gem* ärge palu*ge* ärgu palu*gu*	ärgu palu-*ta-gu*

All verbs having roots of two or more syllables belong to the First Conjugation. These roots undergo no changes whatsoever, either by abbreviation or mutation. This conjugation is the most important in the language, having more verbs than the total for the other five conjugations.

FIRST CONJUGATION

Affirmative speech	Weak conjugations		
	I.	II.	III.
Active Indicative present Singular	(thank)	(sweep)	(die)
1st person	täna*n*	pühi*n*	sure*n*
2d person	täna*d*	pühi*d*	sure*d*
3d person	täna*b*	p6hi*b*	sure*b*
Plural			
1st person	täna*me*	pühi*me* ·	sure*me*
2d person	täna*te*	phi*te*	sure*te*
3d person	täna*wad*	pühi*wad*	sure*wad*
Preterit Singular			
1st person	täna-*si-n*	pühki-*si-n*	sur-*i-n*
2d person	täna-*si-d*	pühki-*si-d*	sur-*i-d*
3d person	täna-*s*	pühki-*s*	sur*i*
Plural			
1st person	täna-*si-me*	pühki-*si-me*	sur-*i-me*
2d person	täna-*si-te*	pühki-*si-te*	sur-*i-te*
3d person	täna-*si-id* (-*si-wad*)	pühki-*si-d*	sur-*i-d*
Conditional Singular			
1st person	täna-*ksi-n*	pühi-*ksi-n*	sure-*ksi-n*
2d person	täna-*ksi-d*	pühi-*ksi-d*	sure-*ksi-d*
3d person ·......	täna-*ks*	pühi-*ks*	sure-*ks*
Plural			
1st person	täna-*ksi-me*	pühi-*ksi-me*	sure-*ksi-mc*
2d person	täna-*ksi-te*	pühi-*ksi-te*	sure-*ksi-te*
3d person	täna-*ksi-d* (-*si-wad*\	pühi-*ksi-d*	sure-*ksi-d*

Imperative
Singular
2d person	täna	pühi	sure
3d person	tänagu	pühkigu	surgu

Plural
1st person	tänagem	pühkigem	surgem
2d person	tänage	pühkige	surge
3d person	tänagu	pühkigu	surgu

Preterit participle
	tänaw	pühkiw	surew
	tänanud	pühkinud	surnud

Affirmative speech	Weak Conjugation	Strong Conjugation	Mixed Conjugation
	IV.	V.	VI.
Active Indicative present	(eat)	(throw)	(lay)
Singular			
1st person	söön	wiska-n	heidan
2d person	sööd	wiska-d	heidad
3d person	sööb	wiska-b	heidab
Plural			
1st person	sööme	wiska-me	heidame
2d person	sööte	wiska-te	heidate
3d person	sööwad	wiska-wad	heidawad
Preterit			
Singular			
1st person	sö-in	wiska-si-n	heit-si-n
2d person	sö-i-d	wiska-si-d	heit-si-d
3d person	söi	wiska-s	heit-i-s
Plural			
1st person	sö-i-me	wiska-si-me	heit-si-mc
2d person	sö-i-te	wiska-si-te	heit-si-te
3d person	sö-i-d	wiska-si-d	heit-si-d
Conditional			
Singular			
1st person	söö-ksi-n	wiska-ksi-n	heida-ksi-n
2d person	söö-ksi-d	wiska-ksi-d	heida-ksi-d
3d person	sööks	wiskaks	heidaks
Plural			
1st person	söö-ksi-me	wiska-ksi-me	heida-ksi-me
2d person	söö-ksi-te	wiska-ksi-te	heida-ksi-tc
3d person	sö-ksi-d	wiska-ksi-d	heida-ksi-d
Imperative			
Singlar			
2d person	söö	wiska	heida
3d person	söögu	wisaku	heitku
Plural			
1st person	söögem	wisakem	heitkem
2d person	sööge	wisake	heitke
3d person	söögu	wisaku	heitku
Preterit participle			
	sööw	wisakaw	heit-e-w
	söönud	wisanud	heitnud

The Second Conjugation contains principally verbs ending in -uma and -ima, with a long initial syllable: õppima, õpin, õppida; loopima, loobin, loopida.

The Third Conjugation includes surema, tuleba, panema, pesena, and the irregular olema and minema. The second infinitives are tulla, panna, pesta, olla, minna.

The Fourth Conjugation includes the following:

saama,	seen,	saada;	sain;	saadakse
jaama,	jään,		jäin;	
joomt,	joon,	juua;	jõin	
looma,			lõin	joodakse, ja juukse, joodama
tooma				
looma,	löön,	lütia;	lõin	
sooma				

Also a number with bisyllabic preterit ending in *-sin*.

The Fifth, or Strong, Conjugation includes verbs of three syllables, with the principal stress on the first syllable, and ending in *-ama* or *-ema*, which undergo mutation in the second infinitive and derivative forms: *hakkama, hakkan, hakata; wõitlema, wõitlen, wõidelda; õmblema, õmblen, õmmelda*.

The Sixth, or Mixed, Conjugation includes verbs which have been reduced to two syllables: *andma*, really *andama*.

There are also some verbs that are irregular.

Compound Verbs

These are formed by adding the auxiliaries *olema*, to be, and *saama*, to become, the latter being seldom used:

	Active		Passive	
		INDICATIVE		
Perfect	*olen lugenud,*	I have read;	*sai loetud.*	it is being read
Pluperfect	*olin ugenud,*	I had read;	*saab loetama,*	it was being read
Future preterit	*sain lugenud,*	I was done reading;	*on loetud,*	it was read
Future	*saan lugema,*	I will read;	*oli loctud,*	it will be read
Future perfect	*saan lubenud (olema),*	I will have read;	*saab loetud (olema),*	it will have been read
		CONDITIONAL		
Preterit	*oleksin lugenud,*	I would have read;	*oleks loetud,*	it would have been read
Future	*saaksin lugema,*	I would have read;	*saaks loetama,*	it would be read
Future perfect	*saaksin lugenud (olema),*	I would have read;	*saaks loetud (olema),*	it will have been read
		IMPERATIVE		
Preterit	——	——	*olgu loetud,*	it must be read
Future perfect	*saagu lugenud,*	stop reading!	*saagu loetud,*	reading must stop!

Adverbs

These are formed mainly by the suffixes *-si, -ti,* and *-sti: tagasi, ööseti, ilusasti;* in the comparative the latter is *ilusamini.*

Note particularly *aga*, only; *alles*, first, yet; *ega*, also not, probably not; the interrogatives *kas* and *eks: ju; juba*, already; *kui*, as; *kuid, (muud kui)*, only; *ometi*, nevertheless; *hoopis*, altogether, actually; *siis*, then, thus; *wast*, in this way, but first; *weel*, yet.

Prepositions and Postpositions

These are (1) simple: *enne, pärast, saadik*, etc.; (2) triple formed: *alla, all, alt; ette, ees. eest*, etc. The first class are those with the partitive: *enne*, before; *pärast*, after; *wastu*, against. The postpositions: *mööda*, along; with the genitive: *pärast*, as postposition (on account of, etc.). Triple formed are those that refer to the questions where to? from where? and where?: *alt*, where?; *alt*, from below; *ette*, before; *ees*, east; *eel* and *eelt*, timely.

The prepositions are taken mainly from substantives.

Conjunctions

aga, but	*et*, that, therewith, while
ehk, or	*kas*, if, when, also
ja, and	*kui*, as, afterward, when
ka, also	*waid*, but
wõi, or	*kas* .... *wõi*, either .... or
kuid, however	*sest et* ⎫ while
kuna, during	*selleparast et* ⎭

Cardinal numbers

üks	one
kaks	two
kolm	three
neli	four
wiis	five
kuus	six
seitse	seven
kaheksa	eight
ühekso	nine
kümme	ten
üksteist (kümmend)	eleven
kaksteist|(kümmend)	twelve
kilmteist (kümmend)	thirteen
neliteist (kümmend)	fourteen
wiisteist (kümmend)	fifteen
kuusteist (kümmend)	sixteen
seitseteist (kümmend)	seventeen
kaheksateist (kümmend)	eighteen
üheksateist (kümmend)	nineteen
kakskümmend	twenty
kaksk mmendüke	twenty-one
kakskümmendkaks	twenty-two
kakskümmendkolm	twenty-three
kolmkümmend	thirty
nelikümmend	forty
sada	hundred
sadanelikümmendüks	one hundred and forty-one
tuhat	thousand
miljon (-ni, -nit)	million

The ordinal numbers are formed by adding *s* to the genitive of the respective cardinals, except in the case of the first three, which are *esimene, teine,* and *kolmas*; also *saada* and *tuhat* do not change when used in connection with 101, 1001, etc.

FINNISH

A	a	*a* in sofa	U	u	*u* in put
E	e	*e* in met	V	v	*v* in vest
H	h	*h* almost German *ch*	Y	y	*ü* in über
I	i	*i* in din	Ä	ä	*a* in at
J	j	*y* in yet	Ö	ö	*er* in herb
K	k	*k*	B	b	*b*
L	l	*l*	C	c	*c* in calm or in cease
M	m	*m*	D	d	*d*
N	n	*n*	F	f	*f*
O	o	*o* in log	G	g	*g* in game
P	p	*p*	Q	q	*cou* in could
R	r	*r* in rose	X	x	*x* in express
S	s	*s*	Z	z	*s* or *ts*
T	t	*t*	Å	å	*aw* in saw

The last nine letters, *b, c, d, f, g, q, x, z,* and *å,* occur only in foreign words and proper names and are never found at the beginning of pure Finnish words.

The Finnish language has been classified as belonging to the Volga-Baltaic group of the Finnic branch of the Ural-Altaic family of languages. This is evidenced by it s agglutinative character, root accentuation, euphonic laws, pronominal suffixes, and other family traits. However, in many respects it resembles the Aryan branch, for in its declensions it resembles Latin and Greek, and in its conjugations it supplements its primitive scanty supply with a number of the auxiliary verb forms after the manner of German and Swedish, from which two languages it has been deeply impregnated with loan-words.

Since 1883 the Suomi, or Finnish language, has, in common with Swedish, been an official language in Finland.

In the following diphthongs the sound of the individual letters must not be lost: *uo, yö, ie, au, eu, iu, ou, äy, öy, ai, ei, oi, ui, yi, äi, öi.*

Phonetics

The characters are sounded as shown in the table, but the following additional remarks should be noted:

1. There are seven so-called "long", or double, vowels which are pronounced as follows:

aa, like *a* in arm	*uu,* like *oo* in boot
ee, like *a* in pale	*ää,* like *a* in man
ii, like *ee* in keen	*öö,* like the French *eu,* lengthened
oo, like *o* in open	

2. There are 16 diphthongs: (*a*) *au, ou, iu, eu, äy öy, ai, oi, ui, ei, äi, öi, yi;* (*b*) *uo, yö, ie* and these combinations may not be separated in forming syllables. In the first group the greater stress is on the first vowel, while in the second group it is on the second. In a diphthong, therefore, each vowel is sounded, but articulated rapidly.

3. The chief stress is always on the first syllable: *tálo, minä, párempi.* There is also a secondary stress falling on the third, fifth, etc., or on the fourth, sixth, etc., syllables: *óp-pi-mát-to-múu-des-san-sa,* in his ability to learn; *ó-pet-ta-mát-to-múu-des-sán-sa,* in his ignorance. In no case is the second or last syllable stressed.

Punctuation

The punctuation marks and their use are similar to those in English.

Syllabication

A syllable consists of a vowel or diphthong with or without one or more consonants, as, *a-pu*, help; *au-rin-ko*, sun.

A consonant between two vowels belongs to the following syllable.

Two consonants may be divided and double consonants, as *kk*, are always divided Diphthongs are not divided.

In words having three consecutive consonants the last will go with the following syllable.

Gender and articles

Finnish, like all cognate languages, has no distinction as to gender and neither definite nor indefinite articles as such, the sense of definitenesss or indefiniteness being inherent in the sentence structure or noun case.

Adjectives

Adjectives are declined exactly like nouns, agreeing with them in number and case. They are also compared as follows:

Positive	Comparative	Superlative
huono, bad	huono*mpa*, worse	huonio*impa*, worst

Nouns

The noun is declined according to cases, of which there are 15; according to number, of which there are 2; according to type of declension, of which there are 3; and according to its pronominal modifier (my, your, etc.). This involves the addition of various definite suffixes, subject, however, to the laws of vowel changes and contractions, of which there are 49. It is the nature of these additions that distinguishes the language as agglutinative. The 15 noun cases are illustrated by *puu* (a tree), of the first declension, singular and plural:

Case	Case relation in English	Substantive	
		Tree	Trees
Nominative	the	puu	puut
Partitive	a (some)	puuta	puita
Genitive	of the	puun	puiden (puiten)
Inessive	in	puussa	puissa
Elative	from (out of)	puusta	puista
Illative	into	puuhun	puihin
Adessive	(done) on or with	puulla	puilla
Ablative	(away) from	puulta	puilta
Allative	to	puulle	puille
Abessive	without	puutta	puitta
Prolative	along	puutse	puitse
Translative	(became) a	puuksi	puiksi
Essive	as a	puuna	puima
Comitative	(together) with	puune	puine
Instructive	by means of	puune	puin

Pronouns

Pronouns are declined almost like nouns, there being personal, demonstrative, interrogative, relative, indefinite, and reflexive pronouns whose functions are like those in the Aryan languages. The possessive pronouns are, as already stated, in the form of affixes to the stem as follows:

kysymyks (stem=kysymykse), a question

	Question			Question
my	kysymykseni		our	kysymyksemme
thy	kysymyksesi		your	kysymyksenne
his	kysymyksensa		their	kysymyksensa

Verbs

The verbs have 3 persons, 2 voices (active and passive), 2 uses (transitive and intransitive) whose significations are like those of the Aryan languages. There are four tenses: Present, imperfect, perfect, and pluperfect, which represent time as in English, except that the present is also used to express future tense: *kirjoitan kirjettä,* I am writing a letter; *kirjoitan kirjettä kirjeen,* I shall write a letter tomorrow. There are also 7 moods: Indicative, imperative, conditional, verbal noun, verbal adjective (whose functions are the same as in English), and optative and concessive, the first being an imperative for the first and third persons, the second expressing probability or likelihood. The negatives of the verb forms are expressed by preplacing a negative verb which may be considered equivalent to our "do not," "does not," since there is no adverb "not" in the language. The following paradigm of the verb *saa* (to receive) in the active voice illustrates the several tenses, moods, and persons in the affirmative and negative forms:

Mood and tense	English equivalent	Affirmative	Negative
Present (indicative)	I receive	saan	en saa
	thou (you) receivest	saat	et saa
	he receives	saa	ei saa
	we receive	saame	emme saa
	you receive	saatte	ette saa
	they receive	saavat	eivät saa
Imperfect	I received	sain	en saanut
Perfect	I have received	olen saanut	en ole saanut
Pluperfect	I had received	olin saanut	en ollut saanut
Concessive	I am not likely to receive	saanen	en saane
Conditional	if I am to receive	saisin	en saisi
Imperative	receive	saa	älä saa
Optative	let him receive	saakoon	älköön saako
Verbal noun	the receiving	saada	
Verbal adjective	(the) received	saapa	

Construction

The following examples illustrate how elements are formed into compounds, phrases, and sentences, the italics indicating sound changes resulting from inflection or agglutination:

	As elements	As constructed
1	pää kaupunki	pääkaupunki
	town head	capital
2	oma tunto	omatunto
	own feeling	conscience
3	isä maa rakkaus	isänmaanrakkaus
	father land love	patriotism
4	vene tämä tuoda	vene täältä tuotanehe
	boat this carry	the boat will be brought
5	vastata sana tuo	vastasi sanalla tuolla
	answer word this	answered with this word
6	joki poikki pääse	joen poikki päästäkseni
	river across pass	for my crossing over the river

Cardinal numbers

yksi	one	yhdeksän	nine
kaksi	two	kymmenen	ten
kolme	three	yksitoista	eleven
neljä	four	kaksitoista	twelve
viisi	five	kolmetoista	thirteen
kuusi	six	kaksikymmentä	twenty
seitsemän	seven	sata	hundred
kahdeksan	eight	tuhat	thousand

Ordinal numbers

ensimäinen	first	yhdeksäs	ninth
toinen	second	kymmenes	tenth
kolmas	third	yhdestoista	eleventh
neljäs	fourth	kahdestoista	twelfth
viides	fifth	kolmastoista	thirteenth
kuudes	sixth	kahdeskymmenes	twentieth
seitsemäs	seventh	sadas	hundredth
kahdeksas	eighth	tuhannes	thousandth

Months

tammikuu	January	heinäkuu	July
helmikuu	February	elokuu	August
maaliskuu	March	syyskuu	September
huhtikuu	April	lokakuu	October
toukokuu	May	marraskuu	November
kesäkuu	June	joulukuu	December

Days

sunnuntai	Sunday	torstai	Thursday
maanantai	Monday	perjantai	Friday
tiistai	Tuesday	lauantai	Saturday
keskiviikko	Wednesday		

Seasons

kevät	spring	syksy	autumn
kesä	summer	talvi	winter

Time

tunti	hour	kuukausi	month
päivä	day	vuosi	year
viikko	week		

FRENCH

A	a			LL	ll	Liquid, as *y* in yellow
Â¹	à	*a* in madam		M	m	*m*
Â¹	â			N	n	*n*
B	b	*b*		O	o	Short, vowel sound in
C	c	*k* in king; *c* in cedar		Ô	ô	law; long *o* in omen
		(before *e, i,* and *y*)		P	p	*p*
Ç	ç	*c* in cedar		Q(U)	q(u)	*k* in kite
CH	ch	*sh* in sham; *ch* in chorus		R	r	*r*
D	d	*d*		S	s	Hard, as in sister; soft,
E	e					as in rose; final, mute
È¹	è	*e* in let; final, mute		T	t	Hard, as in tit; soft,
Ê¹	ê	unless accented				as *c* in cedar
Ë²	ë					
É	é	*a* in mate		U	u	
F	f	*f*		Ù¹	ù	Almost *oo* in pool
G	g	*g* in game; *zh* like sec-		Û¹	û	
		ond *g* in garage (be-		Ü²	ü	
		fore *e, i,* and *y*)		V	v	*v*
H	h	Silent in most cases		W	w	Only in words of for-
I	i					eign origin
Î	î	*ee* in meet		X	x	*k* and *ks; z* and *gz;* like
Ï²	ï					hard *s;* final mute,
J	j	*s* in pleasure				except in borrowed
K	k	*k*				words
L	l	*l;* final *l* sometimes		Y	y	*ee*
		silent		Z	z	*z* in zed

¹ The orthographic signs, grave and circumflex, do not indicate the pronunciation of vowels. For example, *à* in là and *â* in parlâmes are similar.
² The dieresis shows that the vowel bearing it is divided in pronunciation from the preceding vowel, as in Noël.

Phonetics

The characters of the French alphabet are sounded as indicated in the table above; however, there are a few letter combinations which have characteristic sounds of their own.

ai has two sounds: like *a* in fate, when a final in verbs (*parlai,* I speak); like *e* in met, elsewhere (*parlais,* I spoke).

au and *eau* have as the sound of *o* in holy (*autre,* other, *beau,* beautiful).

eu, œ, and *oeu* are pronounced somewhat like the German *ö.*

oi is pronounced like *wa* in water (*moi,* me), *ui* somewhat like *wi* in will (*huille,* oil), *oui* like English we (*oui,* yes).

un has no English equivalent; *an* nearly like *aun* in the English taunt; *ou* like *oo* in food; *in* like *an* in sank; *on* like *on* in long; *gn* like *ni* in onion.

Final consonants, except *c, f, l,* and *r,* and *es* at the end of a word of more than one syllable, also *ent* at the end of the third person plural of verbs are not pronounced.

Capitalization

Capitals are used the same as in English, except that proper adjectives, names of seasons, months, days of the week, titles, and the personal pronoun *je* (I) are not capitalized. In proper names of persons taken from the Italian the article is lower-cased, as *le Dante;* otherwise use the form *La Fayette.* In names of places the article is lower-cased, as *le Havre.*

Use roman small caps for the centuries—example: xix⁰ siècle.

Capitalize the following: Years of the Republican calendar (*l'An IV*), acts of plays (*l'Acte V*), volumes of books (*Tome IX*), titles of rulers (*Louis XIV*), and the numbered divisions of Paris (*le XV⁰ arrondissement*).

Capitalize the first word and all proper nouns in the title of a book. If the title commences with *Le, La, Les, Un,* or *Une,* capitalize also the second word. Examples: *Origines du culte chrétien; Les Origines du culte; La Reine Margot.*

In vivid personifications the nouns personified are capitalized, as *Ici habite la Mort* (Death abides here).

Historical events (*la Révolution*) also take the capital.

The term "street" and its synonyms are lower-cased, as *rue de la Nation, avenue de l'Opéra, route Saint-Denis, boulevard Saint-Laurent.*

Observe the forms used in the following terms: *l'Académie française; la Légion d'honneur; Louis le Grand; son Éminence; l'Église* when referring to the church as an institution, and *l'État* when denoting the nation, as *le Corps d'État, le Conseil d'État.*

Accents

The accent marks are the acute, grave, and circumflex. The first occurs only over *e: cédé,* etc.; the grave mostly over *e: père, mère,* etc., but is also used to distinguish homonyms, as, *la* (the), *là* (there); *ou* (or), *où* (where); it is also used on *dejà* and *jà.* The circumflex may occur over all the vowels, chiefly to indicate the recent elision of some consonant (oftenest *s*): *tête,* formerly *teste,* etc.

The cedilla is placed under *c* to give the sound of *s* before *a, o,* or *u: ça, façon, reçu,* etc.

The dieresis over a vowel indicates that it is to begin a new syllable: *haïr,* pronounced *a-ir.* It is also placed over the final mute *e* to show that the *gu* preceding is a syllable by itself.

The orthographic accents (acute, grave, and circumflex) must not be confused with the tonal accent, which stresses syllables of words. In French there is no mark to indicate stress on any particular syllable, since each is uttered with almost equal force, a very slight stress falling on the last.

Capital letters carry their proper accents unless a protruding accent is likely to interfere with alinement, as in solid matter. Small caps carry all accents where indicated.

Punctuation

Punctuation is practically the same as in English.

Em dashes take a space before and after (—), not closed up as in English, and are also used to denote change of speaker in dialog.

The hyphen is used in compound words and between words closely related: *arc-en-ciel,* rainbow; *avez-vous,* have you?

Geographic names containing the prepositions *en, de,* and *sur* are hyphenated, as *Saint-Valéry-en-Caux.* Hyphens are also used in spelled numbers under 100 with few exceptions. See list on page 84.

The apostrophe indicates elision: *l'ami* for *le ami,* etc.

Syllabication

Division is made on a vowel or diphthong before a consonant, as *jeu-nesse.* The combinations *bl, br, ch, cl, cr, dr, fl, fr, gh, gl, gn, gr, ph, pl, pr, th, tr,* and *vr,* must not be separated, as in *ré-pu-bli-que, dé-peu-ple-ment, cé-lé-brer, dé-cret, au-tre-ment, ou-vrier, qua-drille, dé-pê-cher, ca-tho-lique, té-lé-gra-phique, Vaughan,* but where the *g* and *n* have separate sounds they are divided, as *ag-nus, di-ag-nos-tique.*

Any other two consonants are divided, as *en-suite, im-mense, juil-let, ec-clé-sias-tique, con-struire.*

As a rule, two vowels are not separated: *mi-nuit, théâ-tre.*

It is allowable to divide a monosyllable ending in mute *e,* as *mar-che; hom-me.*

In dividing hyphenated phrases such as *ira-t-il,* and *pré-sente-t-on* the *t* must go over.

No division should be made on *x* or *y,* as in *Alexan-dre, roya-liste.*

Articles

French has two articles: indefinite (*un, une,* masculine and feminine respectively) and definite (*le, la, les,* masculine singular, feminine singular, and masculine or feminine plural, respectively). When these are preceded by the prepositions *à* (to), *de* (of), contraction or elision may take place, as illustrated in the table under "adjectives."

The definite article is used with names of continents, countries, provinces, large European islands, and major political subdivisions, but is omitted after the preposition *en* and sometimes *de*: *en Amérique, de France.* It is also used before *plus* and *moins* to form a superlative: *le plus grand,* the tallest; *la plus jeune,* the youngest; also with possessive force: *ils lavent les mains,* they are washing their hands.

The articles must be repeated before each noun to which they refer: *un livre, une plume, un livre et une plume.* Some idiomatic phrases constitute exceptions to this rule: *les père et mère,* parents.

Adjectives

Adjectives agree with their nouns in number and gender.

The plural of adjectives, and likewise that of nouns, is formed as follows:

(*a*) Regularly, by the addition of *s* to the singular.

(*b*) When the singular ends in *s, x* or *z,* the adjectives (or nouns) remain unchanged in the plural.

(*c*) When ending in *au* or *eu,* they take an *x.*

(*d*) When ending in *al,* they change to *aux.*

The feminine of adjectives is formed as follows:

(*a*) Regularly, by the addition of *e* to the masculine.

(*b*) When ending in *f, x,* or *g,* they change these to *ve, se,* and *gue,* respectively.

(*c*) When ending in *c,* they change this to *che* (sometimes *que*).

(*d*) When ending in *el, eil, ien, on,* and usually *s, t,* they double the final consonant and add *e.*

The following table illustrates inflection, contraction, and elision in articles, and the inflection of adjectives in accordance with the foregoing rules.

| English equivalent | Masculine | | Feminine | |
	Singular	Plural	Singular	Plural
a	un	—	une	—
of a	d'un	—	d'une	—
to a	à un	—	à une	—
the	le	les	la	les
of the	du	des	de la	des
to the	au	aux	à la	aux
large	gros	gros	grosse	grosses
tall, great	grand	grands	grande	grandes
happy	heureux	heureux	heureuse	heureuses
cruel	cruel	cruels	cruelle	cruelles
public	public	publics	publique	publiques

Qualifying adjectives usually follow the noun they modify, the exceptions being—

(*a*) A few common adjectives: *bon* (good), *long* (long), etc.

(*b*) A number of adjectives with variant meanings: *l'homme grand* (the tall man); *le grand homme* (the great man), etc.

The possessive adjectives and the demonstrative *cet* (*ce*) agree with their nouns in gender and number, as follows:

	my	thy	his, her, its	our	your	their	this
Singular (*m.*)	mon	ton	son [1]	notre	votre	leur	ce (cet) [2]
Singular (*f.*)	ma	ta	sa [1]	notre	votre	leur	cette
Plural (*m., f.*)	mes	tes	ses [1]	nos	vos	leurs	ces

[1] Since *son, sa, ses* may each be translated by his, her, its, the meaning in any particular case can be gathered only from the context.

[2] *Ce,* before consonant or aspirate *h*; *cet,* before vowel or mute *h.*

Nouns

French nouns do not inflect as to case, this relation being indicated by the prepositions *de* (of) and *à* (to), but they do inflect as to number and in some cases change for gender.

The genders are masculine and feminine. Names of animate beings follow their natural gender:

le père, the father   la mère, the mother
le mouton, the sheep   la brebis, the ewe

A few nouns are used without change of form according to the sex of the object, as *enfant*, and including some ending in mute *e*, as *camarade*.

In many cases feminine forms exist side by side with the masculine: With the ending *-e*, *ami, amie;* with the ending *-esse, hôte, hôtesse;* with the ending *-euse, chanteur, chanteuse;* more irregular are some such, as *canard, cane*. Most names of animals have but one form, regardless of sex: *l'éléphant, la giraffe*.

The following empirical rules will be useful in determining the genders of words by meaning:

1. Masculine are names of seasons, months, days, cardinal points, most trees, mountains, and metals; other parts of speech used as nouns, as *le pourquoi, le mai*.

2. Feminine are most abstracts and most names of countries: *l'amitié; l'Amérique*.

The gender may also be determined by the ending:

1. Masculine are almost all nouns ending in a consonant (some exceptions in *f, m, n, r, s, t, x*): most ending in a pronounced vowel, *a, é, i, o, u*, and most with the terminations *-age, -ège, -asme, -isme, -iste, -ice, -aire*.

2. Feminine include almost all ending in mute *e* preceded by a vowel or a doubled consonant; most of those ending in mute *e* preceded by *b, c, d, f, h, n, p, s, t, v,* and most terminations *-té, -tié, -ion, -aison, -nce, -nse*.

The plural of nouns is formed in the same way as that of adjectives. The following table illustrates the inflection of nouns according to gender and number:

English	Gender		English	Number	
	Masculine	Feminine		Singular	Plural
friend	ami	amie	king	roi	rois
tutor	gouverneur	gouvernante	arm	bras	bras
negro	nègre	négresse	voice	voix	voix
god	dieu	déesse	journal	journal	journaux
duke	duc	duchesse	castle	château	châteaux
hero	héros	héroïne	work	travail	travaux
ambassador	ambassadeur	ambassadrice	game	jeu	jeux

Pronouns

The personal pronoun inflects in case, number, and person (the third person having masculine and feminine forms), and has a special form to express emphasis, called the disjunctive form. This form is employed in the predicate nominative (*c'est moi*, it is I), or as object of a preposition (*pour moi*, for me).

	I	thou	he (it)	she (it)	we	you	they
Nominative	je	tu ·	il	elle			ils (elles)
Dative	}me	te	{lui {le	lui la	}nous	vous	leur les
Accusative							
Disjunctive	moi	toi	lui	elle			eux (elles)

Verbs

The following table gives the conjugation (simple tenses) of *avoir* (to have), *être* (to be), and the terminations of the three regular conjugations:

Infinitive	avoir	être	— er	— ir	— re
Present participle	ayant	étant	ant	issant	ant
Past participle*	eu	été	é	i	u
Present indicative [1]	ai	suis	— e	— is	— s
	as	es	es	is	s
	a	est	e	it	—
	avons	sommes	ons	issons	ons
	avez	êtes	ez	issez	ez
	ont	sont	ent	issent	ent
Imperfect indicative [2]	avais	étais	— ais	— issais	— ais
	avais	étais	ais	issais	ais
	avait	était	ait	issait	ait
	avions	étions	ions	issions	ions
	aviez	étiez	iez	issiez	iez
	avaient	étaient	aient	issaient	aient
Past definite [3]	eus	fus	— ai	— is	— is
	eus	fus	as	is	is
	eut	fut	a	it	it
	cûmes	fûmes	âmes	îmes	îmes
	eûtes	fûtes	âtes	îtes	îtes
	eurent	furent	èrent	irent	irent
Future [4]	aurai	serai	— erai	— irai	— rai
	auras	seras	eras	iras	ras
	aura	sera	era	ira	ra
	aurons	serons	erons	irons	rons
	aurez	serez	erez	irez	rez
	auront	seront	eront	iront	ront
Conditional [5]	aurais	serais	— erais	— irais	— rais
	aurais	serais	erais	irais	rais
	aurait	serait	erait	irait	rait
	aurions	serions	erions	irions	rions
	auriez	seriez	eriez	iriez	riez
	auraient	seraient	eraient	iraient	raient
Imperative:					
2d person singular	aie	sois	— e	— is	— s
1st person plural	ayons	soyons	ons	issons	ons
2d person plural	ayez	soyez	ez	issez	ez
Present subjunctive [6]	aie	sois	— e	— isse	— e
	aies	sois	es	isses	es
	ait	soit	e	isse	e
	ayons	soyons	ions	issions	ions
	ayez	soyez	iez	issiez	iez
	aient	soient	ent	issent	ent
Imperfect subjunctive [7]	eusse	fusse	— asse	— isse	— isse
	eusses	fusses	asses	isses	isses
	eût	fût	ât	ît	ît
	eussions	fussions	assions	issions	issions
	eussiez	fussiez	assiez	issiez	issiez
	eussent	fussent	assent	issent	issent

[1] This tense is translated by the English present including the progressive and emphatic forms.
[2] Translated usually by the English past or past progressive.
[3] Translated by the English past (preterite) tense.
[4] Translated by the English future.
[5] Translated by the English conditional.
[6] Translated by the English present subjunctive and in most subordinate clauses by the present indicative or potential.
[7] Translated by the past subjunctive and in most subordinate clauses by past indicative or potential. This tense is little used.

*The past participle inflects as to gender and number, agreeing with—

1. The noun of which it is an adjectival modifier:
   Le livre *acheté* hier, the book bought yesterday.
   Les livres *achetés* hier, the books bought yesterday.
   La plume *achetée* hier, the pen bought yesterday.
   Les plumes *achetées* hier, the pens bought yesterday.

2. A direct object that precedes it:
   Quels *livres* a-t-il *achetés?*, what books has he bought?
   But—
   Jai *acheté* bien des *livres*, I bought many books.
   Je *les* ai *achetés*, I bought them.

Each simple tense has a corresponding perfect (or compound) tense, formed by a corresponding form of *avoir* (sometimes *être*) plus the past participle.

The passive voice is formed by the various tenses of *être* plus the past participle.

Abbreviations

Article, titre, chapitre, scène, and *figure* are abbreviated only when they occur in parentheses.

In the following abbreviations superior letters are sometimes used:

a.	accepté, accepted	p.ex.	par exemple, for instance
a.c.	année courante, current year	p.f.s.a.	pour faire ses adieux, to say good-bye
art.	article, article		
av.	avec, with	R.F.	République française, French Republic
B.B.	billet de banque, banknote		
b.à.p.	billets à payer, bills payable	R.S.V.P.	Répondez s'il vous plaît, An answer is requested
b.à.r.	billets à recevoir, bills receivable		
		S.A.R.	Son Altesse Royale, His Royal Highness
c.(pl.c^es)	centime, centimes		
ch.	chapitre, chapter	sc.	scène, scene
ch.de f.	chemin de fer, railway	S.Exc.	Son Excellence, His Excellency
cie [1]	compagnie, company		
c.-à-d.	c'est-à-dire, that is	S.M. (pl. LL. MM.)	Sa Majesté, His (Her) Majesté
Cte	Comte, Count		
E.O.O.E.	erreurs ou omissions exceptées, errors or omissions excepted	Soc.an^e	Société anonyme, limited company
		S.S.	Sa Sainteté, His Holiness
fr., f.	francs, francs	s.v.p.	s'il vous plaît, if you please
h.	heure, hour	t.	tome, book
in-f^o	in folio, folio	tît.	titre, title
J.-C.	Jésus-Christ, Jesus Christ	voy., v.,	voyez, voir, see
M.	Monsieur, Mr.	vve	veuve, widow
Mgr	monseigneur, my lord	&	et, and
MS. (pl. MSS.)	manuscrit, manuscript	1er	premier (*m.*), first
N.-D.	Notre-Dame, Our Lady	1ère	première (*f.*), first
N.-S.	Notre-Seigneur, Our Lord	IIe, 2^e	deuxième, second

Abbreviations of metric signs

mam.	myriamètre	ha.	hectare	g.	gramme
km.	kilomètre	a.	are	dg.	décigramme
hm.	hectomètre	ca.	centiare	cg.	centigramme
dam.	décamètre	das.	décastère	mg.	milligramme
m.	mètre	s., m³	stère	kl.	kilolitre
dm.	décimètre	ds.	décistère	hl.	hectolitre
cm.	centimètre	t.	tonne	dal.	décalitre
mq.	mètre carré	q.	quintal métrique	l.	litre
mm.	millimètre	kg.	kilogramme	dl.	décilitre
mmq.	millimètre carré	hg.	hectogramme	cl.	centilitre
mmc.	millimètre cube	dag.	décagramme	ml.	millilitre

Figures

Numbers are usually spelled in text unless matter is of a statistical nature.

Age and clock time will be spelled, as *huit ans* (eight years); *six heures* (six o'clock).

Dates and figures are spelled in legal documents, as *l'an mil huit cent quatre* (the year one thousand eight hundred and four).

---

[1] It will be noticed that the period is not used where the last letter in the abbreviation is the last letter of the complete word.

Cardinal numbers

un, une	one	soixante et un	sixty-one
deux	two	soixante-dix	seventy
trois	three	soixante et onze	seventy-one
quatre	four	soixante-douze	seventy-two
cinq	five	soixante-treize	seventy-three
six	six	soixante-quatorze	seventy-four
sept	seven	soixante-quinze	seventy-five
huit	eight	soixante-seize	seventy-six
neuf	nine	soixante-dix-sept	seventy-seven
dix	ten	soixante-dix-huit	seventy-eight
onze	eleven	soixante-dix-neuf	seventy-nine
douze	twelve	quatre-vingts	eighty
treize	thirteen	quatre-vingt-un	eighty-one
quatorze	fourteen	quatre-vingt-deux	eighty-two
quinze	fifteen	quatre-vingt-trois	eighty-three
seize	sixteen	quatre-vingt-quatre	eighty-four
dix-sept	seventeen	quatre-vingt-cinq	eighty-five
dix-huit	eighteen	quatre-vingt-six	eighty-six
dix-neuf	nineteen	quatre-vingt-dix	ninety
vingt	twenty	quatre-vingt-onze	ninety-one
vingt et un	twenty-one	quatre-vingt-dix-sept	ninety-seven
vingt-deux	twenty-two	quatre-vingt-dix-huit	ninety-eight
trente	thirty		
trente et un	thirty-one	quatre-vingt-dix-neuf	ninety-nine
quarante	forty		
quarante et un	forty-one	cent	hundred
cinquante	fifty	cent un	one hundred and one
cinquante et un	fifty-one		
soixante	sixty		
		trois cents	three hundred
		mille (mil)	thousand

Ordinal numbers

premier, *m.* \ prem;ère, *f.* /	first	septième	seventh
		huitième	eighth
second \ deuxième /	second	neuvième	ninth
		dixième	tenth
troisième	third	onzième	eleventh
quatrième	fourth	vingt et unième	twenty-first
cinquième	fifth	vingt-deuxième	twenty-second
sixième	sixth	centième	hundredth

Fractions.—The numerator is expressed by a cardinal, the denominator by an ordinal as in English. Half=*moitié* (noun) and *demi* (adjective); $\frac{1}{4}$=*un quart*, $\frac{1}{3}$=*un tiers*. Use *la moitié* (not *demi*), where *the half of* is used in English.
Un huitième; les trois dixièmes=one eighth; the three tenths.
La moitié de l'année=the half of the year.
Une heure et demie=an hour and a half.
Une demi-heure=half an hour.
Les trois quarts de cette somme=three fourths of that sum.

Months

janvier (janv.)	January	juillet (juil.)	July
février (fév.)	February	août	August
mars	March	septembre (sept.)	September
avril (av.)	April	octobre (oct.)	October
mai	May	novembre (nov.)	November
juin	June	décembre (déc.)	December

Days

dimanche	Sunday	jeudi	Thursday
lundi	Monday	vendredi	Friday
mardi	Tuesday	samedi	Saturday
mercredi	Wednesday		

Seasons

printemps	spring	automne	autumn
été	summer	hiver	winter

Time

heure	hour	mois	month
jour	day	saison	season
semaine	week	année	year

Articles to be disregarded in filing

un, *m.*	le, *sing. m.*	la, *sing. f.*	les, *pl. m.*
une, *f.*			*and f.*

GAELIC

Á	á	*a* in call	I	ı	*i*
A	a	*o* in mock	L	l	*l*
B	b	*b* initial; otherwise *p*	M	m	*m*
C	c	*k*	N	n	*n*
D	d	*d;* also *th* in though; also *j* in the Scotch	Ó	ó	*ou* in four
			O	o	*o*
É	é	*a* in fate	P	p	*p*
E	e	*e*	R	r	*r*
F	f	*f*	S	s	*s; sh* before e and ı
G	g	*g;* final, *k*	T	t	*t;* also *ch* in the Scotch
H	h	*h*	Ú	ú	*oo* in wood
Í	í	*ee* in seen	U	u	*u*

The Gaelic is most commonly used in the western counties of Ireland, although, since a measure of independence has been achieved, the Irish Government has made a determined effort to revive the language in all parts of the country. It belongs to the Celtic linguistic family, consisting of five living languages which are divided into two groups, the Gaelic and Cymric. To the first group belongs the Gaelic, the Highland Scotch and the Manx, while the Welsh and Breton (Brittany) belong to the Cymric or Welsh group.

The alphabet was evolved from the Latin and has changed very little since the eighth century. It consists of 18 characters, 5 vowels and 13 consonants; besides these there are a great many vowel combinations, which, however, generally have but a single sound. The most important are:

ei = *ĕ*
ai, ea = *ä*
oi = *ŏ*
io, ui = *ė*
eo = *o*
iu = *o* in who
ái, eá, eái = *ah, aw*
éi, éa = *aye*

ío, áoi = *e* (long)
ói, eó, eói = *o* (long)
úi = *o* in who (long)
áe, ao = *ä* (long)
iúi = *jū*
úa, úai = *ūə*
ía, íai = *īə*

There are two accents, the acute and the dot. The former when placed on vowels indicates that they should be pronounced long. The dot is placed only on consonants and indicates they should be aspirated. The following are especially noticeable:

ḃ, ṁ = *w, v*
ṫ, ṡ = *h*
ċ = *ch*

ġ, ḋ = Modern Greek *γ*, and before e and ı = *y*
ḟ is silent
ṗ = *ph*

Cardinal numbers

aon	one	naoi	nine
ḋá	two	ḋeiċ	ten
trí	three	aon ḋéag	eleven
ceiṫre	four	ḋáḋeag, doḋeag	twelve
cúig	five	tríḋeag	thirteen
sé	six	fiċe	twenty
seaċt	seven	céaḋ	hundred
oċt	eight	míle	thousand

Ordinal numbers

céaḋ	first	naoṁaḋ	ninth
ḋara	second	ḋeaċṁaḋ	tenth
treas	third	aonṁaḋ ḋeag	eleventh
ceaṫramaḋ	fourth	ḋara	twelfth
cúig(ṁ)eaḋ	fifth	treas ḋéag	thirteenth
seireaḋ	sixth	fiċeaḋ	twentieth
seaċtṁaḋ	seventh	ceaḋṁaḋ	hundredth
oċtṁaḋ	eighth	míleaḋ	thousandth

Months

eanaᵱ	January	lúl, -úin, m.	July
feaḃra	February	lúgnasa	August
márta	March	meaḋón fóġmair	September
aḃrán	April	oċtṁí	October
bealtaine	May	samain	November
meiteaṁ	June	mi na nollag	December

Days

omnac, -aiġ, -aiġe, m.	Sunday	ḋiarḋaoin, -e, -nte, f.	Thursday
ḋiluain	Monday	aoine	Friday
márt, -áirt, m.	Tuesday	satarn, -tairn	Saturday
céaḋaoin, -e, f.	Wednesday		

Seasons

earrac	spring	fóġmar	autumn
samraḋ, -aiḋ, m.	summer	geimreaḋ	winter

Time

uaᵱ	hour	mir, míora	month
lá	day	bliaḋain	year
seaċtmain, -e, f.	week		

Articles to be disregarded in filing
an   na

GEORGIC

Name	Mchedruli	Chuzuri		Transliteration	Remarks
An	ა	Ⴇ	ꜰ	a	
Ban	ბ	Ⴁ	ს	b	
Gan	გ	Ⴂ	ჳ	g	
Don	დ	Ⴃ	ჹ	d	
Eni	ე	Ⴄ	ჱ	e	
Win	ვ	Ⴈ	ⴋ	w	
Sen	ზ	Ⴆ	ჼ	z [s]	Weak
He	ჳ	Ⴇ	ჶ	g [e]	Obsolete
Than	თ	Ⴈ	Ꭷ	th	t, strongly aspirated
In	ი	Ⴉ	ꜩ	i	
Kan	კ	Ⴉ	ꜧ	k [kk]	Unaspirated k, long, with final falling inflection
Las	ლ	Ⴊ	Ꭾ	l	
Man	მ	Ⴋ	ჽ	m	
Nar	ნ	Ⴌ	ჶ	n	
Je	ჲ	Ⴐ	Ꭳ	i̤ [y]	Obsolete
On	ო	Ⴍ	ꜵ	o	Short
Par	პ	Ⴎ	Ꭹ	p [pp]	Unaspirated p, long, with final falling inflection
Schan	ჟ	Ⴏ	Ꭽ	ž [sch]	Soft, like j in French journal
Rae	რ	Ⴓ	Ꭽ	r	r, lingual
San	ს	Ⴑ	Ꮈ	s	Hard
Ttan	ტ	Ⴒ	Ꮆ	t [tt]	Unaspirated t, long, with final falling inflection
Un	უ	Ⴍ	Ꮃ	u [w]	
Vi	ჳ	Ⴍ	Ꮅ	ṳ [vi]	Obsolete
Phar	ფ	Ⴔ	ꝑ	ph	p, highly aspirated
Khan	ქ	Ⴕ	Ꭽ	kh	k, highly aspirated
Ghan	ღ	Ⴖ	Ꮄ	ġ [gh]	g, as in Dutch geel; voiced back palatal
Qar	ყ	Ⴗ	Ꮇ	q	Deep guttural
Schin	შ	Ⴘ	Ꮍ	š [sch]	Hard

GEORGIC—Continued

Name	Mche-druli	Chuzuri		Trans-literation	Remarks
Tschin	ჩ	Ⴡ	ⴡ	č [tsch]	
Tßan	Ⴚ	Ⴚ	ⴚ	c	tsz
Dßil	Ⴛ	ⴃ	ⴛ	dz [ds]	
Tsil	ⴅ	Ⴐ	ⴓ	c [z]	Hard, long, with final falling inflection
Dschar	ⴟ	Ⴝ	ⴝ	č [dsch]	Long, with final falling inflection
Chan	ⴙ	Ⴞ	ⴞ	b [ch]	Hard, like German ach
Khar	ⴌ	Ⴗ	ⴗ	h [khh]	Very hard; obsolete
Dschan	ⴌ	Ⴘ	ⴘ	dž [dsch]	Soft
Hae	ⴌ	Ⴇ	ⴓ	h	
Hoe		Ⴠ	ⴠ	ho	Obsolete

This is the language of the successors of the old Kolchian tribes on the southwest slopes of the Caucasus Mountains. It is the remnant of a once prolific language group, of which the Sumerian was the center, and consists of three dialects; the pure Georgic, in the eastern section, was the only one to become a literary language, of which remnants still exist that date back to the fifth century.

The Mchedruli alphabet shown above was generally used, except in ecclesiastical writings where the Chuzuri was employed, hardly a remnant of which exists today.

The text reads from left to right.

Syllabication is entirely phonetical, and punctuation is the same as in English.

Stress is always on the first syllable, but not farther back than the antepenultimate.

There are no diphthongs and all words end in a vowel.

In ancient times the Chuzuri letters were also employed as numerals in religious manuscripts, but the Arabic figures are now used.

Continental sounds are employed in transliterating the alphabet.

GERMAN

𝔄	α	*a* in father	𝔓	p	*p*, or *f* in combination *ph*
𝔅	b	*b*	𝔔	q	*kv*
ℭ	c	*c* in can (before *e*, *i*, and *y*, like *ts* in quarts	ℜ	r	*r* as in wary
𝔇	d	*d*	𝔖	ſ s	*s* in son, or in rose before vowels, or soft *sh* before initial *t* or *p*
𝔈	e	*e* in end (short), or *a* in ale (long)	𝔗	t	*t*
𝔉	f	*f*	𝔘	u	*oo* in coo
𝔊	g	*g* in gay	𝔙	v	*f* in fan
𝔥	h	*h*, initial; otherwise mute	𝔚	w	*v* in van
𝔍	i	*i* in pin (short), *ee* in feeder (long)	𝔛	x	*ks*
			𝔜	y	*y* in lyric ·
𝔍	j	*y* in year	3	ʒ	*ts* in quarts or *ds*
𝔎	k	*k*	𝔄̈	ä	Similar to *a* in fate
𝔏	l	*l*	𝔒̈	ö	*eu* in French feu
𝔐	m	*m*	𝔘̈	ü	Similar to ee in see, with lips protruding
𝔑	n	*n*			
𝔒	o	*aw* in awe (short), *o* in more (long)			

The language has no accent marks; the diacritical marks used are *ä, ö, ü*.

The Latin alphabet is coming into general use in German printing, and all 26 letters are used, with the addition of the ß or *sz*, which is used only in the lower case.

Although modern German dates back to the time of Martin Luther (1483–1546), the language may be said to have entered on a new stage through the influence of the great classical writers of the eighteenth century. Except in some minor details, that is the present-day language of Germany.

Phonetics

The characters of the alphabet are pronounced as shown in the table. However, the following remarks should be noted:

(*a*) There are no silent letters, except medial or final *h*, and *e* in the digraph *ie*.

(*b*) The diphthongs *ai*, *au*, *ei*, *eu*, and *äu* are pronounced as *i* in pine, *ow* in now, *i* in mine, *oi* in oil, *oy* in toy, respectively.

(*c*) The compound character *ch* is a guttural fricative. To pronounce the German word *Dach* properly, utter the English "dock", but instead of the final click, make an audible rubbing or rasping sound.

(*d*) The letter *s* before a vowel is sounded like *s* in rose, before *t* or *p* like *sh*.

(*e*) *Sch* is always pronounced like the English *sh*.

(*f*) *Th* is never pronounced like the English *th*, but always like *t*.

The *th* is always pronounced like *t*, never like the voiced *th* in then, or the voiceless in thin. This combination occurs in modern German only in words of foreign origin, such as *Theater*, *Thema*, *Theodor*, *Balthasar*, and also a few old German names, as *Lothar*, *Mathilde*. In pure German words formerly written with *th* the *h* has been eliminated: *Tür*, *Tor*, *tun*, *Bertold*, *Walter*, *Berta*, etc.

German vowels are either long or short; in the former case the respective sounds are somewhat prolonged, while in the latter they are shortened. In no case, however, does a long vowel assume the distinct vanishing sound possessed by the English long *a*, or does a short vowel change in quality or nature of sound. Vowels are long (1) when doubled: *Aal, Heer, Boot;* (2) when stressed and followed by a single consonant: *le'gen, lo'ben, rot;* (3) when followed by *h*, with or without a consonant: *Kahn, mehr,* Ruh; (4) when stressed and terminal: *wo, je, ja*.

They are short (1) before a double consonant or group of two consonants, unless the last of the group belongs to a flexional ending: *kann, Welt*, but *le'gte* (from *le'gen*); when unstressed: *ha'bĕn, Gĕbe't, dăru'm*.

Compounding

Compounds are much more numerous and extensive in German than in English, especially in official and technical language: *Reichsoberpostamtszeitungsschreiber* (editor of the imperial general post-office journal). The components may, though not usually, be joined by hyphens, dependent on the taste of the writer: *Feuerversicherungs-Gesellschaft, Feuer-Versicherungs-Gesellschaft*, or *Feuer-Versicherungsgesellschaft* (fire insurance company).

When, in compounding, three concurrent consonants result between two vowels, one is dropped, otherwise the three are retained: *Schiffahrt* (navigation), *Brennessel* (nettle), *alliebend* (all-loving), but *stickstofffrei* (free of nitrogen), *Taburettthron* (taburet throne).

In dividing words in which consonantal elision was effected, the letter elided must be restored: *Schiff-fahrt, all-liebend*, etc.

Insert a hyphen where elision may lead to confusion with terms regularly written with a double consonant: *Bettuch* (from *Bett* and *Tuch*), bed sheet, but *Bet-Tuch*, prayer shawl.

Street names

Although, according to rule, adjectives are not capitalized, exception is made when they are used as part of a proper name: *die Breite Strasse*.

Although, in ordinary usage *Breite Strasse*, etc., are often used as one word, or with a hyphen, that is incorrect according to the rule approved by the German Ministry of the Interior and Education. This provides that the basic words *strasse, gasse, platz, allee, chausee, promenade, ufer, graben, gracht, steg, tor, brücke*, etc., shall be joined to the limiting word only when the latter is a noun and forms with the basic word a readily comprehensible compound: *Immanuelkirchstrasse, Schillerstrasse*, etc.

Where the compound would not be easily understood, it shall be hyphenated. This is also true in double compounds where two names, or a title and a name, are used as limiting words and the second is not more closely related to the basic word than is the first: *Friedrich-Wilhelm-Strasse, Prinz-Bismarck-Platz*, etc.

Where the limiting word is an adjective or a derivative from a noun, it will not be compounded with the basic word: *Grosse Strasse, Potsdamer Platz*, etc. But where these adjectives are not derived from the names of cities they will be joined into a single word: *Hohenstaufenplatz*, etc.

Orthography

In words of Latin origin which in the original have a hard *c*, the *k* is regularly employed, especially those beginning with *ko, kol, kom, kon*, etc.: *Kommandeur, faktisch, Publikum*. However, words having a foreign pronunciation, derived especially from the French, retain the *c*: *Coiffeur, Coupe, Courage*, etc. Those which in the original have a soft *c* employ a *z*, as a rule: *Medizin, Offizier*.

The Latin *ti* changes to *zi* when following an accepted syllable, otherwise it remains *ti*: *Gra'zie*, but *Nation', Patient'*. The Latin *cti* is always *kti*: *Aktie*, while the *cc* becomes either *kk* or *kz*, dependent on whether the second consonant is hard or soft: *Akkord, Akzent*.

In transliterating the German ß into roman character, *sz* or the digraph *β* are employed.

If a word ending in ß is followed by another word to form a compound, the ß is retained: losgeben, bisher, dasselbe, Donnerstag. The final ß is also used before a derivative ending which begins with a consonant: Weisheit, Röslein, lösbar; also in foreign words before all consonants, except *t* or *p*: Maske, Discours, Patriotismus.

Capitalize all nouns, both common and proper, including adjectives and infinitives used as nouns: *Der Gute und der Böse*, the good and the wicked; *mit seinem höflichen Grüssen*, with his polite greeting; *zum Schmausen*, for feasting; although we also have *die lutherische Kirche*, the Lutheran church, and *mohammedanische Pilger*, Mohammedan pilgrims.

When used as the polite form of address in the second person, the pronoun of the third person is capitalized in all of its oblique forms and its corresponding possessive, but not its reflexive: *Sie*, you; *Ihnen*, to you; *Ihr*, your, but *sich*, yourself.

Accentuation

The principles of stress are generally like those in English and fall on—
1. The root or significant syllable: *Va'ter*, father; *le'bend*, living;
2. The first term of compound nouns, adjectives and verbs: *Fracht'zug*, freight train; *rot'farbig*, red colored; *los'brechen*, to break loose;
3. The second term of compounds: *dahin'*, thither; *herauf'*, up, up here;
4. The ultima of words of foreign origin: *Nation'*, *Partie'*;
5. The penult of words of foreign origin terminating in a disyllabic suffix or in *ōr*, *er*, *el*: Lemona'de, studie'ren, Prinzes'se, Dok'tor, Kör'per;
6. The negative prefix *un'treu*, faithless.

Stress never falls on inseparable prefixes as *be*, *emp*, *ent*, *er*, *ge*, *ver* and *zer*: *Gesell'schaft*, association; *Erklä'rung*, explanation, etc.

Punctuation

Punctuation marks are practically the same as in English, except that—
1. The comma is used to set off all subordinate clauses, whether restrictive or not: *Ich bin der Geist, der stets verneint*, I am the spirit that always denies;
2. The hyphen is used to indicate a suppressed member of a compound: *Land- und Wassertiere*, land and water animals; *Zahlenreihen und -bilder*, numerical series and symbols;
3. Quotation marks ordinarily appear thus: „*Ende gut, alles gut.*"

Emphasis is usually indicated by letter spacing the stressed words: *Bedenke erst das w i e , dann das w a r u m* , think first of the *how*, then of the *why*.

The digraph *ß* is pronounced like the *ss* and properly should replace the latter; when used th efollowing rules govern:
1. At the end of the word: *Haß*, hatred, but Hasses, of the hatred;
2. Before derivative terminations (not flexional endings): *mußig*, idle;
3. At the end of compounded terms: *Faßreif*, barrel hoop;
4. Before consonants *haßte* (from hassen), hated;
5. With the prefix *miß* (*mis-*, *dis-*, *in-*, etc.);
6. After a double vowel: *genießen*, to enjoy;
7. After a single long vowel: *stößen*, to push; *Mäße*, measures, but *Masse*, mass; *äßen*, ate, but *Asse*, aces; *rüßig*, sooty, but *russisch*, Russian.

There is no simple rule for determining whether a single vowel before the *ss* is long or short. The following lists, with the dictionary, are the only sure guide with respect to the *ß*, except that *e* and *i* are always short before *ss* and take *ss* after them, unless this conflicts with the first six rules above: *wissen*, to know, but *weißt*, knows; *essen*, to eat, but *ißt*, eats.

In the following words the *ß* is preceded by a long vowel and is therefore retained in all inflected forms:

aßen, to graze	Maß, measure
bloß, naked	Muße, leisure
blößen, to expose	Ruß, soot
Buße, compensation	rußen, to blacken
büßen, to make amends	Schoß, lap
Floß, raft	Soße, sauce
flößen, to float	Spaß, jest
Fuß, foot	spaßen, to jest
fußen, to set foot on	Stoß, a push
groß, great	stoßen, to push
Gruß, greeting	Stößel, pestle
grüßen, to greet	Straße, street
Kloß, clod	süß, sweet

The following verbs take a long single vowel in the past indicative and subjunctive and hence change the *ss* to *ß* in all forms of these two tenses:

Infinitive	Past indicative	Past subjunctive
essen, to eat	aß	äße
fressen, to devour	fraß	fräße
messen, to measure	maß	mäße
sitzen, to sit	saß	säße
vergessen	vergaß	vergäße

In poetry, words having medial *ss* do not change to *ß* upon the elision of the final vowel: *Küsse, Küss'* (not *Küß'*); *Fasse, Fass'* (not *Faß'*).

The *ß*, not its equivalent *sz* or *ss*, is never divided.

Modal auxiliaries

This group of verbs constitute a unique class, with irregularities not found in the other auxiliaries and uses that are strange to their English equivalents and thus it is important that these should be understood.

The present and past tenses only will be presented, since these are the only irregularly inflected forms; the other tenses conjugating like the verb *loben*, except that the past participle has two forms, the functions of which will be explained. The principal parts of these auxiliaries are as follows: [1]

durfte	dürfen	gedurft *or* dürfen
konnte	können	gekonnt *or* können
mochte	mögen	gemocht *or* mögen
musste	müssen	gemusst *or* müssen
sollte	sollen	gesollt *or* sollen
wollte	wollen	gewollt *or* wollen

The present and past tenses are inflected as follows (variations for the subjunctive being given in parentheses):

Present	dürfen	können	mögen	müssen	sollen	wollen
ich	darf (dürfe)	kann (könne)	mag (möge)	muss (müsse)	soll(e)	will (wolle)
du	darfst (dürfest)	kannst (könnest)	magst (mögest)	musst (müssest)	soll(e)st	willst (wollest)
er	darf (dürfe)	kann (könne)	mag (möge)	muss (müsse)	soll(e)	will (wolle)
wir	dürfen	können	mögen	müssen	sollen	wollen
ihr	dürf(e)t	könn(e)t	mög(e)t	müss(e)t	soll(e)t	woll(e)t
sie	dürfen	können	mögen	müssen	sollen	wollen
Past						
ich	du(ü)rfte*	ko(ö)nnte	mo(ö)chte	mu(ü)sste	sollte	wollte
du	du(ü)rf-test	ko(ö)nn-test	mo(ö)ch-test	mu(ü)ss-test	solltest	wolltest
er	du(ü)rfte	ko(ö)nnte	mo(ö)chte	mu(ü)sste	sollte	wollte
wir	du(ü)rften	ko(ö)nnten	mo(ö)chten	mu(ü)ssten	sollten	wollten
ihr	du(ü)rftet	ko(ö)nntet	mo(ö)chtet	mu(ü)sstet	solltet	wolltet
sie	du(ü)rften	ko(ö)nnten	mo(ö)chten	mu(ü)ssten	sollten	wollten

As stated, the perfect tenses have two forms:

1. In which the ordinary *ge-* form of the past participle is used, the auxiliary not having any dependent infinitives: *Ich habe es gewollt*, I wanted it; *er hat es nicht gewollt*, he did not want it.

2. The form *-en* is used when the past participle of the auxiliary is preceded by a dependent infinitive: *Ich habe es lesen wollen*, I wanted to read it; *er hat es nicht tun können*, he could not do it.

There are two reasons why these auxiliaries are translated variously:

1. Their English cognates are defective verbs, e. g., the English *must* has but one tense, and thus the various tenses of the German basic equivalent *mussen* can be rendered only by circumlocution.

2. Their original root meanings have ramified into other senses, the most common being as follows:

For *dürfen*:

1. Ordinarily, *may* in present; *might* in past. *Darf ich fragen?* May I ask? *Es dürfte wohl geschehen*, it might happen.

2. Before the adverb *nur* (but). *Du darfst nur sagen*, you need but say;

3. The past subjunctive (to be likely). *Das dürfte wahr sein*, that is likely to be true.

4. The past perfect subjunctive (ought have). *Sie hätten es nicht vergessen dürfen*, they ought not have forgotten it.

---

[1] As these auxiliaries have various translations, the meanings are omitted.

For *können*:
1. Originally, to know. *Ich kann es auswendig*, I know it by heart.
2. Ordinarily, can, be able. *Ich kann es machen*, I can do it.

For *mögen*:
1. Originally, may. *Sie mögen es tun*, they may do it.
2. Ordinarily, to wish, want, care. *Ich mag ihn nicht sehen*, I do not wish to see him.
3. The past subjunctive, should (would) like. *Ich möchte (gern) wissen*, I should like to know.

For *müssen*:
1. Present tense, must. *Ich muss gehen*, I must go.
2. Past tense, had to, was obliged: *Ich musste gehen*, I had to go.
3. Past subjunctive, could need. *Er müsste kommen*, he would need to come.

For *sollen*:
1. Ordinarily, in the present, shall. *Du sollst nicht töten*, thou shalt not kill.
2. Past tense, was to. *Er sollte bald sterben*, he was to die soon.
3. In reporting hearsay, is said to be. *Er soll reich sein*, he is said to be rich.

For *wollen*:
1. Ordinarily, to wish, will. *Ich will gehen*, I wish to go.
2. With perfect infinitive, to claim: *Er will gehört haben*, he claims to have heard.
3. Past subjunctive with *lieber*, had rather: *Ich wollte lieber nichts davon wissen*, I had rather know nothing of it.
4. With impersonals, to mean: *Das will nichts sagen*, that means nothing.

Passive voice

The passive voice is regularly formed by combining the past participle of the verb with the auxiliary *werden*: *Ich werde gelobt*, I am praised; *Er wurde gelobt*. he was praised.

Capitalization

Initial capital letters are used as follows:
(*a*) The first word of a sentence.
(*b*) In poetry, usually, the first word of each line.
(*c*) The first word of a direct quotation; also the first word after a colon. An exception to this rule occurs when the matter following is merely complementary to the preceding. For example, "At home he was seldom, to the Court he never came: if you would find him, you must needs seek him in the forest." Lower case after interrogation and exclamation points if the phrase following is directly connected, as in "Where do we go from here?" the man said; and "Give me liberty or give me death!" cried Patrick Henry. The first word of titles of books also has a capital initial.

All nouns are capitalized, although there is an ever-growing movement in Germany to lower case common nouns.

Pronouns relating to the person addressed, as in letters, etc., as well as titles of honor, are capitalized.

The custom of capitalizing proper nouns used as adjectives is quite variable. We have *Schillersche Trauerspiele*, *Grimmsche Märchen*, but also *die lutherische Kirche* and *mohammedanische Pilger*.

Any word used as a noun (for example, *der Nächste*, *die Armen*, *das Rechte*, *Gutes*, *Böses*, etc.), takes a capital initial.

In solid matter, where the Umlaut (¨) on capital letters is likely to cause trouble in alinement, it will be omitted and a lower-case *e* added after the capital, as *Ae*, (Aerger), *Oe* (Oel), *Ue* (Ueber).

Hyphens

In words made up of two parts, where one part is common to both words, use the hyphen as follows: *Feld- und Gartenfrüchte* (field- and garden produce), the word *früchte* being common to both, and though a noun, is lower-cased; but use *Haftpflicht-Versicherungsgesellschaft und -Versicherte* (liability-insurance company and -insured), because the first is a compound word made up of two nouns.

Combinations of two or more words are printed without hyphens, *Fluss Wasser Stoff Säure* becomes *Flusswasserstoffsäure*.

Where the em dash is used in text in parenthetical phrases, put a space on each side of the dash — , using a thick or thin space, according to the spacing of the rest of the line.

Gender

There are three genders: Masculine (denoting males, or nouns terminating in *ich, ig, ling, rich, er, ler, ner*); feminine (denoting females, or nouns terminating in *ei, heit, keit, schaft, ung, age, ie, ik*, and *(t)ion*); neuter (denoting diminutives, and those nouns ending in *sal, sel, nis, tum*, and infinitives). As there are a great many exceptions in each category, the dictionary must serve as the only dependable guide.

Articles

The articles are *ein, eine, ein* (masculine, feminine, and neuter, respectively), which are indefinite; *der, die, das* (masculine, feminine, and neuter, respectively), are definite. They decline, agreeing with the noun in gender, number, and case. The indefinite article has no plural.

Adjectives

Adjectives used predicatively are indeclinable; when attributive, they decline in agreement with the noun. The comparison of regular adjectives may be observed in the following table. Note suffixes as well as internal changes:

Positive	Comparative	Superlative
reich, rich	reich*er*	reich*st* (am reichsten) [1]
lang, long	läng*er*	läng*st* (am längsten)
kurz, short [2]	kür*zer*	kür*zest* (am kürzesten)

Noun

In the following table the declension of a masculine, a feminine, and a neuter noun (*Kopf*, head; *Seele*, soul; *Herz*, heart) is shown in conjunction with the definite *der*, a pronominal (*kein*, no), and an adjective (*gut*, good), to illustrate their respective inflections:

SINGULAR

Nom.	{ *der* [2] gute / kein guter	} Kopf	{ die / keine	} gute Seele	{ das gute / kein gut*es*	} Herz
Gen.	{ *des* / keines	} guten Kopfes	{ *der* / keiner	} guten Seele	{ *des* / keines	} guten Herzens
Dat.	{ *dem* / keinem	} guten Kopfe	{ *der* / keiner	} guten Seele	{ *dem* / keinem	} guten Herzen
Acc.	{ *den* / keinen	} guten Kopf	{ die / keine	} gute Seele	{ das gute / kein gut*es*	} Herz

PLURAL

Nom.	{ die / keine	} Köpfe		
Gen.	{ der / keiner	} Köpfe	} guten	} Seelen, Herzen
Dat.	{ den / keinen	} Kopfen		
Acc.	{ die / keine	} Köpfe		

[1] The parenthetical superlative form is used predicatively without an article: *Es ist am schönsten in Juni* (It is loveliest in June).
[2] See note (c) on page 96.

NOTES

(a) The plural adjective has the same endings for all genders and cases.

(b) The singular nominative, masculine and neuter, and the accusative neuter have two endings, dependent on whether the adjective is preceded by the definite article or by the pronominal or indefinite article.

(c) The inflection of the adjective is the so-called "weak" inflection. The "strong" inflection is employed when no article or pronominal precedes·it. In that case its endings are as shown in italics in the table.

(d) The declension of the nouns illustrated is that of the strong declension. There are also nouns that belong to the weak or mixed declensions which form the nominative plural with $e(n)$ and a few other terminal changes.

(e) The functions of the four cases shown are similar to the subjective, possessive, indirect object, and direct object, respectively, in English, except that the genitive, dative, and accusative are also governed by certain prepositions.

Pronouns

The personal pronouns are declined as follows:

	I	Thou	He	She	It	We	You	They
Nom.	ich	du	er	sie	es	wir	ihr	sie
Gen.	meiner	deiner	seiner	ihrer	seiner	unser	euer	ihrer
Dat.	mir	dir	ihm	ihr	ihm	uns	euch	ihnen
Acc.	mich	dich	ihn	sie	es	uns	euch	sie

The possessives (including the indefinite article which has only a singular form) are declined like *kein* in the previous table and govern adjective inflections as *kein* does. The pronominals *dies-,-jen-, jed-* and *jeglich* function as *der*.

Verbs

The verbs inflect for voice, mood, tense, person, and number, with functions similar to those in English. Following are paradigms of the regular (weak) verb *loben*, to praise, and of the irregular (strong) verb *fallen*, to fall; the first takes the auxiliary *haben*, to have, the second (being a verb of motion or change of condition) requires the auxiliary *sein*, to be. The parenthetical elements indicate the variation for the subjunctive.

Principal parts {loben, lobte, gelobt (praise, praised, praised)
{fallen, fiel, gefallen (fall, fell, fallen)

Present	ich lobe	ich falle
	du lob(e)st	du fallst (fallest)
	er lobt (lobe)	er fällt (falle)
	wir loben	·wir fallen
	ihr lob(e)t	ihr fall(e)t
	sie loben	sie fallen
Past	ich lobte	ich fiel(e)
	du lobtest	du fiel(e)st
	er lobte	er fiel(e)
	wir lobten	wir fielen
	ihr lobtet	ihr fiel(e)t
	sie lobten	sie fielen

Present perfect	ich habe gelobt	ich bin gefallen
Past perfect	ich hatte (hätte) gelobt	ich war (wäre) gefallen
Future	ich werde loben	ich werde fallen
Future perfect	ich werde gelobt haben	ich werde gefallen sein
Present condi-tional.	ich würde loben	ich würde fallen
Perfect condi-tional.	ich würde gelobt haben	ich würde gefallen sein
Imperative	lobe (praise thou)	falle (fall thou)
	lobt (praise you)	fallet (fall you)
	loben sie[1] (let them praise)	fallen sie[1] (let them fall)
Perfect infini-tive.	gelobt zu haben (to have praised).	gefallen zu sein (to have fallen)

Present parti-   lobend (praising)   fallend (falling)
ciple.

Following are the conjugations of the verbs *haben*, to have; *sein*, to be; *werden*, to become.   The chief auxiliaries in the German conjugations, the present and past tenses being given.   The remainder are formed analogically with the preceding paradigm (subjunctive in parentheses).

Principal parts { sein, war, gewesen (be, was, were).
haben, hatte, gehabt (have, had, had).
werden, wurde, geworden (become, became, become).

	Sein		Haben		Werden	
	Present	Past	Present	Past	Present	Past
Ich	bin (sei)	war (wäre)	habe	ha(ä)tte	werde	wu(ü)rde
du	bist (seiest)	warst (wärest)	ha(be)st	ha(ä)ttest	wirst (werdest)	wu(ü)rdest
er	ist (sei)	war (wäre)	hat (habe)	ha(ä)tte	wird (werde)	wu(ü)rde
wir	sind (seien)	wa(ä)ren	haben	ha(ä)tten	werden	wu(ü)rden
ihr	seid (seiet)	wart (wäret)	hab(e)t	ha(ä)ttet	werdet	wu(ü)rdet
sie[1]	sind (seien)	wa(ä)ren	haben	ha(ä)tten	werden	wu(ü)rden

Word order

Three word orders prevail as regards the position of the finite verb in the sentence: Normal, inverted, and transposed.   The first is used when the subject begins the sentence; the second when an interrogative or adverb begins the sentence; the third in subordinate clauses:

Normal   *Der Knabe ist gefallen*, the boy has fallen.
Inverted   *Wo ist der Knabe gefallen?*   Where has the boy fallen?
Transposed   *Ich weiss wo der Knabe gefallen ist.* I know where the boy has fallen.

Syllabication

The following rules are based on the Prussian "Book of Rules":
I. Polysyllabic words are divided, as a rule, phonetically—i.e., as they naturally divide themselves when pronounced slowly and distinctly, as *Wör-ter-ver-zeich-nis*, *Ge-schlech-ter*, *Ueber-lie-fe-rung*. Syllables consisting of but one letter should not be divided.

NOTE 1.—Avoid the somewhat common division *-ung* in *Lie-fer-ung*, *Schreib-ung*, which is contrary to the above rule.
NOTE 2.—(*a*) If there be but one consonant, carry it over, as *tre-ten*, *nä-hen;* also (*b*), *ch, sch, sz, ph*, and *th* have but a single sound and are therefore indivisible, as *Bü-cher, Hä-scher, Bu-sze, So-phie, ka-tho-lisch; x* and *z* are considered simple consonants, *He-xe, rei-zen*.

Where there are more than one consonant, the last is carried over, as *An-ker*, *Fin-ger, War-te, Rit-ter, Was-ser, Knos-pe, tap-fer, kämp-fen, Karp-fen, Ach-sel*, *krat-zen, Städ-te, Ver-wand-te*.
The *ƌ* or *ck* is changed to *ff* or *kk* when division is necessary, as ßaf=fe, *Bük-ker*
St is never divided, as *ha-sten, be-ste, ko-sten, Klo-ster, mei-ste, Fen-ster, For-ster*, *Pfing-sten*.
(1) These rules are inflexible, but the last does not apply in the case of *äs-the-tisch*, since this is not a separation of *st*, but rather of *s* and *th*.
(2) In simple non-German words the phonetic combinations of *b, p, d, t, g*, and *k* in connection with *l* and *r* are not separated, as *Pu-bli-kum, Me-trum*, *Hy-drant*.

[1] This form is also used for the second person singular and plural, polite form, except that *Sie* is then capitalized.

(3) Retain also the phonetic combination *gn*, since, in most cases, it will be found phonetically correct, as *Ba-gno*, *Ma-gno-lie*, *Ma-gnet*, *Si-gnet*, etc. *Kompag-nie* is, however, an exception because here the *g* is really silent and the last syllable begins with an *n*.

II. Compound words are separated into their physical parts and these are then treated as simple words, as *Diens-tag*, *Tür-an-gel*, *Emp-fangs-an-zei-ger*, *Vor-aus-set-zung*. This rule applies also in certain cases where it appears phonetically incorrect, as *hier-auf*, *hin-aus*, *dar-über*, *war-um*, *wor-an*, *be-ob-ach-ten*, *voll-en-den*.

This is also the case in certain compound words of foreign origin, as *at-mosphä-re*, *Mi-kro-skop*, *In-ter-es-se*, but if the constituent parts of a foreign word are unknown, proceed as directed in (*a*) and (*b*) of Note 2.

Compound geographic names are no exception to this rule, as *Frie-den-au*, *Schwarz-ach*, etc.

III. An old rule prohibiting the division of vowel combinations has been modified to permit division if the vowels do not dissolve, forming a diphthong. This rule also applies in the case of those foreign groups of vowels that cannot be separated into distinct separate sounds in pronunciation, as the French *oi* in *coiffeur*, *oy* in *royalist*, *ay* in *rayon*, *ea* in *orgeade*, as well as the English *ea* in *Lear* and *ee* and *ea* in *beefsteak*. It is also self-evident that in such words as *Trauung* and *Kasteiung* the separation of the final -*ung* is permissible.

Prefixes *be* and *ge* are also separable from words beginning with a vowel, as *be-ar-bei-ten*, *be-er-ben*, *ge-ar-tet*, *ge-eb-net*.

Aside from these exceptions, vowels should not ordinarily be separated, although indicated in the following cases, when unavoidable due to narrow type measure:

(*a*) When the first vowel is stressed, as *Hy-peri-on*, *Mu-se-um*.

(*b*) When both are equal but pronounced separately, as *lini-ie-ren*, *Sper-ma-to-zo-on*, *In-di-vi-du-um*.

(*c*) When a short word cannot possibly be divided otherwise, as *Oze-an*.

(*d*) When each vowel retains its own sound, as *Ela-in*, *Ka-per-na-um*, *kre-iren*, *Zel-lu-lo-id*.

Where the object of the second vowel is merely to lengthen the sound of the first, do not separate them, as *Aachen*, *Moos*.

NOTE 3.—In printing, a two-letter run-over is permissible only in very narrow measure.

IV. Where space is limited there are certain other permissible divisions that are entirely contrary to the foregoing rules. *Glit-sch(e)st* is a case of this kind; the word *glitschst*, having but one syllable, is indivisible, but by adding the *e* it may be divided: *glit-schest*.

V. If a compound noun is run over so that the second or third part of the compound begins the next line, the latter must not be capitalized. Do not use—

        Gepäck-
        Annahme

but

        Gepäck-
        annahme.

With German text the round ẞ is used in dividing only in those cases where it would have been used had the word not been divided—i.e., at the end of a prefix or component part of a compound word and in a few words of foreign derivation, as Blasphemie, Mollusfe, fonfiszieren, Konfisfation, fosmetisch, Kosmogonie, Jschia, Esfimo, viszeral, Escorial, Escapade, Sansfrit, Susquehanna, disputieren; elsewhere the long ſ is used, as Drechsler, Messer, etc.

Abbreviations

The following are some common abbreviations in German:

A.	acceptiert, accepted; Acker, acre	ca.	circa, about
Abk.	Abkürzung, abbreviation	D.R.P.	Deutsches Reichspatent, German patent
a.c.	anni currentis, current year	d.A.,	der Ältere, Sr.
a.D.	ausser Dienst, retired	d.J.	der Jüngere, Jr.; dieses Jahres, the current year
A.G.	Aktiengesellschaft, joint stock company	Dr.	Doktor, doctor
a.M.	am Main, on the Main River	E.V.	Eingang vorbehalten, rights reserved
Art.	Artikel, article		
bez.	bezüglich, respecting	eng.	englisch, English
bezw.	beziehungsweise, respectively (also bzw.)	erg.	ergänze, supply, add
		ff.	folgende, following
Br.	Bruder, Brother	Forts.	Fortsetzung, continuation

fr.	franko, postpaid	s.	siehe, see
Fr.	Frau, Mrs.	sel.	selig, deceased, late
Frl.	Fräulein, Miss	Ser.	Serie, series
geb.	geboren, born, née	S.M.	Seine Majestät, his majesty
gleichbd.	gleichbedeutend, syn- onymous	sog.	sogenannt, so-called
		st.	statt, instead of
G.m.b.	Gesellschaft mit beschränk-	Skt.	Sankt, Saint
H.	ter Haftung, corporation with limited liability	s.o.	siehe oben, see above
		St.	Stück, each
HH.	Herren, Messrs.	s.u.	siehe unten, see below
hrsg.	herausgegeben, published	Thlr.	Thaler, dollar
i.a.	im allgemeinen, in general	U.	Uhr, hour, o'clock
I.G.	Interessengemeinschaft, amalgamation, trust	u.	und, and
		u. a.	unter anderen, among others;
I.M.	Ihre Majestät, your majesty		und andere, and others
Ing.	Ingenieur, engineer	u.A.w.g.	um Antwort wird gebeten,
Kap.	Kapitel, chapter		R.S.V.P.
Komp.	Kompanie, company	u.drgl.	und dergleichen, and the like
kgl.	königlich, royal	unbest.	unbestimmt, indefinite
M.	Mark, mark (coin)	u.s.w.	und so weiter, et cetera
nachm.(nM.)	Nachmittags, afternoon	v. Chr.	vor Christo, before Christ
näml.	nämlich, namely	v. Chr. G.	vor Christi Geburt, before
n.Chr.	nach Christo, anno Domini		birth of Christ
n.Chr.G.	nach Christi Geburt, after birth of Christ	vgl.	vergleiche, compare
		v.H.	vom Hundert, of the hundred
n.F.	neue Folge, new series	v.J.	vorigen Jahres, of the past
no., ntto.	netto, net		year
Nr., Nro.	Numero, number	v.M.	vorigen Monats, ult.; Vormit-
od.	oder, or		tags, a.m.
p.Ct.	pro Cent, percent	Wwe.	Witwe, widow
Pf.	Pfennig, penny	Xber.	Dezember, December (rare)
Pfd.	Pfund, pound, pounds	Xr.	Kreuzer, cruiser; Kreutzer, a
Q.	Quadrat, square		coin
Rab.	Rabatt, discount	z.	zur, to the
resp.	respektiv, respectively	z.B.	zum Beispiel, for example
rglm.	regelmässig, regular(ly)	zk.	zirka
Rm.	Reichsmark, reichsmark (coin	Zs.	Zeitschrift, periodical
S.	Seite, page	Ztr.	Zentner, hundredweight
		zw.	zwischen, between

Chemical signs and symbols are used as in English.

Cardinal numbers

eins	one	zehn	ten
zwei	two	elf	eleven
drei	three	zwölf	twelve
vier	four	dreizehn	thirteen
fünf	five	zwanzig	twenty
sechs	six	ein und zwanzig	twenty-one
sieben	seven	hundert	hundred
acht	eight	tausend	thousand
neun	nine		

Ordinal numbers

erste	first	zehnte	tenth
zweite	second	elfte	eleventh
dritte	third	zwölfte	twelfth
vierte	fourth	dreizehnte	thirteenth
fünfte	fifth	zwanzigste	twentieth
sechste	sixth	ein und zwanzigste	twenty-first
siebente	seventh	hundertste	hundredth
achte	eighth	tausendste	thousandth
neunte	ninth		

After ordinal numbers a period is placed where in English the form would be 1st, 2d, etc., as *1. Heft; 2. Band.*

Months

Januar (Jan.)	January	Juli (Jul.)	July
Februar (Feb.)	February	August (Aug.)	August
März	March	September (Sept.)	September
April (Apr.)	April	Oktober (Okt.)	October
Mai	May	November (Nov.)	November
Juni (Jun.)	June	Dezember (Dez.)	December

Days

Sonntag	Sunday	Donnerstag	Thursday
Montag	Monday	Freitag	Friday
Dienstag	Tuesday	Sonnabend, Samstag	Saturday
Mittwoch	Wednesday		

Seasons

Frühling	spring	Herbst	autumn
Sommer	summer	Winter	winter

Time

Stunde	hour	Monat	month
Tag	day	Jahr	year
Woche	week		

Articles to be disregarded in filing

der (*masculine, nominative case*) ein
die, *f.* eine
das, *n.*

GLAGOLITSA

Old Slavic	Croatian	Numeral values	Name	Transliteration	Old Slavic Cyrillic
Ⰰ	Ⰰ	1	Az	a in father	А
Ⰱ	Ⰱ	2	Buki	b	Б
Ⰲ	Ⰲ	3	Vedi	v	В
Ⰳ	Ⰳ	4	Glagol'	g	Г
Ⰴ	Ⰴ	5	Dobro	d	Д
Ⰵ	Ⰵ	6	Est', jest'	e in men	Є
Ⰶ	Ⰶ	7	Zhivete	h	Ж
Ⰷ	Ⰷ	8	Zelo	z	Ѕ
Ⰸ	Ⰸ	9	Zemĺa, zemlja, zemja	z	З
Ⰹ	Ⰹ	10	Izhe	i in field	Н
Ⰺ	Ⰺ	20	I	$\bar{\imath}$	І
Ⰼ	Ⰼ	30	Derv'	dj	(ђ)
Ⰽ	Ⰽ	40	Kako	k	К
Ⰾ	Ⰾ	50	Ĺudi, ljudi	l	Л
Ⰿ	Ⰿ	60	Mislite	m	М
Ⱀ	Ⱀ	70	Nash	n	Н
Ⱁ	Ⱁ	80	On	o in old	О
Ⱂ	Ⱂ	90	Pokoj	p	П
Ⱃ	Ⱃ	100	R'tsi	r	Р
Ⱄ	Ⱄ	200	Slovo	s	С
Ⱅ	Ⱅ	300	Tvrdo	t	Т
Ⱆ	Ⱆ	400	Uk	$\bar{u}$ in wood	ОУ
Ⱇ	Ⱇ	500	Fert	f	Ф
Ⱈ	Ⱈ	600	Kher	kh; also ch in Scotch loch	Х
Ⱉ	Ⱉ, Ⱛ	700	O	o	Ѡ
Ⱌ	Ⱌ	900	Tsi	$\widehat{ts}$	Ц
Ⱍ	Ⱍ	1000	Cherv'	ch	Ч
Ⱎ	Ⱎ		Sha	sh	Ш
Ⱋ	Ⱋ	800	Shta	sht	Щ
Ⱏ	Ⱏ, Ⰺ		Jery	$y, u, o, \breve{a}, \dfrac{o}{e}$	Ꙑ
Ⱏⱑ	Ⰺ		Jerek	e in bed, $\dfrac{e}{i}$	Ь
Ⱑ	Ⱑ	800	Jet'	j in judge, ja	Ѣ
Ⱓ	Ⱓ		Ju	ju	Ю

GLAGOLI͡SA—Continued

Old Slavic	Croatian	Numeral values	Name	Transliteration	Old Slavic Cyrillic
				$\widehat{ia}$	Ꙗ
				$\widehat{ie}$	Ѥ
Є			Ęs	ę	Ѧ
ҙє			Ąs	ą	Ѫ
ҙє			Jęs	ję	Ѩ
ҩє			Jąs	ją	Ѭ
			Ksi	x; k	Ѯ
			Psi	ps	Ѱ
✛			Thita	f; th	Ѳ
8			Izhi͡sa	y, i	ѵ

NOTE.—When using the above characters as numerals a period is placed before and after the character. In a medial position the jery has the sound of $\breve{u}$ in the German word über.

According to Prof. S. Stanojevitch's Narodna Entsiklopedija, Glagoli͡sa takes its name quite possibly from the Croatian and Dalmatian priests who used it in their liturgical services about the 9th century and came from the Old Slavic word *glagol*, to speak; thus they called the priests *glagolashi*, speakers. There is ample evidence that it was employed especially for liturgical services wherever the Slavs lived. In fact there is evidence of its use in Russia, as shown by the Glagolithic inscriptions in the Novgorod Cathedral.

Aside from the south Slavic sections Glagoli͡sa has also been found on all monumental remains in Moravia and Bohemia, as also possibly in Macedonia. At the beginning of the 10th century it was used also in Bulgaria, but as the Cyrillic was being introduced it soon began to decline in common use and, by the 11th century, we find it confined mainly to Catholic liturgical use in northern Dalmatia, Croatia, and Istria, where it survived until about 1840. Its value now is merely historical, though it also possesses a great wealth of literature.

Its origin is a problem that has engrossed theologians for many years. In 1890 Isaac Taylor advanced the thesis that Glagoli͡sa originated from the Greek hieratic script in the 9th century and that even before the time of SS. Cyril and Methodius the Slavs used Greek letters, combining them with characters Nos. 2 and 3 when it was desired to give a particular sound that was strange to the Greek language. He believed that to be the cause for its similarity to the Greek characters. Prof. Jagich, one of the greatest of Slavic philologists, has probably studied the subject more thoroughly than anyone else and concurs in this view, but further study convinced him that St. Cyril finally developed a style for the entire alphabet, which has a similarity to the Coptic.

The first book printed in Glagoli͡sa came from the press in Venice in 1483 and later was followed by a great mass of printed literature. When the division of eastern Europe into several political units took place the language lost caste, Austria, in particular, doing her utmost to discourage its use. It is interesting to know that in 1903 an Old Slavic academy was found on the beautiful Dalmatian island Krk which was engaged in the publication of books on Glagolithic literature, but all in Cyrillic transcription.

The Cyrillic alphabet, shown in the last column of the table, was originated in the year 863 by the Slavic priests Cyril and Methodius for use in the translation of religious books from the Greek into the Slavic language. With its 44 characters adapted from both the Greek and possibly an extinct Slav-runic alphabet, it became the alphabet of the Slavs who were within the fold of the Greek Orthodox Church. In the 18th century Peter the Great forced upon the Russians, among his many reforms, the modified Russian alphabet, and the use of the Cyrillic was relegated to religious books.

GREEK (Classical)

A	α	alpha	$\bar{a}$ as in father; $\breve{a}$ as in papa	Ξ	ξ	xi	x as in mix
B	β	beta	b as in bad	O	o	omicron	o as in obey
Γ	γ	gamma	g as in go	Π	π	pi	p as in pin
Δ	δ	delta	d as in do	P	ρ	rho	r as in red
E	ε	epsilon	e as in pet	Σ	σ ς	sigma	s as in see
Z	ζ	zeta	Originally as zd; later as z	T	τ	tau	t as in top
H	η	eta	e as in French fête	Υ	υ	upsilon	$\bar{u}$ as in French sûr, German $ü$; $\breve{u}$ as in the German Brücke
Θ	θ	theta	th as in thin				
I	ι	iota	$\bar{\imath}$ as in machine; $\breve{\imath}$ as in pit	Φ	φ	phi	ph as in graphic
				X	χ	chi	ch as in German machen
Κ	κ	kappa	k as in keg				
Λ	λ	lambda	l as in lip	Ψ	ψ	psi	ps as in gypsum
M	μ	mu	m as in mix	Ω	ω	omega	o as in prone
N	ν	nu	n as in now				

The Greek language uses 24 letters. Each letter has at least two forms, the majuscule, or upper-case, and the minuscule, or lower-case. The larger, or capital, letters are very like those used by the Greeks of the classical period; the smaller letters are derived from the cursive script used at a very much later period. The use given herewith is that taught generally in American schools and colleges.

Forms

Five of the lower-case letters have two forms each: α is used in text; α, as a symbol in mathematics; б (beta) and ϑ (theta) are rare, never used as symbols; φ or φ, in text and as symbols; σ, initial or medial; ς, final. For general purposes, however, these variant forms, with the exception of σ and ς, may be used interchangeably.

The later manuscripts had many hundreds of ligatures, a remnant of the shorthand of the period. The earlier printers had a great many of these cast in type, but they are not generally used today. See pp. 105 - 108.

There is the relic of the primitive Greek alphabet remaining in the use of three ancient characters as numerals, Ϝ, digamma, or ς, stigma, used for 6; ϙ, koppa, used for 90, and ϡ, sampi, used for 900. The only other occasion for the use of these characters is in paleography.

Breathings

Attention is called to the breathings, the rough (ʻ) which gives the sound of *h* to the letter on which it is written, and the smooth (ʼ). Every initial vowel takes one or the other of these breathings. It is written over the second letter of a diphthong, and in front of capital letters. Initials υ and ρ take the rough breathing above them, and doubled ρ was formerly written ῤῥ, but modern usage eliminates the breathings. The smooth breathing should not be confused with the apostrophe, which is used at the beginning or end of a word to indicate elision.

Accents

Three stress accents are used in Greek, the acute (ʹ), the circumflex (tilde) (˜), and the grave (ʽ). These may be combined with the breathings to give a number of "sorts", the use of which involves a knowledge of the language. There is also the dieresis, placed over the second of a group of two vowels to indicate separate pronunciation of each.

GREEK DIACRITICAL MARKS

’ lenis	ʼ lenis grave	῏ circumflex asper
ʽ asper	ʼ asper acute	¨ dieresis
ʹ acute	῍ asper grave	῎ dieresis acute
ʽ grave	῀ circumflex	῝ dieresis grave
ʽ lenis acute	῍ circumflex lenis	

Punctuation

The Greek marks of punctuation are the comma (,), the colon-semicolon (·), the period (.), and the mark of interrogation (;). As the ancient Greeks wrote without any breaks, even between words, these marks are of quite recent origin, and are inserted where editors think they should go, generally as in English.

Phonetics

Scholars think that the double consonants φ, χ, θ, ζ, ξ, and ψ, originally sounded both of their component parts, but that later they took on a single sound.

The letter γ before κ, γ, χ, and ζ took the sound of n in ink. The letter ρ, when with a rough breathing, had a sound something like hr.

The pronunciation of the principal diphthongs is:

αι as *ai* in aisle

ει as *ei* in rein

οι as *oi* in toil

υι as *ui* in quit

αυ as *ou* in our

ευ as *eu* in feud

ου as *ou* in you

The diphthong ηυ can only be approximated by the sounds *eh-oo* pronounced quickly together.

The improper diphthongs ᾳ, ῃ, ῳ, are pronounced like a, η, ω, respectively.

There is a division of opinion among modern scholars as to the pronunciation of ancient Greek. Some think that the pronunciation of the modern Greek is more nearly like the ancient than the ordinarily accepted scholastic pronunciation.

Capitalization

As the ancient Greeks did not know the lower-case letters, they had no scheme of capitalization. The modern use is to capitalize proper names and the first word of a sentence. Poetry does not capitalize the first word of a line, unless under the above rule.

Syllabication

Each Greek word has as many syllables as it has vowels or diphthongs. The following rules, based on ancient tradition, are used in divisions:

(a) Single consonants, combinations of consonants which can begin a word, as indicated below, are placed at the beginning of a syllable.

In Greek there are found to be 45 combinations of consonants that are used to begin words. They are:

βδ, βλ, βρ, γλ, γν, γρ, δμ, δν, δρ, θλ, θν, θρ, κλ, κμ, κν, κρ, κτ, μν, πλ, πν, πρ, πτ, σβ. σθ, σκ, σκλ, σμ, σπ, σπλ, σπρ, στ, στρ, σφ, σχ, τλ, τμ, τρ, φθ, φλ, φν, φρ, χθ, χλ, χν, χρ.

(b) Other combinations of consonants are divided.

(c) Compound words are divided into their original parts.

(d) In dividing words ending in κτος, the κ is brought over.

Cardinal numbers

α′	εἷς, μία, ἕν	one		ν′	πεντήκοντα	fifty
β′	δύο	two		ξ′	ἑξήκοντα	sixty
γ′	τρεῖς, τρία	three		ο′	ἑβδομήκοντα	seventy
δ′	τέτταρες, -ρα	four		π′	ὀγδοήκοντα	eighty
ε′	πέντε	five		ϟ′	ἐνενήκοντα	ninety
ϝ′	ἕξ	six		ρ′	ἑκατόν	hundred
ζ′	ἑπτά	seven		σ′	διακόσιοι	two hundred
η′	ὀκτώ	eight		τ′	τριακόσιοι	three hundred
θ′	ἐννέα	nine		υ′	τετρακόσιοι	four hundred
ι′	δέκα.	ten		φ′	πεντακόσιοι	five hundred
ια′	ἕνδεκα	eleven		χ′	ἑξακόσιοι	six hundred
ιβ′	δώδεκα	twelve		ψ′	ἐπτακόσιοι	seven hundred
ιγ′	τρεισκαίδεκα	thirteen		ω′	ὀκτακόσιοι	eight hundred
κ′	εἴκοσι	twenty		ϡ′	ἐνακόσιοι	nine hundred
λ′	τριάκοντα	thirty		͵α	χίλιοι	thousand
μ′	τετταράκοντα	forty		͵ι	μύριοι	ten thousand

Ordinal numbers

πρῶτος	first	ἔνατος	ninth
δεύτερος	second	δέκατος	tenth
τρίτος	third	ἐνδέκατος	eleventh
τέταρτος	fourth	δωδέκατος	twelfth
πέμπτος	fifth	τρίτος καὶ δέκατος	thirteenth
ἔκτος	sixth	εἰκοστός	twentieth
ἕβδομος	seventh	τριακοστός	thirtieth
ὄγδοος	eighth	χιλιοστός	thousandth

These numerals, except the cardinals from 5 to 100, are regularly declinable according to the rules of the language. The exceptions are not declinable.

The numeral characters take an acute accent after them, from 1 to 999. To place an accent below and to the left of a character multiplies it by 1000: e.g., α′=1, ͵α=1000, ͵αϑλγ′=1933.

Chronology

The ancient Greeks divided time into periods of four years, called Olympiads, the first year of the first Olympiad beginning in the middle of the summer of 776 B.C. Each year was divided into twelve months, but there was no division into weeks.

The seasons were called ἦρ, spring; θέρος, summer; ὀπώρα, autumn, and χειμών, winter.

After the rise of the Roman supremacy the Julian calendar was adopted, with the Latin month names transliterated. After the advent of Christianity the weekly system was adopted, with names of the days as in modern Greek.

Months

Ἑκατομβαιών	Hecatombion	About July
Μεταγειτνιών	Metageitnion	August
Βοηδρομιών	Boëdromion	September
Πυανοψιών	Pyanopsion	October
Μαιμακτηριών	Maimacterion	November
Ποσειδεών	Poseideon	December
Ποσειδεών δεύτερος	Second Poseideon	In leap years only (every eight years)
Γαμηλιών	Gamelion	January
Ἀνθεστηριών	Anthesterion	February
Ἐλαφηβολιών	Elaphebolion	March
Μουνιχιών	Mounichion	April
Θαργηλιών	Thargelion	May
Σκιροφοριών	Scirophorion	June

The modern equivalents are, of course, only approximate, as the Greeks had not calculated the year as accurately as more modern mathematicians have. The first day of Hecatombion was intended to fall upon the summer solstice; but it actually varied from the middle of June to the first week in August.

Time

ὥρα	hour	μήν	month
ἡμέρα	day	ἔτος	year
ἑβδομάς	week		

Articles to be disregarded in filing

ὁ	οἱ
ἡ	αἱ
τό	τά

Ligatures, etc.

ϛ = stigma (st)	ϙ = koppa (q)
ϡ = sampi (sch)	ȣ = (ou)

GREEK INCUNABULA

The following old forms of letters, letter combinations, and abbreviations will be helpful to those interested in reading early Greek records or manuscripts. Those under I are individual letters or elements found only in compound characters; under II are such characters as are not immediately obvious and hence are given in an extra-alphabetical order, while in columns III to VI there is an alphabetical arrangement of character combinations, the initial letter of which will be readily ascertained by the aid of those under I.

I

α   γ   ·δ   ε   ε   κ   ν   ν   ν   σ

II

‑ον   γὰρ   γὰρ   ει   εῖ   ελ   ην   ου   τῶ   ῦ   δὲ   καὶ   τι

III	IV	V	VI
αϑι	εἶναι	μετα	ταῦϑα
αλ	ἐν	μω	τὴν
αλλ	ἐπειδὴ	μῶν	τῆς
αν	ἐπευ	οἶον	τῆς
ἀρ	ἐπι	οὐκ	τὸ
αὐτὸ	ἐπὶ	οὗτος	τὸν
γγ	ἐπὶ	παρα	τοῦ
γὰρ	ερ	περ	τοῦ
γὰρ	ευ	περὶ	τοὺς
γελ	κατὰ	πο	τρ
γεν	κεφάλαιον	ρο	τρο
γερ	μάτων	σα	τῶ
γίνεται	μεϑ	σε	τῶν
γο	μὲν	σϑαι	τῶν
γρι	μέν	οο	υι
γρο	μεν	οπ	υν
δεξ	μεν	οσ	ὑπ
δευ	μενος	οω	χϑ
δια	μετὰ	ται	χο
δια		ταῖς	ῶ

INCUNABULA LIGATURES

Many of the old character forms, digraphs, prefixes, and suffixes were conventionalized into ligatures of which there are a very large number in the old editions. Those most frequently used are shown in the following table:

Characters	Value	Characters	Value	Characters	Value	Characters	Value
[lig]	α ι	[lig]	γ χ ε	[lig]	θ ε	[lig]	μ ε λ
[lig]	α λ	[lig]	γ ω	[lig]	θ ε ι	[lig]	μ ε ν
[lig]	α λ λ	[lig]	δ α	[lig]	θ η	[lig]	μ ε τ ά
[lig]	α ν	[lig]	δ α ι	[lig]	θ η ν	[lig]	μ η
[lig]	α ξ	[lig]	δ α ν	[lig]	θ ι	[lig]	μ η ν
[lig]	ά π ο	[lig]	δ α ς	[lig]	Ο ν	[lig]	μ ι
[lig]	α ρ	[lig]	δ α υ	[lig]	θ ο	[lig]	μ μ
[lig]	α ς	[lig]	δ ε	[lig]	θ ρ	[lig]	μ ν
[lig]	α υ	[lig]	δ ἐ	[lig]	θ ς	[lig]	μ ο
[lig]	α ὐ τ ο ῦ	[lig]	δ ε ι	[lig]	θ υ	[lig]	μ υ
[lig]	α ὐ τ ῶ	[lig]	δ η	[lig]	θ ω	[lig]	μ υ ν
[lig]	α ὐ τ ῶ	[lig]	δ η ν	[lig]	κ α	[lig]	μ ω
[lig]	γ α	[lig]	δ ι	[lig]	κ α ι	[lig]	μ ῶ ν
[lig]	γ α ι	[lig]	δ ι α	[lig]	κ α ί	[lig]	ο ἱ ο ν
[lig]	γ α ν	[lig]	δ ο	[lig]	κ α ν	[lig]	ο ν
[lig]	γ α ρ	[lig]	δ ρ	[lig]	κ α ς	[lig]	ο υ
[lig]	γ α ς	[lig]	δ υ	[lig]	κ α τ α	[lig]	ο υ κ
[lig]	γ α υ	[lig]	δ υ ι	[lig]	κ α υ	[lig]	ο ὐ κ
[lig]	γ γ	[lig]	δ υ ν	[lig]	κ ε	[lig]	ο ὗ τ ο ς
[lig]	γ ε	[lig]	δ υ ς	[lig]	κ η	[lig]	π α
[lig]	γ ε ι	[lig]	δ ω	[lig]	κ ι	[lig]	π α ι
[lig]	γ ε ν	[lig]	ε ι	[lig]	κ λ	[lig]	π α ν
[lig]	γ η	[lig]	ε ἰ	[lig]	κ ν	[lig]	π α ρ ά
[lig]	γ η ν	[lig]	ε ῖ ν α ι	[lig]	κ ο	[lig]	π α ς
[lig]	γ ι	[lig]	ἐ κ	[lig]	κ ρ	[lig]	π α υ
[lig]	γ μ	[lig]	ε λ	[lig]	κ ς	[lig]	π ε
[lig]	γ ν	[lig]	ἐ ν	[lig]	κ υ	[lig]	π ε ρ
[lig]	γ ο	[lig]	ε ξ	[lig]	κ ω	[lig]	π ε ρ ι
[lig]	γ ρ	[lig]	ἐ π ι	[lig]	λ λ	[lig]	π η
[lig]	φ ε τ α ι	[lig]	ε ρ	[lig]	μ α	[lig]	π ι
[lig]	γ α ρ	[lig]	ἐ σ τ ι	[lig]	μ α ι	[lig]	π λ
[lig]	γ ρ ι	[lig]	ε υ	[lig]	μ α ν	[lig]	π ν
[lig]	γ ρ ο	[lig]	ἐ υ	[lig]	μ α ρ	[lig]	π ο
[lig]	γ υ	[lig]	ε υ ς	[lig]	μ α τ ω ν	[lig]	π ρ
[lig]	γ υ ι	[lig]	η ν	[lig]	μ α υ	[lig]	π ρ α
[lig]	γ υ ν	[lig]	θ α	[lig]	μ ε	[lig]	π ρ ο
[lig]	γ χ	[lig]	θ α ι	[lig]	μ ε θ	[lig]	π ρ ω
		[lig]	θ α υ				

INCUNABULA LIGATURES—Continued

Characters	Value	Characters	Value	Characters	Value	Characters	Value
	πτ		στλ		σχο		υς
	πυ		στο		σχρ		υσι
	πυν		στυ		σχυ		χα
	πω		στω		σχυν		χαι
	ρα		σσ		σχω		χαν
	ρι		σσα		σω		χαρ
	ρο		σσαν		τα		χας
	σα		σσας		ται		χαυ
	σαι		σσε		ται		χε
	σαν		σσει		ταις		χει
	σαρ		σση		ταν		χν
	σας		σσι		τας		χθ
	σαυ		σσο		ταυ		χθην
	σβ		σσυ		τε		χθω
	σε		σσω		τη		χι
	σει		στ		την		χν
	ση		στα		τηνς		χο
	σθ		σταν		τι		χρ
	σθα		στας		τλ		χς
	σθαι		σταυ		το		χυ
	σθε		στε		τον		χυν
	σθη		στη		τοῦ		χω
	σθην		στι		τρ·		↓α
	σθι		στο		τρι		↓αι
	σθο		στρ		τρο		↓αν
	σθω		στυ		ττ		↓ας
	σι		στω		τυ		↓αυ
	σκ		συ		τυν		↓ε
	σμ		συν		τω		↓ει
	σο		σφ		τῶ		↓η
	σπα		σχ		τῶ		↓ι
	σπαι		σχα		τῶν		↓ο
	σπαν		σχε		υι		↓υ
	σπας		σχει		υν		↓ω
	σπε		σχη		ὑπ		ω̃
	σπει		σχην		ὑπερ		ω̣
	σπη		σχι				
	σπι		σχν				

GREEK (Modern)

A	α	*Aa*	alpha	*a* in father
B	β	*Bb*	beta	*v*
Γ	γ	*Tg*	gamma	Hard *g* aspirated (*gh*) as *g* in the German tragen, before α and o sounds; as *y* (German j), before the vowels ε, η, ι, υ, and the dipthongs αι, ει, οι, and υι. For γγ, γκ, etc., see remarks
Δ	δ	*Dd*	delta	*th* in this; after *r*, *d*.
E	ε	*Ee*	epsilon	A little longer than *e* in well, but not quite as long as *a* in fate; as *e* in German nehmen
Z	ζ	*Zz*	zeta	*z*
H	η	*Hn*	eta	*ee* in eel, German *i*
Θ	θ	*Vd*	theta	*th* in thin
I	ι	*Ii*	iota	*ee* in eel. See under diphthongs
K	κ	*Ku*	kappa	*k*. For γκ, see remarks
Λ	λ	*Ll*	lambda	*l*
M	μ	*Mµ*	mu	*m* (silent before β and π)
N	ν	*Nv*	nu	*n*. For ν before π, see remarks
Ξ	ξ	*Zz*	xi	*x* (*ks*)
O	ο	*Oo*	omicron	*o* in mono
Π	π	*Tω*	pi	*p;* after μ or its sound, as *b*
P	ρ	*Pp*	rho	*r*, somewhat rolled or trilled
Σ	σ ς	*Lσs*	sigma	*s;* before β, γ, δ, μ, ν, ρ, as *z*
T	τ	*Tt (τ)*	tau	*t;* after ν as *d*
Υ	υ	*Vv*	upsilon	*ee* in eel
Φ	φ	*Φφ*	phi	*f*
X	χ	*Xx*	chi	Before α and o, guttural German *ch* in doch; before ε and ι, palatal *ch* in Licht
Ψ	ψ	*Yy*	psi	*ps*
Ω	ω	*Ww*	omega	*o* in note

Modern Greek is very similar to classical Greek, being the direct descendant of that language. There are, at present, two slightly differing forms of modern Greek, the literary, or written form, and the popular or spoken, dialectal form. As practically all printed matter is in the literary form, the following rules concern that form; but certain popular pronunciations are indicated as needed.

The modern alphabet is the same as that used for the older language. The pronunciation of some of the letters differs from that ordinarily used for the ancient Greek. It is given in the table.

Remarks

The character σ is used in initial and medial positions in a word, the character ς in the final position. Variant forms of other letters have no fixed rule for use.

The combinations γγ and γκ are pronounced as *ng* in the word "England", and *nch* in anchor. Before χ and ξ the γ has the sound of *ng* (nasal).

N-final before π-initial is pronounced as *m*, in which case the π is pronounced as *b*.

Diphthongs. — The "improper" diphthongs ᾳ, ῃ, and ῳ are pronounced as α, η, and ω, respectively.

The pronunciation of the diphthongs is as follows: Aι like ε; ει, οι, υι like η (*ee*); ου as *ou* in group. The diphthongs αυ, ευ, ηυ are pronounced before all vowels and the consonants β, γ, δ, ζ, λ, μ, ν, ρ, as *av*, *ev*, *eev*, respectively, before θ, κ, ξ, π, σ, τ, φ, ψ, as *af*, *ef*, *eef*, respectively.

The popular language introduces a number of palatalizations into its pronunciation, notable among which is the prefixing of an ι (or a letter having an ι-sound, generally υ) when the ι takes the consonantal sound of *y*.

Accents and breathings

Modern Greek employs the same accents and breathings as the ancient language, and under practically identical rules. Every word, with a few exceptions, has an accent on one of the three last syllables. Every initial vowel carries a rough or a smooth breathing. The initial letters ρ and υ always carry the rough breathing, and the combination ῤῥ is usually written with a smooth and a rough accent. The rough breathing does not affect the pronunciation in any way.

Capitalization

Majuscules (capital letters) are used on title pages and in headings, much as in English, at the beginning of a sentence, on all proper nouns, on the titles of high-placed officials, and on the designations of corporations, associations, etc. In letters, etc., the pronoun of address is usually capitalized.

Punctuation

The comma, the period, and the exclamation point are the same as in English and are used similarly. The semicolon and the colon are represented by a point above the line. The question mark resembles the English semicolon. The scheme for quotation marks is the same as in the western languages.

Syllabication

In modern Greek the same principles of syllabication apply as in the classic. (See p.104)

A list of the letters which may begin a word can be found under Greek (classical), syllabication, page104. This can be used in modern Greek.

Numerals

Modern Greek uses the Arabic figures for ordinary number work. Where western languages use roman numerals, the modern Greek uses the same scheme of letters as used by classical Greek.

Inflections

In Greek, inflectional endings are employed to indicate cases, of which there are five: Nominative, genitive, dative, accusative, and vocative; genders, of which there are three: masculine, feminine, and neuter; numbers, of which there are two: singular and plural. Classic Greek has also a dual number.

Nouns

Greek nouns are divided into three classes or declensions, each of which have several subdivisions, depending on their case ending.

In the first declension πατέρας, father, and κλέπτης, thief, are representative of the masculine endings; φωνή, voice, and γυναῖκα, woman, of the feminine. In the second declension ἔμπορος, merchant, is masculine, and ξύλον, wood, χέρι, hand, and ἔθνος, nation, are neuter. In the third declension ψωμᾶς, baker, καφετζής, coffee-maker, παππούς, grandfather, and καφές, coffee, represent the masculine endings; ἀλεποῦ, fox, and πρᾶγμα, thing, represent the feminine and neuter endings.

Class or declension	Singular				Plural			
	Nominative	Genitive	Accusative	Vocative	Nominative	Genitive	Accusative	Vocative
First	πατέρ-	ας	α or ου	α(ν)	α	ες	ων	ας	ες
	κλέπτ-	ης	ου	ην	η	αι	ῶν	ας	αι
	φων-	ή	ῆς	ήν	ή	αί	ῶν	ἁς	αί
	γυναῖκ-	α	ας	α(ν)	α	ες	ῶν	ας	ες
Second	ἔμπορ-	ος	ου	ον	ε	οι	ων	ους	οι
	ξύλο-	ν	ου	ον	ον	α	ων	α	α
	χέρ-	ι	ιου	ι	ι	ια	ιῶν	ια	ια
	ἔθν-	ος	ους	ος	ος	η	ῶν	η	η
Third	ψωμ-	ᾶς	ᾶ	ᾶ	ᾶ	άδες	άδων	άδες	άδες
	καφετζ-	ῆς	ῆ	ή (ν)	ή	ῆδες	ήδων	ῆδες	ῆδες
	παππ-	οῦς	οῦ	οῦ	οῦ	οῦδες	ούδων	οῦδες	οῦδες
	καφ-	ἐς	έ	έ	έ	έδες	έδων	έδες	έδες
	ἀλεπ-	οῦ	οῦς	οῦ	οῦ	οῦδες	ούδων	οῦδες	οῦδες
	πρᾶγμ-	α	ατος	α	α	ατα	άτων	ατα	ατα

Adjectives

Like the nouns, adjectives are divided into three classes, the first of which comprises all those which end the nominative singular in -ος, (m), -η (f), -ον (n). These are declined like the nouns ἔμπορος, φωνή, and ξύλον, respectively; the second includes all that end the nominative singular in -ος (m), and -α (f), and -ον (n). These are declined as in the first class, except that the feminine singular is γυναῖκα for the singular. The third class departs somewhat from the declension of the noun and may be represented by φαρδύς, broad, and ζηλιάρης, envious.

		Singular				Plural			
		Nominative	Genitive	Accusative	Vocative	Nominative	Genitive	Accusative	Vocative
Masculine		ύς	υοῦ or ύ	ύ (ν)	ύ	υοί	υῶν (ν)	υούς	υοί
Feminine	φαρδ-	ειά	ειᾶς	ειά (ν)	ειά	ειές	ειῶν (ν)	ειές	ειές
Neuter		ύ	υοῦ, ύ	ύ	ύ	νά	υῶ (ν)	υά	υα
Masculine		ης	η	η	η	ηδες	ηδων	ηδες	ηδες
Feminine	ζηλιάρ-	α	ας	α	α				
Neuter		ικο	ικου	ικο	ικο	ικα	ηκων	ικα	ικα

Adjectives may be placed either before or after the noun:
Good child: καλὸ παιδὶ or παιδὶ καλό.
The good child: τὸ καλὸ παιδὶ or τὸ καλὸ τὸ παιδί.
The comparative is formed by the use of πιὸ or πλιό, more, before the positive or else by changing the ending, as follows:

		Positive	Comparative
Ugly	ἄσχημ·	ος	ὁτερος[1] ὁτατος[2]
Young, new Short, small	νέ-	ος	ώτερος[1] ώτατος[2]
Good	κοντ- καλ-	ός- ός	ήτερος[3] κάλλιστος[3]
Old	γέρ-	ος	οντότερος

[1] Colloquial form.   [2] Literary form.   [3] Irregular form.

Some adjectives compare entirely irregularly: κακός, bad, χειρότερος, worse; πολύς, much, περισσότερος, more. The superlative is expressed by placing the definite article before the comparative. All of these forms inflect regularly for gender and number.

Pronouns

When used substantively, pronouns decline like nouns; used attributively, they decline like adjectives as to case, number, and gender.

		Nominative	Genitive	Accusative
I		ἐγώ	μοῦ	μέ
Thou		ἐσὺ or σύ	σοῦ	σέ
He		αὐτός	(αὐ)τοῦ	(αὐ)τον(ε)
She		αὐτή	(αὐ)τῆς	(αὐ)την(ε)
It		αὐτό	(αὐ)τοῦ	(αὐ)τό
We		ἐμεῖς	(ἐ)μᾶς	(ἐ)μᾶς
You		ἐσεῖς	(ἐ)σᾶς	(ἐ)σᾶς
They	(Masc.)	αὐτοί		(αὐ)τούς
	(Fem.)	αὐτές	(αὐ)τῶν	(αὐ)τές
	(Neut.)	αὐτά		ηαὐ)τά
Who	Masc. sing.	ποιός	ποιοῦ	ποιόν(ε)
Which	Fem. sing.	ποιά	ποιᾶς	ποιαν(ε)
What	Neut. sing.	ποιό	ποιοῦ	ποιό
	Masc. plur.	ποιοί		ποιούς
	Fem. plur.	ποιές	ποιῶν	ποιές
	Neut. plur.	ποιά		ποιά

Adverbs

Adverbs are usually derived from adjectives, in the literary, by dropping the termination and adding ὡς: καλός, good, καλῶς, well. In the popular language merely use the neuter accusative plural of the adjective: καλά, well.

However, a number of adverbs are original root words, as ποῦ, where, πότε, when, etc.

Verbs, footnotes

[1] Used only in literary or classic language to form compound tenses. In ordinary usage, what is the English infinitive is expressed by the conjunction θά, that, with the subjunctive.

[2] Equivalent to the English participle in -ing; used adjectively or substantively, or indeclinably, (in -οντας) to introduce a participial phrase or clause: τοῦτο ἀκούοντας, etc., hearing this, or when he heard this.

[3] Declined like the adjective.

[4] Translated by the English present or present progressive.

[5] Translated by the English past or past progressive.

[6] When of more than two syllables, the prefix ἐ may be dropped.

[7] Translated by the English past only. Verbs whose stem ends in λ, μ, ν, or ϱ do not take the σ in the active voice, but change an ε or αι preceding the λ, μ, ν, or ϱ to ει or α, respectively, and a double λ drops one: στέλλω, I send, ἔστειλα, I sent; ξεραίνω, I dry, ἐξέρανα, I dried.

[8] The form of the verb used with θά is actually the subjunctive and is usually supplanted by the present indicative. This is translated by the English present or present progressive.

[9] This form used with θά is actually the aorist subjunctive, and is translated by the English future, implying a simple absolute act.

[10] Translated by the English present perfect. Formed by the present of the auxiliary ἔχω and the past participle or aorist infinitive. In the active voice the past participle must refer, like an adjective to an object of the action and is, therefore, always in the accusative. In the passive voice ἔχω is used with the passive aorist infinitive and εἶμαι, etc., I am, etc., used with the participle.

[11] Formed by the particle θά with the imperfect of the verb.

[12] Formed by the particle θά with the pluperfect forms of the verb.

[13] Formed by the particle νά followed by the regular subjunctive forms. See future progressive for full conjugation; is translated "that I may loose," etc.

[14] See future absolute for full conjugation of this form; translated "that I might loose," etc.

[15] Translated "that I may have loosed," etc.

[16] Except in the second person, singular and plural, this mood is formed by the subjunctive with ἄς or νά. Present and aorist imperatives are translated alike.

The language is rich in irregular verbs, involving modification of the aorist characteristic and internal vowel and consonantal changes and contractions:

ἁρπάζω	I seize	ἅρπαξα	I seized
φέγγω	I light	ἔφεξα	I lit
ῥάφτω	I sew	ἔρραψα	I sewed
κατεβαίνω	I go down	κατέβηκα	I went down

νά κατεβῶ, that I may go down, etc.

Verbs

The verbs inflect as to person, number, tense, voice, mood, and the participles as to case, number, and gender. The conjugational system of the auxiliary verbs ἔχω, have, and εἶμαι, be, which are defective verbs, and λύω, loose, a regular verb, is shown in the following table:

Person or Case	Tense and Mood	ἐτά ἔχω (have)			εἶμαι (be)			λύω (loose) Active voice			λύω (loose) Passive or reflexive voice
		Mas.	*Fem.*	*Neut.*	*Mas.*	*Fem.*	*Neut.*	*Mas.*	*Fem.*	*Neut.*	
	Pres. Infin.[1] Oarist Inf.[1]	ἔχει			εἶναι			λύσει λύει			λύεσθαι λυθῆ
	Pres. Participle[2]	ἔχων	ἔχουσα	ἔχον	ὤν	οὖσα	ὄν	λύων	λύουσα	λύον	
Singular Nom.		ἔχων	ἔχουσα	ἔχον	ὤν	οὖσα	ὄν	λύων	λύουσα	λύον	
Gen.		—οντος	—σης	—οντος	—όντος	—σης	—όντος	—οντος	—σης	—οντος	
Acc.		—οντα	—σαν	—ον	—τα	—σαν	—ὄν	—οντα	—σαν	—ον	
Plural Nom.		—οντες	—σαι	—οντα	—τες	—σαι	—ὄντα	—οντες	—σαι	—οντα	
Gen.		—οντων	—σών	—οντων	—των	—σών	—των	—οντων	—σών	—οντων	
Acc.		—οντας	—σας	—οντα	—τας	—σας	—τα	—οντας	—σας	—οντα	
Singular Nom.	Past Partic.[3]	ἐχόμενος, -η, -ον									λυμένος, -η, -ον
Plural Nom.		α-, -ς-, -οι									α-, -ς-, -οι
Singular 1. person	Pres. Indic.[4]	ἔχω			εἶμαι			λύω			λύο(υ)μαι
2. person		—εις			—σαι			—εις			—εσαι
3. person		—ει			—ναι, εἶνε			—ει			—εται

For footnotes see page 113

Person or Case	Tense and Mood	εἰα ἔχω (have)	εἰμαι (be)	λύω (loose) Active voice	λύω (loose) Passive or reflexive voice
Plural 1. person		—αμεν	—ʹμασθε (εἴμεθα)	—ο(υ)με	—ο(ύ)μασθε
Plural 2. person		—ατε	—σθε	—ετε	—σθε
Plural 3. person		—ουν(ε), εἰχον	—ναι	—λύουσι	—ο(υ)νται
Singular 1. person	Imperf. Indic.[5]	εἰχα, εἰχον	ἤμουν(α), ἤμην	ἔλυα	(ἐ)λύτο(ύ)μουν(α)[6]
Singular 2. person		—ες	—σουν(α), ἦσο	—ες	—σουνα
Singular 3. person		—ε	—ταν(ε), ἦτο	—ε	—ταν(ε)
Plural 1. person		—ʹ—αμε(ν), εἰχομεν	—μασθε, ἤμεθα	ἐλύαμε[6]	—μασθε
Plural 2. person		—ʹ—ατε, εἰχετε	—σασθε, ἦσθε	—ατε	—σασθε
Plural 3. person		—αν, εἰχον	—ταν(ε), ἦσαν	—αν(ε)	—νταν
Singular 1. person	Aorist Indic.[7]	(defective)	(defective)	ἔλυσα	ἐλύθηκα
Singular 2. person				—σες	—θηκες
Singular 3. person				—σε	—θηκε
Plural 1. person				ἐλύσαμε	—θήκαμε
Plural 2. person				σατε	—θήκατε
Plural 3. person				σαν(ε)	—θήκαν(ε)
Singular 1. person	Future Progr.[8]	θὰ ἔχω	θὰ ἦμαι	θὰ λύω	θὰ λύομαι
Singular 2. person		—ῃς	—σαι	—ῃς	—σαι
Singular 3. person		—ῃ	—ναι	—ῃ	—εται
Plural 1. person		—ομεν	—μεθα	—ομε, λύομε	—όμαστε
Plural 2. person		—ητε	—(σα)σθε	—ετε	—εσθε
Plural 3. person		—ουν(ε)	—ναι	—ουν(ε)	—ονται
Singular 1. person	Fut. Absolute[9]	(defective)	(defective)	θὰ λύσω	θὰ λυθῶ
Singular 2. person				—ῃς	—θῇς
Singular 3. person				—ῃ	—θῇ
Plural 1. person				—σομε	—θοῦμε
Plural 2. person				—σ(ε)τε	—θῆτε
Plural 3. person				—σουν(ε)	—θοῦν(ε)
Plural 1. person	Present Perfect[10]	ἔχω, ἔχεις, etc. ἐχόμενο(ν), -η(ν), -ο, etc.	(defective)	ἔχω, ἔχεις, etc. λυμένο(ν), -ην, -ο or λυμένα, εἰσαι, etc.	
Plural 2. person	Pluperfect	εἰχα, etc. ἐχόμενο	(defective)	εἰχα, etc. λυμένο or λυμένος, -η, -ο ἔχω, ἔχεις, etc., λυθῇ	
Plural 3. person	Future Perfect	θὰ ἔχω, ἔχῃς, ἔχῃ, etc.	(defective)	θὰ ἔχω, ἔχῃς, etc., λύσει εἰχα, etc., λυμένο or λυμένος ἤμουν(α), etc., λυμένος	

For footnotes see page 113

λύω (loose)

Person or Case	Tense and Mood	εἰα / ἔχω (have)	εἰμαι (be)	Active voice	Passive or reflexive voice
Singular 1. person	Present Cond.[11]	ἐχόμενο θὰ εἰχα, etc.	θὰ ἤμουν(α), etc. (defective)	λύσει θὰ ἔχω, ἔχῃς, etc., λυμένο or λύσει θὰ ἔλυα, etc.	or εἰχα λυθῆ θὰ εἰμαι λυμένος or θὰ ἔχω λυθῆ
2. person					
3. person					
1. person	Past Cond.[12]	θὰ εἰχα ἐχόμενο, etc.	(defective)	θὰ εἰχα, etc., λυμένο or λύσει	θὰ (ἐ)λυο(ύ)μουν(α) etc. θὰ ἤμουν(α), etc., λυμένος or θὰ εἰχα, etc., λυθῆ
2. person					
3. person					
1. person	Present Subj.[13] Aorist Subj.[14] Present Perf.[15] Subjun.	νὰ ἔχω, ἔχῃς, etc. (defective) νὰ ἔχω, ἔχῃς, etc., ἐχόμενο	νὰ εἰμαι, etc. (defective)	νὰ λύω, λύῃς, etc. νὰ λύσω, λύσῃς, etc. νὰ ἔχω, ἔχῃς, etc. λυμένο or λύσει	θὰ εἰχα, etc., λυθῆ νὰ λύωμαι, etc. νὰ λυθῶ, λυθῆς, etc. νὰ εἰμαι, etc. λυμένος, -η, -ο or νὰ ἔχω, ἔχῃς, etc.
2. person					
3. person					
1. person	Present Imper.[16]	ἔχε! ἄς (or νὰ) ἔχῃ ἄς ἔχομεν!	νὰ εἰσαι ἔστω (νὰ εἰναι)! ἄς ἤμεθα (εἰμασθε)	λῦε! ἄς (or νὰ) λύῃ! ἄς λύομε!	λύθῆ νὰ λύεσαι! ἄς (or νὰ) λύεται!
2. person					
3. person					
Plural 1. person		ἔχετε! ἄς (or νὰ) ἔχουν(ε)!	ἤσθε (εἰσθε)! ἄς (or νὰ) εἰναι!	λύετε! ἄς (or νὰ) λύουν(ε)!	ἄς λυόμασθε! νὰ λύεσθε! ἄς (or νὰ) λύουνται!
2. person					
3. person					
Singular 1. person	Aorist Imper.[16]	(defective)	(defective)	λῦσε! ἄς (or νὰ) λύσῃ! ἄς (or νὰ) λύσομε!	λύσου (or νὰ λυθῆς)! ἄς (or νὰ) λυθῆ! ἄς λυθῶμε!
2. person					
3. person					
Plural 1. person				λῦσ(ε)τε! ἄς (or νὰ) λύσουν(ε)!	λυθῆτε! ἄς (or νὰ) λυθοῦνε!
2. person					
3. person					

For footnotes see page 113

Articles

The definite article is declined as follows:

	Singular			Plural		
	Mas.	Fem.	Neut.	Mas.	Fem.	Neut.
Nominative	ὁ	ἡ	τό	οἱ	αἱ	τά
Genitive	τοῦ	τῆς	τοῦ	τῶν	τῶν	τῶν
Dative	τῷ	τῇ	τῷ	τοῖς	ταῖς	τοῖς
Accusative	τόν	τήν	τό	τούς	τάς	τά

Ordinarily, the dative is very rarely used, εἰς (to) is employed with accusative instead. Often εἰς τόν (to the) is contracted to στόν. Instead of αἱ, its corresponding singular is frequently and indiscriminately employed.

The indefinite article, as such, is lacking in Greek; the numeral adjective ἔνας or εἷς (one) is used to express its function. Its declension is as follows:

	Masculine	Feminine	Neuter
Nominative	εἷς (ἔνας)	μία (μιά)	ἕν (ἕνα)
Genitive	ἑνός	μίας (μιᾶς)	ἑνός
Dative	εἰς ἕνα	εἰς μίαν	εἰς ἕνα
Accusative	ἕνα	μίαν (μιά)	ἕν (ἕνα)

In place of the numeral adjective, the definite pronoun τις (for masc. and fem.) or τι (neut.) is also, though less generally, employed to express the function of the indefinite article. It must be remembered, however, that the pronoun is invariably placed after the noun, e.g., ἄνθρωπός τις, a man.

Cardinal numbers

ἕις, μία, ἕν	one	ἐννέα	nine
δύο	two	δέκα	ten
τρεῖς, τρία	three	εἴκοσι	twenty
τέσσαρες, -α	four	τριάκοντα	thirty
πέντε	five	ἑκατόν	hundred
ἕξ	six	χίλια	thousand
ἑπτά	seven	ἕν ἑκατομμύριον	hundred thousand
ὀκτώ	eight		

Ordinal numbers

πρῶτος	first	ἔννατος	ninth
δεύτερος	second	δέκατος	tenth
τρίτος	third	εἰκοστός	twentieth
τέταρτος	fourth	τριακοστός	thirtieth
πέμπτος	fifth	ἑκατοστός	hundredth
ἕκτος	sixth	χιλιοστός	thousandth
ἕβδομος	seventh	ἑκατομμυριοστός	hundred thousandth
ὄγδοος	eighth		

Months

Ἰανουάριος	January	Ἰούλιος	July
Φεβρουάριος	February	Αὔγουστος	August
Μάρτιος	March	Σεπτέμβριος	September
Ἀπρίλιος	April	Ὀκτώβριος	October
Μάϊος	May	Νοέμβριος	November
Ἰούνιος	June	Δεκέμβριος	December

Days

Κυριακή	Sunday	Πέμπτη	Thursday
Δευτέρα	Monday	Παρασκευή	Friday
Τρίτη	Tuesday	Σάββατον	Saturday
Τετάρτη	Wednesday		

Seasons

ἄνοξις, ἔαρ	spring	φθινόπωρον	autumn
θέρος, καλοκαῖρι	summer	χειμών	winter

Time

ὥρα	hour	μήν	month
ἡμέρα	day	ἔτος	year
ἑβδομάς	week		

HAWAIIAN

A	a	*a* in father [1]	K	k	*k* [5]
E	e	*e* in obey [2]	L	l	*l*, liquid
I	i	*ee*	M	m	*m*
O	o	*o* in note	N	n	*n*, liquid
U	u	*oo* in too [3]	P	p	*p*
H	h	*h*, aspirated [4]	W	w	Between *w* and *v*

[1] Sometimes when it precedes *k, l, m, n,* and *p* it has the short sound of *u* in mutter, and in a few words it has the sound of *aw* or *au*. The true sound is between *a* in ask and the broad *a* in all.
[2] In an unaccented final syllable it has the sound of *y*.
[3] When preceded by *i* it has the sound of *u* or *yu*.
[4] Sometimes changed to *l*.
[5] In Kauai it has the sound of *t*, but the best usage gives the Hawaiian consonants their unchangeable sounds.

Remarks

In pronouncing the digraphs *ai, ao, au, ei, eu,* or *ou* the stress is on the first letter.

Words taken from the English retain their Latin consonants: *sabati,* Sunday, not *kapaki; buke,* book, not *puke; Baibala,* Bible, not *Paipala.*

Accent

Bisyllabic words are generally accented on the first syllable, but when that is not the case the stressed syllable carries the accent mark: *po-ho,* chalk; *po-hó,* loss.

In words of more than two syllables stress is usually on the penult; if not, the stressed syllable carries the accent: *ka-na-ka,* a man; *ká-na-ka,* men.

Reduplicated words follow the stress of their primitives: *kúhikúhi,* from *kúhi; hólohólo,* from *hólo,* the penult of the reduplicated word taking the primary stress.

The causative *hoo* prefixed to a verb does not change the stress, but receives a secondary stress: *hoóapóno.*

The sign of the passive *i-a* takes a secondary stress: *huná, hunáia.*

Cardinal numbers

hookahi, kekahi	one	umikumamkolua	thirteen
elua	two	iwa kalua	twenty
e kolu	three	kana kolu	thirty
e hā, he kauna	four	kanaha', he kaau	forty
elima	five	kaualima'	fifty
e ono	six	kaua-ono	sixty
e hoku	seven	kauahiku	seventy
ewalu	eight	kauawalu	eighty
eiwa	nine	kauaiwa	ninety
umi	ten	haneri	hundred
umikumamakahi	eleven	kausani, tausani	thousand
umikumamalua	twelve		

Ordinal numbers

ka mua, ka makamua	first	ka walu	eighth
lua	second	hapa-iwa, ka iwa	ninth
ke kolu, hapa-kolu	third	hapa-umi, ka umi	tenth
ka ha, he hapaha'	fourth	ka umikumamakahi	eleventh
ka lima, ka mahele elima	fifth	hapa umikumamalua	twelfth
he hapa-ono, ka ono	sixth	ke kanalima o	fiftieth
ka hiku, he kapahiku	seventh	ka hapa haneri, ka haneri	hundredth

Months

Januari	January	Iulai	July
Feberuari	February	Augate, ka mahina	August
Maraki	March	Sepetemaba	September
Aperila, ka ha o na mahina o ka makahiki	April	Okatoba	October
		Novemaba	November
Mahina o Mei	May	Dekemaba	December
Iune, ka ono o na mahina	June		

Days

la Sabati	Sunday	Poaha'	Thursday
Monede, poaka hi	Monday	Poalima	Friday
Poalua	Tuesday	Poaono, la hoomalolo	Saturday
Poakolu	Wednesday		

Seasons

kai piha	spring	kau haule o na lau	autumn
kau wela	summer	kau hooilo	winter

Time

hora, mahele manawa	hour	he mahina, malama	month
la	day	makahiki	year
hebedoma	week		

Articles to be disregarded in filing

ka, ke	kekahi

HEBREW

Square		Rabbin-ical		Cursive		Name	Phonetic value	Numeral value
א		ħ		ʀ		Aleph	Silent	1
ב		ﬥ		ą		Veth	v	2
ג		ﬞ		ƒ		Gimel	g	3
ד		7		ʔ		Daleth	d	4
ה		ﬣ		﬩		Heh	h	5
ו		ﬠ		ﬠ		Vav	v	6
ז		ﬡ		ﬢ		Zayin	z	7
ח		ﬣ		הּ		Cheth	{ ch, as in German doch	8
ט		ﬦ		ﬨ		Teth	t	9
י		ﬞ		ﬞ		Yod	y	10
כ	ך	ﬞ	ﬞ	ﬞ	ß	Chaph	{ ch, as in German doch	20
ל		ﬥ		ﬧ		Lamed	l	30
מ	ם	﬩	ﬨ	﬩	Ϙ	Mem	m	40
נ	ן	ﬞ	ﬞ	ﬞ	ﬗ	Nun	n	50
ס		ﬞ		ﬞ		Samekh	s	60
ע		ﬞ		ﬞ		Ayin	Silent	70
פ	ף	ﬞ	ﬞ	ﬞ	ß	Feh	f	80
צ	ץ	ﬞ	ﬞ	ß	ﬞ	Tsadi	ts, as in pets	90
ק		ﬞ		ﬞ		Koph	k	100
ר		ﬞ		ﬞ		Resh	r	200
ש		ﬞ		ﬞ		Sin	s	300
ת		ﬞ		ﬞ		Thav	th, as in both	400

The final forms of the letters chaph, mem, nun, feh, and tsadi for the square, rabbinical, and cursive alphabets, respectively, are shown at their immediate right.

The Hebrew alphabet consists of 22 consonants, represented by 22 letters which are also used as numerical signs. Hebrew is read from right to left.

The sound represented by the consonant א (Aleph) is no longer known; ע (Ayin) is a guttural not generally pronounced and is usually transliterated by (').

The characters (ב) Veth, (כ) Chaph, (פ) Feh, and (ת) Thav are hardened with the introduction of a point into (בּ) Beth, (כּ) Caph, (פּ) Peh, and (תּ) Tav. The position of the point also determines the sound of (שׁ) Shin and (שׂ) Sin.

Similarity of certain letters

Veth Chaph	Daleth Chaph (final) Resh	Mem (final) Samekh
ב כ	ד ך ר	ם ס

Gimel Nun	Teth Mem	Ayin Tsadi	Cheth Heh Thav
ג נ	ט מ	ע צ	ח ה ת

Vav Zayin Yod Nun (final)
ו ז י ן

Vowel-signs or points

Besides the letters, which are all consonants, there are ten signs used as vowels, These are the Masoretic points, which, when placed above or below the consonants, indicate the vowel pronunciation. The majority of Hebrew works must be read without the aid of the vowel-points.

LONG VOWELS		SHORT VOWELS	
ָ Kametz	*a* as in father	ַ Patach	*a* as in carry
ֵ Tzere	*ei* as in their	ֶ Segol	*e* as in bed
יִ Chirik gadol	*ie* as in believe	ִ Chirik katon	*i* as in big
וֹ Cholam	*o* as in no	ָ Kametz katon	*o* as in of
וּ Shuruk	*oo* as in moon	ֻ Kubbuts	*u* as in full

The furtive patach

All vowels are pronounced as if they follow the consonant to which they are ascribed with the exception of final ח, which is pronounced, not *cha*, but *ach*. This patach is called "furtive patach."

The sh'va

Two dots placed vertically under a consonant (:) is called Sh'va, and indicates the absence of a vowel. When the Sh'va is united with the following consonant it is vocal, and has the phonetic value of the first *e* in believe, e.g., שְׁמַע (Shema).

When united with the preceding consonant it is silent, e.g., אַבְרָם (Ab-ram).

Certain consonants which may not receive a Sh'va, combine the Sh'va with one of the short vowels, e.g., אֱמֶת, חֲלִי, אֲנִי

The rule is not to divide Hebrew words.

Punctuation and accentuation

Although the principles and marks of punctuation in modern Hebrew are, in the main, as in English, Scriptural Hebrew employs, in addition to the vowel points, 21 accent marks, which are placed either singly or in various combinations above or below the consonantal characters they modify. These have a threefold object: (a) to indicate stress; (b) to direct cantillation—the chanting in which the Scriptures are intoned; and (c) to indicate distinctions in the meanings of words, e.g., בָּנוּ they build, but בָּנוּ in us.

As marks of cantillation, accent marks are divided into two classes: Disjunctives and conjunctives, the former corresponding to marks of separation in English— the period, semicolon, comma, etc.; the latter indicating that the word bearing them is connected in sense with that which follows. The following table presents the forms, names, and classifications of these accents:

DISJUNCTIVES

Forms	EMPERORS (קֵסָרִים).	Names	Forms	PRINCES (מִשְׁנִים).	Names
בְ	Sillūk . .	סִלּוּק	בֿ	Zarka . .	זַרְקָא
בְֽ	Athnach .	אֶתְנָח	בֿ	Pashta . .	פַּשְׁטָא
			ב֒	Yᵉthiv . .	יְתִיב
			בֿ	Tevir .	תְּבִיר
	KINGS (מְלָכִים).		בֿ	Azla . .	אַזְלָא
			בֿ	Geresh . .	גֵּרֵשׁ
בֿ	Segolta . .	סְגוֹלְתָּא	בֿ	Double Geresh .	גֵּרְשַׁיִם
בֿ	Zakeph Katon .	זָקֵף קָטֹן		**COUNTS (שְׁלִישִׁים).**	
בֿ	Zakeph Gadhol .	זָקֵף גָּדוֹל	בֿ	Pazer . .	פָּזֵר
בְ	Tippᵉcha .	טִפְחָא	בֿ	Karne-phara .	קַרְנֵי פָרָה
בֿ	Rᵉvia . .	רְבִיעַ	בֿ	Tᵉlisha Gᵉdolah	תְּלִישָׁה גְדוֹלָה
בֿ	Shalsheleth .	שַׁלְשֶׁלֶת	בֿ	Tᵉlisha Kᵉtonah	תְּלִישָׁה קְטַנָּה
			ב ו	Pᵉsik .	פְּסִיק

CONJUNCTIVES

Forms	Names		Forms		Names
בֿ	Munach . .	מוּנַח	בֿ	Darga . .	דַּרְגָּא
בֿ	Mahpach .	מַהְפַּךְ	בֿ	Mercha . .	מֵרְכָא
בֿ	Kadma . .	קַדְמָא	בֿ	Double Mercha	מֵרְכָא כְּפוּלָה

There are also three supplementary marks of interpunction: The soph-pasuk (:), terminal mark of a verse; the pesik (|), for a pause within the verse; and makkeph (-), the elevated hyphen between words.

Below are reproduced the first five verses of the Book of Genesis, showing the employment of vowel points, accents, and marks of interpunction.

בְּרֵאשִׁית בָּרָא אֱלֹהִים אֵת הַשָּׁמַיִם וְאֵת הָאָרֶץ: וְהָאָרֶץ הָיְתָה תֹהוּ
וָבֹהוּ וְחֹשֶׁךְ עַל־פְּנֵי תְהוֹם וְרוּחַ אֱלֹהִים מְרַחֶפֶת עַל־פְּנֵי הַמָּיִם: וַיֹּאמֶר
אֱלֹהִים יְהִי אוֹר וַיְהִי־אוֹר: וַיַּרְא אֱלֹהִים אֶת־הָאוֹר כִּי־טוֹב וַיַּבְדֵּל
אֱלֹהִים בֵּין הָאוֹר וּבֵין הַחֹשֶׁךְ: וַיִּקְרָא אֱלֹהִים ׀ לָאוֹר יוֹם וְלַחֹשֶׁךְ קָרָא
לָיְלָה וַיְהִי־עֶרֶב וַיְהִי־בֹקֶר יוֹם אֶחָד:

Prefixes

As the definite article, the conjunction "and", and prepositional relations are formed by means of prefixes, these are invariably disregarded in alphabetization and filing. They are—

הַ	the	כ	like, as	ו	and
לְ	to, of, according to	בְ	in, by	מ	from

The calendar

The Hebrew calendar was given its present fixed form by Hillel II about 360 A.D. It is based on a year of 12 months, alternating 30 and 29 days, with an intercalary month of 29 days in an embolismic or leap year. These months, with their corresponding periods in the Gregorian calendar, are as follows:

Tishri	תשרי	September-October
Heshvan	חשון	October-November
Kislev	כסלו	November-December
Tebet	טבת	December-January
Shebat	שבט	January-February
Adar	אדר	February-March
Veadar	ואדר	Intercalary month
Nisan	ניסן	March-April
Iyar	איר	April-May
Sivan	סיון	May-June
Tammuz	תמוז	June-July
Ab	אב	July-August
Elul	אלול	August-September

The year begins on the first day of the month of Tishri, which is the day of the Molad, or appearance of the new moon, nearest the autumnal equinox. The actual date is, however, sometimes shifted one or two days, according to specific regulations; thus, New Year may not fall on either Friday or Sunday, since that would conflict with the observance of the Sabbath; nor, for a like reason, may it come on Wednesday, since that would cause Atonement Day to come on a Friday.

To convert a given year (Anno Domini) into its corresponding Hebrew year (Anno Mundi), add 3,761 to the former, bearing in mind, however, that the year begins in September. As the Hebrew calendar omits the thousands, the year 5696, corresponding to the Christian year 1935, is represented in Hebrew characters by תרצו, 696, these characters, as already explained, denoting 400—200—90—6, respectively.

The days of the week are referred to as First Day, Second Day, etc., the seventh being termed Sabbath (שבת). The holidays, festivals, and fasts, with their dates, are as follows:

Rosh Hashana (New Year, Tishri 1)	ראש השנה
Tsom Gedaliah (Fast of Gedaliah, Tishri 3)	צום גדליה
Yom Kippur (Day of Atonement, Tishri 10)	יום כפור
Sukkoth (Tabernacles, Tishri 15–22)	סכות
Simhath Torah (Rejoicing over the Law, Tishri 23)	שמחת תורה
Hanukkah (Feast of Dedication, Kislev 25)	חנכה
Asereth B'tebet, Fast of (Tebet 10)	עשרת בטבת
Purim (Feast of Lots, Adar 14)	פורים
Pesach (Passover, Nisan 15–21)	פסח
Shabuoth (Feast of Weeks, Sivan 6)	שבועות
Tishah B'ab (Fast of Ab, Ab 9)	תשעה באב

Abbreviations

In Hebrew, abbreviations are set as follows: If of one character, but one prime mark (') is used after the character; if of more than one character, a double prime ('') is used just before the last character. Masoretic points are always omitted. The abbreviations most frequently used are as follows:

Sir, Master, Mr.; thousand	א' אדון; אלף
Aleph Beth (the alphabet)	א"ב, אלף בית
Said our learned ones of blessed memory	אחז"ל, אמרו חכמינו זכרונם לברכה
The land of Israel (Palestine)	א"י, ארץ ישראל
God willing	אי"ה, אם ירצה השם
Synagogue	בהכ"נ, בית הכנסת
Sons of Israel, the Jews	ב"י, בני ישראל
In these words, viz	בוה"ל, בזה הלשון
The author	בע"מ, בעל מחבר
Gaon (title of Jewish princes in the Babylonian exile), His Highness, Majesty.	ג' גאון

Abbreviations—Continued

The laws of Israel	ד״י, דיני ישראל
The Holy One, Blessed be He (the Lord)	הקב ה,הקדוש ברוך הוא
Destruction of the First Temple	חב״ר, חרבן בית ראשון
Destruction of the Second Temple	חב״ש, חרבן בית שני
Exodus from Egypt	יצ״מ, יציאת מצרים
As it was said	כמ״ש, כמו שנאמר
As it was written	כמו שכתב
A.M. (Anno Mundi)	לב״ע, לבריאת עולם
The Holy Language (Hebrew)	להק, לשון הקדש
Good luck; I congratulate you	מז״ט, מזל טוב
The Sacred Books	סה״ק, ספרים הקדושים
The Holy Scroll	ס״ת, ספר תורה
May he rest in peace	ע״ה, עליו השלום
In the hereafter	עוה״ב, עולם הבא
New Year's Eve	ער״ה, ערב ראש השנה
Sabbath Eve	ע״ש, ערב שבת
Verse, chapter	פ׳, פסוק, פרק
The judgment of the court	פב״ד, פסק בית דין
Saint (St.), Zion	צ׳, צדיק, ציון
Recognition of God's justice	צה״ד, צדוק הדין
The reading of the Scroll	קה״ת, קריאת התורה
First of all	קכ״ד, קדם כל דבר
Our Rabbis of Blessed Memory	רו״ל, רבותינו זכרונם לברכה
Rabbi Moses son of Maimon (Maimonides)	רמב״ם, ר׳ משה בן מימון
Catalog	רש״ס, רשימת ספרים
Year, line, hour	ש׳, שנה, שורה, שעה
Sabbath days and holidays	שוי״ט, שבתות וימים טובים
As stated	שנ׳, שנאמר
Babylonian Talmud	ת״ב, תלמוד בבלי
The Books of the Law, the Prophets, and Hagiographa (Old Testament).	תנ״ך, תורה, נביאים, כתובים

Cardinal numbers

one	אחד, אחת	twenty	עשרים
two	שנים, שתים	thirty	שלשים
three	שלשה, שלש	forty	ארבעים
four	ארבעה, ארבע	fifty	חמשים
five	חמשה, חמש	sixty	ששים
six ·	ששה, שש	seventy	שבעים
seven	שבעה, שבע	eighty	שמנים
eight	שמנה	ninety	תשעים
nine	תשעה, תשע	hundred	מאה
ten	עשרה, עשר	thousand	אלף

In forming the numbers from 11 to 19, the terms עשרה in the feminine, and עשר in the masculine are used, preceded by the proper unit number. For 21 and upward, the term corresponding to the proper tenth digit is followed by the proper unit term preceded by the conjunction ו and: twelve שנים עשר, twenty-four עשרים וארבע, etc.

Ordinal numbers

first	ראשון	sixth	ששי
second	שני	seventh	שביעי
third	שלשי	eighth	שמיני
fourth	רביעי	ninth	תשיעי
fifth	חמשי	tenth	עשירי

After ten the ordinals are similar in form to the cardinals with the addition of the definite article ה, thus, העשרים the twentieth.

Seasons

spring	אביב	autumn	סתיו
summer	קיץ	winter	חרף

Time

hour	שעה	month	חדש
day	יום	season	מועד
week	שבוע	year	שנה

HUNGARIAN

A	a	o in dog	N	n	n	
Á	á	a in father	NY	ny	ni (ny) in Virginia	
B	b	b	O	o	o in horn	
C	c	ts	Ó	ó	o in stone	
CS	cs	ch in change .	Ö	ö	u in purr	
CZ[1]	cz	ts in its	Ő	ő	eu in French peur [2][3]	
D	d	d	P	p	p	
E	e	e in lend	R	r	r (trilled)	
É	é	ai in wait	S	s	sh in shut	
F	f	f	SZ	sz	s in silly	
G	g	g in pig	T	t	t	
GY	gy	d in duke, or j in joy	TY	ty	t (ty) in tune	
H	h	h	U	u	oo in good	
I	i	i in bits	Ú	ú	u in brute	
Í	í	i in ravine	Ü	ü	u (y) of French nu, mue [1][2]	
J	j	y in yard				
K	k	k	Ű	ű	(2)	
L	l	l	V	v	v	
LY	ly	l (ly) in lute	Z	z	z	
M	m	m	ZS	zs	French j	

[1] Eliminated since 1910.
[2] No corresponding sound in English.
[3] Really only lengthened form of preceding vowel.

The characters of the alphabet have sounds as shown in the table which never vary, and no character is ever silent.

Punctuation is practically the same as in English.

Capitalization

Forms of address in letters, etc., and titles are capitalized: *Felséges Uram* (Your Majesty); *Méltóságod* (Your Lordship).

Proper names and those referring to God are capitalized.

Adjectives formed from proper names are not capitalized: *budapesti* (of Budapest); *magyar* (Hungarian).

Syllabication

Simple words are divided at the end of a line so that where two vowels follow one another they are separated: *fi-am, mi-enk, ti-e-id.*

Where two consonants follow one another, they also are separated: *nap-pal, er-dő.*

Where a single consonant occurs between two vowels, it goes with the next syllable: *vá-ros, va-dász.* This rule also holds good where the consonant is a double one: *gy, cz, ly, ny, sz, ty, cs, zs* (*a-gyag, e-cset, e-czet, a-nya, a-tya, ró-zsa*).

Two combinations of consonants occurring together in one word are abbreviated: *ssz* instead of *szsz;* but when they are divided, the original spelling is restored: *hosz-szú.*

Compound words are divided according to their construction: *rend-őr, meg-áll.*

Abbreviations

The following will be of interest because of their frequent use:

kir. királyi, royal	p. pengő, 100 filler	szt. szent, Saint
f.é. folyó évi, current year	pl. például, for instance	t.i. tudniillik, that is(i. e.)
fil. fillér, half penny	stb. és a többi, et cetera	
k. korona, crown	sz. szám, number (no.)	

Hungarian belongs to the Finno-Ugrian group of languages—a branch of the Ural-Altaic family which originated in central Asia. In Hungary the language is known as Magyar (pronounced *Madyar*). Its chief literary development dates from the eighteenth century previous to which the official literary language was Latin.

Accentuation

In single (or primary) words the stress is always on the first syllable: *apa* (father), *eleven* (living).

In compounded (or constructed) words the stress still remains on the first syllable.

Word formation

Hungarian words are richly derivative, various ideas being expressed by one root variously modified, whereas in modern languages these ideas are expressed by a dozen quite different words, in which respect the Hungarian language is similar to the Finnish (representing the northern group), the Turkish, and the Manchurian. The following table illustrates how logical and concise is the mode of derivation:

el away	ad give	hat capacity	atlan a negative	Derivative	English equivalent
el+	ad			elad	give away = sell
	ad+	hat		adhat	to be able to give = may give
el+	ad+	hat		eladhat	to be able to give away (or sell)
el+	ad+	hat+	atlan	eladhataᵗlan	not able to give away = inalienable

Gender

There is no grammatical gender.

Articles

There is no indefinite article, but in certain cases the corresponding idea is expressed by *egy* (one).

The definite article is *a* (before a term beginning with a vowel, *az*). The article is indeclinable.

Adjectives

Like the article, the adjectives are indeclinable, nor do they vary for gender or number. However, adjectives may be employed substantively, in which case they are declined in the usual manner.

The comparative of adjectives is formed by suffixing to the positive the particle *bb* (if the term ends in a vowel), *abb* (if ending is in a consonant and the term is deep-sounding [1]), or *ebb* (if the term ends in a consonant and is high-sounding). The superlative is formed by prefixing the particle *leg* to the comparative.

The following table illustrates the comparison of adjectives of the three classes mentioned and gives the comparison of three of the more important irregular adjectives:

English equivalent	Positive	Comparative	Superlative
cheap	olcsó	olcsóbb	legolcsóbb
free	szabad	szabadabb	legszabadabb
sick	beteg	betegebb	legbetegebb
much	sok	több	legtöbb
nice	szép	szebb	legszebb
light, in weight	könnyű	könnyebb	legkönnyebb

Nouns

Nouns inflect according to case (nominative, genitive, dative, accusative), singular and plural; also according to pronominal modification in three persons singular and plural.

[1] By "deep-sounding" are meant terms whose prevailing vowels are hard (*a, o, u*). "High-sounding" terms are those whose prevailing vowels are soft (*e, i, ö, ü*). Vowel harmony being a consistent feature of the language, suffixes must always be of the same nature as the term to which they are attached.

Case	English equivalent	Deep-sounding		High-sounding	
		house	houses	garden	gardens
Nominative	the	a ház	a házak	a kert	a kertek
Genitive [1]	of the	a háznak a	a házaknak a	a kertnek a	a kerteknek a
Dative	to the	a háznak	a házaknak	a kertnek	a kerteknek
Accusative	the	a házat	a házakat	a kertet	a kerteket
Pronominal	my	házam	házaim	a kertem	a kerteim
	thy	házad	házaid	a kerted	a kerteid
	his (her, its)	háza	házai	a kertje	a kertjei
	our	házunk	házaink	a kertünk	a kerteink
	your	házatok	házaitok	a kertetek	a kerteitek
	their	házuk	házaik	a kertjük	a kertjeik

[1] As generally used, the characteristic ending of the genitive is omitted, thus: *a ház kapuja* (the door of the house). There is also what is called a nominative possessive formed by suffixing *é* (plural *éi*) to, ordinarily, the simple form of the case. Its use is predicative, thus: *nem az én házam égett le hanem az orvosé* (not my house burned down, but the doctor's).

Nouns also inflect prepositionally, that is, by suffixing prepositions indicating place, direction, etc.

English equivalent	Deep-sounding	High-sounding	English equivalent	Deep-sounding	High-sounding
	house	garden		table	chair
(Nom.) the	a ház	a kert	(Nom.) the	az asztal	a szék
in the	a házban	a kertben	upon the	as asztalra	a székre
into the	a házba	a kertbe	(down) from the	az asztalról	a székről
out of the	a házból	a kertből	(away) from the	az asztaltól	a széktől
to the	a házhoz	a kerthez	on the	az asztalon	a széken
by (near) the	a háznál	a kertnél	with the [1]	az asztallal	a székkel

[1] The preposition *val (vel)* changes to the final consonant, resulting, in a double consonant.

Pronouns

The pronouns embrace personals, reflexes, reciprocals, possessives, demonstratives, interrogatives, relatives, and indefinites, with functions similar to those in all modern languages which, when used substantively, are declinable analogously with nouns.

The declension of the personal pronoun, including the substantive and prepositional forms of the possessive, is as follows: [1]

	Nominative	Genitive			Dative	Accusative
		Prepositional [2]	Substantive [3]			
			Singular	*Plural*		
I	én	rólam	enyém	enyéim	nekem	engem
Thou	te	rólad	tiéd	tiéid	neked	téged
He (she, it)	ő	róla	övé	övéi	neki	őt
We	mi	rólunk	miénk	miéink	nekünk	minket
You	ti	rólatok	tiétek	tiéitek	nektek	titeket
They	ők	rólok	övék	övéik	nekik	őket
They (inanimate)	azok				azoknak	azokat

[1] Inanimate things use the demonstrative pronoun *az*.
[2] These forms are translated by the aid of the preposition "of", e.g., of me, of thee, of him, etc. They are really not a part of the declension of the personal pronoun, but rather the particle *rol* (of, concerning) suffixed by the pronominal postpositions.
[3] These forms are translated as mine, thine, his (hers), ours, etc., and may be used either as subject, predicate nominative, or following the conjunction "than".

Verbs

The verbs are highly inflective, the conjugation comprising changes for number, person, tense, mood, voice, form, and aspect.

The "form" of the verb refers to being either definite or indefinite. The former is that form of conjugation employed when involving a definite or understood direct object: *látom*, I see (him, it, etc.). The indefinite form is used when no object follows: *látok*, I see (to read, write, etc.). The active voice alone possesses these two forms.

The personal pronouns are usually omitted, the verb ending being sufficient to indicate person.

All endings are affixes to the stem of the verb, which is always represented by the third person singular, indicative, of the verb, which has no ending.

The infinitive always ends in either *ni, ani,* or *eni: vivni,* (to fence); *irtani* (to extirpate); *küldeni* (to send).

The various terminations of a regularly conjugated verb form are shown in the following table:

Number and person	Active				Passive	
	Indicative		Subjunctive		Indicative	Subjunctive
	Indefinite	Definite	Indefinite	Definite		

PRESENT TENSE [1]

Number and person	Indefinite	Definite	Indefinite	Definite	Indicative	Subjunctive
Singular						
First	ok (ek) [2]	om (em) [2]	jak (jek)	jam (jem)	atom [3]	assam
Second	sz	od (ed)	jál (jél)	jad (jed)	atol	assál
Third	—	ja (i)	jon (en)	ja (je)	atik	assék
Plural						
First	unk (ünk)	juk (jük)	junk (ünk)	juk (jük)	atunk	assunk
Second	tok (tek)	játok (itek)	jatok (etek)	játok (jétek)	attok	assatok
Third	nak (nek)	ják (ik)	janak (enek)	ják (jék)	atnak	assanak

IMPERFECT TENSE [4]

(Used mainly in poetry in Old Hungarian)

Number and person	Indefinite	Definite	Indefinite	Definite	Indicative	Subjunctive
Singular						
First	ék	ám (ém)	nék	nám (ém)	atám	atnám
Second	ál (él)	ád (éd)	nál (nél)	nád (éd)	atál	atnál
Third	a (e)	á (é)	na (ne)	ná (né)	aték	atnék
Plural						
First	ánk (énk)	ók (ők)	nánk (nénk)	nók (nők)	atánk	atnánk
Second	átok (étek)	átok (étek)	nátok (nétek)	nátok (nétek)	atátok	atnátok
Third	ának (ének)	ák (ék)	nának (nének)	nák (nék)	atának	atnának

[1] Translated by the English present, including progressive and emphatic.
[2] All terminations in parentheses represent variations for high-sounding words.
[3] High-sounding terminations for the passive are analogous for the active.
[4] Translated by the English past tense.

Terminations of verb.—Continued.

Number and person	Active				Passive	
	Indicative		Subjunctive		Indicative	Subjunctive
	Indefinite	Definite	Indefinite	Definite		

PERFECT TENSE [5]

Number and person	Indefinite (Active Ind.)	Definite (Active Ind.)	Indefinite (Active Subj.)	Definite (Active Subj.)	Indicative (Passive)	Subjunctive (Passive)
Singular						
First	tam (tem)	tam (tem)	(Same as indefinite indicative followed by word *volna*)	(Same as definite indicative followed by word *volna*)	attam	(Same as indicative passive followed by word *volna*)
Second	tál (tél)	tad (ted)			attál	
Third	t	ta (te)			atott	
Plural						
First	tunk (tünk)	tuk (tük)			attunk	
Second	tatok (tetek)	tátok (tetek)			attatok	
Third	tak (tek)	ták (tek)			attak	

PLUPERFECT TENSE [6]

(7)	(7)	(7)	(7)	(7)	(7)

FUTURE TENSE

(8)	(8)	(9)	(9)	(10)	(11)

IMPERATIVE

(Generally the same as the subjunctive present in regard to all verbs.)

PRESENT PARTICIPLE

(Formed by the addition of *o* (*ö*) to stem of verb.)

PAST PARTICIPLE

(Formed by the addition of *tt* (after vowels) and *t* (after consonants) to stem of verb.)

[5] Translated by the English present perfect tense.
[6] Translated by the English pluperfect tense; rarely used.
[7] Formed by the addition of *volt* (or *vala*) to the perfect tense.
[8] Formed by the infinitive and present tense of *fog* (shall): *várni fogok*, etc.
[9] Formed by adding the article *and* (*end*), plus the present indefinite endings: *varandok, varandasz*, etc.
[10] Formed by the passive infinitive plus the present tense of *fog: váratni fogok*, etc.
[11] Formed by the stem of the verb and the particle *and* plus the endings *om, ol, ik, unk, otok, anak: váratandom*, etc.

There are irregular forms of verbs, like those ending in *-ik* in the present, third person singular: *enni* (to eat); singular present: *eszem* (I eat); *eszel* (you eat); *eszik* (he eats).

In addressing, the conventional (polite) form is the third person with *Ön* (singular) and *Önök* (plural) as the personal pronouns; mostly used in addressing men, but not women. For familiar address, use the second person.

Hungarian verbs also have aspects:

(a) Factitive (by adding to the root the particle *at, tat* (*et, tet*): *kér* (he asks), *kéret* (he causes to be asked).

(b) Facultative (by adding the particle *hat* (*het*): *csinál* (he makes), *csinálhat* (he can make).

(c) Frequentative (by the termination *gat* or *ogat* (*get* or *eget*): *kér* (he begs), *kéreget* (he begs often).

There is no verb "to have", but that idea is conveyed by circumlocution with the aid of the verb "to be": *nekem van* (to me is), analogous to the Latin *mihi est*.

Cardinal numbers

egy	one	kilenc	nine
kettő	two	tiz	ten
három	three	tizenegy	eleven
négy	four	tizenkettő	twelve
öt	five	tizenhárom	thirteen
hat	six	húsz	twenty
hét	seven	száz	hundred
nyolc	eight	ezer	thousand

Ordinal numbers

első	first	kilencedik	ninth
második	second	tizedik	tenth
harmadik	third	tizenegyedik	eleventh
negyedik	fourth	tizenkettedik	twelfth
ötödik	fifth	tizenharmadik	thirteenth
hatodik	sixth	huszadik	twentieth
hetedik	seventh	századik	hundredth
nyolcadik	eighth	ezredik	thousandth

Months

január (Jan.)	January	julius (Jul.)	July
február (Feb.)	February	augusztus (Aug.)	August
március (Márc.)	March	szeptember (Szept.)	September
aprilis (Ápr.)	April	október (Okt.)	October
május (Máj.)	May	november (Nov.)	November
junius (Jun.)	June	december (Dec.)	December

Days

vasárnap	Sunday	csütörtök	Thursday
hétfő	Monday	péntek	Friday
kedd	Tuesday	szombat	Saturday
szerda	Wednesday		

Seasons

tavasz	spring	ősz	autumn
nyár	summer	tél	winter

Time

óra	hour	hó, hónap	month
nap	day	év, esztendő	year
hét	week		

Articles to be disregarded in filing

a, az   egy

ICELANDIC (Modern)

A	a	Intermediate between *a* in father and *a* in cat	J	j(joð)	$\begin{cases} y \text{ in yell} \\ j \text{ in hallelujah} \end{cases}$
Á	á	*ow* in cow	K	k(ká)	*k* in kernel
B	b(bje)	*b* in book	L	l(eddl)	*l* in steel, with certain exceptions
D	d(dje)	*d* in day			
Ð	ð(eð)	*th* in bathe	M	m(emm)	*m*
E	e	short: *e* in bet long: *è* in French père	N	n(enn)	*n*, with certain exceptions
É	é(je)	Like Icelandic *í* (short) followed by short *e*	O	o	short: *au* in naught long: *a* in war
			Ó	ó	When long like *oe* in south English toe
F	f(eff)	*f* in file, when initial or when followed by *k*, *s* or *t* *v*, between vowels or at end of words *b*, when followed by *l* or *n*	P	p(pje)	*p*
			R	r(err)	*r* (Scotch)
			S	s(ess)	*s* in house
			T	t(tje)	*t*
			U	u	*eu* in French deux
			Ú	ú	*oo* in moon
			V	v(vaff)	*v*
			X	x(ex)	*x*
G	g(gje)	*g* in gold, with certain exceptions	Y	y(uj)	*i* (Icelandic)
			Ý	ý(új)	*í* (Icelandic)
H	h(há)	*h*	Z	z(seta)	*s* (Icelandic)
I	i	short: *i* in sin long: no English equivalent	Þ	þ(þoddn)	*th* in thin
			Æ	æ(œ)	*i* in mile
Í	í	*ee* in green	Ö	ö	German *ö*

The use of the letter *é*, although retained by many writers, is questionable in modern Icelandic and the letter is now often replaced by *je* which has the same value. The letters *y* and *ý* denote mutation of original *u* and *ú*; *æ* is a mutation of *á* and *ó*; *ö* a mutation of *a*. Z is by some grammarians considered an unnecessary letter and many writers entirely discard it. Diphthongs: *au* (composed of *ö* followed by the sound of *ee* in *seen*), *ei* and *ey* (with the same sound, composed of the French *é* followed by the sound of *ee* in *seen*).

Accent
The accent almost invariably falls on the first syllable.

Articles
There is only one article, the definite article. When used with an adjective employed as a noun, or with a noun further defined by an adjective or an ordinal number, it stands before the adjective, and is then declined as follows:

	Singular			Plural		
	Masc.	Fem.	Neut.	Masc.	Fem.	Neut.
Nom.	*hinn*	*hin*	*hið*	*hinir*	*hinar*	*hin*
Acc.	*hinn*	*hina*	*hið*	*hina*	*hinar*	*hin*
Dat.	*hinum*	*hinni*	*hinu*	*hinum* *hinna* } all genders		
Gen.	*hins*	*hinnar*	*hins*			

If the noun is without any adjectival definition, or if the adjective follows it, the article is suffixed to it, in which case it drops the initial *h*, and if the word ends in a short or unaccented vowel, it drops the *i* also.

Syllabication

Division is made on the last consonant before a vowel: *dag-ar*, *hrafn-ar*, *hepp-in*, *elok-að-i*. Compound words are divided according to their component parts: *vor-draum-ur*.

Cardinal numbers

einn	one	seytján	seventeen
tveir	two	átján	eighteen
þrír	three	nítján	nineteen
fjórir	four	tuttugu	twenty
fimm	five	tuttugu og einn	twenty-one
sex	six	þrjátíu	thirty
sjö	seven	þrjátíu og tveir	thirty-two
átta	eight	fjörutíu	forty
níu	nine	fimtíu	fifty
tíu	ten	sextíu	sixty
ellefu	eleven	sjötíu	seventy
tólf	twelve	áttatíu	eighty
þrettán	thirteen	níutíu	ninety
fjórtán	fourteen	(eitt) hundrað	hundred
fimtán	fifteen	tvö hundruð	two hundred
sextán	sixteen	þúsund	thousand

Ordinal numbers

fyrsti	first	sextándi	sixteenth
annar	second	seytjándi	seventeenth
þriðji	third	átjándi	eighteenth
fjórði	fourth	nítjándi	nineteenth
fimti	fifth	tuttugasti	twentieth
sjötti	sixth	tuttugasti og fyrsti	twenty-first
sjöundi	seventh	þrítugasti	thirtieth
áttundi	eighth	fertugasti	fortieth
níundi	ninth	fimtugasti	fiftieth
tíundi	tenth	sextugasti	sixtieth
ellefti	eleventh	sjötugasti	seventieth
tólfti	twelfth	áttugasti	eightieth
þrettándi	thirteenth	níutugasti	ninetieth
fjórtándi	fourteenth	hundraðasti	hundredth
fimtándi	fifteenth	þúsundasti	thousandth

Months

janúar (mánuður)	January	júlí	July
febrúar	February	ágúst	August
marz	March	september	September
april	April	október	October
maí	May	nóvember	November
júní	June	desember (mánuður)	December

Days

sunnudagur	Sunday	fimtudagur	Thursday
mánudagur	Monday	föstudagur	Friday
þriðjudagur	Tuesday	laugardagur	Saturday
miðvikudagur	Wednesday		

Seasons

vor	spring	haust	autumn
sumar	summer	vetur	winter

Time

klukkustund	hour	mánuður	month
dagur	day	ár	year
vika	week		

ITALIAN

A	a	*a* in far	M	m	*m*	
B	b	*b*	N	n	*n*	
C	c	Before *a*, *o*, or *u*, as *c* in can; before *e* or *i*, similar to but softer than *ch* in chant	O	o	*o* in note; like *aw* in saw	
			P	p	*p*	
			Q	q	*q* in quart	
			R	r	*r* in wary, rolled	
D	d	*d*	S	s	*s*; usually *z* between two vowels	
E	e	*a* in grate; *e* in bell				
F	f	*f*	T	t	*t*	
G	g	Before *a*, *o*, or *u*, as *g* in gay; before *e* or *i* like *j*, but softer	U	u	*oo* in coo	
			V	v	*v*	
			W	w		
H	h	Silent, but makes a preceding *c* or *g* hard	X	x	In foreign words only	
			Y	y	Like the vowel *i*; only in foreign words	
I	i	*e* in me				
J	j	*y*; final, *ee*	Z	z	*ts* in quarts or as *ds* in a few words	
K	k	*k*, only in foreign words				
L	l	*l*				

Phonetics

The pronunciation of the following special combinations of letters should be noted:

cce and *cci* are pronounced *tche* and *tchi*, respectively: *accento* (atchento), accent; *uccidere* (ootchidere), to kill.

cia, *cio*, and *ciu* are pronounced *cha*, *cho*, *choo*, respectively: *ciarlare* (charlare), to prattle.

scia, *scio*, *sciu* are pronounced *sha*, *sho*, *shoo*, respectively: *coscia* (cosha), thigh.

gia, *gio*, *giu* are pronounced *ja*, *jo*, *ju*, respectively: *giorno* (jorno), day.

gl and *gn* are pronounced as liquids *ll* and *ñ*, respectively: *meglio* (melyo), better; *giugno* (joonyo), June.

Syllabication

A single consonant between two vowels is always carried over; in case of two or more consonants, sound combinations must not be separated.

Combinations of two consonants are divisible if the first is a liquid; if one of the liquids, *l*, *m*, *n*, or *r*, is the first of the consonants, divide on these: *Sar-co*, *com-pi-ti*, *quin-di-ci*, *par-la-re*, *dol-cez-ze*. If the first consonant is not a liquid, the entire combination is carried over: *Ri-spo-sta*, *de-sti-no*, *lu-stri*, *se-sto*, *que-sta*.

Do not separate combinations representing a single sound, as *ch*, *gh*, *gl*, *gn*, *sce*, *sci*, *scia*, *scio*: *Po-chi*, *lun-ghez-za*, *fi-glia*, *bi-so-gno*, *cre-sce-re*, *u-sci-re*, *la-scia-re*.

Double consonants and *cq*, are divided: *Quel-lo*, *af-flit-to*, *fac-cio*, *fug-gi-re*, *oc-chi-o*, *vec-chi-o*, *cac-cia*, *ac-qua*.

Combinations of three consonants are divided on the first, except where the first is an *s* not belonging to a prefix: *Sem-pre*, *men-tre*, *in-con-tro*, *com-pren-do*, *dis-gra-zia*, but *lu-stri*, *re-gi-stro*, *co-stret-to*, *me-schi-no*.

Groups of two or more vowels, including *i* as a semivowel, are not separated: *Bea-tri-ce*, *geo-gra-fia*, *miei*, *tuoi*, *mi-glio-re*, *sciol-to*, *vi-sio-ne*, *tea-tro*.

Word groups with an apostrophe must not divide on the apostrophe, as *all'*, *coll'*, etc., but are divided on the first *l*, so that the second *l* and the apostrophe begin the next line, as *del-l'albero*; *un'ar-te*.

The space after the apostrophe is no longer required.

Capitalization

Capitalize all proper nouns, names of the Deity, the initial word of a sentence or a line of poetry, but lower case names of the months and proper nouns when used adjectively.

Capitalize adjectives when forming an integral part of a proper noun, as *Alto Adige*.

In book titles capitalize the first word and all' proper nouns: *Storia della diplomazia europea in Italia*.

Accents

The grave is the only accent used and occurs on the final vowel of a word, indicating that the voice rests on that syllable; it also serves for the distinction of monosyllabic words: *è* (is), *e* (and); *nè* (nor), *ne* (of it).

The apostrophe indicates that a vowel has been elided, which may occur either at the beginning or end of a word, e.g., *sopra 'l letto*, on the bed; *l' opera*, the work, etc.

Gender

There are but two genders: Masculine and feminine, the first including males and the second females, regardless of the terminations of the words. Inanimate objects are either male or female, according to their terminal vowel.

Articles

The indefinite articles are *un, una, un'*, being, respectively, for the masculine, feminine, and feminine terms beginning with a vowel.

The definite articles are *il* (plural *i*), *lo* (plural *gli*), *la* (plural *le*) being, respectively, for the masculine, masculine beginning with *s* or *z*, and for the feminine. The definite article may be coalesced with its preceding preposition as shown in the table.

Coalescence

Monosyllabic case prepositions usually combine with the definite article which they govern, in which case we see the elision of a vowel, or the doubling of a consonant, or some other euphonic modification, as shown in the following table:

	Masculine				Feminine	
	Singular	Plural	Singular	Plural	Singular	Plural
	il (the)	i (the)	lo (the)	gli (the)	la (the)	le (the)
di (of)	del	dei	dello	degli	della	delle
a (at, to)	al	ai	allo	agli	alla	alle
da (from)	dal	dai	dallò	dagli	dalla	dalle
in (in)	nel	nei	nello	negli	nella	nelle
con (with)	col	con i	con lo	con gli	con la	con le
per (by, for)	pel	pei	per lo	per gli	per la	per le
su (on)	sul	sui	sullo	sugli	sulla	sulle

Augmentatives, diminutives, etc.

There are a number of suffixes which, when added to nouns, adjectives, or verbs, modify their meaning augmentatively, diminutively, and in other ways, as follows:

-one (large)	liber (book)	librone (large book)
-etto (small)	liber (book)	libretto (booklet)
-ino, -ello (pretty)	liber (book)	librettino (pretty little book)
-accio (ugly)	liber (book)	libraccio (ugly book)
-otto (sturdy)	giovine (a youth)	giovinotto (a strapping youth)
-acchiare (repeat)	baciare (kiss)	baciucchiare (to kiss repeatedly)

Abbreviations

a.C., avanti Cristo, B.C.
a.D., anno Domini, A.D.
a.f., anno futuro, next year
a.p., anno passato, last year
b.p., buono per, good for
c°., compagno, company
d.C., dopo Cristo, after Christ
d.c., da capo, again
ecc., eccetera, etc.
ferr., ferrovia, railroad
frat., fratello, brother
jun., juniore, junior
L.it., lire italiane, Italian lire
magg., maggiore, major
Med., Medico, Dr.
N°., numero, number

N.S., Nostro Signore, Our Lord
On., Onorevole, Honorable
P., per, for; pagina, page
P.es., per esempio, e.g.
S.A., Sua Altezza, His (Her) Highness
scel., scellino, shilling
S.E., Sua Eccellenza, His Excellency
sez., sezione, section
Sig., Signor, Sir, Mr.
Sigg., Signori, Messrs.
St., San, Santo, Saint
v/, vostra, your
v., vedi, see
V.S., Vostra Signoria, Your Honor

Adjectives

These must agree with their nouns in gender and number.

Adjectives terminate in *o* (plural *i*) and *e* (plural *i*) for the masculine; *a* (plural *e*) and *e* (plural *i*) for the feminine. Those ending in *co, go, ca, ga* change to *chi, ghi, che, ghe*, respectively, in the plural, except a few nouns ending in *ico* or *ica*.

Monosyllabic adjectives and those used figuratively or emphatically precede their nouns as a general rule; all others follow.

Comparison is accomplished by placing *più* (more) before the positive to form the comparative and the definite article + *più* to form the superlative. The superlative may also be formed by placing *molto* (very) before the positive or by inserting *issim* before the terminal vowel.

Nouns

Masculine nouns terminate in *o, e,* and rarely *a,* which terminations change to *i* when forming the plural.

Feminine nouns may end in *a* or *e,* which change to *e* and *i,* respectively, when forming the plural.

Nouns terminating in *co, go, ca, ga,* form the plural like the adjectives with the same terminations. Those ending in an accented vowel do not change their form in the plural.

The feminine is sometimes formed from a corresponding masculine by merely changing the term vowel.

The possessive of nouns is formed by means of the preposition *di* (of).

In the following table are illustrated the inflections of the articles, adjectives, and nouns, with especial reference to the grammatical principles already mentioned:

English	Singular	Plural
a brother	un fratello	fratelli
an uncle	un zio	zii
an aunt	una zia	zie
a friend (feminine)	un' amica	amice
the brother	el fratello	i fratelli
the uncle	lo zio	gli zii
the pretty aunt	la bella zia	le belle zie
the large city	la grande città	le grandi città
the small friend	el piccolo amico	i piccoli amici
a smaller city	una città più piccola	città più piccole
a very pretty goose	una oca molto bella	oche molto belle
the prettiest	le (la) più bello(a)	i (le) più belli(e)
of a brother	d'uno fratello	di fratelli
of the brother	del fratello	dei fratelli

Verbs

The compound tenses of *avere* are formed by adding the past participle *avuto* (had), which always retains the same ending: *Io ho avuto* (I have had); *io aveva avuto* (I had had), etc.

The compound tenses of *essere* are formed by adding *stato* (been), which always agrees in gender and number with the noun or pronoun to which it relates: *ella è stata* (she has been); *noi siamo stato* (we have been), etc.

The negative form is made by adding *non* after the subject: *Io non ho* (I have not); *Io non sono* (I am not), etc.

Examples of the past indefinite: *Io non ho avuto* (I have not had); *Io non sono stato* (I have not been), etc.

Examples of the present interrogative form: *ho io?* (have I?); *sono io?* (am I?); the past indefinite: *ho io avuto?* (have I had?); *sono io stato?* (have I been?).

The present negative interrogative forms add *non* to the interrogative form: *non ho io?* (have I not?) *non sono io?* (am I not?); the past indefinite: *non ho io avuto?* (have I not had?); *non sono io stato?* (have I not been?)

Following are the conjugations of the auxiliary verbs *avere* (to have), *essere* (to be), and of the regular verb *parlare* (to speak) in the simple tenses. *Parlare* belongs to the first (or *a*-stem) conjugation, which varies somewhat from those of the second (or *e*-stem) and third (or *i*-stem) conjugations. Such variations are indicated in parentheses.

Principal parts { avere, avendo, avuto (to have, having, had)
essere, essendo, stato (to be, being, been)
parlare, parlando, parlato (to speak, speaking, spoken)

Tense	Singular			Plural		
	1st person	2d person	3d person	1st person	2d person	3d person
Present	ho	hai	ha	abbiamo	avete	hanno
	sono	sei	è	siamo	siete	sono
	parlo	parli	parla (e, e)	parliamo	parlate (e, i)	parlano
Imperfect	avevo	avevi	aveva	avevamo	avevate	avevano
	ero	eri	era	eravamo	eravate	erano
	parlavo (e, i)	parlavi (e, i)	parlava (e, i)	parlavamo (e, i)	parlavate (e, i)	parlavano (e, i)
Past definite	ebbi	avesti	ebbe	avemmo	aveste	ebbero
	fui	fosti	fu	fummo	foste	furono
	parlai (e, i)	parlasti (e, i)	parlo (è, ì)	parlammo (e, i)	parlaste (e, i)	parlarono (e, i)
Future	avrò	avrai	avrà	avremo	avrete	avranno
	sarò	sarai	sarà	saremo	sarete	saranno
	parlero (e, i)	parlerai (e, i)	parlerà (e, i)	parleremo (e, i)	parlerete (e, i)	parleranno (e, i)
Imperative	—	abbi	abbia	abbiamo	abbiate	abbiano
	—	sii	sia	siamo	siate	siano
	—	parla (i, i)	parli (a, a)	parliamo	parlate (e, i)	parlino (e, i)
Present conditional	avrei	avresti	avrebbe	avremmo	avreste	avrebbero
	sarei	saresti	sarebbe	saremmo	sareste	sarebbero
	parlerei (e, i)	parleresti (e, i)	parlerebbe (e, i)	parleremmo (e, i)	parlereste (e, i)	parlerebbero (e, i)
Present subjunctive	abbia	abbia	abbia	abbiamo	abbiate	abbiano
	sia	sia	sia	siano	siate	siano
	parli (a, a)	parli (a, a)	parli (a, a)	parliamo	parliate	parlino (a, a)
Imperfect subjunctive	avessi	avessi	avesse	avessimo	aveste	avessero
	fossi	fossi	fosse	fossimo	foste	fossero
	parlassi (e, i)	parlassi (e, i)	parlasse (e, i)	parlassimo (e, i)	parlaste (e, i)	parlassero (e, i)

The pluperfect and past definite may in ordinary use be interchangeable, though the second is more literary.   They are both translated by the English past tense. The other tenses are used similarly to ours.

In addition to the above forms, there are compound tenses, past indefinite, pluperfect, past anterior, future perfect, past conditional, perfect subjunctive, and pluperfect subjunctive.   These are formed in each case by the past participle of the verb preceded by the conjugation of the auxiliary *avere* (to have) in the present, imperfect, past definite, future, present conditional, and imperfect conditional, respectively. The compound tenses with *stato* (been) employ *essere* instead of *avere* as the auxiliary.   *Stato* inflects for gender and number, thus: *Egli è stato* (he has been); *ella è stata* (she has been); *eglino sono stati* (they have been).

Pronouns

The following table illustrates the declension of the personal pronoun:

	Singular			Plural		
	1st person	2d person	3d person	1st person	2d person	3d person
Nominative	io	tu	*m.* egli *f.* ella	noi	voi	*m.* essi *f.* esse
Indirect object:						
Preverbal	mi	ti	gli le	ci	vi	} a loro
Prepronominal	me	te	glie	ce	ve	
Direct object .	mi	ti	lo la	ci	vi	li le
Object of preposition	me	te	lui lei	noi	voi	loro
Reflexive	mi	ti	si	ci	vi	si

As the subject of a verb pronouns are used only to prevent misunderstanding or to give emphasis.

The second person singular is used as the familiar form only.

With the infinitive, the gerund, and the imperative the personal pronouns are placed after the verb and united with it: *ditemi* (tell me), *senza dirmi* (without telling me).

Cardinal numbers

uno	one	quattordici	fourteen
due	two	quindici	fifteen
tre	three	sedici	sixteen
quattro	four	diciassette}	
cinque	five	diciasette}	seventeen
sei	six	diciotto	eighteen
sette	seven	diciannove}	
otto	eight	dicianove}	nineteen
nove	nine	venti	twenty
dieci	ten	ventuno	twenty-one
undici	eleven	cento	hundred
dodici	twelve	mille	thousand
tredici	thirteen	duemilla	two thousand

Ordinal numbers

primo	first	decimoprimo}	
secondo	second	undicesimo}	eleventh
terzo	third	dodicesimo	twelfth
quarto	fourth	tredicesimo	thirteenth
quinto	fifth	quattordicesimo}	
sesto	sixth	decimoquarto}	fourteenth
settimo	seventh	ventesimo	twentieth
ottavo	eighth	ventunesimo }	
nono	ninth	ventesimo primo}	twenty-first
decimo}		centesimo	hundredth
decima}	tenth	millesimo	thousandth

Months

gennaio (genn.)	January	luglio	July
febbraio (febb.)	February	agosto	August
marzo	March	settembre (sett.)	September
aprile	April	ottobre (ott.)	October
maggio (magg.)	May	novembre (nov.)	November
giugno	June	dicembre (dic.)	December

Days

domenica	Sunday	giovedì	Thursday
lunedì	Monday	venerdì	Friday
martedì	Tuesday	sabato	Saturday
mercoledì	Wednesday		

Seasons

primavera	spring	autunno	autumn
estate	summer	inverno	winter

Time

ora	hour	mese	month
giorno	day	anno	year
settimana	week	secolo	century

Articles to be disregarded in filing

il, lo	l'
i, gl'; gli	un, uno
la, le	una, un'

JAPANESE

SYLLABARY

Pronunciation	Katakana	Hiragana						Pronunciation	Katakana	Hiragana					
i	イ 伊	い 以	吳 異	伊 伊	意 慮	移 移		yo	ヨ	与	与	与	余	余	
ro	ロ 呂	ろ 呂	呂 呂	呂 呂	呂 慮	路 者		ta	タ 多	太	太	堂	堂	多	
ha	ハ 八	は 波	走 走	左 走	八 八	者	re	レ 禮	れ 禮	禮 禮	禮 禮	禮	連	
ni	ニ 二	に 仁	二 二	耳	本	不	so	ソ 曾	ろ 曾	曾 曾	所 所	曾		
ho	ホ 保	は 保	保 保	保 保	本 本	本 本	tsu	ツ 門	つ 門	門 門	徒	津		
he	ヘ 皿	へ 皿	遍 遍	庵 遍	閉 登	登 登	ne	子 祢	ね 祢	祢 祢	年	然		
to	ト 止	と 止	と 止	止 玄	登 遲	地 理	na	ナ 奈	な 奈	奈 奈	奈 羅	那		
chi	チ 知	ち 知	知 知	知 知	遲 里	理 理	ra	ラ 良	ら 良	良 良	羅 無	辭 雲		
ri	リ 利	り 利	利 利	利 利	里		mu	ム 牟	む 武	武 武	無 雲	雲		
nu	ヌ 奴	ぬ 奴	怒 怒	怒 努	努		u	ウ 宇	う 宇	宇 宇	有			
ru	ル 流	る 留	留 留	留 流	流 乎	果	i	ヰ 井	ゐ 井	井 井				
wo	ヲ 乎	を 遠	遠 遠	乎 王	王 可	家	no	ノ 乃	の 乃	乃 能	能	農		
wa	ワ 和	わ 和	和 和	和 王			o	オ 於	れ 於	於 於	於			
ka	カ 加	か 加	可 可	可 閑	家		ku	ク 久	く 久	久 久	九	俱 俱		

JAPANESE—Continued

Pronun-ciation	Kata-kana	Hiragana				Pronun-ciation	Kata-kana	Hiragana				
ya	ヤ 也	や 也	屋 屋	約 耶	荻 夜		yu	ユ 勇	ゆ 由	ゆ 由	ゆ 由	抝 遊	遊 遊
ma	マ 万	ま 末	末 末	土 末	海 満	田 満	me	メ 女	め 女	免 免	面 面	米 米	馬 馬
ke	ケ 个	け 計	計 計	乡 布	筝 氣	ケ 个 富	mi	ミ 美	み 美	天美	美美	新新	見 見 事
fu	フ 不	ふ 不	石 不	姒 婦	布 布	冒 富	shi	シ 之	し 之	志 志	新 新	事 事
ko	コ 巳	こ 巳	古 古	は 許	故 故		e	エ 慧	ゑ 惠	ゑ 惠	衛 衛	花飛	悲 悲
e	エ 江	江 江	え 衣	え 衣	兄 盈		hi	ヒ 比	ひ 比	ひ 飛	ひ 比	比 比	母 母
te	テ 天	て 天	了 天	豆 豆	帝 帝		mo	モ 毛	も 毛	毛 毛	も 毛	も 毛	
a	ア 阿	あ 安	あ 安	阿 阿			se	セ 世	せ 世	世 世	勢 勢	解 解	
sa	サ 散	さ 左	は 佐	左 左	差 差 佐 佐		su	ス 須	す 寸	春 春	壽 壽	數 數	救 數
ki	キ 幾	き 幾	起 起	幾 幾	支 支 支 支		n	ン 二	ん 旡				

The affinities of the native Japanese language are not yet known. One school relates it to the Ural-Altaic group, while the other to Polynesian tongues. In its early stage, the Chinese ideographs were used for phonetic purposes as well as for their regular ones; but to simplify them, a syllabary, called *iroha*, consisting of 47 abbreviated characters, was selected to represent one Japanese sound each. Its cursive forms represented by several characters are called *hiragana*, and its plain forms represented with one sign for each, *katakana*. Modern Japanese writing is an intermixture of Chinese characters with *kana*.

The first column of the above table contains the English pronunciation; the second, the *katakana*, with the Chinese characters of which they are the abbreviated forms, and the remaining columns, the *hiragana* with their variants, arranged in the order of their most frequent occurrence.

There are actually many thousands of ideographs, though even ordinarily educated Japanese would not be able to read and write more than seven or eight thousand. They were originally used also for phonetic purposes, but, that proving unsatisfactory, the syllabaries were derived, each of which has 48 characters, though the Hiragana (cursive) has many variants. Though the Romaji (roman letter) movement has not been very successful, many words have been adopted from the languages of the occidental world, as *biidoro* (vitrio), glass; *kasūtera* (castilla), sponge-cake; *kōhi* (koffij), coffee; *bōto*, boat; *naifu*, knife, etc.

There are two distinct languages—the colloquial and the written, but the differences between them are rapidly yielding under the influence of the press and the complicated needs of modern life.

Although the Japanese derived the art of writing from the Chinese in the third century, the earliest book now extant dates only from A.D. 712; this is the Kojiki, which is written in archaic style, the script being ideographic and used phonetically.

Phonetics

Generally speaking, both vowels and consonants are softer than in most European languages, the vowel sounds being somewhat similar to the Italian. The long vowels are sounded approximately as follows:

* ā, *a* in father   ō, *o* in cone
  ē, *e* in they   u, *oo* in brood
  i, *ie* in siege

There is hardly any tonic accent in pronunciation.

Grammar

Old grammarians recognized but three parts of speech, substantive, predicative, and the post-position (*teniwoha*).

There is no article, and the noun, which is indeclinable, has neither number nor gender, the latter being expressed by the use of the prefixes o (male) and *me* (female), or by the words *otoko, osu* (male) and *onna, mesu* (female); e.g., *otoko no ko* (a boy), and *onna no ko* (a girl). Abstract nouns are generally expressed by the combination of an adjective or a verb with *koto* (thing).

The place of the English preposition is taken by the post-position.

Case is shown by the post-position *ga* or *wa* for the nominative, *no*, possessive, and *wo*, accusative.

Adjectives have three endings: in *i* (attributive or predicative), in *o*, and in *ku* (adverbial).

There are no inflections to indicate comparison, but there is a secondary inflection, produced by combinations of the verb *aru* (is) with the adverbial form of the adjective, to indicate tense and mood.

The personal pronoun is avoided whenever possible, and person is indicated by the context. "I" is *watakushi*; you, *anata* or *kimi* for polite, and *omae* for deprecatory usage.

The relative pronoun is unknown, its place being taken by a verb used adjectively: *hoeru inu* (barks dog), the dog which barks.

Verbs have two conjugations, the stems of the first ending in *e* or *i* remaining unchanged, while in the second, ending in *i*, changes occur in conjugation. There are a few auxiliary and irregular verbs and many compound verbs. There is also a desiderative form ending in *-tai*, which is really an adjective subject to inflection. The passive voice is rarely used and has no conjugation, passive and potential forms being derived by adding *rareru* to the stem of verbs of the first conjugation, and *reru* to those of the second. Similarly, causative verbs are formed by adding *saseru* and *seru* to the stem, respectively. In all three the *a* is added to the stem in the second conjugation.

Fundamental rules are: (*a*) qualifying words precede the word qualified; (*b*) the object precedes the verb; (*c*) the verb is at the end of the sentence.

The student should note the following points: (*a*) Do not confound long and short vowel; (*b*) avoid the use of personal pronouns; (*c*) apply honorifics to superiors, but not to yourself.

There are no expressions "yes" or "no", and in replying affirmatively to a question such as "it that so?" a Japanese would reply "It is so", and in the negative "It is not so."

ROMANIZED FORM OF JAPANESE PHONETIC SYSTEM

For the purpose of spelling out the language phonetically, the Japanese at an early date classified its sounds into a system of syllables. The following is patterned after the revised Hepburn system as used by A. Rose-Innes and T. Takenobu, with some further modifications:

Consonants								Vowels				
	a	e	i	o	ō	u	ū	ya	yo	yō	yu	yū
b	ba	be	bi	bo	bō	bu	bū	bya	byo	byō	byu	byū
ch	cha	—	chi	cho	chō	chu	chū	—	—	—	—	—
d	da	de	—	do	dō	—	—	—	—	—	—	—
f	—	—	—	—	—	fu	fū	—	—	—	—	—
g	ga	ge	gi	go	gō	gu	gū	gya	gyo	gyō	gyu	gyū
h	ha	he	hi	ho	hō	—	—	hya	hyo	hyō	hyu	hyū
j	ja	—	ji	jo	jō	ju	jū	—	—	—	—	—
k	ka	ke	ki	ko	kō	ku	kū	kya	kyo	kyō	kyu	kyū
m	ma	me	mi	mo	mō	mu	mū	mya	myo	myō	myu	myū
n	na	ne	ni	no	nō	nu	nū	nya	nyo	nyō	nyu	nyū
p	pa	pe	pi	po	pō	pu	pū	pya	pyo	pyō	pyu	pyū
r	ra	re	ri	ro	rō	ru	rū	rya	ryo	ryō	ryu	ryū
s	sa	se	—	so	sō	su	sū	—	—	—	—	—
sh	sha	—	shi	sho	shō	shu	shū	—	—	—	—	—
t	ta	te	—	to	tō	—	—	—	—	—	—	—
ts	—	—	—	—	—	tsu	tsū	—	—	—	—	—
w	wa	—	—	—	—	—	—	—	—	—	—	—

The sounds *che, je,* and *she* are possible, but are not used except in foreign words and a few exclamations.

Any vowel may be followed by an *n.* This *n,* however, almost always should be changed to *m* if the first letter following it is a *b, m,* or *p.* The sound *tsu* before a *k, s, sh, t, ts, ch, h,* or *f,* and the sounds *ku* and *ki* before a *k* are replaced by doubling the following consonant. *sh, ts,* and *ch* become *ssh, tts,* and *tch.* However, this doubling of the consonant is done only for reasons of euphony when the pronunciation of *tsu* preceded by a vowel and followed by a consonant would be difficult or harsh.

Romanization

There are two main styles of romanization. The first, which is widely accepted among the English-speaking people, is called the Hepburn style, named after its originator, James C. Hepburn. The second is called the Nihon style, based primarily on the structure of the Japanese language. The main points of difference in the two are the following:

Hepburn:　shi　ji　chi　tsu　ji　zu　fu
Nihon:　　si　zi　ti　tu　di　du　hu

A committee appointed by the Japanese Department of Education is at present investigating the problem of romanization, and their report will decide which system is to be officially adopted.

The *Romaji Hirome kwai, Romaji kwai,* and others, have been recommending the exclusive use of roman letters for the scholarly and scientific writings, but, on the whole, they have not made much progress.

Accents

Accents in Japanese have but little importance for the student of either the spoken or the written language. Briefly the consonants should be pronounced as in English and the vowels as in Italian; the voice should maintain an even tone, no special emphasis being laid on any but long syllables.

Days

Nichiyō	Sunday	Mokuyō	Thursday
Getsuyō	Monday	Kinyō	Friday
Kayō	Tuesday	Doyō	Saturday
Suiyō	Wednesday		

Seasons

haru	spring	aki	autumn
natsu	summer	fuyu	winter

Time

ji	time	tsuki, getsu	month
nichi, hi	day	toshi, nen	year
shu	week		

Cardinal numbers [1]

ichi	one	niju	twenty
ni	two	hyaku	hundred
san	three	hyakuichi	hundred and one
shi	four	nihyaku	two hundred
go	five	sen	thousand
roku	six	man	ten thousand
shichi	seven	juman	hundred thousand
hachi	eight	hyakuman	million
ku	nine	happyakuman	eight million
ju	ten	senman	ten million
juichi	eleven	ichi oku	hundred million
juni	twelve	cho	billion

For the native characters see the Chinese list of cardinal numbers.

Ordinal numbers

Cardinal forms are converted into ordinals by prefixing *dai*, as *dai ni*, the second.

Certain sets of characters are often used in place of numerals in numbering the volumes of a book, the prints in a set, and the like:

1, 2: 上 *jō*, 下 *ge*; or 前 *zen*, 後 *go*.

1, 2, 3: 上 *jō*, 中 *chū*, 下 *ge*; or 前 *zen*, 中 *chū*, 後 *go*; or 天 *ten*, 地 *chi*, 人 *jin*; or 雪 *setsu*, 月 *getsu*, 花 *kwa* (the order is sometimes *getsu*, *setsu*, *kwa*).

1, 2, 3, 4: 乾 *ken*, 坤 *kon*, 巽 *son*, 艮 *gon*; or 花 *kwa*, 鳥 *chō*, 風 *fū*, 月 *getsu*.

1, 2, 3, 4, 5: *kwa*, *chō*, *fū*, *getsu*, as above, and 雪 *setsu*.

---

[1] The following colloquial numbers are also used: hitsotsu, one; futatsu, two; mitsu, three; yotsu, four; itsutsu, five; mutsu, six; nanatsu, seven; yatsu, eight; kokonotsu, nine; to, ten.

JAVANESE

Normal character	Ligature sign	Transliteration	Normal character	Ligature sign	Transliteration	Normal character	Ligature sign	Transliteration
		hå			djå	Initial letters		
		nå			yå			
		tjå			njå			Nå
		rå			må			Tjå
		kå			gå			Kå
		då			bå			Tå
		tå			ṭå			Så
		så			ngå			På
		wå			rĕ			Njå
		lå			lĕ			Gå
		på						Bå
		ḍå						

Name	Character	Transliteration	Remarks	Character	Transliteration
Vowel and reading signs (Sandangan)				**Arabic sounds**	
Pĕpĕt		ĕ			a
Wulu		i			i
Suku		u			u
Taling		e			e
Taling-Tarung		o			o
Patĕn or Pangkon			Where a letter takes vowel sound	**Isolated vowels**	
Wigñan		h	At end of syllable		h
					k
Tjĕtjak		ng	Do.		δ
Layar		r	Do.		j
Tjåkrå		r	Between a consonant and the following sound		s
Kĕrĕt		rĕ	After a consonant		g
					p
Pingkal		yå	Do.		ng

JAVANESE LIGATURES

Combination with suku					Combination with tjåkrå	
						Other consonantal combinations
					Combination with kĕrĕt	
				Combination with patĕn		
					Combination with pinjkal	

Miscellaneous signs

 A superior begins a letter to an inferior with this character

 Used by equals in rank at beginning of a letter

 Used by an inferior to begin a letter to his superior

Final *suku*

Final *taling*

Used as a sign of separation

Used as a hyphen in poetry

Connected vowel signs

Small reading signs

Javanese is a language spoken in central and eastern Java by some 18,000,000 people. It is a branch of the Malay-Polynesian language family and a direct descendant of the old Javanese, or Kawi, language. It has adopted a considerable number of words from the Sanscrit without, however, making any change in its grammatical construction. The alphabet, also, is derived from the old Kawi, which, in turn, was evolved from a south Indian alphabet. The text reads from left to right.

The ligature character is sometimes used instead of the *patěn* to give the consonant the vowel sound.

Numerals

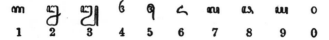

| 1 | 2 | 3 | 4 | 5 | 6 | 7 | 8 | 9 | 0 |

Punctuation

: Comma   \ Half pause   ⟍ Complete pause   ‖ Extract

KANARESE (KANNADA)

Character	Transliteration	Character	Transliteration	Character	Transliteration	Character	Transliteration
ಅ	a	ಓ	ō	ಝು	jha	ಬ	ba
ಆ	ā	ಔ	au	ಞ	ña	ಭ	bha
ಇ	i	೦	ṁ	ಟ	ṭa	ಮ	ma
ಈ	ī	೦	ḥ	ಠ	ṭha	ಯ	ya
ಉ	u	೪	ḥ	ಡ	ḍa	ರ	ra
ಊ	ū	೦೦	ṛh	ಢ	ḍha	ಱ	ṛa
ಋ	ṛ	ಕ	ka	ಣ	ṇa	ಲ	la
ಋೂ	r̄	ಖ	kha	ತ	ta	ವ	va
ಌ	ḷ	ಗ	ga	ಥ	tha	ಶ	śa
ೡ	ḹ	ಘ	gha	ದ	da	ಷ	ṣa
ಎ	e	ಙ	ṅa	ಧ	dha	ಸ	sa
ಏ	ē	ಚ	ca	ನ	na	ಹ	ha
ಐ	ai	ಛ	cha	ಪ	pa	ಳ	ḷa
ಒ	o	ಜ	ja	ಫ	pha	ಱ	ḻa

Kanarese is the language spoken in Mysore, Hyderabad, and the adjoining districts of Madras and Bombay, and it belongs to the Dravidian language group. The irregular forms are similar to the Telugu, but it is closely related to the Tamil. The text reads from left to right and, as shown in the table, has many ligatures.

Besides the vowels shown, there are vowel signs which are placed over or on the sides of the consonants; those for the g are as follows:

ಗ	ga	ಗೄ	gṛ	ಗೇ	gē
ಗಾ	gā	ಗೄಾ	gṝ	ಗೈ	gai
ಗಿ	gi				
ಗೀ	gī	ಗೄ	gḷ	ಗೊ	go
ಗು	gu	ಗೄ	gḹ	ಗೋ	gō
ಗೂ	gū	ಗೆ	gĕ	ಗೌ	gau

Consonantal doubling and combinations are also made by connecting two consonants or using a combination of parts of two consonants, as follows:

$$\text{ಗ್ಗ} = gga, \quad \text{ರ್ಕ} = rka, \text{ etc.}$$

Numerals

೧	೨	೩	೪	೫	೬	೭	೮	೯	೦
1	2	3	4	5	6	7	8	9	0

KOREAN

In 1933 the office of the Governor General of Korea modified and simplified the alphabet and this table follows the new system.

VOWELS[1] TRANSLITERATION AND TONE VALUE

Combinations				Vowel	Transliteration and Tone Value
하 과 타 가 자 아 바 마 사 바				ㅏ (아)	a (as in *ah*)
햐 과 탸 갸 쟈 야 뱌 먀 샤 뱌				ㅑ (야)	ya
허 궈 터 거 저 어 버 머 서 버				ㅓ (어)	u (approximately as in *fur*)
혀 궈 텨 겨 져 여 벼 며 셔 벼				ㅕ (여)	yu (approximately as *you* in *young*)
호 고 토 고 조 오 보 모 소 보				ㅗ (오)	o (equal to the initial sound of long *o* and approximately as in *for*)
효 교 툐 교 죠 요 뵤 묘 쇼 뵤				ㅛ (요)	yo (approximately as in *yo-ho*)
후 구 투 구 주 우 부 무 수 부				ㅜ (우)	oo (long *oo* as in *soon*)
휴 규 튜 규 쥬 유 뷰 뮤 슈 뷰				ㅠ (유)	yoo or u (as in *use*)
흐 그 트 그 즈 으 브 므 스 브				ㅡ (으)	oo (somewhere near short *oo*, as in *book*, though there is really no close English equivalent)
히 기 티 기 지 이 비 미 시 비				ㅣ (이)	i (as in *police*) or ee (as in *see*)
호 고 토 고 조 으 보 므 스 브				· (응)	a (as in *ah*) = ㅏ

DIGRAPHS

ㅘ (와) ㅗ + ㅏ (approximately *wa*)

ㅝ (워) ㅜ + ㅓ (approximately *wo*)

ㅐ (애) *a* (as in *a*s)

ㅒ (얘) *ya* (as in *ya*nkee)

ㅔ (에) *e* (approximately as in *e*nd, and equal to the initial sound of long *a*) = French *è*

ㅖ (예) *ye* (approximately as in *yé*t)

ㅚ (외) no English equivalent (approximately German ö)

ㅙ (왜) no English equivalent (approximately *y* + ö)

ㅟ (위) *we*

ㅞ (웨) approximately *y* + *we*

ㅢ (의) no English equivalent (approximately French *ui* as in *hui*le)

ㅗ + ㅓ no English equivalent; ㅗ + ㅓ (approximately *wa* as in *wa*gon)

ㅘ (왜) no English equivalent; ㅜ + ㅓ approximately *wa* as in *wa*re

CONSONANTS [2]

ㄱ (ㄱ이ㄱ) a sound approximately between *k* and *g* (as in *g*o) [3]; when doubled = *g* (in *g*o)

ㄴ (ㄴ으ㄴ) *n*

ㄷ (ㄷ이ㅌ) a sound approximately between *d* and *t*; when doubled = *d*.

ㄹ (ㅎ으ㄹ) no exact English equivalent; a sound approximately between *l* and *r*.

ㅁ (ㅁ이ㅁ) *m*

ㅂ (ㅂ이ㅂ) no English equivalent; a sound approximately between *b* and *v*. When doubled = *b*.

ㅅ (ㅅ이ㅅ) as initial (처) approximately = *s*; though weaker than *s*; as final (밧잇) approximately = *t*, when doubled (ㅆ) = *s*.

ㅇ (ㅇ이ㅇ) *ng*

ㅈ (ㅈ) no English equivalent; a sound approximately between *j* and *z*; when doubled = *j*.

ㅊ (ㅊ) approximately *ch*.

ㅋ (ㅋ) *k*

ㅌ (ㅌ) *t*

ㅍ (ㅍ) *p*

ㅎ (ㅎ) *h*

COMBINATIONS OF CONSONANTS

ㄲ (= g), ㄸ (= d), ㅃ (= b), ㅆ (= s), ㅉ (= j) are used for both 막 and 밧 잇 . And any other combinations may be made for 밧 잇 .

Examples: ㄺ approximately *lk* or *rk*,
ㄻ approximately *lm* or *rm*,
ㄼ approximately *lb* or *rb*, etc.

[1] The form in the parentheses is the name of the letter (as *b*, in *b*ee). The Korean child, in learning the sounds, recites them as shown in the table; i.e., as a syllabary—each consonant followed in turn by all the vowels.

[2] The form in parentheses is the Korean name of the letter. Since there is a distinction between initial and final uses of the consonants, the name may use the consonant in both positions; but where there is no distinction, the name contains the consonant only once.

[3] We may say that a sound (3) is between two other sounds (1) and (2) when the organs of speech, moving from the position for (1) to that for (2), pass also through an intermediate position which, if paused at, would produce (3). This applies to both vowels and consonants.

The Koreans have a true alphabet, not a syllabary, like that of the Japanese, nor a system of characters representing individual ideas, like that of the Chinese. It doubtless belongs to the Ural-Altaic language family and is at present spoken by some 17,000,000 people, the Chinese characters being used by the upper classes and in technical works. There are dialectic variations in different parts of the country, but these are unimportant. The alphabet, called Önmun, was introduced by the Emperor Sëtjong, with the assistance of some Chinese scholars, during the period embraced in the years 1443–46, and is particularly well adapted for writing the Korean. The characters, of which 14 are consonants and 11 vowels, are quite simple and bear some resemblance to the Sanscrit, although the historical evidence of their origin is lacking.

Korean spelling is very simple, because there are no silent letters and practically all the letters represent invariable sounds. It should be noted, however, that the letters of each syllable are not written in a line but are grouped into one sign, and the final consonant is always placed at the bottom of the sign. Like the Chinese, the text is generally written in columns, from top to bottom, the columns reading from right to left. In modern printing, however, the English style, in lines reading from left to right, has become quite common.

The character for *s* was formerly used after a letter that was to be doubled, but that has now been discontinued and the character is repeated.

The language has neither punctuation, division of syllables, nor distinction as to capital or lower-case letters. If necessary, division may occur after any syllable.

The Chinese figure characters are in use generally.

The lunar month is used, the months being designated "first", "second", etc. In naming the days of the month, the numerals from 1 to 10 are used, and thus the 11th would be designated "second first", the 21st, "third first", etc.

LADINO

Ladino (Judaeo-Spanish) is a dialect composed of a mixture of Spanish and Hebrew elements. It is used as the vernacular as well as literary language by the Sephardim or "Spagnioli", descendants of the Jews expelled from Spain and now scattered throughout Turkey, Jugoslavia including Bosnia, Bulgaria, and Morocco. The so-called Rabbinical cursive characters are used in writing Ladino, but it is printed generally in Rabbinical, though sometimes in the square Hebrew characters (see 120), and also quite frequently in Latin letters.

It is most nearly like the Old Spanish, or Castilian, of the 15th century, containing about 80 percent of Spanish words, and is frequently called "idioma castellana" or "lengua vulgar." Students of Old Spanish should first familiarize themselves with Ladino. It resembles the Yiddish in that it includes many old Hebrew and Talmudic words, particularly such as have been transmitted from generation to generation or cannot be exactly translated into another language; e.g., *chen, rachmonuth, zedackah.* It differs from modern Spanish in that it contains many forms and words now obsolete which were still current in Castile toward the close of the 15th century when the Jews were expelled from Spain; e.g., *fruchiguar, ermollecer, escuentar, muchiguar, podestania, pecilgo* (=*pellizco*), *espandir,* etc.

One of the characteristics of Ladino is that it contains words taken from the Hebrew that have become Spaniolized; e.g., *meldar,* to read; *meldador,* the reader; *melda,* school; *darsar* (from the Hebrew root דרש), to investigate, to instruct; *chanufer* (from חנף), the flatterer, etc. Some of these words from the Hebrew have become current in the Iberian Peninsula; i.e., *malshin*=Spanish *malsin,* and Portuguese *malsim,* accuser, slanderer, and its derivatives *malsinar* and *malsindad;* the Rabbinical *get* became the Spanish *guet,* etc.

In Ladino, as also in the Old Spanish, *f* and *g* are each used instead of *h;* e.g., *fijo* instead of *hijo; fablar* instead of *hablar; fambre* instead of *hambre; fermosa* instead of *hermosa; agora* instead of *ahora.* The *h,* whether initial or median, is frequently omitted, as in *ermano* for *hermano,* and *conortar* for *conhortar.* Often *m* takes the place of *n,* as in *muestros* for *nuestros, mos* and *muevo* for *nos* and *nuevo; m* and *n* are sometimes inserted, as in *amvisar* for *avisar,* and *munchos* for *muchos.* Metastasis of *d* before *r* also takes place, as *vedrad, vedre, acodro,* and *pedrer* for *verdad, verde, acordo,* and *perder;* or of *r* before *o,* as *probe* for *pobre,* and *proberia* (still used in Galicia) for *pobreria.* The *b* is quite frequently used for *v,* as *biuda, bolar,* instead of *viuda* and *volar.* The Ladino has also absorbed a considerable number of Turkish words. One of its phonetic characteristics is the change of the Spanish *ll* to *y;* e.g., *cabayero* for *caballero,* and *estreya* for *estrella.* In printing with Hebrew square or Rabbinical characters this sound is represented by a lamed and double yod (לי); e.g., לייאמאר for *llamar;* לייבאר for *llevar;* קאלי for *calle* (street). For the letter *q* preceding *e* and *i,* ק is used, as קי for *que;* אקי for *aqui;* קיין for *quien.* The *s* is used instead of *c* and *z,* as in *sielo* and *cabeson* for *cielo* and *cabezon;* while ׳, pronounced *j,* is used instead of *yod* and *gimel* before *e* and *i,* as מוזער for *mujer,* and איזו for *hijo.* The *r* is never doubled in Ladino.

The language has a comparatively rich literature, the origin of which dates back to the beginning of the 16th century, and this has in recent years been augmented by translations from the best in the literature of the leading countries of the world.

LANGUAGES AND MONIES OF THE WORLD

Country	Language	Commercial language	Monetary unit
Aden	Arabic	Arabic	Indian rupee
Alaska	English; Eskimo dialects	English	Dollar
Albania	Albanian, Italian	Albanian, Italian	Gold franc
Algeria	Maghreb, French	French	French franc
Angola	Portuguese, Dutch; Kisi Kongo (north); Kimbundu (north-central); Umbundu (eastern highlands); Luchazi (south)	Portuguese	Escudo
Arabia	Arabic	Arabic	Indian rupee
Argentina	Spanish, French, Italian	Spanish	Gold peso
Ashanti	Twi	English	British pound
Australia	English; native dialects	English	Australian pound
Austria	German	German, English	Schilling
Azores	Portuguese	Portuguese	Gold escudo
Bahamas	English	English	British pound
Barbados	English	English	British pound
Basutoland ...	Susuto, Xosa, Afrikaans	English	British pound
Bechuanaland.	Sechuana, Afrikaans	English	British pound
Belgian Congo.	Various Bantu languages; English in Katanga mining district	French	Belgian franc
Belgium	French, Flemish	French, Flemish	Belgian franc
Bermuda Islands	English	English	British pound
Bolivia	Spanish, Aymasa, Quichua, Mojo, Chiquito, Guarani, Toba, Lengua	Spanish, English	Boliviano
Borneo	Malay, Chinese	Malay, Chinese, Dutch in Dutch Borneo	Straits dollar; Dutch currency
Brazil	Portuguese, German, Spanish, Italian and Indian languages	Portuguese (Spanish and English to some extent)	Gold cruzeiro
British Cameroons ..	Duala, Fula, Hausa	English	British pound; silver shilling
British Columbia ...	English	English	Canadian dollar
British Guiana	Arawak, Carib, Wapisiana, Warraw, English	English	British Guiana dollar
British Honduras ...	Maya, Carib, English	English	U. S. gold dollar
British Malaya	Malay dialects	English	Straits dollar
British North Borneo	Malay, Chinese	Malay, Chinese	British pound; Mexican peso
British Oceania	Malay dialects	English	British pound
British Solomon Islands.	Malay dialects, "pidgin English"	French	British pound
British Somaliland ..	Somali, Arabic	French	Indian rupee
British West Africa..	Wolof and other Bantu dialects	English	British pound; siver shilling
Brunei	Malay	Malay	Straits dollar
Bulgaria	Bulgarian	German, Spanish, French, English	Lev
Burma	Hindu	English	Indian rupee

Country	Language	Commercial language	Monetary unit
Canada	English, ⅔; French, ¼; remainder, German, Scandinavian, Slavic	English, French	Canadian dollar
Canary Islands	Spanish	Spanish	Gold peseta
Celebes	Mainly Malay, also Toala, Tozaga, Buginese, Macassar, and other dialects	English, French, German; Malay indispensable with Malay and Chinese dealers	Indian rupee
Ceylon	Singalese, Tamil; English amongst middle and upper classes	English	Indian silver rupee
Chile	Spanish	Spanish; some exporters use German	Chilean peso
China	Chinese (very many dialects)	English	Yuan dollar; also many other coins
Chosen (Korea)	Korean	Japanese	Japanese yen
Colombia	Indian dialects, Spanish	Spanish	Gold peso
Costa Rica ...	Spanish, English in Limon province	Spanish	Colon
Cuba	Spanish	Spanish	Cuban gold peso
Curaçao	Papamiento (composite dialect); Dutch	Spanish	Florin (gulden)
Cyprus	Dialect of Modern Greek, Osmanli Turkish by Moslems; French by educated classes; English is gaining ground	Modern Greek (corrupt dialect)	British pound
Cyrenaica	Modern Greek, Italian	Italian	Italian lira
Czechoslovakia	Bohemian, Moravian, Ruthenian, Slovak	Bohemian, Slovak, German	Koruna
Danzig	German, Polish	German	Gulden
Denmark	Danish	Danish; English may be freely used	Krone
Dominican Republic	Spanish	Spanish	U. S. gold dollar
Dutch Guiana.	Dutch, English	Dutch	
East Africa¹ ..			
Ecuador	Otavalo, Quechua, Spanish	Spanish	Sucre
Egypt	Arabic	Arabic, English, French, Italian, Modern Greek	Egyptian gold pound
Ellice Islands .	Samoan	Samoan	British pound
El Salvador ..	Spanish, English	Spanish, English	Colon
Equatorial Africa	Arabic	Arabic	French franc
Estonia	Estonian, German, Russian; English compulsory in schools	Estonian	Gold kroon
Ethiopia (Abyssinia) ..	Amharic, Tigre, Tigriña, and Guragua and Harar dialects	Arabic, Italian	Italian lira
Falkland Islands	English	English	British pound
Federated Malay States ...	Malay	English, Malay, Tamil, Chinese	Straits dollar
Fiji	Bauan dialect	Bauan dialect	British pound
Finland	Finnish, Swedish, German, English	Finnish, Swedish	Markka

¹ See Kenya, Northern Rhodesia, Nyasaland, Tanganyika, Uganda, Zanzibar

Country	Language	Commercial language	Monetary unit
France	French	French	Franc
French Guiana	Indian dialects, French patois	French	French franc
French India..	Hindu	French	Silver piastre
French Indo-China	Annamese, Cambodian, Thais, Chinese	French	Silver piastre
French Morocco	Maghreb	French	French franc
French Oceania	Malay dialects	French	French franc
French West Indies	French	French	French franc
Gambia	Wolof		French franc
Germany	German	German	Deutsche mark (gold)
Gibraltar	English	English	British pound; Spanish coins in common use
Gilbert Islands	Melanesian dialects	English	British pound
Gold Coast ...	Awune, Fanti, Gã, Twi	English	British pound; special silver coinage
Great Britain.	English, Scotch, Welsh	English	Pound sterling
Greece	Modern Greek	Modern Greek	Drachma
Greenland	Eskimo dialects, Danish	Danish	Danish krone
Grenada	French patois	English	British pound
Guadeloupe Islands	French	French	French franc
Guar	Malay dialects, English	English	U. S. currency
Guatemala ...	Carib and Quiché (altogether 18 different languages); Spanish	Spanish	Quetzal
Haiti	French; patois in interior	French, English	Gourde
Hawaiian Islands	English, Hawaiian	English	U. S.. currency
Holland [2]			
Honduras	Carib, Spanish	Spanish	Peso (silver)
Hong Kong ...	Chinese, English	English	Hong Kong dollar
Hungary	Hungarian	Hungarian, German; (use of English increasing)	Forint
Iceland	Icelandic	Icelandic; (English is understood)	Krona
India	[3]	Hindu, Bengali	Silver rupee
Indo China ...	Annamese, Cambodian, Thais	French	Silver piastre
Indonesia	Malay, Javanese	Dutch, English	Dutch florin (gulden)
Iraq	Arabic	Arabic	Indian rupee
Irish Free State	Gaelic, English	Gaelic, English	Saorstát pound
Italian Africa.	Arabic dailect, Nyika, Swahili	Arabic, Italian	Italian lira
Italy	Italian	Italian	Lira
Jamaica	English	English	British pound
Japan	Japanese	Japanese; English and Esperanto used to some extent	Yen

[2] See Netherlands.
[3] Arsami, Awadhi, Bengali, Bhili, Bhojpuri, Bihari, Braj Basha, Bundeli, Dakhini, Dasi, Eastern Hindu, Gujurati, Hindu, Hindustani, Jaipuri, Jarki, Kabul, Kanauji, Kandahar, Kashmiri, Kohistani, Konkani, Lahudo, Lari, Magahi, Maharashtri, Maithili, Marathi, Marwarri, Multani, Nepali, Pahari, Punjabi, Rajashani, Raverty, Sindhi, Urdu, Uriya.

Country	Language	Commercial language	Monetary unit
Kenya	Swahili	Swahili	East African shilling;
Korea [4]			
Kwangtung ..	Chinese	Japanese	Japanese yen; Chinese currency
Labrador	English	English	Canadian dollar
Latvia	Lettish, German, Russian, English	Lettish, English	Lat
Leeward Islands	English	English	British and U. S. currencies legal tender
Liberia	Mandingo, Mendi, Vai and other negro dialects	English	Liberian dollar; British currency
Lithuania	Lithuanian, Russian, Yiddish, German	Lithuanian	Lit
Luxembourg ..	French, German	French, German	Belgian franc
Macao	Chinese, Portuguese	Portuguese	Tael
Madagascar ..	Malagasy, French	French	French franc
Madeira	Portuguese	Portuguese	Portuguese escudo
Malta	Maltese, Modern Greek, English	English	British pound
Martinique ...	French	French	French franc
Mauritius	Indian dialects French, English	English, French	British pound; Rupee
Mexico	Spanish, Mayan and other Indian dialects	Spanish	Peso
Morocco:			
French zone	Maghreb and Berber dialects	French	French franc
Spanish zone	Maghreb, Spanish	Spanish	Spanish peso; Hassani (silver)
Tangier zone	Maghreb, French, Spanish	Maghreb, French, Spanish	Moroccan francs; Spanish currency
Mozambique ..	Kua (Mozambique)	Portuguese	Escudo
Netherlands ..	Dutch	Dutch, English, French, German	Florin
Netherland East Indies [5] .			
New Zealand..	English	English	British pound
Newfoundland.	English	English	Standard is gold Newfoundland dollar, (not coined); Canadian, U. S. and British currency used
Nicaragua	Carib, Spanish patois English	Spanish, English	Córdoba
Nigeria	Hausa	English	Shilling; British currency
Northern Rhodesia ...	Afrikaans, Mashona (Chiswina), English	English, Afrikaans	British pound
Norway	Norwegian	Norwegian, English	Krone
Nyasaland ...	Nyanja	Nyanja	British pound
Palestine	Arabic, Hebrew, Yiddish, English and various European languages	English, French, German, Arabic, Hebrew	Palestine pound
Panama Canal Zone	Spanish, English	English, Spanish	U. S. dollar

[4] See Chosen.
[5] See Indonesia.

Country	Language	Commercial language	Monetary unit
Panama Republic	Spanish, Indian dialects, English	Spanish, English	Balboa
Paraguay	Guarani, Spanish	Spanish	Paper peso
Persia	Persian	French, English	Silver kran
Peru	Spanish, Quechua dialects	Spanish	Sol
Philippine Islands	Spanish, English, Moro, Tagalog, and many other Malayan dialects	English, Spanish	Philippine peso (silver)
Poland	Polish	Polish, French, German, some English	Zloty
Porto Rico	Spanish, English	Spanish, English	U. S. dollar
Portugal	Portuguese	Portuguese	Gold escudo
Portuguese East Africa	Thonga, Arabic dialects	Portuguese, English	Portuguese escudo
Rhodesia	Mashona (Chiswina)	English	British pound
Roumania	Roumanian	Roumanian, German, French, Russian	Leu
Russia	Russian [6]	Russian, some French	Chervonets
Saint Lucia	English, French patois.	English, French	British pound
Samoa	Samoan	English	U. S. currency
Seychelles Islands	Chinese, Hindu, Bantu, English, French patois	English	Indian rupee
Siam	Siamese	English, Siamese	Baht
Sierra Leone	Mendi, Sulima, Sasu, Timne	English	Shilling
Somaliland	Somali, English, Arabic, Hindustani	Somali, English, Arabic, Hindustani	Indian rupee
South Africa, Union of	English, Afrikaans	English, Afrikaans	South African pound
South West Africa (British)	Bantu dialects	English, German	British pound
Southern Rhodesia	English, Afrikaans	English, Afrikaans	South African pound
Spain	Spanish	Spanish, some French	Peseta (gold)
Straits Settlements	Malay, English	English, Malay	Straits dollar
Sudan	Arabic, Acholi, Bari, Dinka, Kanuri, Latuko, Madi, Shilluk, Zande	Arabic	Egyptian pound
Sumatra	Malay	Dutch, Malay	Guilder
Surinam	East Indian dialects, Dutch patois	Dutch	Dutch florin (gulden)
Swaziland	Swazi, Afrikaans	English, Afrikaans	South African pound
Sweden	Swedish	Swedish, English, German, French	Krona
Switzerland	German, French, Italian, Romansol	German, French, Italian	Swiss franc
Syria	Syriac dialects, Arabic	Arabic, French, English	Syrian pound

[6] The various national minorities have their own language.

Country	Language	Commercial language	Monetary unit
Tanganyika ..	Arabic dialects, Hindu patois, Kiswahili and many other Bantu dialects	Arabic	East African shilling
Tangier [7]			
Tobago	English	English	British currency U. S. gold
Togoland	Ewe, Twi, English	English	Shilling; French franc in French sphere
Tonga Islands.	Tonga, Malay dialects, English	English	British pound
Trinidad	English	English	British currency; U. S. gold
Tripolitania ..	Arabic, Berber, Italian, Jewish, Maghreb	Italian, French	Italian lira
Tunisia	Maghreb	French	French franc
Turkey	Turkish	Turkish, French, English	Turkish paper pound
Uganda	Kiswahili, Luganda, Swahili	Kiswahili, Luganda, Swahili	East African shilling
Unfederated Malay States.	Malay, English	Malay, English	Straits dollar
United States .	English [8]	English	U. S. dollar
Uruguay	Spanish	Spanish	Peso
Venezuela ...	Arawak, Carib, Spanish	Spanish	Bolivar
Virgin Islands	English, Danish	English	U. S. dollar
Weihaiwei ...	Mandarin Chinese	English	Yuan dollar; tael
Yugoslavia (Serb, Croat and Slovene Federation) ..	Serbo-Croatian, Slovenian, German Magyar, Turkish	German, French	Dinar
Zanzibar	Arabic, Swahili Guajarati, Kutchi	English, Arabic	British Indian rupee

[7] See Morocco.
[8] German, Italian, French, the Scandinavian and all of the Slavic tongues and the languages of practically all of the civilized countries of the world are in common use.

LATIN

Ā	ā	*a* in father	N	n	*n*	
Ă	ă	*a* in Cuba	Ō	ō	*o* in old	
B	b	*b*	Ŏ	ŏ	*o* in obey	
C	c	*k* in king	P	p	*p*	
D	d	*d*	Q	q	*q*	
Ē	ē	*e* in prey	R	r	*r*	
Ĕ	ĕ	*e* in net	S	s	*s* in son	
F	f	*f*	T	t	*t* in time	
G	g	*g* in get	Ū	ū	*u* in rule	
H	h	*h*	Ŭ	ŭ	*u* in full	
Ī	ī	*i* in machine	V	v	*w* in we	
Ĭ	ĭ	*i* in cigar	X	x	*x*	
J	j	*y* in yet	Y	y	*ü* in German (only in foreign words)	
K	k	*k*				
L	l	*l*	Z	z	*z* in zone (only in foreign words)	
M	m	*m*				

i preceded by an accented *a, e, o,* or beginning a word, and followed by another vowel, becomes a semivowel, with.the sound of *y* in yet. This semivowel use of the *i* has been replaced by the letter *j*, which was introduced in the seventh century post Christum, but is still rejected by some modern editors.

u in *qu*, and generally in *gu* and *su*, has the sound of *w*, when preceding a vowel: e.g., *quo, suaviter*.

The combination *ch* has nearly the pronunciation of the German *ch*. This, with certain other combinations, and the letters *y* and *z* were introduced in the second century B.C. for the purpose of transliterating Greek words.

The digraphs *æ* and *œ* are not to be considered separate letters, any more than the English *fi* or *fl*. The present tendency is away from the use of these characters.

The so-called "English" and "Continental" methods of pronunciation are no longer in use by scholars. There is an ecclesiastical pronunciation that approximates Italian.

Diphthongs

The pronunciation of diphthongs was to sound each vowel rapidly with the other: as *ae*=aye, *oe*=boy, *au*=our, *ei*=feint, *ui*=we, almost; *eu* can be represented by eh-oo.

Capitalization

Inasmuch as the Romans used only one form of letter, they had no rules for capitalization. Modern editors usually begin the first word of a sentence and proper names with capital letters, but not the first word of a line of poetry.

Accent

Words of two syllables are always accented on the first: *men'-sa*.

Words of more than two syllables are accented on the penult (next to last syllable) if that be long, otherwise on the antepenult: *ho-nō'-ris, cŏn'-su-lis*.

Syllabication

The number of syllables is governed by the number of vowels or diphthongs in the word: *a-mi-ci-ti-am, se-ri-o, car-du-us*.

When a single consonant occurs between two vowels or between a diphthong and a vowel, division is made before the consonant, excepting the letter *x: Caesar, fre-num*, but *max-i-mus*.

When two or more consonants occur together, division is before the last consonant; *inep-ti, nar-cis-sus, ves-ti-gia, emp-tus;* but the following groups of consonants, *bl, br, ch, cl, cr, dl, dr, fl, fr, gh, gl, gr, ph, pl, pr, th, tl,* and *tr* should always remain intact: *nos-trum, pan-cra-ti-um,* etc.

ch, ph, and *th* may be treated as single consonants and keep *l* and *r* with them. *gu* and *qu* should be kept together.

Compounds are separated into their component elements: *prod-est.*

Calendar

The Romans numbered their years from the foundation of the city of Rome (*a.u.c.*), which corresponded with the year 753 B.C.

The first day of each month was called *kalendæ* (calends).

The seventh day of March, May, July, and October, and the fifth day of the other months were the *nonæ* (nones).

The fifteenth day of March, May, July, and October, and the thirteenth day of the other months were the *idus* (ides).

This is the scheme of the Julian Calendar, which was put into effect in 46 B.C.

After the introduction of Christianity and the 7-day week *Dominica dies* was adopted in place of *dies solis,* and the other days were numbered *feriæ.* For Friday the Greek term *parasceve* was sometimes employed, and for Saturday *vigilium.*

Cardinal numbers

unus, una, unum	one	decem	ten
duo, duæ, duo	two	undecim	eleven
tres, tria	three	duodecim	twelve
quattuor	four	tredecim	thirteen
quinque	five	viginti	twenty
sex	six	viginti unus	twenty-one
septem	seven	centum	hundred
octo	eight	mille	thousand
novem	nine		

Ordinal numbers

primus	first	decimus	tenth
secundus	second	undecimus	eleventh
tertius	third	duodecimus	twelfth
quartus	fourth	tertius decimus	thirteenth
quintus	fifth	vicesimus, vigesimus	twentieth
sextus	sixth	vicesimus primus	twenty-first
septimus	seventh	centesimus	hundredth
octavus	eighth	millesimus	thousandth
nonus	ninth		

Months

Januarius	January	Julius	July
Februarius	February	Augustus	August
Martius	March	September	September
Aprilis	April	October	October
Maius	May	November	November
Junius	June	December	December

Days

dies solis	Sunday	dies Mercurii	Wednesday
dies dominica	Sunday	dies Jovis	Thursday
dies lunæ	Monday	dies Veneris	Friday
dies Martis	Tuesday	dies Saturni	Saturday

Seasons

ver	spring	autumnus	autumn
æstas	summer	hiems	winter

Time

hora	hour	mensis	month
dies	day	annus	year
hebdomas	week	centuria	century

LATIN ABBREVIATIONS

[The use of the ligatures æ and œ is not in as much favor in American printing as formerly]

A., absolvo, I acquit; antiquo, I abrogate

a., annus, year; ante, before

A.A.C., anno ante Christum, in the year before Christ

A.A.S., Academiæ Americanæ Socius, Fellow of the American Academy [Academy of Science and Arts]

A.B., artium baccalaureus, bachelor of arts

ab init., ab initio, from the beginning

abs. re., absente reo, the defendant being absent

A.C., ante Christum, before Christ

A.D., anno Domini, in the year of our Lord

a.d., ante diem, before the day

ad capt., ad captandum, for the purpose of catching

ad fin., ad finem, at the end, to one end

ad h.l., ad hunc locum, to this place, on this passage

ad inf., ad infinitum, to infinity

ad init., ad initium, at the beginning

ad int., ad interim, in the meantime

ad lib., ad libitum, at pleasure

ad loc., ad locum, at the place

ads., ad sectam, at the suit

adv., adversus, against

ad val., ad valorem, according to value

æq., æquales, equal, equals

æt., ætatis, of age, aged

Ag., argentum, silver

A.H., anno Hegiræ, in the year of Hegira, or flight of Mohammed

a.h.l., ad hunc locum, on the passage, to this place

A.H.S., anno humanæ salutis, in the year of human salvation

a.h.v., ad hunc vocem, at this word

A.I., anno inventionis, in the year of the discovery

al., alia, alii, other things, other persons

A.L., anno lucis, in the year of light

A.M., anno mundi, in the year of the world; Annus mirabilis, the wonderful year [1666]; Ave Maria, Hail Mary; a.m., ante meridiem, before noon

an., anno, in the year; ante, before

angl., anglice, in English

ann., annales, annals; anni, years; annona, yearly produce

ap., apud, according to

A.P.C.N., anno post Christum natum, in the year after the birth of Christ

A.P.R.C., anno post Romam conditam, in the year after the building of Rome [753 B.C.]

A.R.R., anno regni regis or reginæ, in the year of the king's or queens' reign

A.R.S.S., Antiquariorum Regiæ Societatis Socius, Fellow of the Royal Society of Antiquaries

A.S., anno salutis, in the year of salvation

a t., or a tem., a tempo, in time

Au., aurum, gold

a.u., anno urbis, in the year of the city [Rome]

A.U.C., anno urbis conditæ, in [the year from] the building of the city [Rome], 753 B.C.

a.v., annos vixit, he, or she, lived [so many] years

B.A., baccalaureus artium, bachelor of arts

bals., balsamum, balsam

bibl., bibliotheca, library

B.M., beatæ memoriæ, of blessed memory; b.m., bene merenti, to the well deserving

b.p., bonum publicum, the public good

B.Q., bene quiescat, may he, or she, repose well

B.Sc., baccalaureus scientiæ, bachelor of science

B.V., Beata Virgo, the Blessed Virgin; b.v., bene vale, farewell

C., centum, a hundred; condemno, I condemn

c., circa, about

cap., capiat, let him, or her, take; caput, head; capitulum, section, head

c.a.v., curia advisare vult, the court desires to consider; curia advisari vult, the court desires to be advised

c.d., cum dividendo, with dividend

cent., centum, a hundred

cet. par., ceteris paribus, other things being equal

cf., confer, compare

circ., circa, circiter, circum, about

C.M., chirurgiæ magister, master of surgery; c.m., causa mortis, by reason of death

coch., cochlear, a spoon, spoonful

coch. amp., cochlear amplum, a tablespoonful

coch. mag., cochlear magnum, a large spoonful

coch. med., cochlear medium, a dessert spoonful

coch. parv., cochlear parvum, a teaspoonful

con., contra, against; conjunx, wife

cont. bon. mor., contra bonos mores, contrary to good manners

C.P.S., custos privati sigilli, keeper of the privy seal

C.R., civis Romanus, a Roman citizen; custos rotulorum, keeper of the rolls

C.S., custos sigilli, keeper of the seal

Cs., communis, common

C.Ss.R., Congregatio Sanctissimi Redemptoris, Redemptorist Fathers

Cu., cuprum, copper

cuj., cujus, of which

cwt., c. for centum, wt. for weight, hundredweight

D., Deus, God; Dominus, Lord; d., decretum, a decree; denarius, a penny; da, give

D.D., divinitatis doctor, doctor of divinity; D.d., Deo dedit, gave to God

D.D.D., dat, dicat, dedicat, he gives he devotes, he dedicates; dono dedit, dedicavit, he gave and dedicated as a gift

de d. in d., de die in diem., from day to day

del., delineavit, he, or she, drew it

des., designatus, indicated, described

D.F., defensor fidei, defender of the faith

D.G., Dei gratia, by the grace of God; Deo gratias, thanks to God

D.N., Dominus noster, our Lord

D.N.P.P., Dominus Noster Papa Pontifex, our Lord the Pope

D.O.M., Deo optimo maximo, to God, the best, the greatest

D.P., Domus Procerum, the House of Lords

dram. pers., dramatis personæ, the persons of the drama

D.S., de suo, from his own

D.Sc., doctor scientiæ, doctor of science

d.s.p., decessit sine prole, died without issue

D.S.P.P., de sua pecunia posuit, laid out from his own money

D.T.D., detur talis dosis, give of such dose

D.V., Deo volente, God willing

d.v.p., decessit vita patris, died during his, or her, father's lifetime

dwt., d. for denarius, wt. for weight, pennyweight

e.g., exempli gratia, for example

ejusd. gen., ejusdem generis, of the same kind

E.M., Equitum Magister, Master of the Horse

E.R., Eduardus Rex, King Edward

E.R. et I., Eduardus Rex et Imperator, Edward King and Emperor

et al., et alibi, and elsewhere; et alii, or aliæ, and others

etc., et ceteri or cetera, and others, and so forth

et seq., et sequentes, and those that follow

et ux., et uxor, and wife

exc., excudit, he, or she, engraved it

ex div., ex dividend, without next dividend

F., filius, son, f, forte, strong

f., fiat, let it be made

fac., factum similis, facsimile; an exact copy

fasc., fasciculus, a bundle

f.c., fidei commissum, bequeathed in trust

F.D., fidei defensor or defensatrix, defender of the faith

Fe., ferrum, iron

fec., fecit, he, or she, made it or did it

ff. fecerunt, they made it or did it

fict., fictilis, made of clay

fi. fa., fieri facias, a writ

fl., flores, flowers; floruit, flourished; fluidus, fluid

f.l., falsa lectio, a false reading

flòr., floruit, flourished

F.R., Forum Romanum, the Roman Forum

f.r., folio recto, right-hand page

F.R.S., Fraternitatis Regiæ Socius, Fellow of the Royal Society

f.v., folio verso, on the back of the leaf

gen., genus, kind; genera, kinds

ger., gerund, a part of the Latin verb expressing the carrying on of the action of the verb

gl., gloria, glory

G.P., gloria Patri, glory be to the Father

G.P.R., genio populi Romani, to the genius of the Roman people

G.R., Georgius Rex, King George

G.R.I., Georgius Rex et Imperator, George King and Emperor

guttat., guttatim, by drops

H., hora, hour

h.a., hoc anno, in this year; hujus anni, this year's

hab. corp., habeas corpus, have the body—a writ

h.e., hic est, this is; hoc est, that is

her., heres, heir

H.I., hic iacet, here lies

H.I.S., hic iacet sepultus, here lies buried

h.m., hoc mense, in this month; hujus mensis, this month's

H.M.P., hoc monumentum posuit, he, or she, erected this monument

h.q., hoc quære, look for this

H.R.I.P., hic requiescat in pace, here rests in peace

H.S., hic sepultus, here is buried; hic situs, here lies; h.s., hoc sensu, in this sense.

H.S.S., Historiæ Societatis Socius, Fellow of the Historical Society

h.t., hoc tempore, at this time; hoc titulo, in or under this title

I., Idus, the Ides; imperator, emperor; imperium, empire; i., id, that; immortalis, immortal

ib. or ibid., ibidem, in the same place

I.C., Iesus Christus, Jesus Christ

I.C.N., in Christi nomine, in Christ's name

I.C.T., Iesu Christo Tutore, Jesus Christ being our protector

Id., idem, the same

i.e., id est, that is

ign., ignotus, unknown

i.h., iacet hic, here lies

I.H.S., Iesus hominum Salvator, Jesus, Saviour of men

Ill., illustrissimus, most distinguished

imp., imperium, empire; imprimatur, sanction: let it be printed

Impx., Imperatrix, empress

I.N.D., in nomine Dei, in the name of God

in f., in fine, at the end

inf., infra, below

inf. dig., infra dignitatem, undignified

infus., infusus, an infusion

I.N.I., in nomine Iesu, in the name of Jesus

init., initio, in the beginning

in lim., in limine, on the threshold, at the outset

in loc., in loco, in its place

in loc. cit., in loco citato, in the place cited

in pr., in principio, in the beginning

I.N.R.I., Iesus Nazarenus Rex Iudæorum, Jesus of Nazareth, King of the Jews

I.N.S.T., In nomine Sanctæ Trinitatis, in the name of the Holy Trinity

in trans., in transitu, on the way

I.P.D., In præsentia Dominorum, in the presence of the Lords [of Session]

i.p.i., in partibus infidelium, in the regions of the unbelievers

i.q., idem quod, the same as

i.q.e.d., id quod erat demonstrandum, what was to be proved

I.S.M., Iesus Salvator mundi, Jesus Saviour of the world

J., judex, judge

J.C., juris consultus, jurisconsult, justice-clerk

J.C.D., juris civilis doctor, doctor of civil law

J.D., jurum doctor, doctor of laws

J.R., Jacobus Rex, King James

J.U.D., juris utriusque doctor, doctor of both civil and canon law

L., liber, a book; locus, a place

£, libra, pound; placed before figures, thus £10; if l., to be placed after, as 40l.

L.A.M., liberalium artium magister, master of the liberal arts

L.B., baccalaureus litterarum, bachelor of letters; lectori benevolo, to the kind reader

lb., libra, pound; singular and plural

l.d., littera dominicalis, dominical letter

leg., legit, he, or she, reads; legunt, they read; legendum, to be read

L.H.D., litterarum humaniorum doctor, approximately doctor of the more humane letters

Lit. Hum., litteræ humaniores, classics

Litt.D., litterarum doctor, doctor of letters

ll., see loc. laud.

ll., leges, laws

LL.B., legum baccalaureus, bachelor of laws

LL.D., legum doctor, doctor of laws

LL.M., legum magister, master of laws

loc. cit., loco citato, in the place cited

loc. laud., loco laudato, in the place cited with approval

loq., loquitur, he, or she, speaks

L.S., locus sigilli, the place of the seal

l.s.c., loco supra citato, in the place above cited

£ s. d., libræ, solidi, denarii, pounds, shillings, pence

M., magister, master; manipulus, handful; medicinæ, of medicine; m., meridies, noon

M.A., magister artium, master of arts

M.B., medicinæ baccalaureus, bachelor of medicine

M.Ch., magister chirurgiæ, master of surgery

M.D., medicinæ doctor, doctor of medicine

m.d., manu dextra, with the right hand

mem., memento, remember, a souvenir

m.m., mutatis mutandis, with the necessary changes

m.n., mutato nomine, the name being changed

M.P., mille passus, 1,000 paces, the Roman mile

MS., manuscriptum, manuscript; pl. MSS., manuscripta

M.S., memoriæ sacrum, sacred to the memory

Mus.B., musicæ baccalaureus, bachelor of music

Mus.D., musicæ doctor, doctor of music

Mus.M., musicæ magister, master of music

N., Nepos, grandson; nomen, name; nomina, names; noster, our; n., natus, born; nocte, at night

N.B., nota bene, mark well

n.e.i., non est inventus, he has not been found

nem. con., nemine contradicente, unanimously

nem. dis., nemine dissentiente, no one dissenting

ni. pri., nisi prius, unless before

nob., nobis, for, or on, our part

nol. pros., nolle prosequi, will not prosecute

non cul., non culpabilis, not guilty

n.l., non licet, it is not permitted; non liquet, it is not clear; non longe, not far

non obs., non obstante, notwithstanding

non pros., non prosequitur, he does not prosecute

non seq., non sequitur, it does not follow logically

N.S.I.C., Noster Salvator Iesus Christus, our Saviour Jesus Christ

O., octarius, a pint

ob., obiit, he, or she, died; obiter, incidentally

ob.s.p., obiit sine prole, died without issue

o.c., opere citato, in the work cited

omn.hor., omni hora, every hour

O.P., ordinis prædicatorum, of the order of preachers

op., opus, work; opera, works

op. cit., opere citato, in the work cited

o.p.n., ora pro nobis, pray for us

P., papa, pope; pater, father; pontifex, bishop; populus, people; p., partim, in part; per, by, for; pius, holy; pondere, by weight; post, after; primus, first; pro, for

p.a., or per ann., per annum, yearly; pro anno, for the year

p.æ., partes æquales, equal parts

pass., passim, everywhere

Pb., plumbum, lead

P.B., Pharmacopœia Britannica, British Pharmacopoeia

percent., per centum, by the hundred

pil., pilula, pill

Ph.B., philosophiæ baccalaureus, bachelor of philosophy

pl., plebis, plebeian

P.M., post mortem, after death

p.m., post meridiem, afternoon

pnxt., pinxit, he, or she, painted it

p.p., or per proc., per procurationem, by procuration

PP.C., patres conscripti, conscript fathers

P.R., populus Romanus, the Roman people

P.R.C., post Romam conditam, after the building of Rome [753 B.C.]

p.r.n., pro re nata, as the occasion arises

pr. pr., præter propter, about, nearly

pro tem., pro tempore, for the time being

prox., proximo, in or of the next [month]

prox. acc., proxime accessit, he, or she, came very near

P.S., postscriptum, postscript; pl., P.SS., postscripta

q., quære, inquire

q.d., quasi, dicat, as if one should say; quasi dictum, as if said; quasi dixisset, as if he had said

q.e., quod est, which is

Q.E.D., quod erat demonstrandum, which was to be demonstrated

Q.E.F., quod erat faciendum, which was to be done

Q.E.I., quod erat inveniendum, which was to be found out

q.l., quantum libet, as much as you please

q.m. quo modo, by what means

g.pl., quantum placet, as much as seems good

q.s., quantum sufficit, sufficient quantity

q.v., quantum vis, as much as you will; quod vide, which see; pl., qq.v.

R., regina, queen; recto, right-hand page; respublica, commonwealth; rex, king

℞., recipe, take

rel., reliquiae, relics

R.I.P., requiescat, or requiescant, in pace, may he, she, or they, rest in peace

R.P.D., rerum politicarum doctor, doctor of political science

rr., rarissime, very rarely

R.S.S., Regiæ Societatis Sodalis, Fellow of the Royal Society

S., sepultus, buried; situs, lies; societas, society; socius or sodalis, fellow; s., semi, half; solidus, shilling

s.a., sine anno, without date; secundum artem, according to art

S.A.S., Societatis Antiquariorum Socius, Fellow of the Society of Antiquaries

sc., scilicet, namely; sculpsit, he, or she, carved or engraved it

S.C., senatus consultum, a decree of the senate

scan. mag., scandalum magnatum, defamation of high personages

Sc.B., scientiæ baccalaureus, bachelor of science

Sc.D., scientiæ doctor, doctor of science

schol., scholium, a note

S.D., salutem dicit, sends greetings

s.d., sine die, indefinitely

sec., secundum, according to

sec. art., secundum artem, according to art

sec. leg., secundum legem, according to law

sec. nat., secundum naturam, according to nature, or naturally

sec. reg., secundum regulam, according to rule

seq., sequens, sequentes, sequentia, the following

S.H.S., Societatis Historiæ Socius, Fellow of the Historical Society

s.h.v., sub hac voce or sub hoc verbo, under this word

s.l.a.n., sine loco, anno, vel nomine, without place, date, or name

s.l.p., sine legitima prole, without lawful issue

S.M.E., Sancta Mater Ecclesia, Holy Mother Church

S.M.M., Sancta Mater Maria, Holy Mother Mary

s.m.p., sine mascula prole, without male issue

s.n., sine nomine, without name

s.p., sine prole, without issue

S.P.A.S., Societatis Philosophiæ Americanæ Socius, Fellow of the American Philosophical Society

S.P.Q.R., Senatus Populusque Romanus the Senate and Roman people

s.p.s., sine prole superstite, without surviving issue

S.R.I., Sacrum Romanum Imperium, the Holy Roman Empire

S.R.S., Societatis Regiæ Socius or Sodalis, Fellow of the Royal Society

ss., scilicet, namely, in law .

S.S.C., Societas Sanctæ Crucis, Society of the Holy Cross

SS.D., sanctissimus dominus, most holy lord, i.e., the Pope

stat., statim, immediately

S.T.B., sacræ theologiæ baccalaureus, bachelor of theology

S.T.D., sacræ theologiæ doctor, doctor of theology

S.T.P., sacræ theologiæ professor, professor of sacred theology

sub, subaudi, understand, supply

sup., supra, above

sus. per coll., suspensio per collum, hanging by the neck

S.V., Sancta Virgo, Holy Virgin; Sanctitas Vestra, your holiness; s.v., sub voce or sub verbo, under a specified word

t. or temp., tempore, in the time of

tal. qual., talis qualis, just as they come; average quality

text. rec., textus receptus, the received text

U.J.D., utriusque juris doctor, doctor of both civil and canon law

ult., ultimo, last month; may be abbreviated in writing but should be spelled out in printing

ung., unguentum, ointment

u.s., ubi supra, in the place above mentioned °

ut dict., ut dictum, as directed

ut sup., ut supra, as above

ux., uxor, wife

v., versus, against; vide, see; voce, voice

v.a., vixit . . . annos, lived [so many] years

var.lect., varia lectio, variant reading

V.D.M., Verbi Dei minister, preacher of the Word of God

verb.sap., verbum [satis] sapienti, a word to the wise suffices

v.g., verbi gratia, for example

viz, videlicet, namely

v.l., varia lectio, a variant reading

V.R.P., vestra reverendissima paternitas, your most reverend paternity

v.s., vide supra, see above

V.T., Vetus testamentum, Old Testament

vv. ll., variæ lectiones, variant readings

LATIN INCUNABULA

Special typographical characters and abbreviations most commonly used in 15th and 16th century books:

ꝑ 9 9 ꝛ ꞇc̓ p p̄ ꝑ ꝓ q̇ q ꝙ ꝙ̃ ꝗ ꝛ ᶻ ſ ſm ß ꝺ ꝺ̃ t̃ ẏ ȝ ꜩ ꜩ ꞃ ꝙ

’ (apostrophe) after any letter extending above the line stands for omitted letter or letters.

’ (apostrophe) over letters not extending above the line for *i* or *r* with or without other letters.

⁓ over letters for *a* with or without other letters.

° over letters for *o* with or without other letters.

‒ ⁓ ⌐ ⁓ over one or more letters in a word are used for omissions in general (*e. g.* dñi ñri = *domini nostri*; c̄oē ſc̄oꝛ = *commune sanctorum;* ōro = *oratio;* īpēſ = *impenſis*)

ꝑ = *com, con, cum, cun* (*e. g.* ꝑpelli = *compelli;* ꝑtꝛa = *contra;* quiꝛqꝫ = *quicunque*) at end = *us* (*e. g.* quibꝫ = *quibus*)

⁹ above the line = *us* (*e. g.* fili⁹ = *filius*)

9 on the line at beginning of a word = *con* (*e. g.* 9iugio = *conjugio*)

   ꝛ = *et*

   ꞇc = *etcetera*

   p = *per, par, por*

   p̄ = *pre*

ꝑ, ꝓ = *pro*

   q̇ = *qui* (*e. g.* q̇ſqꝫ = *quiſque*)

   q = *qui, quae* (*e. g.* qſqꝫ = *quiſque*)

   ꝙ = *que, quod*

ꝙ̃, q̃ꝫ = *quam, quan* (*e. g.* q̃ꝫtus = *quantus*)

   qꝫ = *que*

   ꝛ = *r*

   ᶻ = *rum* (*e. g.* ſu⁹ ſuoꝛ d’i = *servus servorum dei*)

   ſ = *sis,* also = *sz* or *ss,* also = *ser* (*e. g.* īpēſ = *impenſis;* ſmo = *sermo*)

  ſm = *secundum*

   ß = *sed*

   ꝺ = *is*

   ꝺ̃ = *de, dis, dum, der*

   t̃ = *tra*

   ẏ = *vir, ver*

   ȝ at end of word = *m,* also *us,* also *et* (*e. g.* īpreſſuȝ = *impressum;* tpibȝ = *temporibus;* decederȝ = *decederet;* videlȝ = *videlicet*)

ꜩ, ꜩ = *et*

   ꞃ = *rum, rubr* (*e. g.* ꞃica = *rubrica;* humoꞃ = *humorum*)

   ꝙ = *quum*

Numerals:

1	2	3	4	5	6	7		8	9	0	CIↃ = M
1	2	3	ꝺ	ꜩ	6	7	ᴧ	8	9	0	IↃ = D

LATVIAN

A	a	*a* in father	L	l	*l*
Ā	ā	*a* in fate	Ļ	ļ	*ly* in lyonnaise
B	b	*b*	M	m	*m*
C	c	*ts*	N	n	*n*
Č	č	*ch* in church	Ņ	ņ	*ny* in canyon
D	d	*d*	O	o	*ua,* in foreign words *o*
DZ	dz	*dz* in adze			in lotto
DŽ	dž	*j*	P	p	*p*
E	e	*e*	R	r	*r*, rolled
Ē	ē	*e, ä*	Ŗ	ŗ	*ry* in country
F	f	*f*	S	s	*s*, soft; final *s* is sharp,
G	g	*g*, hard			as *ss*
Ģ	ģ	*gy* with consonantal *y*	Š	š	*sh* in shut
H	h	*h,* only in foreign words	T	t	*t*
I	i	*i* in pin	U	u	*u* in shut
Ī	ī	*i* in mine	Ū	ū	*oo* in fool
IE	ie	*ia* in Philadelphia	V	v	*v;* final *v* has *u* sound
J	j	*y*, consonantal	Z	z	*z*
K	k	*k*	Ž	ž	*j* in French journal
Ķ	ķ	*ky*			

The following variations are also found in old Latvian prints:
G g (ǵ), K k (ķ), Ł ł (ļ), N n (ņ), R r (ŗ), and S ſ (s and š).

In 1921 the old German text was superseded by the Latin in Latvia.
The language is purely phonetic and makes use of the diacriticals *č*, *š*, and *ž* to indicate the *tch*, *sch*, and *tsch* sounds, respectively.

Accents

The accents are as follows: ^ indicates a long vowel; ‾ indicates that the syllable is to be pronounced clearly and not slurred, as *devās;* the apostrophe indicates the elision of a vowel. The new orthography customarily uses but one sign of prolongation, the ‾.

The stress is always on the first syllable, but the others are also pronounced distinctly, whether long or short; sometimes the unaccented long syllable has a ^ or ˇ, and thus receives a secondary accent.

In a few cases the second syllable has the accent, as *labrīt* (good morning).

In words having the negative *ne*, the accent is on the first syllable of the stem word: *nekā* (nothing), *nekūr* (nowhere).

Syllabication

Letters forming but a single sound must not be separated, nor will the *h* be separated from the preceding vowel.

Divide on a vowel followed by a consonant.

A single consonant goes with the vowel, two may be divided, but the consonant combinations *dz* and *dž*, must not be divided.

Cardinal numbers

viens, viena, *f.*	one	desmit (desmits)	ten
dvas, *f.*	two	vienpadsmit	eleven
trīs	three	divpadsmit	twelve
četri, četras, *f.*	four	trīspadsmit	thirteen
pieci, -as	five	divdesmit (dividesmit)	twenty
seši, -as	six	divdesmit viens	twenty-one
septini, -as	seven	simt(s)	hundred
astoni, -as	eight	tūkstošs (tūkstots)	thousand
devini, -as	nine		

Ordinal numbers

pirmais, pirmā, *f.*	first	desmitais, desmitā	tenth
otrais (otrs), otrā	second	vienpadsmitais, -tā	eleventh
trešais, trešā	third	divpadsmitais, -tā	twelfth
ceturtais, ceturtā	fourth	trīspadsmitais, -tā	thirteenth
piektais, piektā	fifth	divdesmitais, -tā	twentieth
sestais, sestā	sixth	divdesmit pirmais or	twenty-first
septītais, septītā	seventh	pirmā	
astotais, astotā	eighth	simtais, simtā	hundredth
devītais, devītā	ninth	tūkstošais, -šā	thousandth

Months

jānvaris, -ra, *m.*	January	julijs, -ija, *m.*	July
februaris, -ra, *m.*	February	augusts	August
màrts, -a, *m.*	March	septembris, -ra, *m.*	September
aprilis, -ļa, *m.*	April	oktobris, -ra, *m.*	October
maĩjs, -a, *m.*	May	novembris, -ra, *m.*	November
junijs, -ija, *m.*	June	decembris, -ra, *f.*	December

Days

svètìena, -as, *f.*	Sunday	ceturdiena, -as, *f.*	Thursday
pìrmdìena, -as, *f.*	Monday	pìektdìena, -as, *f.*	Friday
ùotrdìena, -as, *f.*	Tuesday	sestdìena, -as, *f.*	Saturday
vidus	Wednesday		

Seasons

pavasaris, ra, *m.*	spring	rudens	autumn
vasar	summer	zìema, -as, *f.*	winter

Time

stunda, -as, *f.*	hour	mēnesis, -ša, *m.*	month
diena, -as, *f.*	day	gads, -a, *m.*	year
nedeļa, -as, *f.*	week		

LITHUANIAN

A	a	*a* in father	J	j	*y,* almost
Ą[1]	ą	*a,* long	K	k	*k*
B	b	*b* in boy	L	l	*l,* before *e, i,* and *y*
C	c	*ts*	Ł[2]	ł	Almost open *o*
Č CZ č cz[1]		*tsch*	M	m	*m*
CH	ch	*k,* only in foreign words	N	n	*n*
			O	o	*o*
D	d	*d*	P	p	*p* in pay
E	e	Open *e,* almost *a*	R	r	*r,* stressed
Ę[1]	ę	*e,* long, nasal	S	s	*s*
Ė	ė	Closed long *e*	Š SZ	š sz[2]	*sh,* almost
Ė[2]	ë	*ie*	T	t	*t*
F	f	*f,* only in foreign words	U	u	*oo*
			Ų[1]	ų	*oo*
G	g	*g,* in gay	Ū	ū	*ōō*
H	h	*h,* only in foreign words	Ů[2]	ů	*uò*
			V W	v w[2]	*w* in way
I	i	*e*	Z	z	*z* in zeal
Į[1]	į	*i,* long, nasal	Ž, Ż	ž, ż[2]	*sh* voiced
Y	y	*ea* in pease			

[1] Only in etymological works.
[2] Used mainly in German and Polish works.

Syllabication

Syllabication is the same as in the German and punctuation is the same as in English.

Diphthongs

ai	*i* in fire	oi	*oy* in boy
au	*ow* in now	ui	Like the vowels combined in *do we*
ei	*ei* in they	uo	*wa* in war

There is no article.

There are two genders: masculine and feminine. Substantives of masculine in the nominative singular end in *us, ys, as,* or *is,* those of the feminine in *a* or *e*. In speaking of persons, regardless of sex, there is also a common gender ending in *a*. A good rule is always to remember the gender of the substantive.

There are three numbers: Singular, dual, and plural, and seven cases: Nominative, genitive, dative, accusative, instrumental, and locative.

Adjectives

The adjectives have but two genders: Masculine and feminine. The nominative singular of masculine adjectives end in *as, ias, is,* or *us,* and the definitive form in *asis, ysis,* or *usis;* the same case in the feminine gender end in *a, ia, e,* or *i,* and the definitive form in *oji* or *ioji*.

Add *esnis* and *esne* for the comparative, and *iausias* or *iausis* and *iausia* or *iausi* for the superlative.

Pronouns

Aš	I	ši'tas (*m*) ši'ta (*f*)	this	Kas	who / what
Męs	we	Tas (*m*) Ta (*f*)	that	Ta'vo	thine
Tu	thou			Tokis' (*m*) Tokia' (*f*)	such
Jūs	you	Mūsų	ours		
Nie'kas	nobody	Ju	theirs	Kiekvie'nas (*m*) Kiekvie'na (*f*)	every-one
Jo	his	Kuri's (*m*) Kuri' (*f*)	which	Jūsų	yours
Jis	he				
Ji	she				
Jie / Jos	they (*f*)				
Ma no	mine				
Jos	hers				

Verbs

The forms of the third person singular and plural are alike in all verbs. The conjugation of only the commonest tenses and forms of the verbs *su'kti*, to turn; *myle'ti*, to love; *maty'ti*, to see, and *žino'ti*, to know, are given in the following table:

Present				
Aš	suku'	myliu'	matau'	žinau'
Tu	suki'	myli'	matai'	žinai'
Jis	su'ka	my'li	ma'tova	ži'no
Mu'du	su'kava	my'liva	ma'to	ži'nova
Ju'du	su'kate	my'lite	ma'tote	ži'note
Męs	su'kame	my'lime	ma'tome	ži'nome
Jūs	su'kate	my'lite	ma'tote	ži'note
Imperative				
Tu	suk	mylē'k	maty'k	žino'k
Mu'du	su'kiva	mylē'kiva	maty'kiva	žino'kiva
Ju'du	su'kite	mylē'kite	maty'kite	žíno'kite
Męs	su'kime	mylē'kime	maty'kime	žino'kime
Jūs	su'kite	mylēkite	maty'kite	žino'kite

Cardinal numbers

vienas	one	devyni	nine
dvu	two	dešimt	ten
trys	three	vienuolika	eleven
keturi	four	dvylika	twelve
penki	five	trylika	thirteen
šeši	six	dvidešimt	twenty
septyni	seven	šimtas	hundred
aštuoni	eight	tukstantis	thousand

Ordinal numbers

pirmas	first	devintas	ninth
antras	second	dešimtas	tenth
trečias	third	vienuoliktas	eleventh
ketvirtas	fourth	dvyliktas	twelfth
penktas	fifth	tryliktas	thirteenth
šeštas	sixth	dvidešimtas	twentieth
septintas	seventh	šimtinis, šimtoji, *f.*	hundredth
aštuntas	eighth	tukstantinis	thousandth

Months

sausis	January	liepos mēnuo	July
vasaris	February	rugpiutis	August
kovas	March	rugsējas	September
balandis, karvelis	April	spalinis, spalius	October
gegužis	May	lapkritys	November
sējos mēnuo, birželis	June	gruodis	December

Days

nedēlia, nedēldienis, -io, *m.*	Sunday	sereda	Wednesday
		ketvergas	Thursday
panedēlis	Monday	pētničia	Friday
utarninkas	Tuesday	subata	Saturday

Seasons

pavasaris, -io, *m.*	spring	ruduo	autumn
vasara	summer	žiema	winter

Time

valanda	hour	mēnesis, mēnuo	month
diena	day	metai	year
sanvaitē, nedēlia	week		

MALAY

Name	Iso-lated	Final	Me-dian	Ini-tial	Translit-eration	Name	Iso-lated	Final	Me-dian	Ini-tial	Translit-eration
Alif	ا	ا			'	Zā [1]	ظ	ظ	ظ	ظ	dl
Bē	ب	ب	ﺒ	ﺑ	b	Ain [1]	ع	ع	ﻌ	ﻋ	'
Tē	ت	ت	ﺘ	ﺗ	t	Ghain [1]	غ	غ	ﻐ	ﻏ	gh
Sē [1]	ث	ث	ﺜ	ﺛ	th	Nga	غ	غ	ﻐ	ﻏ	ng, n
Jīm	ج	ج	ﺠ	ﺟ	j	Fē [1]	ف	ف	ﻔ	ﻓ	f
Chīm	ج	ج	ﺠ	ﺟ	ch	Pa	ف	ف	ﻔ	ﻓ	p
Ḥē [1]	ح	ح	ﺤ	ﺣ	h	Qāf, Kāf	ق	ق	ﻘ	ﻗ	k, q
Khē [1]	خ	خ	ﺨ	ﺧ	k	Kēf	ک	ک	ک	ک	k
Dāl	د	د			d	Ga	گ	گ	گ	گ	g [2]
Ẓāl [1]	ذ	ذ			dż	Lām	ل	ل	ﻠ	ﻟ	l
Rē	ر	ر			r	Mīm	م	م	ﻤ	ﻣ	m
Zē [1]	ز	ز			z	Nūn	ن	ن	ﻨ	ﻧ	n
Sīn	س	س	ﺴ	ﺳ	s	Wāw	و	و			u, w
Shīn [1]	ش	ش	ﺸ	ﺷ	sh	Hē	ه	ﻪ	ﻬ	ﻫ	h
Sād [1]	ص	ص	ﺼ	ﺻ	s	Yē	ى	ى	ﻴ	ﻳ	y
Dād [1]	ض	ض	ﻀ	ﺿ	dl	Nja	ڽ	ڽ	ﯿ	ﯾ	ny, ñ
Tā [1]	ط	ط	ﻄ	ﻃ	t						

[1] Characters alien to the Malay and found only in foreign, mainly Arabic, words.
[2] Often n.

A distinct connection is apparent between most of the languages which prevail from Madagascar to Easter Island, in the Pacific, and from Formosa, on the China coast, to New Zealand, the most wide-spread in the history of rude languages. One of the most important of these languages is the Malay, which, however, has been strongly impregnated by alien languages, most important of which is the Arabic, the exact extent of which is rather difficult to determine.

There are also some 50 or 60 Persian words, mainly nouns and names of objects.

The few Portuguese words found in the language represent objects and ideas new to the Malays before their contact with Europeans.

Remarks

Where two vowels come together both must be sounded, but the first coalesces with the second: *au*, nearly *ow* in cow.

The consonants have the English sound, with the exception of the *r*, which is sounded more clearly and with a more decided roll than in English.

The final *k* is not sounded, and thus the word ends with an *n* sound.

An apostrophe at the end of a syllable indicates an abrupt shortening of sound; between two vowels it indicates that they are pronounced separately.

Final *h* shortens the syllable.

The *jazm* (ˇ) indicates that the vowel over which it is placed closes the syllable.

Cardinal numbers

satu or s-	one	ĕnam	six
dua	two	tujoh	seven
tiga	three	dĕlapan	eight
ĕmpat	four	sĕmbilan	nine
lima	five	s-puloh	ten

By adding *bĕlas* to the numerals from 1 to 9 those from 11 to 19 are formed: *s-bĕlas*, 11; *dua-bĕlas*, 12, etc.

Multiples of 10 are formed by the addition of *puloh: dua-puloh*, 20; *tiga-puloh*, 30, etc.

Units are placed after the tens to form the intermediate numbers above 20: *dua-puloh-satu*, 21; *tiga-puloh-satu*, 31, etc.

sa-ratus	hundred	sa-ribu	thousand

Ordinal numbers

The ordinals are formed by adding to the cardinals the word *yang*, which corresponds to the English definite article, and prefixing *ke* to the cardinal: *yang kĕdua*, second, etc.; it should be noted, however, that *yang pertama*, first, is an exception to this rule.

Year

The Mohammedan year is lunar, consisting of approximately 354 days and 9 hours. The Arabic names for the months are used in the Malay.

Muharram [1]	first month	Rajab	seventh month
Safar	second month	Sh'aban	eighth month
Rabi'u 'l-awwal	third month	Ramadlan	ninth month
Rabi'u 'l-akhir	fourth month	Shawwal	tenth month
Jumadi 'l-awwal	fifth month	Dhu 'l-k'adah	eleventh month
Jumadi 'l-akhir	sixth month	Dhu 'l-hijjah	twelfth month

Week

Ahad	first day	Sunday
Ithnain, Isnein, Snin	second day	Monday
Thalatha, Salasa	third day	Tuesday
Arba, Rabu	fourth day	Wednesday
Khamis	fifth day	Thursday
Jum'ah, Jum'at	the congregation [2]	Friday
Sabatu	sabbath	Saturday

The colloquial names for the days of the week are Hari minggo, Hari satu, Hari dua, Hari tiga, Hari ampat, Hari lima, and Hari anam.

Seasons

rebia	spring	ákir moosim	autumn
kâmarau, moo-sim pauras	summer	moosim dingin	winter

Time

jam	hour	bulan	month
hari	day	täun, tahun	year
juma'at, minggu	week		

---

[1] According to the best calculation this month approximately corresponds to the English July.
[2] Celebrated instead of Sunday.

MANCHU

Initial	Median	Final	Isolated	Transliteration	Initial	Median	Final	Isolated	Transliteration
ſ	◂	ᰋ	ᰋ	a	ᰋ	ᰋ	ᰋ		l
ᰋ	◂◂	ᰋ	ſ	e	ᰋ	ᰋ	ᰋ		m
ᰋ	ᰋ	ᰋ	ᰋ	i	u	u			cl
ᰋ	ᰋ	ᰋ	ᰋ	ô	ᰋ	ᰋ			j
ᰋ.	ᰋ.	ᰋ.	ᰋ.	u	ᰋ	ᰋ			y
ᰋ	ᰋ	ᰋ	ᰋ	ó	ᰋ	ᰋ	ᰋ		(k
ᰋ	◂◂¹ ◂²	ᰋ		n	ᰋ·	ᰋ·		(⁶)	{ g
ᰋ	ᰋ¹ ᰋ²	ᰋ		(k	ᰋ	ᰋ			(kh
ᰋ	ᰋ·		(³)	{ g	ᰋ	ᰋ	ᰋ		r
ᰋ	ᰋ·			(kh	ᰋ	ᰋ		(⁷)	f
ᰋ	ᰋ	ᰋ		b	ᰋ	ᰋ			w⁸
ᰋ	ᰋ			p	ᰋ	ᰋ			ts
ᰋ	ᰋ	ᰋ		s	ᰋ	ᰋ			ths
ᰋ	ᰋ ᰋ	ᰋ		sh	ᰋ				sh
ᰋ	ᰋ	ᰋ	(⁴)	{ t / d	ᰋ	ᰋ			ss
ᰋ	ᰋ·				ᰋ	ᰋ			chᶜ
ᰋ	ᰋ		(⁵)	{ t / d	ᰋ				jᶜ
ᰋ	ᰋ·								

Ligatures   **Diphthongs**

⟋ } b	⟋ ba	⟋ } k	⟋ } g	⟋ } h
⟋ } p	⟋ be			
	⟋ bi	⟋ ke	⟋ ge	⟋ he
	⟋ bo	⟋ ki	⟋ gi	⟋ hi
	⟋ bu	⟋ ku	⟋ gu	⟋ hu
⟋ ⟋ ⟋ an		⟋ ⟋ ng		

ai

oi

Manchu belongs to the Tungus group of languages and was doubtless in use by the Tungus people, in what is now called Manchuko, already in the 3d century B.C.   It is an adaptation of the Mongolian and the text is arranged in columns, reading from the top down, the columns being arranged from left to right.

Books were already printed in Manchu in 1647, and soon the Chinese and Mongolian classics were translated and published, which fact accounts for the present-day interest in the language on the part of scholars, since these accurate translations have greatly facilitated the interpretation of those classics.

The vocalic harmony is not very strictly observed in the Manchu, and there are no alternative hard and soft forms in the case of grammatical suffixes (postpositions), which are as follows:

Accusative,	be
Genitive instrumental,	i, ni
Dative locative	de
Ablative,	chi

The verb does not distinguish either person or number, and the tenses are only imperfectly expressed, general notions being expressed by adverbial and participial forms.

There is no relative pronoun and participles are employed to express relative prepositions.

Affixes are added to the verbal root to express some extended meaning; thus *bu* added to *ara* (to write), becomes *arabu* (to cause to write), and *ja* added to *wa* (to kill), becomes *waja* (to kill oneself).

The vowel *a* is changed to *e* to distinguish gender, or between strong and weak; thus *ama* (father), becomes *eme* (mother); even foreign words are treated in this manner as we find the Turkish *arsalan* (lion), changed to *erselen* for the female of the species, and the Sanscrit *garudai* (male phoenix) becomes *gerudei* (female phoenix).   We also have *ganggan* (strong), changed to *genggen* (weak), and *wasima* (descend) becomes *wesime* (climb), etc.

MONGOLIAN

Initial	Median	Final	Transliter- ation	Initial	Median	Final	Transliter- ation
			a				k
			e				g
			i				m
			o				l
			u				r
			ö				t
			ü				d
			n				y
			b				s, ds
			kh				ts
			gh				s
							sh
							w

1 Used only in first syllable.   4 Used before vowels.
2 Used after a soft vowel.   5 Used before consonants.
3 Used after a hard vowel.   6 Used only in foreign words.

The Mongolian, dating back to the 14th century, belongs to the Altaic language group. The three principal dialects are the Khalkha, Kalmuk, and Buriatic, which differ only slightly. The alphabet is very imperfect, and, as a result, many words of widely different meaning are written alike.

The language is written vertically downwards, the columns running from left to right.

Future participles or infinitives are -qu, kü.

Various adjunctive forms and the gerund ending in -jü, -ged, -tele, -rün, etc., are used.

Negation is expressed by the adverbs ülü, ese, ügei, and the imperative buu, while uu expresses the interrogation.

There are no prepositions, and sentences are joined by certain adjunctive and participial forms of the verb.

Following are the forms of the so-called "*oi* diphthongs" as used in the various positions:

Initial	Median	Final	Transliteration
᠊ᡠ	᠊ᡠ	᠊ᠣ	*ai*
᠊ᠣ	᠊ᠣ	᠊ᠣ	*oi*

Ligatures

Final	Median		
᠊ᠪ *ba, be*	᠊ᡦ *bi*	᠊ᠪ *bo, bu*	
᠊ᠺ *ke, ge*	᠊ᡴ *ki, gi*	᠊ᠺ { *kö, kü* *gö, gü*	
᠊ᠩ *ng*			

In the literary language the word order is almost the reverse of the English. The nouns have six oblique cases:

Genitive	-*yin, ü* (*n*)
Dative locative	-*dür, -e*
Accusative	-(*y*) *i*
Ablative	-*eče*
Instrumentative	-*ber, -iyer*
Cooperative	-*lüge*

With certain modifications this is also true of the pronouns:

bi	I	*ta*	ye
či	thou	*ene*	this
bide	we	*tere*	that

The nominative case of a noun is usually indicated by *inu, anu,* or *ber,* and the plural by -*ner,* -(*ü*)*d, s,* etc.

Adjectives do not deflect for comparison and are often used substantively.

Person and number are not expressed by verbs, but these are conjugated for tense and mood:

Indicative present and future	-*mü*(*i*), etc.
Indicative past	-*be*(*i*), etc.
Optative	-*sü*(*gei*), etc.
Conditional	-*basu, -besü*
Present participle	-*gči*
Past participle	-*gsen*

NORWEGIAN

A	a	a in father, short or long	P	p	p in pay
B	b	b [1]	Q	q	kv; as a rule kv is substituted for q
C	c	k before a, o, u; s before other vowels [2]	R	r	r
D	d	d, sometimes mute [3]	S	s	s, sharp
E	e	a in care, also e in met	T	t	t
F	f	f	U	u	u in full, also u in true
G	g	g in give; y [4] in yet before soft vowels	V	v	v, also f in some words, often mute after l
H	h	h, mute before j and v	W	w	w or v; usually v is used instead
I	i	i in flit, also ee in flee			
J	j	y in yet	X	x	ks, which is usually substituted for x
K	k	k, before i and y like ch in German ich	Y	y	ü in German über
L	l	l, mute when initial before j	Z	z	s, which is used instead
			Æ	æ	a in care [5]
M	m	m	Ø	ø	ö in German Götter or eu in French peu [6]
N	n	n			
O	o	o in rot, also o in globe	Å	å	aw in law [7]

[1] In older spelling b was often used for the sound p; now p is used.
[2] k and s are now usually substituted for c.
[3] Many mute d's found in older spelling are now omitted; d was also formerly used in many words to express the sound t where t is now used.
[4] In former spelling g was used for k in many words, where k is now used.
[5] The letter e is now often used where æ was formerly used.
[6] Usually written ö and printed ø.
[7] The form aa was formerly used, but å is now preferred.

The Latin alphabet is universally used in Norway, with addition of the letters æ, ø or ö, and å or aa. Æ and ø are not diphthongs but separate letters, likewise å, although it may be written aa, is not a double a but the 29th letter in the alphabet, and usually found in that place in dictionaries. C, q, w, x, and z are used only in foreign words and proper names. Even in words of foreign origin they are preferably avoided by substituting k or s for c, kv for q, v for w, ks for x, and s for z.

The Norwegian language belongs to the Scandinavian group of Teutonic languages, which comprises also Danish, Swedish, Icelandic, rural Norwegian, and the language of the Faeroe Islands. With the languages of Iceland, Greenland, the islands north and west of Scotland, and the Faeroe Islands, it forms the western group of Scandinavian languages, which still have the true diphthongs as diphthongs and have also retained the old voiceless stops.

There are two official languages, "riksmål" and "landsmål". The former was in the past generally known as "Dano-Norwegian", because, under strong Danish influence, its written form was almost identical with the Danish. Development, however, has been and still continues to be in a distinctly nationalistic direction, and there are already wide divergences in grammar, spelling, and vocabulary between the two languages. The "landsmål" is based upon the dialects which have developed from the Old Norse, free from Danish influence; it is taught in the public schools and is used jointly with "riksmål" in the Government service. As a matter of fact, from the two languages there is now evolving a new language which is a combination of the two.

Capitalization

Capital letters are used only at the beginning of a sentence, or after a full stop, after colon and quotation marks, in proper names, and in the personal pronouns De, Dem, Deres, I, Dykk, and Dykkar. Proper names used as adjectives and the names of months and the days of the week are not capitalized.

Syllabication

Where one consonant stands between vowels, divide before the consonant. Of one or more consonants, the last only is carried over, but sk, sp, st, and str are inseparable. Compound words are divided so that the component parts remain intact, regardless of the consonant rule.

Punctuation

English rules for punctuation will apply.

Diphthongs

The sounds are as follows:

ai	*i* in mile	öi	*eui* in feuilleton
æi	*ei* in Marseille	œu	*au* sound almost Cockney pro-
oi	*oy* in boy		nunciation of "house"

In all diphthongs the first element is generally considerably shorter than in the appropriately corresponding English sounds.

Accentuation

The principles of accentuation are subject to numerous arbitrary rules; however, in general, it may be stated that—

(*a*) Stress rests on the radical syllable: *ren'lig* (clean), *uren'lig* (unclean);

(*b*) In words of foreign origin, the stress is on the last syllable: *General'*, *Kollegium'*;

(*c*) The prefixes of Germanic origin, *be, er, for* (German *ver*), are never stressed, but those of native origin are: *begri'be* (to comprehend), but *ved'blive* (to continue);

(*d*) Compound words stress the leading component.

Distinction must be made between accent-stress and the musical accent, the former, as a rule, being on the first syllable, with sometimes a secondary stress, especially in compound words, laid in most cases on the first syllable of the second part of the compound.

The musical, of which there are two kinds, the monosyllabic (´) and the dissyllabic (`), differs from the stress accent. The first is used in monosyllabic and the latter in dissyllabic or polysyllabic words. Many pairs of otherwise consonous words are distinguished only by the difference in musical accent: *am'en*, amen; *am`men*, the wet nurse.

Articles

The following table illustrates the forms and uses of the articles:

	Common gender		Neuter gender	
	Singular	Plural	Singular	Plural
Indefinite	en	—	et	—
Definite:				
Substantive [1]	-en (-n)	-ene (-ne)	-et (-t)	-ene (-ne)
Adjective [2]	den	de	det	de

[1] Employed as suffix to noun when not modified by adjective, sometimes called postpositive.
[2] Precedes the adjective modifying a noun, called also prepositive.

The definite article is required, contrary to English usage, by abstract nouns (*livet er langt*, life is long) and in places where the English uses the possessive if possessiveness is self-understood (*gutten satte hatten på hovedet*, the boy placed *his* hat upon *his* head).

Gender

There are two genders, common and neuter, and, while no hard and fast rules for gender exist, the following will be helpful:

The former includes words denoting most living beings; trees, plants, and stones; seasons, months, days, and other divisions of time; names of winds and weather; rivers and lakes; and names of sciences. Exceptions are *kvæget*, the cattle; *et lam*, a lamb; and *et blad*, a leaf; also *regn*, rain, and *hagl*, hail, which may be either gender.

The neuter gender includes most collective nouns and names of substances; countries and cities; names of mountains, and nouns having the same form as the stems of verbs. Exceptions: Names of letters of the alphabet and names of languages when combined with the substantive article.

Compound words usually have the gender of the last component part.

Some words have a different meaning according to the gender used, and in other cases originally different words have the same sound but differ in gender: *en stift*, a tack; *et stift*, a diocese.

The natural genders of animals are usually denoted by *han*, he, and *hun*, she.

Adjectives

Adjectives agree with their nouns in gender and number, whether attributive or predicative.

When preceded by a definite article, they always end in *e*, both in the singular and the plural.

When preceded by the indefinite article, or used predicatively, they end in *t* in the neuter singular, and in *e* for both genders in the plural.

Adjectives are compared by adding *ere* (or *re*) for the comparative, and *est* (or *st*) for the superlative. Many adjectives are compared by preplacing *mere* (more) and *mest* (most). Some, also, compare irregularly: *god* (good), *bedre* (better), *best* (best), etc.

The following table illustrates the articles, nouns, and adjectives in their various forms and relations:

English	Norwegian	
	Singular	Plural
a man	en mann	menn
a man's	en manns	menns
a good man	en god mann	gode menn
the man	mannen	mennene
the man's	mannens	mennenes
the good man	den gode mann(en)	de gode menn
a house	et hus	hus
of a house	et huses	huses
a good house	et godt hus	gode hus
the house	huset	husene
of the house	husets	husenes
the good house	det gode hus(et)	de gode huse(ene)

Nouns

The nouns have three cases and two numbers. The cases are nominative and objective, which are always alike in form, and possessive (genitive), the latter being formed by adding *s* to the nominative:

	Singular	Plural
Nominative	mann (mand), [man]	menn (mænd), [men]
Possessive	manns	menns

When the noun has the substantive definite article, the *s* is added to the latter:

	Singular		Plural	
Nominative	mannen [the man]	huset [the house]	mennene	husene
Possessive	mannens	husets	mennenes	husenes

Nouns ending in *s* (*x*, *z*) form their possessive by adding *es*: *paradis, paradises.* Possession may also be expressed by the preposition *av* (of): *eieren av huset* (the owner of the house). Proper nouns in *s* form the possessive usually by adding *'s*: *Valders's,* of Valders.

The plural is formed as follows:

1. By adding *r* or *er* to the singular, with or without mutation.[1]

	Indefinite singular	Definite singular	Indefinite plural	Definite plural
Nominative	flåte [fleet]	flåten	flåter	flåtene
Possessive	flåtes	flåtens	flåters	flåtenes

[1] Mutation means a change of the vowel of a stem syllable caused by assimilation to a following vowel (*i, u*) or consonant (*j*).

2. By adding *e* to the singular, in a few cases with mutation:

	Indefinite singular	Definite singular	Indefinite plural	Definite plural
Nominative	egn [region]	egnen	egne	egnene
Possessive	egns	egnens	egnes	egnenes

3. No change of form in the plural, except that in a few cases the vowel is changed by mutation:

	Indefinite singular	Definite singular	Indefinite plural	Definite plural
Nominative	ord [word]	ordet	ord	ordene
Possessive	ords	ordets	ords	ordenes

Some words such as proper and collective nouns, names of substances, and abstract nouns indicating quality, have no plural: *foreldre*, parents.

Personal pronouns

The following table gives the declension of the personal pronoun with the landsmål variants in parentheses:

English equivalent	Singular			Plural		
	Nominative	Genitive	Objective	Nominative	Genitive	Objective
I	jeg (eg)	min [1]	mig (meg)	vi (vi, me)	vår [1]	oss
thou (familiar)	du	din [1]	dig (deg)	I, de (de)	deres (dykkar)	dere dykk
you (polite)	De	Deres (Dykkar)	Dem (Dykk)	De	Deres (Dykkar)	Dem (Dykk)
he	han	hans	ham (honom, han)	de (dei)	deres (deira)	dem (deim, dei)
she	hun (ho)	hennes (hennar)	henne (henne, ho)			
it { common [2]	den	dens	den			
{ neuter	det	dets	det			

[1] *Min, din,* and *vår* are merely possessive adjectives which agree with their nouns in number and gender, as follows:

English equivalent	Singular			Plural, all genders
	Common (Masculine)	(Feminine)	Neuter	
my	min	(mi)	mitt	mine
thy	din	(di)	ditt	dine
our	vår	(vår)	vårt	våre

[2] New Norwegian (*Landsmål*) does not employ the common gender, but it has a feminine gender as shown in footnote 1.

Verbs

The Norwegian verb forms are functionally remarkably analogous to the English. The tenses and moods may be translated by the corresponding English verb forms, except that the present participle is not employed as in English for the progressive aspects. The following table shows the conjugation of the two auxiliaries and the irregular verb *to give* and the regular verb *to love:*

Tense and mood	to have	to be	to give	to love
Present infinitive	å ha	å være	å gi	å elske
Perfect infinitive	å ha hatt	å ha vært	å ha gitt	å ha elsket
Future infinitive	å skulle ha	å skulle være	å skulle gi	å skulle elske
Present participle	haende	værende	giende	elskende
Past participle	hatt	vært	gitt	elsket
Present indicative	ha	er	gir	elsker
Past indicative	hadde	var	gav	elsket
Perfect indicative	ha hatt	ha vært	ha gitt	ha elsket
Pluperfect indicative	hadde hatt	hadde vært	hadde gitt	hadde elsket
Future [1]	skal ha	skal være	skal gi	skal elske
Future perfect [1]	skal ha hatt	skal ha vært	skal ha gitt	skal ha elsket
Present subjunctive	ha	være	gi	elske
Present conditional	vilde ha	vilde være	vilde gi	vilde elske
Past conditional	vilde ha hatt	vilde ha vært	vilde ha gitt	vilde ha elsket
Imperative	ha	var	gir	elsk

[1] As in English, *skal* is the auxiliary in the first person and *vil* in the second and third persons.

Word order

The word order in a sentence is, subject, predicate, and object: *mannen kommer*, the man comes; *hesten bar rytteren*, the horse carried the rider. In the first sentence, if the words are transposed, the sentence will read, *kommer mannen?*, does the man come?

The indirect object precedes the direct object; *far gav Johan boken*, father gave John the book.

In an independent interrogative sentence, or where the question is the main proposition, only the subject and predicate are transposed: *gav far Johan boken?*, did father give John the book? However, in subordinate interrogative sentences the subject precedes the predicate: *fortel mig, hvor du kommer fra*, tell me, where you come from. If the predicate is a compound form of the verb, the subject goes immediately after the auxiliary: *hvor har du været?*, where have you been? An attributive adjective precedes the noun: *en stor hund*, a big dog; this is also true of the genitive: *mannens hus*, the man's house. An adverb modifying an adjective or another adverb, precedes the word which it modifies (*en meget smuk mann*, a very handsome man), but an adverb modifying a verb is placed after it: *Karl gik meget hurtig*, Charles walked very fast.

In relative sentences the subject follows immediately after the relative word, if that is not itself the subject: *det hus, som du har kjøpt, er meget dårlig*, the house, which you have bought, is a very poor one; *overalt, hvor han har været, har han gjort sig forhatt*, wherever he has been he has made himself disliked.

The usual order occurs after conjunctions: *nar jeg kommer til byen, skal jeg kjøpe mig nye klær*, when I go to town, I shall buy myself new clothes.

Cardinal numbers

Riksmål	Landsmål		Riksmål	Landsmål	
en, ett	ein, ei, eit	one	seksten	sekstan	sixteen
to	tvo	two	sytten	syttan	seventeen
tre	tre (tri)	three	atten	attan	eighteen
fire	fire	four	nitten	nittan	nineteen
fem	fem	five	tyve	tjuge	twenty
seks	seks	six	en og tyve	ein og tjuge	twenty-one
syv	sju	seven	tredve	tretti	thirty
otte	åtte	eight	firti	fyrti	forty
ni	ni	nine	femti	femti	fifty
ti	ti	ten	seksti	seksti	sixty
elleve	elleve	eleven	sytti	sytti	seventy
tolv	tolv	twelve	otti	åtti	eighty
tretten	trettan	thirteen	nitti	nitti	ninety
fjorten	fjortan	fourteen	hundrede	hundrad	hundred
femten	femtan	fifteen	tusen	tusund	thousand

Ordinal numbers

Riksmål	Landsmål		Riksmål	Landsmål	
første	fyrste	first	tiende	tiande	tenth
annen,	andre	second	ellevte	ellevte	eleventh
annet			tolvte	tolvte	twelfth
tredje	tridje	third	trettende	trettande	thirteenth
fjerde	fjorde	fourth	tyvende	tjugande	twentieth
femte	femte	fifth	enogty-	ein og	twenty-first
sjette	sjette	sixth	vende	tjugande	
syvende	sjuande	seventh	tredevte	trettiande	thirtieth
ottende	åttande	eighth	firtiende	fyrtiande	fortieth
niende	niande	ninth			

Months

januar (jan.)		January	juli		July
februar (feb.)		February	august (aug.)		August
mars		March	september (sept.)		September
april (apr.)		April	oktober (okt.)		October
mai		May	november (nov.)		November
juni		June	desember (des.)		December

Days

Riksmål	Landsmål		Riksmål	Landsmål	
søndag	sundag	Sunday	torsdag	torsdag	Thursday
mandag	mondag	Monday	fredag	fredag	Friday
tirsdag	tysdag	Tuesday	lørdag	laurdag	Saturday
onsdag	onsdag	Wednesday			

Seasons

Riksmål	Landsmål		Riksmål	Landsmål	
vår	vår	spring	høst	haust	autumn
sommer	sumar	summer	vinter	vinter, vetter	winter

Time

Riksmål	Landsmål		Riksmål	Landsmå	
time	time	hour	måned	månad	month
dag	dag	day	år	år	year
uke	vike (veke)	week			

Articles to be disregarded in filing

en	ein	den	den
et	{ei, e / eit	det	det
		de	dei

Abbreviations

The most common abbreviations used in Norwegian·commercial correspondance are:

a (French preposition e.g. 10 à 20 kr.: from 10 to 20 kr.; 4 kasser à 4 kg. à kr. 2.00: 4 cases of 4 kgs. at kr. 2.00.

adr. (adresse), address.

A/S (aksjeselskap), joint-stock company (Ltd.).

aug. (august), August (Aug.).

a/v (a vista) ,at sight, on demand (o/d).

bet. (betalt), paid (Pd.).

btb. (betalbar), payable

bl.a. (blandt annet), amongst other .things, inter alia.

ca. (cirka), about (abl.), approx.

cm (centimeter), centimetre (cm).

cif., c.i.f.

cf., c.&f.

90 d/d, at 90 days' date.

d.e. (det er), that is (i.e.).

des. or desbr. (desember), December (Dec.).

3 dg./s, at 3 days' sight (at 3 d/s).

disk. (diskonto), discount.

d.m. (denne måned), instant (inst.).

ds. (dennes, denne måned), instant (inst.).

D.s. (den samme), the same, idem.

d/s (dampskib), steamship (s/s).

d.v.s. (det vil si), that is, that is to say.

d.å. (dette år), this year

28. febr. d.å.

{ 1) 28th Feb. last / 2) 28th Feb. next.

eftf. (efterfølger), successor.

eftm (eftermiddag), after noon (p.m.).

emball. (emballasje), packing.

febr. (februar), February (Feb.).
f.eks. (for eksempel), for example (e.g.).
ff (forfallen, forfallent, forfalne), due, payable.
fhv. (orhenværnde), former, late, ex-.
f.m. (forrige måned), ultimo (últ.).
fob., f.o.b.
for., f.o.r:
form. (formiddag), before noon (a.m.).
frk. (frøken), Miss.
f.å. (forrige år), last year.
gr. (gram), gramme.
gt. (gate), street (st.).
hl (hektoliter), hectolitre.
hr. (herr), Mr.
hrr. (herrer), Messrs.
inkl. (inklusiv), including, inclusive of.
jfr. or jvf or jvfr. (jevnfør), cf., cp.
jun. or jr. (junior), junior.
kfr. (konferer), cf., cp.
kg (kilo, kilogram), kilogramme.
kl. 7 (klokken 7), 7 o'clock.
km (kilometer), kilometre.
kr. (krone), Norwegian unit of coinage is 100 øre.
K/S (kort sikt, i.e. due 14 days from of issue)—short sight.
1/ (last), to be placed before the name of the drawee)—on.
l (liter), litre.
lev. (levert), delivered.
l/s (lang sikt, i.e. due 2 or 3 months or more from date of issue), long date.
ltr./ (litra), to be placed before the name of the drawer), drawn by.
novbr. (november), November (nov.).
nr. (nummer), numero (No.).
n.å. (nestre år), next year.
o/, to be placed before the name of the payee (ordre), to the order of (o/o).
oktb. (oktober), October (oct.).
omkr. (omkring), about (abt.).
o.s.v. (og så videre), and so on, etc.
pct. (procent), percent.
p.g.a. (på grunn av), on account of, owing to.
m (meter), metre.
1 md./d (one month after date of issue), at 1 month's date (at 1 m/d).

mdr. (måneder), montrs [mdrs. (måneders), the genitive case.]
medio april, middle April.
m.fl. (med flere), et alii, et al.
mrk. (merket), marked.
m/s (motorskib), motor-ship.
n.m. (neste måned), next (prox.).
p.p.
pp.
p.pr. } prokura (per prokura), per
pr.pr. } procuration (per pro.).
p.pa.
pr.pro.

pr. kontant }
pr. kont. } for cash.
pr. kassa }

primo April, early April.
pr., per: pr. år, per year(per annum, per anm.), a year; ff. pr. 31. (30.) ds., due end of this month; pr. omgående, by return of post; Notodden pr. Skien, N. near S. (via S.); pr. brev, by letter; bestilling pr. brev, letter order; sendt (avlevert) pr. bud, sent by hand, by messenger; saldo pr. idag i min favør, balance due this day in my favour, balance per to-day for my credit; pr. stk., a piece.
Rek. (rekommandert), by registered post.
s.d. (samme dato), the same date.
septbr. (september), September (Sept.).
sen. (senior), senior.
sk. (sekk), bag.
stk. (stykke), piece; pr. stk., a piece.
S.U. (svar utbes), R.S.V.P. (repondez s'il vous plâit, please reply).
sukcess. (sukcessivt), gradually, by degrees.
tlf. or telef. (telefon), telephone.
ultimo april, end April.
÷, less, e.g. ÷2½ pct., less 2½ per cent.
Ordinal numbers are formed by putting a point after the cardinal numbers, e.g. 21. mars, 21st March; 20. årr., 20th century.

OSSETTE

Name	Character	Script	Transliteration and tone value
A	A a		a; medium long a
Ae	Æ æ		a; short a
Bie	Б б		b
Wie	В в		v; w
Gie	Г г		g
Ghie	Б̆ б̆		g; Dutch g
Die	Д д		d
Je	Е е		e; long closed e
I	I i		i
Jot	J j		j
Ka	К к		k; aspirated as in German
El	Л л		l
Em	М м		m
En	Н н		n
Oh	О о		o; long closed o
Pie	П п		p; aspirated as in French pein
Qa	Q q		q; back palatal, like Arabic qâf
Er	Р р		r
Es	С с		s; sharp
Tie	Т т		t; aspirated as in terror
U	У у		u
Ef	Ф ф		f
Cha	Х х		x
Y	ў ÿ		w; as in English
Sie	З з		z; soft Dutch z
Dse	Дз дз		dz; ds
Dsche	ДжС джс		dž; dsh
Tsze	Ц ц		c; ts
K'a	Ќ ќ		k; guttural ending
P'e	ҧ ҧ		p; guttural ending
T'e	ҭ ҭ		t; guttural ending
Tsz'e	Ц̆ ц̆		c; ts
Tsche	Ч ч		č; tsch
Tsch'e	Ч̆ ч̆		c ; tsch, hard
3	V v		ə; like u in sun
Hæ	b b		h

The Ossettes are an Indo-Germanic people descended from the ancient Massagetae and Alani which were a branch of the Ostrogoths, portions of which moved on into northern Africa. They live mainly in the middle Caucasus, and there are two principal dialects, the Iron and the Digor. The similarity of some of the words indicates a possible connection with the Hungarian.

The language was first reduced to writing toward the close of the 18th century, when the Russian alphabet was used with the addition of several characters to represent sounds foreign to the Russian. At the present time the Latin text is employed; and while some newspapers and books have been printed, literacy is very low among the people.

Syllabication and punctuation are like the German.

PERSIAN (Nestalic)

Name	Isolated	Final	Median	Initial	Transcription	Pronunciation
Alef	ا	ـا ـل			'	Soft breathing [1]
Bē	ب	ـب	ـبـ	بـ	b	*b*
Pē	پ	ـپ	ـپـ	پـ	p	*p*
Tē	ت	ـت	ـتـ	تـ	t	Italian *t*
Ṣē	ث	ـث	ـثـ	ثـ	ṣ	*s*
Jīm	ج	ـج	ـجـ	جـ	j	*j*
Chē	چ	ـچ	ـچـ	چـ	ch	*ch* in church
Ḥē	ح	ـح	ـحـ	حـ	ḥ	*h*
Khē	خ	ـخ	ـخـ	خـ	kh	*ch* in Scotch loch
Dāl	د	ـد ـد			d	Italian *d*
Ẕāl	ذ	ـذ ـذ			ẕ	*z*
Rē	ر	ـر ـر			r	Italian *r*
Zē	ز	ـز ـز			ž	*z*
Žē	ژ	ـژ ـژ			zh	French *j* in jour
Sīn	س	ـس	ـسـ	سـ	s	*s*
Shīn	ش	ـش	ـشـ	شـ	sh	*sh*

PERSIAN (Nestalic)—Continued

Name	Isolated	Final	Median	Initial	Transcription	Pronunciation
Sād	ص	ص	ـصـ	صـ	ṣ	s
Ẓād	ض	ض	ـضـ	ضـ	ẓ	z
Ṯā	ط	ط	ـطـ	طـ	ṯ	Italian t
Ẕā	ظ	ظ	ـظـ	ظـ	ẕ	z
Ain	ع	ع	ـعـ	عـ	ʿ	Soft breathing [2]
Ghain	غ	غ	ـغـ	غـ	gh	Like German ch.
Fē	ف	ـف	ـفـ	فـ	f	f
Qāf	ق	ـق	ـقـ	قـ	q	Hard, guttural k
Kāf	ک	ـک	ـکـ	کـ	k	k
Gāf	گ	ـگ	ـگـ	گـ	g	g in go (soft)
Lām	ل	ـل	ـلـ	لـ	l	l
Mīm	م	ـم	ـمـ	مـ	m	m
Nūn	ن	ـن	ـنـ	نـ	n	n
Vāv	و	ـو			v	v [3]
Hē	ه	ـه	ـهـ	هـ	h	h
Ye	ی	ـی	ـیـ	یـ	y, i	Consonantal y

[2] It has exactly the same sound as the initial alef.

[3] Vāv preceded by zammeh (expressed or understood) sounds like the Italian u; when preceded by fateh and not followed by another vowel the two form a diphthong au pronounced as the English long o.

NOTE.—The characters Ain and Ghain appear to be hard gutturals; Ghain is always *g*, but from a grammatical standpoint Ain cannot be well defined in any of the three Near Eastern languages. While at best it has only a very short sound, it cannot be omitted from the alphabet because of the effect it has on the proper pronunciation of the words.

It is also considered a vowel, especially at the beginning of words, taking the place of *a*, *ā*, *i*, *ī*, *u*, *ū*. In a median position it generally takes the place of *i* or *ii*, depending mainly on the proper relation of the words and its nearest transcription and pronunciation into the Latin alphabet.

Ligatures

But one example is given of the characters that differ only in the diacritical sign

	l-a		*h-d*		*t-r*		*h-r*		*k-m-r*		*b-h-h*		*b-j*
	k-a		*h-r*		*ġ-r*				*l-m*		*ġ-h*		*k-j*
	m-a		*š-r*		*f-r*		*k-l*		*l-m-r*		*q-h*		*l-j*
	h-a		*d-r*		*m-r*		*k-m*		*h-h*		*m-h*		*h-j*

Cardinal numbers

yak	one	nuh	nine
dū	two	dah	ten
sih	three	yazdeh	eleven
chahār	four	davāzdeh	twelve
panj	five	sīzdah	thirteen
shash	six	bist	twenty
haft	seven	sad	hundred
hasht	eight	hazār	thousand

Ordinal numbers

yakum, nukhustīn [1]	first	shashum	sixth
duvum	second	haftum	seventh
sivum	third	hashtum	eighth
chahārum	fourth	nuhum	ninth
panjum	fifth	dahum	tenth

Year

The Iranian (Persian) year is a solar one, beginning and ending in the spring, March 21, and is divided into 12 months of 30 days each, 5 days being added to the twelfth month to bring the total up to 365, and every fourth year there is a leap year as with us.

Since the Arabic conquest the Mohammedan calendar has been in use in Iran (Persia) for all ordinary purposes.

Persian	Arabic	Afganistan
Farvardīn [2]	Muharram	Hamal
Urdībihisht	Safar	Saūr
Khurdad	Rabi'ul avval	Jaūza
Tīr	Rabi'ussani	Saratān
Murdād	Jumadiyu'lavval	Asad
Shahrīvar	Jumadiyu'ssani	Sombulah
Mihr	Rajab	Mīzān
Ābān	Sha'ban	Aqrab
Azur	Ramazān	Qaūs
Dai	Shavvāl	Jadī
Bahman	Zu'l Qa'deh	Dalw
Isfand	Zu'l Hijjeh	Hūt

[1] The Arabic word *awwal* is also sometimes used

[2] This does not correspond exactly with Muharram, one being solar and the other lunar.

Days

yakshanbeh	Sunday	panj-shanbeh	Thursday
dōshanbeh	Monday	jum'eh	Friday
sih-shanbeh	Tuesday	shanbeh	Saturday
chahār-shanbeh	Wednesday		

Seasons

bahār	spring	pāiz	autumn
tābistān	summer	zamīstān	winter

Time

sā'at	hour	māh	month
rūz, yaum	day	sāl, saneh	year
hafteh	week		

POLISH

A	a	*a* in ah	M	m	*m* in him
Ą	ą	*on*[g] (nasal)	N	n	*n* in new
B	b	*b* in bah	Ń	ń	in French gn
C	c	*ts* in hoots	O	o	*o* in boy
Ć	ć	*ch* in child	Ó	ó	*oo* in goose
CH	ch	*ch* in loch	P	p	*p* in poor
CZ	cz	*c*, hard	R	r	*r* in rare
D	d	*d* in dough	RZ	rz	*zh, r* mute
DZ	dz	*ds*	S	s	*s* in salt
DŹ	dź	*dzj* (voiced)	Ś	ś	*ś*
DŻ	dż	*j*	ŚĆ	śĆ	
E	e	*e* in ever	SZ	sz	*sh* in shall
Ę	ę	*en*[g] (nasal)	SZCZ	szcz	*shch,* in fresh cherry
F	f	*f* in favor	T	t	*t*
G	g	*g* in good	U	u	*u*
H	h	*h* in half	W	w	*v* in vaudeville; *f,* final
I	i	*e;* before vowel, *y*			
J	j	*y* in yell	Y	y	*y* in pity
K	k	*c* in cost	Z	z	*z* in zebra
L	l	*l* (trilled)	Ź	ź	*s*[1]
Ł	ł	([1])	Ż	ż	*j,* French

[1] This sound can be learned only from a native; *oo* has been suggested as an equivalent: *Władysław* (*Vooadysooav*) in three syllables, *Vooa* and *sooav* being each pronounced as one syllable.

Punctuation is practically the same as in English.

The Polish has six words consisting of but one letter each: *w*, in; *z*, with; *i*, and, also; *a*, and; *o*, about; *u*, by, at, among, with, near, in.

Accent

Stress is invariably on the next to the last syllable.

Syllabication

1. Divide on a vowel followed by a single consonant (*ch, cz, dz, dź, dż, rz, sz,* and *szcz* being treated as single consonants, cannot be divided), as *chło-pak, cho-dak.* Vowels are *a, ą, e, ę, i, o, ó, u,* and *y* (*ą, ę,* and *ó* not properly accentual).

2. Divide on the first of two or more consonants (*szcz, zd,* and *zg* are not separable), as *an-te-nat, jutrz-nia.*

3. The following vowel and consonant combinations are inseparable: *bi, fi, gi, gie, ki, kie, mi, ni, pi,* and *wi.*

Abbreviations

The following frequently used abbreviations will be helpful:

i.t.d.	i tak dalej, et cetera	r.	rok, year
n.p.	na przykład, for instance	św.	święty, Saint
p.	pan, pani, Mr., Mrs.	w.	wiek, century
por.	porównaj, compare with	ś.p.	świętej pamięci, deceased

The Polish title *Pan* is equivalent to Mr. and sir, and is used immediately before the surname, but it may also be employed either before a baptismal name alone or a baptismal name together with a surname: *Pan Wajerski, Pan Jan, Pan Jan Wajerski; Tak Panie,* Yes, sir; *Czy Pan idzie?* Are you going, sir? The feminine of *Pan* is *Pani* (Mrs.) and *Panna* (Miss).

Prepositions

Prepositions are used with genitive, dative, accusative, instrumental and locative cases. The prepositions are *u*, at; *od*, from; *do*, to; *dla*, for; *bez*, without.

Adjectives

Adjectives must agree with the nouns they modify in number, gender, and case. In the singular the masculine termination in the nominative case is *y* or *i*, the feminine *a*, and the neuter *e*. In the plural the masculine personal has *y* or *i*, and the other genders *e*.

Nouns

There are three genders in Polish: Masculine, feminine, and neuter.

Nouns before which the word *ten* can be used, are masculine, as *ten ojciec*, the father; *ten kwiat*, the flower; *ten koń*, the horse.

Nouns before which the word *ta* can be used, are feminine; as *ta matka*, the mother; *ta woda*, the water; *ta sarna*, the deer.

Nouns before which the word *to* can be used are neuter; as *to dziecko*, the child; *to imię*, the name; *to krzesło*, the chair.

The words *ten, ta, to*, do not correspond to the English definite article, serving to indicate merely the gender of nouns.

Generally speaking, most nouns ending in a consonant are masculine, those ending in the vowel *a*, feminine, and those ending in *o*, neuter.

The names ending in *g* or in a syllable beginning with *g* form their feminines as follows: (Mr.) *Waliga*, (Mrs.) *Waligowa*, (Miss) *Waliżanka*; (Mr.) *Mertig*, (Mrs.) *Mertigowa*, (Miss) *Mertiżanka*.

It is possible to distinguish, by the form of the family name, whether it is applied to a man, a married woman, or a spinster. The feminine forms of the name are always derived from that of the masculine, according to the following rules:

When the masculine name ends in *ski* or *cki* the feminine forms terminate in *ska* or *cka*. (Mr.) *Wajerski*, (Mrs.) *Wajerska*, (Miss) *Wajerska;* (Mr.) *Malecki*, (Mrs.) *Malecka*, (Miss) *Malecka*.

When the masculine form ends in any other letter or syllable (but not in *g* or a syllable beginning with *g*) than *ski*, the feminine endings are as follows: (Mr.) *Nurkiewicz*, (Mrs.) *Nurkiewiczowa*, (Miss) *Nurkiewiczówna;* (Mr.) *Kowal*, (Mrs.) *Kowalowa*, (Miss) *Kowalówna*.

There are two numbers: The singular and the plural, and seven cases: Nominative, genitive, dative, accusative, vocative, instrumental, and locative.

There are three declensions: masculine, feminine, and neuter.

The following table shows the endings of each of the three declensions:

Case	Masculine		Feminine		Neuter	
	Singular	Plural	Singular	Plural	Singular	Plural
Nom.	$-(^1)$	owie (i, y, e)	a, i (or ^{2})	e (i, y)	e (ę, o)	a (ęta, ona)
Gen.	a (u)	ów (i, y)	i (y)	$(^3)$ i (y)	a (ęcia)	$(^3)$, ów
Dat.	owi (u)	om	e (i, y)	om	u (ęciu)	om (ętom, onom)
Accus.	$(^4)$	$(^4)$	ę, ą $(^5)$	e (i, y)	e (ę, o)	a (ęta, ona)
Voc.	e (u)	owie (i, y, e)	o (u, i)	e (i, y)	e (ę, o)	a (ęta, ona)
Instr.	em	ami	ą	ami	em (eciem)	ami (onami)
Locat.	e (u)	ach	e (i)	ach	u (e, ęciu)	ach (onach)

¹ Ending in a hard or soft consonant.
² Ending in a soft consonant.
³ Without any termination.

⁴ Same as genitive for living beings; as nominative for inanimate objects.
⁵ Or as nominative.

The first includes nouns of the masculine gender which end in a consonant, as *wól*, an ox; *plot*, a fence; *król*, a king; *piec*, a stove; *Amerykanin*, an American; and diminutives ending in *o*, as *Józio*, Joey; *Franio*, Frankie, etc.

The second declension includes feminine nouns ending in *a* or *i*, as *baba*, an old woman; *pani*, a lady, or in soft consonants as *kość*, a bone; *twarz*, the face.

The third declension includes neuter nouns ending in *o* preceded by a hard consonant, and in *e* or *ę* preceded by a soft consonant.

Irregular forms.—The noun *tydzień*, week, is declined as follows: Singular *tydzień*, plural *tygodnie*. *Dziecko*, child, has as plural *dzieci*, children. *Człowiek*, man, has as plural *ludzie*, men, people. *Rok*, year has for its plural *lata*, years.

Pronouns

Personal pronouns, first and second persons: First person singular is *Ja*, I; second person singular is *ty*, you (thou); third person, *on* (he), *ona* (she), *ono* (it). Plural first person is *my*, we; second person, *wy*, you; third person, *oni* (*m.* and *n.*), *one* (*f.*), they.

Verbs

The Polish verb is highly inflective. Not only does it conjugate according to mood, voice, tense, person, number, and gender, but its participles, which take the nature of nouns or adjectives, in turn decline according to case, number, and gender.

The following table shows the conjugations of the important verbs *być* (to be) and *mieć* (to have), which are irregular, and of *kochać* (to love), *pisać* (to write), *czynić* (to make, do), and *jęczeć* (to sigh, groan), of the first, second, third, and fourth regular conjugations, respectively.

	być	mieć	kochać	pisać	czynić	jęczeć
Infinitive	być	mieć	kochać	pisać	czynić	jęczeć
Present participle [1]	będący, -a, -e	mający, -a, -e	kochający, -a [2]	piszący [2]	czyniący [2]	jęczący [2]
Perfect participle [3]	były, -a, -e	miany, -a, -e	kochany, -a [2]	pisany [2]	czyniony [2]	(lacking)
Future participle [4]	(mający, -a, -e		-a, -e plus the infinitive of the verb)			
Present gerund [5]	będąc	mając	kochając	pisząc	czyniąc	jęcząc
Perfect gerund [6]	bywszy	miawszy	kochawszy	pisawszy	czyniwszy	jęczawszy
Present indicative:						
Singular—						
1st person	jestem	mam	kocham	pisze	czynię	jęczę
2d person	jesteś	masz	asz	esz	isz	ysz
3d person	jest	ma	a	e	i	y
Plural—						
1st person	jesteśmy	mamy	amy	emy	imy	ymy
2d person	jesteście	macie	acie	ecie	icie	ycie
3d person	są	mają	ają	ą	ią	ą
Perfect indicative: [8]						
Singular—						
1st person	byłem, -am, -om	miałem, -am, -om	ałem [2]	pisałem [2]	iłem [2]	ałem [2]
2d person	byłeś, -aś, -oś	miałeś, -aś, -oś	ałeś	ałeś	iłeś	ałeś
3d person	był, -a, -o	miał, -a, -o	ał	ał	ił	ał
Plural—						
1st person	byliśmy, łyśmy [9]	mieliśmy, miałyśmy	aliśmy [2]	aliśmy [2]	iliśmy [2]	eliśmy [2]
2d person	byliście, łyście [9]	mieliście, miałyście	aliście	aliście	iliście	eliście
3d person	byli, -ły [9]	mieli, miały	ali	ali	ili	eli
Pluperfect indicative	(Same as perfect plus the auxiliary był, -a, -o, -li, -ły)					

	(10)	(10)	(10)	(10)	(10)	(10)
Future:						
Singular—						
1st person	będę					
2d person	będziesz					
3d person	będzie					
Plural—						
1st person	będziemy					
2d person	będziecie					
3d person	będą					
Imperative:						
Singular—						
2d person	bądź	miej	kochaj	pisz	czyn	jęcz
3d person	niech będzie	niech ma	niech kocha	niech pisze	niech czyni	niech jęczy
Plural—						
1st person	bądźmy	miejmy	kochajmy	piszmy	czyńmy	jęczmy
2d person	bądźcie	miejcie	kochajcie	piszcie	czyńcie	jęczcie
3d person	niech będą	niech mają	niech kochają	niech piszą	niech czynią	niech jęczą

1 Equivalent to our *ing* verb form, but is preferably translated as "one who is, one who has, etc." The three forms are for the masculine, feminine, and neuter, respectively.
2 Varies for gender analogously to *być.*
3 Translated as "who has been, who has had, who has been loved," etc.
4 Translated as "who is to be, who is to have," etc.
5 Translated as "while being, while having," etc.
6 Translated as "after having been, after having had," etc.
7 Translated by English simple present, progressive, or emphatic.
8 Equivalent to English past tense or present perfect.
9 The second form applies to both feminine and neuter.
10 Formed by the future of *być* (to be) preceded by infinitive: *kochać będę*, etc.

There is also a subjunctive and a conditional. The first is formed by the aid of *módz* (may) as auxiliary: *Ja mogę żyć* (I may live), *ja mogłem żyć* (I might live), etc. The conditional is formed by the perfect of "have" as an auxiliary and the infinitive of the verb preceded by *był, bym, byś,* or *by: Ja miałem był żyć* (I should have lived).

Adverbs

The adverb is used to modify the meaning of a verb, an adjective or another adverb. Most adverbs are formed from adjectives, but there are also many that are formed from nouns, verbs, prepositions, and numerals.

Cardinal numbers

jeden, -na, -no	one	czterdzieści	forty
dwa, dwie, dwa	two	pięćdziesiąt	fifty
trzy	three	sześćdziesiąt	sixty
cztery	four	siedmdziesiąt (sie-	seventy
pięć	five	demdziesiąt)	
sześć	six	ośmdziesiąt (osiem-	eighty
siedm (siedem)	seven	dziesiąt)	
ośm (osiem)	eight	dziewięćdziesiąt	ninety
dziewięć	nine	sto	hundred
dziesięć	ten	dwieście	two hundred
jedenaście	eleven	trzysta	three hundred
dwanaście	twelve	czterysta	four hundred
trzynaście	thirteen	pięćset	five hundred
czternaście	fourteen	sześćset	six hundred
piętnaście	fifteen	siedmset (siedemset)	seven hundred
szesnaście	sixteen	ośmset (osiemset)	eight hundred
siedmnaście (siedemna-	seventeen	dziewięćset	nine hundred
ście)		tysiąc	thousand
ośmnaście (osiemnaście)	eighteen	dwa tysiące	two thousand
dziewiętnaście	nineteen	trzy tysiące	three thousand
dwadzieścia	twenty	pięć tysięcy	five thousand
dwadzieścia jeden	twenty-one	sto tysięcy	hundred thousand
trzydzieści	thirty	miljon	million

Ordinal numbers

pierwszy, -sza, -sze	first	trzydziesty	thirtieth
drugi, -ga, -gie	second	czterdziesty	fortieth
trzeci	third	pięćdziesiąty	fiftieth
czwarty	fourth	sześćdziesiąty	sixtieth
piąty	fifth	siedmdziesiąty	seventieth
szósty	sixth	(siedemdziesiąty)	
siódmy	seventh	ośmdziesiąty	eightieth
ósmy	eighth	(osiemdziesiąty)	
dziewiąty	ninth	dziewięćdziesiąty	ninetieth
dziesiąty	tenth	setny	hundreth
jedenasty	eleventh	sto pierwszy	hundred and first
dwunasty	twelfth	dwusetny	two hundredth
trzynasty	thirteenth	trzysetny	three hundredth
czternasty	fourteenth	czterechsetny	four hundredth
piętnasty	fifteenth	pięćsetny	five hundredth
szesnasty	sixteenth	sześćsetny	six hundredth
siedmnasty (siedem-	seventeenth	siedmsetny	seven hundredth
nasty)		ośmsetny	eight hundredth
ośmnasty (osiem-	eighteenth	dziewięćsetny	nine hundredth
nasty)		tysiączny	one thousandth
dziewiętnasty	nineteenth	dwutysięczny	two thousandth
dwudziesty	twentieth	miljonowy	millionth
dwudziesty-pierwszy	twenty-first		

Months

Styczeń (Stycz.)	January	Lipiec (Lip.)	July
Luty	February	Sierpień (Sierp.)	August
Marzec (Mar.)	March	Wrzesień (Wrzes.)	September
Kwiecień (Kwiecz.)	April	Październik (Paźdz.)	October
Maj	May	Listopad (Listop.)	November
Czerwiec (Czerw.)	June	Grudzień (Grudz.)	December

Days

Niedziela	Sunday	Czwartek	Thursday
Poniedziałek	Monday	Piątek	Friday
Wtorek	Tuesday	Sobota	Saturday
Środa	Wednesday		

Seasons

wiosna	spring	jesień	autumn
lato	summer	zima	winter

Time

godzina	hour	miesiąc	month
dzień	day	rok	year
tydzień	week	wiek	century

PORTUGUESE

A	a	} *a* in mar	M	m	*m;* final, nasal
Ã	ã		N	n	*n;* final, nasal
ÃE	ãe	*a*, nasal	NH	nh	*ni* in minion
ÃO	ão	*a*, nasal	O	o	*o* in more
B	b	*b*	ÕE	õe	French *on*
C	c	*c* in car before *a, o,* or *u;*	P	p	*p*
		s in mason before *e* and *i*	Q	q	*k; qu=kw*
Ç	ç	*s*	R	r	*r* in wary or trilled
CH	ch	*sh*	RR	rr	Spanish *rr*
D	d	*d*	S	s	*s, z* between vowels
E	e	*a* in fate	T	t	*t*
F	f	*f*	U	u	*oo*, silent in combinations
G	g	*g* in gay, *z* in azure before			gui, gue, qui, que
		e and *i*	V	v	*v*
H	h	*h,* mute	W	w	*w* in wind; used only in
I	i	*e* in he			foreign words
J	j	*j*	X	x	*sh, x*
K	k	*k*	Y	y	*e* in me
L	l	*l*	Z	z	*z, zh;* final, *s*
LH	lh	Liquid; nearly *ly*			

Remarks

Do not put a space after the apostrophe, as in *d'aquelle, n'estas.*

The sign $ is used as follows in Brazil: 234:583$120, meaning 234 *contos*, 583 *milreis*, and 120 *reis* and in Portugal, 234,583$12, meaning 234 *contos*, 583 *escudos*, and 12 *centavos.*

Punctuation marks are used in the same manner as in English.

Capitalization

Capital letters are used for proper names, titles of books, plays, etc., and the first word of a sentence.

Adjectives derived from proper nouns are lower-cased.

Syllabication

A single consonant begins a new syllable, as also *ch, lh, nh, ps, sc,* and *sp,* which are indivisible. The *l* and *r* are not separable from a preceding *b, c, d, f, g, p, t,* or *v.* However, when there are two consonants between vowels, they are divided. In nasal syllables, *m* and *n* belongs to the preceding vowel: *bem-dito, parlamen-to.* In the case of three or more consonants the usage is irregular, but, as a rule, the first two are kept together. Two consecutive vowels are inseparable, even when they do not form a diphthong. Whether silent or not, *u* after *g* or *q* is not separated from the consonant: *ar-guir, mi-quo.*

Except in the case of *ex,* prefixes are now divided according to the above rules.

Adjectives

The adjectives agree in number and gender with the noun they modify. Those ending in *o* of the masculine singular change the ending to *a* to form the feminine singular. Other adjectives, except as noted below, have the same ending for both masculine and feminine:

    o aluno aplicado, the industrious pupil (*m.*)
    a aluna aplicada, the industrious pupil (*f.*)
    o aluno inteligente, the intelligent pupil (*m.*)
    a aluna inteligente, the intelligent pupil (*f.*)

Exceptions are adjectives ending in *or* (except comparatives), and adjectives of nationality which add *a* to form the feminine:

o homem hablador, the talkative man
a mulher habladora, the talkative woman
o homem português, the Portuguese man
a mulher portuguesa, the Portuguese woman.

The rules which apply to the formation of the plural of nouns also apply to adjectives.

Limiting adjectives usually precede the noun they modify, while descriptive adjectives usually follow their noun: *o senhor tem muitos livros*, you have many books; *o livro azul*, the blue book.

Some adjectives have different meanings, dependent on whether they precede or follow the noun: *o pobre homem*, the poor fellow; *o homem pobre*, the poor (indigent) man.

The comparative is usually formed by placing *mais* (more) before the adjective, and the superlative by use of the definite article: *ligeiro*, light; *mais ligeiro*, lighter; *o mais ligeiro*, lightest. There are a number of adjectives which have irregular comparison, as *bom*, good; *melhor*, better; *o melhor*, best.

Articles

There are four forms of the definite article: *o*, masculine singular; *os*, masculine plural; *a*, feminine singular; *as*, feminine plural. The article must agree with the noun in number and gender.

The indefinite article *a(n)*, some, also has four forms: *um*, masculine singular; *uns*, masculine plural; *uma*, feminine singular; *umas*, feminine plural.

Nouns

Nouns ending in *o* are usually masculine, while those ending in *a* are usually feminine, though names of masculine persons are of the masculine gender even though they end in *a: o dia, o mapa*, and also certain words of Greek origin having endings *ma* and *ta: o poema, o planeta*, etc. The gender of other nouns must be learned separately.

Possession is denoted by the preposition *de*, or by the contraction of *de* with the definite article:

O amigo de Carlos, Charles' friend
O livro do (de+o) senhor, the man's book

To form the plural of nouns ending in—

a vowel, add -*s*, galinha, galinhas
ão change to *ãos, ões*, or *ães*,[1] orgão, orgãos; patrão, patrões; pão, pães
r, s, or *z*, add -*es*; flor, flores; país, países; luz, luzes
al, substitute -*ais*, sinal, sinais
el, substitute *eis*, níquel, níqueis
ol, substitute -*ois*, anzol, anzois
ul, substitute -*uis*, paúl, paúis
stressed *il*, substitute -*is*, barril, barris
unstressed, *il*, substitute -*eis*, fóssil, fósseis
m, substitute *ns*, viagem, viagens

Personal pronouns

SINGULAR

Subject	Direct object	Indirect object
eu, I	me, me	me, to me
tu, thou	te, thee	te, to thee
êle, he, it	o, him, it	lhe {to him, to her, to it
ela, she, it	a, her, it	

PLURAL

Subject	Direct object	Indirect object
nós, we	nos, us	nos, to us
vós, you	vos, you	vos, to you
êles, they, *m.*	os, them, *m.*	lhes {to them, *m.* to them, *f.*
elas, they, *f.*	as, them, *f.*	

[1] The plural of these must be learned separately.

In direct adddress "you" is expressed by *o senhor, a senhora*, or, when speaking to a child, *o menino, a menina*. In Brazil *senhorinha* is used for Miss, instead of *menina*.

Personal pronoun objects are usually suffixed to the verb with a hyphen. When the final letter of the verb is *r, s,* or *z*, this letter is dropped and the *o, os, a, as* change to *lo, los, la, las: lêmos-o* becomes *lêmo-lo*, we read it. When the final letter is *m*, they are changed to *no, nos, na, nas: aprendem-as* becomes *aprendem-nas*, they learn them.

In the future and conditional forms, where the infinitive is used as the stem, the direct object, indirect object, and reflexive pronouns are placed in hyphens between the stem and the ending, the direct object pronouns change from *o, os, a, as* to *lo, los, la, las*, and the *r* of the infinitive is dropped: *aprender-o-ei* becomes *aprende-lo-ei*, I will learn it.

In negative sentences the personal pronoun object precedes the verb, but when there are two personal pronoun objects following a verb the indirect object precedes the direct. In this case the pronouns *me* or *te* and *o, os, a, as* become *mo, mos, ma, mas, to, tos, ta, tas; nos* before *o* becomes *no-lo, vos* and *o* become *vo-lo*, etc.; *lhe* or *lhes* and *o, os, a, as* become *lho, lhos, lha, lhas*.

Special forms of the personal pronoun for use with a preposition are:

(a) mim, to me

(a) ti, to you

(a) o senhor ⎱ to you
(a) a senhora ⎰

(a) êle, to him, it

(a) ela, to her, it

(a) nós, to us

(a) vós, to you

(a) os senhores ⎱ to you
(a) as senhoras ⎰

(a) êles, to them, *m*.

(a) elas, to them, *f*.

Possessive pronouns agree in number and gender with the thing possessed. They take the definite article, except when used in direct address, before the names of relatives, or in the predicate: *o meu, os meus; a minha, as minhas.*

The demonstrative pronouns agree in number and gender with their antecedents: *êste, êstes; esta, estas.*

The prepositions *de* (from, of, etc.) and *em* (in) contract with *êste*, etc., to form *deste(s), desta(s), nêste(s), nesta(s),* etc. The preposition *a* contracts with *aquele*, etc., and *aquilo* to form *àquele(s), àquela(s), àquilo.*

The relative *que* is the most commonly used of its class and does not require inflection. It may be used as subject, direct object, or indirect object. After a preposition *que* (meaning whom) changes to *quem*. The other relative pronouns must agree in number and gender with their antecedent:

que, which, who, whom, that

quem, who, whom

o qual, os quais, a qual, as quais ⎱ who, whom, which
o que, os que, a que, as que ⎰

cujo, cujos, cuja, cujas, whose

quanto, quantos, quanta, quantas, all that, all who

Contractions

A peculiarity of the Portuguese is the contraction of prepositions with the following articles:

de+o, do (dos)

de+a, da (das)

de+um, dum (duns),

de+ uma, duma (dumas)

a+o, ao

a+a, à

em+o, no (nos)

em+a, na (nas)

em+um, num (nuns)

em+uma, numa (numas)

por+o, pelo

por+a, pela

Auxiliary verbs

Those most used are *ser* and *estar* (to be), and *ter* and *haver* (to have). The simple forms are as follows.

Auxiliary verbs

	ser	estar	ter	haver
Indicative:				
Present	sou (I am, am being)	estou	tenho (I have, am having)	hei
	es	estas	tens	hás
	e	esta	tem	há
	somos	estamos	temos	havemos, (h)emos
	sois	estais	tendes	haveis, (h)eis
	são	estão	te(e)m or tem	hão
Future	serei (I shall or will be)	estarei	terei (I shall or will have)	haverei
	seras	estaras	terás	haverás
	sera	estara	terá	haverá
	seremos	estaremos	teremos	haveramos
	sereis	estareis	tereis	havereis
	seráo	estarão	terão	haverão
Imperfect	era (I was being)	estava	tinha (I had, was having)	havia, (h)ia
	eras	estavas	tinhas	havias, (h)ias
	era	estava	tinha	havia, (h)ia
	eramos	estavamos	tinhamos	havíamos, (h)íamos
	ereis	estaveis	tinheis	havíeis, (h)íeis
	eram	estavam	tinham	haviam, (h)iam
Conditional	seria (I should or would be)	estaria	teria (I should or would have)	haveria
	serias	estarias	terias	haverias
	seria	estaria	teria	haveria
	seríamos	estaríamos	teríamos	haveríamos
	seríeis	estaríeis	teríeis	haveríeis
	seriam	estariam	teriam	haveriam
Preterite	fui (I was)	estive	tive (I had)	houve
	foste	estiveste	tiveste	houveste
	foi	esteve	teve	houve
	fomos	estivemos	tivemos	houvemos
	fostes	estivestes	tivestes	houvestes
	foram	estiveram	tiveram	houveram
Pluperfect	fôra (I had been)	estivera	tivera (I had had)	houvera
	foras	estiveras	tiveras	houveras
	fôra	estivera	tívera	houvera
	fôramos	estiveramos	tiveramos	houvéramos
	fôreis	estivereis	tivereis	houvéreis
	foram	estiveram	tiveram	houveram
Subjunctive:				
Present	seja (that I may be)	esteja	tenha (that I may have)	haja
	sejas	estejas	tenhas	hajas
	seja	esteja	tenha	haja
	sejamos	estejamos	tenhamos	hajamos
	sejais (sejaes)	estejais (estejaes)	tenrais (tenhaes)	hajais (hajaes)
	sejam	estejam	tenham	hajam

Auxiliary verbs

	ser	estar	ter	haver
Future	fôr (I may or shall be)	estiver	tiver (I may or shall have)	houver
	fores	estiveres	tiveres	houveres
	fôr	estiver	tiver	houver
	formos	estivermos	tivermos	houvermos
	fordes	estiverdes	tiverdes	houverdes
	forem	estiverem	tiverem	houverem
Imperfect	fosse (that I might be)	estivesse	tivesse (that I might have)	houvesse
	fosses	estivesses	tivesses	houvesses
	fosse	estivesse	tivesse	houvesse
	fôssemos	estivéssemos	tivéssemos	houvéssemos
	fôsseis	estivésseis	tivésseis	houvésseis
	fossem	estivessem	tivessem	houvessem
Personal infinitive	ser	estar	ter	haver
	seres	estares	teres	haveres
	ser	estar	ter	haver
	sermos	estarmos	termos	havermos
	serdes	estardes	terdes	houverdes
	serem	estarem	terem	houverem
Present participle (gerund)	sendo (being)	estando	tendo (having)	havendo
Past participle	sido (been)	estado	tido (had)	havido
Imperative:				
Sing., 2d per.	sê (be)	está	tem (have)	há
Pl., 2d pers.	sêde	estai	tende	havei

[1] The present subjunctive is used for the other persons.
[2] *tem* is used instead when followed by an object pronoun, *o, a, os, as* (*lo, la, los, las*).

Verbs

Portuguese verbs are inflected for mood, tense, number, and person. This is accomplished by substituting different endings to a stem which in the future and conditional tenses of the indicative mood is the infinitive, and in the remaining tenses, the infinitive without the infinitive ending. There are three conjugations with endings of *ar*, *er*, and *ir*, respectively.

Since most verbs are conjugated regularly, the following specimen will be a useful guide for the conjugation of all regular verbs; however, there are many irregular verbs, and these must be learned separately.

Infinitive	fal-ar	aprend-er	part-ir
Present participle	fal-ando	aprend-endo	part-indo
Past participle	fal-ado	aprend-ido	part-ido
Imperative { Singular	fal-a	aprend-e	part-e
Imperative { Plural	fal-ai	aprend-ei	part-i

INFINITIVE MOOD

	Singular			Plural		
	First person	Second person	Third person	First person	Second person	Third person
Present personal	fal-ar aprend-er part-ir	fal-ares aprend -eres part-ires	fal-ar aprend-er part-ir	fal-armos aprend -ermos part -irmos	fal-ardes aprend -erdes part -irdes	fal-arem aprend -erem part-irem

INDICATIVE MOOD

Present	fal-o	fal-as	fal-a	fal-amos	fal-ais	fal-am
	aprend-o	aprend -es	aprend-e	aprend -emos	aprend -eis	aprend -em
	part-o	part-es	part-e	part-imos	part-is	part-em
Imperfect	fal-ava	fal-avas	fal-ava	fal -ávamos	fal-aveis	fal-avam
	aprend-ia	aprend -ias	aprend-ia	aprend -íamos	aprend -íeis	aprend -iam
	part-ia	part-ias	part-ia	part -íamos	part-íeis	part-iam
Preterite	fal-ei	fal-aste	fal-ou	fal-ámos	fal-astes	fal-aram
	apprend-i	aprend -este	aprend -eu	aprend -emos	aprend -estes	aprend -eram
	part-i	part-iste	part-iu	part-imos	part-istes	part-iram
Pluperfect (simple)	fal-ara	fal-aras	fal-ara	fal -áramos	fal-áreis	fal-aram
	aprend -era	aprend -eras	aprend -era	aprend -êramos	aprend -êreis	aprend -eram
	part-ira	part-iras	part-ira	part -íramos	part-íreis	part-iram
Future	falar-ei	falar-ás	falar-á	falar-emos	falar-eis	falar-ão
	aprender -ei	aprender -ás	aprender -á	aprender -emos	aprender -eis	aprender -ão
	partir-ei	partir-ás	partir-á	partir -emos	partir-eis	partir-ão
Conditional	falar-ia	falar-ias	falar-ia	falar -íamos	falar-íeís	falar-iam
	aprender -ia	aprender -ias	aprender -ia	aprender -iamos	aprender -ieis	aprender -iam
	partir-ia	partir-ias	partir-ia	partir -íamos	partir -íeis	partir-iam

SUBJUNCTIVE MOOD

Present	fal-e	fal-es	fal-e	fal-emos	fal-eis	fal-em
	aprend-a	aprend-as	aprend-a	aprend -amos	aprend -ais	aprend -am
	part-a	part-as	part-a	part-amos	part-ais	part-am
Imperfect	fal-asse	fal-asses	fal-asse	fal -ássemos	fal-ásseis	fal-assem
	aprend -esse	aprend -esses	aprend -esse	aprend -êssemas	aprend -êsseis	aprend -essem
	part-isse	part-isses	part-isse	part -íssemos	part -ísseis	part-issem
Future	fal-ar	fal-ares	fal-ar	fal-armos	fal-ardes	fal-arem
	aprend-er	aprend -eres	aprend-er	aprend -ermos	aprend -erdes	aprend -erem
	part-ir	part-ires	part-ir	part -irmos	part-irdes	part-irem

Abbreviations

cm	centimetro, centimeter	m	metro, meter
D.	dona, lady	p.	pagina, page
Dr.	doutor, doctor	pp.	paginas, pages
Dra.	doutora, doctress	S.Excia.	Sua Excelencia, Excellency
EE.UU.da A., E.U.A.	Estados Unidos da America; United States of America	S.	São (contraction of santa), saint
Exmo.	Excelentissimo, Most Excellent	Snr., Sr.	senhor, Mr.; also Lord
hect.	hectare, hectare	Snra., Sra.	senhora, Mrs.
Illmo.	Ilustrissimo, Most Illustrious	Snrta., Srta.	senhorita, Miss
kilo., kg.	kilograma, kilogram	Sta.	santa, saint
km.	kilometro, kilometer	V.E., V.Excia	Vossa Excellencia, Your Excellency
l.	litro, liter	V.Você,	you (in familiar style)

Cardinal numbers

um, -a	one	dez	ten
dois, dous, duas	two	onze	eleven
tres	three	doze	twelve
quatro	four	treze	thirteen
cinco	five	vinte	twenty
seis	six	vinte e um	twenty-one
sete	seven	cem	hundred
oito	eight	mil	thousand
nove	nine		

Round millions used adjectively are followed by *de: Um milhão de contos*, or *1,000,000 de contos.*

Ordinal numbers

primeiro	first	decimo	tenth
segundo	second	undecimo}	
terceiro	third	onzeno }	eleventh
quarto	fourth	duodecimo, decimo	twelfth
quinto	fifth	segundo	
sexto	sixth	decimo terceiro	thirteenth
setimo	seventh	vigesimo	twentieth
oitavo	eighth	centesimo	hundredth
nono	ninth	millesimo	thousandth

Months

janeiro (jan.)	January	julho (jul.)	July
fevereiro (fev.)	February	agosto (agto.)	August
março (mço.)	March	setembro (set.)	September
abril (abr.)	April	outubro (obro)	October
maio	May	novembro (nov.)	November
junho (jun.)	June	dezembro (dez.)	December

Days

domingo	Sunday	quinta-feira	Thursday
segunda-feira	Monday	sexta-feira	Friday
terça-feira	Tuesday	sabbado	Saturday
quarta-feira	Wednesday		

Seasons

primavera	spring	outomno	autumn
verão	summer	inverno	winter

Time

hora	hour	mez	month
dia	day	anno	year
semana	week		

Articles to be disregarded in filing

o   a   os   as   um   uma

REFORMED PORTUGUESE ORTHOGRAPHY

On September 1, 1911, the commission appointed on February 15 of the same year for the purpose of revising the national language, made its report to the Minister of the Interior. The commission recommended the adoption, with very slight changes, of "Ortografias Portuguesas," a volume containing 183 pages, which had been published by the Academy of Sciences of Lisbon in 1902, and further that it be adopted for all governmental publications and institutions of learning.

On June 15, 1931, the Provisional Government of the Republic of Brazil, the largest and most important Portuguese-speaking country in the world, issued a decree making extensive and somewhat radical changes in the orthography of the language "for the purpose of securing uniformity in the national language." The new orthography had been adopted previously by the Brazilian Academy of Letters, and the decree directs that it be used in all public departments, educational institutions, the Official Journal, and in all other official publications. A decree dated August 3, 1933, provided that after January 1, 1935, only those textbooks conforming to the decree of June 5, 1931, will be used in the public schools. However, its official use has since been abandoned.

The following is a free translation of the essential portions of the decree:

MUTE CONSONANTS

Do not use any consonant that is not sounded:

autor *not* auctor	aluno *not* alumno
sinal *not* signal	salmo *not* psalmo
adesão *not* adhesão	

but do not change the words—

abdicar	recepção	egipcio	espectador
acne	caracteres	egipciaco	espectativa
gnomo	optar	egiptologo	mnemonica

or any other words in which the letters *bd, cn, gn, pç, ct, pt, pc,* or *mn* are sounded separately and distinctly.

Double letters.—Do not double consonants:

sabado *not* sabbado	belo *not* bello
acusar *not* accusar	chama *not* chamma
adido *not* addido	pano *not* panno
efeito *not* effeito	aparecer *not* apparecer
sugerir *not* suggerir	atitude *not* attitude

Exceptions.—(*a*) The letters *r* and *s* are doubled for emphasis:

barro	parra	passo	russo, etc.
carro	cassa		

(*b*) The *c* is doubled or used with the *ç* when each is sounded separately:

secção	seccionar	infeccionar	sucção, etc.
seccional	infecção	infeccioso	

(*c*) The letters *r* and *s* are doubled in words having a prefix ending in a vowel:

prorrogar	prorromper	arrasar	assegurar
prerrogativa	pressentir	(from raso)	(from seguro)

THE LETTER H

Retain the initial, median, and final *h*, (*a*) when it conforms to the etymology of the word:

hoje	homem	hora	honorario, etc.

(*b*) In words having a prefix and a complete Portuguese word:

deshabitar	deshumano	inhumano	rehaver, etc.
deshonra			

(*c*) When used in combination as *ch, lh,* or *nh* to form arbitrary sounds:

chave	malha	lenho	manha, etc.
chapéu	velho		

(*d*) In interjections: *oh! ah!*

Drop the *h*, (*a*) when it occurs in the middle of a word, except as above noted:

sair *not* sahir	cair *not* cahir
compreender *not* comprehender	exumar *not* exhumar
coorte *not* cohorte	proibir *not* prohibir

(*b*) In future and conditional pronominal forms of verbs:

dever-se-á *not* dever-se-há	dir-se-ia *not* dir-se-hia, etc.
escrever-se-á *not* escrever-se-há	

Where it occurs at the end of a word:

Jeova *not* Jehovah	raja *not* rajah

CHANGES FROM INITIAL SC

The initial *s* has been dropped in words like—

ciencia	cetro	cisão	cintilar
cena	cetico	centelha	ciatico

also when used with a prefix:

precientifico   preciencia, etc.

USE OF THE APOSTROPHE

Drop the apostrophe, (*a*) in the contraction of the preposition *de* with the personal pronoun of the third person:

dêle	dela	dêles	delas

with the demonstrative pronouns:

disto	disso	daquilo

with the article:

do	dos	dum	dumas
da	das	duns	

with the demonstrative adjectives:

dêsse	dessa	dêsses	dessas
dêste	desta	dêstes	destas
daquele	daquela	daqueles	daquelas

with the adverbs:

aí *as in* daí	onde *as in* donde
aqui *as in* daqui	aquem *as in* daquem
ali *as in* dali	além *as in* dalêm
antes *as in* dantes	

with the preposition:

entre *as in* dentre

(*b*) Drop it in the combinations *em*, with the pronoun in the third person: *nele*, etc., and with the demonstrative pronoun: *neste*, etc.

(*c*) In forms composed of the demonstrative adjectives:

essoutro	destoutro	aqueloutro	outrora
nestoutro			

THE LETTERS K, W, AND Y

These letters are not used in the Portuguese nor in translated words, but are replaced: (*a*) the *k* by *qu* before *e* and *i*:

querosene	quilo	quilômetro	faquir
quiosque			

and by *c* in every other case:

calendar	caleidoscopio	cleptomania	cleptofobia
cágado			

NOTE.—Retain the *k* in abbreviations of *quilo, quilogramo, quilolitro,* and *quilômetro,* as *k, kg, kl, km.* Although it does not belong to the Portuguese alphabet, the *k* is used in foreign proper names and foreign words which have been adopted into the language. Limit its use to—

kantismo	kantista	kaiser	kaiserista
kappa (Greek)	Kepler	kepleria	kepleriana
kermesse	Kiel	Kiew	kummel
kiries			

(*b*) The *w* is replaced by *u* or *v*, according to its pronunciation:

vigandias	vagão	valsa	Osvaldo

NOTE.—Retain the *w* as a symbol for *oéste* (west).

(*c*) The *y* is replaced by *i:*

juri	mártir	tupí	Andaraí

THE COMBINATIONS CH (HARD), PH, RH, AND TH

(*a*) Substitute *qu* for *ch* (hard) before *e* and *i:*

traquéa *not* trachéa	querubim *not* cherubim
quimera *not* chimera	quimica *not* chimica

Elsewhere it is replaced by *c:*

caldeu *not* chaldeu	cromo *not* chromo
caos *not* chaos	Cristo *not* Christo
corografia *not* chorographia	cloro *not* chloro
catecumeno *not* catechumeno	

(*b*) The digraphs *ph, rh,* and *th* are replaced by *f, r,* and *t,* respectively:

filosofia *not* philosophia	reumatismo *not* rheumatismo
fosforo *not* phosphoro	tesouro *not* thesouro
retorica *not* rhetorica	ortografia *not* orthographia

THE COMBINATION MP

Substitute *n* for *m* in the words which etymologically carry the *p:*

pronto *not* prompto	isento *not* isempto
assunto *not* assumpto	

USE OF THE LETTER S

Use the final *s* and not *z*, (*a*) in the pronouns *nós* and *vós;*

(*b*) In the second person singular of the future indicative:

amarás	ofenderás	irás	porás

(*c*) In the second person singular of the present indicative of the monosyllabic verbs and their compounds:

dás	vês	revês	ris
desdás	crês	descrês	sorris

(*d*) In the plural of words ending in a long vowel:

pás	frenesís	teirós	perús
cafés			

(*e*) In foreign adjectives and other words formed with the suffix *ês* (Latin, ense):

aragonês	inglês	turquês	cortês
barcelonês	iroquês	veronês	pedrês
berlinês	javanês	marquês	baionês
borgonhês	português	burguês	garcês
finês	siamês	camponês	tamarês
francês	sudanês	montanhês	tavanês, etc.
holandês	turquianês	montês	

(*f*) In Latin words in common use which maintain their original form:

bis	plus	virus	pus (substantive)
jus			

(g) In the monosyllables and the following stressed words:

aliás	carajás	freguês	piós
ananás	catrapús	gilvás	princês
após	convés	grós	rês
arnês	cós	linaloés	res
arrás	cris	luís (money)	resvés
arriós	daruês	macis	tornês
ás	dês (since, from)	mês	trás
atrás	detrás	obús	tris
através	enapupês	pardês	viés
calcês	enxós	paspalhós	zás-trás, etc.
camoês	filhós	pavês	

USE OF THE MEDIAN S

(a) In the feminine forms (substantive) which take the ending *esa* or *isa:*

baronesa	consulesa	sacerdotisa	diaconisa
duquesa	prioresa	poetisa	profetisa
princesa			

(b) In adjectives formed from the substantives with the augmentative suffix *oso:*

animoso	formoso	populoso	teimoso
doloroso			

(c) In the different tenses of the verbs *querer* and *pôr*, with their components:

quis	quisemos	puseram	compôs
quisestes	pus	pusemos	dispusestes
quiseram	pusestes	compús	

(d) In the words ending in *esa* or *eso*, which are not truly Portuguese, in harmony with the language of their origin, also their derivatives in conformity with them:

empresa	surpresa	represa	defeso
despesa	framboesa	poesa	obeso
defesa	presa	aceso	teso
mesa	devesa	ileso	

(e) In the verbs of Latin origin ending in *sar:*

acusar (acusare)   recusar (recusare)   refusar (refusare)

(f) In the substantives, adjectives, and the participles terminating in (or consisting of) *aso asa, iso, isa, oso, osa, uso, usa:*

caso	paraiso	divisa	uso
aso	siso	esposo	abuso
vaso	guiso	glosa	luso
asa	liso	rosa	fuso
casa	friso	raposa	escuso
brasa	narciso	grosa	infuso
viso	brisa	entrosa	concluso
conciso	frisa	tosa	contuso
aviso	camisa	prosa	musa
graniso			

(g) In the prefix *trans*, as well as the forms *tras* and *tres*, and also their derivatives:

transação	transandino	transoceanico	traseiro
transiguir	transição	trasante-hontem	trasordinario
tresandar			

(h) In the nouns ending in *ase, ese, ise,* and *ose:*

crase	fase	génese	apófise
frase	perípase	diurése	bacilóse
acroase	diátese	síntese	diagnóse
apófase	tése		

(i) In composite words derived from the Greek with *isos:*

khrysos	stasis	crisóstomo	quersoneso
lysis	thesis	crisántemo	fisiologia
mesos	isocolo	analise	ptoseonomia
nesos	isodico	mesartérite	êxtase
physis	isodinamico	mesaulio	sintese
ptosis	crisóptero		

(j) In verbs terminating in *isar* whose roots terminate in *s* formed with the suffix *ar:*

avisar	precisar	analisar	irisar
(avis ar)	(precis ar)	(analis ar)	(iris ar)

USE OF THE Z

Use final *z* in stressed words ending in *az, ez, iz, oz,* or *uz:*

assaz	perdiz	veloz	arcabuz
xadrez			

NOTE.—See exceptions given in the rules governing the use of the letter *s.*

USE OF THE MEDIAN Z

(a) Use *z* in words of Latin origin in which the *z* displaces the *c, ci,* or *ti:*

azêdo (acetum)	vizinho (vicinus)	prezar (pretiare)
fiuza (fiducia)	razão (rationem)	mezinha (medicina)
juizo (judicium)	prazo (placitum)	

(b) In verbs ending in *zer* or *zir* and their components:

aprezer	jazer	conduzir	luzir
dizer	cozer	induzir	produzir
fazer	(to cook)		

NOTE.—Spell *coser* (with *s*) when it means to sew, and also in the variations *descoser, recoser,* etc.

(c) In the terminations (*z*)*inho* and (*z*)*ito* of the diminutives:

florzinha	paizinho	avezita	pobrezito
maezinha			

(d) In words of Arabic, oriental, and Italian origin and their derivatives which have been adopted into the language:

azáfama	azar	gazúa	bizantino
azeite	azeviche	vizir	bizarro
azul	bazar	bezante	gazeta
azouge	ogeriza		

(e) In verbs ending in *izar* (Latin izare):

autorizar	batizar	civilizar	colonizar

(f) In substantives formed from the adjectives with the suffix *eza* (Latin itia):

beleza	firmeza	moleza	pobreza
fereza	madureza		

(g) In words derived from those ending in *z:*

apaziguar	cruzado	dezena	felizardo
avezar			

PROPER NOUNS

Portuguese or translated proper nouns, whether personal or locative, are written with the final *z* when terminating in a long syllable:

Quieroz	Luiz	Tomaz	Andaluz
Garcez	Queluz		

When the last syllable is short use the final *s:*

Alvares	Dias	Fernandes	Nunes
Peres	Pires		

NOTE.—The name *Jesus* and *Paris* retain the *s.*

Retain the corresponding vernacular forms of spelling already in use in the case of foreign proper names:

Antuerpia	Berna	Bordéus	Cherburgo
Colonia	Escandinavia	Escalda	Florença
Londres	Marselha	Viena	Algeria

NOTE.—Wherever such exist, vernacular names for those in foreign languages are to be preferred.' Retain, however, the original forms of those that are not adapted to the Portuguese language:

Anatole France	Byron	Conte Rosso	Carlyle
Carducci	Musset	Shakespeare	Southampton

DUAL FORMS OF SPELLING

Where two forms have been in use, adopt the following (also in their derivatives and compounds):

(a) Brasil *not* Brazil

(b) idade *not* edade   igreja *not* egreja   igual *not* egual

(c) assucar *not* açucar   alvissaras *not* alviçaras   sossegar *not* socegar
pessego *not* pecego   dossel *not* docel   jovem *not* joven
rossio *not* rocio   criar (to raise)   crear (to create)
almaço *not* almasso   maciço *not* massiço   solene *not* solemne

(d) ansia *not* ancia   ascensão *not* ascenção   cansar *not* cançar
dansar *not* dançar   farsa *not* farça   pretensão *not* pretenção

ENDINGS IN Ã, ÃO, AM

Use *ã* and not *an* in words where the last syllable is stressed:

amanhã   maçã   talismã, etc.

in the feminine of words ending in *ão* in the masculine—

aldeã   cristã   irmã, etc.

and the monosyllables—

lã   vã   sã, etc.

Use *ão*, and not *am*, in the case of monosyllables:

cão   chão   vão

in the stressed words—

coração   verão   alcorão

in the future form of the verbs—

amarão   deverão   farão

and in other words which are now written either *ão* or *am*—

acórdão	bénção	órgão	órfão
sótão			

NOTE.—The tonic syllable of words ending in *ão* must carry an acute accent as shown in the case of the five examples given above.

Use *am* in the unstressed terminations of the verbs:

amam	amavam	amaram	disseram
fizeram	expuseram		

DIPHTHONGS

The diphthongs *ae* and *ao* will be written with *i* and *u:*

pai	cai	sai	amais, etc.
grau	mau	pau	

The diphthong *eo* is replaced by *éu* or *eu:*

céu	véu	teu, etc.
chapéu	meu	

The diphthong *iu* replaces *io:*

feriu	partiu	**viu**

The diphthong *oi* replaces *oe:*

anzois	doi	heroi, etc.

NOTE.—When these vowels do not form a diphthong, no change is made:

aérides	aéreo	cáos	caótico
teologia	rio	tio	oeste
oeta	teleologia		

Write *ao* and not *au* when it is a combination of the preposition *a* with the article *o.*

Retain the diphthongs *ãe, õe,* and *ue:*

mãe	anões	dispões	**pões**
tabeliães	azues		

USE OF THE LETTER G

Retain the median *g* in the following, also in their components and derivatives:

imagem	eleger	legitimo	fugir
pagem			

THE PRONOUN LO

Retain the forms *lo, la, los, las:* (*a*) with the infinitives of the verbs:

amá-lo	ofendê-la	possuí-los	repô-las

(*b*) With the verbal forms ending in *s:*

ama-lo, etc.

and also when they end in *z*—

di-lo	fá-los

(*c*) With the pronouns *nós, vós,* and the form *eis:*

vo-lo	no-la	ei-lo

NOTE.—These pronouns are connected by a hyphen and the tonic vowel of the verb is accented.

THE LETTER X

In words taking *x, s, z, cs, ss, ch,* their prosodic values (*s, z, cs, ss,* and *ch*) are retained:

excelente	exato	fixe	proximo
luxo			

SYLLABICATION

Divide words phonetically according to the spelling, and do not separate them into the elements of derivation, composition, or formation:

subs-cre-ver	sec-ção	de-sar-mar	in-ha-bil
bi-sa-vô	e-xer-ci-to	ex-ce-der	cons-ti-tui-ção

In order to do this readily, observe the following rules:

(*a*) Separate double letters:

ar-ras-trar	pas-sa-gem	suc-ção

(*b*) The *s* of the prefixes *des, dis* remains with the first syllable when followed by a consonant:

des-di-zer	dis-con-ti-nu-ar

If followed by a vowel, it is carried over to the next syllable:

de-sen-ga-nar	de-sen-vol-ver	de-si-lu-são

(*c*) Where two consonants are pronounced separately, the first is retained with the preceding syllable:

con-tac-to	re-cep-ção	es-pec-ta-ti-va

(*d*) Do not separate diphthongs:

neu-tro   nai-pe   rei-na-do   au-to
i-gual (i-guais)

(*e*) Separate vowels of equal force:

co-or-te   co-or-de-na-da

as well as consecutive vowels that do not form a diphthong—

vo-ar   po-ei-ra   pro-e-mio   me-ú-do
ci-ú-me

THE HYPHEN

Separate compound words whose different elements retain their phonetic independence with a hyphen:

para-raios   guarda-pó   contra-almirante

NOTE.—Do not use a hyphen between the elements in the made-up words:

claraboia   parapeito   malmequer   malferido

RULES FOR ACCENTS IN PORTUGUESE
Decree of February 23, 1938 [1]

1. Usar-se-ão o acento agudo, o acento circunflexo e o acento grave. Não será usado o trema.
2. Levam o acento conveniente, agudo ou circunflexo, as palavras esdrúxulas: Pássaro, Pêssego.
3. Levam o acento conveniente, agudo ou circunflexo, as formas verbais agudas ou monossilábicas tônicas, que ficam terminando em vogal por ter caído a consoante final: dí-lo, pô-lo, dí-lo-ei.
4. Levam o acento competente, agudo ou circunflexo, os oxítonos terminados em *a, e, i, o, u*, tônicos, seguidos ou não, de *s*: tupí, tupís.
5. Tomam acento agudo as palavras cuja vogal tônica é *e* ou *o* abertos dos ditongos éi, éu, ói: fiéis, chapéu, sóis, jibóia, idéia.
6. Tem acento agudo o *i* tônico da sequência vocálica aía: saía, baía, caía.
7. Levam o acento conveniente, agudo ou circunflexo, os monossílabos tônicos terminados nas vogais *a, e, o*, seguidas, ou não, de *s*: pá, Brás.
8. Leva o acento circunflexo o *o* tônico fechado, seguido de *o* ou *os*: perdôo, vôos.
9. Usa-se o acento grave na contração da preposição *a* com o artigo definido ou pronome demonstrativo feminino átono *a*, e com os demonstrativos *aquele, aquela, aquilo*.

1. The accents used in the Brazilian Portuguese language are the acute, grave and circumflex. Do not use the dieresis.
2. Use either the acute or the circumflex on polysylabic words: Pássaro, Pêssego.
3. Use the proper accent, acute or circumflex, in acute verbs or monosylabic tonics, when they end in a vowel after the final consonant: dí-lo, pô-lo, dí-lo-ei.
4. Use the proper accent, acute or circumflex, in liquids terminating *a, e, i, o, u*, tonics (with or without the *s*): tupí, tupís.
5. Those words take the acute whose tonic vowel is *e* or *o*, in order to indicate there is no diphthong in éi, éu, or ói: fiéis, chapéu, sóis, jibóia, idéia.
6. The acute accent is used on the tonic *i* in the combination aía: saía, baía, caía.
7. Use either the acute or circumflex in tonic monosyllables terminating in the vowels *a, e,* or *o*, whether or not followed by *s*: pá, Brás.
8. Use the circumflex on the first of double *o*'s, whether or not it ends in *o, os*: perdôo, vôos.
9. Use the grave accent on the contracted preposition *a* with the definite article or the demonstrative feminine active *a*, and also with the demonstratives *àquele, àquela, àquilo*.

[1] Diario Oficial, Brazil, Feb. 28, 1938.

ACCENTUATION IN REFORMED PORTUGUESE

Use the acute accent on bisyllabic or polysyllabic words where the stress is on the last syllable, and which terminate in *i* or *u*, whether or not followed by *s*:

| aquí | tupí(s) | colibrí(s) |
| perú(s) | urubú(s) | |

RULES GOVERNING THE USE OF WRITTEN ACCENTS

1. Differentiate between stressed and unstressed words and distinguish the predominant syllable where there are more than one.
2. Distinguish words that are spelled the same, but differ in either pronunciation or meaning and grammatical function.

There are monosyllabic, bisyllabic, and polysyllabic words:

| pá | pára | parada |

There are monosyllabic and bisyllabic stressed words:

| dá | pára |

as well as unstressed words:

| da | para |

In bisyllabic words the first syllable usually receives the stress: *mares*, but if the second, that carries the accent mark: *marés*.

In polysyllabic words when the stress is on the last syllable the accent mark is used: *falará;* when on the penultimate, the mark is omitted: *falara*, but when on the antepenultimate, it is used: *faláramos*.

Words in which the last syllable is predominant are called "acutes" or "ultimates." If the next to the last syllable is predominant, they are called "grave", "perfect", or "penultimate." If the predominant syllable is that next to the penultimate, it is called "antepenultimate" or "prepenultimate."

No Portuguese word carries the stress on a syllable preceding the antepenultimate syllable, except in cases of pronouns connected by hyphens, where the stress will remain as in the original verbal form, regardless of how many syllables there are: *dávamos-to, dávamo-vo-lo.*

Where a written accent is necessary, use an acute on the stressed vowel in *i* and *u* and in the case of *a, e, o,* when open:

| fará | maré | portaló |
| difícil | útil | |

Use the circumflex on *a, e,* and *o,* closed:

| câmara | mercê | avô |
| ânsia | indulgência | brônzeo |

but—

| fímbria | núncio |

The tilde serves to indicate the stress in words not otherwise indicated:

| varão | maçã | capitães |
| órgão | órfã | |

The grave accent serves to designate, wherever convenient or necessary to the correct pronunciation of a word, the value of the vowels *a, e,* and *o,* regardless of whether or not they are stressed, but especially where they are not:

| à | pègada | mòlhada |
| sòzinho | fàcilmente | |

The dieresis over unstressed *i* or *u* indicates that it does not form a diphthong with the preceding vowel:

| saïmento | saüdar |

But if the vowel should be stressed, use the acute—

| saída | saúde |

Use the dieresis also on the *u*, if followed by *e* or *i*, in combinations of *gu* and *qu* where the *u* is to be sounded—

| freqüência | agüentar | argüir |

WORDS THAT DO NOT TAKE THE WRITTEN ACCENT

(a) Unstressed monosyllabic and bisyllabic words:

o(s)	a(s)	lo(s)	la(s)	no(s)	na(s)
do(s)	da(s)	ao(s)	pelo(s)	pela(s)	polo(s)
pola(s)	me	mo(s)	ma(s)	te	to(s)
ta(s)	lhe(s)	nos	no-lo(s)	no-la(s)	vo-lo(s)
vo-la(s)	lho(s)	lha(s)	se	de	por
sem	sob	com	mas	que	porque

(b) Monosyllabic stressed words ending in *em* or *ens:*

bem	bens	tem	tens	cem

(c) Verbal forms ending in *am* or *em* where the penultimate is the prominent syllable:

louvam	louvem	contem (of the verb contar)

Also in bisyllabic and polysyllabic substantives ending in *em* or *ens* where the penultimate is the stressed syllable:

ordem	ordens	viagem	viagens	ferrugem	ferrugens

(d) Stressed monosyllabic words with a final *i* or *u*, whether or not followed by *s:*

vi(s)	cru(s)

(e) Stressed monosyllabic and bisyllabic words, and polysyllabic words terminating in a nasal vowel, diphthongs, whether or not followed by *s:*

lã(s)	maçã(s)	sai(s)	arrais	mau(s)	sarau(s)
som	sons	atum	atuns		

Also those followed by any other consonant where the stress is on the last syllable:

mar	der	ser	dor	mal	canal
painel	funil	farol	azul	cruz	Artur
mão(s)	verão	varões			

(f) Bisyllabic and polysyllabic words terminating in *a(s)*, *e(s)*, or *o(s)*, where the penultimate syllable is stressed:

casa(s)	camada(s)	camarada(s)	trave(s)	parede(s)
vicissitude(s)	desaire(s)	modo(s)	devoto(s)	lume(s)

This applies to a majority of Portuguese words, including most of the verbal forms:

louvo	louva(s)	louve(s)	louvava(s)
louvara(s)	louvaria(s)	louvare(s)	

(g) Bisyllabic and polysyllabic words, having the stress on the penultimate syllable, which end in *i* or *u*, whether or not followed by *s:*

juri(s)	quasi	tribu(s)	iris
Amarilis	oasis	Venus	onus

WORDS THAT TAKE THE WRITTEN ACCENT

(a) Those ending in *a*(*s*), *e*(*s*), or *o*(*s*) with stress on the last syllable:

pá(s)	sé(s)	vê(s)	mês	pó(s)
pôs	fará(s)	maré(s)	avó(s)	avô(s)
mercê(s)	alvará(s)	jacaré(s)	português	portaló(s)

(b) Bisyllabic and polysyllabic words with stress on the last syllable and ending in *i*(*s*) or *u*(*s*):

alí	aquí	escreví	tupí(s)	colibrí(s)	anís	funís (pl. of funil)
perú(s)		urubú(s)				

(c) Bisyllabic and polysyllabic words ending in *em* or *ens* with stress on the last syllable:

vintém	vinténs	armazém	armazéns
cecém	cecéns	contém	conténs (fr. verb
porém	Jerusalém	Belém	conter)

(d) Bisyllabic and polysyllabic words ending in a nasal vowel, diphthong, whether or not followed by *s*, or by any other consonant, with stress on the penultimate syllable:

órfã(s)	órfão(s)	louváveis	louváreis
fácil	fáceis	têxtil	tésteis
cônsul	sável	sáveis	cadáver
éter	mártir	sóror	alcáçar
Sófar	açúcar	gérmen	líquen
Félix	córtex	sílex	

(e) The diphthongs *éi*, *éu*, *ói*, with open *e* or *o* are always stressed:

réis	batéis [1]	véu(s)	chapéu(s)	sóis [2]
róis	herói(s)	jóia	gibóia	

(f) The *a* of the suffix *ámos* of the first person, plural of the preterit, to distinguish it from the first person, present:

louvámos (cf., louvamos=louvâmos).

(g) Monosyllabic and bisyllabic words stressed to distinguish them from other unstressed homographs:

quê	porquê	pôr [3]	pára [4]	péla
pélo	pêlo [5]	pólo [6]	pêra	

(h) All words stressed on the antepenult:

prática	ânimo	ânsia	férvido
gênero	gêmeo	gênio	pêssego
fêmea	concêntrico	tísico	tirocinio
fímbria	próximo	próprio	antimônio
lôbrego	brônzeo	úbere	lúgubre
único	núncio	cadáveres	árvore(s)
multíplice(s)	múltiplo(s)	quádruplo(s)	

Also the verbal forms stressed on the antepenult—

louvávamos	louváramos	louvaríamos	devíamos
devêramos	deveríamos	puníamos	puníramos
puniríamos	louvássemos	devêssemos	puníssemos
saíssemos	fizéssemos		

---

[1] Cf., reis, bateis.
[2] Cf., verb sois.
[3] Cf., *por*, a preposition.
[4] Cf., *para*, a preposition.
[5] Cf., *pelo, pela*, prepositions for the articles *lo, la.*
[6] Cf., *polo*, preposition for the article *lo.*

(*i*) Use the circumflex on the *e* and *o* when stress is on the penult, ending in *a*(*s*), *e*(*s*), or *o*(*s*), closed, as well as in those having the same spelling where the vowels are open:

Substantives		Verbs	
rêgo	rôσο	rego	rogo
Present		Preterit	
dêmos		demos	
Closed_____sêde		côrte côr	mêdo
Open_____sede		corte cor	medo

(*j*) Use the acute accent on stressed *i*, *e*, *o*, and *u* where they do not form a diphthong with the preceding vowel:

país	saída	faísca	Taígeto
saúde	balaústre	baú	

(*k*) Do not use the accent before *nh*, *nd*, and *mb*, nor before any consonant, except *s*, which does not begin a syllable:

bainha	ainda	Coimbra	juiz
ruim	paul	cair	sair

but

juízes	caíres	saíres

(*l*) Where *o*, *i*, or *u* do not form a diphthong with the preceding vowel and are unstressed use the dieresis instead of the acute:

saïmento	païsagem	saüdar	abaülado

(*m*) The dieresis is also used in the combinations *gu* and *qu*, where the *u* is to be sounded:

conseqüência	agüentar	argüir

But if the *u* is the predominant vowel, use the acute:

apazigúe

(*n*) Use the grave accent to indicate that the unstressed *a*, *e*, or *o* are open:

àquele(s)	àquela(s)	àparte (substantive)
aquele(s)	aquela(s)	aparte (verb)

Also in homographs where a vowel is mute:

prègar	pregar (de prego)
molhàda (de molho)	molhada (de molhar)

(*o*) To avoid mistakes in reading, the acute accent is replaced by the grave as follows:

1. In derivatives, whether augmentatives or diminutives, formed with the letter *z:*

má, màzinha, màzona	avó, avòzinha
órfã, òrfãzinha	anéis, anèizinhos

2. In those adverbs ending in *mente* in whose primary form the vowel carries the acute accent:

rápido, ràpidamente	benéfico, benèficamente
exótico, exòticamente	lícito, lìcitamente
último, ùltimamente	fácil, fàcilmente
só, sòmente	

but—

contraído, contraïdamente	miúdo, miüdamente

The circumflex designates the closed *e* and *o* and is used in monosyllabic, as well as bisyllabic and polysyllabic homographs; it is, however, omitted in *dor, poço* and *cera*, for example, since there are no such words as *dór* and *céra*, and the verb *posso* is spelled with the *ss* which distinguishes it from *poço.*

Cortês, cortêsmente	sêco, sêcamente
sôfrego, sôfregamente	cômico, cômicamente
cristã, cristãmente	vã, vãmente

Omit the written accent in homographs where there is no question as to the meaning; thus we use the circumflex on—

séco   sêca   lôgro

to distinguish them from the corresponding verbal forms—

seco   seca   logro

With the *e* or *o*, open, omit the written accent in the plural, as—

secos   logros

but retain it in *sêcas* to distinguish it from the verbal form *secas.*

Also use *vaidoso(s)*, *vaidosa(s)* without the accent on the penultimate syllable, even though the pronunciation is *vaidôso, vaidósos, vaidósa(s)*.

The open *o* in the plural of the different substantives is the same as the closed *o* in the singular:

tijolo (tijôlo)   tijolos (tijólos)

but—

trôco   trocos   troco (verb)

The words *espôso, espôsa(s)* take the written accent because of the verbal forms with the open *o, esposo, esposa(s)*, but the plural *esposos* does not take the accent because it is not a homograph.

Write *pôr* with the circumflex to distinguish it from the preposition *por*, but—

dispor   propor   expor

dispense with the written accent.

The circumflex is used on the *e* in the following because the stress is on the last syllable:

português   cortês   têm

In the following the written accent is omitted because the stress has passed from the last to the next to the last syllable:

portugeses   portuguesa(s)   corteses

The accent is placed on *árvore(s)* because stress is on the antepenultimate syllable; *arvore(s)* (verb) does not take it because stress is on the penultimate.

The imperfect and conditional verb forms, as

louvaria   deveria   puniria
louvava   devia   punia

take the accent if the stress is on the antepenult, as—

louvaríamos   louvávamos   deveríamos
devíamos   puniríamos

also on the penult of a form ending in a diphthong—

louváveis   louvaríeis   devíeis
deveríeis   puníeis   puniríeis

but—

saía   tê-lo-á

The accent is used in all persons of the imperfect tense:

saía   saías   saía   saíamos
saíeis   saíam

because the *i* does not form a diphthong with the preceding *a*.

Use the written accent in proper nouns under the same conditions as in common nouns:

Pôrto   pôrto (to distinguish it from the verb porto)
Setúbal   Pontével   Pedrógão   Antônio
Tomé   Nazaré   Belém   Águeda

Compound words retain their appropriate accents:

mãe-d'agua   pára-raios   pesa-papéis

RUMANIAN

Ą	a	*a* in far	J	j	*s* in measure
Ă	ă	*e* in her; also *ö*	K	k	*k,* only in foreign words
Â	â	*u* in cur	L	l	*l* in lemon
B	b	*b* in bell	M	m	*m* in member
C	c	*c* hard, but before *i* and	N	n	*n* in natural
		e as *ch* in chin, church;	O	o	*o* in horse
		before *h* like *k* in king	P	p	*p* in pantry
D	d	*d* in Delaware	R	r	*r* in remedy
E	e	*e* in hen; *ye*	S	s	*s* in sex
F	f	*f* in federal	Ş	ş	*sh* in shelf
G	ġ	*g* in gem before *e* and *i;*	T	t	*t* in ten
		g in get before *h;*	Ţ	ţ	*ts* in hats
		otherwise like *g* in	U	u	*oo* in wood; also *w*
		gate	V	v	*v* in value
H	h	Almost *kh*	X	x	*cs* in relics
I	i	*i* in machine	Y	y	Only in foreign words
Î	î	*u* in cur	Z	z	*z* in maze

This language sharply reflects the history of the Roumanian people. The basis of the language is a vulgate Latin, introduced by Trajan's legions when they occupied Dacia 101-107 A.D.

In the sixth century, however, the Slavs and Bulgarians made conquests, and their influence bore heavily upon the language, altering sounds, introducing novel forms, and in other ways affecting the composition and derivation of the vocabulary; thus the Latin *dis-* was displaced by the Slavonic *ragu-,* the negative *in-* by the corresponding Slavonic *ne-,* etc.

In later years, the Albanians, Byzantines, Hungarians, Poles, and Turks, peoples with whom they lived on friendly or hostile terms, also impregnated the language with word-forms from their own stock, so that the language acquired characteristics that distinguish it from the other Romance languages.

The orthography also has undergone a number of successive changes beginning with 1866, when the Roumanian Academy was first established. Other radical changes were made in 1869, 1879, 1881, 1895, and, finally, in 1904 the Academy abandoned the etymological principles based on Latin orthography and adopted the phonetic principles in use today.

Accentuation

Words ending in a single vowel receive the stress on the penult: *ma'mă* (mother), *părin'te* (male parent). Exceptions: Words ending in a diphthong or tripthong, or accented vowel: *gălbiniu'* [1] (yellowish), *gunoiu'* (rubbish), *cureà'* (strap), *hotărî* (conclude).

Words ending in one or more consonants have the stress on the ultima: *bolnav'* (ill), *pământ'* (earth). Exceptions: A number of words ending in *-ăt,* *-ec,* *-ic,* *-ed,* *-es,* *-et* and *-ot:* *su'net* (sound), *singura'tic* (solitary), etc.

Some words of Slavic or Latin origin retain their original antepenult stress: *prive'lişte* (view), *bise'rică* (church).

Nouns retain the stress on the same syllable throughout the declension: *ma'mă* (mother), *ma'melor* (to the mother), etc.

[1] The final *u* in a tripthong is silent.

Punctuation

Punctuation is practically the same as in English.

The apostrophe is used to show elision of the vowel in the words *nu* (not), *mă* (me), *să* (that), *intre* (in) when occurring before words beginning with a vowel: *m'aşteaptă* (wait for me), *intr'adevăr* (indeed), etc.

Syllabication

A consonant between vowels is joined to the vowel following: *că-la-re* (riding), *mi-nu-ne* (wonder).

Two consonants between vowels are divided, unless the second is *e* or *r*, in which case both are joined to the vowel following: *par-te* (portion), *pa-tru* (four).

Three consonants divide on the first: *cus-cru* (parent-in-law), *măn-dru* (proud). Diphthongs can not be divided: *impre-siune* (impression), not *impresi-une*.

Derivatives are divided into their component parts: *trans-scriere* (transcribing).

Phonetics

When stressed, *ă* becomes almost the German *ö*.

When unstressed before a vowel, *e* and also *i* are almost *y*, and in this position ase nearly mute after *c* (soft) and *g* (soft).

When unstressed before *a*, the *o* has almost the sound of *w*.

Article

The definite article takes the form of suffixes to the substantive: *-l*, *-ul*, and *-le* for masculine, and *-a* for the feminine.

The suffixes *-lui* (masculine) and *-ei* (feminine) indicate the genitive singular with the definite article.

Articles

The indefinite article is *o* (feminine), and *un* (masculine and neuter), in the singular number, and *unele* (feminine), and *unii* (masculine and neuter), plural. It precedes the substantive it modifies and is declined as shown in the table of the indefinite declension of nouns.

The definite article is a suffix to the noun or adjective modified: *-a* or *-ua* (feminine), and *l-* or *-l* (for the masculine and neuter gender when they terminate in *u* or a consonant, respectively), *-le* (for masculines terminating in *e*), for the singular, and *-le* (feminine and neuter), and *-i* (masculine) in the plural: *o lege*, a law; *legea*, the law; *un socru*, a father-in-law; *socrul*, the father-in-law; *un frate*, a brother; *fratele*, the brother. These endings are also inflected according to case, as shown in the table of the definite declension of nouns.

Nouns

Nouns are classed according to their termination and their natural gender.

All nouns ending in a consonant or in the vowel *u* denote males, names of peoples, mountains, months, winds, trees, and the letters of the alphabet are of masculine gender, otherwise, neuter.

Nouns ending in *a*, *ea*, *ă*, and *i* are feminine, except a few denoting males: *papă*, pope; *vlădică*, bishop; *popă*, priest; *tată*, father; *vodă*, prince; *agă*, commander.

Nouns ending in *e* may be either masculine, feminine, or neuter, and the dictionary must be used to ascertain which.

The plural of nouns is formed as follows:

Masculine nouns ending in a consonant add *i*; those ending in a vowel, drop the vowel and add *i*: *nepot*, nephew, *nepoti*; *socru*, *socri*; *popă*, *popi*; but nouns ending in *l* drop it as a rule before adding the *i*: *cal*, horse, *cai*; *copil*, child, *copii*.

Feminine nouns ending in *à* drop that and add *ale*: *basmà*, kerchief, *basmale*; those ending in *eà* drop the *à* and add *le*: *steà*, star, *stéle*; those ending in *ià* drop the *à* and add *ele*: *nuià*, rod, *nuiele*; those ending in *ă* drop that and add *e* or *i*, there being no simple rule as to whether it shall be *e* or *i*: *casă*, house, *case*; *vacà*, cow, *vaci*.

Neuter nouns terminating in a consonant add *e* or *uri*, again without a simple rule as to which, to form the plural; if ending in *u* this is dropped before adding the *e* or *uri*: *fruct*, fruit, *fructe*; *corp*, body, *corpuri*; *lucru*, work, *lucruri*. Neuters ending in *iu* change the *u* to *i* to form the plural: *studiu*, study, *studii*.

In addition to these, many nouns also take internal changes, such as changing the internal *a* to *ă* or *e*, the *d* to *z*, and the *t* to *ţ*: *rană*, wound, *răni*; *bandă*, band, *bende*; *vodă vozi*; *frate*, *fraţi*.

Other nouns form their plural irregularly and some have a double plural: *zi*, day, *zile*; *cap*, head, *capi* or *capete*.

Adjectives

Adjectives inflect as to gender, number, case, and degree, as shown in the following table:

English equivalent	Singular		Plural	
	Masculine	Feminine	Masculine	Feminine
Sour	acr*u*	acr*ă*	acr*i*	acr*e*
Old	vech*iu*	vech*ie*	vech*ii*	vech*ie*
Sweet	dulce	dulce	dulc*i*	dulce
Tiny	mitit*el*	bitit*ica*	mitit*eli*	mitit*ice*
Industrious	sili*tor*	sili*toare*	sili*tori*	sili*toare*
Good	bun	bun*ă*	bun*i*	bune
The good	bun*ul*	bun*a*	bun*ii*	bun*ele*
Of the good	a bun*ului*	a bun*ei*	a bun*ilor*	a|bun*elor*
To the good	bun*ului*	bun*ei*	bun*ilor*	bun*elor*
Better	*mai* bun	*mai* buna	*mai* buni	*mai* bune
Best	*cel mai* bun	*cel mai* bun*ă*	*cel mai* buni	*cel mai* bune

The following inflect irregularly as to gender: *Bad, rău (m), rea (f)*; difficult.
greu (m), grea (f); new, *nou (m), nouă (f)*.

The following phrases show the versatility in which adjectives may be used with nouns:

Un mare viteaz
A great hero

Ochi negri
Eyes black = Black eyes

Tot satul
Whole the country = The entire country

Satul   intreg
The country entire = The entire country

Cartea   cea nouă
The book the new = The new book

Unui·băiat sărac
To a boy poor = To a poor boy

Omului   leneş
To the man lazy = To the lazy man

Nouns

Nouns are inflected according to cases (of which there are 5: Nominative, genitive, dative, accusative, and vocative, whose functions are similar to the same in all modern languages), and according to declension, of which there are three. To the first declension belong all nouns terminating in *ă, à,* and *eà*; to the second, those ending in *u* or a consonant; to the third, those ending in *e*.

A declension may be either indefinite, if accompanied by the indefinite article, or definite, when it carries the definite terminations. The following table shows the indefinite declension of the nouns *mamă, socru,* and *nume,* name, being of the feminine, masculine, and neuter genders and of the first, second and third declensions, respectively. Note that the neuter noun takes the masculine article in the singular and the feminine in the plural.

Number and case	Mother	Father-in-law	Name
Singular:			
Nominative	o ma,mă	un socru	un nume
Genitive	a unei mame	a uni socru	a unui nume
Dative	unei mame	unui socru	unui nume
Accusative	o mamă	un socru	un nume
Vocative	o ma,mă	o socru!	o nume!
Plural:			
Nominative	unele mame	unii socri	unele nume
Genitive	a unor mame	a unor socri	a unelor nume
Dative	unor mame	unor socri	unelor nume
Accusative	unele ma,me	unii socri	unele nume
Vocative	mame!	socri!	nume!

The following table shows the definite inflection of nouns of the three declensions, including the various types embraced by each. As the nominative and accusative are always alike, as are also the genitive and dative, except that the former is preceded by the particle *a*, only the nominative and dative are given. The vocative, which sometimes takes the form of the nominative, at other times that of the dative, is indicated by an asterisk.

| | Singular | | Plural | |
	Nominative	Dative	Nominative	Dative
1st Declension:				
The mother	mamă*	mamei	mamele	mamelor*
father	tata*	tatălui	tații	tatilor*
priest	popa*	papei	popii	popilor[1]
kerchief	basmaua*	basmalei	basmalele	basmalelor*
star	steaua*	stelei	stelele	stelelor
2d Declension:				
father-in-law	socrul	socrului	socrii	socrilor*
youth	puiul[2]	puiului	puii	puilor*
boy	băiatul[2]	băiatului	băieții	băieților*
song	cântecul[2]	cântecului	cântecele	cantecelor*
song	focul[2]	focului	focurile	focurilor*
3d Declension:				
brother	fratele[2]	fratelui	frații	fraților*
law	legea[2]	legei	legile	legilor*
name	numele	numelui	numele	numelor

[1] The vocative plural is *popi*.
[2] The vocative singular is *socrule, puiule, băiete, cantecule, focule, frato, lege,* and *nume,* respectively.

Pronouns

The personal pronouns are inflected as follows:

| English | Nominative | Possessive [1] | | | | Dative | Accusative |
| | | Singular | | Plural | | | |
		Masculine	Feminine	Masculine	Feminine		
I	eu	(al) meu	(a) mea	(ai) mei	(ale) mele	mie, mi, imi	pe mine, mă
Thou (you)	tu	(al) tău	(a) ta	(ai) tăi	(ale) tale	ție, ți, iți	pe tine, te
He	el	(al) său, lui	—	(ai) răi, lui	—	lui, î, ii	pe el, 'l
She	ea	—	(a) sa, ei	—	(ale) sale, ei	ei, ii	pe ea, o
We	noi	(al) nostru	(a) noastra	(ai) noștri	(ale) noastre	nouă, ne, ni	pe noi ne
You	voi	(al) vostru	(a) voustră	(ai) voștri	(ale) vostre	vouă, vă, vi	pe voi, vă
They (*m*)	ei }	(al) lor	(a) lor	(ai) lor	(ale) lor	{ lor, le	pe ei, îi
They (*f*)	ele }					{ le, li	pe ele, le
Self	—	—	—	—	—	sie, își, și	pe sine, se

[1] Possessive pronouns may also be used as adjectives, when they drop the *al, a, ai,* or *ale* and agree with the noun in gender and number.

The personal pronouns of respect are formed by the word *Dumnia* (abbreviated D-), followed by the proper possessive adjective: *Dumnia-ta* (D-ta), you; *Dumnia-lui* (D-lui), he; *Dumnia-lor* (D-lor), they, etc.

The following table gives the inflections of the demonstratives:

	Nominative and accusative				Genitive and dative			
	Singular		Plural		Singular		Plural	
	Masculine	Feminine	Masculine	Feminine	Masculine	Feminine	Masculine	Feminine
This	acest¹	acestă	aceşti	aceste	acestui	acestei	acestor	acestor
	acesta²	aceasta	aceştia	acestea	acestuia	acesteia	acestora	acestora
	ăst³	astă	ăşti	aste	ăstui	ăştii	ăstor	ăstor
	ăsta⁴	asta	ăştia	astea	ăstuia	ăştiia	ăstora	ăstora
That	acel¹	acea	acei	acele	acelui	acelei	acelor	acelor
	acela²	aceea	aceeia	acelea	aceluia	acelei	acelora	acelora
	ăl³	a	ăi	ale	ălui	alei(ăi)	ălor	ălor
	ăla⁴	aia	ăia	alea	ăluia	aleia(ăia)	ălora	ălora

¹ Literary form used before the noun.
² Literary form used after the noun.
³ Colloquial form used before the noun.
⁴ Colloquial form used after the noun.

Verbs

The following table gives the conjugation of the auxiliary verbs a aveà, to have, a fi, to be, and the terminations of the four regular conjugations: a jurà, to swear; a taceà, to be silent; a bate, to beat; a fugi to run:

Infinitive	a aveà	a fî	-à	-eà	-e	-ì
Present participle	având	fiind	-ând	-ând	-ănd	-ind
Past participle	avut	fost	-at	-ut	-ut	-it
Present indicative¹	am	sânt, (sunt, îs, -s)	(¹)	(¹)	(¹)	(¹)
	ai	eşti	-i	-i	-i	-i
	are	este (e, îi, -i)	-ă	-e	-e	-e
	avem	sântem (suntem)	-am	-em	-em	-im
	aveţi	sânteţi (sunteţi)	-aţi	-eţi	-eţi	-iţi
	au	sânt (sunt, îs, -s)	-à	—	—	—
Imperfect²	aveam	eram	-am	-eam	-eam	-iam³
	aveai	erai	-ai	-eai	-eai	-iai
	aveà	erà	-à	-eà	-eà	-ià
	aveam	eram	-ăm	-eam	-eam	-iam
	aveaţi	eraţi	-aţi	-eaţi	-eaţi	-iaţi
	aveau	erau	-au	-eau	-eau	-iau
Preterite²	avui	fui	-ai	-ui	-ui	-ii
	avuşi	fuşi	-aşi	-uşi	-uşi	-işi
	avù	fù	-ă*	-ù	-ù	-ì
	avurăm	furăm	-arăm	-urăm	-urăm	-irăm
	avurăti	furăţi	-arăţi	-urăţi	-urăţi	-irăţi
	avură	fură	-ară	-ură	-ură	-iră
Past indefinite⁴	am, ai, etc avut	am, ai, etc. fost	am, etc. -at	am, etc. -ut	am, etc. -ut	am, etc. -it
Pluperfect⁵	avusem*	fusem*	-asem	-usem	-usem	-isem
	avuseşi	fuseşi	-aseşi	-useşi	-useşi	-iseşi
	avuse	fuse	-ase	-use	-use	-ise
	avusem	fusem	-asem	-usem	-usem	-isem
	avuseţi	fuseţi	-aseţi	-useţi	-useţi	-iseţi
	avuse	fuse	-ase(ră)	-use (ră)	-use(ră)	-ise
Future	voiu, vei, va, vom, veţi, vor } aveà	fi	-à	-eà	-e	-i

Future perfect	voiu, etc. avut	fi	-at	-ut	-ut	-it
Present subjunctive	ca să { am ai aibă avem aveți aibă	fiu fi fie fim fiți fie	— -i -e -ăm -ați -e	— -i -ă -em -eți -ă	— -i -ă -em -eți -ă	— -i -ă -im -iți -ă

Perfect subjunctive[6]	ca să fi avut	fost	-at	-ut	-ut	-it
Present conditional	aș ai ar am } aveà ați ar	fi	-à	-eà	-e	-ì
Perfect conditional	aș, etc. fi avut	fost	-at	-ut	-ut	-it
Imperative	aibi (să) aibi (să) avem aveți (să) aiba	fi (să) fie (să) fim fiți (să) fie	-ă (să) -e (să) -ăm -ați (să) -e	-i (să) -a (să) -em -eți (să) -ă	-e (să) -ă (să) -em -eți (să) -ă	-i (să) -ă (să) -im -iți (să) -ă

* For all persons.
[1] The present indicative may also be translated by the English present or personal progressive.
[2] I had, I was, I swore, etc.
[3] This has a variant form : *fugeam, fugeai,* etc.
[4] Translated as I have had, have been, have sworn, etc. Notice that this tense is not compounded and also has variant forms : *cruscsem, fuscscm,* etc.
[5] Translated as I had had, etc. Notice that this tense is not compounded and also has variant forms : *avusesem, fuscsem,* etc.

The passive voice takes the auxiliary *a fi,* to be, in its various tenses, followed by the past participle: *sânt laudat,* I am praised; *eram laudat,* I was praised; *fii laudat,* be praised, etc. The passive conditionals and subjunctives are the same as their respective active forms.

There are also many irregular verbs, such as:

Those that add *-ez* or *-eaz-* to the terminations of the present indicative, subjunctive, and imperative: lucr*ez*, lucr*ezi*, lucr*ează*, I work, thou workest, he works.

Those adding *u* in the first person singular, and *i* in the second person singular, present indicative and subjunctive, the stems ending in *bl, fl, pl, rl* and *tl*: afl*u*, I find; afl*i*, thou findest.

Those adding short *u* in the first person singular indicative and subjunctive, the stems ending in a vowel: da*u*, I give; scri*u*, I write.

Those ending in *-esc, -eşti, -eşte* in all persons of the singular and the third person plural, respectively, which includes many verbs belonging to the fourth conjugation: priv*esc*, I look; priv*eşti*, thou lookest, etc.

Those whose past participles take *-s* or *-t* instead of *-ut*, belonging to the third conjugation whose preterite ends in *-sei* instead of *-ui*: ales*ci*, I chose; ale*s*, chosen; spar*sei*, I broke; spar*t*, broken.

Adverbs

Adverbs may be formed from adjectives, nouns, and verbs by replacing the terminations of the various parts of speech and adding those of the adverbs. The following table illustrates their formation, including the comparative and superlative degrees:

English	Rumanian equivalent	Adverbial forms		
		Positive	Comparative	Superlative
Rumanian	românesc	românește	—	—
Princely	domnesc	tomnește	mai domnește	foarte domnește
Insane	nubunesc	nebunește	mai nebunește	foarte nebunește
Cross	csuce	cruciș	mai crucis	foarte cruciș
To steal	a furà	furiș (fur-tively)	mai furiș	foarte fnriș
But—				
Darkness	beznă	—	—	—
Pitch dark	—	întunerec bezna		

Cardinal numbers

un, unul, una	one	nouă	nine
doui, două	two	zece	'ten
trei	three	unsprezece	eleven
patru	four	douăsprezece	twelve
cinci	five	doisprezece	thirteen
șase	six	treisprezece	twenty
șapte, șeapte	seven	douăzeci	hundred
opt	eight	sutǎ	thousand
		mie	

Ordinal numbers

întâiu	first	nouălea	ninth
doilea	second	zecelea	tenth
treilea	third	unsprezecelea	eleventh
patrulea	fourth	doisprezecelea	twelfth
cincilea	fifth	treisprezecelea	thirteenth
șaselea	sixth	douăzecilea	twentieth
șaptelea	seventh	sutelea	hundredth
optulea	eighth	mielea	thousandth

Months

ianuarie	January	iulie	July
februarie	February	august	August
martie	March	septembrie	September
aprilie	April	octombrie	October
mai	May	noembrie	November
iunie	June	decembrie	December

Days

duminecă	Sunday	joi	Thursday
luni	Monday	vineri	Friday
marți	Tuesday	sâmbâtă	Saturday
miercuri	Wednesday		

Seasons

primăvară	spring	toamnă	autumn
vară	summer	iarnă	winter

Time

oră } ceas }	hour	săptămână	week
		lună	month
zi	day	an	year

Articles to be disregarded in filing

un, o　　　　　　lu, le, lu, oa, i

RUNES

	Nordic		Old Germanic	
Name	Char-acter	Transliteration	Char-acter	Transliteration
Fê	ᚠ	*f*	ᚠ	*f*
Ûr	ᚢ	*oo*	ᚢ	*oo*
Thurs, Thorn	ᚦ	*th* [1]	ᚦ	*th* [2]
Ôs	ᚨ	*o*	ᚨ	*a* in father
Reith	R	*r*	R R	*r*
Kaun	ᚴ	*k, g,* hard	ᚲ	*k*
			ᚷ	*g*
			ᛈ ᛈ	*w*
Hagal	ᚼ ᚻ ᚺ	*h*	ᚺ ᚻ	*h*
Nauth	ᚾ ᚿ	*n*	ᚾ ᚾ	*n*
Îs	ᛁ	*e*	ᛁ	*e*
Âr	ᛆ ᛅ	*a* in father	ᛋ	*y*
Ŷr	ᛣ	*r*	ᛉ	
			ᛃ	*ts* [3]
Sôl	ᛍ	*s*	ᛋ ᛉ	*s* [4]
Týr	ᛏ ᛐ	*t, d*	ᛏ	*t*
Bjarkan	ᛒ	*b, p*	ᛒ	*b*
			ᛗ	*a* in way
Mathr	ᛉ	*m*	ᛗ	*m*
Lögr	ᛚ	*l*	ᛚ	*l*
			◊ ◇	*ng* in singe
			ᛗ	*d*
			ᛦ	*o*

[1] As *th* in thing; also *th* in there.   [3] Soft *s*.
[2] Labial *th*.   [4] Hard *s*.

As the Nordic alphabet has only 16 characters, kaun, týr, and bjarkan each have two sounds.

The runes, the earliest form of Teutonic writing, are believed to have come originally from southeastern Europe as they exhibit Gothic influence. They were, therefore, in contact with both Greek and Latin culture, and it is believed they had their origin in one of these classical alphabets, or possibly both. They have the same signs for the vowels *a*, *e*, and *o*, and the runes for *f*, *h*, and *r* are clearly taken from the Latin alphabet. They may, possibly, have come via some late Northern Etruscan alphabet, most of whose letters came from the Latin. In this connection, it is interesting to note the possible influence of the runes in the formation of the Cyrillic alphabet.

The original runes found in western Europe consisted of 24 letters divided in groups (*oett*) of 8. The first evidences of them are found in Denmark and date from the 3d century. They flourished all through the Anglo-Saxon period in England, for five centuries, but there they varied somewhat from the continental alphabet. From Denmark they were introduced into Sweden at the beginning of the 11th century and there they continued in use for centuries, in fact in some remote districts almost up to the present day.

The relics found consist mainly of inscriptions on monuments, weapons and ornaments.

RUSSIAN

А	а	𝒜 a	a	a in far
Б	б	ℬ б	b	b in bed
В	в	ℬ в	v	v in vague
Г	г	𝒯	g (h)	g in gay [5]
Д	д	𝒟 д	d	d in day
Е	е	ℰ е	e, ĩe	ye in yell
Ж	ж	ℳ ж	zh	z in azure
З	з	ℨ з	z	z in zeal
И [12]	и	𝒰 и	i	i in machine
I [13]	i	𝒥 i	i	i in élite
Й [4]	й	й	ĭ	y in boy
К	к	𝒦 к	k	k in kite
Л	л	ℒ л	l	l in long
М	м	ℳ м	m	m in man
Н	н	𝒩 н	n	n in no
О	о	𝒪 о	o	o in mother
П	п	𝒫 п	p	p in pay
Р	р	𝒫 р	r	r in error
С	с	𝒞 с	s	s in say
Т	т	𝒯 т m̄	t	t in tea
У	у	𝒴 у	u	oo in boot
Ф	ф	𝒻 ф	f	f in fold
Х	х	𝒳 х	kh	kh (as German ch)
Ц	ц	𝒰 ц	t͡s	ts in hoots
Ч	ч	𝒞 ч	ch	ch in church
Ш	ш	𝒰 ш ш	sh	sh in shawl
Щ	щ	𝒰 щ	shch	shch, somewhat like sti in Christian
Ъ [1]	ъ [67]	ъ		Mute
Ы	ы	ы	y	y in nymph
Ь [89]	ь	ь	'	Mute
Ѣ [1]	ѣ	ℬ ѣ	ĩe	ye in yea
Э	э	𝒟 э	ė	e in Emma
Ю	ю	𝒥𝒪 ю	ĩu	u in union
Я	я	𝒥 я	ĩa	ya in yard
Ѳ [1]	ѳ	𝒪 ѳ	f	ph in philosophy
Ѵ [10]	ѵ	𝒱 ѵ	ẏ	y in rhythm

[1] See "Reformed orthography."
[2] Vos'merichnoe.
[3] Desĩaterichnoe (s tochkoĭ).
[4] S kratkoĭ (kratkoe).
[5] Used also in place of Latin h.
[6] Tverdyĭ znak.
[7] Indicates that preceding consonant is hard.
[8] Mĩagkiĭ znak.
[9] Indicates that preceding consonant is soft.
[10] Now replaced by и.

The Russians use the Cyrillic alphabet, which has been modified so that it bears some resemblance to the Latin alphabet.

Russian, or, more precisely, Great Russian, belongs to the eastern group of the Slavonian subfamily of languages. It is the chief literary language of Russia, with records dating to the tenth or eleventh century. It is a highly inflected language, and its most curious mechanism—and this is true to a certain extent of all Slavonic languages—is the so-called "aspects" of its verbs, by means of which not only the shades of most of our compound tenses, which are lacking in Russian, but also a variety of other shades of meaning—shades which even English is incapable of conveying—are tersely expressed. The Moscow dialect, which combines some of the northern or o-group and some of the southern or a-group characteristics, is the foundation of the literary tongue. ·

Punctuation and capitalization

Punctuation is very similar to the English usage. In regard to capitalization, it follows the French style.

The letters б, в, г, д, ж, and з, when terminating a word are often transliterated by English p, ff, k, t, sh, and s, respectively. (See note 4, under "Phonetics.")

Syllabication

1. A single vowel, with or without one or more consonants, constitutes a syllable.

2. Where a vowel is followed by but one consonant, the syllable ends on the vowel, the consonant beginning the next syllable. Example: ца-ри-ца.

3. Where a vowel is followed by more than one consonant, the syllable ends with the first consonant. Example: зав-тра; сол-дат.

4. The semiconsonants ъ, ь, and й, when they occur within a word, terminate a syllable.

5. The prepositional prefixes без, до, пере, вы, на, не, от, за, пре, чрез, раз, and воз must remain intact.

6. The consonant combinations ств, ст, стр, бл, вл, мл, пл must not be separated.

7. Where two or more words are used to form a compound, divide so as to keep each component part intact.

Transliteration

The Russian language being phonetic, transliteration is simply a matter of substituting the proper English values for the respective Russian letters, as Полтава = Poltava.

The following important points should, however, be carefully observed:

1. ъ and ь are mute and indicate only that the consonant preceding such letter is, respectively, hard or soft.

    былъ = byl = he was.

    быль = byl' = a tale.

Note.—The apostrophe (') is used to indicate the soft consonant.

2. ѣ and е are to be transliterated by e only when hard, by îe when soft:

    весь = ves' = all.

    поле = polîe = field.

    ѣмъ = îem = I eat.

Phonetics

The characters of the alphabet are sounded as indicated in the table; however, the following additional remarks should be noted:

1. The letter e occurs also as ё, used only when the syllable is accented, in which case its sound is that of yo in yolk.

2. The letter й is employed to form diphthongs only: ай, яй, sounded like i in mine; ей, ѣй, like ey in grey; ій, ый, like ey in key; ой, ёй, like oy in toy; and уй, юй, like ui in bruin.

3. The letter г before к, т, or ч is sounded somewhat like ch in loch. мягкій (miachkey), soft. In the genitive endings—aro, ero, oro, яго—the г is pronounced like v: кого (kovo), whose.

4. The voiced consonants (б, в, г, д, ж, з), when final, are pronounced unvoiced, i.e., like English p, ff, k, t, sh, s, respectively: Литвинов (Litvinoff).

Accentuation

Tonal stress, or syllabic accentuation, must remain in general, a puzzling problem to the student of Russian. No definite simple rule has been formulated whether to place stress either on the root word or on any of its inflected forms.

Articles

There are no definite or indefinite articles, as such, in Russian. The equivalent idea must be grasped from the context.

The copula

The copulas, like the English "am", "is", "are", are not used, e.g., the expression онъ солдатъ means he [is a] soldier.

Genders

Russian has three genders: Masculine (nouns terminating in ъ, ь, й), feminine (nouns terminating in а, я, ь), neuter (nouns terminating in о, е, мя). However, all male living beings, whatever their ending, are masculine and female living beings are likewise always feminine in gender, though they decline according to their terminational classification. An analogy of this may be found in Latin (*poeta*, a masculine noun though feminine in declension).

Nouns

The noun declines in six cases: Nominative (like English subjective); genitive (English possessive); dative (indirect object, after prepositions къ, to, по, on), accusative (direct object); instrumental (denoting means by which, and after prepositions надъ, on, подъ, under, etc.); locative (denoting place in which, after prepositions въ, in, на, on, etc.). There are two numbers and three declensions. The following table indicates the terminal inflections of nouns in their various cases and declensions:

Representative noun (rule indicates stem)	First declension				Second declension		Third declension	
	Masculine		Neuter		Feminine		Feminine	Neuter
	Hard	Soft	Hard	Soft	Hard	Soft		
	зубъ (tooth)	конь (horse) бой (battle)	село (village)	море (sea)	рыба (fish)	пуля (bullet)	кость (bone)	имя (name,
SINGULAR								
Nominative	ъ	ь, й	о	е	а	я	ь	мя
Genitive [1]	а	я	а	я	ы	и	и	мени
Dative	у	ю	у	ю	ѣ	ѣ	и	мени
Accusative	(²)	(²)	о	е	у	ю	ь	мя
Instrumental	омъ	емъ	омъ	емъ	ою	ею	і̇ю	менемъ
Locative	ѣ	ѣ	ѣ	ѣ	ѣ	ѣ	и	мени
PLURAL								
Nominative	ы	и	а	я	ы	и	и	мена
Genitive	овъ	евъ, ей	ъ	ей	ъ	ь, ей	ей	мёнъ
Dative	амъ	ямъ	амъ	ямъ	амъ	ямъ	ямъ	менамъ
Accusative	(²)	(²)	а	я	(²)	(²)	и	мена
Instrumental	ами	ями	ами	ями	ами	ями	ьми	менами
Locative	ахъ	яхъ	ахъ	яхъ	ахъ	яхъ	яхъ	менахъ

[1] The genitive, in addition to showing possession, is used to express direct object if the verb is negative. This case is also governed by many prepositions, such as безъ (without), отъ (from, etc.)

[2] If treating of an animate object, the accusative is identical with the genitive; if inanimate it is the same as the nominative.

Adjectives

Attributive adjectives are fully declinable and agree with their nouns in gender, number, and case:

Gender	Singular			Plural		
	Masculine	Feminine	Neuter	Masculine	Feminine	Neuter
Nominative	ый, ій, ой,	ая, яя	ое, ее	ые, іе	ыя, ія	ыя, ія
Genitive	a(о,я)го	ой, ей	ое, ее	ы(и)хъ	ы(и)хъ	ы(и)хъ
Dative	о(е)му	ой, ей	о(е)му	ы(и)мъ	ы(и)мъ	ы(и)мъ
Accusative	(¹)	ую, юю	ое, ее	(¹)	(¹)	ыя, ія
Instrumental	ы(и)мъ	ой, ей	ы(и)мъ	ы(и)ми	ы(и)ми	ы(и)ми
Locative	о(е)мъ	ой, ей	о(е)мъ	ы(и)хъ	ы(и)хъ	ы(и)хъ

¹ See footnote 2, under preceding table.

Adjectives used predicatively are indeclinable and usually have a shortened form.

The comparative of adjectives is formed by adding to the stem ѣе (ѣй, е) and is indeclinable. The superlative is formed by adding to the stem ѣйшій (айшій, шій) and is declinable as a regular adjective.

Pronouns

The personal and reflexive pronouns are declined as follows:

	Nominative	Genitive	Dative	Accusative	Instrumental	Locative
I	я	меня	мнѣ	меня	мною(й)	мнѣ
Thou	ты	тебя	тебѣ	тебя	тобою(й)	тебѣ
He	онъ	его	ему	его	имъ	ёмъ
She	она	ея	ей	её	ею	ей
It	оно	его	ему	его	имъ	ёмъ
We	мы	насъ	намъ	насъ	нами	насъ
You	вы	васъ	вамъ	васъ	вами	васъ
They	они(ѣ)	ихъ	имъ	ихъ	ими	ихъ
Self ¹	—	себя	себѣ	себя	собою(й)	себѣ

¹ For all persons and genders, singular or plural; this form is translatable, as myself, thyself, himself, ourselves, etc.

The pronominal adjectives and intensive pronoun самъ (self) are declinable like adjectives.

Russian appellatives

Russians have three names: The Christian name (имя), the patronymic, i.e., the father's name (отчество), and the family name (фамилія): Лёвъ Николаевичъ Толстой, (Lyoff Nikolaevich Tolstoy), the middle name meaning the son of Nicholas.

These patronymics end in -овичъ (-евичъ), for the masculine and -овна (-евна) for the feminine.

Family names ending in юй, ой, ій in the masculine change to ая in the feminine, and those terminating in ъ, to а, e.g., Петровъ (masculine), Петрова (feminine).

When relationship is not distant, Russians address each other by the Christian name and patronymic only.

Verbs

The conjugation of the Russian verb inflects according to: (a) person (of which there are three), (b) number (of which there are two), (c) gender (masculine, feminine, neuter, occurring in past tense and participles only), (d) tense (present past, future), (e) mood (infinitive, indicative, conditional, imperative, and participle), (f) voice (active, passive, reflexive, and reciprocal), and (g) aspect (imperfective and perfective with subaspects into abstract, concrete, instantaneous, iterative, causative, inceptive, and diminutive.

In the following table the inflection is indicated by underscoring.

Inflections of verb

	Russian form	English equivalent	Explanation
Infinitive (present)	жела́ть нести́	to wish to carry	The past and future infinitives are expressed by various aspects or the participle
Gerund	жела́ніе	the wishing (wish)	A verbal noun, declinable in the neuter gender
Present gerundive	жела́я	wishing	Like indeclinable adjectives; modify the subject only
Past gerundive	жела́въ (вши)	having wished	
Present participle active	жела́ющій	the wishing (the one who wishes)	
Past participle active	жела́вшій	the afore-wishing (the one who wished or had wished)	Declined like adjectives in case, gender, and number; modify a noun or are used substantively
Present participle passive	жела́емый	the wished-for (at present)	
Past participle passive	жела́нный	the wished-for (in the past)	
Present indicative	жела́ю, ешь, етъ, емъ, ете, ютъ	I, thou, he (she, it), we, you, they wish	The flection vowel varies according to conjugation
Past indicative	жела́лъ, ла, ло, ли	I, thou, he (she, it), we, you, they wished	лъ m. singular ла f. singular ло n. singular
Future indicative	бу́ду, ешь, етъ, емъ, ете, утъ жела́ть	I, thou, he (she, it), we, you, they will (shall) wish	Formed by the present of "to be" plus infinitive.
Imperative	жела́й жела́йте	wish (thou) wish (you)	
Passive voice	я люби́мъ, былъ, буду люби́мъ	I am loved, was, shall be loved	Inflects as to gender, number, and tense
Reflexive	мы́ться,	to wash oneself	Conjugated like transitive indicative plus ся or сь
Reciprocal	встрѣ́чаться	to meet each other	
Aspects			
Imperfective: Abstract	пла́вать	to swim (in general)	Verbal idea as a fact
Concrete	плы́ть	to swim (at the instant)	Verbal idea as an act
Inceptive	слабѣ́ть	to become ill	Intransitive
Causative	слаби́ть	to render ill	Transitive
Iterative	попи́сывать	to write from time to time	From писа́ть (to write)
Perfective: Instantaneous	написа́ть напишу́ написа́лъ	to have written I shall have written I wrote (had written)	Perfectives have no present tense
Inceptive	записа́ть	to write in (down)	
Diminutive } Depreciatory }	попи́сать	to write a little (or scribble a little)	

Adverb

The adverbs may be formed from adjectives, and inflect as follows:

сильны̄й	strong	сильнѣйше	most strongly
сильно	strongly	русскій	Russian
сильнѣе	more strongly	по русски	(in) Russian

ORGANIZATION OF THE UNION OF SOVIET SOCIALIST REPUBLICS (U.S.S.R.)

POPULATION AND GEOGRAPHY

The Union of Soviet Socialist Republics is made up of 16 Union (or Constituent) Republics, 16 Autonomous Republics, 9 Autonomous Regions and 10 National Areas. It covers an area of 8,597,100 square miles, and has an estimated population of 196,800,000.

Constituent Republics	Population*	Area (square miles)	Capital
1. Russian Soviet Federated Socialist Republic	112,800,000	6,531,900	Moscow
2. Ukrainian Soviet Socialist Republic	40,800,000	222,000	Kiev
3. Belorussian Soviet Socialist Republic	9,300,000	80,100	Minsk
4. Uzbek Soviet Socialist Republic	6,000,000	157,300	Tashkent
5. Kazakh Soviet Socialist Republic	6,000,000	1,003,000	Alma-Ata
6. Georgian Soviet Socialist Republic	3,600,000	29,000	Tbilisi
7. Azerbaidzhan Soviet Socialist Republic	3,300,000	33,000	Baku
8. Lithuanian Soviet Socialist Republic	3,000,000	25,100	Vilnius
9. Moldavian Soviet Socialist Republic	2,700,000	13,000	Kishinev
10. Latvian Soviet Socialist Republic	2,100,000	24,900	Riga
11. Kirgiz Soviet Socialist Republic	1,500,000	76,000	Frunze
12. Tadzhik Soviet Socialist Republic	1,500,000	55,000	Stalinabad
13. Armenian Soviet Socialist Republic	1,200,000	12,500	Erevan
14. Turkmen Soviet Socialist Republic	1,200,000	187,100	Ashkhabad
15. Estonian Soviet Socialist Republic	1,200,000	17,400	Tallin
16. Karelo-Finnish Soviet Socialist Republic	600,000	68,900	Petrozavodsk

*Estimated on basis of 1946 USSR election figures.

Cardinal numbers

одинъ, одна, одно *m., f., n.*	one	двѣнадцать	twelve
		тринадцать	thirteen
два, двѣ *m. & n., f.*	two	четырнадцать	fourteen
три	three	пятнадцать	fifteen
четыре	four	шестнадцать	sixteen
пять	five	семнадцать	seventeen
шесть	six	восемнадцать	eighteen
семь	seven	девятнадцать	nineteen
восемь	eight	двадцать	twenty
девять	nine	двадцать одинъ	twenty-one
десять	ten	сто	hundred
одиннадцать	eleven	тысяча	thousand

Ordinal numbers

первый [1]	first	седьмой	seventh
второй	second	восьмой	eighth
третій	third	девятый	ninth
четвёртый	fourth	десятый	tenth
пятый	fifth	одиннадцатый	eleventh
шестой	sixth	двѣнадцатый	twelfth

[1] The ordinal numbers here given are of the masculine gender. To convert them to feminine or neuter, it is only necessary to effect the proper gender changes: For the feminine change ый to ая, ій to ья, ой to ая. For the neuter change ый to ое, ій to ье, and ой to ое.

Ordinal numbers—Continued

тринадцатый	thirteenth	девятнадцатый	nineteenth
четырнадцатый	fourteenth	двадцатый	twentieth
щятнадцатый	fifteenth	двадцать первый	twenty-first
пестнадцатый	sixteenth	сотый	hundredth
семнадцатый	seventeenth	тысячный	thousandth
восемнадцатый	eighteenth		

Months

Январь (Янв.)	January	Іюль	July
Февраль (Февр.)	February	Августъ (Авг.)	August
Мартъ	March	Сентябрь (Сент.)	September
Апрѣль (Апр.)	April	Октябрь (Окт.)	October
Май	May	Ноябрь	November
Іюнь	June	Декабрь (Дек.)	December

Days

Воскресенье	Sunday	Четвергъ	Thursday
Понедѣльникъ	Monday	Пятница	Friday
Вторникъ	Tuesday	Суббота	Saturday
Среда	Wednesday		

Seasons

весна	spring	осень	autumn
лѣто	summer	зима	winter

Time

часъ	hour	мѣсяцъ	month
день	day	годъ	year
недѣля	week		

REFORMED ORTHOGRAPHY AND GRAMMAR

The movement to reform the Russian orthography and grammar had its origin long before the Revolution. It was sponsored by many of the scientific and scholastic academies and institutions of the Empire, but resulted in no official action until after the Revolution. The old style is presented in this Manual, however, because of the great number of the old works that are still extant. The student will bear in mind the various changes given below when dealing with present-day literature.

By the decree of the Council of the People's Commissars of October 10, 1918, relating to the introduction of the new orthography (Collection of Laws and Decrees of the Workers' and Peasants' Government no. 74, of October 17, 1918, item 804) all governmental publications, periodicals (newspapers and magazines) and nonperiodical publications (learned works, collections, etc.), and all documents and legal papers must, beginning with October 15, 1918, be printed according to the new rules of spelling given below. This spelling has also been introduced in all schools.

1. Replace the letter ѣ by е (колено, вера, семя, в избе). (Cf. nos. 9, 10.)
2. Replace the letter ѳ everywhere by ф (Фома, Афанасий, кафедра).
3. Drop the letter ъ at the end of words and parts of compound words (хлеб, посол, меч, контр-адмирал), but retain it in the middle of words as a sign of division (съемка, разъяснять, адъютант).

Note.—The apostrophe (') in the middle of words is also used instead of ъ.
4. Replace the letter i everywhere by и (учение, Россия, пиявка, Иоанн, высокий).
5. Write prefixes из, воз, вз, раз, роз, низ, без, чрез, через before vowels and hard consonants with з but replace з before mute consonants (к, п, т, х, ц, ч, ш, щ, ф) also before с (расставаться, чрессельник, беспокойство, чересполосица).

Note.—This rule differs from the old one in that the prefixes без, роз, чрез, через were also added to this group and that з is now replaced by с before с.
6. In the genitive case of adjectives, participial adjectives, and pronouns of masculine gender write oro, ero instead of aro, яro (доброго, пятого, которого, синего).

Note.—Adjectives whose roots end in ж, ч, ш, щ, have in the genitive case ero instead of oro (высшего, текущего, свежего, кипучего).

7. In the nominative and accusative plural of feminine and neuter adjectives, participial adjectives, and pronouns write ые, ие instead of ыя, iя (добрые, старые, синие, какие). (Cf. no. 4.)

8. Use они instead of онѣ in the feminine nominative plural.

9. Write in the feminine одни, одних, одними instead of однѣ, однѣх, однѣми.

10. Use ее instead of ея in the feminine genitive singular personal pronoun.

NOTE.—In connection with the discontinuance of ѣ, the letter ё is sometimes used to designate the fluctuating e sound (ёлка, всё).

11. Of all the rules on syllabication only the following are retained: When dividing words a consonant (one or the last in a group of consonants) immediately preceding a vowel must not be separated from this vowel; likewise a group of consonants at the beginning of a word must not be separated from a vowel; the letter й before a consonant must not be separated from the preceding vowel; also a final consonant, final й, and a group of consonants at the end of words must not be separated from the preceding vowel. In dividing words having prefixes, a consonant at the end of the prefix, if preceding another consonant, is not to be carried over to the next line.

SAMARITAN

Name	Character	Transliteration and tone value	Name	Character	Transliteration and tone value
Aleph	𐤀	—, '	Lamedh	𐤋	*l*
Beth	𐤁	*b, bh*	Mem	𐤌	*m*
Gimel	𐤂	*g, gh*	Nun	𐤍	*n*
Daleth	𐤃	*d, dh*	Samekh	𐤎	*s*
Heh	𐤄	*h*	Ayin	𐤏	‘
Vau	𐤅	*v, w*	Pe	𐤐	*p, ph*
Zayin	𐤆	*z,* soft *s*	Sadhe	𐤑	*ṣ, s* sharp
Cheth	𐤇	*ḥ, ch*	Koph	𐤒	*q, k*
Teth	𐤈	*ṭ*	Resh	𐤓	*r*
Yod	𐤉	*j*	Shin	𐤔	*š, sh*
Caph	𐤊	*k, kh*	Tav	𐤕	*t, th*

This language is a dialect of the Aramaic of Palestine, the best examples of which are found in the literature belonging to the 4th century A.D., in which the alphabet derived from the old Hebrew was used. This had been used by the Jews up to the time of the Babylonian Captivity. The alphabet is still employed for writing Aramaic, Hebrew, and even Arabic. The literature is chiefly of a religious character.

The alphabet consists of 22 characters, and the text reads from right to left. Since there are neither vowels nor diacritical marks above or below the characters, the following consonants are employed as vowel characters:

$$𐤕 = a, e, \qquad 𐤉 = e, i,$$
$$𐤄 = a, \qquad\qquad 𐤅 = o, u.$$
$$𐤏 = a,$$

Punctuation

The last letter of a word is surmounted by a point; : or · or ·: are used at the end of a sentence; .. at the end of a phrase; =·: or —<: at the end of a paragraph; and < ·:· = ·:· > at the end of a chapter.

SAMOAN

A	a	*a* in father; also *a* in mat [1]	M	m	*m*	
E	e	*a*	N	n	*n*	
I	i	*ee* in keep	P	p	*p*	
O	o	*o*	S	s	*s*, not sibilant as in English	
U	u	*oo* in book	T	t	*t*	
F	f	*f*	V	v	*v*	
G	g	*ng* in sing				
L	l	*l;* soft *r* before *i* or after *a, o* or *u*				

[1] The distinction between long and short *a* is very important as a great many words spelled the same way have very different meanings: *tamā*, father; *tăma*, boy; *tina*, mother; *tinā*, wedge; *fai*, to do; *fāi*, to abuse.

The Samoan is a Malay language which became highly impregnated with Arabic centuries ago, and again in the last century absorbed a great many English and other European words.

The Samoan names for the consonants are *fa, nga, la, mo, nu, pi, sa, ti, vi.*

In addition to the above letters there is a sound somewhat between *h* and *k* which has the value of a consonant and represents the *k* sound of other kindred dialects. It is called a "break" and is represented by an inverted comma: *n'a,* paper-mulberry. The word is in Niuean *uka.* It is a very important distinction between words that are otherwise similar in spelling and must be carefully observed: *fua*, fruit; *fu'a*, flag. It is also a general rule that two similar vowels cannot occur without a "break" between them.

Every letter is distinctly sounded, so that there are no improper diphthongs. The proper diphthongs are *au, ai, ae, ei* and *ou.*

The *k* and *r* are retained in foreign words introduced into the Samoan language: *Keriso* (Greek, Christon), but *d* becomes *t: Tavita*, David; *ph* becomes *f: Ferukia*, Phrygia; *g* and hard *c* become *k: Kanana*, Canaan; *h* is also retained at the beginning of some proper names: *Herota*, Herod; *z* becomes *s: Sakaria; w* becomes *u* or *v: Uiliamu*, William; *b* becomes *p: Petania*, Bethany. In some foreign names *h* is changed to *s: Sapai* for Hapai.

Syllabication

Every syllable must end in a vowel and no syllable can have more than three letters, a consonant and two vowels, the vowels forming a diphthong: *fai, mai, tau.* There must be a vowel between any two consonants.

Accent

As a general rule the accent is on the penultimate syllable, but there are many exceptions to this rule; where the accent is on the last, which take it on more than one syllable, or which take no accent whatever.

Reduplicated words take two accents: *pălapăla*, mud. In this way compound words may have three or four accents.

Cardinal numbers

e tasi	one	e iva	nine
e lua	two	e sefulu	ten
e tolu	three	e sefulu ma le tasi	eleven
e fa	four	e sefulu ma le lua	twelve .
e lima	five	e sefulu ma le tolu	thirteen
e ono	six	e luafulu, e luasefulu	twenty
e fitu	seven	e selau	hundred
e valu	eight	e afe	thousand

Ordinal numbers

'o le ulua'i ⎫ 'o le muamua⎭	first	'o le iva	ninth
		'o le sefulu	tenth
'o le lua	second	'o le sefuluma letasi	eleventh
'o le tolu	third	'o le sefulu ma lua	twelfth
'o le fā	fourth	'o le sefulu ma tolu	thirteenth
'o le lima	fifth	'o le luafulu ⎫ 'o le lua sefulu⎭	twentieth
'o le ono	sixth		
'o le fitu	seventh	'o le selau	hundredth
'o le valu	eighth	'o le afe	thousandth

Distributives are formed by prefixing *ta'i* to the cardinal: *ta'itasi*, one by one. The adverbial numerals are expressed by prefixing *atu*: *'o le atutasi*, one by one; by prefixing *fa'a*: *Ua'ou sau fa'alua,* I have come twice; or by prefixing *fo'i* as well as *fa'a*: *Ua fo'i fa'afa ona'ou alu,* I went back four times.

Months

Januari	January	Iulai	July
Fepuari	February	Aokuso	August
Mati	March	Setema	September
Aperila	April	Oketopa	October
Me	May	Novema	November
Iuni	June	Tesema	December

Days

Aso Sa	Sunday	Aso Tofi, Asotuloto	Thursday
Aso Gafua	Monday	Aso Falaile	Friday
Aso Lua	Tuesday	Aso To'ona'i	Saturday
Asolulu, Asomanu	Wednesday		

Seasons

taisuusu'e, tai-ofeití	spring	ò le tau inu'uile Sone fa'aleogalua e ma-maeaila'au	autumn
vaitoelau	summer		
		vai palolo tau ma'alili	winter

Time

ituaso, itulā, itupo	hour	masina	month
aso	day	tausaga, usuitau	year
vāi'asosa, vaiaso	week		

Articles to be disregarded in filing

le, se

SANSCRIT

Sanscrit, though no longer a spoken language, is still the classical language of India and the key to her religious; philosophical, and legal literature, as well as the source of many of her modern languages. The earliest Sanscrit compositions date back as far as 1500 B.C., and it became the official language of the Indo-Aryan people in the 4th century A.D.

There are two principal periods in the history of Sanscrit literature, the Vedic and the Classical, which overlap somewhat; the first extending from 1500 to 200 B.C., and the second from 500 B.C. to 1000 A.D.

The alphabet comprises the following letters:

I. Five short and five long vowels, viz:

Short: अ *a,* इ *i,* उ *u,* ऋ *ṛi,* ऌ *ḷi,*

Long: आ *â,* ई *î,* ऊ *û,* ॠ *rî,* ॡ *ḷî.*

II. Four diphthongs: ए *e,* ऐ *ai,* ओ *o,* औ *au.*

Note that ए *e* is in most cases a combination of *a* and *i,* ऐ *ai* of *â* and *i,* ओ *o* of *a* and *u,* and औ *au* of *â* and *u.*

III. 1. Two slight nasals; the one, called *anusvâra,* is denoted by a dot ◌̇ placed above the letter after which it is to be pronounced, e.g. अं *am̐;* the other, called *anunâsika,* is denoted by a half-moon with a dot in it ◌̐ and placed either above or after the preceding letter, in the latter case with an oblique dash under it, e.g. अँ or अꣳ *aꝏ.*

2. An aspirate, called *visarga,* which is denoted by two dots, placed one above the other (:), e.g. अः *aḥ.*

IV. Thirty-three consonants:

1. Five gutturals: क *ka,* ख *kha,* ग *ga,* घ *gha,* ङ *ṅa,*

2. Five palatals: च *cha,* छ *chha,* ज *ja,* झ *jha,* ञ *ṅa,*

3. Five linguals: ट *ṭa,* ठ *ṭha,* ड *ḍa,* ढ *ḍha,* ण *ṇa,*

4. Five dentals: त *ta,* थ *tha,* द *da,* ध *dha,* न *na,*

5. Five labials: प *pa,* फ *pha,* ब *ba,* भ *bha,* म *ma,*

6. Four semivowels: य *ya,* र *ra,* ल *la,* व *va,*

7. Three sibilants: श *ça,* ष *sha,* स *sa,*

8. The soft aspirate: ह *ha.*

It is not possible to state positively what the original sounds of the letters were. However, the transcription of Hindu proper names in Greek and Latin literature, as well as some other facts bearing on this subject, enable us to give the following rules with considerable confidence: *a* as in apt; *â* as in far; *i* as in pin; *î* like *ee* in feeble; *u* as in full; *û* like *o* in move; *ṛi* like *ri* in rid; *rî* like *ree* in reed; *ḷi* as in lid; *ḷî* like *lea* in to lead; *e* like *a* in fate; *ai* as in the Italian mai; *o* as in note; *au* like *ou* in our.

Before the semivowels *ya, ra, la, va,* the sibilants *ça, sha, sa,* and the aspirate *ha,* the *anusvâra* is pronounced like *ng* in king. Before all other consonants it sounds like the nasal of the class to which the following letter belongs. The *anunâsika* seems to have been almost inaudible, and the *visarga* like the Greek spiritus lenis

The *ka* was like *k* in king; *kha* as in khan; *ga* like *g* in gun; *gh* as in afghan; *na* like *ng* in sing; *cha* like *ch* in church; *chha* like *ch*+*h* in Churchhill; *ja* like *j* in jet; *jha* like *j*+*h; ña* like *n* in singe.

The unaspirated dentals and labials, the *sa* and the *ha* are all pronounced like the corresponding English letters; in the aspirated dentals and labials an *h* sound must be added: *sha* to be pronounced like *sh* in shun, and *ça* like a sharp *s* in sit.

The forms of the vowels and diphthongs, if preceded by a consonant, are as follows:

ा *â,* ि *i,* ी *î,* ु *u,* ू *û,* ृ *ṛi,* ॄ *ṛî,* ॢ *ḷi,* ॣ *ḷî,* e.g.

का *kâ,* कि *ki,* की *kî,* कु *ku,* कू *kû,* कृ *kṛi,* कॄ *kṛî,* कॢ *kḷi,* कॣ *kḷî.*

े *e,* ै *ai,* ो *o,* ौ *au,* e.g.

के *ke,* कै *kai,* को *ko,* कौ *kau.*

Some consonants also change their forms when combined with vowels. Thus

र *ra*	with	ु *u*	becomes	रु *ru*
—	„	ू *û*	„	रू *rû*
ह *ha*	„	ु *u*	„	हु *hu*
—	„	ू *û*	„	हू *hu*
—	„	ृ *ṛi*	„	हृ *hṛi*
श *ça*	„	ु *u*	„	शु *çu*
—	„	ू *û*	„	शू *çû*
—	„	ृ *ṛi*	„	शृ *çṛi*

The declensions of nouns comprise three numbers: Singular, dual, and plural; and eight cases: Nominative, accusative, instrumental, dative, ablative, genitive, locative, and vocative.

The verb has the following stems: Present, aorist, perfect, and future, the latter being rare in the old language. The present stem is predominant in classical Sanscrit.

There are three genders, as in English.

Accent

The accent was mainly a musical or tonic, not a stress. Three different types are distinguished: *Udâtta* (raised), *anudatta* (unraised), and *svarita* (rising-falling), following the *udâtta.*

Numerals

The system was constructed on a decimal basis; there are two separate names for the numbers up to 10, while up to 19 there are compounds of the units with the word for 10: *d(û)yadsá,* 12; 20, 30, etc., are compounds that express a number of tens, and the intermediate numbers are formed by adding the various units: *páñca,* 5; *páñcâsat,* 50; *páñcapáñcâsat,* 55. There are separate words for 100, 1,000, and 100,000, the latter, *lakṣah,* being post-Vedic. The numerals from 1 to 19 are adjectives, while the rest are substantives.

SERBO-CROATIAN

Serbian		Croatian		
А	а	A	a	*a* in father
Б	б	B	b	*b*
В	в	V	v	*v*
Г	г	G	g	*g* in go
Д	д	D	d	*d*
Ђ	ђ	Dj, Đ / Gj	dj, đ / gj	Between *d* in dune and *j* in John
Е	е	E	e	*e* in end
Ж	ж	Ž	ž	*j* in jour / *s* in measure
З	з	Z	z	*z*
И	и	I	i	*i* in machine
Ј	ј	J	j	*y* in you
К	к	K	k	*k*
Л	л	L	l	*l*
Љ	љ	Lj	lj	*li* in million
М	м	M	m	*m*

Serbian		Croatian		
Н	н	N	n	*n* in new
Њ	њ	Nj	nj	*ni* in opinion
О	о	O	o	*o* in note
П	п	P	p	*p*
Р	р	R	r	*r* in very
С	с	S	s	*ss* in glass
Т	т	T	t	*t*
Ћ	ћ	Ć	ć	Between *t* in tune and *ch* in church
У	у	U	u	*oo* in room
Ф	ф	F	f	*f*
Х	х	H	h	*ch* in Scotch loch [1]
Ц	ц	C	c	*ts* in cats
Ч	ч	Č	č	*ch* in church
Џ	џ	Dž	dž	*j* in James
Ш	ш	S	š	*sh* in sheep

[1] Before a vowel like English *h*.

In the western part of the country the language is written with Latin characters, while in the eastern part the Cyrillic are used. The language may be written equally well with either. The important differences are that in the Croatian diacritical marks are used to indicate phonetic values, and the letters follow the regular order of the English, while the Serbian follows the order of the Greek on which it was founded.

There are three dialects: the Southern, or jekavski; the Eastern, or ekavski, and the Western (Dalmatian), or ikavski, but only the first two have any literary value.

Phonetics

It will be noticed that in several cases the Croatian Latin alphabet employs double letters where the Serbian Cyrillic employs only a single character, and it even has alternative signs to represent certain sounds. This is due to the fact that uniformity in spelling has not yet been achieved in Croatia. For example, the Serbian ђ can be represented in Croatian by gj, đ, or dj, the first two being most common. The lj is commoner than ļ, nj than ń, and dž than ģ.

The pronunciation of each individual letter is the same in all cases, and it is thus necessary merely to learn the value of each letter.

The vowels и, e, a, o, and y are all pronounced "openly" as in Italian; p is also considered a vowel when standing between two consonants or at the beginning of a word before a consonant; it is then strongly rolled as in the Scotch.

The Serbian p very seldom occurs as a vowel sound before or after a vowel and carries a dieresis where it does: rpóңe (3 syllables) = throat.

Most of the consonants present no difficulty whatever, and the only ones that call for special remark are ш and ж, ч and ц, ћ and ђ. The first in each case is the voiceless [1] and the second the corresponding voiced consonant.

Rather more difficult are ћ and ђ. To pronounce them the teeth must be brought close together and the lips slightly opened; the blade of the tongue must cleave to the inside of the gums of the upper teeth and be slightly retracted at the time the stream of air issues from the chest through the mouth.

[1] A voiceless consonant is one that is pronounced with breath from the mouth only, while in the case of a voiced consonant a stream of breath from the chest is necessary.

It is also well to notice the difference between л and љ and between н and њ; љ and њ are the softened or palatal forms of л and н, just as ħ and ђ are of т and д. They seldom occur at the ends of words, and in the middle of words they have the sound of *l* and *n* in million and new.

All vowels including p, may be either short or long.

At the end of Serbian words only the following groups of consonants are possible: ст, шт, зд, жд; when a word would end in any other group, an a is inserted in the nominative singular as well as in the genitive plural, its use in the latter being due to the fact that the invariable long a of this case is of comparatively modern origin.

Final л of a syllable, and especially of a word, frequently becomes o; where the original nominative singular ending was -ол, the oo combine in one long o, but the л reappears in the other cases.

There is no article: цвет, (*m*.), a flower or the flower; соба (*f*.), a room or the room; дете (*n*.), a child or the child.

Punctuation is practically the same as in English.

The accent is musical, and there are four different kinds: two long and two short. Of the former, the first is a rising inflection, marked by the acute sign ('), while the second is a falling inflection which is marked by the circumflex sign (ᴧ). Of the short accents the first also has a rising inflection which is marked by the grave sign (`), while the second has a falling inflection and is either marked by a double grave sign (``) or is not marked at all. The stress is invariably on the first syllable.

Syllabication

A consonant between two vowels goes with the next syllable.

Where two or more consonants occur between two vowels, they are separated, provided it is a combination with which no Serbian word can be begun.

The following consonants must not be divided: бл, бр, вл, вр, гв, гд, гл, гр, дв, др, зб, зв, зл, зм, зн, зр, кл, кљ, кн, књ, кр, мл, мн, мр, пл, пр, пч, п, ш, рђ, св, ск, сл, см, сн, сп, ср, ст, ств, стр, тв, тр, фл, фр, хл, хр, хт, цв, цр, чл, чр, џб, шк, шљ, шт.

Abbreviations

The following abbreviations will be helpful:

Г., Господин	G., Gospodin	Mr.
ГГ., Господа	GG., Gospoda	gentlemen
Г-ђа, Госпођа	G-đa, Gospođa	Mrs.
Г-ђица, Госпођица	G-đica, Gospođica	Miss
Г-де, Госпо_де	G-de, Gospode	ladies
и т.д., и тако даље	i t.d., i tako dalje	and so forth (etc.)
н.пр., на пример	n.pr., na primer	for example
ов.год., ове године	ov.god., ove godine	the current year
т.ј., то јест	t.j., to jest	that is

Cardinal numbers

један	jedan, -dna, -dno	one
два	dva	two
три	tri	three
четири	četiri	four
пет	pet	five
шест	šest	six
седам	sedam	seven
осам	osam	eight
девет	devet	nine
десет	deset	ten
једанаест	jedanaest	eleven
дванаест	dvanaest	twelve
тринаест	trinaest	thirteen
двадесет	dvadeset	twenty
сто	sto	hundred
хиљада	hiljada, tisuća	thousand

Ordinal numbers

први	prvi	first
други	drugi	second
трећи	treći	third
четврти	četvrti	fourth
пети	peti	fifth
шести	šesti	sixth
седми	sedmi	seventh
осми	osmi	eighth
девети	deveti	ninth
десети	deseti	tenth
једанаести	jedanaesti	eleventh
дванаести	dvanaesti	twelfth
тринаести	trinaesti	thirteenth
двадесети	dvadeseti	twentieth
стоти	stoti	hundredth
хиладити	hiljaditi, tisući	thousandth

Months

јануар (јан.)	siječanj (siječ.)	January
фебруар (фебр.)	veljača (velj.)	February
март	ožujak (ožuj.)	March
април (апр.)	travanj (trav.)	April
мај	svibanj, maj (svib.)	May
јуни	lipanj (lip.)	June
јули	srpanj (srp.)	July
аугуст (ауг.)	kolovoz (kol.)	August
септембар (септ.)	rujan (ruj.)	September
октобар (окт.)	listopad (list.)	October
новембар (нов.)	studeni (stud.)	November
децембар (дец.)	prosinac (pros.)	December

Days

недеља	nedelja	Sunday
понедељак	ponedeljak	Monday
уторак	utorak	Tuesday
среда	srieda	Wednesday
четвртак	četvrtak	Thursday
петак	petak	Friday
субота	subota	Saturday

Seasons

прољеће	proleće	spring
лето	ljeto	summer
јесен	jesen	autumn
зима	zima	winter

Time

сат	ura, sat	hour
дан	dan	day
недеља	sedmica	week
месец	mesec	month
година	godina	year

SIAMESE [1]

Character	Transliteration	Character	Transliteration	Character	Transliteration	Character	Transliteration
ก	ko	ฑ	tho	ย	jo	ู	u
ข	kho	ฒ	tho	ร	ro	ฤ	rŭ'
ฃ	khó	ณ	no	ล	lo	ฤๅ	rŭ
ค	kho	ด	do	ว	vo	ฦ	lŭ'
ฅ	kho	ต	to	ศ	só	ฦๅ	lŭ
ฆ	kho	ถ	thó	ษ	só	เ	e
ง	ngo	ท	tho	ส	só	แ	ĕ
จ	cho	ธ	tho	ห	hó	ไ	ăi
ฉ	xó	น	no	ฬ	lo	ใ	ăi
ช	xo			อ	o	โ	ó
ซ	so	บ	bo	ฮ	ho	เ...า	ăo
ฌ	xo	ป	po	า	a	ำ	ăm
ญ	jo	ผ	phó	ิ	ĭ	ะ	a:
		ฝ	fó	ี	i		
ฎ	do	พ	pho	ึ	ŭ		
ฏ	to	ฟ	fo	ื	u'		
ฐ	thó	ภ	pho	ุ	ŭ		
		ม	mo				

[1] Continental sounds are used in the transliteration.

This language belongs to the Tai group, and the alphabet was derived from a south Indian source. The language is purely monosyllabic, each true word consisting of a single vowel sound, preceded or followed by a consonant. There are less than 2,000 of these monosyllables and, consequently, many of them serve for the expression of more than one idea, the variations being indicated, as in the Chinese, by the tone employed.

Siamese is written from left to right, and in the old manuscripts there was no spacing, although in modern writings it is used.

There are 44 consonants, each having inherent the vowel sound *aw*, and 32 vowels which are not indicated by individual letters but by signs that are placed either above, below, before, or after the consonants. Only vowel or diphthong sounds, or the letters *m*, *n*, *ng*, *k*, *t*, and *p* are permissible at the end of words, and where, as in foreign words, some other letter is final it is not sounded.

There are five simple tones: Even, circumflex, descending, grave, and high, and any one of these placed on a word will change the meaning radically. Four of these tones are indicated by signs placed over the consonant affected, while the absence of a sign indicates that the fifth tone is to be used.

The consonants are grouped in three classes, each having a special tone, and thus the application of a tonal sign to a letter has a different effect, dependent on the class to which the letter belongs.

The person, number, tense, and mood of a verb are indicated by auxiliary words when they cannot be inferred from the context. There are a great many adverbs, both single and compound. The prepositions are mainly nouns.

The subject of the sentence precedes the verb and the object follows it. In compound sentences the verbs are placed together.

Accents and other signs

1. Accent *ă*
2. Accent *thăntha : khat*
3. Accent *lek pët*
4. Accent

Numerals

๑	1	๖	6
๒	2	๗	7
๓	3	๘	8
๔	4	๙	9
๕	5	o	0

SLOVAK

A	a	*a* in father	N	n	*n*
Á	á	*aa* in German Haar	Ň	ň	*ñ* in Spanish cañon
B	b	*b*	O	o	*o* in long
C	c	*ts*	Ó	ó	*o* in low
Č	č	*ch* in church	P	p	*p*
D	d	*d*	Q	q	*qu* in question
Ď	ď ď	*dj* in Hedjaz	R	r	*r*
E	e	*a*	Ř	ř	*rsh*
É	é	*ee* in German Seele	S	s	*s* in sing
Ě	ě	*ye* in yesterday	Š	š	*sh* in show
F	f	*f*	T	t	*t*
G	g	*g* in gay	Ť	t' ť	*tj*
H	h	*h*	U	u	*u*
CH	ch	*ch* in Scotch loch	Ú	ú	*oo* in stool
I	i	*e*	Ů	ů	*ōō*
Í	í	*ie* in field	V	v	*w* in wand
J	j	*y*	X	x	*ks*
K	k	*k*	Y	y	*i* in silt
L	l	*l*	Ý	ý	*ie* in field
Ĺ	ĺ	*l*, trilled	Z	z	*s*
Ľ	ľ	*ly* in lyric	Ž	ž	*s* (zh sound in French journal)
M	m	*m*			

The *ó*, *q*, and *x* are used only in foreign words.
Stress is consistently on the first syllable.

Capitalization

Begin sentences with a capital letter, but after exclamation and interrogation points only if these complete the previous sentence. Capitalize after the colon, as a general rule. Capitalize all proper nouns, including God and any word used to designate the Deity.

Syllabication

Divide on a vowel, but bear in mind that *l*, *r*, and *v*, often have the characteristics of vowels. The consonants *sk*, *št*, *st*, and *sd* are inseparable and begin the following syllable. Division between two vowels is permissible. Compound words are treated as two separate words in regard to syllabication.

Punctuation is practically the same as in English.

Cardinal numbers

jeden, -dna, -dno	one	desat'	ten
dva, dve	two	jedenást'	eleven
tri	three	dvanást'	twelve
štyr-i	four	trinást'	thirteen
pät'	five	dvadsat'	twenty
šest'	six	dvadsat' jeden	twenty-one
sedem	seven	sto	hundred
osem	eight	tisíc	thousand
devät'	nine		

Ordinal numbers

prvy	first	deviaty	ninth
druhý	second	desiaty	tenth
tretti	third	jedonásty, -a, -e	eleventh
šivrtý	fourth	dvanásty	twelfth
piaty	fifth	trinásty	thirteenth
šiesty	sixth	dvadsiaty	twentieth
siedmy	seventh	stotý, stý	hundredth
ôsmy	eighth	tisíci	thousandth

Months

l'adeň (l'ad.)	January	červenec (červen.)	July
únor (ún.)	February	srpen (srp.)	August
brezeň (brez.)	March	zári	September
dubeň (dub.)	April	rujeň (ruj.)	October
kveteň (kvet.)	May	listopad (list.)	November
červen (červ.)	June	prosinec (pros.)	December

Days

nedel'a	Sunday	štvrtok	Thursday
pondelok	Monday	piatok	Friday
utorok	Tuesday	sobota	Saturday
sreda	Wednesday		

Seasons

jaro	spring	jaseň	autumn
leto	summer	zima	winter

Time

hodina	hour	mesiac	month
deň	day	rok	year
týdeň	week		

SLOVENIAN

A	a	*a*		N	n	*n*	
B	b	*b*		NJ	nj	*nj*, as the French *gn*	
Ç	c	*ts*		O	o	*o*	
Č	č	*ch*		Ô	ô	*ō*	
D	d	*d*		P	p	*p*	
DJ	dj	*dj*		R	r	*r*	
E	e	*e*		RJ	rj	*rj*	
Ê	ê	*ē*		S	s	*s*	
F	f	*f*		Š	š	*sh*	
G	g	*g*		T	t	*t*	
H	h	*h, ch,* as in German Dach		TJ	tj	*tj*	
				U	u	*u*	
I	i	*i*		V	v	*v*	
J	j	*y*		KS	ks	*ks*	
K	k	*k*		Z	z	*z*	
L	l	*l*		Ž	ž	*zh* sound in French journal	
LJ	lj	*lj* as Italian *gl* in egli					
M	m	*m*					

The Slovenian language is related to the Serbo-Croatian language, with which it forms the Yugoslavic language group.

The one-letter words, *s, z, k* and *v*, must not be placed at the end of a printed line.

Syllabication

Division is phonetical, though compound words are divided as though they were separate words, as, *po-mlád* (spring); the consonantal combinations *dj, lj, nj, rj, tj,* and *ks* must not be separated.

Proper nouns only are capitalized and punctuation is as in English.

Abbreviations

dr.	doktor, doctor	itd.	in tako daljo, et cetera	n.pr.	na primer, for instance
i.dr.	in drugi, and others	itn.	in tako napredj, and so forth	p.K.	po Kristusu. A.D.

Cardinal numbers

édĕn jedĕn	one	devet	nine
dva	two	desét	ten
tri	three	jednajst	eleven
štiri	four	dvanájst	twelve
pét	five	trinájst	thirteen
šest	six	dvajset	twenty
sedem	seven	sto, stotina	hundred
osĕm	eight	tisoč, tisočina	thousand

Ordinal numbers

prvi	first	devéti	ninth
drugi	second	deséti	tenth
tretji	third	enajsti, jednajsti	eleventh
četŕti	fourth	dvanájsti	twelfth
péti	fifth	trinájsti	thirteenth
šesti	sixth	dvájseti	twentieth
sedmi	seventh	stoti, stotni	hundredth
osmi	eighth	tisočni	thousandth

Months

januar, janvar (jan.)	January	julij (jul.)	July
februar, februvarij (feb.)	February	avgúst (avg.)	August
marĕc (mar.)	March	septémbĕr (sept.)	September
april (apr.)	April	októbĕr (okt.)	October
maj	May	novémbĕr (nov.)	November
junij (jun.)	June	decembĕr (dec.)	December

Days

nedélja	Sunday	četftĕk	Thursday
ponedéljĕk	Monday	petĕk	Friday
torĕk	Tuesday	sobóta	Saturday
sreda	Wednesday		

Seasons

pomlád, spomlad	spring	jesén	autumn
leto, polétje	summer	zima	winter

Time

ura	hour	mesec, mesĕc	month
dan, den	day	leto	year
tedén	week		

Articles to be disregarded in filing

a   k   s   v   z

SPANISH

A	a	*a* in art	P	p	*p*
B	b	(¹)	Q	q	*q* in quart
C	c	Preceding *e* or *i*, as *th* in Martha. Otherwise, as in car	R	r	*r* in wary, trilled
			RR	rr	*r* forcibly rolled
CH	ch	*ch* in chart	S	s	*s* in saw
D	d	Initial and following *l* and *n*, *d;* elsewhere, shading heavily toward *th* in breathe	T	t	*t*
			U	u	*oo* in coo²
			V	v	Between *b* and *v*, with the *v* sound slightly stronger
E	e	*a* in ale	W	w	*w* only in foreign words
F	f	*f*	X	x	*x* in axle
G	g	Preceding *e* or *i*, as *kh* energetically pronounced; otherwise as in gate	Y	y	*e* in he, initial, *y* in yet
			Z	z	*th* in Martha; *z*
			Á	á	⎫
			É	é	⎪
H	h	Mute	Í	í	⎬ As same letters unaccented
I	i	*e* in he	Ó	ó	⎪
J	j	*h,* strongly aspirated	Ú	ú	⎭
K	k	*k* (only in foreign words)	Ü	ü	*oo* (dieresis indicates that the *u* is pronounced as in *güeldo* (gwaildo) where otherwise it would be gaildo
L	l	*l*			
LL	ll	*llio* in million			
M	m	*m*			
N	n	*n*			
Ñ	ñ	*ni* in onion			
O	o	*o* in note			

¹ Softer than in English, produced by joining the lips without pressure; between vowels, almost *v*.
² Between *g* and *e* or *i*, silent, rendering the *g* hard.

Punctuation

Punctuation is practically the same as in English, and, in addition, inverted interrogation and exclamation marks are used at the exact beginning of the question or exclamation.

Si es así, ¿qué he de hacer?   Pero, ¡ay de mí! no es posible.

Quotation marks begin the first paragraph of a dialogue. The succeeding paragraphs sometimes start with em dashes instead of quotation marks, and the latter are not used until the dialogue ends.

"¿Es así, señor?
—Sí; es verdad.
—¿Cómo se puede averiguarlo?
—No sé; pero es la verdad."

Capitalization

The English style of capitalization is followed, with few exceptions.

Adjectives derived from proper nouns are lower-cased, as *las mujeres colombianas* (the Colombian women) and *los cruceros brasileños* (the Brazilian cruisers).

The first word of a question occurring within a sentence is lower-cased, as:

Cuando venga la noche, ¿cómo se puede ver?

Note the following forms of capitalization:
El señor Enrique Palava; el señor don Enrique Palava.
Days of the week and months begin with a lower-case letter.

In titles of books only the initial and proper nouns, are capitalized: Historia crítica de España y de la cultura española.

Accents

(1) Words ending in *n*, *s*, or a vowel, and emphasized normally on the last syllable but one (penultimate), dispense with the accent mark.

(2) Words ending in a consonant except *n* or *s*, and emphasized normally on the last syllable, dispense with the accent mark.

(3) Words not included in (1) and (2) require an accent on the syllable carrying the emphasis, as *é-po-ca*, *se-gún*, *in-cóg-ni-to*. This includes verbs to which pronouns are appended, as *págaselo* and certain verb tenses.

Words having a dual meaning, as *mas* (but) and *más* (more), do not fall under these rules, and the proper accent should be carried.

Usually but one accent is used in a word, regardless of the number of syllables.

Formerly the words, *a*, *e*, *o*, and *u* were accented, but this has become obsolete. However, changes should not be made without authority, as some authors follow the old custom.

When the word *o* (or) is used adjoining numerals, as *14 ó 15*, the accent should be used to prevent confusing the *o* with a cipher.

Syllabication

Words are usually divided on a vowel: *a-si-mi-la-ción*, *pa-la-bras*.

The letter *y* is considered a vowel when standing alone, or at the end of a word. At the beginning of a word or syllable it is treated as a consonant.

The following combinations must not be divided: *ai*, *au*, *ei*, *eu*, *ia*, *ie*, *io*, *iu*, *oi*, *ou*, *ua*, *ue*, *ui*, *uo*, *iai*, *iei*, *uai*, *uei* (*a-li-via-dor*). This does not apply when either letter carries an accent (*pa-ís*, *rí-o*), which permits the vowels to be separated, but exceptions are made in certain cases.

The combinations of *ay*, *ey*, *oy*, and *uy* may be separated only when followed by a vowel, but must not be separated when followed by a consonant or when occurring at the end of a word.

| | *ha-ya* | *re-yes* | *a-rro-yo* | *cu-yo* |
| but— | *rey-na* | *voy-me* | *Go-doy* | *muy* |

A consonant occurring between two vowels should be carried over: *com-po-si-ción*.

Two separable consonants standing between vowels are divided: *ac-ta*, *chas-co*, *cuer-da*, *pron-to*.

The letters *ch*, *ll*, and *rr* are never divided and always begin a syllable, as *ria-chue-lo*, *gue-rri-lla*, *fe-rro-ca-rril*.

Prepositional prefixes form a separate syllable, as: *des-agradable*, *pre-colom-biano;* but when the prefix is followed by *s* and another consonant, the *s* is joined to the prefix. Examples: *abs-tener*, *cons-trucción*, but *ab-solver*.

A syllable cannot begin with *s* followed by a consonant, as *cir-cuns-tan-cia*.

The liquid consonants *l* and *r*, when preceded by a consonant, other than in the combinations *rl*, *sl*, *tl*, and *sr*, must not be separated from that consonant, except in the case of prefixes or compound words. Examples: *ha-blar*, *po-dría*, *sub-lu-nar*, *ab-ro-gar*, *es-la-bon*.

| *bl* | *br* | *cl* | *cr* | *dr* | *fl* | *fr* |
| *gl* | *gr* | *pl* | *pr* | *tr* | | |

Double *c* and *n* may be divided as in English: *ac-ce-so*, *in-na-to*.

Articles

The definite article, singular and plural, is expressed as follows: Masculine, *el* and *los;* feminine, *la* and *las*. When *el* follows *de* (from, of) the two combine, *del*, and after *a* (to), *al*. Abstract phrases and words take the neuter article, *lo: lo mismo*, the same. Feminine singular nouns beginning with a stressed *a* or *ha* take the definite article *el*, but their gender remains unchanged:

el agua, the water	el hacha, the ax
las aguas, the waters	las hachas, the axes

The indefinite article, singular and plural, is expressed by *un*, *unos*, *una*, *unas:*

un caballo, a horse	una vaca, a cow
unos caballos, some horses	unas vacas, some cows

Adjectives

Adjectives must agree with the nouns they modify in both number and gender. Those ending in *o* change the ending to *os*, *a*, or *as* in order to agree with the noun they modify. The rules which apply to the formation of the plurals of nouns also apply to the adjectives.

Most adjectives form their comparative by prefixing *más* (more) to the positive, and the superlative is formed by employing the definite article before the comparative: *El más barato*, the cheapest. There are many adjectives of irregular comparison which must be learned separately.

Descriptive adjectives usually follow and limiting adjectives usually precede the noun modified. Some adjectives, *bueno*, *malo*, *uno*, *ninguno*, *alguno*, *primero*, *tercero*, drop the final *o* of the masculine singular when they precede the noun they modify.

Gender

Nouns are either masculine or feminine, those ending in *o* being usually masculine while those ending in *a*, *d*, *ión*, *umbre*, or *ie* are usually feminine:

carro, *m.*, cart	carta, *f.*, letter
soldado, *m.*, soldier	criada, *f.*, maid.
hermano,[1] *m.*, brother	hermana, *f.*, sister
verdad, *f.*, truth	lumbre, *f.*, light
creación, *f.*, creation	serie, *f.*, series

Exceptions to the above rule are *mano*, *f.*, hand; *día*, *m.*, day, and a number of words of Greek origin, as—

telegrama, *m.*, telegram	cometa, *m.*, comet
poema, *m.*, poem	planeta, *m.*, planet

Nouns having other endings may be either masculine or feminine, and the gender must be learned separately:

fogón, *m.*, fireplace	vez, *f.*, time
ascensor, *m.*, elevator	sinopsis, *f.*, synopsis

There are a number of neuter adjectives, pronouns, and adverbs which may be used as abstract nouns, taking the neuter form of the definite article:

Es siempre lo mismo, it is always the same.
Eso es lo bueno de vivir, that is the good of living.

Nouns

Singular nouns ending in an unstressed vowel add *s* to form the plural: *tintero*, inkstand; *tinteros*, inkstands.

Nouns ending in a consonant, or a stressed vowel (except *e*) or diphthong, add *es*: *árbol*, tree; *árboles*, trees: *maní*, peanut; *maníes*, peanuts. Exceptions are: *sofá*, sofa; *sofás*, sofas; *canapé*, couch; *canapés*, couches. Stressed diphthong: *rey*, king; *reyes*, kings.

Final *c* changes to *qu* and final *z* to *c* when *es* is added to form the plural:

frac, dress coat	fraques, dress coats
luz, light	luces, lights

The possessive is expressed by—

(1) *de* + an article and a noun:

Los libros del (de el) muchacho, the boy's books
Las plumas de la señora, the lady's pens

(2) By the possessive adjectives:

a. Short form, used before the noun:

Singular	Plural	English
mi	mis	my
tu	tus	your
su	sus	his, her, its, your, their
nuestro, -a	nuestros, -as	our
vuestro, -a	vuestros, -as	your
su	sus	his, her, its, your, their

---

[1] Some nouns, as *hermano*, may change gender by substituting the feminine ending *a* for the masculine *o*.

Nouns—Continued

The possessive is expressed by—Continued

b. Long form, used after the noun:

Singular	Plural	English
mío, -a	míos, -as	my
tuyo, -a	tuyos, -as	your
suyo, -a	suyos, -as	his, her, its, your, their
nuestro, -a	nuestros, -as	our
vuestro, -a	vuestros, -as	your
suyo, -a	suyos, -as	his, her, its, your, their

(3) By the possessive adjective+the definite article:

el (libro) mío, mine (book)   los (libros) míos, mine (books)
la (carta) suya, your (letter)   las (cartas) suyas, your (letters)

The indirect object takes the preposition *a: Doy el libro a Juan,* I give John the book.

Dative of the person is used with verbs meaning to take from, ask of, etc.: *Pedí una bicicleta a mi padre,* I asked my father for a bicycle.

The direct object does not require a preposition, unless it is a proper noun, or a noun or pronoun that denotes a definite person or a personified thing:

Veo un automóvil, I see an automobile   Veo a ella, I see her
Veo a Georgina, I see Georgina   Hablo al (a el) perro, I speak to
                                         the dog

The object personal pronoun usually precedes the verb; however, if the verb is an infinitive, present participle, affirmative imperative, and usually if the subjunctive is used in the imperative sense, the pronoun follows the verb and is attached to it: *Usted me habla,* you are speaking to me; *quiero hablarte,* I wish to speak to you.

Personal pronouns

Personal pronouns have four cases, as shown below. *Ello* (it) is used only in referring to an intangible antecedent, and its accusative *lo* is differentiated from *lo,* accusative of masculine pronoun *él,* which is similar in form.

			Nominative	Dative	Accusative	Prepositional
Singular	1st person		yo	me	me	mí
	2d person		tú	te	te	tí
	3d person	masculine	él	le	le, lo	él
		feminine	ella	le	la	ella
		neuter	ello	—	lo	ello
Plural	1st person	masculine	nosotros	nos	nos	nosotros
		feminine	nosotras	nos	nos	nosotras
	2d person	masculine	vosotros	os	os	vosotros
		feminine	vosotras	os	os	vosotras
	3d person	masculine	ellos	les	los	ellos
		feminine	ellas	les	las	ellas
Reflexive substitute for 3d person, common to both numbers.			—	se	se	sí

Usted (you), like nouns, is invariable, except for number.

Auxiliary verbs

Estar (to be) [*estoy,* I am] expresses a transitory condition as to location, health, state of mind, etc.

Ser (to be) [*soy,* I am] expresses permanency, as sex, nationality, religion, existence, etc.

Yo estoy en América porqué soy americano.

I am in America because I am an American.

Infinitive, *ser*   Gerund, *siendo*   Past participle, *sido*

Auxiliary verbs

Present stem: phases of *es*

	Singular			Plural		
Present:						
Indicative	soy	eres	es	somos	sois	son
Subjunctive	sea	seas	sea	seamos	seáis	sean
Imperative	—	sé	—	—	sed	—
Imperfect	era	eras	era	éramos	erais	eran
Aorist stem: *fu*						
Aorist indicative	fui	fuiste	fué	fuimos	fuisteis	fueron
Imperfect subjunctive	fuera	fueras	fuera	fuéremos	fuerais	fueran
Aorist subjunctive	fuese	fueses	fuese	fuésemos	fueseis	fuesen
Future subjunctive	fuere	fueres	fuere	fuéremos	fuereis	fueren
Future stem: Regular (*ser*)						
Indicative	seré	serás	será	seremos	seréis	serán
Conditional	sería	serías	sería	seríamos	seríais	serían

Infinitive: *estar*   Gerund, *estando*   Past participle, *estado*

Present stem: *est*

	Singular			Plural		
Present:						
Indicative	estoy	estás	está	estamos	estáis	están
Subjunctive	esté	estés	esté	estemos	estéis	estén
Imperative	—	está	—	—	estad	—
Imperfect	estaba	estabas	estaba	estábamos	estábais	estaban
Aorist stem: *estuv*						
Aorist indicative	estuve	estuviste	estuvo	estuvimos	estuvisteis	estuvieron
Imperfect subjunctive	estuviera	estuvieras	estuviera	estuviéramos	estuvierais	estuvieran
Aorist subjunctive	estuviese	estuvieses	estuviese	estuviésemos	estuvieseis	estuviesen
Future subjunctive	estuviere	estuvieres	estuviere	estuviéremos	estuviereis	eestuvieren
Future stem: Regular (*estar*)						
Indicative	estaría	estarás	estará	estaremos	estaréis	estarán
Conditional	estaría	estarías	estaría	estaríamos	estaríais	estarían

Hacer (to do, make) (Latin *facere*[1])

Infinitive, *hacer*   Gerund, *haciendo*   Past participle, *hecho*

Present stem: *hag* (strong); *hac* (weak)

	Singular			Plural		
	1st person	2d person	3d person	1st person	2d person	3d person
Present:						
Indicative	hago	haces	hace .	hacemos	haceis	hacen
Subjunctive	haga	hagas	haga	hagamos	hagáis	hagan
Imperative	—	haz	—	—	raced	—
Imperfect	racía	hacías	hacía	hacíamos	hacíais	hacían
Aorist stem: *hic*						
Aorist indicative	hice	hiciste	hizo	hicimos	hicisteis	hicieron
Imperfect subjunctive	hiciera	hicieras	hiciera	hiciéramos	hicierais	hicieran
Aorist subjunctive	hiciese	hicieses	hicicse	hiciésemos	hicieseis	hiciesen
Future subjunctive,	hiciere	hicieres	aiciere	hiciéremos	hiciereis	hicieren
Future stem: *har*						
Future:						
Indicative	haré	harás	hará	haremos	haréis	harán
Conditional	haría	harías	haría	haríamos	haríais	harían

[1] Three of the compounds of *hacer* have not changed the Latin *f* to *h*: *liquefacer*, *rafefacer* and *satisfacer*.

Verbs

Spanish verbs are divided into three conjugations; those ending in *ar* belong to the first, those ending in *er* to the second, and those ending in *ir* to the third: *Hablar*, to talk; *comer*, to eat; *vivir*, to live. Different endings to show distinctions of person, number, tense, and mode are added to the stem of the verb.

Infinitive

habl-ar, to speak	com-er, to eat	viv-ir, to live

Gerund

habl-ando, speaking	com-iendo, eating	viv-iendo, living

Past participle

habl-ado, spoken	com-ido, eaten	viv-ido, lived

INDICATIVE MOOD

	Singular			Plural		
	First person	Second person	Third person	First person	Second person	Third person
Present	habl-o	habl-as	habl-a	habl-amos	habl-áis	habl-an
	com-o	com-es	com-e	com-emos	com-éis	com-en
	viv-o	viv-es	viv-e	viv-imos	viv-ís	viv-en
Imperfect	habl-aba	habl-abas	habl-aba	habl-ábamos	habl-ábais	habl-aban
	com-ía	com-ías	com-ía	com-íamos	com-íais	com-ían
	viv-ía	viv-ías	viv-ía	viv-íamos	viv-íais	viv-ían
Past definite	habl-é	habl-aste	habl-ó	habl-amos	habl-asteis	habl-aron
	com-í	com-iste	com-ió	com-imos	com-isteis	com-ieron
	viv-í	viv-iste	viv-ió	viv-imos	viv-isteis	viv-ieron
Future	habl-aré	habl-arás	habl-ará	habl-aremos	habl-aréis	habl-arán
	com-eré	com-erás	com-erá	com-eremos	com-eréis	com-erán
	viv-iré	viv-irás	viv-irá	viv-iremos	viv-iréis	viv-irán
Conditional	habl-aría	habl-arías	habl-aría	habl-aríamos	habl-aríais	habl-arían
	com-ería	com-erías	com-ería	com-eríamos	com-eríais	com-erían
	viv-iría	viv-irías	viv-iría	viv-iríamos	viv-iríais	viv-irían

SUBJUNCTIVE MOOD

Present	habl-e	habl-es	habl-e	habl-emos	habl-éis	habl-en
	com-a	com-as	com-a _f._	com-amos	com-áis	com-an
	viv-a	viv-as	viv-a	viv-amos	viv-áis	viv-an
Imperfect	habl-ase	habl-ases	habl-ase	habl-ásemos	habl-aseis	habl-asen
	_or_ -ara	_or_ -aras	_or_ -ara	_or_ -áramos	_or_ -arais	_or_ -aran
	com-	com-	com-	com-	com-	com-
	iese _or_	ieses _or_	iese _or_	iésemos _or_	ieseis _or_	iesen _or_
	-iera	-ieras	-iera	-iéramos	-ierais	-ieran
	viv-	viv-	viv-	viv-	viv-	viv-
	iese _or_	ieses _or_	ieses _or_	iésemos _or_	ieseis _or_	iesen _or_
	-iera	-ieras	-iera	-iéramos	-ierais	-ieran

There are many irregular verbs the conjugations of which must be learned separately.

Abbreviations

Spell out names of countries, States, and Provinces, whether town is given or not.

Titles preceding names are usually spelled out, but both forms are permissible; uniformity should be adopted when possible. Observe the following form: _el Sr._ (or _señor_) _Enrique Palava._

A.	autor, author	Hnos.	hermanos, brothers
AA.	autores, authors	íd.	ídem, the same
ab.	abril, April	íb.	íbidem, in the same place
agto.	agosto, August	Ilmo.	ilustrísimo, most illustrious
art.	artículo, article		
B.	beato, blessed	jul.	julio, July
B.S.M.	beso sus manos, with great respect (_lit._ I kiss your hands)	jun.	junio, June
		Lic., Lcdo.	licenciado, licenciate
		L.S.	lugar del sello, place of the seal
C.A.	Centroamérica, Central America	Méx.	México, Mexico
cap.	capítulo, chapter	mzo.	marzo, March
Cía.	compañía, company	m/n.	moneda nacional, national currency
C.M.B.	cuyas manos beso, very respectfully (_lit._ whose hands I kiss)	n.a.	nota del autor, author's note
c/l.	curso legal, legal procedure (legal currency)	nbre.	noviembre, November
		No., Nº, núm.	número, number
D.	don, Mr.		
dbre.	diciembre, December	N.Y.	Nueva York, New York
D.F.	Distrito Federal, Federal District	obre.	octubre, October
		P.R.	Puerto Rico
Dña.	doña, Mrs.	pág.	página, page
Dr.	doctor, doctor	pár.	párrafo, paragraph
Dra.	doctora, doctress	R.A.	República Argentina, Argentine Republic
eno.	enero, January		
EE. UU., E.U.	Estados Unidos, United States	Q.E.P.D.	que en paz descanse, may he (she) rest in peace
E.U.A.	Estados Unidos de América, United States of America	S.A.	Sociedad Anónima, stock company; Su Alteza, His Highness; Sudamérica, South America
fbro.	febrero, February		
Gral.	general, general		
hh.	hojas, leaves		

Abbreviations

sbre.	septiembre, September		faithful servant
S.E.u.O.	salvo error u omisión, errors and omissions excepted	Sto., Sta.	santo, santa, saint
		t.	tomo, volume
		tip.	tipografía, printing office
S.E.	Su Excelencia, His Excellency	Ud., V., Vd.	usted, you
		Uds., VV.	ustedes, pl. of you
S.M.	Su Majestad, His Majesty	V.	véase, see
		V.A.	Vuestra Alteza, Your Highness
sec.	sección, section		
Sr.	señor, sir; also God	V.B.	visto bueno, O. K.
Sra.	señora, lady	V.E.	Vuestra Excelencia, Your Excellency
Sres.	señores, sirs		
Srio.	secretario, secretary	V.M.	Vuestra Majestad, Your Majesty
Srita., Srta.	señorita, young lady, miss		
S.S.	Su Señoría, His Lordship	Vm.	Vuestra Merced, Your Worship
S.Atto.S.S.,	su atento y seguro servidor, your obedient and		
S.A.S.S.		&	y, and

Figures

Arabic and roman numerals are used as in English.
The following form is used in numbering paragraphs and sentences.

(1°) Todos los días, etc.   (2°) Los hombres, etc.

Note that a superior lower-case o (°), not a degree mark, is used.

Cardinal numbers

un, -o, -a	one	diez	ten
dos	two	once	eleven
tres	three	doce	twelve
cuatro	four	trece	thirteen
cinco	five	diez y seis	sixteen
seis	six	veinte	twenty
siete	seven	veintiuno (veintiun)	twenty-one
ocho	eight	cien, ciento	hundred
nueve	nine	mil	thousand

Round millions preceding units of quantity are followed by the preposition *de: tres millones de pesos, 3,000,000 de pesos.*

Ordinal numbers

primero, -a (1°)	first	décimo	tenth
segundo, -a (2°)	second	undécimo	eleventh
tercero, tercer	third	duodécimo	twelfth
cuarto	fourth	décimotercio	thirteenth
quinto	fifth	vigésimo	twentieth
sexto	sixth	vigésimo primero	twenty-first
séptimo	seventh	centésimo	hundredth
octavo	eighth	milésimo	thousandth
noveno, nono	ninth		

Months

enero (eno.)	January	julio (jul.)	July
febrero (fbro.)	February	agosto (agto.)	August
marzo (mzo.)	March	septiembre (sbre.)	September
abril (ab.)	April	octubre (obre.)	October
mayo	May	noviembre (nbre.)	November
junio (jun.)	June	diciembre (dbre.)	December

Days

domingo	Sunday	jueves	Thursday
lunes	Monday	viernes	Friday
martes	Tuesday	sábado	Saturday
miércoles	Wednesday		

Seasons

primavera	spring	otoño	autumn
verano	summer	invierno	winter

Time

hora	hour	mes	month
día	day	año	year
semana	week		

Articles to be disregarded in filing

un, uno	una, unas	el, los	la, las

SWEDISH

A	a	*a* in father
B	b	*b*
C	c	*k* before *a, o, u* or consonants; *s* in foreign words and before *e, i, ä* and *y*
D	d	*d*
E	e	*e* in felt
F	f	*f*, but *v* at end of word
G	g	*g* before *l, r, t, a, o, u* and *å; y* before *e, i, j, y, ä, ö;* before *n* the French *en*
H	h	*h* aspirated, except before *j* and *v*
I	i	*ee* in tree
J	j	*y* in yellow
K	k	*k*[1]
L	l	*l;* silent before *j*
M	m	*m*

N	n	*n;* before *k* has sound of *ng*
O	o	*o* in folio, also *oo* in boon
P	p	*p*
Q	q	*k*
R	r	*r*, strongly enunciated
S	s	*s*, hard[2]
T	t	*t*
U	u	*u* in value (no *y* sound); when short, *u* in up
V	v	*v*
W	w	*v*
X	x	*x*
Y	y	*ü* in German über
Z	z	*s* hard
Å	å	*aw* in saw
Ä	ä	*ä* in German Fährte; when short, *e* in wren
Ö	ö	*ö* in German Götter

---

[1] Before *l, r,* and *v,* and before the hard vowels *a, å, o, u,* as well as at the end of words. Before the soft vowels *ä, e, i, y,* and *ö* it has what is called the "*tje*" sound, nearly equivalent to *ch.*
[2] Before *e, i, j, y, ä,* and *ö, sh, sk,* and *stj* are pronounced as *sh.*

The Latin alphabet is universally used in Sweden, with the addition of the letters *å, ä,* and *ö.* The *a, o, u* and *å* are hard vowels; *e, i, y, ä,* and *ö* soft vowels. *C, q, w, x,* and *z* are used only in words of foreign origin and in proper names.

Swedish belongs to the Scandinavian group of languages, constituting a branch of the Teutonic class of the northern division of the Aryan. Previous to 1200 A. D. it was recorded only in runic inscriptions, the modern standard having begun its development in the fourteenth century.

Accentuation

Accent marks are used only in foreign loan words (*resumé*) and in certain proper names (*Tegnér*).

As a general rule word stress falls as follows:

1. On the root syllable in all simple native words: *ba'ka* (bake), *fa'der* (father).
2. On the first syllable in all compound words of native origin: *av'stand* (distance), *prat'sam* (talkative).
3. On the last syllable in all words ending in *eri: tryckeri'* (printing office), *slaveri'* (slavery).
4. Foreign words usually retain their original stress.
5. In addition to stress accentuation, there is a so-called "musical" accent, of which there are high, low, and normal tones. These can be learned best from a native.

Phonetics

The characters of the alphabet are pronounced as shown in the table, but the following additional remarks are pertinent:

ch has the sound of *sj*, used mainly in words of foreign origin: *choklad* [sjoklad] (chocolate).

k is pronounced as in English before consonants and hard vowels, *a, o, u,* and *å;* also before the soft vowels *e* and *i* when in unaccented suffixes, and in foreign words: *klocka* (clock), *rynkig* (wrinkled), *arkiv* (archive). It is pronounced like the English *ch* before all soft vowels, *e, i, y, ä,* and *ö: kylig* (chilly); it is not silent before *n: kniv* (knife).

sch, sj, skj, ssj, and *stj* before a vowel have the sound of *sh*, though somewhat rougher.

The suffixes *sion* and *ssion* have the sound of *tion* in English, while the suffix *tion* has the sound of *tsion*.

The combination *tj* is equivalent to the English *ch* in chair.

Capitalization

Capitals are used almost as in English: At the beginning of a sentence, in proper names, but not in the case of adjectives derived from them. The names of the months and the days of the week are not capitalized.

Syllabication

A consonant between two vowels usually goes with the following vowel (*lä-ra-re*); when two or more consonants occur between two vowels, the last consonant generally goes with the following vowel (*fladd-ra*); *sch* and *sk* when used for the *sj* sound are not separated, but added to the following vowel (*mar-schera, männi-ska*); *ng* remains with the preceding vowel unless *n* and *g* belong to different parts of a compound word. Compound words are divided according to their component parts.

Punctuation

The rules of punctuation are essentially the same as in English, although the Swedish punctuation is perhaps somewhat closer, the comma, especially, being used more freely.

Articles

		Common gender	Neuter gender
Indefinite article		*en*	*ett*
Definite article:			
Postpositive	Singular	*-en, -n*	*-et, -t*
	Plural	*-na* (rarely *-ne*)	*-na, -a, -en*
Prepositive	Singular	*den*	*det*
	Plural	*de*	

The postpositive article, which is suffixed to the noun, is always used when the noun is definite in sense; the prepositive article is used together with the postpositive article when the noun is modified by an adjective.

Adjectives

These agree with the noun in gender and number, but not in case.

In declining, they add *t* to the stem for the neuter singular, and *a* for the plural of all genders when used attributively with the indefinite article or predicatively; *a* (or *e*), singular or plural, when used attributively with the definite article.

Comparatives and superlatives are formed by adding *are* and *ast*, respectively, to the stem, but there are also irregular forms.

The following table shows the use of the articles, nouns, and adjectives in their more significant constructions and collocations:

	Singular	Plural
English	(girl)	(girls)
(a)	en flicka	flickor
the	flickan	flickorna
of the	flickans	flickornas
(a) pretty	en vacker flicka	vackra flickor
the pretty	den vackra flickan	de vackra flickorna
of the pretty	den vackra flickans	de vackra flickornas
for the	för flickan	för flickorna
the prettier	den vackrare flickan	de vackrare flickorna
the prettiest	den vackrasta flickan	de vackrasta flickorna

Genders

There are four genders: masculine (all living beings of the male sex), feminine (all living beings of the female sex), common (comprising such nouns as foot, goose, hand), and neuter (comprising abstract and geographic terms; also miscellaneous nouns having certain endings). The first three are sometimes termed "common" genders.

Nouns

The plural is formed by adding the endings *or, ar, er,* or *n* to the stem of the noun, depending on its class, or by internal modification.

The five declensions differ in the formation of the nominative plural of the indefinite form:

First.—Ending in *or*: flicka (girl), flickor (girls);
Second.—Ending in *ar*: fågel (bird), fåglar (birds);
Third.—Ending in *er*: bild (picture), bilder (pictures);
Fourth.—Ending in *n*: hjärta (heart). hjärtan (hearts);
Fifth.—Without ending: bagare (baker), bagare (bakers).

The possessive is formed by adding *s*, singular or plural. If the word ends in *s*, it takes only an apostrophe: *flickornas blommor* (the girls' flowers); *Johannes' evangelium* (the Gospel of St. John).

Pronouns

The use of pronouns is in the main similar to that in English. The declension of the personal pronouns is as follows:

	Singular			Plural		
	Nom. (I)	Poss. (my)	Obj. (me)	Nom. (we)	Poss. (our)	Obj. (us)
I	jag	min	mig	vi	vår	oss
Thou	du	din	dig	ni	eder, er	eder, er
He	han	hans	honom			
She	hon	hennes	henne	}de	deras	dem
It	det	dess	det			

Auxiliary verbs

There are three classes of auxiliary verbs:

1. "Temporala," those which help to form compound tenses. *hava* (to have), and *skola* (shall or will).

2. "Modala," those which serve to express different moods: *skola* and *lär* (shall); *må* and *måtte* (may, might); *måste* (must); *böra* (ought); *månde* (should); *kunna* (can); *vilja* (will); *tör* (may); *töras* (dare); *få* (may), and *låta* (let).

3. "Passive," those which serve to conjugate the passive: *vara, varda* (be); blifva (become).

Auxiliary verbs —Continued.

	Singular	Plural	Singular	Plural	Singular	Plural
Indicative:						
Present	Jag har [1]	vi ha (hava)	är [2]	äro	skall [3]	skola
	du har	Ni hava	är	äro	skall	skola
	han har	de ha (hava)	är	äro	skall	skola
Imperf.	hade	hade	var	voro	skulle	skulle
	hade	haden	var	voro	skulle	skulle
	hade	hade	var	voro	skulle	skulle
Perfect	har haft		varit		har skolat	
	har haft		varit		har skolat	
	har haft		varit		har skolat	
Pluperf.	hade haft		hade varit		hade skolat	
	hade haft		hade varit		hade skolat	
	hade haft		hade varit		hade skolat	
Future	skall ha(va)		skall vara			
	skall ha(va)		skall vara			
	skall ha(va)		skall vara			
Future perf.	skall ha(va) haft		skall hava varit			
	skall ha(va) haft		skall hava varit			
	skall ha(va) haft		skall hava varit			
Subjunctive:						
Present	have (må or måtte ha(va))	hav (må. ha(va))	vare (må vara)	vare (må vara)		
	"	.hava (må ha(va))	"	varen (må vara)		
	"	hav (må ha(va)	"	vare (må vara)		
Imperf.	hade (skulle (matte) ha(va))	hade (skulle (matte) ha(va))	vore (måtte (skulle) vara)	vore (måtte (skulle) vara)		
	"	hade (skulle (matte) ha(va))	"	vore (måtte (skulle) vara)		
	"	hade (skulle (matte) (ha(va))	"	vore (måtte (skulle) vara)		
Perfect	må ha(va) haft		må hava varit			
	må ha(va) haft		må hava varit			
	må ha(va) haft		må hava varit			
Pluperf.	hade haft (skulle ha(va) haft)		skulle hava varit			
	"		"			
	"		"			
Imperative	—	havom (låt(om) oss ha(va))	—	varo (låt(om) oss vara)		
	hav!	hav	var!	vare		
	—	—	—	—		
Infinitive:						
Present	hava (ha) ,		vara		skola	
Perfect	ha (va) haft		hava varit		hava skolat	
Participle						
Present	(havande)		varande		skolande	
Perfect	havd (uncommon)		—		—	
Supine	haft		varit		skolat	

[1] Forms in parentheses are almost, if not entirely obsolete. Only the present, imperfect, future, infinitive, and present participle are used as auxiliary verbs.

[2] 1. The verb *vara* (endure) belongs to the regular 4th conjugation.
2. With a perfect participle, *vara* means "to be": *Jag är älskad* (I am loved).
3. *Varande* (participle) is used infrequently.

[3] For *skall* and *skola* current usage is *ska*.

Buva (to become) is entirely regular of the 4th conjugation.

Lar occurs only in the present indicative. The plurals are *vi lära, I lären, de lära.*

The plurals of *må* and *måtte* are *vi må, I mån, de må; vi måtte, I måtten, de måtte; må (så) vara* (maybe).

The forms *måga* and *mågen* are obsolete, and *måtte* is never used in the past tense. It rather emphasizes a desire, as "would that I might."

Do not confuse *må (mår, mådde, måtte)* = to find oneself, which belongs to the 3d conjugation.

The plurals of *måste* are *vi måste, I måsten, de måste;* supine, *måst (Det måste så vara* = it must be).

Although imperfect, *måste* is also used for the present; occasionally the perfect and pluperfect are the same *(har, hade måst).* The infinitive in the Swedish used in Finland is *måsta,* and the supine *måstat.*

Mande (imperfect) is almost obsolete though occasionally found as in *Vad månde det vetyda?* (What might that signify?) It has been generally displaced by *månne: Månne han vil?* (will he want to?) *Mån* is also used: *Mån tro det* (Is it possible? Really! I would never have believed it!)

Verbs

The so-called "weak verbs" belong to the first, second and third conjugations, which form their imperfect by adding an ending to the unchanged root. The "strong verbs" belong to the fourth conjugation and form their imperfect by merely changing the vowel of the root.

I. The first conjugation takes the following endings:
-*a* in the infinitive;
-*ar* in the singular of the present indicative;
-*a* elsewhere in the plural present indicative;
ade in both numbers of the imperfect indicative;
-*ande* in the present participle;
-*at* in the supine [1];
-*ad* in the gender form of the past participle;
-*at* in the neuter form of the past participle.

II. The second conjugation takes the following endings:
-*a* in the infinitive;
-*er* in the singular of the present indicative;
-*a* elsewhere in the plural present indicative;
-*de* or -*te* in both numbers of the *imperfect* indicative;
-*ande in the present participle;*
·*t* in the supine;
-*d* or -*t* in the gender form of the past participle;
-*t* in the neuter form of the past participle.

III. The third conjugation takes the following endings:
any vowel other than *a* in the infinitive;
-*r* in the singular of the present indicative;
same as the infinitive, in the plural present indicative;
-*dde* in both numbers of the imperfect indicative;
-*ende* in the present participle;
-*tt* in the supine;
-*dd* in the gender form of the past participle;
-*tt* in the neuter form of the past participle.

IV. The fourth conjugation takes the following endings:
-*a* in the infinitive;
-*er* in the singular of the present indicative;
-*a* elsewhere in the plural present indicative;
no termination in the imperfect indicative;
-*ande* in the present participle;
-*it* in the supine;
-*en* in the gender form of the past participle;
-*et* in the neuter form of the past participle.

---

[1] The "supine" has been evolved from the neuter form of the past participle, and with the auxiliary verb *hava* forms the compound perfect tenses.

The following is the conjugation of the verb *kalla* (call) in the active form:

Indicative	Singular	Plural
Present	kallar kallar kallar	kalla kallen kalla
Imperfert	kallade kallade kallade	kallade kalladen kallade
Perfect	kallat kallat kallat	ha *or* hava kallat han *or* haven kallat ha *or* hava kallat
Pluperfect	hade kallat hade kallat hade kallat	hade kallat haden kallat hade kallat
Future	komer att (skall) kalla komer att (skall) kalla komer att (skall) kalla	komma (&c.) att (skola, &c.) kalla komma (&c.) att (skola, &c.) kalla komma (&c.) att (skola, &c.) kalla
Future perfect	kommer att (skall) hava kallat kommer att (skall) hava kallat kommer att (skall) hava kallat	komma (&c.) att (skalla, &c.) hava kallat komma (&c.) att (skall, &c.) hava kallat komma (&c.) att (skall, &c.) hava kallat

att kalla (to call), *kallas* (to be called)

Cardinal numbers

en, ett, ene (a)	one	sjutton	seventeen
två	two	aderton	eighteen
tre	three	nitton	nineteen
fyra	four	tjugu (tjugo)	twenty
fem	five	tjuguen (tjuguett)	twenty-one
sex	six		
sju	seven	trettio	thirty
åtta	eight	fyrtio	forty
nio	nine	femtio	fifty
tio	ten	sextio	sixty
elva	eleven	sjuttio	seventy
tolv	twelve	åttio	eighty
tretton	thirteen	nittio	ninety
fjorton	fourteen	hundra	hundred
femton	fifteen	tusen	thousand
sexton	sixteen		

Ordinal numbers

(den) förste(a)	first	sextonde	sixteenth
andre(a)	second	sjuttonde	seventeenth
tredje	third	adertonde	eighteenth
fjärde	fourth	nittonde	nineteenth
femte	fifth	tjugonde	twentieth
sjätte	sixth	tjuguförsta	twenty-first
sjunde	seventh	trettionde	thirtieth
åttonde	eighth	fyrtionde	fortieth
nionde	ninth	femtionde	fiftieth
tionde	tenth	sextionde	sixtieth
elfte	eleventh	sjuttionde	seventieth
tolfte	twelfth	åttionde	eightieth
trettonde	thirteenth	nittionde	ninetieth
fjortonde	fourteenth	hundrade	hundredth
femtonde	fifteenth	tusende	thousandth

Months

januari (jan.)	January	juli	July
februari (feb.)	February	augusti (aug.)	August
mars	March	september (sept.)	September
april (apr.)	April	oktober (okt.)	October
maj	May	november (nov.)	November
juni	June	december (dec.)	December

Days

söndag	Sunday	torsdag	Thursday
måndag	Monday	fredag	Friday
tisdag	Tuesday	lördag	Saturday
onsdag	Wednesday		

Seasons

vår	spring	höst	autumn
sommar	summer	vinter	winter

Time

timme	hour	månad	month
dag	day	år	year
vecka	week		

Abbreviations

Where the last letter of the abbreviation is the last letter of the complete word the period is not used.

a.-b.	aktiebolag, joint-stock company	ex.	exempel, example (illustration), e.g.
adr.	adress, address, c/o	f.	född, born
ang.	angående, concerning	f.d.	för detta, before this, formerly
anm.	anmärkning, remark, observation		
		f.m.	förmiddagen, before noon, a.m.
b., bd	band, volume, volumes	frk.	fröken, Miss
bl.a.	bland annat, bland andra, among other things, or others	förf.	författare, author; författarinna, authoress
d.	död, dead	f.ö.	för övrigt, besides
d:o	dito, ditto	H.M. H.Maj:t	Hans Majestät, His Majesty
dr, d:r	doktor, doctor	hr	herr, Sir, Mr.
d.v.s.	det vill säga, that is, that is to say	i st.f.	i stället för, in place of
d.y.	den yngre, junior	jfr	jämför, compare
d.ä.	den äldre, senior; det är, that is	kap.	kapitel, chapter
		kl.	klockan, o'clock
e.m.	eftermiddagen, afternoon, p.m.	kr.	krona, crown; kronor, crowns (coin)
etc.	et cetera, and so forth	kungl.	kunglig, royal

Abbreviations—Continued

m.a.o.	med andra ord, in other words	o.s.a.	om svar anhålles, an answer is requested
m.fl.	med flera, with others, and others	o.s.v.	och så vidare, and so forth
m.m.	med mera, etc., and so forth	p.s.	postskriptum, postscript
n.b.	nota bene, mark (notice) well	red.	redaktör, editor
		s., sid.	sida, page; sidor, pages
nr, n:o	nummer, numro, number	s.d.	samma dag, the same day
näml.	nämligen, namely, viz, to wit	s.k.	så kallad, so called
		t.ex.	till exempel, for instance
obs.	observera, observe	t.o.m.	till och med, even
o.d.	och dylikt (dylika), and the like	und.	undantag, exception

TAGALOG

A	a	ah	O	o	o
B	b	b	P	p	f
C	c	c, k	R	r	r
D	d	d	S	s	s
E	e	a	T	t	t
G	g	g, hard	U	u	oo
H	h	h	V	v	b
I	i	e	W	w	ua (wa); ao (aw)
K	k	Often used for hard c and q	X	x	h, initial; only in Spanish words
L	l	l	Y	y	ay (ai); also initial consonant
M	m	m			
N	n	n	Z	z	s, only in Spanish words
NG	ñg	ng in ringing			

The Tagalog is the most important of the Philippine languages, of which there are some three score.

The vowels *e* and *i* are very often confused, but *e* does not exist in pure Tagalog.

Syllabication

Division is on the vowel and a consonant goes with the following vowel; two consonants between vowels are separated, but *ñg* being a single letter must not be separated.

Capitalization

The capital letters are used for initials of proper names and at the beginning of a sentence.

Accents

The Tagalog uses three accents, the acute, grave and circumflex.

The acute may fall on any syllable, but usually the last or next to the last. In a word ending with a vowel the accent indicates that the vowel has a broad sound and that the suffixed particles *an* and *in* prefix an *h* when joined to such words: *Umútang*, to borrow; *magútang*, to lend; *magpaútang*, to lend freely. In some cases the suffixing of *han* or *hin* draws the accent one syllable nearer the end of the word.

As a rule words not carrying an accent take the stress on the last syllable if ending with a consonant, except in the case of *n* or *s*, when stress is on the next to the last syllable.

The grave accent marks words ending in a vowel which take *an* or *in*, instead of *han* or *hin*, and the stress is on the preceding syllable: *Batà*, child, pronounced "báhta." The grave accent is not used in words ending with a consonant.

The circumflex is used only on the final vowel of words ending with an abrupt, obscure vowel sound on which the stress is placed, and permits only *an* or *in* as a suffix: *Dumalitâ*, to endure.

Proper accentuation is very important as many words are only distinguished by the accent, differing entirely in meaning: *Gátas*, milk; *gatás*, trail; *sumílang*, to rise; *sumilang* (stress on last syllable), to pass between.

Articles

The article of proper nouns is *si* and is generally prefixed to nouns designating persons related or well known to the writer, as well as terms of endearment; it may also be used with the proper name of an animal belonging to the speaker. It is declined as follows:

Nom.	Joseph	*si José*
Gen.	Joseph's; of Joseph	*ni José; kay José*
Dat.	To, for Joseph	
Acc.	Joseph	*kay José*
Abl.	From, with Joseph	

The plural article for names when coupled with words is declined as follows:

Nom. Joseph and his ———— *siná José*
Gen. The field of Joseph and his family *ang búkid nina José*
Dat. To, for Joseph and his ————
Acc. The field of Joseph and his family ⎱ *ang kaná José búkid*
Abl. From, by Joseph and his ———— ⎰

The article of common nouns is *ang*, and is declined as follows:

	Singular	Plural	
Nom.	*ang*	*ang mañgá*	the
Gen.	*nang, sa*	*nang mañgá, sa mañgá*	of the
Dat.	*sa*	*sa mañgá*	to, for the
Acc.	*nang, sa*	*nang mañgá, sa mañgá*	the
Abl.	*nang, sa*	*sa mañgá, nang mañgá*	from, with the

There is no indefinite article, though the numeral *isá* (one) may be used.

Numerals

In Tagalog there are four classes: Cardinals, ordinals, adverbials, and distributives.

Cardinal numbers

isá	one	dalawang pouó't isá	twenty-one
dalawá	two	tatlong pouó	thirty
tatló	three	apat na pouó	forty
apat [1]	four	limang pouó	fifty
limá	five	anim na pouó	sixty
anim [1]	six	pitong pouó	seventy
pitó	seven	walong pouó	eighty
waló	eight	siyam na pouó	ninety
siyam	nine	isang dáan, sangdáan	hundred
sangpouó	ten	sangdáa't isá	hundred and one
labing isá	eleven		
labing dalawá	twelve	sanglibo	thousand
dalawang pouó	twenty		

Ordinal numbers [2]

naóna	first	ikasiyam	ninth
ikalawá	second	ikapouó, ikasang pouó	tenth
ikatló	third	ikalabing isá	eleventh
ikápat	fourth	ikalabing dalawá	twelfth
ikalimá	fifth	ikadalawang pouó	twentieth
ikánim	sixth	ikadalawang pouo't isá	twenty-first
ikapitó	seventh	ikasangdáan	hundredth
ikawaló	eighth	ikasanglibo	thousandth

Adverbial numbers

minsan, ninsan (rare)	once	makasiyam	nine times
		makasangpouó	ten times
makalawá	twice	makalabing ápat	fourteen times
makatatló	thrice	makadalawang pouó	twenty times
makaápat, makaípat (rare)	four times	makadalawang pouó't limá	twenty-five times
makalimá	five times	makasangdáan	hundred times
makaánim	six times	makasanglibo, maka libo	thousand times
makapitó	seven times		
makawaló	eight times		

Distributive numbers

isáisá	one by one	sangposangpouó	ten by ten
daladalawá	two by two	labilabing isá	eleven by eleven
tatlótatló	three by three	labilabing dalawá	twelve by twelve
apatápat	four by four	daladalawang pouó	twenty by twenty
limálimá	five by five		
animánim	six by six	sangdasangdáan	hundred by hundred
pitópitó	seven by seven		
walówaló	eight by eight	sanglisanglibo	thousand by thousand
siyamsiyam	nine by nine		

[1] Stress on the first syllable.
[2] Ordinals are used for all the days of the month as in English.

Months

enero (eno.)	January	julio (jul.)	July
febrero (fbro.)	February	agosto (agto.)	August
marzo (mzo.)	March	septiembre (sbre.)	September
abril (ab.)	April	octubre (obre.)	October
mayo	May	noviembre (nbre.)	November
junio (jun.)	June	diciembre (dbre.)	December

Days

lingo	Sunday	jueves	Thursday
lunes	Monday	viernes	Friday
martes	Tuesday	sábado	Saturday
miércoles	Wednesday		

Seasons

ang tagárao	the dry season	ang tagulán	the wet season

Time

ora	hour	buán	month
árao	day	taón	year
lingo	week		

TAMIL

Character	Transliteration	Character	Transliteration	Character	Transliteration	Character	Transliteration	Character	Transliteration	Character	Transliteration
அ	a	உள்	ŭ	ஐ	ai, ei	ஞ	ña	ப	pa, ba	வ	va
ஆ	ā	எ	e	ஔ	au	ட	ṭa	ம	ma	ழ	ṛa
இ	i	ஏ	ē	க	ka, ga	ண	ṇa	ய	ya	ள	ḷa
ஈ	ī	ஒ	o	ங	ṅa	த	ta	ர	ra	ற	ṛa
உ	u	ஓ	ō	ச	śa	ந	na	ல	la	ன	ṇa

COMBINATIONS

	a	ā	i	ī	u	ŭ	e	ē	o	ō	aì	au
k	க	கா	கி	கீ	கு	கூ	கெ	கே	கொ	கோ	கை	கௌ
ṅ	ங	ஙா	ஙி	ஙீ	ஙு	ஙூ	ஙெ	ஙே	ஙொ	ஙோ	ஙை	ஙௌ
ś	ச	சா	சி	சீ	சு	சூ	செ	சே	சொ	சோ	சை	சௌ
ñ	ஞ	ஞா	ஞி	ஞீ	ஞு	ஞூ	ஞெ	ஞே	ஞொ	ஞோ	ஞை	ஞௌ
ṭ	ட	டா	டி	டீ	டு	டூ	டெ	டே	டொ	டோ	டை	டௌ
ṇ	ண	ணா	ணி	ணீ	ணு	ணூ	ணெ	ணே	ணொ	ணோ	ணை	ணௌ
t	த	தா	தி	தீ	து	தூ	தெ	தே	தொ	தோ	தை	தௌ
n	ந	நா	நி	நீ	நு	நூ	நெ	நே	நொ	நோ	நை	நௌ
p	ப	பா	பி	பீ	பு	பூ	பெ	பே	பொ	போ	பை	பௌ
m	ம	மா	மி	மீ	மு	மூ	மெ	மே	மொ	மோ	மை	மௌ
y	ய	யா	யி	யீ	யு	யூ	யெ	யே	யொ	யோ	யை	யௌ
r	ர	ரா	ரி	ரீ	ரு	ரூ	ரெ	ரே	ரொ	ரோ	ரை	ரௌ
l	ல	லா	லி	லீ	லு	லூ	லெ	லே	லொ	லோ	லை	லௌ
v	வ	வா	வி	வீ	வு	வூ	வெ	வே	வொ	வோ	வை	வௌ
ṛ	ழ	ழா	ழி	ழீ	ழு	ழூ	ழெ	ழே	ழொ	ழோ	ழை	ழௌ
ḷ	ள	ளா	ளி	ளீ	ளு	ளூ	ளெ	ளே	ளொ	ளோ	ளை	ளௌ
ṛ	ற	றா	றி	றீ	று	றூ	றெ	றே	றொ	றோ	றை	றௌ
ṇ	ன	னா	னி	னீ	னு	னூ	னெ	னே	னொ	னோ	னை	னௌ

Tamil is the language spoken in the Madras Presidency, Tanjore, Tinnevelly, Coimbatore, Chittoor, and the Nilgris, as also in the coffee and tea districts of northern Ceylon. It is the oldest, richest, and most thoroughly organized of the Dravidian languages, and has also the distinction of having fewer Sanscrit words than any of the others.

Tamil has borrowed words from the Hindustani, Arabic, Persian, and, more recently, English, while a few Tamil words have crept into the English, as curry (*kaṛi*), mulligatawny (*milagu*, pepper, and *tannîr*, cool water), cheroot (*suruttu*), and pariah (*paṛeigan*).

The characters shown in the table have changed but little in the past 500 years. They differ from the other Dravidian alphabets, both in shape and phonetic value.

The alphabet is well adapted to express the 12 vowels of the language (a, $\bar{a}$, i, $\bar{\imath}$, u, $\bar{u}$, e, $\bar{e}$, o, $\bar{o}$, ei, and au), but the consonantal sounds are very meagerly served; the character k must also serve for kh, g, and gh, and, occasionally, h, while ch also serves for s; of the other surd consonants, ch, $\underline{t}$, t, and p, each represents the remaining three sounds of its class. Each of the consonants k, ch, $\underline{t}$, t, and p has its own nasal.

The short a remains with the consonant, but, if it should separate, a point will be placed above the letter. All the other vowels will remain either before or after the consonant.

In addition to the four semivowels, there are a cerebral r and l, as also a liquid l, that was formerly a feature of all Dravidian languages, the sound, however, varying in different districts. There is also a peculiar n, differing in function though not in pronunciation, from the dental n.

Vowel ligatures

ஷ	வ	ஹ	ஜ	க்ஷ	ஂ	உ	மீ	வரு
sha	*sa*	*ha*	*ja*	*ksha*	χ or Visarga	Day	Month	Year

The consonants are classified as follows:

1.	Hard	k	$\acute{s}$	$\underline{t}$	t	p	r
2.	Soft (nasal)	$\dot{n}$	$\tilde{n}$	$\underline{n}$	n	m	n
3.	Medium (semivowels)	y	r	l	v	r	l

Divide words on any syllable, but do not separate a consonant from its vowel. The period is the only punctuation mark used.

Numerals

க	உ	ங	ச	ரு	சா	எ	அ	கூ	ய	யக	ாா	த
1	2	3	4	5	6	7	8	9	10	11	100	1000

TELUGU

Character	Transliteration	Character	Transliteration	Character	Transliteration	Character	Transliteration
అ	a	ఒ	o	ఞ	ña	ఫ	pha
ఆ	ā	ఓ	ō	ట	ṭa	బ	ba
ఇ	i	ఔ	au	ఠ	ṭha	భ	bha
ఈ	ī	ం	ṅ	డ	ḍa	మ	ma
ఉ	u	ః	ḥ	ఢ	ḍha	య	ẏa
ఊ	ū	క	ka	ణ	ṇa	ర	ṙa
ౠ	ṛ	ఖ	kha	త	ta	ల	la
ౠ	ṝ	గ	ga	థ	tha	వ	va
ఎ	e	ఘ	gha	ద	da	శ	śa
ఏ	ē	ఙ	ṅa	ధ	dha	ష	ṣa
ఐ	ai	చ	ca	న	na	స	sa
		ఛ	cha	ప	pa	హ	ha
		జ	ja			ళ	ḷa
		ఝ	jha			క్ష	kṣa

Consonantal combinations
The second is often placed under the first, often in widely variant form; some forms are shown here:

గ్ర gra · త్క tkā · స్తి sti · త్న tna · క్వ kva · మ్న ṁna

Numerals
౧ 1 · ౨ 2 · ౩ 3 · ౪ 4 · ౫ 5 · ౬ 6 · ౭ 7 · ౮ 8 · ౯ 9 · ౦ 0

Punctuation
౷ ౦ ౩ ౹ ౼ ॥ ।

COMBINATIONS

	ā	i	ī	u	ū	e	ē	o	ō	au	ai
k	కా	కి	కీ	కు	కూ	కె	కే	కొ	కో	కౌ	కై
kh	ఖా	ఖి	ఖీ	ఖు	ఖూ	ఖె	ఖే	ఖొ	ఖో	ఖౌ	ఖై
g	గా	గి	గీ	గు	గూ	గె	గే	గొ	గో	గౌ	గై
gh	ఘా	ఘి	ఘీ	ఘు	ఘూ	ఘె	ఘే	ఘొ	ఘో	ఘౌ	ఘై
ṅ	ఙా	ఙి	ఙీ	ఙు	ఙూ	ఙె	ఙే	ఙొ	ఙో	ఙౌ	ఙై
c	చా	చి	చీ	చు	చూ	చె	చే	చొ	చో	చౌ	చై

COMBINATIONS—Continued

	ā	*i*	*ī*	*u*	*ū*	*e*	*ē*	*o*	*ō*	*au*	*ai*
ch	చా	చి	చీ	చు	చూ	చె	చే	చొ	చో	చౌ	చై
j	జా	జి	జీ	జు	జూ	జె	జే	జొ	జో	జౌ	జై
jh	ఝా	ఝి	ఝీ	ఝు	ఝూ	ఝె	ఝే	ఝొ	ఝో	ఝౌ	ఝై
ñ	ఞా	ఞి	ఞీ	ఞు	ఞూ	ఞె	ఞే	ఞొ	ఞో	ఞౌ	ఞై
ṭ	టా	టి	టీ	టు	టూ	టె	టే	టొ	టో	టౌ	టై
ṭh	ఠా	ఠి	ఠీ	ఠు	ఠూ	ఠె	ఠే	ఠొ	ఠో	ఠౌ	ఠై
ḍ	డా	డి	డీ	డు	డూ	డె	డే	డొ	డో	డౌ	డై
ḍh	ఢా	ఢి	ఢీ	ఢు	ఢూ	ఢె	ఢే	ఢొ	ఢో	ఢౌ	ఢై
ṇ	ణా	ణి	ణీ	ణు	ణూ	ణె	ణే	ణొ	ణో	ణౌ	ణై
t	తా	తి	తీ	తు	తూ	తె	తే	తొ	తో	తౌ	తై
th	థా	థి	థీ	థు	థూ	థె	థే	థొ	థో	థౌ	థై
d	దా	ది	దీ	దు	దూ	దె	దే	దొ	దో	దౌ	దై
dh	ధా	ధి	ధీ	ధు	ధూ	ధె	ధే	ధొ	ధో	ధౌ	ధై
n	నా	ని	నీ	ను	నూ	నె	నే	నొ	నో	నౌ	నై
p	పా	పి	పీ	పు	పూ	పె	పే	పొ	పో	పౌ	పై
ph	ఫా	ఫి	ఫీ	ఫు	ఫూ	ఫె	ఫే	ఫొ	ఫో	ఫౌ	ఫై
b	బా	బి	బీ	బు	బూ	బె	బే	బొ	బో	బౌ	బై
bh	భా	భి	భీ	భు	భూ	భె	భే	భొ	భో	భౌ	భై
m	మా	మి	మీ	ము	మూ	మె	మే	మొ	మో	మౌ	మై
y	యా	యి	యీ	యు	యూ	యె	యే	యొ	యో	యౌ	యై
r	రా	రి	రీ	రు	రూ	రె	రే	రొ	రో	రౌ	రై
l	లా	లి	లీ	లు	లూ	లె	లే	లొ	లో	లౌ	లై
ḷ	ళా	ళి	ళీ	ళు	ళూ	ళె	ళే	ళొ	ళో	ళౌ	ళై
v	వా	వి	వీ	వు	వూ	వె	వే	వొ	వో	వౌ	వై
ś	శా	శి	శీ	శు	శూ	శె	శే	శొ	శో	శౌ	శై
ṣ	షా	షి	షీ	షు	షూ	షె	షే	షొ	షో	షౌ	షై
s	సా	సి	సీ	సు	సూ	సె	సే	సొ	సో	సౌ	సై
h	హా	హి	హీ	హు	హూ	హె	హే	హొ	హో	హౌ	హై
kṣ	క్షా	క్షి	క్షీ	క్షు	క్షూ	క్షె	క్షే	క్షొ	క్షో	క్షౌ	క్షై

Telugu is one of the most important of the five great Dravidian languages, and is spoken by the non-Aryan subjects of the nizam of Hyderbad as well as some who are under British rule.   These occupy the territory extending from a point north of the city of Madras and extending northwestward to Bellary (where the Telugu meets the Kanarese), and northeast nearly to Orissa.   It is the only descendant of the Āndhra dialect of the Old Dravidian and is strongly impregnated with Sanscrit.

The text reads from left to right.   Vowel signs are very similar to the Devanāgarī.

Vowel signs

The consonant is inherent with the short *a*, even where the "hook" √ is missing, while the other vowel ligatures are as shown in the table.

TIBETAN

Character	Transliteration	Character	Transliteration	Character	Transliteration	Character	Transliteration
ཀ	ka	ཐ	t'a	ཛ	dza	ས	sa
ཁ	k'a	ད	da	ཝ	wa	ཧ	ha
ག	ga	ན	na	ཞ	z'a	ཨ	a
ང	nga	པ	pa	ཟ	za	ཏ	ta
ཙ	ċa	ཕ	p'a	འ	'ha	ཐ	t'a
ཚ	ča	བ	ba	ཡ	ya	ད	da
ཇ	ja	མ	ma	ར	ra	ན	na
ཉ	nya	ཙ	tsa	ལ	la	ཥ	s'a
ཏ	ta	ཚ	ts'a	ཤ	s'a		

Ligatures

Character	Transliteration	Character	Transliteration	Character	Transliteration	Character	Transliteration	Character	Transliteration	Character	Transliteration
	kya		gva		rju		rna		bla		stsa
	kra		rga		lja		sna		rba		rdsa
	kla		rgya		rña		snra		lba		żu
	kva		lga		sña		pu		sba		zu
	rka		sga		tra		pya		sbya		zla
	rkya		sgya		rta		pra		sbra		u
	lka		sgra		lta		lpa		mu		yu
	ska		ṅu		sta		spa		mya		ru
	skya		rṅa		thra		spya		mra		hu
	skra		sṅa		dra		spra		rma		rla
	khya		lṅa		dva		phu		rmya		śra
	khra		cu		rda		phya		sma		su
	khva		lca		lda		phra		smya		sra
	gya		chu		sda		bu		smra		sla
	gra		ju		sdu		bya		tsu		hra
	gla		rja		nra		bra		rtsa		lha
											rtsva

There are a number of dialects in the three groups which, with the Burmese, comprise the Burman language family. This language was first reduced to writing in the middle of the 7th century A.D., and the letters, which are really a variation from those of the Indian Sanscrit of that period, follow the same arrangement as the Sanscrit. The text reads from left to right..

The Sanscrit cerebrals were introduced later and are turned to face in the opposite direction as shown in the table.

There are also a large number of ligatures made by combining two or more letters, and each ligature will form a syllable. The continental sounds of the ligatures are given in the table.

The vowels are *a, i, u, e,* and *o* which are not distinguished as either long or short, except in loan words.

A number of letters are written in words, but are not pronounced. This is also true of some initial as well as final letters.

The all-important feature of the language appears to be euphony.

The cases of the nouns are indicated by suffixes, and the plural is indicated by adding one of several words of plurality.

The language has personal, demonstrative, interrogative, and reflexive pronouns, as well as an indefinite article which is also the numeral "one".

The verb is really a kind of noun or participle and has no element of person, denoting the tense and mood by an external inflection or the addition of auxiliary verbs and suffixes when the stem cannot be inflected.

The Tibetans have developed tones along the same lines as the Chinese. It is quite improbable that any of the original consonants were hard, since many of these old soft consonants, which are hardened in the modern language, are preserved in the Tibetan classics of the period extending from the 7th to the 9th centuries.

The table shows the older text, known as the *dbu-can,* which has been preserved in the sacred literature. Later this was followed by an italic-like face, known as *dbu-med,* as well as a more flowing text: *akhyug-yig.*

Super- and subscripts

	i		*tse*	
	u		*tso*	
	e		*r*	
	o		*y*	
	ts		*v*	
	tsi		*m*	

Numerals

?	1	S	6
?	2	V	7
?	3	L	8
?	4	?	9
?	5	o	0

Punctuation

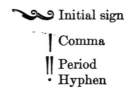 Initial sign

| Comma

|| Period

· Hyphen

TURKISH (Ryk'a)

Name	Isolated	Final	Median	Initial	Name	Isolated	Final	Median	Initial
Elif	ا	ا			Sad	ص	ـص	ـصـ	صـ
Be	ب	ـب	ـبـ	بـ	Dad	ض	ـض	ـضـ	ضـ
Pe	پ	ـپ	ـپـ	پـ	Ti	ط	ط	ط	ط
Te	ت	ـت	ـتـ	تـ	Zi	ظ	ظ	ظ	ظ
Se	ث	ـث	ـثـ	ثـ	'Ain	ع	ع	ـعـ	عـ
Djim	ج	ـج	ـجـ	جـ	Ghain	غ	ـغ	ـغـ	غـ
Chim	چ	ـچ	ـچـ	چـ	Fe	ف	ـف	ـفـ	فـ
Ha	ح	ـح	ـحـ	حـ	Qaf	ق	ـق	ـقـ	قـ
Kha	خ	ـخ	ـخـ	خـ	Kef	ك	ـك	ـكـ	كـ
Dal	د	ـد			Lam	ل	ـل	ـلـ	لـ
Zal	ذ	ـذ			Mim	م	ـم	ـمـ	مـ
Re	ر	ـر			Nun	ن	ـن	ـنـ	نـ
Zs	ز	ـز			Waw	و	ـو		
Zhe	ژ	ـژ			He	ه	ـه	ـهـ	هـ
Sin	س	ـس	ـسـ	سـ	Ye	ى	ـى	ـىـ	يـ
Shin	ش	ـش	ـشـ	شـ					

Ligatures

(Of characters that are distinguished by diacritical marks but one example is given)

لالا	l-a	گ	k-ḥ	ضر	ḥ-r	لم	l-m	خوضه	ḥ-h	ضی	ḥ-j
ٮٮ	k-a	لخنج	l-ḥ	لمر	l-r	ڡ	f-m	ـ	s-h	عی	·-j
ككك	k-l	ٮ	m-ḥ	سر	m-r	م	m-m	لمد	l-h	کیکی	k-j
كلاكلا	k-l-a	﴾	m-ḥ-m	ضح	ḥ-m	ٮ	p-n-m	للّه	l-l-h	لیلی	l-j
ٮٯٮٮٮٯ	t-b	محمد	m-ḥ-m-d	ككم	k-m	لولو	l-w	٧	m-ḥ	می	m-j

The Osmanic-Turkish language is the most important member of the Turko-Tartar language group.   It is highly impregnated with both Arabic and Persian words, but its grammar is both clear and simple.

The language has a fixed rule that a strong vowel (*a*, *o*, and *u*), must be followed by a similar vowel, and, likewise, a weak vowel is followed by a weak vowel; e.g., *dere* (valley), *dereler* (valleys), *ada* (island) and *adalar* (islands).

Until the introduction of the modified Latin alphabet the Turks used the Arabic alphabet with the addition of three Persian characters.   Of the many different styles formerly in use the one that was the most popular was the Ryk'a, which is here reproduced.

The text was written and read from right to left.

While Turkey has adopted the Latin alphabet it is well to bear in mind, before taking up the Latinized form, that it is very important from a philological standpoint to acquire a knowledge of the old Arabic script, its grammar, spelling, and pronunciation before taking up the New Turkish.

TURKISH (New)

A	a	*a* in fat; also *a* in far	L	l	*l*	
B	b	*b* [1]	M	m	*m*	
C	c	*j* in joint	N	n	*n*; often nasal	
Ç	ç	*ch*, in church	O	o	*o* in or; also *o* in note	
D	d	*d* [1]	Ö	ö	*oe* in Goethe	
E	e	*e* in red; also *ê* in fête	P	p	*p* [1]	
F	f	*f* in fay	R	r	*r*	
G	g	*g*, hard, sometimes mute between consonants	S	s	*s* in sun	
			Ş	ş	*sh* in shape	
Ğ	ğ	*g*, soft, nearly *gh* in eight	T	t	*t*	
H	h	*h*, always	U	u	*u* in push; long as in through	
İ	i	*i* in ring; long, as in machine				
			Ü	ü	*ü* in German über, or *u* in French musée	
I	ı	*i* in sir				
J	j	*j* in French journal	V	v	*v* in vain	
K	k	*k*, hard	Y	y	*y* in yet	
Ǩ	ǩ [2]	*k*, soft	Z	z	*z* in zero	

[1] In using the new alphabet *p* is sometimes substituted for *b*, as *edip* instead of *edib*, *kutuphane* instead of *kutubhane;* this is also the case where *t* is substituted for *d*, as *alaettin* instead of *alaeddin*. However, this is not always the case.
[2] Takes the place of the Arabic *q*.

The Turkish language has been revolutionized by the reform in the alphabet instituted by Moustafa Kemal Pasha in 1928, which swept away the use of the old Arabic characters and substituted the Latin alphabet. The pronunciation has been simplified and the construction, even though different from English, is both logical and simple. A truly phonetic language has been evolved where every syllable is pronounced exactly as it is written. There are no silent letters and every letter must be pronounced even where the effect sounds unusual to English ears: saba*h*, ny*k*u, saat, (sa'at).

There is as yet no uniformity in the spelling; grammars and scholars are still at variance, while the generality of people spell as the word was pronounced in the days before the Latin script was adopted, regardless of rules—in fact there are as yet no perfected rules. Many changes will doubtless be made and, since the Turkish, like all Oriental languages, is a difficult one, it is questionable whether a perfect uniformity in spelling and pronunciation will ever be attained.

Remarks for transliterators

The language is practically phonetic; there being no silent letters, diphthongs or compound consonants, each is invariably the symbol of but one sound.

The soft vowels are *e, ö, ü,* and *i.*

The soft *ğ* cannot be used as the initial or final letter of a word.

The *y* is not always a consonant, as it sometimes takes the place of *i*, usually at the end of a word.

When the circumflex is used over *a, i,* or *u,* the sound is long, but *â* and *û* after *g, k,* and *l* are used for softening these consonants.

There is no silent *e* in the Latin transliteration, nor has the Turkish a vowel sound corresponding to *a* in man, *e* in her, *i* in bird, and *o* in not.

An infallible table for transliterating from the Arabic into the New Turkish is out of the question, as only a thorough knowledge of the Turkish will enable one to determine whether a vowel is hard or soft, or whether words are correctly spelled or pronounced.

Accent

There is practically no accent, the long vowels replacing, to some extent, the accent in other languages, but without stress.

Capitalization

Capitalize proper names, both personal and geographic, but lower case the latter when used adjectively.

Capitalize the first word of a sentence, but lower case, as a rule, after a colon

Capitalize the name of the Deity as also the first word in a line of poetry.

Syllabication

Divide on a vowel, but diphthongs must not be separated.

A consonant goes with the following vowel, but if there be two consonants, they are separated.

Articles

There is no definite article, "the" being understood: *adam*, the man; *ev*, the house.

The indefinite article is expressed by *bir*, one: *bir hanım*, a lady.

Personal pronouns

First person				
Nominative	ben	I	biz	we
Accusative	beni	me	bizi	us
Genitive	benim	my, of me	bizim	our, of us
Dative	bana	to me	bize	to us
Locative	bende	in me	bizde	in us
Ablative	benden	from me	bizden	from us

Second person				
Nominative	sen	thou	siz	you
Accusative	seni	thee	sizi	you
Genitive	senin	thy, of thee	sizin	your, of you
Dative	sana	to three	size	to you
Locative	sende	in thee	sizde	in you
Ablative	senden	from thee	sizden	from you

Third person				
Nominative	o	he, she, it	on lar	they
Accusative	onu	him, her, it	on ları	them
Genitive	onun	of him, her, it	ononların	of them
Dative	ona	to him, etc.	onlara	to them
Locative	onda	in him, etc.	onlarda	in them
Ablative	ondan	from him, etc.	onlardan	from them

It will be noted that there are irregularities in the above declension, but that of the second person plural is entirely regular and may be used as a model for the declension of all nouns.

The genitive forms, *benim*, *senin*, etc., must never be used independently as possessive pronouns, their places being taken by pronominal affixes to the nouns: *ev-im*, my house; *gözler-in*, thy eyes.

When the noun ends in a vowel, modified forms of the affixes are used: *-m*, my; *-n*, they; *-si*, *sı*, his, hers, its; *-miz*, our; *-niz*, your; *leri*, *ları*, their.

When other possessive pronouns, *benim*, *senin*, are used in conjunction with the affixes the latter are emphasized; *benim evim*, my house, etc.

The pronoun *kendi* (self) is usually used instead of *o* for the third person singular form where it is used to mean "he" or "she".

o de-di	it said
kendi de-di	he or she said
gördüm onu	I saw it, or that
gördüm kendini	I saw him, or her

Euphony

ç, f, h, k, p, s, ş, and t are hard consonants, and the others are soft or neutral, as a result of which we have two rules:

1. When an inflection or particle with an initial d (dir) follows a word ending in a hard consonant, the d changes to t: sıcak-tır, it is hot.

2. When the consonantal ending of a syllable or word is either ç, k, p, or t and is followed by a vowel, the result is the substitution of a soft consonant for the hard: c, ğ, b, or d, respectively: yok-udu becomes yoğ-udu.

Nouns

There is but one declension for all nouns; any variations found being merely due to the rules governing hard and soft vowels and hard and soft consonants.

The nominative case is the simple stem of the noun and the following are th various other case endings:

	After e or i	After a or ı	After o or u	After ö or ü
Accusative	-i	-ı	-u	-ü
Genitive	-in	-ın	-un	-ün
Dative	-e	-a	-a	-e
Locative[1]	-de	-da	-da	-de
Ablative[1]	-den	-dan	-dan	-den

When the stem of a noun ends in either ç, k, p, or t, these are changed to the corresponding soft consonants, c, ğ, b, or d if immediately followed by a vowel:

ayak	foot	ayağ-ın	of the foot
kitap	book	kitab-ın	of the book

When the stem ends in a vowel, a so-called "buffer letter" precedes the case ending where that also begins with a vowel. y is used in the accusative and dative cases, and n in the genitive.

oda	room	oda-ya	to the room
kedi	cat	kedi-nin	of the cat

The same case endings are used for the plural after the characteristic plural ending -ler or -lar.

The case endings are added after the pronominal affixes where these are used; in the third person singular, ending in -si or sı, an n serves as the buffer letter in all cases.

Noun construction

The following table will illustrate the construction of nouns:

Singular		Plural		
el	hand	el-ler	hands	
el-im	my hand	el-ler-im	my hands	[Possessive added]
el-im-de	in my hand	el-ler-im-de	in my hands	[Case ending added]

Auxiliary verbs

The verb ol-mak (to be) is the only irregular verb in the language:

Infinitive: ol-mak, to be, to become

	Singular		Plural	
Present	im	I am	iz	we are
	sin	thou art	siniz	you are
	dir	he is	dir-ler	they are
Past	idim	I was	idik	we were
	idin	thou wert	idiniz	you were
	idi	he was	idi-ler	they were
Future	olur-um	I will be	olur-uz	we will be
	olur-sun	thou wilt be	olur-sunuz	you will be
	olur	he will be	olur-lar	they will be
Conditional	isem	if I am	isek	if we are
	isen	if thou art	iseniz	if you are
	ise	if he is	ise-ler	if they are
Imperative	—		ol-a-lım	let us be
	ol	be thou	ol-un, ol-unuz	be ye
	ol-sun	let him be	ol-sun-lar	let them be

[1] When the stem of a noun ends in a hard consonant (ç, f, h, k, p, s, ş, or t), the d changes to t: tabak-ta not tabak-da (in the plate).

The position of the verb is usually at the end of the sentence.

The personal pronoun is usually implied by the form of the verb (*iyi sin*, thou art good), and that is suffixed to the preceding word: *güzelim*, I am beautiful.

The negative is expressed by prefixing *değil* to the verb; *değil-im*, I am not.

There is a special verb ('to have," the meaning of which is usually expressed by means of the imprsonal verb *var-dır*, *var-ıdı*, *yok-tur*, etc., with the genitive case of the personal pronouns:

benim var-dır	I have
benim var-ıdı	I had
benim yok-tur	I have not
benim yoğ-udu	I had not
benim var-ısa	if I have
benim yoğ-ısa	if I have not

The object possessed remains in the nominative case, but takes the proper possessive affix to denote that it is the object possessed: *benim bir ev-im var-dır*, which is literally translated, "*of me a house-of-me there is*" = I have a house.

The locative case of the personal pronoun is sometimes used instead of the genitive, but in that case the possessive affix is omitted, and there is then also a slightly different shade of meaning: *ben-de bir kitap vardır*, literally translated, "there is a book" = I have a book.

The verb "to be" may be used where the object possessed is a particular definite article, and here the object is placed at the beginning of the sentence for emphasis: *kitap ben-de dir*, literally translated, "the book is in me" = I have the book.

Vowel agreement

The vowel sounds of the auxiliary verb conform to the sounds of the pre-dominant vowel of the words to which they are attached. A complete list of these forms is as follows:

After *e* or *i*	After *a* or *ı*	After *o* or *u*	After *ö* or *ü*
im	ım	um	üm
sin	sın	sun	sün
dir	dır	dur	dür
iz	ız	uz	üz
siniz	dırlar	sunuz	sünüz
dirler	sınız	durlar	dürler

The participle *mi* (which must agree in form as shown in the above table) changes a simple statement to a question, and is suffixed to the word whiih the question ioncerns, being usually followed by the auxiliary suffix: *iyi-sin* (thou art well), *iyi mi-sin* (art thou well?). This particle conforms to the above rule for vowel agreement.

Impersonal verbs

The impersonal verbs "there is", "there are", etc., are expressed by the use of the adjectives *var* (present) and *yok* (absent) with the verb "to be":

var-dır	there is, or are
var-ıdı	there was, were
var-ısa	if there is, are
yok-dur	there is (are) not
yok-udu	there was (were) not
yok-ısa	if there is (are) not
su var-dır	there is water
su yok-dur	there is no water

The simple form of the imperative mood is the stem of a verb, and the infinitive is formed by adding -*mek* and -*mak* for soft and hard stems, respectively:

gel	come!	gel-mek, to come
bak	look!	bak-mak, to look

Aside from the auxiliary verbs, all verbs are conjugated in accordance with the Standard Conjugation, giving due allowance, as in the case of nouns, to the rules governing hard and soft vowels and consonants and the use of buffer letters.

PRESENT TENSE

Every verbal tense has its characteristic sign (syllable) which is attached to the verbal stem, and thus the third person singular is formed. If the stem ends in a consonant rules of euphony require a vowel (usually i or $\imath$, though sometimes u or $\ddot{u}$) between the stem and the characteristic sign. When the stem ends in the vowel e, that will change to i before the characteristic sign -*yor*:

ko-mak	to put	ko	put	ko-yor	he is putting
de-mek	to say	de	say	di-yor	he is saying
gel-mek	to come	gel	come	gel-i-yor	he is coming
bak-mak	to look	bak	look	bak-ı-yor	he is looking
otur-mak	to sit	otur	sit	otur-u-yor	he is sitting
gör-mek	to see	gör	see	gör-ü-yor	he is seeing

The other persons of the present tense take personal endings to the above forms; these endings being simply modified forms of the auxliary verb.

The -*yor* suffers no vowel change, and thus the conjugation of all verbs in the present tense, whether the stem be hard or soft, conform to the following standard model:

geliyor-um	I am coming	geliyor-uz	we are coming
geliyor-sun	thou art coming	geliyor-sunuz	you are coming
geliyor	he is coming	geliyor-lar	they are coming

To change the present tense statement to a question, the interrogative particle is added after the sign -*yor*, which, being invariable, makes the particle *mu* in this tense.

For the negative, which is -*mi* or *mı* with soft and hard stems, respectively, in order to harmonize with the sign -*yor*, the particle is added immediately after the stem.

geli-yor	he is coming	bakı-yor	he is looking
geli-yor mu	is he coming?	bakı-yor mu	is he looking?
gel-mi-yor	he is not coming	bak-mı-yor	he is not looking
gel-mi-yor mu	is he not coming?	bak-mı-yor mu	is he not looking?

The conjugation of these forms is as follows:

geliyor muyum	gelmiyor-um	gelmiyor muyum
geliyor-musun	gelmiyor-sun	gelmiyor musun
geliyor mu	gelmiyor	gelmiyor mu
geliyor muyuz	gelmiyor-uz	gelmiyor muyuz
geliyor musunuz	gelmiyor-sunuz	gelmiyor musunuz
geliyor-lar mı	gelmiyor-lar	gelmiyor-lar mı

The aorist tense has a somewhat different meaning than the present tense, as will be seen from examples given. Its sign is r which is usually added directly to the stem, unless that ends in a consonant, when a vowel is intervened. The particular vowel varies and must be learned from experience:

	Infinitive				Aorist
de-mek	to say	de	say	der	he says
gel-mek	to come	gel	come	gel-ir	he comes
yaz-mak	to write	yaz	write	yaz-ar	he writes
gör-mek	to see	gör	see	gör-ür	he sees

The proper personal endings are added to the above to form the other persons of this tense as shown in the table of conjugations.

The negative of the aorist is irregular and there are two forms, one for soft and the other for hard stems:

gel-mem	I come not	bak-mam	I look not
gel-mezsin	thou comest not	bak-mazsın	thou lookest not
gel-mez	he comes not	bak-maz	he looks not
gel-meğiz	we come not	bak-mağız	we look not
gel-mezsiniz	you come not	bak-mazsınız	you look not
gel-mez-ler	they come not	bak-maz-lar	they look not

The interrogative forms are obtained as usual by means of the interrogative particle:

	Soft			Hard
gelir miyim	do I come?		bakar mıyım	do I look?
gelir misin	dost thou come?		bakar mısın	dost thou look?
gelir mi	does he come?		bakar mı	does he look?
gelir miyiz	do we come?		bakar mıyız	do we look?
gelir misiniz	do you come?		bakar mısınız	do you look?
gelir-ler mi	do they come?		bakar-lar mı	do they look?
gelmez miyim	do I not come?		bakmaz mıyım	do I not look?
gelmez misin	dost thou not come?		bakmaz mısın	dost thou not look?
gelmez me	does he not come?		bakmaz mı	does he not look?
gelmez miyiz	do we not come?		bakmazmıyız	do we not look
gelmez misiniz	do you not come?		bakmaz mısınız	do you not look
gelmez-ler mi	do they not come?		bakmaz-lar m	do they not look?

The future tense is formed by adding *e-cek* to soft and *a-cek* to hard stems, thus furnishing the third person singular; a buffer letter *y* is inserted where the stem ends in a vowel.

gel-e-cek	he will come	de-ye-cek	he will say
bak-a-cak	he will look	ko-ya-cak	he will put

As in the present tense, the remaining persons are formed by adding the proper personal endings, as shown in the table.

The *k* is hard and where it is followed by a vowel it changes to a *ğ*; the *ğ* has the hard *gh* sound with vowels and the *y* sound with consonants.

Interrogative forms are obtained by using the interrogative particle (*mi* after -*e-cek* and *mı* after -*a-cak*) after the characteristic sign: *gelecek mi*, (will he come?).

Placing the negative particle (*mi* and *mı* for soft and hard stems, respectively) immediately after the stem given the negative form: *gel-mi-ye-cek* (he will not come).

Although the interrogative and negative signs are identical in form, confusion is avoided by suffixing the negative to the stem, while the interrogative follows the characteristic sign of the tense: *gelmiyecek mi* (will he not come?).

The sign of the past tense is the suffix *di*, which takes the various forms *di*, *dı*, *du*, *dü*, and *ti*, *tı*, *tu*, *tü*, in conformity with the rules governing vowel and consonantal agreement:

gel-di	he came	git-ti	he went
yaz-dı	he wrote	bak-tı	he looked
bul-du	he found	tut-tu	he held
gör-dü	he saw	düş-tü	he fell

Since the tense sign ends in a vowel, modified personal endings are used to form the other persons, as shown in the table.

The negative particle comes, as usual, immediately after the stem.

The conjugations are as follows:

geldim mi	gelmedim	gelmedim mi
geldin mi	gelmedin	gelmedin mi
geldi mi	gelmedi	gelmedi mi
geldik mi	gelmedik	gelmedik mi
geldiniz mi	gelmediniz	gelmediniz mi
geldiler mi	gelmediler	gelmediler mi

The following is the Standard Conjugation in the various tenses of *gel-mek* (to come) in the present; *gel-mek* and *bak-mak* (to look), in the future; *gel-mek*, *bak-mak*, and *bul-mak* (to find), in the past; and *de-mek* (to say), *gel-mek*, *yaz-mak* (to write), and *gör-mek* (to see), in the aorist.

See notes on tenses for further details.

	PRESENT	FUTURE	
		Soft	Hard
Singlar:			
1st person	geliyor-um	geleceğ-im	bakacağ-ım
2d person	geliyor-sun	gelecek-sin	bakacak-sın
3d person	geliyor	gelecek	bakacak
Plural			
1st person	geliyor-uz	geleceğ-iz	bakacağ-iz
2d person	geliyor-sunuz	gelecek-siniz	bakacak-sınız
3d person	geliyor-lar	gelecek-ler	bakacak-lar

PAST

Singular:			
1st person	gel-dim	git-tim	bul-dum
2d person	gel-din	git-tin	bul-dun
3d person	gel-di	git-ti	bul-du
Plural			
1st person	gel-dik	git-tik	bul-duk
2d person	gel-diniz	git-tiniz	bul-dunuz
3d person	gel-di-ler	git-ti-ler	bul-du-lar

AORIST

Singular:				
1st person	gelir-im	yazar-ım	der im	görür-üm
2d person	gelir-sin	yazar-sın	der-sin	görür-sün
3d person	gelir	yazar	der	görür
Plural:				
1st person	gelir-iz	yazar-ız	der-iz	görür-üz
2d person	gelir-siniz	yazar-sınız	der-siniz	görür-sünüz
3d person	gelir-ler	yazar-lar	der-ler	görür-ler

The infinitive and imperative moods, combined with the subjunctive and optative moods, will cover all necessities of ordinary conversation.

The characteristic sign of the subjunctive is *se* or *sa* immediately after the stem. It corresponds to the English subjunctive, commencing with "*if*":

gel-sem	if I come	bak-sam	if I look
gel-sen	if thou comest	bak-san	if thou lookest
gel-se	if he comes	bak-sa	if he looks
gel-sek	if we come	bak-sak	if we look
gel-seniz	if you come	bak-sanız	if you look
gel-se-ler	if they come	bak-sa-lar	if they look

The sign of the optative mood is *e* or *a*, which is translated "that I may":

gel-e-yim	that I may come	bak-a-yım	that I may look
gel-e-sin	that thou mayest come	bak-a-sın	that thou mayest look
gel-e	that he may come	bak-a	that he may look
gel-e-lim	that we may come	bak-a-lım	that we may look
gel-e-siniz	that you may come	bak-a-sınız	that you may look
gel-e-ler	that they may come	bak-a-lar	that they may look

Past tenses of the subjunctive and optative moods are formed by combining the past tense of the auxiliary verbs with their respective characteristic signs, with a buffer letter between the two adjacent vowels. Thus —

gel-se idim	becomes	gelseydim	if I had come
gel-e idim	becomes	geleydim	that I might come

Only a few of the man yother moods of the Turkish language will be given.

The sign of the dubitative mood is *-miş*, and it serves to express a doubtful statement:

gel-miş	(I believe) he has come
geliyor-muş-sunuz	(I understand) you are coming
para çok sever miş	(I think) he is very fond of money

The sign of the necessitative mood is *-meli* or *-mali*, and it corresponds to the English "must":

gel-meli-yim	I am obliged to come, I must come
gel-meliydim	I had to come; I was obliged to come

POTENTIAL VERBS

To express "can" (to be able) it is, necessary to combine *bil-mek* (to know) with the optative stem of the verb:

gel-mek	to some	gel-e-bil-mek	to be able to come
bak-mak	to look	bak-a-bil-mek	to be able to look

"Cannot" (to be unable) is obtained by adding the negative patricle *-me* or *-ma*:

gel-mek	to come	gel-me-mek	not to come
		gel-e-me-mek	to be unable to come
bak-mak	to look	bak-a-ma-mak	to be unable to look

To express speedier action, the verb *ver-mek* (to give) is used as an auxiliary: *gel* (come!); *gel-i-ver* (come quickly!).

PASSIVE VOICE

The passive voice is derived by adding a short syllable, ending in *l* or *n*, to the active form:

sev-mek	to love	to be loved	sev-il-mek
kes-mek	to cut	to be cut	kes-il-mek
yaz-mak	to write	to be written	yaz-ıl-mak
bul-mak	to find	to be found	bul-un-mak
yıka-mak	to wash	to be washed	yıkan-mak

COMPOUND VERBS

Ol-mak (to be) and *et-mek* (to make), and other simple verbs are frequently used as auxiliaries with nouns and adjectives:

sus	silent	sus-ol-mak	to be silent
rica	request	rica et-mek	to make request
nefes	breath	nefes al-mak	to breathe

PARTICIPLES

There are five subjective participles: (1) Present, which is formed by adding -*en* or -*an* to the verb stem, preceded by *y* when the stem ends in a vowel:

gel-en	who comes, the coming
yaz-an	who writes, the writing
anla-yan	who understands, the understanding

(2) The past participle is the same as the first person plural of the past tense:

gel-dik	who has come, having come
yaz-dık	who has written, having written

(3) The future participle is the same as the third person singular of the future tense:

gel-e-cek	who will come
yaz-a-cak	who will write

(4) The aorist participle is the same as the third person singular of the aorist tense:

gel-ir	who comes, is accustomed to come
yaz-ar	who writes, is accustomed to write

(5) The past dubitative participle is the same as the third person singular of the dubitative mood:

gel-miş	who has come
yaz-mış	who has written

There are but two objective participles, the past and the future, and these are merely derivatives of the same subjective participles, with the addition of personal affixes.

    (1) Past:

yazdığım	which I wrote
yazdığın	which thou wrotest
yazdığı	which he wrote
yazdığımız	which we wrote
yazdığınız	which you wrote
yazdıkları	which they wrote

    (2) Future:

yazacağım	which I shall write
yazacağın	which thou shalt write
yazacağı	which he shall write
yazacağımız	which we shall write
yazacağınız	which you shall write
yazacaklari	which they shall write

NOTES ON USE OF PARTICIPLES

The present past, and future subjective participles may be used without a noun (as pronominal adjectives), when they may take personal affixes and be declined like nouns.

The aorist participle is seldom used; when used, it expresses customary action very definitely.

The dubitative participle is practically equivalent to the English past participle.

A participle always precedes the noun which it qualifies, while a verb is always placed at the end of the sentence.

NOTES

The plural of nouns is formed by adding *-ler* if the vowels are *e, i, ö,* or *ü,* or *-lar* if the vowels are *a, ı, o,* or *u: el,* hand, *eller,* hands; *adam,* man, *adamlar,* men.

There is no alteration of nouns, pronouns, or adjectives to correspond with gender.

The position of the adjectives is before the nouns, as in English, and they are indeclinable.   When used with the indefinite article, the adjective usually precedes the article: *güzel bir gün,* beautiful a day.   The adjectives are also used as adverbs: *iyi,* good, also means well (adverb).

The comparative and superlative of all adjectives are formed by placing before them the words *daha* (more) and *en* (most).

The position of the verb is usually at the end of the sentence.   The present pronoun is generally omitted, being implied by the form of the verb itself: *güzel im,* beautiful (I) am.   This verb is often a suffix of the preceding word, making *güzelim.*

Nouns

The stem of a noun is its simplest form, the nominative singular.   The various derivatives, the plural, the possessive forms, and the various cases are obtained by adding certain syllables to the stem itself, which is known as agglutination. The various parts of verbs are also formed in this way.   In the case of nouns the stem comes first, then the syllable for plural (*-ler* or *-lar*), then a possessive affix, and finally the case ending:

el, the hand	eller, hands
elim, my hand	ellerim, my hands
elimde, in my hand	ellerimde, in my hands
eliniz, your hand	elleriniz, your hands
elinize, to your hand	ellerinizden, from your hands

Cardinal numbers

bir	one	dokuz	nine
iki	two	on	ten
üç	three	on bir	eleven
dört	four	on iki	twelve
beş	five	on üç	thirteen
altı	six	yirmi	twenty
yedi	seven	yüz	hundred
sekiz	eight	bin	thousand

Ordinal numbers

birinci	first	dokuzuncu	ninth
ikinci	second	onuncu	tenth
ücüncü	third	on birinci	eleventh
dordüncü	fourth	on ikinci	twelfth
beşinci	fifth	on üçüncü	thirteenth
altıncı	sixth	yirminci	twentieth
yedinci	seventh	yüzüncü	hundredth
sekizinci	eighth	bininci	thousandth

Months

Ocak	January	Ağustos (Ağust.)	August
Şubat (Şub.)	February	Eylûl (Evl.)	September
Mart	March	Ekım	October
Nisan (Nis.)	April	Kasım	November
Mayıs (May.)	May	Aralık	December
Haziran (Haz.)	June		
Temmuz (Tem.)	July		

Note: The names of the months of January, October, November, and December have been modernized, and the current usage is as indicated. Previously, these months were as follows:

Kânunsani, January	Teşrinsani (Teşrins.), November
Teşrinevel (Teşrinev.), October	Kânunevel (Kânunev.), December

Days

Pazar günü	Sunday	Perşembe	Thursday
Pazarirtesi	Monday	Cuma	Friday
Salı	Tuesday	Cumairtesi	Saturday
Çarşamba	Wednesday		

Seasons

ilkbahar	spring	sonbahar	autumn
yaz	summer	kiş	winter

Time

saat	hour	ay	month
gün	day	yil, sene	year
hafta	week		

UIGHURIC

Final	Median	Initial	Transliter-ation	Ligature	Transliter-ation	Ligature	Transliter-ation
					kä, gä,		ym
			ä, a		kn, gn,		ymä
					ka, ga,		
					kr, gr		mz
			i, ï				
			o, ö, u, ü (ʼand w)		ki, gi		mkä, mgä
							miš, miš
			γ, q, χ				ml
			k, g		kü, gü, kö, gö, ku, gu		pä, bä, pa, ba, pn, bn, pr, br
			y; ï. i		kü, gü, kö, ki.		
			r		kd, gd		pi, bi
			l		kz, gz		pu, bu, po, bo, pü, pö etc.
			t		kγ, gγ		
			d		kq, gq		
			č		kt, gt		pd, bd
					kkä, gkä, ggä		pz, bz
			s		kki, gki		pγ, bγ
			š		kl, gl		pq, bq
			z, ž		km, gm		pt, bt
			ñ		ks		pkä, bkä, bgä
			b, p				pki, bgi
			v		kš, gš		pkl
			w		da, dä		pl, bl
			m		di·		pm, bm
			h		do, dv, dö, dü		ps, bs
					dkü, dgü		pš, bš
							čmbu
							so, su, sö, sü

The Uighurs were a Turkish people who reached a high state of culture only in the time of their descendants who inhabited the region comprising the Provinces of Kashgar and Khotan, and extending from the Orkhon to what is now Eastern Turkestan during a period beginning about the eighth century. Their chief city, Chotscho, which is now merely a ruin, lies some 19 miles east of the present city of Turfan.

The alphabet was not, as formerly commonly believed, derived from the Syriac Estrangela but owes its origin to an unknown Semitic text. The Manchu, Mongolian, and Kalmuck alphabets have their origin in the Uighuric.

The existing literature is entirely of a religious character, and a great many of the works are Buddhistic, some are Manichaeistic, while the minority are Christian. The authors, following a Manichaeistic custom, were very fond of decorating the pages of their books with a great profusion of miniatures and ornamental scrolls, and the existing remnants are a perpetual source of admiration to book lovers. In the main they were printed from blocks after the manner of the Chinese and were often embellished with wood cuts. The text reads from right to left although, at times, probably under Chinese influence, it was written in columns, reading from the top downward, the columns, unlike the Chinese, reading from left to right. The striking similarity of a number of the letters to one another adds to the difficulty in reading the language.

Syllables must not be separated; and if there remains any space at the end of a line, a space is inserted between the last and next to the last letters, or else an extended final letter is used. These letters are shown in the table.

The following punctuation marks are used:

UKRAINIAN

Character		Transliteration and tone value	Remarks on tone value
А	а	*a*	
Б	б	*b*	
В	в	*v (w)*	After vowels and at close of syllable has weak *u* sound
Г	г	*g (h)*	Before unvoiced consonants and at close of syllable it becomes a weak x
Ґ	ґ	*ġ (g)*	Softened to *gi* before *e-* and *i*-sounds
Д	д	*d*	
Е	е	*e*	Open *e* as in ever
Є	є	*je*	After p like *ie*
Ж	ж	*ž* (voiced)	Like *j* in French journal
З	з	*z (s)*	Voiced as in zeal
И	и	*i* or *y* (closed)	As *i* in police, approximately
І	і	*i*	
Ї	ї	*ji*	
Й	й	*j*	Before *o* like German *j*
К	к	*k*	
Л	л	*l*	Like Polish *ł*; before є, ї, ю, я, b, like *łᴶ*
М	м	*m*	
Н	н	*n*	
О	о	*o*	Mainly open *o* as in loss
П	п	*p*	
Р	р	*r* (lingual)	
С	с	*s (ss)*	Unvoiced as in German das; softened before є, ї, ю, я, b
Т	т	*t*	Becomes *tᴶ* before є, ї, ю, я, b
У	у	*u*	
Ф	ф	*f*	
Х	х	*ch*	As in German ach; before unvoiced consonants as also after e, и, i, and in the initial sound of these vowels like *ch* in German ich
Ц	ц	*c (ts)*	
Ч	ч	*č (tsh)*	
Ш	ш	*š (sh)*	
Щ	щ	*šč*	
Ю	ю	*ju*	} After p like *ᴵu* or *ᴵa*
Я	я	*ja*	
Ь	ь	*'*	Soft sign

The Ukrainian language group is also known as Ruthenian, and its territory is bounded on the west by the Polish and Czech, and extends eastward over southern Russia to the districts of Kharkov and Woronesch. In the north it extends to Minsk and Tschernigov where White Russian is used.

The language is remarkably uniform when we take into consideration the great variation in conditions in the widely separated portions of its realm. The number of dialects is very small.

In ordinary literature the Russian alphabet introduced by Peter the Great is used, though the Cyrillic alphabet is still employed in religious books. The characters г, ґ, and ї have been added, while the Russian letters ъ, ы, ѣ, э, ѳ, and v are not used.

Syllabication is the same as in Russian and punctuation as in English.

Cardinal numbers

один	one	десять	ten
два, дві	two	одинадцять	eleven
три	three	дванадцять	twelve
чотирі	four	тринадцять	thirteen
пять	five	двадцять	twenty
шість	six	двадцять один	twenty-one
сім	seven	сто	hundred
вісім	eight	сто один	hundred and one
девять	nine	тисяч, тисяча	thousand

Ordinal numbers

перший	first	десятий	tenth
другий	second	одинадцятий	eleventh
третій	third	дванадцятий	twelfth
четвертий	fourth	тринадцятий	thirteenth
пятий	fifth	двадцятий	twentieth
шестий	sixth	двадцять перший	twenty-first
семий	seventh	сотний	hundredth
восьмий	eighth	стоперший	hundred and first
девятий	ninth	тисячній	thousandth

Months

Січень	January	Липець	July
Лютий, Лютень	February	Серпень	August
Марець	March	Вересень	September
Цвитень	April	Жовтень	October
Май	May	Листопад	November
Червець	June	Грудень	December

Days

Неділя	Sunday	Четвер	Thursday
Понеділок	Monday	Пятниця	Friday
Вівторок	Tuesday	Субота	Saturday
Середа	Wednesday		

Seasons

весна	spring	осінь	autumn
літо	summer	зима	winter

Time

час, година	hour	місяць	month
день	day	рік	year
тиждень	week	вік	century

URDU (HINDUSTANI)

Name	Iso-lated	Final	Medi-an	Ini-tial	Transliteration and tone value	Name	Iso-lated	Final	Medi-an	Ini-tial	Transliteration and tone value
Alef	ا	ا			—, ' (', a)	Shīn	ش	ش	ش	ش	š; sh
Bē	ب	ب	ب	ب	b	Sād	ص	ص	ص	ص	s; German sz
Pē	پ	پ	پ	پ	p	Zad	ض	ض	ض	ض	ḍ; soft s
Tē	ت	ت	ت	ت	t	Tō	ط	ط	ط	ط	t; as in Italian
Te	ٹ	ٹ	ٹ	ٹ	t; cere-bral	Sō	ظ	ظ	ظ	ظ	z; soft s
Sē	ث	ث	ث	ث	t; sz	Ain	ع	ع	ع	ع	'; gut-tural
Jīm	ج	ج	ج	ج	ǧ; j in joy	Ghain	غ	غ	غ	غ	ġ; g in Wagen
Chē	چ	چ	چ	چ	č; tsh	Fē	ف	ف	ف	ف	f
Ḥe	ح	ح	ح	ح	h; highly as-pirat-ed	Qāf	ق	ق	ق	ق	q; gut-tural
Khē	خ	خ	خ	خ	ḵ; ch in loch	Kāf	ک	ک	ک	ک	k
Dāl	د	د			d	Gāf	گ	گ	گ	گ	g
Ḍa	ڈ	ڈ			d'; cere-bral	Lām	ل	ل	ل	ل	l
Ẕal	ذ	ذ			ḏ; soft s	Mīm	م	م	م	م	m
Rē	ر	ر			r	Nūn	ن	ن	ن	ن	n
Ṛā	ڑ	ڑ			ṛ; cere-bral		ن	ن			ñ; nasal
Zē	ز	ز			z; soft s	Wāw	و	و			w; w, o, u [1]
Žē	ژ	ژ			French j	Hē	ه	ه	ه	ه	h
Sīn	س	س	س	س	s; sz in Ger-man	Ye	ی	ی	ی	ی	y, i, e [1]

[1] Depending on its location in the word.

Urdu is an Indo-Aryan dialect spoken by some 25,000,000 people. Its history dates back to the early part of the nineteenth century.

With the exception of some dialectic differences, its grammar is like that of the Hindī but differs from the latter in its extensive vocabulary, which contains large numbers of Persian and Arabic words, so that it might well be termed the Per-sianized Hindustani of the educated Moslems. Some European words have also been incorporated, especially English technical terms. Because of the large number of Persian words, it can be written best in the Arabic characters, with the addition of some characters used to represent non-Arabic sounds.

Syllabication is the same as in the Arabic.

Vowel and reading signs

Sukūn ° or ˆ is sometimes written ˇ, but all the other signs are as in the Arabic.

Punctuation (used only in modern prints)

  ؟ Interrogation mark,

  — Period.

  + End of an extract.

WELSH

A	a	*a* in father	LL	ll	*thl* sound
B	b	*b* in ban			
C	c	*k;* final like *q*	M	m	*m*
CH	ch	*ch* in Scotch loch	N	n	*n,* liquid and nasal
D	d	*d*	O	o	*o*
DD	dd	*th* in they	P	p	*p*
E	e	*a* in race	PH	ph	*ph* in phimosis
F	f	*v* in van, and *f* in of	R	r	*r,* liquid, as in err
FF	ff	*f* in for or *ff* in effort	RH	rh	*r,* breathed
G	g	*g* in log	S	s	*s,* sibilant, not as in rose
H	h	*h* in hand, not *h* in hour	T	t	*t*
I	i	*ee* in fee	TH	th	*t* aspirate, as in Beth
J	j	*ia* sound; in foreign words only	U	u	*eu*
			W	w	*oo* in wooing
K	k	*c;* seldom used	Y	y	*u* in fur; also a sound between *e* and *i*
L	l	*l,* liquid			

Cardinal numbers

un	one	naw	nine
dau	two	dēg	ten
tri	three	unarddeg	eleven
pedwar	four	deuddeg	twelve
pump (pimp)	five	triarddeg	thirteen
chwech	six	ugain	twenty
saith	seven	cant	hundred
wyth	eight	mil (meal)	thousand

Ordinal numbers

cyntaf	first	nawfed	ninth
ail	second	degfed	tenth
trydydd	third	unfedarddeg	eleventh
pedwerydd	fourth	deuddegfed	twelfth
pumed	fifth	trydyddarddeg	thirteenth
chweched	sixth	ugainfed	twentieth
saithfed	seventh	cantfed	hundredth
wythfed	eighth	milfed	thousandth

Months

Ionawr (Ion.)	January	Gorffenaf (Gorf.)	July
Chwefror (Chwe.)	February	Awst	August
Mawrth (Mawr.)	March	Medi	September
Ebrill (Ebr.)	April	Hydref (Hyd.)	October
Mai	May	Tachwedd (Tach.)	November
Mehefin (Meh.)	June	Rhagfyr (Rhag.)	December

Days

Dydd Sul	Sunday	Dydd Iau	Thursday
Dydd Llun	Monday	Dydd Gwener	Friday
Dydd Mawrth	Tuesday	Dydd Sadwrn	Saturday
Dydd Mercher	Wednesday		

Seasons

gwanwyn	spring	hydref	autumn
haf (have)	summer	gaeaf	winter

Time

awr	hour	boreu	morning
dydd	day	canol dydd	mid-day (noon)
wythnos (eight nights)	week	hwyrnos	evening
mis (mease)	month	gwawr	dawn
blwyddyn	year	nos	night

WENDISH

A	a	*a* in far	Ḿ	ḿ	*mj*, soft
B	b	*b*	N	n	*n*
Ḃ	b'	*bj*	Ń	ń	*nj*, soft
Ç	c	*c*, hard	O	o	*o*
Ć	ć	*tsz*, soft	Ó	ó	*ō*, long
Č	č	*ch*, hard	Ò	ò	*oa*
D	d	*d*, hard	P	p	*p*
DŹ	dź	*dz*	Ṕ	ṕ	*pj*, soft
DŽ	dž	*dzh*, soft	R	r	*r*
E	e	{Open *e* in ten / Closed *a* in day	Ŕ	ŕ	*rj*, soft
			S	s	*s*, hard
Ě	ě	*ie* in field	Ś	ś	*sh*, soft
F	f	*f*	Š	š	*sh*, harder: Pasha
G	g	*g*, soft	T	t	*t*, hard
H	h	*h*, soft	TS	ts	*ts*
CH	ch	*ch*, soft; also *kh*	U	u	*oo*
I	i	*e*	W	w	*v* in value
J	j	*j*, soft	Ẃ	ẃ	*vj*, soft
K	k	*k*, soft	Y	y	*i* in irritate
L	l	*l*, soft	Z	z	*z*, hard
Ľ	ľ	*lj*	Ź	ź	*z*, very soft
Ł	ł	Guttural	Ž	ž	*zh* (like *j* in French journal)
M	m	*m*			

Q, *v*, and *x* are used only in foreign words, and for the first *kw* is quite generally used, while *ks* takes the place of *x*; *f* is always used for the *ph* sound, as *fosfor*, phosphorus.

Stress is invariably on the first syllable.

Capitalization

Capitalization is practically as in English.

Syllabication

The general rules of the west Slavic languages are followed in the division of words.

Cardinal numbers

jeden	one	dwanasćo	twelve
dwa	two	tśinasćo	thirteen
tśo, tśi	three	dważasća	twenty
štyfo, štyfi	four	jeden a dważasća, dwaz a jeden }	twenty-one
pěś	five		
šěsć	six	sto	hundred
sedym	seven	żaześ stow }	
wósym	eight	żaześ hundertow }	thousand
żewes	nine	towzynt }	
żaześ	ten	tysac }	
jědnasćo	eleven		

Ordinal numbers

prědny	first	žasety	tenth
drugi	second	jadnasty	eleventh
tśeśi	third	dwanasty	twelfth
stwórty	fourth	tśinasty	thirteenth
pěty	fifth	dwažasty	twentieth
šesti	sixth	jeden a dwažasty	twenty-first
sedymy	seventh	hundertny	hundredth
wósmy	eighth	towzyntny	thousandth
žewety	ninth		

Months

januar (jan.)	January	julij (jul.)	July
februar (feb.)	February	awgust (awg.)	August
měrc	March	september (sept.)	September
hapryl (hapr.)	April	oktober (okt.)	October
mej	May	november (nov.)	November
junij (jun.)	June	december (dec.)	December

Days

njedźela	Sunday	štwórtk	Thursday
pónežele	Monday	pjatk	Friday
wutora	Tuesday	sobota	Saturday
srjeda	Wednesday		

Seasons

naléćo	spring	nazyma	autumn
lětnje	summer	zyma	winter

Time

góźina	hour	měsac	month
dźeń	day	lěto	year
tydźeń	week		

YIDDISH

Yiddish, or Judaeo-German, is the language spoken by Polish and Russian Jews whose forbears, early in the Middle Ages, emigrated to Poland from the Rhineland. They carried the German language with them, but soon absorbed words from the languages of the countries in which they lived as well as Hebrew words.

The Yiddish uses the same letters as the Hebrew (see 120), with the Ashkenazic pronunciation; it also is read from right to left.

All Hebrew letters are consonants, but when employed in Yiddish ע, ו, י, א are made to represent vowel-sounds.

The vowel-sounds *a* and *o* are represented by א e.g., נאר nar, דאס dos; *e* is represented by ע e.g., ער er; *i* is represented by י e.g., פיר fir; *u* is represented by ו e.g. שול shul; *ei* and *ai* are represented by ײ e.g., בײן bein, פײן fain; *oi* is represented by ױ e.g. לױב loib.

In addition to the vowel-letters, the Hebrew vowel-points are also frequently employed.

Syllabication

A single consonant between two vowels belongs to the next syllable: נו־ציג nu-tsig, קא־פא־טע ka-po-te.

Of two consonants between two vowels one belongs to the preceding, the other to the following syllable e.g., זין־קען sin-ken, שפאל־טונג spal-tung.

The letter י preceded by א, אָ (אַ,אָ) and followed by a vowel, belongs to that vowel: נא־רא־יען na-ra-yen, װאָ־יע־װען vo-ye-ven; when followed by a consonant, it belongs to the preceding syllable: באַי־קע bai-ke, סטאָי־קע stoi-ke.

The combinations טש, זש, טה, ך representing simple sounds, are inseparable and belong to the next syllable: קאַ־װירען ka-vi-ren, הו־זשען hu-zhen, ראַ־טהען ra-then, פאַ־טשען pa-tshen.

Prefixes and suffixes are distinct syllables: גע־דריקט ge-drikt, פער־שטאַנד fer-stand, גליק־ליך glik-lich, פרײנד־שאַפט freind-shaft.

In dividing words at the end of a line the rules of syllabication *must* be observed.

At the end of a line, compound words should be divided into the simple words of which they consist: דרײ־פוס drei-fus, האַנד־טוך hand-tuch, װינש־פינגערל vinsh-fingerl.

AMERICAN INDIAN LANGUAGES

295

INTRODUCTION

Before European contact the Indians north of Mexico had not evolved any system or systems for recording their languages by means of either phonetic or syllabic signs. In 1809–21, a Cherokee named Sequoyah invented a syllabary, based on the characters in our own alphabet, which was well suited to his language, was rapidly adopted by his people, and was used in the printing of parts of the Bible and a native weekly newspaper, *The Cherokee Phoenix.*

With this exception, systems of writing and printing Indian tongues in this portion of North America have been devised either by missionaries desiring to convert the natives to Christianity or by linguists whose interests were purely scientific.

In the former case (consult in the subjoined material Chippewa, Cree, Eskimo, Kalispel, and Muskokee) the characters used were simpler and some of the systems attained a certain amount of currency for a time, being used more particularly in religious works, but all, as well as that of the Cherokee, soon began to fall into disuse as the younger generations of Indians acquired a knowledge of English, and without exception they will be entirely discontinued within a relatively short time.

Aside from the Cherokee syllabary, systems of representation used most widely were those of the Chippewa, Muskokee, and Choctaw. The Muskokee or Creek alphabet was officially adopted by the Creek Nation, and many Creeks are still able to employ it. The Choctaw alphabet is that upon which the one contained in the present work is based, and differed from it principally in using r for ł, v for ạ, and an underscore with the vowels (a, i, o, u) instead of the superior n (a^n, i^n, o^n, u^n) to represent nasalized vowel sounds. The Dakota system here given, founded on the widely used alphabet of S. R. Riggs, came nearest of all to enjoying both missionary and scientific currency.

The systems devised solely by students of language are not, of course, intended for popular usage but merely as contributions to a scientific study of the languages in question. In some cases, owing to the extinction of a dialect or because the work has been done in an exceptionally thorough manner, the system of a single student will persist for all time, but if several investigators have studied a variety of speech, the phonetic signs may be progressively amplified or one or more conflicting systems may arise. Numerous and serious efforts have been made, both in the United States and abroad, to introduce a uniform series of characters, and special mention may be made of the system of the International Phonetic Association and that suggested by a committee of the American Anthropological Association for use in recording Indian tongues. This last was published by the Smithsonian Institution as volume 66, number 6, of the *Smithsonian Miscellaneous Collections,* Washington, 1916. But Indian languages vary so widely and investigators themselves approach the study of them from such different angles that there seems to be no prospect of avoiding a considerable diversity of usage.

The languages in the accompanying sketch, other than those mentioned above, illustrate almost entirely the alphabets and phonetic devices used by scientific students of Indian tongues. That of Olbrechts, a painstaking modern worker in Cherokee, may be contrasted with the syllabary of Sequoyah, invented for practical use, in order to appreciate the varied forms linguistic representations may take in response to differing demands.

Unless otherwise indicated, the vowel values of the various languages are those of the continental system, and consonantal sounds are approximately those of the same characters in English.

Diacritical marks over or after letters merely indicate the position of the stress, unless otherwise indicated in tables of phonetic values.

CADDOAN

a	As in father	r	r trilled, in Pawnee and Arikara [2]	
a	As u in but			
b	b	s	A surd, more sibilant than in English	
c	sh in show			
d	Sonant	t	t, intermediate [3]	
e	a in fate	tc	Affricative in Caddo; more intermediate in Arikara	
ε	e in met [1]			
h	h	ts	Affricative intermediate; in Caddo it is surd	
i	ee in feet			
ι	i in hit	u	oo in hoot	
k	Intermediate, neither sonant nor surd	w	Slightly more rounded than in English	
m	m	x	Almost ch in German ich	
n	n	y	y	
o	o in go	ω	aw in law; in Wichita	
p	p	ai	ei in height; in Caddo	

[1] In the Pawnee this sound is made with the lips very wide, the aperture between them forming a very narrow slit, and the e does not have the usual diphthongal quality.

[2] In Kitsai and Wichita, where a distinct n occurs, the r more nearly approximates the English r, but is not made as far back in the mouth nor trilled as strongly.

[3] Pawnee final t is nasalized, indicated by superior n (t^n). Caddo t is a surd.

The above phonetic system is used by Drs. Lesser and Weltfish for the languages of the Caddoan stock.

The Caddoan linguistic stock is composed of four major languages: Pawnee, Wichita, Kitsai (Kichai), and Caddo. The Pawnee now occurs in three dialects; the Wichita and Caddo probably each included several dialects, though but one form is known, while the Kitsai has never developed dialectic differentiation. Pawnee, Wichita, and Kitsai are mutually unintelligible, and Caddo is the most divergent of the four languages.

Diacritical marks

The glottal catch (') and the aspiration (') are used in the usual way. Stress is indicated by the prime (') after the syllable: a'. Vowel length is indicated by a raised period (·) after the vowel: a·; vowel shortness, by a breve (˘) under the vowel: ă. Pitch accents are, á for high tone, and a̤ for middle high. Tone combinations occurring in Pawnee are, â· high to middle high, ā· normal to middle high, ā· middle high to normal, and â·, middle high to high.

Whispered or faintly articulated sounds are indicated by superior symbols: t°.

CHEROKEE

a   Long, open, as in far
ā   Long, closed, as in German Wahl
c   Unvoiced, as in shut
ᴀ   Voiceless, oral vowel
â   Open vowel, as in far
ą ⎰ Nasalized vowels, but more commonly with less pronounced
ǫ ⎱   nasalization
d   Voiced, as in dawn
dj   Voiced, as in George
dz   Voiced, as in hands up
ᴅ   Intermediate between voiced and unvoiced dental
$ᴅ_n$ Voiced nasal, as in near, but preceded by a hardly audible d sound
$ᴅ_l$ Voiced, as in lid, but preceded by a hardly audible d sound
e   Closed vowel, as *a* in baby[1]
ə   Vowel of indefinite quality, as *e* in father
ɛ   Long open vowel, as in air
ɛ·   Long nasal, as in French pain
g   Voiced consonant, as in go
i   Closed vowel, as in pin
ɪ   Voiceless, oral vowel
ɩ   Open vowel, as in seat
j   Voiced, as in French jambe
k   Unvoiced, as in back
ķ   Unvoiced, but pronounced farther back than k
k'   Unvoiced, aspirated, as in come, but more emphatic
l   Voiced as in lid
ł   Unvoiced *l*
m   Voiced, as in mother
n   Voiced nasal, as in can
ɴ   Voiceless nasal, followed by a strong nasal aspiration
ŋ   Voiced, as in sing
o   Closed vowel, occurs only in songs
ö·   Nasalized (usually long), as in French un
ɔ   Open vowel, as in not
ö   Very short vowel, as in German Götter
ɔ   Voiceless, oral vowel
ɔ·   Nasalized vowel (usually long), as in French bon
öⁿ   Nasalized vowel (very short), as in German Götter [2]

[1] This sound is rarely heard in Cherokee, and then always finally; it seems to be a contraction of ɛ· (nasalized long ɛ+i).

[2] When only a slight degree of nasalization is heard a superior ⁿ is used after the vowel, instead of a hook under it, as in cases where nasalization is more pronounced.

CHEROKEE—Continued

s   Unvoiced fricative, as in sing

t   Unvoiced as in hit

t'   Unvoiced, aspirated, as in tin, but with aspiration more emphatic

tc   Prepalatal affricative, unvoiced, as in China

ts   Dental affricative, unvoiced, as in ants

tł   Lateral affricative, unvoiced *l*, preceded by unvoiced dental stop

u   Closed vowel, as in nook

u̇   A short vowel sound between *a* and *ö*

ᴜ   Voiceless, oral vowel

υ   Open vowel as in spoon

w   Semiconsonant [3]

ꭓ   Unvoiced palatal, as in German nicht

y   Semiconsonant [3]

z   Dental, voiced fricative, as in gaze

---

[3] This letter may be strongly aspirated, when it is followed by a spiritus asper ('), but it may be voiceless when it is rendered by a small-capital letter. The w is often preceded by a barely audible u sound, and the phoneme is written ᵘw.

NOTE.—Phonemes that are scarcely audible and occur frequently as weakly articulated vowels are indicated by small superior letters: ɔˑᵘ, ɛˑⁱ, ᵘw, ⁱy, etc.

Diacritical marks

ᶜ   Indicates aspiration.

'   Indicates glottalization.

ą   Indicates nasalization.

ą̓   Combination of the spiritus asper and nasalization hook indicates strong nasal aspiration.

ⁿ   Indicates slight nasalization.

·   After a vowel indicates that it is a long vowel.

:   After a vowel indicates very long quantity.

˘   After a vowel indicates an abnormally short vowel.

;   After a vowel or consonant indicates a very slight pause.

ˊ   After a phoneme, indicates primary stress.

ˋ   After a phoneme, indicates secondary stress.

ˊ   Over a vowel, indicates rising pitch.

ˋ   Over a vowel, indicates falling pitch, but this and the preceding mark can be combined to ˇ, ie., "falling-rising," or to ˆ, i.e., "rising-falling" pitch.

CHEROKEE SYLLABARY

In old prints this is erroneously called "Cherokee Alphabet"

D *a*		**R** *e*	**T** *i*	**Ꮰ** *o*	**Ꮕ** *u*	**i** *v*
Ꮪ *ga*	**Ꭴ** *ka*	**Ᏻ** *ge*	**Ꭹ** *gi*	**A** *go*	**J** *gu*	**E** *gv*
Ꮙ *ha*		**Ꭾ** *he*	**Ꭿ** *hi*	**Ꮂ** *ho*	**Ꮎ** *hu*	**Ꮐ** *hv*
W *la*		**Ꮄ** *le*	**Ꮅ** *li*	**Ꮶ** *lo*	**M** *lu*	**Ꮑ** *lv*
Ꮉ *ma*		**Ꮊ** *me*	**H** *mi*	**Ꮝ** *mo*	**Ꮻ** *mu*	
Ꮓ *na*	**Ꮤ** *hna*	**Ꮕ** *nah*	**Ꮑ** *ne*	**Ꮒ** *ni*	**Z** *no*	**Ꮕ** *nu*	**Ꮕ** *nv*
Ꮖ *qua*		**Ꮗ** *que*	**Ꮘ** *qui*	**Ꮙ** *quo*	**Ꮚ** *quu*	**Ꮛ** *quv*
Ꮜ *sa*	**Ꮝ** *s*	**4** *se*	**Ꮟ** *si*	**Ꮠ** *so*	**Ꮡ** *su*	**R** *sv*
Ꮣ *da*	**W** *la*	**Ꮥ** *de* **Ꮦ** *te*	**Ꮧ** *di* **Ꮨ** *ti*	**Ꮩ** *do*	**S** *du*	**Ꮯ** *dv*
Ꮸ *dla*	**Ꮬ** *tla*	**L** *tle*	**C** *tli*	**Ꮬ** *tlo*	**Ꮭ** *tlu*	**P** *tlv*
Ꮶ *tsa*		**Ꮴ** *tse*	**Ꮲ** *tsi*	**K** *tso*	**Ꮷ** *tsu*	**C** *tsv*
Ꮹ *wa*		**Ꮺ** *we*	**Ꮻ** *wi*	**Ꮼ** *wo*	**Ꮽ** *wu*	**6** *wv*
Ꮿ *ya*		**Ᏸ** *ye*	**Ᏹ** *yi*	**Ᏺ** *yo*	**Ᏻ** *yu*	**B** *yv*

Vowel sounds

a *a* in father; short, as *a* in rival
e *a* in hate; short, as *e* in met
i *i* in pique; short, as *i* in pit

o *aw* in law; short, as *o* in not
u *oo* in fool; short, as *u* in pull
v *u* in but, nasalized

Consonant sounds

g *g*, nearly, but approaching *k*
d *d*, nearly, but approaching *t*
h, k, l, m, n, q, s, l, w, and y as in English

Syllables beginning with g, except f, sometimes have the power of *k*; Ꭽ, Ꮝ, Ꮯ are sometimes sounded *to*, *tu*, and *tv*, and those written with tl, except g, sometimes change to dl.

CHINOOK

The Chinookan stock embraces a number of closely related dialects which were spoken on both sides of the Columbia River from the Cascades to the sea, and some distance up the Willamette Valley. There were two principal dialects, Upper Chinook and Lower Chinook. These were again subdivided into slightly different dialects. The Chinook proper of the Lower Chinook is treated here.

The phonetic system is characterized by a superabundance of consonants and consonant-clusters, combined with a great variability of vowels.

The series of consonants may be represented as follows:

	Sonant	Surd	Fortis	Spirant	Semi-nasal	Nasal	Lateral	Semi-vowels
Glottal_____	ε	—	—		—	—	—	—
Velar_____	(g?)	q	q!	x	—	—	—	—
Palatal_____	g	k	k!	x̣	—	—	—	—
Anterior palatal_____	(g·?)	k	k·!	x·	—	—	—	—
Alveolar_____	(d?)	t	t!	s, c	—	n	(l)	(y)
Dento-alveolar affricative_____	—	ts, tc	ts!, tc!	—	—	—	—	—
Labial_____					—	p p!	—	m m —	(w)
Lateral_____					ʟ̣	ʟ ʟ!	ɫ, l	—	— · —

The system of vowels and semivowels may be written as follows:

Diphthong	Semi-vowel		Vowels						Semi-vowel	Diphthong
				E						
	w	U	o	ô	A	ê	(E)	î	y	
au		u	o	(ô)	a	ê	(e)	i		ai
		ū	ō	â	ā	ä	ē	(ī)		

The accent affects the character of the vowel upon which it falls and modifies consonants insofar as certain consonants or consonantic clusters are not tolerated when they precede the accent.

The small-capital letter indicates an obscure sound.

The circumflex is often used instead of the breve.

ä   Has the sound of ai in hair.

ô   Like o in top.

â   Like aw in law.

u   oo in soon.

hw   wh in who; when final, this sound is pronounced less distinctly.

c   sh sound, quite generally.

x   Like ch in the German ich.

tc   Similar to tch or ch in English.

Laterals (ʟ) similar to dl; ʟ, similar to tl or kl; ɫ, a surd, somewhat similar to thl.

Fortis = Explosive.

The glottal stop is a sonant stop.

CHIPPEWA (Ojibway)[1]

A	a	*a* in fate	O	o	*o* in note
B	b	*b*	P	p	*p*
D	d	*d*	Q	q	*q*
E	e	*e* in met	S	s	*s* in so
G	g	*g* in go	T	t	*t*
I	i	*i* in mit	U	u	*u* in but
J	j	*j* in judge	W	w	*w*
K	k	*k*	Y	y	*y*
M	m	*m*	Z	z	*z*
N	n	*n*			

DIPHTHONGS AND DOUBLE CONSONANTS

AH	ah	As *a* in father, fast, mahjah	QU	qu	As in queen, equa
AU	au	As in laugh, odenáun	NG	ng	As in king, neebing
EE	ee	As in feet, opineeg	NS	ns	Almost *nce* in prince, muhkukoons
OO	oo	As in foot	SH	sh	As in wish, kookósh
UH	uh	As in but, muhkuk	WH	wh	Like *w* in cow, owh
UY	uy	As in buy, chébuy	ZH	zh	Like French *j*, meezh
CH	ch	As in much, cheemaun			

The Chippewa (Ojibway) are a large group of the Algonkian family of Indians, occupying the wooded country about Lake Superior and westward as far as northern Minnesota. They now number some 30,000 souls.

Cardinal numbers

pázhig	one	medáhswe	ten
neezh	two	medahswe'zhe pazhig	eleven
neswé	three	medahswe'zhe neezh	twelve
néewin	four	medahswe'zhe neswe	thirteen
náhnun	five	néezhtuhnuh	twenty
ningodwáuswe	six	neezhtuhnuh'zhe pazhig	twenty-one
néezhwahswe	seven	ningodwáuk	hundred
ishwáhswe	eight	medauswauk	thousand
sháunguswe	nine		

Ordinal numbers

netúm, nátumesing	first	ako-medáuching	tenth
ako-néezhing	second	ako-'zhe pázhig	eleventh
ako-nesíng	third	ako-'zhe néezhing	twelfth
ako-néewing	fourth	ako-'zhe nesing	thirteenth
ako-náhuing	fifth	ako neezhtuhnuhwag	twentieth
ako-ningodwáuching	sixth	ako neezhtuhnuhwag 'zhe pazhig	twenty-first
ako-néezhwauching	seventh		
ako-ishwáuching	eighth	ako ningodwáukwuk	hundredth
ako-sháunguching	ninth	ako medáuswáukwuk	thousandth

[1] "The Ojebway Language," by the Rev. Edward F. Wilson, Toronto, 1874.

NOTE.—The Otchipwe is practically the same language with a variant transliteration.

Months

muhnedoo-keezis	January	misquéemene-keezis	July
nuhmábene keezis	February	meen-keezis	August
onáhbune-keezis	March	muhnóomene-keezis	September
babooquadáhgeming keeziss }	April	penáhque keezis	October
		kushkúdene-keézis	November
wáhbegoone-keezis	May	múhnedoo-kéezisoons	December
odáemene-keezis	June		

Days

uhnuhmeakézhegud [1]	Sunday	ahbetóosa	Wednesday
ke-ishquah-uhnúhmea-kézheguk, netum-kezhegud }	Monday	neeo-kezhegud	Thursday
		nahno-kezhegud	Friday
		ningodwáusokezhegud	Saturday
neezho kezhegud	Tuesday		

Seasons

séegwun, menókumme	spring	túhgwáhge	autumn
néebin	summer	pebóon	winter

Time

tebúhegun	hour	kéezis (*pl.* -oog)	month
kézhegud (*pl.* -oon)	day	pebóon [2]	year
uhnuhmeakézhegud	week		

[1] This word, meaning Sunday, is also used for week, thus: two weeks would be neezho-uhnuhmeakézhegud, two Sundays.

[2] As in the case of week, year is expressed by "number of winters", thus: neezhopebóon.

CHIPPEWA (Otchipwe)[1]

A	a	*a* in father	M	m	*m* in man
B	b	*b* in bad	N	n	*n* in name
C	c	*c* in watch	O	o	*o* in note
D	d	*d* in den	P	p	*p* in part
E	e	*a* in same	S	s	*z* in zeal
G	g	*g* in go	SS	ss	*ss* in mass
H	h	*h* in hoe	T	t	*t* in top
I	i	*i* in pin or like *ee*	W	w	*w* in wet
J	j	*j* in jour (French)	DJ	dj	*j* in judge
K	k	*k* in kite			

Except in foreign proper names there are neither *f, l, q, r, u, v, x, y* or *z*, as the Chippewa cannot pronounce these letters correctly; he will therefore substitute *p* or *b* for *f* and *v*, thus *Dabid* instead of *David*; for *l* and *r* they use *n*, as *Mani* instead of *Marie; Maginit* for *Margaret; Nouis* for *Louis; Sanswi* or *Soswen* for *Francis*, etc.

Every letter must be distinctly pronounced, as *sagaam, sa-ga-am; sagiin, sa-gi-in.*

Cardinal numbers

bejig (ningot)	one	midāsswi	ten
nij	two	midasswi ashi bejig	eleven
nisswi	three	midasswi ashi nij[2]	twelve
niwin	four	midasswi ashi nisswi	thirteen
nānan	five	nijtana	twenty
ningotwāsswi	six	nijtana ashi bejig	twenty-one
nijwāsswi	seven	ningotwak	hundred
nishwāsswi (ishwasswi)	eight	midāsswak	thousand
jāugasswi	nine		

Ordinal numbers

netāmissing, nitam	first	eko-midatching	tenth
eko-nijing	second	eko ashi bejig	eleventh
eko-nissing	third	eko ashi nijing	twelfth
eko-niwing	fourth	eko ashi nissing	thirteenth
eko-nananing	fifth	eko-nijtanaweg	twentieth
eko-ningotwatching	sixth	eko ashi bejig	twenty-first
eko-nijwatching	seventh	eko-ningotwakwak	hundredth
eko-nishwatching	eighth	eko-midasswakwak	thousandth
eko-jangatching	ninth		

Days

anamiégijigad	Sunday	abitosse	Wednesday
anwebiwinigijigad	Sabbath	niogijigad	Thursday
gi-ishkwa-anamiegijigak	Monday	([3])	Friday
([3])	Tuesday	mariegijigad	Saturday

[1] "Grammar of the Otchipwe Language," by the Rt. Rev. Bishop Baraga, Montreal, 1878.
[2] In counting from 11 to 20, midāsswi (10) is usually omitted, as ashibejig, ashi nij, ashi nissiwi, etc.
[3] We have no record of the Chippewa terms for Tuesday and Friday [probably well-known to the Chippewa, however, who form a large tribe]. In Lemoine's dictionary of the Algonkian dialect, which is closely allied to Chippewa, Tuesday is given as Anjeni Kijik and Friday as Tcipaiatiko Kijik. In these terms, *j* is pronounced as in French, and *tc* is equivalent to English *ch*.—Report Bureau of American Ethnology.

Months

Manito-gisiss	January	Miskwimini-gisiss	July
Namebini-gisiss	February	Min-gisiss	August
Onābani-gisiss	March	Manominike-gisiss	September
Bebokwedagiming-gisiss	April	Binākwi-gisiss	October
		Gashkadino-gisiss	November
Wabigoui-gisiss	May	Manito-gisissons	December
Odeimini-gisiss	June		

Seasons

sigwan, minôkami	spring	tagwâgi	autumn
nibin	summer	bibôn	winter

Time

gijig, gijigad	day	gisiss	month
ningo anamiegijigad	week	bibon, bibonagad	year

CHOCTAW

A	a	*a* in father	Ł	ł	*l* aspirated
Ạ	ạ	*u* in tub and *a* in around	M	m	*m*
B	b	*b*	N	n	*n*
CH	ch	*ch* in church	O	o	*o* in note
E	e	*e* in they and short *e* in met	P	p	*p*
			S	s	*s* in sir, never *s* in his
F	f	*f*	SH	sh	*sh* in shall
H	h	*h*	T	t	*t*
I	i	*i* in marine and short *i* in pin	U	u	*oo* in wool
			W	w	*w* in war
K	k	*k*	Y	y	*y* in you
L	l	*l*			

DIPHTHONGS

AI   ai   *i* in pine   AU   au   *ow* in how

NASALIZED VOWELS

Aⁿ	aⁿ ⎫	These are pure nasals, and retain the vowel sounds, except
Iⁿ	iⁿ ⎪	before the letter k, when they are like the long *ang, ing,*
Oⁿ	oⁿ ⎬	*ong, ung.* The usual sound is softer than *ang*, and like
Uⁿ	uⁿ ⎭	that of the French vowel followed by *n* in the same syllable.

Each consonant has but one sound and the sounds ascribed to the vowels are as indicated in accented syllables, while in unaccented syllables they have the sound of short vowels. Do not give the English sound to the vowels, except as indicated in the alphabet.

The Choctaws were a prominent Indian tribe of Muskhogean stock. They are now located in eastern Oklahoma and in Mississippi and officially number about 18,000 pure bloods.

CREE

Ā	ā	*a* in hate	M	m	*m*	
A	a	*a* in far	N	n	*n*	
C	c	*ch* in church	O	o	*o* in note	
E	e	*e* in me	P	p	*p*	
G	g	*g*, hard	S	s	*s* [4]	
H	h	*h*, aspirated	T	t	*t*	
ʿ		(¹)	U	u	*u* in but	
Ī	ī	*i* in thine	W	w	*w*	
I	i	*i* in pin [2]	Y	y	*y*	
K	k	*k*	OO	oo	*oo* in soon	
KW	kw	*q*	EW	ew	*u* in pure	
L	l	*l* [3]	OW	ow	*ow* in now	

¹ Some syllables are strongly aspirated for which the *h* is not always adapted, and so the Greek asper (ʿ) has been adopted, usually at the end of the syllable aspirated. Some words depend on the asper for their signification: *ukochin*, he hangs, but *uko'chin*, he hangs in a liquid, he floats.

² The pronoun *I* is *nela* at Moose Factory; *nena* at Albany, Severn, and York Factory; *neya* on the east main coast; *netha* at English River, and *nera* at Isle à la Crosse.

³ Used at Moose Ferry only; elsewhere *n, y, th,* or *r* are substituted.

⁴ The *sh* sound is confined principally to Moose Factory and vicinity, and we have *sheshep*, duck; *sheshepish*, small duck, while elsewhere *sesep* and *sesepis* are used.

The Cree is an Algonkian Indian tribe occupying a large territory in Canada, extending from Hudson Bay west to Manitoba and Saskatchewan. They are in the main a forest people, though one branch is known as the Plains Cree. They number about 15,000, including mixed breeds, which was probably about their original number.

Cardinal numbers

pāyuk	one	neshoshap	twelve
nesho	two	nistoshap	thirteen
nisto	three	neshitanow	twenty
nāö	four	neshitanow pāyukoshap	twenty-one
neyalul	five	nisto-mitanow	thirty
nekotwas	six	nāmitanow	forty
neswas, tāpuko'p	seven	neyalilo-mitanow	fifty
yananāö	eight	nekotwaso-mitanow	sixty
shaketat, payukostāö	nine	neswaso-mitanow	seventy
kākat metat		yananā-mitanow	eighty
metat	ten	shaketato-mitanow	ninety
pāyukoshap, metat	eleven	metato-mitanow	hundred
pāyukoshap		kiche mitato-mitanow	thousand

There are no ordinals in the Cree language.

Months

Kisāpowatukinumoowepesim, Oosāaskoonepesim	January
Kisāpesim	February
Mikisewepesim	March
Niskepesim	April
Une'kepesim	May
Wawepesim, Oopināawepesim, Pinawāwepesim, Asimoakoopesim	June
Puskoohoowepesim, Puskoowepesim Oopuskoowepesim	July
O'opuhoowepesim	August
Nimit'ahumoowepesim, Mit'ahumoowepesim, Ooskuhoowepesim, Wesakoopesim	September
Powatukinusesewepesim, Misekamāyowoopesim	October
'Akwutinoowepesim, Kuskutinoowepesim	November
Yeyekwutinoowepesim. Yeyekoopewepesim	December

Days

Ayum'eākesikow, Ayum'eāwekesikow	Sunday
Nistum kesikow, Pooneayum'eākesikow	Monday
Nesookesikow	Tuesday
Nistoo kesikow, ā ap'etowipuyik	Wednesday
Nāoo kesikow, ā ap'etowipuyik	Thursday
Neyanunoo kesikow	Friday
Matinuwā kesikow, Nikootwasikoo kesikow	Saturday

Seasons

sekwun	early spring	tukwakin	autumn
meyooskume	late spring	pipoon	winter
nepin	summer		

Time

tipp'uhikun, pesimooka-netipp'uhikun tipp'uhipesimwan	hour	pāyukwow ā ispuyik	week
		pesim	month
kesikow	day	pipoon, uske, uskewin	year

DAKOTA (Sioux)

A	a	*a* in far
B	b	*b*
C	c	*ch* in chin
Cʻ	cʻ	*ch*, aspirated
Ç	ç	Exploded *ch*, not in English
D	d	*d*
E	e	*e* in they
G	g	*g* in give
Ġ	ġ	*g*, velar fricative, voiced, not in English
H	h	*h*
Ḣ	ḣ	velar fricative, unvoiced
I	i	*i* in machine
K	k	*k*, medial
Kʻ	kʻ	Aspirate
Ḳ	ḳ	Exploded *k*, not in English
L	l	*l*
M	m	*m*
N	n	*n*

Ŋ n	ŋ	*n* in ink (nasal) Follows a nasalized vowel
O	o	*o* in go
P	p	*p*, medial
Pʻ	pʻ	Aspirate
Ṗ	ṗ	Exploded *p*, not in English
S	s	*s*
Ṡ	ṡ	*sh* in she
T	t	*t*, medial
Ṭ	ṭ	Exploded *t*, not in English
U	u	*oo* in ooze
W	w	*w*
Y	y	*y*
Z	z	*z*
Ż	ż	*z* in azure
Ą	ą	Nasalized vowels
Į	į	(Riggs used ŋ after the
Ų	ų	vowels)
'		Glottal stop[1]

[1] Following s, ṡ, and ḣ (not glottalized s, ṡ, and ḣ).

The Dakota is the largest confederation of Siouan tribes, occupying the north-western plains of the United States. Numbering about 25,000, they now occupy 10 reservations in several States.

NOTE.—Glottalized p', t', and k' must be distinguished from p, t, and k followed by a vowel which opens with glottal closure.

Syllabication

As a rule every vowel ends a syllable, but the following are exceptions:
1. The nasal ŋ always closes a syllable, as ka-hiŋ-ta, sweep.
2. A syllable, contracted by dropping the vowel, is attached to the preceding syllable, thus making it close with a consonant, as: i-piḣ-ya, cause to boil, from i-pi-ġa, boil, and ya, cause.
3. The words en, in, and is (he, she, it) and their compounds do not close the syllable with a vowel.

Accents

A misplaced accent is as bad as a mispronounced letter, for it often changes the meaning of a word; as má-ga means field and ma-ġá means goose.
Most words are accented on the second syllable and thus accent marks are not usually printed; also all words beginning with *wo* are accented on the first syllable, and the accent marks are not printed. In all other cases the accent is printed and should be carefully noted.

Cardinal numbers

waŋźi	one	napciwaŋka	nine
noŋpa	two	wikcemna	ten
yámni	three	akewaŋźi	eleven
tópa	four	akenoŋpa	twelve
záptaŋ	five	akeyamni	thirteen
śákpe	six	wikcemnanoŋpa	twenty
śakowiŋ	seven	opawiŋge	hundred
śahdoġaŋ	eight	kektopawiŋge	thousand

Ordinal numbers

tokaheya	first	iśakowiŋ	seventh
inoŋpa, icinoŋpa,⎱ iyokihe ⎰	second	iśahdoġaŋ	eighth
		inapciwaŋka	ninth
iyamni	third	iwikcemna	tenth
itopa, tópayuśpapi	fourth	iakewaŋżi	eleventh
izaptaŋ	fifth	iakenoŋpa	twelfth
iśakpe	sixth	iakeyamni	thirteenth

Months

Witeȟi	January	Mdokecokawi	July
Wicatawi	February	Wiiśahdoġaŋ	August
Máni	March	Wiinapciŋwaŋka	September
Wiitopa	April	Wi iwikcemna	October
Wożupiwi	May	Tahecapśuŋwi	November
Ważuśtecaśawi	June	Wiiakenoŋpa	December

Days

Aŋpetuwakaŋ	Sunday	Aŋpetuitopa	Thursday
Aŋpetutokaheya	Monday	Aŋpetu Izaptaŋ	Friday
Aŋpetuinoŋpa	Tuesday	Owaŋkayużażapi	Saturday
Aŋpetuiyamni	Wednesday		

Seasons

wétu	spring	ptaŋyetu	autumn
mdoketu	summer	waniyetu	winter

Time

wíhiyaya	hour	wi wiyawapi	month
aŋpetu	day	wiiakenoŋpa	year
uŋpetuwakaŋ oko	week		

ESKIMO

Ā	ā	a in fate	O	o	o in not	
A	a	a in far	Ō	ō	o in note	
B	b	b	P	p	p in poor	
D	d	d	R	r	r [3] (palatal)	
Ē	ē	e in me	R'	r'	Like a deeply palatal	
E	e	e in pen			ch in German	
F	f	f in if	S	s	s [3] in so	
G	g	g	SS	ss	sh in short	
H	h	h (rarely used)	T	t	t in ten	
Ī	ī	i in thine	U	u	u in but	
I	i	i in pin	V	v	v in event	
J	j	y in yard	W	w	w	
K	k	([1])	Y	y	y	
L	l	l in holy	OO	ōō	oo in soon	
M	m	m in me	OU	ou	ou in sound	
NG	ng	n [2]	AU	au	au in caught	

[1] K has often a deep guttural sound something like we would pronounce rk or ak, and it is then represented by a q.
[2] Ng is a deep nasal sound frequently heard amongst the natives.
[3] S and r are often pronounced forcibly.

There are peculiarities in the pronunciation of the Eskimo language that cannot be described, but must be acquired by intercourse with the natives.

The accents are: ', short and sharp; ‾, long and sharp; ʌ, long and dull.

While the above is the generally accepted alphabet, the vocabularies from Labrador westward to the Aleutian Islands, including Greenland, differ very widely.

Cardinal numbers [1]

attausuk	one	tedlemaurooktoot	ten
maggook	two	tedlemaurooktoot attausuglo	eleven
pingashoot	three		
sittamut	four	tedlemaurooktoot maggooglo	twelve
tedlemut	five		
pingashoorooktoot, iggaktoot, (arkvenelēt in Baffin Land)	six	tedlemaurooktoot pingashoolo	thirteen
pingashoorooktoot attausuglo	seven	avatoongegaktoot, tedlemaurooktoolo sittamaurooktoolo attausuglo	twenty
sittamaurooktoot	eight	avate tedlemāt	hundred
tedlemulo sittamulo	nine		

Ordinal numbers

sivordluk	first	pingashoorooktoongāt	sixth
ipunga	second	maggoongnut ikaktoongāt	seventh
pingarooāt	third	sittamaurooktoongāt	eighth
sittamungāt	fourth	tedlemulogāt	ninth
tedlemungāt	fifth	tedlemaurooktoongāt	tenth

[1] There are names for only the first five numerals, after which a cumbersome system of addition and multiplication is used, which is poorly adapted for large numbers. It is used and understood by only the most intelligent of the natives on the eastern shore of Hudson Bay and Baffin Land.

ESKIMO (No. 2)

(Bureau of American Ethnology)

A	*a* in far
a	*a* in father
ȧ	*a* in man (about)
ä	*e* in German denn
c	Stopped front palatal, voiceless; transcribed *tj* or *kj*
ç	*c* in German ich
e	*e* in French été, but more closed; when long, like a long i
E	*e*, uvularized
ϵ	*e*, uvularized, farther back than E
ə	*ə*, uvularized; short mid-vowel
F	Bilabial fricative
g̡	*g* in North German Bogen
h	*h*; sometimes heard in interjections
i	*i* in French fini
I	Between i and e
j	*y* in yard
q	(1)
r	(1)
E	(1)
N	(1)
k	*c* in French cas, unaspirated
l	(2)
L	(2)
r	*r* [3]
n	*n*
ŋ	*ng* in sing [4]
N.	See q̃
o	*o* in French rose, but slightly more closed
oo	Like a long U
O	([5])
ɔ	*o* in more
p	*p* in French pas, unaspirated
q̃	Uvular nasal
r	Uvular fricative, voiced [6]
rq	*q*, long (modified form) [7]
R	*r* voiceless, short or long
ɹ	([3])
s	Usually voiceless [8]
t	As in French, especially between a and o [9]
T	See t
ɋ	See c
u	*ou* in French jour
U	*u*, long, between o and u
w	Voiced sound corresponding to F
x	See c.
ü	Between u and y in French jour, rue
Y	Related to ü as I to i, U to u
z	*s* voiced, rare

1 These are uvular consonants, so called because they are articulated at the uvula; q is a stopped voiceless consonant.

2 These are articulated nearly alike, bilaterally, with the tip of the tongue against the back of the upper teeth.

3 In some sections becomes an untrilled palatal r, as in Arab, but with a firmer pressure against the palate.

4 Frequently this sound is so loosely articulated that it may be described rather as a nasalized g̡ fricative.

5 Uvularized o is rather closed like o in so, followed by the Eskimo fricative r or q.

6 Rather different than the English r, but somewhat similar to the German back r, when untrilled. Its articulation is especially tense when it is followed by q.

7 When the r stands alone between vowels, its place of articulation is often somewhat advanced, and the friction is not very tense; in some districts it is nasalized.

8 In rs it resembles the English s; in ts the articulation of the s is tenser.

9 Before i, e, and u it is often aspirated, especially when the t is long.

Accent and quantity

Two or more sounds may follow each other in a word without being shortened, and every sound, whether consonant or vowel, may be short or long, apart from the fact that the voiced consonants, in case they are lengthened, become unvoiced (except the nasals). Thus four types of combinations are possible: Short vowel + short consonant, short vowel + long consonant, long vowel + short consonant, and long vowel + long consonant.

FOX

Consonants

	Stops	Spirants	Affricatives	Nasals	Semivowels
Glottal............	ʻ	ʻ	—	—	—
Palatal............	k ʻk g g^k	—	—	—	y^y
Alveolar..........	—	c ʻc	tc ʻtc ^{d}tc	—	—
Dental............	t ʻt (d)	s ʻs	—	n^n	—
Labial............	p ʻp (b)	—	—	m^m	w^w

Vowels and diphthongs
Full sounding:

a ʌ e i o u
ā â ä ē ī ō[1]

(ē is always a terminal as a rhetorical lengthening of e or i, and then has an i-vanish; ō in a similar position has a u-vanish; â is found only after w.)

ai (only before y) •
au (only in the exclamation ʻau ʼ)

Voiceless and aspirated (terminally only):
ᴀʻ aʻ eʻ iʻ oʻ

The sibilants s and c occur only initially, elsewhere they are replaced by ʻs and ʻc, respectively. The spirant ʻ after back vowels is nearly intermediate between a surd velar spirant and our h, although after front vowels the effect is more palatal. It always occurs before initial vowels and ai. The stops g, d, and b are articulated more forcibly than in English and never occur initially; before terminal voiceless vowels g becomes g^k; d and b (both rare), do not occur in final syllables. Voiceless ⁿ, ᵐ, ʸ, and ʷ are phonetic modifications of n, m, y, and w, respectively, before terminal voiceless vowels. The affricative ^{d}tc occurs initially and medially, except in final syllables; ^{d}tc occurs mostly in final syllables, though also in medial ones. ʻk, ʻt, ʻp, and ʻtc are given as a series, because (outside of verbal compounds after ʻä-, nī-, kī-, and wī-, where they are transformations of k, t, p, and tc), they correspond in Cree to a sibilant followed by k, t, p, and tc, or, more rarely, followed by k, t, p, tc; ʻp, ʻt, and ʻtc never occur in terminal syllables nor initially. The surds k, t, p, and tc are unaspirated, and k never occurs in terminal syllables, p and tc rarely.

---

[1] ä, e. i, and u are open; ī and ō are closed.

HUPA

The Hupa belongs to the Pacific Coast division of the Athapascan linguistic stock and is spoken by Indians living on the lower portions of Trinity River in northern California.

Consonantal continuants predominate among the sounds composing this language, resulting in an absence of the definiteness produced by a predominance of stops as well as the musical character imparted by full, clear vowels standing alone or scantily attended by consonants.

The complete system of consonants is as follows:

| | Stops | | Continuants | | | |
	Sonant	Surd	Spirant	Affricative	Nasal	Liquid
Glottal____	—	ʻ	h (ʻ)	—	—	—
Velar_____	—	q	x	—	—	—
Palatal____	—	k (k̲)	hw̲ (w̲)	—	ñ	—
Anterior Palatal }	-- g, gy	k, ky	ʟ (lateral)	{tc, tcw, dj} {ʟ (lateral)}	—	l (lateral)
Dental_____	d	t (t̲)	s	ts, dz	n	—
Labial_____	—	—	hw̲ (w̲)	—	m	—

The consonantal sounds are the same as in Chinook, except gy, and ky are used instead of g and k; k̲ and t̲ are the same as k! and t!.

The nine vowel sounds and two semivowels are represented as follows:

y, ī, i, ē, e, a, û, o, ō, ū, w

The vowels are formed with much less movement of the lower jaw and lips than is employed in the corresponding sounds in English.

Words or syllables rarely begin with a vowel, but semivowels and consonants are frequent initially. Many syllables end in vowels, and when final in the word, and bearing the accent, some vowels, under certain conditions, seem to develop semivowels after themselves, becoming diphthongs. This is especially true of the vowel a in the roots of verbs.

IROQUOIAN

a	*a* in father	ñ	*ng* in ring
ā	Same sound prolonged	o	*o* in note
ă	*a* in what	q	*ch* in German ich
ä	*a* in hat	r	*r*, slightly trilled
ā̈	Same sound prolonged	s	*s* in see
â	*a* in law	t	*t* [1]
ai	*i* in fine	u	*u* in rule
au	*ou* in out	ŭ	*u* in rut
c	*sh* in shall	w	*w* in wit
ç	*th* in health	y	*y* in yes
d	*th* [1]	dj	*j* in judge
e	*e* in they	hw	*wh* in what
ĕ	*e* in wet	tc	*ch* in church
f	*f* in waif	ⁿ	Marks nasalized vowels [2]
g	*g* in gig	'	Indicates aspiration [3]
h	*h* in has	'	Indicates glottal closure [4]
i	*i* in machine	'	Marks accented syllable of
ī	Same sound prolonged		every word
ĭ	*i* in pick	th	In this combination both let-
k	*k* in kick		ters are pronounced sep-
n	*n* in nun		arately

[1] Pronounced in all cases with the tip of the tongue touching the upper teeth as in enunciating the English th.

[2] eⁿ, oⁿ, aiⁿ, ĕⁿ, ä̈ⁿ.

[3] This is either in initial or final: 'h, ĕⁿ', o'.

[4] This mark precedes or follows a sound: 'a, o', ä', ä̈ⁿ'.

The term Iroquois was originally applied to a group of five tribes at the time united in a strong confederacy, both for offense and defense, and inhabiting what is now central and eastern New York State. Other names were: Five Nations, the League of the Iroquois, and the Six Nations after they adopted the Tuscaroras in 1722. They were never numerically very strong but reached a commanding position by an incisive and unexcelled diplomacy, an effective political organization founded on maternal blood relationship, both real and fictitious, and by an aptitude for coordinate political action, all due to a mentality superior to that of the neighboring tribes. In fact they dominated the greater part of the Great Lakes region during the latter part of the seventeenth century.

KALISPEL

A	a	*a* in arm	M	m	*m* in my
CH	ch	*ch* in church	N	n	*n* in not
E	e	*e* in bet	O	o	*o* in hot
G	g	*h* in Hebrew heth	P	p	*p* in par
H	h	*h* in home	S	s	*s* in sack
I	i	*i* in river	T	t	*t* in toll
K	k	*k* in kettle	U	u	*u* in bull
L	l	*l* in lad	Z	z	*ts* not *ds*
Ł	ł	*w* in wood			

The Kalispel were related to the Flathead Indians and spoke a similar dialect but the tribe was distinct. The Flathead were also known as Salish and the latter name, in the form Salishan, has been given to the linguistic family to which both the Kalispel and Flathead belong.

Cardinal numbers

chináksi	one	ganút	nine
esél	two	open	ten
chełés	three	ópen-eł-nko	eleven
mús	four	ópen eł esel	twelve
zil	five	ópen eł chełés	thirteen
tákan	six	eselópen	twenty
sispel	seven	nkokèin	hundred
hanm	eight		

Ordinal numbers

l'es-shìt	first	łu ks-tàkani	sixth
łu ks-esél	second	łu ks-sispel	seventh
łu ks-chełés	third	łu ks-héenem	eighth
łu ksmùs	fourth	łu ksganut	ninth
kłchzilzil	fifth	łu ks'ópen	tenth

Seasons

skepz, tiimulegu	spring	s'cheéi	autumn
saánłka	summer	siístch	winter

Time

s'lichch	hour	spakaní	month
sgalgàlt	day	spèntich, smogóp	year
spelcháskat	week		

KWAKIUTL

This is one branch of the two languages of the Wakashan stock which is spoken by a number of tribes inhabiting the coast of British Columbia and extending southward to Cape Flattery in the State of Washington. It has three main dialects, each of which is divided into subdialects which differ somewhat in phonetics, form, and vocabulary. That spoken by the Kwakiutl tribe of Vancouver Island will be treated here.

The phonetic system is very rich, abounding in sounds of the k and the l series. The system is represented as follows:

	Sonant	Surd	Fortis	Spirant	Nasal
Velar	g	q	q!	x	—
Palatal	g(w)	k(w)	k!(w)	x̣ᵘ(w)	—
Anterior palatal	g·	k·	k·!	x·	n
Alveolar	d	t	t!	s(y)	—
Affricative	dz	ts	ts!	—	—
Labial	b	p	p!	—	m
Lateral	ʟ	L	L!	ɬ, l	—
Glottal stop,ᶜ					

h, y, w

The vowels are quite variable, the indistinct ᴇ being very frequent. The two pairs i e and o u probably represent each a single intermediate sound. The entire series is represented as follows:

		E		
i e	î	ê	a	ô	o u
ī ē	ë		ā	â	o u

By certain grammatical processes, consonants may be weakened or hardened, and these processes reveal a number of unexpected relations of sounds. For example:

Spirants	Hardened	Weakened
x	xᶜ	x
x̣ (w)	ꞌw	w
x′	n	ꞌn
s	ts!	y or dz
ɬ	ᶜl	l

ᵘ Indicates a u position of the lips. The others are the same as in Chinook.

ë is an intermediate between ē and êī.

(w) = w quality accompanying the sound.

MAIDU

The Maidu (or Pujunan) stock comprises the various dialects of the language spoken by a body of Indians in northeastern California. The dialect spoken in the mountain valley extending from Big Meadows south to the Sierra Valley is given here.

The phonetic system is only moderately extensive. The glottal catch is but little used. A peculiar feature is the existence of two weak inspirational sonant stops в and ᴅ, the exact formation of these sounds not being clear. They occur, as a rule, only before ö, and the difference between them and the ordinary b and d is, in some cases, very slight, while in others it is very marked.

The consonant system is presented as follows:

	Sonant	Surd	Fortis	Spirant	Inspirant	Nasal
Palatal	g	k	k!	x	—	ñ
Alveolar	d	t	t!	—	ᴅ (ö)	n
Dento-alveolar	—	ts	—	s, c	—	—
Labial	b	p	p!	—	в (ö)	m
Lateral	l	—	—	—	—	—
Glottal catch	(')					
		h	y	w		

The vowels are quite variable, and one of the most characteristic features of the use of vowels is the fondness for ö, ä, and ü sounds. The vowels are as follows:

ü
u ū
i ī
e ē
ä ᴇ ö
a   o
ā   â   ō

Words may begin with a vowel, h, y, or w, or with any consonant except x or ñ, though most of them begin with a consonant, most commonly t, k, b, or p. The most frequent initial vowels are a, o, and e.

MUSKOKEE (Creek)

A	a	*a* in far	S	s	*s*	
C	c	*che*, for *tch*	T	t	*t*	
E	e	*i* in pin	U	u	*oo* in wood	
F	f	*f*	V	v	*u* in tub	
H	h	*h*	W	w	*w*	
I	i	*i* in pine	Y	y	*y*	
K	k	*k*	Æ	æ	*ae* in Aenid	
L	l	*l*	AU	au	*au* in Milwaukee	
M	m	*m*	EU	eu	*eu* in Euripides	
N	n	*n*	OE	oe	*oe* in Oestreich	
O	o	*o* in note	OU	ou	*ou* in houri	
P	p	*p*	UE	ue	*ue* in Nuevitas	
R	r	*hle* for *hl*				

The Muskokee or Muskogee Indians were the dominant tribe of the Creek Confederacy, and their language is usually called Creek, but the confederation included some peoples speaking related dialects and some speaking unrelated, or only distantly related, dialects. They have given their name to the Muskhogean linguistic family which includes several other languages, including Choctaw (q.v.). The Muskokee language is also spoken by the greater part of the Seminole Indians.

Cardinal numbers

hvm'ken	one	pálen	ten
hokkólen	two	pálen-hvmkvntvláken	eleven
tut-cénen	three	pálen-hókkolóhkáken	twelve
o'sten	four	pálen-tutcénóhkáken	thirteen
cah'kēpen	five	pálē-hokkólen	twenty
epáken	six	pále-hokkólen-hv'm	twenty-one
kulvpáken	seven	kvntvláken	
cenvpáken	eight	cúkpē-hv'mken	hundred
óstvpáken	nine	cúkpē-rákko	thousand

Ordinal numbers

hv'tecéskv	first	es'kulvpákē	seventh
svhókkólv	second	svcénvpákat	eighth
svtucénat	third	es-ostoh-pákat	ninth
sv-óstat	fourth	espálat	tenth
résv-cáhképat	fifth	espálē-hvmkvntvláken	eleventh
esēpákē	sixth		

Months

Rv'fo-cúsē	January	Híyucē	July
Hótvlē-hv'sē	February	Hiyo-rakko	August
Tasáhcucē	March	Oto-wóskucē	September
Tasáce-rákko	April	Oto-wáskv-rak'ko	October
Kē-hv'sē	May	Ehólē	November
Kv'co-hvsē	June	Rv'fo-rak'ko	December

Days

Net'tv-cáko	Sunday	Rv'ste, Nvr-kv'-	Thursday
Mv'ntē	Monday	pvenhiyv'tkē	
Tústē, Mvn'tē-	Tuesday	Flitē	Friday
enhíyvtkē		Sátvtē, netty-cákocúsē	Saturday
Net'tv-cákucē-	Wednesday		
ennvrkvp'v			

Seasons

tasáhcē	spring	rafo-hakof	autumn
mes'kē, hiyo	summer	rvf'o	winter

Time

hv'sē-vkérkv	hour	hvs'e-hv'mken	month
nettv	day	oh rólopē, méskē	year
net'tv-cákucē	week		

NAVAHO

a	*a* in art	l	*l* in lad
æ	*a* in lather	ł	Surd of *l;* no English equivalent
b	*b*		
c	Composite of *t* and *s*	m	*m* in man
d	*d* in dig	n	*n* in name
e	*a* in fate	ń	Indicates ellipsis of a vowel; also stress
g	*g* in get		
ǧy	*g,* followed by a glide	o	*o* in more
ǧh	*g,* soft	q	*ch* in German Licht
ǧw	*gw,* labialized	s	*s*
h	*h* in her	sh	*sh* in shall
'	Glottal spirant	t	*t,* strongly aspirated
i	*e* in peer	t'	*t-is* in it is
j	*j* in judge	u	*oo* in foot
k'	*k* in kirk, aspirated	w	*w* in wart, a semivowel
kw	*qu* in quick	x	Interchangeable with q
k	*k-it* in tack it	y	Palatal
ky	Denotes absence of aspiration, sometimes *kq*	z	*z* in zigzag

The Navaho Indians are an Athapascan people living in northern Arizona, related to the Apache and probably like them of northern origin. They now number some 25,000 pure bloods.

Remarks

Capital letters are not used.

A long vowel is indicated by an inverted period after the vowel: a·, e·, i·, o·, u·, æ·.

An unusually short vowel is indicated by a breve after the vowel: aˇ, eˇ, iˇ, oˇ, uˇ, æˇ.

Nasalized vowels are indicated as follows: ą, ę, į, ǫ, ų, ǽ: these may also carry the long or short signs: ą˙, ąˇ.

The colon is used to indicate the absence of a diphthong: a:i, e:i, a:o.

Punctuation is the same as in English, with the exception of the colon just mentioned.

Accent

Syllables are not regularly stressed as in English according to some rule, but the Navaho either raises or lowers the tone, and thus syllables may have either level, raised, or lowered tones.

When used, the acute accent usually indicates a rising inflection of the voice. In polysyllabic words its position will indicate the point of rising inflection and show that both preceding and following syllables require an even or slightly lowered tone. When the acute accent occurs twice the tone is either even, or waving from high to low to high.

Syllabication

The vowel or diphthong sounded by itself forms a syllable: æ, ai, but aa, a'i, a:i, ąi, having two distinct impulses, represent two syllables. The syllable may, therefore, begin with a vowel and end there, or it may begin with a vowel and end with a consonant, or a consonant may begin the syllable, followed by a vowel. The usual rule, therefore is a succession of consonants combined by a single impulse exerted in their utterance, and two consecutive syllables require two impulses which are separated in some manner: cxą:ats' os (a-ts' os).

Cardinal numbers

dałai, łái	one	tsebįdzáda	eighteen
nak'i	two	naast'aidzada	nineteen
txa·	three	nádi·n	twenty
dį·	four	nádin dó'baą dałai,	twenty-one
ašdlá	five	nádin ła	
hastxą́	six	nádin dó'baą naki,	twenty-two
tsosts·ed	seven	nádin naki	
tsebį́	eigʜt	txádi·n	thirty
naast·aí	nine	dísdi·n	forty
nææzná	ten	ašdládi·n	fifty
ładzá'·da	eleven	xastxádi·n	sixty
nakidzáda	twelve	tsosts'edi·n	seventy
txa'dzá·da	thirteen	tsebį́˘di·n	eighty
dįdzada	fourteen	naastádi·n	ninety
ašdlaáda	fifteen	nææznádi·n	hundred
xastxaáda	sixteen	mi·l, dałaí di mi·l	thousand
tsosts'edzáda	seventeen		

There are no ordinals.

Months

yásnłt'es	January	nææešjástso	July
atsá biya·ž	February	bini·nt'ą́·ts'osi	August
ǧwošc'įd	March	bini·nt'ą·tso	September
t'ą́·c'il	April	ǧą·ji	October
t'ą́·tso	May	nłts'i ts'osi	November
yaiš jášc'ili	June	nłts'i tso	December

Days

damí·go	Sunday	damou na·biskáne	Tuesday
damígo biskáni	Monday	iskągo damógoyæædą·	Saturday

These names are all modern and reference to the other days is usually made
by numbering the days to and from Sunday.

Seasons

dą	spring	ak'æd	autumn
šį	summer	xai	winter

Time

ó·la	hour	na˘hidizi·di, ndi˘zi·d	month
jį, ša bí·ga	day	náxai	year

There is no word for week.

NEW NAVAHO [1]

The Navaho belongs to the southern division of the Athapascan linguistic stock and is spoken by Indians living on a reservation in northwestern New Mexico, northeastern Arizona, and southwestern Utah. It is also spoken by an isolated group of 50 families in the settlement of Canyoncito, in Valencia County, New Mexico, and by another small group of 50-60 families living in a settlement called Puertecito, in Socorro County, New Mexico. All told the Navahos number between 45,000 and 50.000

The series of consonants are represented by single symbols of phonemes for the various sounds:

Labial:

w	*w* in window
b	*b* in bun
m	*m* in man

Dental:

d	*d* in did
t	Always followed by a strong guttural aspiration not found in English, thus *tin* must be sounded *t*ˣ*in*
t'	Never followed by an aspiration, but glottalizes t', more so than *t-is* in English "it is"
n	*n* in name. Syllabic *n*, that is, when *n* implies a following vowel which is suppressed in pronunciation, may be either low toned, or high toned. When high toned it is indicated like any high toned vowel: ń (instead of suppressed *ni*)
ń	Indicates a glottal closure preceding *n* as one sound, approximating *dn* in Dnieper

Guttural:

x	*ch* in German Dichter, Dach, Loch
h	*h* in here, but is frequently "rubby", approximating the preceding *x*-sound
g	*g* in get, git, got
γ	Is a trilled *g*-sound, not found in English
k	*k* in kirk
k'	Is a glottalized *k*-sound, as if we separated k-irk
y	*y* in yes, yam
'	Is a distinct phoneme; the glottal stop

es = sibilants:		s	z	ʒ	c	c' (or ć)
esh = sibilants:		š	ž	ʒ	č	č' (or č)

s	*s* in sit
š	*sh* in shall
z	*z* in zeal
ž	*z* in azure
ʒ	*dz* in adze
ʒ	*j* in join, or as *g* in gin
c	*z* in German zechen, or *tz* in Pretzel
c'	Glottalizes *c*, approximately the German zanken
č	*ch* in chin
č'	glottalized ch-in

---

[1] By Fr. Berard Haile, O. F. M., in charge of the Indian schools on the Navaho Indian reservation.

Laterals:

l   *l* in lard
ł   Forces the breath out laterally with tongue in *l*-position; no equivalent in English
λ   as *dl*, as if we pronounced English lard: *dlard*
λ   Is a combination of *t* and *ł*; no English equivalent
λ'   Is the glottalized form of the preceding, accompanied by a strong lateral explosion; no English equivalent

Labialized gutturals.—At times gutturals are labialized, which we indicate by a superior ^{w}:

$$k^w \quad h^w \quad \gamma^w \quad x^w \quad g^w \text{ (infrequent)}$$

Emphasized sibilants.—In a similar manner ^{x} indicates emphasis placed in sibilants by individuals:

$$c^x o \quad \check{c}^x a \quad \mathfrak{z}^x a \text{ (rarely)}$$

The vowels have values as follows:

a   *a* in far
e   *e* in they and short *e* in let
i   *i* in marine and short *i* in bin
o   *o* in note
u   *u* in full, or *oo* in wool

Vowels are normally short. At times half-long quantity is added and indicated by a superior period following the vowel: $a\cdot, e\cdot, i\cdot, o\cdot$.

Length and glottal closure at the end of vowels is indicated by the superior period plus glottal stop: $a\cdot', e\cdot',$

Choked or abruptly closed vowel sounds are indicated by the glottal stop following the vowel: a', e'. The breath is here forcibly interrupted, instead of its natural release.

The glottal stop should, consistently, be indicated before syllables beginning with a vowel. Yet this rule is so general that it has been dispensed with: $a\cdot \dot{a}\cdot n$, instead of $'a\cdot \dot{a}\cdot n$, a burrow.

Nasal quality of vowels is indicated by the nasal hook:

$$q \quad e \quad i \quad o \quad u$$

In turn nasal vowels may be half long: $q\cdot$, or long $q\cdot'$.

Diphthongs

The following diphthongs are formed by combinations of vowels:

ai, ei, oi (or ui)
ao, eo, io
oa (usually ^{w}a: k^{w}a)

The first component of the diphthong may be half long at times, in $a\cdot i, e\cdot i, \cdot o\cdot i$, or nasalized qi. Tone of diphthong is again indicated on the first component only: $\acute{a}i, \hat{e}i, \check{a}\cdot i$.

Tones

There is no accent, except in foreign words: *wášindo·n*. Such accents can be treated here as tone quality. We have two registers of tone: high and low tones of syllables. All syllables (including syllabic *n*) not marked by the acute accent are low toned, all others high toned: *ké·yah*, the land, shows *ké·*, high, and *yah*, low toned.

The two tones may be combined for a drop from high to low, or a rise from low to high, hence a falling tone: *da· nê·lá·'*? How many? a rising tone: *šinǎ·i*, my older brother.

The syllable may be formed by a simple vowel: *a·á·n*, a burrow, is a word of two syllables. Or by a vowel and a consonant: *at'q·* various; or a consonant and a vowel: *dibé yǎžé*, a lamb.

Punctuation marks (comma, period, exclamation point, question mark) have English values. The colon is employed to indicate exceptional length of vowels: *i:ye·'*.

Capital letters are not used.

Cardinal numbers

ła' ťá·łá'í }	one	ła'c'á·da	eleven
na·ki	two	na·kic'á·da	twelve
tá·'	three	tá·c'á·da	thirteen
dí·'	four	dí·c'á·da	fourteen
ašλa'	five	ašλa'á·da	fifteen
xastą́	six	xastą́'á·da	sixteen
cosc'id	seven	cosc'i'c'á·da	seventeen
cebí·	eight	cebí·c'á·da	eighteen
ná·xásťái	nine	ná·xásťáic'á·da	nineteen
ne·zná	ten	nadi·n	twenty

nadi·n ła'
nadi·n na·ki•   twenty-one
nadi·n tá·'   twenty-two
tádi·n ła' or tágí ła'   twenty-three
dísdi·n ła' or dízí ła'   thirty-one
ašλadi·n   forty-one
ašλadi·n ła' }   fifty
ašλadi·n do· bi'ąh ťá·łá'í }   fifty-one

For numbers above 50, dó· bi'ąh is preferred, excepting that ła', one, may be
used with tens up to hundred, thus:

xastádi·n ła'   sixty-one
cosc'edi·n ła'   seventy-one
cebídi·n ła'   eighty-one
náxásťádi·n ła'   ninety-one

Above hundred use dó· bi'ąh (plus): ne·znádi·n dó· bi'ąh ťá·łá'í, one hundred
one; ne·znádi·n dó· bi'ąh na·ki, one hundred and two, etc.

The hundreds are multiplied by the addition of di (times):

na·kidi ne·znádi·n   two hundred
tâ·di ne·znádi·n   three hundred
dí·di ne·znádi·n   four hundred
ašλadi ne·znádi·n   five hundred
xastą́·di ne·znádi·n   six hundred
cosc'idi ne·znádi·n   seven hundred
cebí·di ne·znádi·n   eight hundred
ná·xásťáidi ne·znádi·n   nine hundred
ne·znâ·di ne·znádi·n, }
mí·l, }   one thousand
ťá·łá'í di mí·l }

Then repeat as with the hundreds.

Ordinal numbers

A regular series of ordinal numbers is unknown, but the following and
similar makeshifts are employed:

alą́·ʒi' in the lead, first
na·ki gúne' second
tá·'gúne third, etc.

The second may also be designated as:

ťá· aké'égo   the very following one, or the next one
ťá· ata'gi   at the very between, the middle one
c'ídá aké·dę·'   very last

Months

yas niłťes	January	ya 'išʒásco	July
acá biyá·ž	February	bini' anťą́ c'ózí	August
γʷožč'í·d	March	bini' nťą́ co	September
ťą́· č'il	April	γa·ʒi'	October
ťą́· co	May	ńłc'i c'ósí	November
ya 'išʒá·sčilí	June	ńłc'i co	December

Seasons

dą·go	in spring	aǩe·go	in fall
šį·go	in summer	xaigo	in winter
dí· dą·ní	this spring	dą·dą́·'	last spring
dí· žíní	this summer	šį·dą́·'	last summer
di· aǩe·dí	this autumn	aǩe·dą́·'	last autumn
dí· γa·í	this winter	xaidą́·'	last winter

Days

damí·go (*or* damó·go) Sunday, from which others days are reckoned:
damó·go biskání "day after Sunday", Monday
damó·go ná·biskání "day again after Sunday", Tuesday

Some use *damó·go tá·' biskání*, three days after Sunday, but most Navahos prefer to employ "this number of days ago" or "in so many days". One also hears:

na·kiská·go damó·go yę́·dą́·, last Friday
yiská·go, tomorrow
adą́·dą́, yesterday
na·ki yiská·go *or* na·ki·ská·go, day after tomorrow
na·ki·skáńdą́·', two days ago
tá·' yiskáńdą́·', three days ago, etc.
kóxoʒa·dą́·', this time yesterday
kóxoʒa·go, this time tomorrow
kóxoťé·dą́·', this time yesterday
kónáxoťéhé *or* kónáxoʒa·í, this time next year
ʒį·go, in daytime
ƛ'é·go, at night
xos'į·dgo, at daylight
dí· ʒį, this day (today)
ʒį·dą́·', this past day
dí· ƛ'é·', this (coming) night
xa'í·'á·go, at sunrise
ałníná'ą́, noon
'i'í·'ą́, sunset
ƛ'é·'íłní·', midnight

OSAGE

A	a	*a* in father	HN	hn	(¹)	
B	b	*b* in bad	O	o	*o* in note	
Ç	ç	*th* in thin	'O	'o	*o*, exploded	
D	d	*d* in dog	Oⁿ	oⁿ	*o*, nasalized	
E	e	*e* in prey	P	p	*p* in pipe	
'E	'e	*e*, exploded	Ƥ	ᵽ	*p*, medial; between *p* and *b*	
G	g	*g* in go				
H	h	*h* in he	S	s	*s* in sit	
I	i	*i* in pierce	SH	sh	*sh* in shun	
'I	'i	*i*, exploded	T	t	*t* in ten	
Iⁿ	iⁿ	*i*, nasalized	Ṭ	ṭ	*t*, medial; between *t* and *d*	
'Iⁿ	'iⁿ	*i*, exploded, nasalized				
K	k	*k* in kin	TH	th	*th* in then	
Ḳ	ḳ	*k*, medial; between *k* and *g*	U	u	*u* in rule	
			'U	'u	*u*, exploded	
M	m	*m* in man	W	w	*w* in wet	
N	n	*n* in no	X	x	*ch*, German	
	ⁿ	*n*, nasalized	ZH	zh	*z* in azure	

¹ The sound of the initial letter is scarcely audible.

The Osage Indians lived in Missouri and Arkansas prior to their removal to the present State of Oklahoma. Their speech belongs to the Siouan family. While their original population consisted of 5,000, they now number in the neighborhood of 2,200.

The accent is the most important item to be considered in the Osage words.

Cardinal numbers

wiⁿ	one	gthe'-bthoⁿtse wiⁿ thiⁿ-ge	nine
thoⁿ-ba	two	gthe'-bthoⁿ	ten
tha'-bthiⁿ	three	a-gthiⁿ' wiⁿ xtsi	eleven
do'-ba, du'-ba	four	a-gthiⁿ thoⁿ-ba	twelve
ça'-toⁿ	five	a-gthiⁿ-tha-bthiⁿ	thirteen
sha'-pe	six	gthe'-bthoⁿ thoⁿba	twenty
pe'-thoⁿ-ba	seven	gthe'-bthoⁿ-hu-zhiⁿ-ga	hundred
ḳi-e'-do-ba	eight	zhoⁿ-ḳu-ge	thousand

Ordinal numbers

pa-hoⁿ'gthe-the	first	we'-ḳi-e-do-ba	eighth
u-thu-a'-toⁿ	second	we'-gthe'-bthoⁿtse wiⁿ-thiⁿge	ninth
we'-tha-bthiⁿ	third		
we' do-ba	fourth	we'-gthe-bthoⁿ	tenth
we'-ça-ṭoⁿ	fifth	we'-a'-gthiⁿ wiⁿ xtsi	eleventh
we'-sha-pe	sixth	we'-a'-gthiⁿ thoⁿ-ba	twelfth
we'-pe-thoⁿ-ba	seventh	we'-a'-gthi'-tha-bthiⁿ	thirteenth

Months

Mi'-uḳoⁿ-dsi	January	Ṭseḳi'-the-xa bi	July
Hoⁿ'-ba-stse-dse	February	Xtha-çi'-bi	August
Mi u'-ḳ'oⁿ thiⁿ-ge	March	Xtha-çi'btho ga-çi	September
I'-wa-bi	April	Ṭa-ḳi'-thi-xa-bi	October
Hiu'-wa-thi-xtha-xtha-zhu-dsa bi } Xtha-çká zhiⁿ-ga ṭs'e-the }	May	Ṭa-he'-ba-xoⁿ bi } Mi-ḳa'-ḳi-thi-xa bi }	November
Hiu'-wa-thi-xtha-dse zhu-dsa bi	June	Wa-ça'-be we-da-tha-bi	December

Days

Hon'-ba Wa-ḳon-da-gi On'-ba-wa-ḳon-da-gi }	Sunday	Hon'-ba we-tha-bthin	Wednesday
		Hon'-ba we-do-ba	Thursday
Hon'-ba pa-hon-gthe	Monday	Ṭa-tha'-ṭa-zhi hon-ba	Friday
Hon'-ba we-thonba	Tuesday	Hon'-ba u-ga-xe-thin-ge	Saturday

Seasons

be	spring	ṭon	autumn
do-ge'	summer	ba'-the	winter

Time

mi-u'-tha-ga u-ṭa-non	hour	mi'-on-ba	month
hon'-ba	day	u-mon'-in-ḳa	year
hon'-ba wa-ḳon-da-gi	week		

PIMA

a	*a* in father	r	*r*, initial uvular
â	*a* in law	s	*s* in sauce
ă	*a* in what	t	*t* in touch
ä	*a* in hat	td	Between t and d
ʋ	Indeterminate, between a and ä	u	*u* in rule
		ŭ	*u* in pull
c	*sh* in shall; rare	û	*u* in but
d	*d* in dread	ɑ	*ö* in German Göthe
e	*e* in they	v	*v* in valve
ě	*e* in then	ʌ	Synthetic sound, *v* + *w*
f	*f* in fife	w	*w* in wish
ɟ	Mere breathing	y	*y* in you
g	*g* in good; in foreign words	hy	*hu* in hue
ȝ	Between k and g	ñg	*ng* in finger
h	*h* in he	ny	*ny* in canyon
i	*i* in pique	tc	*ch* in church
ĭ	*i* in pick	t'	
k	*k* in kick	d'	
l	*l* in lull	k'	Exploded breathing
ł	*l* as with a faint ꝗ following	p'	
m	*m* in mum	x	*k* sound with expulsion of breath before sounding it
n	*n* in nun		
ñ	*ng* in sing	ɪ̈	*m*, with lips closed
o	*o* in note	'	Exploded breathing
ŏ	*o* in whole	'	Laryngeal closure
p	*p* in pipe		

The Pima Indians are a semi-civilized tribe living on their reservation in southern Arizona.

TAKELMA

This language was spoken in the southwestern part of the present State of Oregon, along the middle portion of the Rogue River and certain of its tributaries.

The consonant system is represented as follows:

	Aspirated tenuis	Voiceless media	Fortis	Spirant v. unv.	Lateral	Nasal
Labial	p	b	p!	w -ᶜw	—	m
Dental	tᶜ	d	t!	—	l	n
Sibilant	—	—	ts!, ts·!	s, s·	—	—
Palatal	—	—	—	y	(ł)	—
Guttural	kᶜ	g	k!	x	—	—
Faucal	—	—	ᶜ	h		

In the above table the spirants have been arranged in two columns, the voiced and the unvoiced. The rare palatal lateral ł is also voiceless. Any of the above consonants may occur initially, except the voiceless labial spirant -ᵂ, which occurs only with k at the end of a syllable. The catch (ᶜ) as an organic consonant occurs only medially or finally, the ł only initially. The pronunciation of w, s, y, h, l, m, and n does not differ materially from the English.

The simple vowels appear, quantitatively considered, in two forms, short or long, or, quite appropriately called, pseudodiphthongal, meaning that a long vowel normally consists of the corresponding short vowel plus a slight rearticulation of the same vowel (indicated by a superior letter), the whole giving the effect of a diphthong without material change of vowel-quality in the course of production.

Vowels

Short	Long		Short diphthong		Long diphthong	
a	āᵃ, (ā)	ai, au,	al am, an	āi, āu,	āᵃl, āᵃm, āᵃn	
e	eᵉ, (è)	ei, eu,	el, em, en	èi, èu,	ēᵉl, ēᵉm, eᵉn	
i	īⁱ, (ĭ)	iu,	il, im, in	īu,	īⁱl, īⁱm, īⁱn	
o,(u)	ōᵘ, (ō)	oi, ou,	ol, om, on	ōi, ōᵘ(w),	ōᵘl, ōᵘm, ōᵘn	
		(ōᵘ),	(ul), (um), (un),			
ū	ūᵘ, (ū)	ui, ūw,	ūl, ūm, ūn	ūi, ūᵘ(w),	ūᵘl, ūᵘm, ūᵘn	
		(ūᵘ)				
ü	üᵅ, (ǖ)	üi, üw,	ül, üm, ün	üi, üᵅ(w),	üᵅl, üᵅm, üᵅn	
		(üᵅ)				

The ü has a sound between that in the German Mütze and muss. O is the same as u in rude.

Under proper syllabic conditions, i and u may, respectively, appear in semivocalic form as y and w; thus ōᵘ and ūᵘ appear as ōw and ūw when followed by vowels. Similarly ai, au, āi, and āu may appear as ay, aw, and aᵃw, and correspondingly for the other vowels. Sometimes, though rather unusually, a diphthong may appear in the same word either with a semivowel or vowel as its second element, depending on whether or not it is followed by a connecting inorganic a.

TSIMSHIAN

This language is spoken on the Skeena River in northern British Columbia and on the islands farther to the south.

Its phonetic system is in many respects similar to that of other languages on the north Pacific Coast, abounding, particularly, in k and l sounds.

The system of consonants is represented as follows:

	Stops			Affricatives			Continued		Nasals	
	Sonant	Surd	Fortis	Sonant	Surd	Fortis	Sonant (trill?)	Surd	Sonant	Fortis
Labial_____	b	p	p!	—	—	—	—	—	m	m!
Dental_____	d	t	t!	dz	ts	ts!	—	s	n	n!
Anterior palatal_____	g·	k·	k·!	—	—	—	—	—	—	—
Middle palatal_____	ĝ	k	k!	—	—	—	r	—	—	—
Velar_____	ġ	q	q!	—	—	—	(ṛ)[1]	x	—	—
Glottal_____	ʻ	—	—	—	—	—	—	—	—	—

Lateral continued	Voiced_____	l
	Voiced fortis_____	l!
	Voiceless posterior_____	ł
Breathing_____		h
Semivowels_____		{ y / w
Semivowels, fortis_____		{ y! / w!

The series of vowels is presented as follows:

Short_____	u	o	ô		ê	e	î	i
Long_____	—	ō	â		ä	ē	—	ī
With parasitic vowel_____	—	ōu	âô	āa	äê	ēê	—	iî

---

[1] Has the sound of y.

ZUÑI

a	*a* in father	ŋ	*ng*, before k only
ä	*a* in hat	o	*ō*
ai	*i* in high	p	*p* in French père
c	*sh*	p̑	*p*, slightly glottalized
e	*a* in may	s	*s*
h	*h*, but more affricative	t	As in French té
ʼ	Glottal stop	t̑	*t*, slightly glottalized
i	*e* in me	ts	*z* in German Zeit, without aspiration
k	*c* in Spanish boca	t͡s	*dz* almost; glottalized
k̭	*k*, palatalized, unaspirated	tc	*ch* in church
k̭̑	*k*, palatalized, glottalized	t͡c	*ch*, glottalized with slight force of articulation
k̑	*k*, glottalized	u	*oo* in mood
l	*l*	w	*w*; vowel
ł	*l*, voiceless	y	*y*; vowel
m̀	*m*		
n	*n*		

Note.—Both vowels and consonants may be long, and the length is indicated by a point following the letter. All accented syllables are lengthened, some of the length being accorded to the terminating consonant. Unless otherwise indicated, the primary accent is on the first syllable and the secondary accent, in words of four or more syllables, on the penult. Compound words retain their original accents.

The Zuñi Indians, numbering less than 2,000 individuals, live on their reservation in western New Mexico.

AFRICAN LANGUAGES

INTRODUCTION

From a language standpoint Africa is still an unexplored world. Its numerous languages and dialects offer a wide field, the cultivation of which will not fail to reward the persistent philologist with many interesting discoveries concerning the life and languages of the people. The African linguist has not only an excellent opportunity for extending the bounds of philological science, but, at the same time, he will materially assist in preparing channels for spreading knowledge and civilization throughout the Dark Continent.

Confining ourselves to native languages, we find in Africa four principal families: *Bantu* (Negro), which consists of the *Sudanic* and true *Bantu* groups, both closely united and with clearly defined features, and by far the most important, covering practically the southern half of the continent; *Hamitic*, which is used in northern and northeastern Africa; *Semitic*, which is spoken in Egypt and Ethiopia; and the *Bushman*, a small group which includes a number of languages all closely allied. Numerical strength as to languages comprised in each group is as follows: Sudanic, 264; true Bantu, 182; Hamitic, 47; Bushman, 11; Semitic, 10.

In northern Africa and parts of eastern Sudan a modified Arabic has become the ruling language and, through Islamic influence, it is a literary idiom throughout all of east Africa.

However, Prof. T. J. Tucker, in his Introduction to the Natural History of Languages, has divided the African languages into six groups: (1) The Semitic, comprising such languages as Amhāric, Hebrew, and a host of variant dialects. These are both inflectional and agglutinative [1] in character, their changes being determined by vowel modifications, and all have in common the following striking traits: Trilateral stems, agreement of noun and verb, and restriction of verbal tense to completed and incompleted action. (2) The Hamitic, whose chief representatives are the ancient Egyptian, Coptic, and the various Berber and Cushite languages. Though these differ one from the other in degree of development—from monosyllabic crudity to involved inflection—they nevertheless have decided points of resemblance: the pronominal system, formation of the feminine, certain roots, and poverty of tense and mode. These are classed as agglutinatives. (3) The Bantu, constituting the most important linguistic family south of the Sahara, which may be best represented by the Hausa, Kongo, and Swahili languages. These are also agglutinative, their syntax being effected entirely by prefixes and suffixes, though infixes are unknown. Although they show no trace of inflection, except in the preterite formation of the verb, they do have a considerable flexibility. (4) The Negro, the most prominent language of this group being the Ewe. This family is perhaps the least developed of all the African groups, approaching a form of monosyllabication. (5) The Nubian-Fulah, comprising preeminently the Fulani. This also is a family of suffix-agglutinating speeches. Though the people are of Hamitic stock with some negroid admixture, the languages are decidedly non-Hamitic. Their genealogical relationship, however, is uncertain. This group recognizes no masculine or feminine gender, but classifies all things as of human (or rational) and brute (or

---

[1] Forming or modifying their root words by means of prefixes, suffixes, or infixes which were originally root words themselves.

irrational) gender. (6) The Hottentot, also an agglutinative tongue, shows remarkable grammatical and phonetic development, considering the low order of the mixed races that speak it. It possesses four of the "clicks" characteristic of the Bushman, "tones" such as are encountered in Indo-Chinese languages, and what resembles inflections, in its grammatical genders and relation suffixes. We can thus assume that agglutination is the common denominator of all African languages.

In the following section are found the alphabets, outstanding characteristics, and incunabula of some of the African languages. Those selected are probably most representative, most highly developed, and, we trust, of greatest interest philologically as well as commercially.

PAN AFRICAN TONGUES

The problem of evolving a practical and uniform method of writing the great number of African languages and dialects has been a matter of interest to philologists for many years. In Africa necessity sometimes compels large numbers of inhabitants to leave their own tribal districts and settle either temporarily or permanently among those whose language is different from their own, and thus, in daily intercourse, they in time learn another language. It would be greatly to their advantage if, in the orthography of the newly acquired language, the phonetic value of the letters were similar to those of their mother tongue, and among teachers and merchants throughout the African Continent even an approach to uniformity would be of incalculable benefit.

Some 10 years ago the International Institute of African Languages and Cultures suggested a system of orthography which has already been accepted for the Ewe, Fante, Gã, and Twi, on the Gold Coast; Efik, Hausa (partly), Ibo, and Yoruba, in Nigeria; Konno, Limba, Mende, Sosa (Xosa), and Temne, in Sierra Leone; Bari, Dinka, Latuko, Madi, Nuer, Shilluk, and Zande, in the Sudan; for Mashonaland a written language, to be called Shona, is proposed, which is based on the closely related dialects of Karanga, Korekore, Manyika, Ndau, and Zezuru; while in the Union of South Africa the introduction of the new orthography is under discussion.

Simplification of orthography is also under consideration, and this is of great importance, since the number of ways in which speech-sounds are represented in Africa is overwhelming. For daily use, diacritical marks constitute a practical difficulty and a potential danger, since they are liable to be altered beyond recognition, or even omitted altogether.

Considerations such as these led the Institute to recommend the introduction of a few new letters, which, in view of their greater simplicity, are to be preferred to ordinary roman letters with diacritical marks.

REPRESENTATION OF SOUNDS

Consonants.—b, d, f, h, k, l, m, n, p, s, t, v, w, and z shall have English values subject to the following special conditions:

(a) To distinguish between aspirated and unaspirated p, t, k, these letters shall be used to represent the unaspirated sounds, while the aspirated shall be represented by ph, th, and kh, the first to be pronounced as in *loophole* (not like *f*), the as in *at home* (not as in *thin*), and kh as in *bockhand*.

(*b*) To distinguish between dental and cerebral d and t, the ordinary letters are used for the dental and t and d for the cerebral sounds. In the Ewe dialect the words du (town) and du (powder), da (snake) and da (hair) must be distinguished.

(*c*) g has its hard value as in *get*.

(*d*) r has the rolled lingual Scottish pronunciation.

(*e*) x has the *ch* sound as in the German *ach*.

(*f*) y is sounded as in *yet*.

(*g*) ty, dy, ny, ly, sy, and zy are used to represent the palatal *t*, *d*, *n*, *l*, *s*, *z*, while ky and gy are used to represent the palatal *k* and *g*.

ky and gy are used to represent the palatal *k* and *g*.

When a palatal consonant is preceded by a vowel, a kind of *i*-sound can often be heard between the two; thus the sound-group *anya* is often heard and written as *ainya*, but this is unnecessary and should be avoided.

kp and gb are used for the labio-velar consonants in many of the Sudanic languages.

(*h*) The following special consonants are added:

ŋ for the sound of *ng* in *sing*.

ƒ for bilabial ƒ, as in Ewe, ƒu (bone), ƒo (to beat) to distinguish them from fu (feather), fo (to tear off).   For this purpose the f is also used.

ʋ for the bilabial *v* for the sound of German in *schweben*.   In Ewe the words ʋu (boat), ʋɔ (python) are thus distinguished from vu (to tear), and vɔ (to be furnished).

ʃ for English sound of *sh*.

ʒ for the sound of *s* in *pleasure*.   The character ɤ may also be employed for this purpose.

ɣ for the sound of *g* in the German *Lage*.

' for the glottal stop, as in the Hausa a'a (no).

pf is used for the same sound in the German *hüpfen* and bv for the corresponding voiced sound; ts like the German *z*, and dz the corresponding voiced sound; tʃ, the sound of English *ch*, and dʒ the sound of English *j*.

(*i*) Consonants pronounced with simultaneous glottal stop are represented as follows: p', t', k', s', ts', etc.; that is, like (in the Hausa), k'ofa (door).   Write the ' before the y in the Hausa, as in 'ya'ya (children).

(*j*) The sounds of consonants caused by sucking in of the air are called implosive and these are represented by the ordinary consonants preceded by an apostrophe, as 'b, 'd, 'g.   It frequently happens that a language has only one implosive sound, the implosive *b*, and the special letter ɓ is used for the purpose, while ɗ is used in those languages where implosive *d* occurs.   In Ibo gb has been adopted for the implosive *b*.

(*k*) In the new orthographies for Bari, Nuer, Dinka, Shilluk, and other Sudanese languages where a distinction is found between dental and alveolar *t*, *d*, and *n*, th, dh, and nh have been adopted for the dental sounds, but this is possible only in languages which do not have an aspirated *t*.

(*l*) The following methods for writing the lateral sounds and "clicks" which occur in South African languages are given:

Present spelling	Suggested spelling	
tl	tl	for laterally exploded t.
tlh	tlh	for aspirated tl.
hl	ɬ	for lateral s (voiceless fricative l).
dhl	ɮ	for lateral z (voiced fricative l).

(*m*) c is used in South Africa for the dental click, q for the retroflex click, and x for the lateral click.

The following click combinations are also found:

c_____	ch	nc	nch	gc	ŋc	ŋgc
q_____	qh	nq	nqh	gq	ŋq	ŋgq
x_____	xh	nx	nxh	gx	ŋx	ŋgx

In the third column we find n followed by a click, while the sixth column shows clicks completely nasalized.

As the letters c and x are used in other languages for quite different sounds, the following letters are used for the clicks: ʇ for c, c for q, and ʖ for x.

In the Zulu and Soso, if x represents the lateral click, the χ is used for the Scotch loch-sound.

In the Hottentot dialect Nama the following symbols for clicks are in use: / for the dental, ǂ for the alveolar, ! for the retroflex, and // for the lateral.

(n) ş and ʒ have been adopted to represent the labialized s and z in the new alphabet for the Shona dialects.

The ɥ has been adopted as the symbol for "front labialization", which is quite important in the grammar for the languages of the Suto-Chwana language group.

Vowels.—The a, e, i, o, and u have the values of the Italian vowels. (See p. 104.) Where it is necessary to distinguish between a closed and open e (as between the French é and è) the ε is used for the open vowel, and where it is necessary to distinguish between a closed and an open o (as between the French vowels in *Baumé* and *bonne*) the latter is represented by ɔ; while in languages like the Ibo, where there is a middle o it is represented by ǝ.

Central vowels.—There are neutral vowels, neither front (like i and e), nor back (like u and o), being a sound similar to the initial vowel in *about, along*. When this is e-like, the ǝ is used to represent it, while the letter ö is used to represent the o-like sound. In Nuer there are three central vowels besides o, ɔ, and a, which are represented by ö, ɔ̈, and ä.

Diphthongs.—ai, εi, ei, au, and ɔi represent diphthongs; ya and wa may also be considered diphthongs and may be written ia and ua, though the spelling ya and wa are in common use.

Nasalization.—This is represented by the tilde (~) over the vowel. However, this is not necessary where it is preceded or followed by a nasal consonant (m, n, ny, or ŋ).

Long sounds.—These are represented by doubling the letter in the case of both vowels and consonants. For example, in Luganda we have the verb siga (to sow) and sigga (scorpion); in Akan, ɔmá (he gives) and ɔmmá (he does not give), and in Ewe, godo (yonder) and godoo (around). In some cases where the lengthening of a vowel can be used for expressing two different meanings the · is used to denote length. But, like nasalization, vowel length need not always be marked.

Tones.—An accent above the vowels is used for marking tones: á for a high and à for a low tone; rising and falling tones are represented by ǎ and â, respectively, and midtones by ā.

GENERAL PRINCIPLES

Phonemes.—This term is used to denote any small family of sounds which may be regarded as a single entity for reasons given below. Frequently in a language the sound represented by a letter is modified by the letter immediately following. Thus in English the k sound in *keep* and *kola* are different, hence we regard them as two varieties. This applies also to the differences in the French *qui* and *quoi* and the German *Kiel* and *Kuh*.

In some languages the sound ŋ occurs only in the groups ŋk, ŋg, ŋw, and ŋh, but not in any other case. In that case the ŋ may be treated as a variety of n, and these combinations may be written nk, ng, nw, and nh. In some languages there is a tendency to give the velar pronunciation to every final consonant; i.e., to substitute ŋ for every final m or n, and where the ŋ does not exist as a separate phoneme, write m and n and ignore the velar pronunciation. But if ŋ is found in a language as a separate phoneme, write ŋ wherever it occurs, not only before vowels but also before k, g, etc.

The Zulu has both a closed and an open e, which are used in accordance with a certain principle of vowel harmony. For practical purposes these are regarded as one speech unit and may be written with the single letter e. In the Akan language of western Africa the w in wu, wo, and wɔ is quite distinct from that in wi, we, and wɛ but, since the following vowel determines its use, for practical purposes a single character is sufficient. In Kikuyu the *g*-sound occurs only in the combination ŋg, but the related sound ɣ occurs in other positions, though never after ŋ, and thus g and ɣ may be treated as a single entity. In Chwana there is a *d*-like variety of l before i and u, but the ordinary l is used before the other vowels.

Closed and open e and o (e and ɛ, o and ɔ) distinguish words in most west African languages, as also those of the Chwana, Suto, and many others in various parts of the continent, and there they are separate phonemes.

Orthography.—Observe the following general principles in fixing the orthography of any language:

Base it on the principle of one letter for each phoneme of that language. Thus, whenever two words differ in sound, they must also be spelled differently.

In Akan the syllable di is pronounced *dzi* and ti as *tsi*; but the di and ti are sufficient for both pronunciations. In the Hausa some dialects pronounce the *f* as labio-dental, in others as a bi-labial *ʃ* and also p, but the f is usually sufficient in writing.

Departures from a strict phonetic system are not uncommon, for in Luganda soka oleke (wait a bit) is written, although the pronunciation is sok oleke; in Akan ɔ hwɛ no (he saw him), although in many districts the final o is not pronounced, and hwɛ notwithstanding it is actually pronounced hwe when followed by a syllable containing i or u (ɔ hwɛ mu).

Rules governing vowel harmony and assimilation in Akan and some other languages are numerous and complicated, and their influence on current spelling must depend on the special phonetic and grammatical usages of each particular language.

When the sound denoted by a roman letter does not occur in a language, that letter is used instead of one of the special characters. Thus f is used in writing Sechwana instead of *ʃ*, and in the Oshikuanyama s is used instead of *ʃ*.

SOUND CHART

	Bi-labial	Labio-dental	Dental and alveolar	Post-alveolar	Retroflex (cerebral)	Palatal	Velar	Laryngal
CONSONANTS								
Explosive_ _ _ _ _ _ _ _ _ _	p b	_ _ _ _ _ _	t d	_ _ _ _ _ _	ʈ ɖ	ty dy kg gy	k g	'
Implosive_ _ _ _ _ _ _ _ _ _	ɓ	_ _ _ _ _ _	ɗ					
Affricative_ _ _ _ _ _ _ _ _	pf bv	_ _ _ _ _ _	ts dz	tʃ dʒ (= c j)	_ _ _ _ _ _	_ _ _ _ _ _	k x	
Nasal_ _ _ _ _ _ _ _ _ _ _ _	m	_ _ _ _ _ _	n	_ _ _ _ _ _	_ _ _ _ _ _	ny	ŋ	
Lateral—								
Explosive_ _ _ _ _ _ _ _ _	_ _ _ _ _ _	_ _ _ _ _	tl dl	_ _ _ _ _	_ _ _ _ _ _	_ _ _ _ _	_ _ _ _ _	
Fricative_ _ _ _ _ _ _ _ _	_ _ _ _ _ _	_ _ _ _ _	ɬ ɮ	_ _ _ _ _	_ _ _ _ _ _	_ _ _ _ _	_ _ _ _ _	
Frictionless_ _ _ _ _ _ _	_ _ _ _ _ _	_ _ _ _ _	l	_ _ _ _ _	_ _ _ _ _ _	ly	_ _ _ _ _	
Rolled and flapped_ _ _	_ _ _ _ _ _	_ _ _ _ _	r	_ _ _ _ _	_ _ _ _ _ _		_ _ _ _ _	
Fricative_ _ _ _ _ _ _ _ _ _	fʋ	f v	s z	ʃʒ	_ _ _ _ _ _	sy zy	x ɣ	h
Semivowel_ _ _ _ _ _ _ _ _	w			_ _ _ _ _	_ _ _ _ _ _	y	(w)	
VOWELS								
Closed_ _ _ _ _ _ _ _ _ _ _	(u)	_ _ _ _ _	_ _ _ _ _	_ _ _ _ _	_ _ _ _ _ _	i	u	
Half closed_ _ _ _ _ _ _ _	(o)	_ _ _ _ _	_ _ _ _ _	_ _ _ _ _	_ _ _ _ _ _	e	o	
Half open_ _ _ _ _ _ _ _ _	(ɔ)	_ _ _ _ _	_ _ _ _ _	_ _ _ _ _	_ _ _ _ _ _	ɛ ɔ		
Open_ _ _ _ _ _ _ _ _ _ _ _	_ _ _ _ _ _	_ _ _ _ _	_ _ _ _ _	_ _ _ _ _	_ _ _ _ _ _	a		

THE ALPHABET

Roman	Name	Italic	Cursive	Roman	Name	Italic	Cursive
a A		*a A*	*a A*	l L	el	*l L*	*l L*
b B	be	*b B*	*b B*	m M	em	*m M*	*m M*
ɓ Ɓ	ɓa	*ɓ Ɓ*	*ɓ ƒ*	n N	en	*n N*	*n N*
c C	ce(tʃe)	*c C*	*c C*	ŋ Ŋ	iŋ	*ŋ Ŋ*	*ŋ Ŋ*
d D	de	*d D*	*d Ð*	o O		*o O*	*o O*
ɖ Ɖ	ɖa	*ɖ Ɖ*	*ɖ or ɖ Ð*	ɔ Ɔ		*ɔ Ɔ*	*ɔ Ɔ*
e E		*e E*	*e ℰ*	p P	pe	*p P*	*p P*
ɛ Ɛ		*ɛ Ɛ*	*ɛ Ɛ*	r R	ra	*r R*	*r or r R*
ə Ə		*ə Ə*	*ə Ə*	s S	es	*s S*	*s or s S*
f F	ef	*f F*	*f F*	ʃ Σ	iʃ	*ʃ Σ*	*ʃ ʃ*
ƒ Ƒ	iƒ	*ƒ Ƒ*	*ƒ ƒ*	t T	te	*t T*	*t T*
g G	ga	*g G*	*g G*	u U		*u U*	*u U*
ɣ Ɣ	ɣe	*ɣ Ɣ*	*ɣ Ɣ*	v V	ve	*v V*	*v V or v V*
h H	ha	*h H*	*h H*	ʊ Ʊ	ʋi	*ʋ Ʊ*	*ʊ or ʋ Ʋ*
x X	ex	*x X*	*x X*	w W	wa	*w W*	*w W*
i I		*i I*	*i I*	y Y	ya	*y Y*	*y Y*
j J	je(dʒe)	*j J*	*j J*	z Z	ze	*z Z*	*z Z*
k K	ke	*k K*	*k K*	ʒ Ʒ	ʒi	*ʒ Ʒ*	*ʒ ʒ*

The following is the alphabetical arrangement:

a b ɓ c d ɖ ɗ e ɛ ə f ƒ g ɣ h x i j
k l m n ŋ o ɔ p r s ʂ ʃ t u v ʋ w y
z ʐ ʒ '

Nasal vowels should follow ordinary vowels, and central [1] vowels should follow nasal vowels: o, õ, ö.

SPECIMENS OF THE STANDARD ORTHOGRAPHY

GÃ

Dʒata ko hi ʃi yɛ dʒeŋ a·hu. Agbɛnɛ egbeɔ hewɔ lɛ enyɛ̃ emomo hewalɛ na· doŋŋ. Enɛ hewɔ lɛ eyakã ʃi yɛ ebu le mli akɛ ehe mi· ye. Koloi lɛ ba· eŋɔ ekome-kome ni amɛbasra· lɛ yɛ ebu lɛ mli. Osɔ le enɛ fɛ̃ hewɔ lɛ ete koni eyasra dʒata helatʃɛ nɛ. Beni ete lɛ ebotee bu lɛ mli. Edamɔ sɛ ʃoŋŋ ni ebi dʒata lɛ akɛ, 'Helatʃel te oyɔ teŋŋ?'

EWE

Asime. Asi ɖina le tefe geɖewo le ŋkeke ene sia ŋkeke ene megbe. Ame geɖewo va ƒoa ƒu de aƒima. Wãtsɔa bli, te, mɔli, agbeli, fofoŋ, fetri, agbitsa atida kple kutsetse bubu geɖewo, ɖetifu, de, nɛfi, amidzẽ, nemi, yɔumi kple nu bubu geɖewo va dzrana.

MENDE

Mu gɔnɛi gbe, ngi mayomboi manyɛingɔ, tɛli lɔhu ke kolei. Ngi yamɛisia gbe kea ta vo dão.

ZULU

Aɓelungu ɓahamba ngemikhumbi, ɓayizingele. Ɓaphatha imikhonto eminingi emikhulu enezintlenɠa, nezintambo nemiphongolo emingi. Ɓathi qedi ɓafike elwanɠe, umkhomo ubonakae, ɓasondela kaɬe ɓathekelezele intambo emk-hontweni ɓawugwaze.

---

[1] Neutral or intermediate, being neither front (*i, e*), nor back (*u, o*), like the initial English vowel in *about, along.*

ACHOLI

a	*a* in father	n	*n* in now
b	*b* in bend	ŋ	*ng* in singer
c	*ch* in chair	o	*o* in gone, also bone, or *au*
d	*d* in down		in caution
e	*a* in make or *e* in tether	p	*p* in pain
g	*g* in gather, never soft	r	*r* in rent
i	*ee* in been	t	*t* in tent
j	*j* in jolt	u	*u* in moon, always
k	*k* in keep	w	*w* in went
l	*l* in lane	y	*y* in yard
m.	*m* in mend		

The Acholi belong to a large group of tribes of Uganda and a small portion of the southern Sudan, where the more than a million people occupy a tract of some 14,000 square miles. Their language is very similar to that of the Alur on the northwestern shore of Lake Albert.

NOTES

ny is sounded like the Spanish *ñ*, but when final as in *piney*.

y and *w* are semivowels and may come together, as *yweko*, *nywalo*.

The final *c* has various shades of pronunciation in different districts; sometimes *ts*, or again *sh*, but usually *ch*.

When followed by a vowel, *p* and *k* sometimes change to *b* and *g*, respectively. Acholi vowels combine *ai* and *oi* to form diphthongs.

Since *f*, *v*, *h*, *s*, *z*, *th*, and *ph* do not occur in Acholi, these sounds are represented as follows:

f (or ph) by p	s by c	th by t
h by k	z by j	v by b

The nasal *n* before another consonant, so common in Bantu, is absent when initial, though present when preceded by a vowel.

The verb supplies adjectives, adverbs, and abstract substantives, besides fulfilling the functions of a verb.

Cardinal numbers

acel	one	apar wiye adek	thirteen
aryo	two	pyerayo	twenty
adek	three	pyeradek	thirty
aŋwen	four	pyeraŋwen	forty
abic	five	pyerabic	fifty
abicel	six	pyerabicel	sixty
abiro	seven	pyerabiro	seventy
aboro	eight	pyeraboro	eighty
abuŋwen	nine	pyerabuŋwen	ninety
apar	ten	miya	hundred
apar wiye acel	eleven	tuntumiya	thousand
apar wiye aryo	twelve		

Ordinal numbers

meacel, meati, mukwoŋo	first	me abiro	seventh
		me aboro	eighth
me aryo, me arcnye	second	me abuŋwen	ninth
me adek	third	me apar	tenth
me aŋwen	fourth	me apar wiye acel	eleventh
me abic	fifth	me apar wiye aryo	twelfth
me abicel	sixth		

The article

There is no indefinite article: saw (a) man; faras (a) horse.   When, however, it is desired to emphasize the article *and* (one) is used: *thewāth and baklo ayyahu*, I saw one mule yesterday.

The definite article is represented by the suffix ū for the masculine and wā for the feminine singular; ū is used for the plural of both genders:

bēth	(a) house	bēthōch.	houses
bēthū	the house	bēthōchū	the houses
sēth	(a) woman	sēthōch	women
sēthwā	the woman	sēthōchū	the women

It will be noted that the suffix -ōch indicates the plural.

It is also worthy of note that the ū and wā are also used as pronominal suffixes:

faras	horse	faraswā	her horse
farasū	his horse		

Adjectives must agree with the noun they qualify, both in gender and number.

AFRIKAANS

Character	Tone value and remarks
a	When closed,[1] like *a* in sat; open, like *a* in farthing
b	*b;* final, sounded like *p*
c	*c,* hard; used only in proper names
ch	*ch* in Scotch loch
d	*d;* final, sound of *t;* preceded by *l, n,* or *r.* sound is assimilated with preceding consonant
dj	*tj*
e	*e;* closed, as in get; open in accented syllable, as in merely, but in unaccented syllable as in manner
f	In inflected forms sounds like *w*
g	*ch* in loch, but when preceded by *r* (and sometimes *l*) and followed by semiaccented *e,* like *g* in go
gh	*g* in go
ghw	*gu* in guano
h	*h,* voiced
i	*i* in wit in accented syllable; *e* in unaccented syllable
ie	*ea* in speak, but much shorter
j	*y* in year; never *j*
k	*k*
l	*l*
m	*m*
n	*n*
ng	*ng* in singer
o	*o* in pot, when in closed syllable; *oo* in moor, in open syllable
ô	*aw* in law
oe	*oo* in foot, but shorter; when followed by *r,* as *u* in rule
p	*p*
r	Always well trilled
s	*s* in so
sch	*sk,* except final when it is *s;* used in proper names only
sj	*sj* in the English sjambok (shām′ bek)
t	*t*
u	*u* in thus, when closed; *ü* in German über when open
v	*f; w* is substituted where its syllable does not have the principal stress
w	*v* in very; never *w*
x	*ks;* used only in proper names
z	*s;* used only in proper names
ai	*i* in might
aai	*y,* long, in why

[1] A syllable ending in a consonant is closed; in a vowel or diphthong, open.

By act of the Parliament of the Union of South Africa, Afrikaans has been adopted as the official language.

Capitalization

Use capitals as initials of geographic names, except when used adjectively; names of religions, sects, and church organizations; any name referring to the Deity; principal words in names of books, periodicals, and newspapers; principal words in titles of articles, etc.; titles of honor; names of months, weeks, and feast days, and also any word to which the writer wishes to direct special attention.

The article *'n* is not capitalized, even though it occurs at the beginning of a sentence.

Pronouns

PERSONAL

	Subjective		Objective
Ek	I	my,[1] u	me
jy,[1] u	you, thou	you,[1] u	you, thee
hy	he	hom	him
sy	she	haar	her
dit	it	dit	it
one	we	ons	us
julle,[1] u	you	julle,[1] u	you
hulle	they	hulle	them

POSSESSIVE

	Adjective		Substantive
my	my	myne	mine
jou	your, thy	joue, joune	yours, thine
sy	his	syne	his
haar	her	hare	hers
sy	its	syne	its
ons	our	ons s'n	ours
julle,[1] u	your	julle s'n, u s'n	yours
hulle	their	hulle s'n	theirs

Nouns

Nouns are inflected for number, forming the plural generally by adding *e* or *s* (rarely by *ere* or *ers*) to the singular form. Where stress is on the last syllable, it is formed by adding *e*, which rule includes all monosyllabic nouns. If the last syllable is unstressed, the plural is formed by adding *s*: *been* (leg), *bene* (legs), and *eier* (egg), *eiers* (eggs). Exceptions are monosyllables ending in *im* or *rm*: *arm* (arm), *arms* (arms). Nouns denoting relationship also take *s*: *broer* (brother), *broers* (brothers). Finally, the following monosyllabic nouns also take *s*: *saal, spreeu, leeu, kok, maat, smied*.

Nouns having more than one syllable usually have two forms: *wandeling* (walk), *wanderlinge* or *wandelings* (walks).

Foreign nouns usually take *s*.

Nouns ending in a stressed *a* or *o* take an apostrophe before the *s*: *pa* (father), *pa's* (fathers).

Nouns ending in *aris* add *se*: *notaris* (notary), *notarisse* (notaries). Those ending in *heid* change this to *hede*: *geleentheid* (opportunity), *geleenthede* (opportunities).

There are, however, many irregular plurals.

There are three genders: living beings are either masculine or feminine, according to sex, while those referring to inanimate objects are neuter.

Feminine nouns are inflected by adding a suffix to the masculine: *beer* (bear), *berin* (she bear). Gender is also indicated by prefixing or suffixing the words *mannetjie* (male) *wyfie* (female): *Mannetjie-gans* (gander), *ganswyfie* (goose). In other cases entirely different words are used to distinguish gender: *man* (man, husband), *vrou* (woman, wife).

Verbs

There are comparatively few changes in the inflection of the verb. It does not change for number or persons:

Ek	is	I am	het	have
jy (u)	is	thou art, you are	het	hast
hy	is	he is	het	has
sy	is	she is	het	has
dit	is	it is	het	has
ons	is	we are	het	have
julle (jul)	is	you are	het	have
hulle (hul)	is	they are	het	have

[1] *jy, jou, jul,* and *julle* are used in ordinary conversation among equals or friends, while *u* is the polite form used in addressing superiors or strangers.

The noun or pronoun preceding the verb indicates whether the verb is singular or plural, first, second, or third person. Auxiliaries are frequently used to express time and mood. Thus the future of *loop* is *ek sal loop* (*sal* + the present); the simple past: *ek het geloop* (*het* + the past participle); the imperative: *jy moet loop*. The form changes, however, in the case of *het*, which aids to form the past tense: *ek sal loop* (I shall go), *ek wil loop* (I want to go).

Prepositions and other small words are used to attain what older languages have attained by inflections.

The verb can be either separably or inseparably compounded. Thus *uitsel* (postpone) is separable because it is a compound of two complete words, while *bestel* (to order) is inseparable, since *be* is merely a prefix. Among other prefixes used are *ge-, er-, her-, ont-, ver-* (but not *ver* (far)). It is well to remember this rule even though it does not apply in every case.

The following examples will be helpful in this respect:

Separable:

Present:	Ek *stel* die vergadering *uit* (I postpone the meeting)
Future:	Ons *sal* die vergadering *uitstel* (we shall postpone the meeting)
Past:	Ons *set* die vergadering *uitgestel* (we postponed the meeting)
Infinitive:	Ons *set* besluit om die vergadering *uit te stel* (we decided to postpone the meeting)
Imperative:	*Stel* die vergadering *uit* (Postpone the meeting)

Inseparable:

Present:	Ek *bestel* die goedere (I order the goods)
Future:	Ek *sal* die goedere *bestel* (I shall order the goods)
Past:	Ek *het* die goedere *bestel* (I ordered the goods)
Infinitive:	Ons *het* besluit *om* die goedere *te bestel* (we decided to order the goods)
Imperative:	*Bestel* die goedere dadelik (order the goods immediately)

For inflection as to voice (active and passive) *word* and *is* are used: *Ek skryf 'n brief* (I write a letter), and *'n brief word deur my geskryf* (a) letter is (being) written by me).

Of moods there are, as in English, the indicative, imperative, subjunctive, and infinitive. A proper use of the latter is very difficult to acquire.

In the following table the form of the first person only is given, as we have seen that the form of the verb does not change for persons: *ek kies, jy kies, hy kies, sy kies, one kies, julle kies, u kies, hulle kies*. Though there is no difference in form between the present perfect, past incomplete or pluperfect (*ek het gekies*), when these tenses are used in conjunction with so-called "form words" like *nou net, alreeds,* etc., it is quite obvious which tense is implied.

Conjugation of kies (choose):

INDICATIVE MOOD

	Active voice	Passive voice
Present incomplete	ek kies	ek word gekies
Present perfect	ek het gekies	ek is gekies (geword)
Past incomplete	ek het gekies	ek is gekies (geword)
Pluperfect	ek het gekies	ek was gekies
Future:		
Incomplete	ek sal kies	ek sal gekies word
Complete	ek sal gekies het	ek sal gekies geword het
Past future:		
Incomplete	ek sou kies	ek sou gekies word
Complete	ek sou gekies het	ek sou gekies geword het

IMPERATIVE MOOD

Second person	kies, jy moet kies	word gekies, jy moet gekies word
Third person	laat hom kies, hy moet kies	hy moet gekies word

SUBJUNCTIVE MOOD

Present tense	ek sou (mag) kies	eek sou (mag) gekies word
Past tense	ek sou (mag) gekies het	ek sou (mag) gekies geword het

INFINITIVE

| Present | kies, te kies, om te kies | (om) gekies te word |
| Past | (om) te gekies het | (om) gekies te geword het |

PARTICIPLE

| Present | — | kiesende |
| Past | gekies | — |

Word order

In simple sentences having an auxiliary verb, that takes its place after the subject, as in English, but the other part of the predicate is placed at the end of the sentence: Ek *het* my vader *gesien* (I have my father seen); Ek *moet* my werk *doen* (I must my work do).

When a sentence begins with an introductory phrase, the auxiliary precedes the subject: *In die aand sal* ek my moeder *sien* (In the evening shall I my mother see).

Adjectives

Adjectives are inflected by adding *e* (positive): *Jan is 'n flukse seun* (John is a diligent boy); by adding *er* (comparative): *Jan is flukser as Piet* (John is more diligent than Peter); by adding *ste* (superlative): *Van die twee seuns is Jan die fluksste* (of the two boys John is the most diligent).

All polysyllabic and those monosyllabic adjectives ending in *d, f, g,* or *s* add *e* when used attributively, and in a similar use nearly all those having more than one syllable add the *e*:

Predicative use	Attributive use
Die plan is *geod* (good)	Dis 'n *goeie* plan
Sy hande was *grof* (rough)	Hy het *growwe* hande
Die muur is *hoog* (high)	Daar is 'n *hoë* muur om die tuin
Hier die stories is *snaaks* (funny)	Ek het 'n *snaakse* storie gelees
Ek is *besig* (busy)	Ek is 'n *besige* man

When a long vowel precedes *d*, the latter is usually dropped when the word is inflected by the addition of *e*. Under similar circumstances, the *f* changes to *w* after a long vowel or consonant, and to *ww* after a short vowel: *laf, lawwe*.

The *g* is usually dropped in inflection, except in the case of words derived from the High Dutch, which usually have a short vowel and, where the word ended in *t*, retain that letter when the *e* is added. As already noted, the *e* takes the dieresis if there is any danger of it being considered a diphthong with the previous vowel.

In words ending in *s* that came from the High Dutch and which previously ended in *t*, that letter is inserted before the attributive *e*: *vas, vaste*.

There are, however, some monosyllabic adjectives ending in *s* and preceded by a short vowel that do not take the *e*: *fris, los, vars*.

Polysyllabic adjectives ending in *er* or *el* sometimes retain the same form when used attributively: *ander, edel*.

In the comparative degree, which always ends in *er*, the *e* is seldom used.

The following have special forms:

Predicative	Atributive
jonk (young)	jong
lank (long)	lang
oud (old)	ou
nuut (new)	nuwe

When used attributively, adjectives formed from proper nouns end in *e* (usually *se*): Die Amerikaan*se* Volk (the American people).

When past-participles are used as adjectives, the attributive ending is *te* or *de*:

| verlig | (to light) | verlig*te* | (lighted) |
| verniel | (to spoil) | verniel*de* | (spoiled) |

Double negative

The use of the double negative is very common and really, in most cases, essential:

Ek kan *nie* (not) candag kom *nie* (not)	I cannot come today not
Ek het *geen* (no) geld *nie* (not)	I have no money not .
Hy het *nooit* (never) die see gesien *nie* (not)	He has never the sea seen not

Niemand (no one) het my pa gesien *nie*	No one has seen my father not
Hy het *niks* (nothings) *nie*	He has nothing not
Nimmer (never) *sal ek dit weer* doen *nie*	Never shall I that weather do not
Ek kan hom *nêrens* (nowhere) sien *nie*	I can him nowhere see not.

Diacritical marks, etc.

Where in compounding words too many vowels would come together, the hyphen is used: *see-eend* (sea duck); *drie-uur* (3 o'clock). It is also used in reduplication: *sing-sing* (singing) as also in compound numerals: *twee-en-twinting* (twenty-two).

The dieresis is used to indicate that two vowels do not form a diphthong: *hoë* (inflected form of *hoog*, high), which without the dieresis would be *hoe* (row).

The circumflex is occasionally found: *wie* (wedges); *môre* (to-morrow), which is also written *more*; *brûe* (bridges); *rûens* (rugs); it is more often used with *e*: *hê* (to have); *sê* (to say); *nêrens* (nowhere).

The grave accent is found in *nè* (eh? Is it not?); *dè* (take it).

The acute accent is found in *dié* (an abbreviation of *hierdie* or *daardie*); *sál* (will, shall; an expression of determination), and in a few other cases.

The apostrophe indicates the omission of a vowel: *'n* (a, an); *s'n* (his), and also to form the plurals of nouns ending in accented *a* or *o*: *pa's* (fathers); *buro's* (bureaus).

Syllabication

Each syllable has either one vowel or a diphthong: *re-de* (cause).

A single consonant goes with the following vowel: *wa-ter* (water); *moe-der* (mother).

Two consonants between vowels are separated: *wat-tes* (which); *mod-der* (mud).

Division occurs after a prefix: *ge-maak* (made); *be-taal-bar* (payable); *mak-lik* (easy).

Division occurs before a vowel having a dieresis: *re-ën* (rain); *o-ë* (eyes).

Component parts of a compound word are treated separately: *hoof-in-spek-teur* (chief inspector); *hoog-e-de-le* (right honorable).

NOTE

An "open" syllable is one that ends in a vowel, while a "closed" syllable is one that ends in a consonant. This distinction is important, since the long vowels *a*, *e*, *o*, and *u* are doubled in closed syllable, whereas they appear singly to represent the same sounds in words ending in open syllables. At the end of a word the long *e* always appears in its doubled form (*ee*):

maan (moon)	mane
been (leg, bone)	bene
boom (tree)	bome
muur (wall)	mure
nasionaal (national)	nasionale (people)
gemeen (common)	gemene (common people or things)

Prepositions

Some of the more common prepositions are given below. It is only by careful observation and constant use that one can hope to master the preposition in its idiomatic context.

na, to; *-toe* is also used as a suffix to the noun: *dorp-toe* (to the town)

aan, at, to, on; also used for the present continuous tense: *Ek is aan skriwe* (I am (was) writing)

aangaaende, concerning

agter, behind (place)

anderkaant, on the other side

behalwe, except

benewens, besides

betreffende, concerning

binne, within (time), inside

binnekant, inside

bo, above

bokant, above (place)

bo-op, on top of

buite-kant, outside

buiten, except

by, at (nearness), by (with), by (nearness of time)
deeskant, on this side of
deur, through (place), by (agency), throughout (time)
digteby, close to
gedurende, during
in, in, at
in . . . in, motion into a place
inplaas van, instead of
in weerwil van, in spite of
langs, langse, alongside of, beside
met, with
na, after (time)
na or *na . . . toe*, to, towards (place)
naby, near
naas, naas aan, next to
namens, in the name of
nieteenstaande, notwithstanding
om, at (time), around (place), for the sake of
omtrent, omstreeks, ongeveer, about
ondanks, trots, in spite of
onder, underneath, among
oor, over, about
op, on, upon (place), on (time), at (place)
per, by (instrument)
regoor, opposite
rondom, around, round about
saam met, with, together with
sedert, sinds, since
sonder, without
te, by (instrument)
teen, against (place), to (against), by (time), at (price or rate)
teenoor, toward, over against
ten spyte van, in spite of
terwille van, for the sake of
ten behoewe van, on behalf of
tot, till, until (time), to
tussen, between
tydens, at the time of, during
uit, out of (place), because of, as a result of
van, of, from (time, place)
vir, with indirect object in the dative: *Gee vir my die boek* (give to me the book); for (time); purpose: *Hy werk vir geld* (he works for money)
verby, past, beyond
voor, in front of, before (time)
volgens, according to
weens, on account of

Cardinal numbers

een	one	tien	ten
twee	two	elf	eleven
drie	three	twaalf	twelve
vier	four	dertien	thirteen
vyf	five	twintig	twenty
ses	six	een-en-twintig	twenty-one
sewe	seven	honderd	hundred
ag(t)	eight	duisend	thousand
nege	nine		

Ordinal numbers

eerste	first	tiende	tenth
twede	second	elfde	eleventh
derde	third	twaalfde	twelfth
vierde	fourth	dertiende	thirteenth
vyfde	fifth	twintigste	twentieth
sesde	sixth	een-en-twintigste	twenty-first
sewende	seventh	honderdste	hundredth
ag(t)ste	eighth	duisendste	thousandth
negende	ninth		

Months

Januarie	January	Julie	July
Februarie	February	Augustus	August
Maart	March	September	September
Aprilmaand	April	Oktober	October
Mei	May	November	November
Junie	June	Desember	December

Days

Sondag	Sunday	Donderdag	Thursday
Maandag	Monday	Vrydag	Friday
Dinsdag	Tuesday	Saterdag	Saturday
Woensdag	Wednesday		

Seasons

lente	spring	herfs	autumn
somer	summer	winter	winter

Time

uur	hour	maand	month
dag	day	jaar	year
week	week	jaarhonderd	century

Articles to be disregarded in filing

die   'n

AMHARIC

I. order, äh, as *a* in eat	II. order, ā, as *a* in father	III. order, ĕ, as *e* in medal	IV. order, i, as *i* in pin	V. order, o, usually sharp as in *so*	VI. order, u as in *put*	VII. order final short *i* or *ĕ*, as *i* in since, and *e* in summer	Remarks on sounds
ha	hā	he	hi	ho	hu	h, hi *or* he	As in English
la	lā	le	li	lo	lu	l, li *or* le	As in English
ha	hā	he	hi	ho	hu	h, hi *or* he	As in English
ma	mā	me	mi	mo	mu	m, mi *or* me	As in English
sa	sā	se	si	so	su	s, si *or* se	As in English
ra	rā	re	ri	ro	ru	r, ri *or* re	As in English
sa	sā	se	si	so	su	s, si *or* se	As in English
sha	shā	she	shi	sho	shu	sh, shi *or* she	As in English
ka	kā	ke	ki	ko	ku	k, ki *or* ke	Soft guttural clicks often omitted
ba	bā	be	bi	bo	bu	b, bi *or* be	As in English
tha	thā	the	thi	tho	thu	th, thi *or* th	Soft *t* followed by soft *th*
cha	chā	che	chi	cho	chu	ch, chi *or* che	As in English
ha	hā	he	hi	ho	hu	h, hi *or* he	As in English
na	nā	ne	ni	no	nu	n, ni *or* ne	As in English
iña	iñā	iñe	iñi	iño	iñu	iñ, iñi *or* iñe	Spanish ñ
a	ā	ĕ	i	o	u	e *or* i	As in English

ከ k'a	ካ k'ā	ኬ k'e	ኪ k'i	ኮ k'o	ኩ k'u	ክ k', k'i or k'e	k followed by slight aspirate
ኸ kha	ኻ khā	ኼ khe	ኺ khi	ኾ kho	ኹ khu	ኽ kh, khi or khe	As in German ach
ወ wa	ዋ wā	ዌ we	ዊ wi	ዎ wo	ዉ wu	ው w, wi or we	As in English; see Notes
ዐ a	ዓ ā	ዔ e	ዒ i	ዖ o	ዑ u	ዕ e or i	As in English
ዘ za	ዛ zā	ዜ ze	ዚ zi	ዞ zo	ዙ zu	ዝ z, zi or ze	As in English
ዠ zha	ዣ zhā	ዤ zhe	ዢ zhi	ዦ zho	ዧ zhu	ዥ zh, zhi or zhe	As in azure
የ ya	ያ yā	ዬ ye	ዪ yi	ዮ yo	ዩ yu	ይ y, yi or ye	As in English
ደ da	ዳ dā	ዴ de	ዲ di	ዶ do	ዱ du	ድ d, di or de	As in English
ጀ ja	ጃ jā	ጄ je	ጂ ji	ጆ jo	ጁ ju	ጅ j, ji or je	As in English
ገ ga	ጓ gā	ጌ ge	ጊ gi	ጎ go	ጉ gu	ግ g, gi or ge	Always hard
ጠ ta	ጣ tā	ጤ te	ጢ ti	ጦ to	ጡ tu	ጥ t, ti or te	t hard; see Notes
ጨ cha	ጫ chā	ጬ che	ጪ chi	ጮ cho	ጩ chu	ጭ ch, chi or che	See notes
ጰ pa	ጳ pā	ጴ pe	ጲ pi	ጶ po	ጱ pu	ጵ p, pi or pe	As in English
ጸ tsa	ጻ tsā	ጼ tse	ጺ tsi	ጾ tso	ጹ tsu	ጽ ts, tsi or tse	In Shoa replaced by ta
ፀ tsa	ፁ tsā	ፄ tse	ፂ tsi	ፆ tso	ፀ tsu	ፅ ts, tsi or tse	Rare
ፈ fa	ፋ fā	ፌ fe	ፊ fi	ፎ fo	ፉ fu	ፍ f, fi or fe	As in English
ፐ pa	ፓ pā	ፔ pe	ፒ pi	ፖ po	ፑ pu	ፕ p, pi or pe	As in English
ቈ kwo	ቋ kwā	. . . .	kwi	. . . .	. . . .	ቍ kwi	DIPHTHONGS As in English
ኈ hwo	ኋ hwā	. . . .	hwi	. . . .	. . . .	ኍ hwi	As in English
ኰ k'wo	ኳ k'wā	. . . .	k'wi	. . . .	. . . .	ኵ k'wi	As in English
ጐ gwo	ጓ gwā	. . . .	gwi	. . . .	. . . .	ጕ gwi	As in English

The Ethiopians, who became independent of Egypt about the eleventh century B.C., appear to have derived their civilization from that country, as the royal inscriptions are written with the hieroglyphic characters in the Egyptian language. About the time of Ergamenes, a contemporary of Ptolemy Philadelphus, a vernacular came into use in inscriptions written in a new alphabet of 23 signs in square hieroglyphic as well as cursive forms. The latter were read from right to left, while the hieroglyphics were placed in the direction in which the figures face, which is contrary to the Egyptian usage. However, even here the forms and values of the signs are largely based on the Egyptian. The employment of the Geez, as the language is called, for literary purposes dates to a time not long before the introduction of Christianity in the fifth century. Although none of the literature is of first rank, being to a great extent merely translations from the Greek and Arabic, it can lay claim to a translation of the Bible in 81 volumes, 46 for the Old Testament and 35 for the New. In the fourteenth century Amhāric displaced it as the prevailing language of the country, and at present it is merely the ecclesiastic language. In the table the continental sounds are used in the romanization of the alphabet.

Amhāric may be termed a syllabic language; it has an alphabet consisting of 247 characters, each representing a syllable, not a single letter. These are not all intrinsically different, but consist of 37 consonantal characters, each having seven variations, orders, or shapes, the character being slightly varied in shape according to the syllable required. For a vivid illustration of this, note the seven shapes of what corresponds to our *m* sound in the fourth line of the table.

NOTES

The different words are separated by colons, and the only punctuation used is a double colon for a full stop.

There is no indefinite article; the numeral *and* (one) is used in place of the English article *a*.

In the transliterated Amhāric the consonants are pronounced as in English and the vowels as in Italian, except as noted below:

c This is replaced (except ch as in English) by k or s according to the sound

ch Midway between ch and ty

g Always hard

k' k, slightly aspirated

kk ch, guttural as in loch

k k, slightly guttural, often omitted by the uneducated; the Egyptian kaf

ñ ni in minion, almost

ph ph as in loophole, not as in phoenix

t t, hard

th t soft, followed by a th sound, as th in at the

y Is always a consonant

zh French j, or s in pleasure

w Terminal w is not sounded as in English: saw (man) is sounded almost as sao

Vowels are pronounced indistinctly by the natives, and it is often difficult to distinguish an *a* from an *e* mute (as English *er*) or an *i*.

a is pronounced as a in cat, and a in father;
e is pronounced as e in medal, and e in whey;
i is pronounced as i in pin, and i in marine;
o is pronounced as o in folly, and o in pole;
u is pronounced as u in pull, and u in rule.

Numerals

𝔁	1	𝟕	6	𝕴𝖒𝖘	11	𝖅	60	𝖗𝖗		200
𝖊	2	𝟕	7	𝕬	20	𝖖	70	𝕴𝖞		1 000
𝕮	3	𝖅	8	𝖦	30	𝕿	80	𝖀		10 000
𝖦	4	𝖇	9	𝖌	40	𝟙	90	𝕴𝖀		100 000
𝖆	5	𝕴	10	𝖖	50	𝖟	100	𝖞𝖀		1 000 000

Cardinal numbers

and	one	heyā and	twenty-one
hulath	two	salāsā	thirty
sōsth	three	arbā	forty
arāth	four	amsā	fifty
ammisth	five	sidsā	sixty
siddisth	six	sabā	seventy
sabbāth	seven	simānya	eighty
simminth	eight	zatana	ninety
zataiñ	nine	mathō	hundred
asar	ten	hulath mathō	two hundred
asrā and	eleven	shī	thousand
asrā hulath	twelve	sōsth shī	three thousand
heyā	twenty		

Numbers between the hundreds are formed by prefixing k'a, as mathō k'a-sōsth, hundred and three.

Ordinal numbers are formed by adding aiñā to the cardinal, or to the last of a string of cardinal numbers:

hulathaiñā	second	asar shī k'a-siddisth mathō	ten thousand six hundred
sōsthaiñā	third	k'a-zatana si-minthaiñā	and ninety-eight
mathō k'a-sōs-thaiñā	hundred and third		

Fithaiñā and majmaryā are also used for first, but in a historic sense kadāmi (first) and dāgmāwī (second) are used: Dāgmāwī Minilik', Minilik the Second.

Months

The Abyssinian year does not begin at the same time as ours, their year 1896 "Lukas" beginning on the 12th of September of our year 1903. Each year is named after one of the Evangelists. The year consists of 12 months of 30 days each, and at the end of the year 5 days, leap years 6, are added; these being called Pagwimē and are generally considered holidays. Approximately the names of the months are—

Tir	January	Hāmlē	July
Ek'atīth	February	Nahāsī	August
Magābīth	March	Mask'aram	September
Miyāzyā	April	Tikimth	October
Gimbōth	May	Hidār	November
Sannē	June	Tahsas	December

Week

Ehud	Sunday	Amus	Thursday
Saiñō	Monday	Arb	Friday
Māk'hsaiñō	Tuesday	Kidāmī	Saturday
Rōb	Wednesday		

Seasons

tsadāī, from September 26 to December 26.
k'aramth, from December 26 to March 26.
matsau (matau), from March 26 to June 26.
hagai, from June 26 to September 26.

There are actually but two seasons: k'aramth, which is the rainy season, from June to September, and bagā, the dry season.

Time

saāth	hour	war	month
kan	day	amath	year
sāminth, simōn	week		

BANTU LANGUAGE FAMILY

a	*a* in father	n	*n* in nail
b	*b* in bone	o	*o* in boy
c or ch	*ch* in church	p	*p* in pass
d	*d* in done	q	A "click" sound [1]
e	*ai* in chair	r	*r* in rude
f	*f* in fall	s	*s* in see
g	*g* in gone	t	*t* in tin
h	*h* in home; never used in Tonga	u	*u* in rude
		v	*v* in over
i	*i* in ravine; also in tin	w	Not so full as English *w*
j	*j* in juice	x or sh	*sh* in shall
k	*k* in key	y	*y* in year
l	*l* in lamb	z	*z* in zone
m	*m* in mine		

[1] The *q* sound is produced by drawing a hard sound as if from the palate downward; this sound is sometimes heard in Suto.

This group of languages is the most important of those spoken in South Africa, and those included here comprise the idioms used by all the agricultural black tribes of the country. Languages that are distinctly Bantu are heard in all the well-watered parts of South Africa from the Keiskamma River, in Cape Colony, to the Equator in the east and from Walfish Bay to the Old Kalabar River, on the fifth parallel, north latitude, in the west. In most parts of central Africa the Bantu field extends but little north of the Equator. It must not be inferred that the variation between the many languages comprising the Bantu family is as great as that existing between the Indo-European languages. Bantu as a whole is quite clearly divided into 31 groups; and while considerable similarity exists within each group, the difference is sufficiently great for each to be classed as a separate language. Notwithstanding the existence of a considerable amount of literature, the study of the language is still in its infancy. Writing is still almost unknown, except among the coast tribes under foreign influence. The roman letters alone are known on the West Coast, while elsewhere the Arabic characters have been long in use and still prevail.

REMARKS

In Zulu and Xosa the *c* and *x* are used to represent clicks, or peculiar sounds found in these dialects. In Chwana the simple *c* has the sound of *ch* in church, while *ch* adds an aspiration to the same sound.

In Tonga and several other languages, *b* before *u* and *o* is almost the Dutch *w* in *wijn*: *mu-bua* (a dog) is pronounced nearly like *mu-wua*.

In Chwana *d* has a sound midway between *d* and *r*, which in others is represented by *l*.

In Kafir, *e* followed by a syllable which contains *i* or *u* sounds like the French *é* in *bonté*. It also represents slightly different sounds in different positions in the Chwana.

In Chwana *f* is almost like the Dutch *v* in *vader*, while in certain dialects of that language it is more nearly a labial *h*.

When *g* is not immediately preceded by *n* in Chwana it sounds like the Dutch *g* in *goed*.

Except in the Kafir language, *j* is the counterpart of *c*, having a sound midway between *j* in juice and *d* in due. In Angola, Karanga, and Chwana this sound (the same as in the French *jour*) is represented by a *j* without a dot.

After the vowels *a*, *e*, and *o*, the *l* has nearly its true sound, while after the vowels *i* and *u* it sounds more like *r*. In Kafir, *l* has the pure English sound.

In Kafir, *o* followed by a syllable which contains *u* is sounded like *o* in rope. In Chwana this letter has slightly different sounds in different positions.

In Tonga, *r* is merely a phonetic modification of *l*, while in Kafir a sound more guttural than the German *ch* in ach is given to it.

In Karanga, Kamba, Herero, and elsewhere, *s* has a sound midway between *th* in think and *s* in see.

In Kafir, *tsh* is used to render the sound *ch* in church.

Bétween a consonant and a vowel, *u* is frequently replaced by *w*.

When *n*, *d*, or *t* precedes *y*, the two sounds are combined as one, thus producing the three sounds *ny*, *dy*, and *ty*, which have no exact equivalents in English, the nearest approach being *ni* in onion, *d* in duty, and *t* in tune. In Herero *ty* sounds very much like the Tonga *c*.

ADDITIONAL SOUNDS IN CHWANA (SUTO, TIHAPING, ROLONG, AND KOLOLO)

The *tl* approximates the same letters in bottle, while *tlh* is more strongly aspirated.

ADDITIONAL SOUNDS IN KAFIR (XOSA, ZULU, AND TEBELE)

hl is sometimes spelled *kl* and *sl*; it approximates the Greek combination χλ.

In Kafir, *tl* represents a sound almost of *hl*, but preceded by *t*, it is a mere modification of *hl*, owing to the *n* before it: *in-tlalo* (a sitting).

dl has two soft sounds like *hl* and *tl*. When not preceded by *n*, it approximates *gl* in the Dutch *glorie*, but when preceded by *n* the sound is more like the spelling.

The click sounds are difficult of description, being produced by drawing in, rather than by expressing, sound and are analogous to *k* and *g*. They are as follows:

c, which is produced by drawing a hard sound from the front teeth inward.

q, produced by drawing a hard sound from the palate downward. This click is sometimes heard in Suto.

gq is a soft sound corresponding to *q*.

x, produced by drawing a hard sound inward from the side teeth.

gx is a soft sound corresponding to *x*.

CHARACTERISTIC FEATURES

1. Concord is established by means of prefixes which are, as a rule, expressed before the substantives and then repeated in various forms before every expression that must agree with it.

2. In nearly all of the Bantu languages monosyllabic stems of verbs and nouns (substantives, adjectives, and pronouns) are subjected to special rules tending to prefixes or suffixes where other stems have none. This principle of avoiding monosyllables or single sounds may be compared with triliterality in the Semitic languages.

3. Phonetic changes affect consonants more than vowels, which is a novelty in philology. Those changes which affect vowels bear mostly on vowels which begin a stem, as *i* in *-injila* (enter), and the weaker of two vowels which are adjacent, as *u* (alias *w*) in *-fua*, *-fwa*, or *-fa* (die). The most of the changes that affect consonants may be traced to differences in the conformation of lips and nose, with the additions or absence of lip rings, nose rings, and the various artificial gaps in the teeth. The nasals *n* and *m* frequently have the beneficial effect of retaining consonants which, according to general laws, should have been weakened or dropped altogether, though, in other cases, those same nasals apparently have the contrary effect of modifying the consonants which they precede.

COMPARATIVE PHONETICS

In Tonga, which is considered the standard Bantu language, the most striking feature is the regular *ji* and *ci* where most of the others have the sharper sounds *gi* and *ki*. The sounds *s* and *z* are more common here than in any of the others, not even excepting Kafir. The *p* is not heard or is replaced by *w*.

In Yao, spoken on the tableland between Lake Nyassa and the coast, many of the words which are common to Tonga and Yao are greatly reduced in form in the latter: *im-vula* (rain) in Tonga becomes *ula* in Yao. On the other hand, stems which are monosyllabic in Tonga are found to have richer forms in Yao: *i-ji* (an egg) becomes *li-jele* in Yao.

The two Nya-mwezi dialects best known are the Nya-nyembe and Sukuma, which have a decided tendency to weaken certain consonants after nasals, going even further than the Yao. It is interesting to note that this is the opposite of many of the other Bantu languages where the same nasals have the very opposite effects. These dialects often use *g* where Tonga has *f*. In many cases they drop certain vowels which, in the other languages, are either contracted or assimilated with those which follow them.

The Shambala and Boondei, which are spoken inland opposite Pemba Island, are very similar, and both are closely allied to the Sagara, though the consonants which follow the nasal *n* are firmer and occur much oftener than in Sagara, generally strengthening those which it precedes. *S* is sounded *x* (English *sh*) in Shambala, though not in Boondei, this being the most important difference between these two languages.

Taita is distinguished by the large number of its words that are not found in the more southern Bantu languages.

In Kamba, which is spoken west from Mombasa to Mount Kenia, not only *b* but also *l*, *z*, and *j* are usually dropped or weakened, causing a decided shortening of many stems. The *s* is sounded similar to *th* in this. The nasal *n* preceding *l* changes to *d*, *w* and *v* to *b*, and also *t* to *z*.

Swahili exhibits the greatest amount of Arabic influence of any of the Bantu languages. It often drops the Tonga *l*, and there are other remarkable phonetic differences between it and the generality of Bantu languages, which space will not permit us to enumerate.

Nyika is spoken inland from Mombasa, and Pokomo on the Pokomo River, and, while differing considerably, have a remarkable feature in common in that they generally use the consonant *h* where most Bantu languages have a *t*. They also have the sound *dz* where Tonga has *s*. The principal difference between Nyika and Pokomo is that the latter weakens the *l* or *r* of the other languages in many cases and drops it in others.

The most prominent feature of Senna, which includes Tette and Nyassa, as compared with the others is that, where most of these have a sharp *z*, *v*, or *f*, it in many instances has compound sounds, most of which result from a suppressed *i* or a suppressed nasal.

A close relative to the Senna is the Karanga (Kalaka), the features of the former just mentioned being applicable to the Karanga, though the latter has some remarkable features which distinguish it from the Senna. In Karanga we find the *j* (French *j*) and *x* (English *sh*). Karanga has many contractions and elisions unknown in Tonga and thus cannot be considered an agglutinative language.

In comparing Ganda, which is spoken on the shores of the Victoria Nyanza, with the languages which have been mentioned, the most noticeable feature will be the repeated use of the vowel article *a*, *e*, or *o* before substantives, and the conjunction *na* (and) before verbs used in a historic sense. This usage indicates possible Semitic influence. Another feature is the use of *g*, sometimes *b*, between vowels, as if to avoid a hiatus. Phonetic permutations of consonants indicate a tendency to labial and palatal sounds in opposition to the dental and principally to the sibilant sounds of Tonga. A notable fact is that a number of common substantives are of a different class from that in which they belong in nearly all of the other Bantu languages.

The distinctive features of the Kafir, which includes the Xosa, Zulu, and Tebele, are: The use of the click sounds which are probably borrowed from the Hottentot; the use of the compound liquid dentals *hl*, *tl*, and *dl*, which, like the clicks, have penetrated merely into the verbal roots; a marked tendency to drop vowels before vowels, or to combine them with other sounds.

Herero, spoken in Damaraland, has a marked tendency to weaken several consonants, especially *s*, *z*, *k*, and *l*, even where there is a nasal sound.

Bihe, spoken on the upper Kwanza, appears to be an amalgamation of several other languages. Its most important features are: In many words the syllable *mu* of the other languages is changed to *u*, and *mi* to *vi* or *i;* the change of the Tonga sound *b* in some cases to *m*, in others to *v;* the change of the Tonga sound *z* to *l*.

Mbunda, Lojazi, Nano, and Ndonga, which are spoken from Benguella to the upper Zambesi, differ materially from each other, but are purer than the Bihe and are midway between Herero and Karanga.

In Runda (Lunda) and Luba, the first spoken on the upper and the second on the lower Kasai, the most remarkable feature is that final vowels are almost inaudible, while some others are broadened or weakened. It is also apparent that the Tonga *zi* is sounded *ji* or *ci* in Lunda.

Apparently the most noticeable phonetic feature of Rua, spoken on the Lualaba, south of Nyangwe, is the change from *li* to *ji*, but there are exceptions to this rule in some of the dialects.

In many respects Angola, Mbamba, and Fiote (lower Kongo) differ considerably, but they are in agreement in most points in which they differ from the Tonga. In the classification of nouns generally, Kongo recedes further from Tonga and from most of the Bantu languages than Angola does. Mbamba approaches Tonga more nearly than either Angola or Kongo.

In Nywema, spoken north of Lukuga River, the Tonga *z* before *i* is replaced at times with *l*, and the sound of *v*, when not influenced by a nasal, changes to *p* when influenced by one.

In Kua (Mozambique) and Chwana we must distinguish carefully between consonantal sounds which include a nasal and those which contain none: In the latter group the correspondence of *r* and *t* is especially noticeable, the general tendency being to guttural sounds; in the first group the nasal is apparently suppressed except before monosyllabic stems when, in Chwana, the remaining consonant is either hardened or strengthened, or, if possible, dentalized; this nasal influence on other consonants results in a great many words having two forms each, at times widely different; contrary to Mozambique, the Chwana often changes *o* to *u* and *e* to *i;* another remarkable feature of the latter being a series of combinations of consonants and vowels which occur before suffixes that begin with a vowel.

Tshagga is one of the languages spoken near Kilima-njaro, and Hinzua is one of those used on the Comoro Islands, both of which have some of the features of Mozambique, especially in respect to dental and liquid sounds.

Mpongwe, spoken on the lower Ogowe, is more closely allied to Chwana and Mozambique than to the lake-region languages.

Dualla, the principal language of the Cameroons, has a great deal in common with Mpongwe, and the Bantu grammatical elements are better preserved in it than in the latter.

Fan, spoken on the upper Gabun River, is very closely related to Kele and reminds one forcibly of Chwana, and even more so of Mozambique. Here we find many words dropping their final vowel, especially after *n*, and also that several accented vowels themselves have an uncertain pronunciation; this probably explains why in Fan the *a* = the Tonga *o* or *u*, the *e* sometimes the Tonga *o* or *a*, and the *o* often the Tonga *u*.

A remarkable feature of Fernandian (Fernando Po) is the frequent use of *b* where the other languages have *m*.

The languages of the Congo Forest were probably borrowed from the adjacent agricultural tribes, since a large number of the words belonging to the languages of the dwarfs are unmistakably of Bantu origin.

Numerals

Among the Bantu counting is done principally with the fingers, but there are also words and expressions for the different numbers; these are partly adjectives and partly substantives. Among the Tonga and other tribes of the interior there are numeral adjectives up to 5, but 6 is 5-and-1, 7 is 5-and-2, etc.; 10 is expressed by the substantive *ikumi*, 100 by *ma-kume-kumi*, which is a superlative of 10; beyond that there is *makumi a-ta balui*, or "tens without number." In most of the other languages there are numeral adjectives up to 6 and substantives or foreign words for the other numbers.

BOBANGI

a		As *a* in father	n	ne	As *ne* in net
b	be	As *be* in bell	o		As *ou* in brought
c	ce	As *tse* in itself	ô	(¹)	
d	de	As *de* in den	p	pe	As *pe* in pet
e		As *a* in bale	s	se	As *se* in set
ê	(¹)		t	te	As *te* in tell
g	ge	As *ge* in get	u	u	As *oo* in pool
i	i	As *ee* in peel	w	we	As *we* in wet
k	ke	As *ke* in keg	y	ye	As *ye* in yet
l	le	As *le* in let	z	ze	As *dze* in adze
m	me	As *me* in met			

¹ There is no equivalent in the English language for the sound of *ê*, it being exactly midway between *e* and *i*, as noted in the above alphabet. The *ô* is pronounced like *o* in note or *oa* in coat.

As the representatives of the original tribe are almost extinct, the history of the Bobangi can be gotten only from the folklore. The strangers who came to dwell in their midst and who speak their language live along the south bank of the Congo from the junction of the Kasai to Irebu, as well as along the banks of the Mobangi River, and on the north bank at Bakutu. Other neighboring tribes use the language as a common means of intercommunication, and more or less among themselves. It is also the basis of the trade language used by the officers of the Congo Independent State, as well as traders and other travelers.

NOTES

Double consonants occur only when the nasal *m* and *n* are prefixed to other consonants, as *mbula*, or when the semiconsonants *b*, *w*, and *y* are affixed to other consonants, as *ligbu*, *bwa*, and *nyala*.

A consonant may have a nasal prefix as well as a semiconsonant affix: *mbwa*, *ngbe*, *ngwala*.

The natives invariably divide a double consonant with the vowel that may seem to be most euphonious for the consonants or in harmony with the remaining vowels of the word; among the most common are the divisions of *l*, *r*, and *s* from other consonants with which they are compounded, and the most common vowel used is *u: pūlankī*.

The semiconsonants *w* and *y* represent vowels reduced for the sake of euphony; *w* represents *o* or *u*, and *y* represents *i*, the former being pronounced as in *twenty*, and *y* as *i* in *com-pa-nion*.

Any of the vowels may receive a raised or lowered tone, irrespective of accent. This raising and lowering is similar to the English use of long and short vowels.

Vowel combinations should not be regarded as diphthongs, as each vowel receives its true alphabetical value. The language is strictly phonetical, and the phonetic value of each letter is as has been indicated in the table.

Every syllable ends in a vowel.

Accent in nouns is invariably on the first syllable when stripped of its alliterative prefix. For verbs it is on the first syllable of the root.

d and *g* usually have a nasal prefix.

Vowels are frequently dropped before the same and other vowels: *māmbi* for *māāmbi*, *mëngô* for *māëngô*, etc.

Numerals

mpambā	zero	(mī)tanô	five
(m)oko	one	môtëba	six
(mī)bālë	two	ncāmbô	seven
(mī)satô	three	mwāmbī, *pl.* mīāmbī	eight
(mī)nêī	four	lībwa	nine

zömu, *pl.* mömū	ten	nyuncåmbô	seventy
mākwabālë	twenty	lôāsī, *pl.* ndwāɛī	eighty
bwēlī, *pl.* mēlī	thirty	môbwa	ninety
nyumīnêī	forty	mônkama	hundred
nyumītanô	fifty	nkötô	thousand
nyumôtöba	sixty	êpūna	million

Ordinal numbers are expressed by qualifying the noun stated or understood with an adjectival clause containing the numeral.

Days

eyêngā	Sunday	masalā ma manêī	Thursday
masalā ma bôsö	Monday	masalā ma matanô	Friday
masalā ma mabālë	Tuesday	ncono ek'-eke	Saturday
masalā ma masatô	Wednesday		

Seasons

esīmbīsêlā	}spring	moca mō manyītêlā	autumn
eyumbīwīsêlā		moca mō mpīō	winter
moca mö masôlêlā	summer		

Time

lobetē	hour	eyelī, ncöngë	month
busa	day	mobu, eböngô	year
ncono	week		

BULUBA-LULUA

a	a	As in father	k	kay	As in king
ă	a	As in hat	l	lay	As in long
ä	a	As in fall	m	may	As in man
b	bay	As in bone	n	nay	As in not
c	chay	As *ch* in choose	o	o	As in note
d	day	As in day	p	pay	As in pay
e	e	As in they	s	say	As in sit
ĕ	e	As in met	t	tay	As in tone
f	fay	As in fat	u	u	As in rule
g	gay	As in king	ŭ	u	As in but
h	hay	(¹)	v	vay	As in vine
i	i	As in machine	w	way	As in water
ĭ	i	As in hit	x	shay	As *sh* in shall
ī	i	As in pine	y	yay	As in yonder
j	jay	*j* in French jeune	z	zay	As in zone

¹ This letter is used to represent a peculiar breathing sound found in no European language, being between *f* and *p*, though clearly distinct from either. The sound is produced by placing the lips as if to whistle, not protruding them too much, nor pressing the lower lip against the teeth, then expelling the breath and allowing the lips to fall apart.

The Baluba and Lulua people belong to the great Bantu family, both in language and race. This family occupies, roughly speaking, all of Africa south of the fifth parallel, with the exception of the Hottentot-Bushmen in the extreme south. The different dialects of this family have much in common, though some of them are as widely different as English and Greek; others are so nearly alike that the differences are really nothing more than a brogue. This is true of the language under discussion. These tribes, occupying a large area on the healthful highlands of southern Africa, are remarkably peaceable and eager for civilization.

NOTES

The governing principle of the alphabet is that it is phonetic, each sound being represented by a distinct letter, though *m* and *n* in double consonant are apparent exceptions. There the division of the syllable is between the two consonants and *m* retains its ordinary sound. When *n* and another consonant come at the beginning of a word a peculiar sound is given the combination: The end of the tongue is brought up against the roof of the mouth, as in the pronunciation of *n*, the initial sound passes through the nose, and the breath is expelled.

The *a*, *ă*, and *ä* must not be regarded as different sounds of the same letter, but as different letters. This is true also of the other vowels.

The *j*, *v*, and *z* are used mostly by the Baluba, while the Lulua people generally use *x*, *f*, and *s*, respectively, little confusion being caused because the sounds are so similar.

In spelling, each vowel is given its exact sound, and each consonant is followed by the sound of *e* in they.

The long vowels are *a*, *e*, *i*, *ī*, *o*, and *u*, as well as the broad *a*, while *ă*, *ĕ*, *ĭ*, and *ŭ* are short.

The *c* has frequently the sound of *ts* in nuts.

The *g* is always found in combination with *n*.

The letter *y* is always a consonant, though in certain cases it is closely related to *i*.

The pronunciation of *ny* is like the Spanish *ñ* in cañon.

Syllabication

Syllables are formed to represent the pronunciation rather than the etymology. Where the syllable begins with a single consonant it ends with a vowel or diphthong. When double consonants occur, division is between them.

Euphony

This is a most important subject, requiring careful study. A vowel is dropped when it comes before its like in the same word, and *a* is always dropped before all other vowels in the word; thus—

$a+a$ becomes *a:* *ba+ana* becomes *bana* (children);
$i+i$ becomes *i:* *bi+impe* becomes *bimpe* (seed);
$u+u$ becomes *u:* *ku+umuka* becomes *kumuka* (to go out);
$a+e$ becomes *e:* *ka+ele* becomes *kele* (small knife);
$a+i$ becomes *i:* *ba+ipi* becomes *bipi* (thieves);
$a+\bar{\imath}$ becomes *ī:* *ba+inyi* becomes *bīnyi* (my)
$a+o$ becomes *o:* *ba+onso* becomes *bonso* (all);
$a+u$ becomes *u:* *badi ba+ula* becomes *badi bula* (they are buying).

The remaining vowel usually has a long sound.

When *u* begins a word and is followed by another vowel in the same syllable, also when it occurs between two other vowels, it is changed to a *w*; in a similar position *i* becomes *y*.

Before *i* or under the influence of *n*, *l* becomes *d*.

Before *i*, *t* becomes *c*, and *s* becomes *x*.

Before *p* or *b*, *n* becomes *m*.

When *h* follows *n*, the former changes to *p* and the latter becomes *m*.

A final *n* occurring before an initial vowel becomes *ng*.

Certain consonants sometimes serve to separate vowels, as when *v* is inserted between *i* and the following vowel, and also between *n* and *l* in certain inflections. The *n* is also used between *u* and *e* as well as double *a*.

Accent

In simple words the accent usually falls on the penult, with a secondary accent on the fourth syllable from the end in polysyllabic words. In inflected words stress is on the initial syllable of the root.

Cardinal numbers [1]

-mue (-mo)	one	onemakumi abidi	twenty-two
-bidi	two	ne-bidi	
-sătu	three	makumi asătu	thirty
-nī	four	makumi asătu ne-mue	thirty-one
-tanu	five	makumi ani	forty
-sambombo	six	makumi atanu	fifty
muanda mutekete	seven	makumi asam-	sixty
muanda mukulu	eight	bombo	
citema	nine	makumi muanda	seventy
dikumi	ten	mutekete	
dikumi ne-mue	eleven	makumi muanda	eighty
(-mo)		mukulu	
dikumi ne-bidi	twelve	mukumi citema	ninety
dikumi ne muan-	seventeen	lukama	hundred
da mutekete		lukama ne-mue	hundred and
dikumi ne muan-	eighteen	(-mo)	one
da mukulu		lukama ne dikumi	hundred and
dikumi citema	nineteen		ten
makumi abidi	twenty	nkama ibidi	two hundred
makumi abidi ne-	twenty-one	nkama isătu	three hundred
mue (-mo)		cinunu	thousand

Ordinal numbers

The ordinals second to sixth are inflected as regular adjectives, taking the primary prefixes, while the substantive forms from seventh on have an adjective phrase with *-a*. The form for first also has this construction.

-a kumudilu	first	-isambombo	sixth
-ibidi	second	-a muanda mutekete	seventh
-isătu	third	-a dikumi	tenth

---

[1] Note the hyphen where the numbers are used after nouns with the force of adjectives.

Days

Lumingu (Lubingu)	Sunday	dituku disătu	Wednesday
dituku dia mpatu-	Monday	dituku dinī	Thursday
kilu wa Lumingu		dituku ditanu	Friday
dituku dibidi	Tuesday	dituku disambombo	Saturday

Months (adapted from the English)

Januale	January	Juli	July
Febluale	February	Augusite	August
Malasa	March	Sepetemba	September
Apila	April	Okotoba	October
Maya	May	Novemba	November
Junyi	June	Disemba	December

Seasons

| cidimu cia munya | summer | cidimu cia maxika | winter |

Time [2]

| diba | hour | ngondo | month |
| munya | day | | |

² I have been unable to find any terms for either week or year.—EDITOR.

CHIKARANGA

a	*a* in father	m	*m* in mine
b	*b* in bag	n	*n* in no
ch	*ch* in cherry; never hard	o	*o* in bold; also in boy
d	*d* in do	p	*p* in pass
e	*e* in they; also in jest	r	*r* in rude
f	*f* in fan	s	*s* in see
g	*g* in grain; never soft	t	*t* in tin
h	*h* in hen	u	*u* in rude
i	*i* in ravine; also in tin	v	*v* in over
j	*j* in juice [1]	w	*w* in win
k	*k* in key	y	*y* in year
l	*l* in late [2]	z	*z* in zinc

[1] It often has a sound more nearly that of *j* in the French jour
[2] *l*, *d*, and *r* are often interchangeable.

This is one of the languages of the Mashona people; in fact, it might be said to be the language, since there is no more difference between the different Mashona dialects than between those of the United States. There is ground for crediting to a certain extent ancient Portuguese tales of a large native kingdom some 600 years ago. That it was powerful is indicated by the ruins still extant.

NOTES

a before *i* becomes *e*.
i before another vowel is replaced by *y*; after another vowel it becomes *yi*.
kw is used for the *qu* sound in queer.
m is frequently used for *mu;* and *mu* before *e* or *i* becomes *mw*, and before *o* loses the *u* altogether.
There are no diphthongs, two succeeding vowels being pronounced separately.
ng has the sound of those letters in longing.
ny has the sound of *ni* in onion.
w and *y* are merely the vowels *u* and *i* pronounced as consonants.
j is sounded *swi*, *tsw*, and *zw*.
Every syllable ends with a vowel, and formerly every syllable began with a consonant, which is still true of all but the initial syllable, though the consonantal sounds in the middle of words is often barely audible.
Stress is invariably on the penultimate syllable.

Numerals

posi, potsi	one	makumi mabiri ne imwe	twenty-one
piri, biri	two		
tatu	three	makumi mabiri ne mabiri	twenty-two
china	four		
shanu	five	makumi matatu, makumatatu	thirty
tanatu	six		
chinomwe	seven	makumasere	eighty
sere	eight	makumafemba	ninety
femba, fembamwe	nine	zana	hundred
gumi	ten	zana ne potsi	hundred and one
gumi ne potsi	eleven		
gumi ne biri	twelve		
makumi mabiri, makumabiri	twenty		

Cardinal numbers

These are treated as adjectives in requiring the prefix of the governing noun:

-mwe	one	-tanatu	six
-biri	two	-nomwe	seven
-tatu	three	-sere	eight
-na	four	-femba, fembamwe	nine
-shanu	five	-gumi	ten

Ordinal numbers

In the singular these are treated as genitives having the preposition *ya* (of), *yapotsi*, first. In the plural *pa* is placed between the preposition and the root, *dza-pa-mve*. First is also expressed by the verbs *ku-tanga* and *ku-wamba* (to begin). The ordinals are also expressed by the prefixes *ka* and *chi*, *katatu*, third.

Week

Sabata	Sunday	zuwa re kacina	Thursday
zuwa re chipotsi	Monday	zuwa re chishanu	Friday
zuwa re kabiri	Tuesday	Gobero	Saturday
zuwa re katatu	Wednesday		

Seasons

kupumha	spring	rupohi	autumn
mayinza	summer	chandu	winter

Time

chinguwa	hour	mwedzi	month
zuwa	day	gore	year
viki	week		

COPTIC

Charac-ter	Name	Nu-meral	Sound
Ⲁ ⲁ	alpha	1	*a* in man
Ⲃ ⲃ	beta	2	*b* in babe; also used for *v* sound
Ⲅ ⲅ	gamma	3	*g;* never found in pure Coptic
Ⲇ ⲇ	delta	4	*d;* in foreign words; sometimes *t* sound
Ⲉ ⲉ	ei	5	*ĕ* in pet
Ⲍ ⲍ	zeta	7	*z;* only in foreign words; sometimes *s*
Ⲏ ⲏ	heta	8	*e* in fête
Ⲑ ⲑ	theta	9	*th;* sometimes *f*
Ⲓ ⲓ	iota	10	*ee* in feet
Ⲕ ⲕ	kappa	20	*k* in keg
Ⲗ ⲗ	lauda	30	*l*
Ⲙ ⲙ	mi	40	*m*
Ⲛ ⲛ	ni	50	*n*
Ⲝ ⲝ	xi	60	*x;* mainly in foreign words
Ⲟ ⲟ	ou	70	*ŏ*
Ⲡ ⲡ	pi	80	*p;* modern Egyptian *b*
Ⲣ ⲣ	ro	100	*r;* sometimes changed to *l*
Ⲥ ⲥ	sima	200	*s*
Ⲧ ⲧ	tau	300	*t*
Ⲩ ⲩ	hu	400	*u*
Ⲫ ⲫ	phi	500	*f;* initial has *b* sound
Ⲭ ⲭ	chi	600	*ch*
Ⲯ ⲯ	psi	700	*ps* in gypsum
Ⲱ ⲱ	ou	800	*ō* in prone
Ϣ ϣ	shei	900	*sh*
Ϥ ϥ	fei	90	*f;* sometimes *b*
Ϧ ϧ	khei		*kh*

Character	Name	Numeral	Sound
Ⳁ ⳁ	hori		h, aspirate
Ⲭ ⲭ	gangia		g in go
Ⳃ ⳃ	shima		s, sh
Ϯ ϯ	dei		ti, di

Although the living language of the Egypt of today is a modification of the Arabic, the Egyptian language still retains its interest not only to the Egyptologist and the student of the Septuagint but also to the antiquary and the tourist who would read the inscriptions on the ancient monuments of that land and the mementoes of that civilization. Old Egyptian, as represented by hieroglyphics, still remains, however, merely a vague consonantal skeleton as far as pronunciation is concerned. It is only through the Coptic, its final lineal descendant, that we can gain an approach to its vocalization. It is, therefore, this language with its enchorial alphabet that is presented in this manual.

Coptic is the latest form of the ancient Egyptian and, with an admixture of Semitic and Greek, continued to be the spoken tongue of the land until three centuries ago. Its employment today is only in connection with some of the liturgy of the Coptic church. Its alphabet consists of 31 characters, the names of which and the English equivalents, together with their numerical values, being given in the table.

Cardinal numbers

The Coptic numbers are generally expressed by the letters of the alphabet with a superimposed line.

	Masculine	Feminine		Masculine	Feminine
Ⲁ̄	ⲞⲨⲀⲒ,	ⲞⲨⲈ.	ⲟ̄	ⲰⲂⲈ,	
	ⲞⲨⲰⲦ		ⲡ̄	ⲂⲀⲘⲚⲈ,	
Ⲃ̄	ⲤⲚⲀⲨ,	ⲤⲚⲞⲨϮ,	ⲫ̄	ⲠⲒⲤⲦⲀⲨ,	ⲠⲒⲤⲦⲈⲞⲨⲓ,
Ⲅ̄	ϢⲞⲘⲦ,	ϢⲞⲘϮ,	ⲣ̄	ϢⲈ,	
Ⲇ̄	ϤⲦⲰⲞⲨ,	ϤⲦⲞⲈ,	ⲥ̄	ⲤⲚⲀⲨⲚ̀ϢⲈ,	ⲤⲚⲀⲨϢⲈ,
Ⲉ̄	ϮⲞⲨ,	ϮⲈ, Ϯ,	ⲧ̄	ϢⲞⲘⲦⲚ̀ϢⲈ,	
Ⲋ̄	ⲤⲞⲞⲨ,	ⲤⲞ,	ⲩ̄	ϤⲦⲞⲞⲨⲚ̀ϢⲈ,	
Ⲍ̄	ϢⲀϢϤ,	ϢⲀϢϤⲒ,	ⲫ̄	ϮⲞⲨⲚ̀ϢⲈ,	ϮⲞⲨϢⲈ,
Ⲏ̄	ϢⲘⲎⲚ,	ϢⲘⲎⲚⲒ,	ⲭ̄	ⲤⲞⲞⲨⲚ̀ϢⲈ,	ⲤⲞⲞⲨϢⲈ,
Ⲑ̄	ⲮⲒⲦ,	ⲮⲒϮ,	ⲯ̄	ϢⲀϢϤⲚ̀ϢⲈ,	
Ⲓ̄	ⲘⲎⲦ,	ⲘⲎϮ,	ⲱ̄	ϢⲘⲎⲚⲚ̀ϢⲈ,	
Ⲕ̄	ⲬⲰⲦ,	ⲬⲞⲨⲰⲦ,	Ⳁ̄		
Ⲗ̄	ⲘⲀⲠ,		Ⲁ̿	ϢⲞ,	
Ⲙ̄	ⳘⲘⲈ,		Ⲃ̿	ϢⲞⲤⲚⲀⲨ,	
Ⲛ̄	ⲦⲀⲒⲞⲨ,		Ⲧ̿	ⲐⲂⲀ,	
Ⲝ̄	ⲤⲈ,				

EGYPTIAN

[See Coptic]

HIEROGLYPHICS		DEMOTIC	
A	𓄿 (glyphs)	A	(glyphs)
I, E	(glyphs)	I	(glyphs)
U, OU	(glyphs)	OU	(glyphs)
B	(glyphs)	B	(glyphs)
F, V	(glyphs)	F, V	(glyphs)
K	(glyphs)	K	(glyphs)
R, L	(glyphs)	R	(glyphs)
M	(glyphs)	L	(glyphs)
N	(glyphs)	M	(glyphs)
P	(glyphs)	N	(glyphs)
S	(glyphs)	P	(glyphs)
Sh	(glyphs)	S	(glyphs)
T	(glyphs)	SH	(glyphs)
T (x)	(glyphs)	T	(glyphs)
KH	(glyphs)	x, ϭ	(glyphs)
H	(glyphs)	KH, ⳓ	(glyphs)
		H	(glyphs)

The little that we know of the language of ancient Egypt has come to us through the medium of the Coptic language, which consists of three dialects: true Coptic, also known as Memphitic, because it was indigenous to Lower Egypt, of which Memphis was the capital; the Sahidic, meaning upper or superior, was spoken in Upper Egypt, of which Thebes was the capital, and so it is also called Thebaïc; a third was spoken in the Delta province, the inhabitants of which were described by Thucydides as "wild beasts, leading a wandering life, and living by robbery and plunder, whom the Persians, Greeks, and Romans could hardly subdue". This will account in a measure for the Bashmouric, as it is called, being ruder than the Sahidic. It is not possible to state which dialect is the oldest.

It cannot be stated positively at what date hieroglyphs were first used in Egypt, though inscriptions dating back to almost 4000 B.C. have been found. There are from 60 to 70 alphabetic signs, i.e., representing simple vowel and consonantal sounds, and nearly 200 more that are syllabic, representing a combination of simple sounds. Quite probably all were syllabic at one time, and those which subsequently became pure consonants had at first a complementary vowel. The enchorial or demotic system of writing was derived from the hieratic, which was a conventionalization of the hieroglyphs, the characters retaining only some of the original characteristics. This system was instituted about 600 B.C. and, like the original alphabets, has a limited number of purely alphabetical characters, as well as many syllabic ones. Those shown in the table may all be considered purely alphabetic.

The hieroglyphic characters are sometimes read from right to left, at others from left to right, or from the top downward. It would not be practicable always to observe strictly an order of sequence in placing the characters. It is interesting to note that the characters are always read from the side toward which the animals look. The query (?) before characters in the table indicates that the sound is not fully determined, while an asterisk denotes that the character is found on late inscriptions.

HIEROGLYPHIC NUMERALS

1	I.	21	∩∩I·
2	II.	22	∩∩II·
3	III.	30	∩∩∩·
4	IIII.	40	∩∩∩∩·
5	IIIII. ᵻᵼᵻ	50	∩∩∩∩∩·
6	III III.	60	∩∩∩·
7	IIII III. ᵻᵼᵻᵻ.	70	∩∩∩∩·
8	IIII IIII. IIII IIII·	80	∩∩∩∩·
9	IIIII IIII. ᵻᵼᵻᵼᵻ.	90	∩∩∩∩∩·
10	∩. ⊓.	100	𝟿.
11	∩I·	200	𝟿𝟿·
12	∩II·	300	𝟿𝟿𝟿·
13	∩III·	400	𝟿𝟿𝟿𝟿·
16	∩IIIIII·	500	𝟿𝟿𝟿𝟿𝟿·
20	∩∩·	1000	⚓. ⚓

DEMOTIC NUMERALS

1	ɣ ⅃ I	60	⤬ =
2	५	70	ʔ
3	Ƅ Ƅ Ⱳ	80	⤳
4	ᐁ V ⱴ ƞ Ⱳ	90	Ƕ
5	ʔ ʔ	100	)
6	⪜ ⪜ ⟆	200	⤳
7	ʒ ⱴ	300	ⱳ
8	ⱜ ⱜ	400	ⱳ
9	ⱜ ʔ I	500	→ʒ
10	ʌ	600	→ⱳ
20	ʃ	700	→ʔ
30	ʒ	800	→ⱳ
40	ⱜ	900	→ʒ
50	ʒ	·1000	Ḷ

ETHIOPIC

a	ŭ	ĭ	ā	ĕ	e	ō
ሀ ha	ሁ hŭ	ሂ hĭ	ሃ hā	ሄ hē	ህ he	ሆ hō
ለ la	ሉ lŭ	ሊ lĭ	ላ lā	ሌ lē	ል le	ሎ lō
ሐ ḥa	ሑ ḥŭ	ሒ ḥĭ	ሓ ḥā	ሔ ḥē	ሕ ḥe	ሖ ḥō
መ ma	ሙ mŭ	ሚ mĭ	ማ mā	ሜ mē	ም me	ሞ mō
ሠ ša	ሡ šŭ	ሢ šĭ	ሣ šā	ሤ šē	ሥ še	ሦ šō
ረ ra	ሩ rŭ	ሪ rĭ	ራ rā	ሬ rē	ር re	ሮ rō
ሰ sa	ሱ sŭ	ሲ sĭ	ሳ sā	ሴ sē	ስ se	ሶ sō
ቀ qa	ቁ qŭ	ቂ qĭ	ቃ qā	ቄ qē	ቅ qe	ቆ qō
በ ba	ቡ bŭ	ቢ bĭ	ባ bā	ቤ bē	ብ be	ቦ bō
ተ ta	ቱ tŭ	ቲ tĭ	ታ tā	ቴ tē	ት te	ቶ tō
ኀ ḫa	ኁ ḫŭ	ኂ ḫĭ	ኃ ḫā	ኄ ḫē	ኅ ḫe	ኆ ḫō
ነ na	ኑ nŭ	ኒ nĭ	ና nā	ኔ nē	ን ne	ኖ nō
አ ʼa	ኡ ʼŭ	ኢ ʼĭ	ኣ ʼā	ኤ ʼē	እ ʼe	ኦ ʼō
ከ ka	ኩ kŭ	ኪ kĭ	ካ kā	ኬ kē	ክ ke	ኮ kō
ወ wa	ዉ wŭ	ዊ wĭ	ዋ wā	ዌ wē	ው we	ዎ wō
ዐ ʽa	ዑ ʽŭ	ዒ ʽĭ	ዓ ʽā	ዔ ʽē	ዕ ʽe	ዖ ʽō
ዘ za	ዙ zŭ	ዚ zĭ	ዛ zā	ዜ zē	ዝ ze	ዞ zō
የ ja	ዩ jŭ	ዪ jĭ	ያ jā	ዬ jē	ይ je	ዮ jō
ደ da	ዱ dŭ	ዲ dĭ	ዳ dā	ዴ dē	ድ de	ዶ dō
ገ ga	ጉ gŭ	ጊ gĭ	ጋ gā	ጌ gē	ግ ge	ጎ gō
ጠ ṭa	ጡ ṭŭ	ጢ ṭĭ	ጣ ṭā	ጤ ṭē	ጥ ṭe	ጦ ṭō
ጰ pa	ጱ pŭ	ጲ pĭ	ጳ pā	ጴ pē	ጵ pe	ጶ pō
ጸ ṣa	ጹ ṣŭ	ጺ ṣĭ	ጻ ṣā	ጼ ṣē	ጽ ṣe	ጾ ṣō
ፀ ḍa	ፁ ḍŭ	ፂ ḍĭ	ፃ ḍā	ፄ ḍē	ፅ ḍe	ፆ ḍō
ፈ fa	ፉ fŭ	ፊ fĭ	ፋ fā	ፌ fē	ፍ fe	ፎ fō
ፐ pa	ፑ pŭ	ፒ pĭ	ፓ pā	ፔ pē	ፕ pe	ፖ pō

Ligatures

ኰ kuā	ኵ kuĭ	ኴ kuĕ	ኳ kuā	ኴ kuē
ጐ guā	ጕ guĭ	ጔ guĕ	ጓ guā	ጔ guē
ቈ quā	ቍ quĭ	ቌ quĕ	ቋ quā	ቌ quē
ኈ ḫua	ኍ ḫuĭ	ኌ ḫuĕ	ኋ ḫuā	ኌ ḫuē

Name	Transcription	ă	ū	ī	ā	ē	ĕ	ō	Hebrew equivalent
Hōi	h								ה
Lawe	l								ל
Ḥaut	ḥ								ח, German *ch*
Māi	m								מ
Shaut	sh								שׁ
Re'es	r								ר
Sāt	s								ס
Ḳaf	ḳ								ק, emphatic
Bēt	b								ב
Tawe	t		For names, transcrip-						ת
Ḥarm	h		tions and Hebrew equiv-						Emphatic
Nahās	n		alents of Ethiopic vow-						נ
'alf	'a		els, correlate table on						א, slight impulse
Kāf	k		preceding page herein.						כ
Wāwī	w								ו
'ain	'a								ע
Zai	z								ז, soft
Yaman	y								י, German *j*
Dant	d								ד
Gaml	g								ג
Tait	ṭ								ט, emphatic
Pait	p								פ, *ts*, emphatic
Sadāi	ṣ								צ, emphatic
Dappā	ḍ								Emphatic
Af	f								
Pa	p								*pˢ*, slightly assibilated

The transliteration in the table gives continental sounds.

Punctuation

: Hyphen ፤ Comma ፤ Semicolon ፡፡ Period

NOTES

Reduplication of consonants.—In the Ethiopian text the doubled-consonant sound is written with but a single consonant, and, unlike the Hebrew, the character has no sign to show that it is doubled.

Reading of ĕ.—It is very similar to *shewa* in Hebrew and, if accented or before a reduplication, is always vocal, *wĕ'ĕtū, wălĕbbū;* otherwise it is always vocal in the first syllable, *lĕb;* at the end of a word it is usually silent, while in the middle of a word it is silent after a vocal ĕ, *wĕstā,* and vocal after a silent ĕ, *tĕktĕlī.*

Syllabication.—Every syllable must have either a vowel or a diphthong; an open syllable ends in a vowel, while a closed one ends in a consonant. A syllable must begin with a consonant, and no syllable can begin with two consonants. A syllable may end in either a vowel or a consonant, and the final syllable of a word may end in two consonants.

Tone.—Authoritative data are nonexistent. Philologists assume that the tone depends on the number of syllables or the nature of the vowels in a root word. It rests usually upon one of the last three syllables, but may be still farther back, *bărăkătă.* Most often the tone avoids the final syllable, being on the antepenult, *'antĕmmūsă;* but most often on the penult, *kămă.* There are elaborate rules governing the tone, but also very many exceptions to the rules.

Adjective.— The adjective must agree with the participle in gender and number, and with the noun in case.

The ancestors of the people who now occupy Abyssinia came originally from Yemen, in Arabia; they were a pure Semitic people who spoke a pure Semitic language. They were converted to Christianity in the third century, and the Ethiopian language, as it is now called, remained the spoken tongue until the seventeenth century, when it was displaced by the Amhāric, Tigre, and Tigriña. It has, however, retained its position as the language of the church and of literature, the majority of which, aside from some inscriptions, is in manuscript form, the most important being versions of the Old and New Testaments. This language is more closely related to the Arabic than to any other Semitic language, but is also very similar to the Assyrian and Hebrew.

The language is known as Geez by the natives and belongs to the southern group of the Semitic languages. It is very much like the dead Arabic dialect known as Himjaritic.

The alphabet is itself a development of the Himjaritic and formerly read from right to left, like all Semitic languages, and consisted of consonants only. Since the introduction of Christianity it has been changed to read from left to right and, with the addition of hooks and circles on certain consonants, has obtained vowel sounds.

The alphabet or syllabary—for each sign represents a syllable—consists of 26 signs written from left to right, though formerly from right to left.

The vowels are $\check{a}$, $\check{e}$, $\bar{a}$, $\bar{\imath}$, $\bar{u}$, $\bar{e}$ $\bar{o}$, the fundamental one being $\check{a}$. Short $\check{e}$ is like the vocal shewa in Hebrew, the shortest and most colorless of the vowel sounds, being pronounced like the first e in believe; it represents the short sound of all vowels but a. Before ee the $\bar{a}$ changes to $\check{a}$, except when the first e belongs to a semi-vowel.

The $\check{u}$ is changed to $\bar{a}$ before gutturals with $\check{e}$ in all verbs with final gutturals, in some causative reflexive forms of verbs whose initial consonant is a guttural, and in most substantives with a guttural. The $\check{e}$ changes to $\bar{e}$ before some gutturals.

The $\check{a}$ changes to $\check{e}$ before a guttural with $\check{e}$ in nouns as well as verbs; before a final guttural with $\check{a}$; and in the imperfect of all intensive forms. The $\check{e}$ changes to $\check{a}$ before a primal or medial guttural with $\check{a}$, except in the personal prefixes of the reflexive passive. The $\bar{u}$ and $\bar{\imath}$ change to $\bar{e}$ when followed by ee. When two consecutive syllables in the same word contain $\bar{\imath}$, the $\bar{\imath}$ in the first syllable is changed to $\check{e}$.

Crasis

When the final vowel of a word is followed by an initial vowel of a suffix, $\check{e}$ becomes $\check{a}$; $\check{e}$ becomes $\check{a}$, and $\bar{\imath}$ becomes $\bar{e}$.

Gender

These are masculine, feminine, and common, the first having no distinctive ending, while the feminine usually ends in $\check{a}$.

Number

These are singular and plural, the strong plural being formed by means of the termination $\bar{a}$ (m), and $\bar{a}$ (f); the broken plural is formed by vocal modification and by prefixes and suffixes.

Case

There are four cases: Nominative, vocative, genitive and accusative; the nominative and genitive have no distinctive ending, while the vocative is the same as the nominative, and the accusative is formed by vocal change, where it differs from the nominative.

Conjunctions

These are independent and dependent; among the latter some are suffixed, others affixed.

Definiteness

There is no article, but words which are the sole representative of their class and proper names are definite. Definiteness is expressed by the context, by an appended pronoun, or by periphrasis. A common noun is usually indefinite.

Verbs

The root of the strong verb has three radicals: *kătălă*, he killed.

Each stem has three forms to express (1) the simple act, *kătălă*, he killed; (2) intensity, *kăttălă*, he certainly killed, and (3) a frequentative act, *kătălă*, he used to kill.

Each of these forms may further express (1) a causative, (2) a reflexive, passive, or reflexive-passive, and (3) causative-reflexive ideas.

EWE

a	*a* in want	ny	*ni* in companion
b	*b*	ŋ	*ng* in sing
d	*d* in harder	o	Closed, as French beau
ɖ	*d*, trilled	ɔ	*o* in cost
ε	*e* in French père	p	*p*, rare
e	*e* in get	r	*r*, liquid
f	*f*	s	Voiceless, as in hiss
ƒ	*f*, bilabial	t	*t*, French
g	*g* in gold	ts	*ts* in hits
γ	Voiced velar fricative	u	*oo* in cool, also *u* in put
gb	*kp*, but softer	v	*v*
h	*h*, voiced	w	*w* in wall; semivowel
i	*ie* in believe	ⱳ	*w* in German schwimmen
k	French *c* before *a, ọ, u*	x	*ch* in loch
kp	*p* labial	y	*y*
l	*l*	ỹ	*y*, nasalized
m	*m*	z	*z* in azure
n	*n*		

The Ewe are a numerous people occupying an extensive district east of the Volta River in the Gold Coast colony and in Togoland. An important feature of the language is the complicated system of tones, a thorough knowledge of which is absolutely essential if one would acquire any real knowledge of the language. Many of the words whose roots have entirely different origin have tones of equal value, which adds to the difficulty of acquiring the language.

NOTES

As a rule the vowels are short, and lengthening is indicated by doubling the vowel. Whether long or short, all can be nasalized, the tilde being used to indicate nasalization. If a nasalized vowel is preceded by a nasalized consonant (*m, n*), the tilde is generally omitted.

There are five tone marks: ´ indicates a high tone, ' a middle tone, ` a low tone, ^ a falling tone, and ˇ a rising tone. The first three are known as "simple tones"; the last two, "compound tones". A syllable without a tone mark takes the tone of the nearest preceding syllable which has a tone mark. An initial syllable without a tone mark is low, as well as those following which have no tone mark.

With few exceptions, every vowel can combine with every other one as a diphthong, and the combination of a semivowel with a vowel is also in the nature of a diphthong: *wa, ya*, etc.

Numerals

ɖeká, ɖé	one	bláavè vɔ́ ɖekɛ	twenty-one
eve	two	bláavè vɔ́ve	twenty-two
etɔ̌	three	bláàtɔ̌	thirty
ene	four	bláanè	forty
atɔ̌	five	blaatɔ̌	fifty
adé, andé	six	bláàde	sixty
adré, ádre, andré	seven	bláàdre, blâdré	seventy
enyi	eight	blàanyí, blânyí	eighty
enyiɖe, asiékè, asi-dèkɛ	nine	bláàsiékè, blâsiékè	ninety
		alafá ɖeká, blaawó	hundred
ewó	ten	alafá ɖeká kplé ɖeká	hundred and one
wúiɖekɛ	eleven		
wúìeve	twelve	alafá eve	two hundred
bláavè	twenty	akpé	thousand

The ordinals are formed by suffixing *-leá* or *-liá* to the cardinals: *eveleá, eveliá* the second; *etɔleá, etɔliá*, the third, etc. The first is *gbátɔ*.

Days

These days of the week, as well as the custom of using them as proper names, are not native to the Ewe, but have become thoroughly naturalized.

Kwásiɖa	Sunday	Yámòɖa	Thursday
Dzóɖa	Monday	Fiɖa	Friday
Bráɖa	Tuesday	Mémleɖa	Saturday
Kúɖa	Wednesday		

An indigenous reckoning, which is connected either with farming or the days of the markets, is as follows:

agbletóègbe, the day on which work begins.
agbleveegbe, the second workday.
domegbe, tɔgbe, middle or third day.
viegbè, a lucky day, for weddings, etc.
vietoègbe, an unlucky day, on which spirits are driven out.
agbleamiegbe, feast of the god Amiyi (Tagbamiyi).
afénɔegãgbè, rest day.

A division of time into months and years is unknown.

FULANI-ADAMAWA DIALECT

a	*a* in father	n	*n* in nest; voiced
ạ	*u* in but	ng	*ng* in bang
b	*b* in boy; voiced	o	*o* in no
ḅ	*b* final in superb	ọ	Between *oo* in good and *o* in hot
ch	*ch* in church; voiceless	p	*p* in post; voiceless
d	*d* in dust	r	*r*, rolled, in Scotch heard [3]
ḍ	*d* in wind	ṛ	Voiceless, trilled, palatal
e	*è* in père	s	*s* in some; voiceless
ẹ	*e* in pen	ṣ	Voiceless, palatal
f	*f* in fan; voiceless	t	*t* in tale; voiceless
g	*g* in gun; voiced	u	*oo* in food
h	*h* in hand; voiceless [1]	w	*w* in wide; voiced [4]
i	*ee* in meet	ẉ	Almost *hu* in *huile;* voiceless palatal
j	*j* in judge; voiced	y	*y* in you; voiced
k	*k* in kit; voiceless	ẏ	Almost *h* in huge; voiceless
ḳ	Voiced [2]	z	*s* in rose; voiced
l	*l* in lid; voiced		
m	*m* in mad; voiced		

[1] Must be sounded if final.
[2] This sound is not found in English, and in the Fulani occurs in only a few words borrowed from the Arabic.
[3] If initial, care must be taken that the breath does not escape before the rolling commences.
[4] In a final syllable, before *o* and *u*, it is often only a strong rounded glide between the two vowels, almost as that heard in "do it".

This language, used by the people of Nigeria, has been claimed both as a Hamitic and a Bantu language, with a preponderance of evidence in favor of the former. There is evidence that it might be the parent Hamitic language, bearing the same relationship to the other Hamitic languages—and perhaps Bantu—that the Indo-Germanic language does to the languages of Europe and western Asia.

Diphthongs.—*ai* as *gh* in high; *au* as *ou* in house; *ei* as *ay* in say; *eu*, the first element, having less force than the second, there is a tendency to leave it out, with the result that the *u* is lowered and becomes *o*; *oi* as *oy* in boy; *ou* as the *o* in guano; *ui*, which has a sound similar to that of the native *ya*.

Nasalization.—*b, d, g, j,* and *y* are frequently nasalized. Where this is distinct, as at the beginning of words, and sometimes in the middle of a word, the *n* or *m* will be used, while the tilde serves where nasalization is weak.

Accent.—This is predominantly a stress accent and, generally speaking, depends on the long vowels.

Numerals

Cardinals	Ordinals	
hounde, *pl.* kouḍe; sifri		cipher
goṭẹl, go'o, go	go'owo, go'ojo aranowo	one
diḍi	diḍaḅo, diḍawo	two
tati	tataḅo	three
nai	nayaḅo	four
jowi	jowaḅo	five
jowego	jowego'ojo	six
jowediḍi	jowedidaḅo	seven
jowetati	jowetataḅo	eight
jowenai	jowenayaḅo	nine

Numerals—Continued

Cardinals	Ordinals	
sappo	sappojo	ten
sappo ẹ go'o	sappo ẹ go'owo	eleven
sappo ẹ ḍiḍi	sappo ẹ ḍiḍabo	twelve
nogas	nojasjɔ	twenty
nogas ẹ go'o	nogas ẹ go'owo	twenty-one
temerre	temerrejo	hundred
ujinere	ujinerejo	thousand

Months

The Mohammedan calendar is used as follows: Hāram, Sendanda Hāram, Hāram mirawo, Banjāru arandu, Banjāru tumbindu, Banjāru raginindu, Sumatendu wauḅe, Wairordu sumaye, Sumayr or Ramabana, Julandu, Siutorandu, Laihaji.

Days

Alad	Sunday	Alhamīsa	Thursday
Altine	Monday	Jum'are	Friday
Salāsa	Tuesday	‑Asawe	Saturday
Alarba	Wednesday		

Seasons

dabunda	cold season	chedu	hot season
seto,	{tornado season,	yamde	harvest
ndungu	{rainy season		

GÃ

a	vowel	*a* in hat	
ã	nasal vowel	*a* in and	
b	labial	*b*	
d	lingual	*d*	
e	vowel	*e* in prey	
ẹ	vowel	*e* in let	
ẽ	nasal vowel	*e* in mend	
f	labial	*f*	
ſ	labial	(¹)	
g	palatal	*g*, weak, always hard	
h	palatal	*h*, weak, always hard	
i	vowel	*i* in sit	
ĩ	nasal vowel	*i* in sing	
k	labial	*k*, weak	
l	lingual	*l*, strong	
m	labial	*m*, strong	

n	lingual	*n*, strong	
ṅ	palatal	*ng* in sing ²	
o	vowel	*o* in go	
ọ	vowel	*o* in cot	
õ	nasal vowel	*o* in gone	
p	labial	*p*, weak	
r	lingual	*r*	
s	lingual	*s*, weak	
š	lingual	*sh* in bush; weak	
t	lingual	*t*, weak	
u	vowel	*u* in put	
ŭ	nasal vowel	*oo* in moon	
v	labial	*v*, strong	
w	labial	*w*, strong	
w̌	labial	(³)	
y	lingual	*y*, strong ⁴	
z	lingual	*z*	

---

¹ ſ is an *s* with which an English *w* has been united: while the tongue produces the sound of *š* the lips go to the position required for sounding *w*. This is also true in the case of *dſ, tſ* which equals *dšw, tšw; ŭ* equals *wy*.

² It is sometimes doubled at the end of a syllable to indicate a long sound, as *faṅṅ*, plain; *soṅṅ*, far off. Alone or before a consonant, *n, ṅ,* and *m* have all the properties of vowels, though defective in sound.

³ The compound letters *wy* occurring before *ẹ, ẹ,* and *ṅ* are expressed by *w̌*.

⁴ In proper names *y* is used, instead of *ſ*, which is not in the alphabet.

NOTES

Except in foreign names, consonants do not occur at the end of a syllable or word.

All the vowels are short, being lengthened only by way of inflection. Very short vowels are marked by a breve. In order to avoid too many diacritical marks, the long vowels are not always marked as such, which is also true of the nasal vowels.

Diphthongs.—*ai, ọi, oi, ui, ẹi,* and *ei* are closely combined, while *ao, ọo, ou, eo, ẹo,* and *iu* approach two syllables.

tš, dš, tſ, dſ, ny, kp, gb, ṅw, gbl, ṅmi, nt, nd, nk, ṅš, mp, mb, nw, and *nſ* are frequently combined.

Capitalization.—This is employed as follows: In case of the first word of a book, chapter, letter, note, or in any piece of writing, but not necessarily the first word of every line of poetry; the first word after a full stop, an exclamation, or an interrogation mark, provided the clauses before and after these signs are independent of each other; the first word of a direct quotation; proper names of persons, places, streets, rivers, ships, mountains, and days; nouns and principal words in titles of books and the heads of their principal divisions, and names of divine persons.

Accents, intonations, and stress.—The acute accent denotes a high tone of the vowels, but if a second acute follows, without the interposition of a grave accent or point, the second denotes a lowering into a middle tone. The grave accent denotes a low tone, but if it is followed by the definite article *lẹ*, the low tone is raised. Long vowels, diphthongs, and syllables ending in *m* or *ṅ* may have two tones and the accent for the second tone is placed after the long vowel or semivowel, or on the second vowel of the diphthong. The stress (word accent) is either connected with the first high tone of a word or with the first or second of several low-toned syllables, or else it lies on the low-toned syllable immediately before a high-toned one, in which case the grave accent is placed on account of stress, though not necessarily on account of the tone. Sometimes there is a secondary stress.

Articles.—The article *the* is translated by the word *le̞* placed after the noun. The indefinite article *a* or *an* is never used, but is included in the noun.

Numerals

eko, ékòmé, kome	one	kpawo		seven	
enyǫ	two	kpānyǫ		eight	
ete	three	nẹhū		nine	
édfẹ	four	nyoṅma		ten	
énumǫ	five	ɔhá		hundred	
ekpạ	six	akpé		thousand	

The numerals up to and including 19 are formed by prefixing *nyoṅma ke̞* to the first nine numerals, after which the following procedure occurs:

nyoṅmai-ényǫ	twenty	nyoṅmai-kpawo	seventy
nyoṅmai-étẽ	thirty	nyoṅmai-kpānyǫ	eighty
nyoṅmai-édfẹ	forty	nyoṅmai-nẹhū	ninety
nyoṅmai-énumǫ	fifty	ohá ke̞ ékòmé	hundred
nyoṅmai-ékpā	sixty		and one

Ordinal numbers are unknown, being replaced usually by verbal phrases.

Days of week

Hǫgbā	Sunday	Sō	Thursday
Dšu	Monday	Sohā	Friday
Dšufǫ	Tuesday	Hǭ	Saturday
Šo	Wednesday		

Seasons [1]

fẽibe	winter	latšābe	summer
gbò	autumn		

[1] I have been unable to find a word for spring.—EDITOR.

HAUSA

Character and name	Isolated	Final	Median	Initial	Transliteration	Sound
اَلِف Alif	ا	ل	. . .	. . .		
بَآء Ba	ب	ب	ﺒ	ﺑ	p,b	*b*
تَآء Ta	ت	ت	ﺘ	ﺗ	t	*t*
ثَآء Cha	ث	ث	ﺜ	ﺛ	ch	*ch* in church
جِيم Jim	ج	ج	ﺠ	ﺟ	j	*j*
حَآء Hha	ح	ح	ﺤ	ﺣ	h	*h*, strong
خَآء Kha	خ	خ	ﺨ	ﺧ	kh	*kh*, or hard as in Scotch loch
دَال Dal	د	د	. . .	. . .	d	*d*
ذَال Zal	ذ	ذ	. . .	. . .	ẓ	*z*
رَآء Ra	ر	ر	. . .	. . .	r	*r*
زَآء Za	ز	ز	. . .	. . .	z	*z*, same as Zal
سِين Sîn	س	س	ﺴ	ﺳ	s	*s*
شِين Shîn	ش	ش	ﺸ	ﺷ	sh	*sh*
صَاد Sâd	ص	ص	ﺼ	ﺻ	ṣ	*s*, same as Sin
ضَاد Dâd	ض	ض	ﻀ	ﺿ	ḷ	*l*
طَآء Ta	ط	ط	ﻂ	ﻃ	ts	*ts*, sometimes *t*
ظَآء Tsa	ظ	ظ	ﻆ	ﻇ	ṭs	*ts*, seldom used
عَين Ain	ع	ع	ﻌ	ﻋ		
غَين Ghain	غ	غ	ﻐ	ﻏ	g	*g* always hard
بَآء Fa	ب	ب	ﻔ	ﻓ	f	*f* (dot sometimes above the letter)
قَاب Kâf	ف	ف	ﻔ	ﻓ	ḳ	*k* (two dots are occasionally used)

HAUSA—Continued

Character and name	Isolated	Final	Median	Initial	Transliteration	Sound
گَاب Kâf	ك	ك	ک	ک	k	k (same as preceding character)
لَام Lâm	ل	ل	ل	ل	l	l
مِيم Mîm	م	م	ﻤ	ﻣ	m	m
نُون Nun	ن	ن	ﻨ	ﻧ	n	n
هَآﺀ Ha	ه	ﻪ	ﻬ	ﻫ	ḥ	h, same as Kha
وَاو Wâ	و	ﻮ	. . .	. . .	w	w as in win
يَآﺀ Ya	ى	ى	ﻴ	ﻳ	y	y in yard; always a consonant

The vowel sounds are ◄ Fatha sounded *a* or *e;* Kesre ◄ *i* or *e;* ◄ *u* or *o.* The diphthongs are ى◄ *ai,* as *i* in ice, and و◄ *au,* as *ow* in cow.

• This is probably the most widely spoken language on the African Continent. The Hausas occupy about a million square miles, and, of the approximately 25,000,000 inhabitants, some 15,000,000 speak this language. This is about 1 percent of the earth's inhabitants. In attempts to classify the modern languages of Africa they are usually placed in three groups: the Semitic, Hamitic, and Bantu, Hausa belonging probably to the second group. The Hausa people, however, are not a Hamitic race, and the language must have been brought in by immigrants from the north.

The literature is written in Ajami, a species of Arabic, which has certain distinctive peculiarities that render it very difficult to read by one familiar with the Arabic script only. Great quantities of native manuscripts exist, very few of which have been printed. Some religious poems and several volumes of native tales have been printed both in transliteration and in the original Ajami. There are also prints of a great many folk stories as well as schoolbooks.

All vowels are pronounced as in Italian, all consonants as in English; every letter is sounded, and no redundant letters are introduced.

This language possesses a regular gender formation, the rule being that words denoting the feminine end in *a,* and likewise all words ending in *a* are feminine, though in several instances the feminine is formed by prefixing a *t, nágari* (good), feminine *tágari.*

The genitive is denoted by *n* or *na;* thus "the door of the house" would be *kofan gidda* or *kofa na gidda.*

The noun is formed by prefixing *ma* or *mai* to a verb, substantive or adjective; thus *gudu* (to run) becomes *maigudu* (a fugitive); *gidda* (house), *maigidda* (owner of a house), and *girima* (great), *maigirima* (one who is great).

Cardinal numbers

daia	one	bokkoi	seven
biu	two	tokkos	eight
uku	three	tara	nine
fudu, hudu	four	goma	ten
biar, bial, biaṭ	five	goma sha daia	eleven
shidda	six	goma sha biu	twelve

Cardinal numbers—Continued

goma sha uku	thirteen	hamsin	fifty
ashirin, ishirin	twenty	settin	sixty
ashirin da daia	twenty-one	sebbaïn	seventy
ashirin da biu	twenty-two	tamanin	eighty
tallatin	thirty	tissaïn	ninety
tallatin da daia	thirty-one	dari, zango, mia	hundred
arbaïn	forty		

Ordinal numbers

These are formed by prefixing *na*, masculine, or *ta*, feminine, to the cardinal numbers, except in case of the first three, as follows:

Masculine	Feminine	
nafari	tafari	first
nabiu	tabiu	second
naüku	taüku	third

After tenth, the cardinal numbers are usually employed.

The adverbial numerals "once", "twice", etc., are formed by prefixing *so* to the cardinal numbers: *sodaia*, once; *sobiu*, twice, etc.

The distributive numerals are formed by repeating the cardinals: *ya bada biu biu*, "he gave two to each of the men."

Fractional numbers.—Half is expressed by *shashi* or *rabi* (from *raba* to divide); *sulusi*, third; *rubaï*, a quarter; *sudusi*, sixth; *subuï*, seventh, and *sumuni*, eighth. The word *zaka*, a tenth, is applied to the tithe given as alms.

Punctuation.—The only sign of punctuation is ∴, which corresponds to a full stop or semicolon. No mark of interrogation is used.

Days of the week

rana lahadi	Sunday	rana alhamis	Thursday
rana latini	Monday	rana aljimua	Friday
rana talata	Tuesday	rana assubat	Saturday
rana laraba	Wednesday		

Time

saa, lokachi	hour	wata	month
rana, kwana	day	shekkara	year

KĀNURĪ

a	*a* in cart	n	*n*
a̦	Almost *i* in fir	ṅ	*ng* in king
b	*b* in be	o	*o* in bone
d	*d* in do	o̦	*a* in water
e	*e* in pen	p	*p* in pain
e̦	*i* in girl	r	*r*, liquid
e̱	*a* in hat	s	*s* in see
f	*f* in father	š	*sh* in show
g	*g* in go	t	*t* in tool
h	*th* in hothouse	u	*oo* in coo; often *w* [1]
i	*i* in pin; often *y* [1]	w	*w* in wood
k	*k* in key	y	*y* in yes
l	*l*, liquid	z	*z* in zeal
m	*m*		

[1] When, according to grammatical rules, *i* would be followed by *y*, or *u* by *w*, the *y* and *u* are omitted.

The Kānurī, or Beriberi, is the leading tribe of the large province of Gazir in Bornu, which is situated in the central Sudan south and west of Lake Chad. The history of these people, though quite fragmentary, goes back to the ninth century; they gained the height of their glory some four centuries ago. The language has expressions and phrases very similar to those of European languages and is also connected with Indo-European and Semitic languages by a large number of roots. Besides these, many parent words came from the Arabic on the introduction of Mohammedanism.

NOTES

The diphthongs are *ai, ei, oi,* and *ui; au* and *ou.* Like the Greek, when there is an accent it falls on the second vowel: *meīrō.*

There are three compound consonants: *dz, ts,* and *tš.* The first of these is rare and is generally replaced by *z,* having the sound of *j* in join. The *ts* and *tš* are quite common, the first having the sound of *z* in the German word *Zeit,* while the latter is like *ch* in church.

Long vowels are usually marked(¯), and all others are short. The tilde (˜) indicates nasalization.

Cardinal numbers

tilō, tulō	one	wusge̦n	eighteen
ndi	two	le̦gārri	nineteen
yāsge̦	three	pindi	twenty
dēge̦	four	pindin tatā tilon	twenty-one
ūgu, ūge	five	pindin tatā ndin	twenty-two
ārasge̦	six	piāsge̦	thirty
tulur	seven	pidēge̦	forty
wusge̦	eight	pīūgu	fifty
le̦gar	nine	pīrasge̦	sixty
mēgu, mēogu	ten	pītūlur	seventy
laga̦rē	eleven	pītusgu	eighty
nduri	twelve	pīle̦gār	ninety
yāsge̦n	thirteen	miă, yoru	hundred
dēri	fourteen	miăn tatā tilon	hundred and one
ūri, wūri	fifteen		
arasge̦n	sixteen	dubu	thousand
tulurri	seventeen		

Ordinal numbers

tilō, burgōbē	first	kẹnārasgẹ	sixth
deregēbē, ńgāfōbē	second	kẹntulur	seventh
kẹnyāsgẹ	third	kẹnwusgẹ	eighth
kẹndēge	fourth	kẹnlẹgār, kẹllẹgar	ninth
kẹnwūgu, kẹnūgu	fifth	kẹnmēgu, kẹmmēogu	tenth

After tenth the cardinals are used.

KONGO

a	*a* in father	o	*o* in boy, *a* in call, or *ou* in bought
b	*b* in boy		
d	*d* in do	p	*p* in park
e	*a* in fate	s	*s* in so
f	*f* in for	t	*t* in town
g	*g* in get	u	*oo* in fool
i	*i* in machine	v	*v* in very
j	*z* in azure	w	*w* in we
k	*k* in kind	x	*sh* in she
l	*l* in let	y	*y* in yet
m	*m* in man	z	*z* in zeal
n	*n* in no		

The Kongo language, a branch of the Bantu family, is one of those spoken by the natives of the basin of the Congo (Kongo) River. In the interior the language is uninfluenced by any of the other great language families, although along the coast the Portuguese language has left its impress. Students of African languages have been impressed by the richness, flexibility, subtilty of idea, and nicety of expression of this language. These points indicate a very high-class parent stem, as in the case of the languages in which were written the early Vedic hymns chanted in ceremonials at the time when Moses was growing up in Pharaoh's court.

NOTES

There are two diphthongs: *au* with the sound of *ow* in cow, and *ai* as *i* in pine. The sound of *ti* is as *chee* in cheese, although some dialects give it the same sound as the word tea in English.

The nasals *m* and *n* are the only true consonants that can be combined with other consonants, and *m* only before labials, *b*, *f*, *p*, and *v*, and before *w; mw* is actually a combination of *m+o* or *m+u* before another vowel, the only position in which it will be found; *n* is used before *d*, *g*, *j*, *k*, *l*, *s*, *t*, *v*, *w*, *x*, *y*, and *z*.

Combinations of nasals with other consonants at the beginning of a word appear difficult at first sight, but are not so in reality except in the case of *ny* or *nw*. There is no vowel sound before nasal combinations, and the pronunciation can be illustrated by an unusual division of some English words: *nke* is pronounced as in donkey when divided do-*nkey*, *nso* as in co-*nso*-nant. The following list will be helpful:

mb has the sound of *mb* in co-*mb*ine
mf has the sound of *mf* in co-*mf*ort
mp has the sound of *mp* in ca-*mp*ing
nd has the sound of *nd* in la-*nd*ing
ng has the sound of *ng* in fi-*ng*er
nj has the sound of *nj* in A-*nj*ou

nk has the sound of *nk* in do-*nk*ey
nl has the sound of *nl* in thi-*nl*y
ns has the sound of *ns* in co-*ns*onant
nt has the sound of *nt* in hu-*nt*ing
nx has the sound of *nsh* in moo-*nsh*ine
nz has the sound of *ns* in clea-*ns*ing

The articles are *a*, *e*, and *o*. Those nouns whose archaic prefixes contained the vowel *i* (*in*, *zin*, *mi*, *ki*, *di*, and *fi*) take *e*, those which contained *u* (*mu*, *ku*, *lu*, *tu*, *u*, or *bu*) as also the prefixes *ma* and *va*, take *o*, but *a* or *b* requires the article *a* in the plural.

Euphony is an absolute essential of the language: Every syllable must end with a vowel, and no two consonants can ever come together, except the nasals prefixed to other consonants, as *kanda*, *nkanda*, or the semivowels *w* and *y*, which may also follow a consonant, as *bwa*, *nygala*. The vowel *a*, when standing at the end of a word is elided before any other *a* that may follow it: *Mbwa a mfumu* becomes *Mbw'a mfumu;* when there *a*'s come together the first two are dropped: *Nsadisanga a abunji* becomes *Nsadisang' abunji ame*. The *a* is also dropped before *e* and *o*, and *e* standing alone as a particle elides before an initial *e*.

Of course these elisions do not occur when the vowels referred to belong to different sentences. When *a* comes before *i* they combine and *e* results, as *mengi* for *ma-ingi*.

Year

The Kongo year is short and indefinite, being rather a season.

Numerals

moxi	one	kumi ye sambanu	sixteen
ole	two	kumi ye nsambwadi	seventeen
tatu	three	kumi ye nana	eighteen
ya	four	kumi ye vwa	nineteen
tanu	five	makumole	twenty
sambanu	six	makumatatu	thirty
nsambwadi	seven	makumaya	forty
nana	eight	makumatanu	fifty
vwa	nine	makumasambanu	sixty
kumi	ten	lusambwadi	seventy
kumi ye moxi	eleven	lunana	eighty
kumi ye zole	twelve	luvwa	ninety
kumi ye tatu	thirteen	nkama	hundred
kumi ye ya	fourteen	ezunda	thousand
kumi ye tanu	fifteen		

Week

The week consists of but four days:

nkandu	nkenge
konzo	nsona *or* mpangala

The names for the foreign week days are as follows:

lumingu	Sunday	kietanu	Thursday
kiezole	Monday	kiesambanu	Friday
kietatu	Tuesday	kiansabula	Saturday
kieya	Wednesday		

Time

ola	hour	ngond	month
lumbu	day	mvu	year
lumingo	week		

LU-GANDA

a	*a* in father	ng'	*ng* in singer
b	*b*, soft	ny	(²)
c	*ch* in church	o	*o* in bold
d	*d*	p	*p*, soft
e	*e* in were	r	*r*, more cerebral than English [1]
f	*fw* or *vw* sound		
g	*g*	s	*s*
i	*i* in ravine	t	*t*
j	*j*, light	u	*u* in rule
k	*k*	v	Bilabial, see *f*
l	*l*, more cerebral than English [1]	w	*w*, soft [3]
		y	*y*, soft [3]
m	*m*, nasal	z	*z*
n	*n*, nasal	ai	*ai* in aisle

[1] The *l* and *r* sounds are considered as one sound by the natives, *l* being used after *a*, *o*, and *u*, and *r* after *e* and *i*.

[2] This sound is considered only one of a series of palatalized consonants.

[3] The *w* replaces the *u* before a vowel other than *u*, and *y* is found only in combination with *n*, making the syllable *nyi* in about a dozen words; in all other cases *y* before *i* is dropped.

Ganda is an original Bantu language uncontaminated by the clicks of the Bushmen or the awkward Sudan *kp* and *gb* sounds. The Ganda have attained a higher degree of civilization than any of their neighbors in Uganda. Their language is one of the purest and most archaic types of Bantu. Aside from the publications of the missionary stations, which include a native monthly paper, there is very little native literature, but the thought of the people is preserved orally in proverbs, the principal parts of which are quoted in every conversation by way of enforcing a point or clinching an argument.

NOTES

The language is called Lu-Ganda, the people are Ba-Ganda, and an individual is a Mu-Ganda; finally the name of the country is Bu-Ganda. Thus the root Ganda may mean a language, a people, or a country, according to the prefix used; also the prefix distinguishes between a single individual, Mu-Ganda, and a number of such persons, Ba-Ganda. In other words, the plural is formed by a change in the prefix.

Every syllable ends in a vowel or is itself a vowel, and under certain conditions these may be prolonged for emphasis, but the English custom of stressing syllables for emphasis is unknown.

Each sentence is uttered in a monotone, and jerky, impassioned utterance would be quite unintelligible.

A question is asked by raising the tone on the principal syllable necessary to give point to the question.

A vowel is usually short between two simple consonants, which is also true of the final vowel in a word.

The following emphatic consonants are pronounced with explosive force: '*k*, '*g*, '*t*, '*d*, '*p*, '*b*, '*s*, '*z*, '*f*, '*v*, '*j*, '*m*, and '*n*.

Numerals

omuko	one	mukaga	six
babiri	two	musamvu	seven
basatu	three	muana	eight
bana	four	mwenda	nine
batano	five	'kumi	ten

Numerals—Continued

'kumi na -mu	eleven	nkaga	sixty
'kumi na -biri	twelve	nsamvu	seventy
(amakumi) abiri	twenty	kinana	eighty
(amakumi) abiri mu	twenty-one	kyenda	ninety
-mu		kikumi	hundred
(amakumi) asatu	thirty	kikumi mu -mu	hundred and
(amakumi) ana	forty		one
(amakumi) atano	fifty	lukumi	thousand

Ordinal numbers are formed by prefixing the genitive particle *a* (of) to the cardinals, though the first five have a special form:

-oluberyeberye	first	-okuna	fourth
-okubiri	second	-okutano	fifth
-okusatu	third		

MAGHREB

Name	Isolated	Final	Median	Initial	Transliteration and tone value
Alif	ا	ـا			—, ’, Spiritus lenis, smooth breathing, without *h* sound
Bē	ب	ـب	ـبـ	بـ	*b*
Tē	ت	ـت	ـتـ	تـ	*t*, sometimes *ts*
Sē	ث	ـث	ـثـ	ثـ	*t*, English hard *th;* also *t* and *s*
Jīm	ج	ـج	ـجـ	جـ	*ġ;* generally French *j;* isolated, *g*
Hē	ح	ـح	ـحـ	حـ	*h*, strongly aspirated
Khē	خ	ـخ	ـخـ	خـ	*h; ch* in German ach
Dāl	د	ـد			*d*
Zāl	ذ	ـذ			*d;* soft English *th*
Rē	ر	ـر			*r*, lingual
Zē	ز	ـز			*z;* like *s* in saw
Ṡīn	س	ـس	ـسـ	سـ	*s;* like *sz* in the German grüszen
Shīn	ش	ـش	ـشـ	شـ	*sh;* as in shell
Ṣād	ص	ـص	ـصـ	صـ	*ṣ;* emphatic, sharp *s*
Dād	ض	ـض	ـضـ	ضـ	*ḍ;* emphatic, soft English *th* or emphatic *d*
Tā	ط	ـط	ـطـ	طـ	*ṭ*
Zā	ظ	ـظ	ـظـ	ظـ	*ẓ*
Ain	ع	ـع	ـعـ	عـ	‘; equivalent to English *h*
Ghain	غ	ـغ	ـغـ	غـ	*ġ*
Fē	ڢ	ـڢ	ـڢـ	ڢـ	*f*
Qāf	ڧ	ـڧ	ـڧـ	ڧـ	*q;* guttural
Kēf	ك	ـك	ـكـ	كـ	*k*
Lām	ل	ـل	ـلـ	لـ	*l*
Mīm	م	ـم	ـمـ	مـ	*m*
Nūn	ن	ـن	ـنـ	نـ	*n*
Hē	ه	ـه	ـهـ	هـ	*h*
Wāw	و	ـو			*w;* as in English
Yē	ى	ـى	ـيـ	يـ	*y;* as in yet

Maghreb is the name applied to the language-in use at present in northern Africa, from the Egyptian border to Morocco, which may also include the Maltese, as well as the old Spanish Arabic.   The various dialects show a strong Berber influence as well as some trace of the Romance languages, the Maltese being highly impregnated with Italian.

As shown in the table of the Moroccan alphabet, the Maghreb has developed from the Arabic alphabet a unique type face of its own, which is particularly noticeable in the *fē*, *qāf*, and *ye*.   Eastward from Tunis it is displaced by the Arabic alphabet, while in Malta the Latin characters are employed.

The Arabic numerals are in general use.

MASAI

a	*a* in father	n	*n* in no [2]
ä	*a* in way	o	*o* in more
ai	*ai* in fair	ö	*a* in day
b	*b* [1]	oi	*oy* in hoyden
c	*c*	p	*p* [1]
d	*d*	r	*r*
e	*e* in end; *a* in ale	rr	A marked burr sound
g	*g* [1]	s	*s*
h	*h*	ss	*ss*, sharp as in hissing
i	*e* in he	t	*t*
j	*j* in join	u	*oo* in moo
k	*k* [1]	ü	*e* in we
l	*l*	w	*w*
m	*m* in mutter [2]	y	*y*

[1] *b* and *p* and *g* and *k* are very similar in pronunciation and are practically interchangeable.
[2] As initials, followed by a consonant, these letters have sounds similar to those in the most of the African languages.

The Masai are the most important of the Nilo-Hamitic group, but, unlike some other members of that group, they are still nomadic.

NOTES

Spelling is practically phonetic and the accents are either short or long. Without using accents, any clear idea of pronunciation of many of the words is impossible.

In bisyllabic words the accent is usually on the first syllable; in words of three syllables, on the second, but occasionally on the last; in polysyllabic words, usually on the second, though accentuation is very irregular.

The numeral adjectives always follow the substantive and usually end the sentence. Counting is usually done on the fingers, the closed fist representing 5 and the two closed fists 10. For higher numbers the fists are moved up and down until the desired number is indicated.

Numerals

nabu	one	tomon oimiet	fifteen
ari, are	two	tomon oiille	sixteen
üni	three	tomon nabishäna	seventeen
ungwun	four	tomon oissiet	eighteen
miet	five	tomon nawdo	nineteen
elle	six	tigitum	twenty
nabishäna	seven	tigitum obbo	twenty-one
issiet	eight	ossom	thirty
nawdu, endörroi	nine	ossom obbo	thirty-one
tomon	ten	arrtam	forty
tomon obbo	eleven	orrnom	fifty
tomon are	twelve	ïp [1]	sixty
tomon ogüni	thirteen	ïpari	two sixties
tomon ungwun	fourteen		

The following are the only ordinals:

tangasino	first	korom	last

[1] This takes the place of our 100, since the Masai count in sixties.

MASHONA (CHISWINA)

a	*a* in father [1]	m	*m*
b	*b*	n	([2])
ch	*ch*	o	*o*
d	*d*	p	*p*
e	*a* in day	r	*r*
f	*f*	s	*s*
g	*g* in goat	t	*t*
h	Aspirated when joined with *l* or *w*	u	*oo* in boot
i	*ee* in feet	v	*v*
j	*j*	w	*w*
k	*k*	y	*y*
l	*l*	z	*z*

[1] Equals the diphthong *ai* when followed by *y*.
[2] When followed by *g*, hard *ng* as in anger, but sometimes soft *ng* as in singing.

The Mashona are a pastoral people living in southern Rhodesia.
The accent is always on the antepenult except when followed by *zwe*, when it falls on the last syllable.

Numerals

potsi	one	gumi ne nomwe	seventeen
piri	two	gumi ne tsere	eighteen
tatu	three	gumi ne pfumbamwe	nineteen
china	four	makumi mayiri (two tens)	twenty
shanu	five		
tanhatu	six	makumi matatu	thirty
chinomwe	seven	makumi mana	forty
rusere	eight	makumi mashanu	fifty
pfemba, pfumbamwe	nine	makumi matanhatu	sixty
gumi	ten	makumi manonwe	seventy
gumi ne imwe	eleven	makumi masere	eighty
gumi ne biri	twelve	makumi mapfumbamwe	ninety
gumi ne nhatu	thirteen	zana	hundred
gumi ne ina	fourteen	gumi re mazana	thousand
gumi ne shanu	fifteen	hakuna chiro	zero
gumi ne nanhatu	sixteen		

Ordinals

we chipotsi, kutanga	first	rwe chinomwe	seventh
ye chipiri	second	ye rusere·	eighth
we chitatu	third	re pfumbamwe, re chipfumbamwe	ninth
re china	fourth		
we chshanu	fifth	we gumi	tenth
che chitanhatu	sixth		

Days

Musi we Sondo	Sunday	Musi we china	Thursday
Musi we chipotsi	Monday	Musi we chishanu	Friday
Musi we musumbunuko	Tuesday	Musi we chitanhatu	Saturday
Musi we chipiri		Musi we mugobera	
Musi we chitatu	Wednesday		

Seasons

mwakani, ka kupumha	spring	matsutso	autumn
mayenza (wet)	summer	chirimo (dry)	winter

Time

musi, zuwa	day	mwedzi (moon)	month
viki	week	gore	year

MŌLE

a	*a* in fat	l	*l* [1]	
ā	*a* in father	m	*m*	
ã	Nasal	n	*n*	
b	*b*	ṅ	*ng* in sing	
c	*ch* in church	o	*o* in tobacco	
d	*d*	o̲	*o* in or	
e	*a* in fate	õ	Nasal	
e̲	*e* in there	p	*p*	
ē	Nasal	p'	Explosive *p*	
f	*f*	r	*r;* interchangeable with *l*	
g	*g* in get, always	s	*s*	
g'	Explosive *g*	t	*t*	
h	*h*	t'	Explosive *t*	
i	*i* in fill	u	French *ou*	
ī	*e* in English	v	*v*	
ḭ	Nasal	w	*w*	
j	French *j* in jour, always	y	*y*	
k	*k*	z	*z*	

[1] Before *o* and *iu*, as *l* in French lui.

The Mōle, the language of the Moshi, is quite the most important of the languages of the Northern Territories of the Gold Coast Colony. Moshiland is situated between 11° and 13° north latitude and 2° to 5° west longitude and is a part of the French African colonial empire. The language is one of a group which comprises Dagomba, Dagarti, Mamprussi, Wala, and Fura-Fura, all of which are so similar to Mōle that anyone conversant with the latter will be able to learn to speak them all with but little difficulty. The language belongs to that class which is agglutinative.

NOTES

Vowels may be nasal, open, or close, and some of the consonants also have two different sounds.

Elision, apocope, syncope, and assimilation are marked features of the language. The first is the suppression of a final vowel (*a, ie, e*) or syllable before a letter in the word following: *zams' mam Mōle* for *zamse mam Mōle*. Apocope is the elision of the final letter or syllable in a word: Where the final letter is a consonant, *ko'* for *kom;* where it is a vowel, *f'* for *fo, bamm'* for *bamma;* where the elision is a syllable, *fu' pim* for *fugu-pim.* Syncope is the elision of a letter or letters from the middle of a word; *yal'ma* for *yalema.* Assimilation, *nyetta* for *nyetda, yetta* for *yedda, yelda,* etc.

Many letters are interchangeable: *k* with *p, b* with *p, t* with *d, d* with *r* and *l, s* with *r, d* with *n, r* with *l,* etc.

When a consonant is doubled in a word the syllables are pronounced distinctly: *dilla* is *dil-la.*

Cardinal numbers

ayimle, yimle, ye'	one	ayopoi, yopo'	seven
ayību, yību	two	anī, nī	eight
atābo, tābo	three	awai, wai	nine
anāse, nāse	four	pīga (*one ten*)	ten
annu, nnu	five	pi la yimle (*or* ye)	eleven
ayōbe, yōbe	six	pi la yību (*or* yi)	twelve

Cardinal numbers—Continued

pishi (pishi yi) (*two tens*)	twenty	pishyopoi	seventy
		pishnI	eighty
pish la yimle (*or* ye)	twenty-one	pishwai	ninety
pishta	thirty	kwobaga	hundred
pishnase	forty	kwobaga la yimle	hundred and one
pishnnu	fifty		
pishyŏbe	sixty	tusuli	thousand

Ordinal numbers

The ordinals are expressed by adding *sǫba*, plural *ramma*, to the cardinals, the words for first being irregular:

pipisǫba, pipiramma taursǫba, tauramma }	first	pishisǫba, pishiramma	twentieth
yibsǫba, yibramma	second	kwobagsǫba, kwobagramma	hundredth
tabsǫba, tabramma	third		
nasesǫba, naseramma	fourth	tusulsǫba, tusulramma	thousandth
nnusǫba, nnuramma	fifth		
pigsǫba, pigramma	tenth		

Time

nyingtogo	day	yumde	year
chiugu	month		

NAMAQUAH-HOTTENTOT

a	*a* in father	n	*n* in no
b	*b* in band	o	*o* in bone
c	Click [1]	p	*p* in put
d	*d* in day	q	Click [1]
e	*a* in may	r	*r* in run
f	*f* in far	s	*s* in sun
g	*g* in go	t	*t* in too
gh	Guttural, as in the Dutch	u	*oo* in moon
kh	Deep guttural	v	Click [1]
h	*h* in hand	w	*w* in we
i	*i* in pin	x	Click [1]
k	*k* in keep	y	*y* in ye
l	*l* in love	z	*ts* in hats
m	*m* in man		

[1] There are no exact corresponding English sounds for the clicks. The hard and soft sounds of *c* may also be expressed by *k* and *s*.

The history of the Hottentots is intimately connected with the rise and progress of Cape Colony. Their language, owing to its harsh and peculiar sounds, has until quite recently been much neglected by philologists. However, it will prove of interest to anyone wishing to preserve some record of the language spoken by a people so peculiar and once so numerous; it may also assist in tracing their descent. Of the four original Hottentot dialects spoken by the tribes who dwelt near the present Cape Colony, one, considered the purest, has practically disappeared. The remaining three still are in use: the Corunna being spoken by those inhabiting the banks of the Orange River and some stragglers in the interior; the Namaquah dialect, which is spoken by the tribes of Little and Great Namaquahland; and the Bushman, which is spoken by many roving bands in the desert and mountainous districts of the interior.

NOTES

The English sounds of *f*, *l*, and *y* are not found in the Namaquah dialect, but are included for use in foreign words: *Faro, Ghalilea,* and *Yohanip.*

A circumflex indicates a strong nasal accent: *mâ, tê, xnâ.*

The vowels, which are either long or short, always preserve the same radical sound, differing only in the enunciation; as a rule they are long in accented syllables, and all vowels are invariably sounded.

There are the following diphthongs:

ae as *a* in bay	oi as *y* in boy
ai as *y* in my	ou as *ow* in sow
au as *ou* in thou	ui as *ui* in tuin (Dutch)
ei as *ey* in they	

The *y* is used as a consonant only at the beginning of a sentence or word, its vowel sound being represented by the diphthongs *ai* and *ei*.

The *w* is a semivowel and at the beginning of syllables and words has the sound of the English *w*.

The clicks are the most peculiar feature of the language. They occur frequently and form an important part in the roots of many words. In pronouncing them, without any supplementary vowel or consonantal sound, the breath, instead of being ejected as is usual with other articulations, is checked, or drawn inward, and as soon as it is combined with any other sound it is forcibly emitted. A dental click, *c* is sounded by pressing the tip of the tongue against the front upper teeth and then suddenly and forcibly withdrawing it; *v*, a palatal, is sounded by pressing the tip of the tongue with as flat a surface as possible against the end of the palate at the gums, and removing it as for *c; q*, a cerebral, is sounded by curling up the tip of the tongue against the roof of the palate, and withdrawing it as for the first two; *x* is either a lateral or a cerebral, and may be sounded either by placing the tongue against the side teeth or covering the entire palate with it and producing the sound as far back in the palate as possible. The clicks can be combined with any of the vowels as well as *h, k, g, kh*, and *n* and occur only at the beginning of syllables.

Numerals

cqui	one	qnani	six
ckam	two	hû	seven
qnona	three	xkhaisi	eight
haka	four	goisi	nine
kore	five	disi	ten

There are no facilities for a very extensive numeration; in fact, counting is a very difficult process above a hundred. Combinations of tens, and also of tens and units, are expressed as follows.

disi ckui ckha	eleven	ckam disi disi	two hundred
disi ckam ckha	twelve	qnona disi disi	three hundred
ckam disi	two tens	kore disi disi, qnona disi, haka ckha	five hundred and thirty-four
cham disi ckui	twenty-one		
ckam disi ckam ckha	twenty-two		
qnona disi	three tens	kei vgou disi	thousand
haka disi	four tens	ckam kei vgou disi-kha	two thousand
disi disi	hundred		
disi disi ckui ckha	hundred and one	qnona kei vgou di-sika	three thousand
disi disi ckam disi ckui ckha	hundred and twenty-one		

Only one numeral, *vkuro*, first, is used to express an ordinal adjective, the rest being formed by adding the particle *xêi* to the cardinal numbers:

ckam xêi	second	qnani xêi	sixth
qnona xêi	third	disi xêi	tenth
haka xêi	fourth	ckam disi xêi	twentieth
kore xêi	fifth	ckam disi ckui ckha xêi	twenty-first

NYIKA

a	*a* in father, always	m	m^4	
b	*b;* sometimes used for *p*	n	*n*	
ch	*ch* in church[1]	o	*oo* in foot	
d	*d*[2]	p	*p*	
dz	([3])	r	*r*	
e	*a* in gate, always	s	*s*	
f	Almost *v*	t	*t,* soft; also *th* in thy and thigh	
g	*g* in go, always			
h	*h,* aspirate	u	*u* in full	
i	*ee* in feel, always	v	*v*	
j	*dj*	w	*w*	
k	*k* in king	y	*y*	
l	*l*	z	*z*	

[1] The *ch* is sometimes used for *j,* and is sometimes replaced by *k.*
[2] Sometimes used for *ch, j, t,* or *th* in thy.
[3] A compound sound which must be represented by both letters.
[4] Often used as a prefix to words.

This is the language of some nine tribes of eastern Bantu people who in the sixteenth century moved down the eastern coast of Africa from the steppes on the left bank of the Tana River.

NOTES

The accent is invariably on the penultimate syllable.
Two vowels do not form a diphthong: *Rabai* is pronounced *Ra-ba-i.*

Cardinal numbers

umenga	one	fungahe	seven
mi iri, vairi	two	nane	eight
tahu	three	wai	nine
minane, nane, naɲe	four	kumi	ten
adzano	five	mirongo	twenty
tandahu	six	gana	hundred

Ordinal numbers

The first ordinal is *ansa* or *kwansa,* and the others are formed by prefixing the word *cha: cha iri,* second; *cha tahu,* third, etc.

Time

saa	hour	muesi	month

SHUNA

a	*a* in father	p	*p* in pat
b	*b* in bone [1]	r	*r* in rat
d	*d* in dale [2]	s	*s* in sat [4]
e	*e* in fête	t	*t* in tat
f	*f* in fat; often with *p: pf*	u	*oo* in tool
g	*g* in get; always hard	v	*v* in vat; often with *b: by*
h	*h*, aspirate [3]	w	*w* in was
i	*i* in machine	y	*y* in yet
j	*j* in join	z	*z* in zone; often with *d*
k	*k* in kill		and *w: dz, zw*
l	*l* in lot	tj	*ch* in church
m	*m* in may	zh	*z* in azure [5]
n	*n* in nail	mñw	
ñ	*ng* in king	mñr	(6)
o	*o* in no		

[1] In some dialects *b* becomes *w* or disappears: *bona, wona, ona* (see).
[2] Some dialects have a nasal *d*, like *dn*, combined in a single sound and spoken through the nose.
[3] The *h* is guttural only after *b, m*, and *r*.
[4] The *s* has a peculiar hissing sound (*sw*) in some words.
[5] Among the various tribes, the *zh* sound oscillates between *z, zh*, and *j*.
[6] These are forms of *mu* into which an *ñ* has been inserted: *mñwana* for *mu-ana* (child) and *mñrandu* for *mu-andu* (wind).

The Shuna is still practically an unknown tongue used by the Mashuna people in the Zambesi. It is divided into a number of dialects.

NOTES

It is often impossible to distinguish between *p* and *b*, *t* and *d*, *k* and *g*, *f* and *v*, *pf* and *bv*, *s* and *z*.

With the exception of *h*, each letter has but one sound, and every letter in a word is sounded. The stress always occurs on the penultimate syllable, and the article is absent.

Numerals

mñwe	one	tanatu	six
biri	two	nomñwe	seven
natu	three	tsere	eight
na	four	fumbamñwe	nine
shanu	five	gumi	ten

SWAHILI

a	*a* in father	m	*m* in man
b	*b* in bare	n	*n* in no
ch	*ch* in cherry [1]	o	*o* in boy; very near *au*
d	*d* in do [2]	p	*p* in paint
e	*ai* in chair	r	*r* in raise
f	*f* in fine	s	*s* in sun [5]
g	*g* in gate; always hard	t	*t* in ten [6]
h	*h* in hat	u	*oo* in fool
i	*ee* in feet	v	*v* in very
j	*j* in joy [3]	w	*w* in win
k	*k* in kalsomine	y	*y* in yonder [7]
l	*l* in long [4]	z	*z* in zone [8]

[1] Italian *c* before *i* or *e*.
[2] This letter occurs very frequently in the Mombas dialect where *j* is used in that of Zanzibar.
[3] Sometimes more like *dy*, or *di* in cordial.
[4] *l* and *r* are generally treated as the same letter.
[5] Never like *z*; *s* and *sh* are interchangeable.
[6] This letter frequently occurs in the Mombas dialect where *ch* is used in Zanzibar.
[7] This letter frequently occurs in the Lamoo dialect where *j* is used in Zanzibar.
[8] This letter frequently occurs in the Lamoo dialect where *v* is used in Zanzibar.

The Swahili is the language used by the mixed race of Arabs and Negroes on the East Coast of Africa, especially in the country extending from Lamoo southward to Cape Delgado, and belongs to the middle branch of the Bantu language family. Like all Bantu tongues, it is very rich in verbs and poor in adjectives and prepositions. There is no difficulty in writing Swahili in roman characters, there being no sound in this language that is not duplicated in some European language.

NOTES

The following sounds are obtained from the Arabic and are not found in purely African sounds:

gh is a guttural similar to the Dutch *g*, and may be produced by pronouncing *g* with the mouth as nearly wide open as possible.

kh is a very rough form of the German *ch*, and may be replaced by an *h*, but never by *k*.

th has four different sounds: the first like *th* in think, the second like that in they; the third and fourth are thicker varieties of the second; the first sound is indicated by italics.

The following compound consonantal sounds are also noted:

ch is a very common sound used instead of a *t*, and sometimes *ki*, in other languages.

kw has the sound of *qu* in queen.

m frequently equals *mu*, and is then pronounced with a half-suppressed *u* sound. Where *m* occurs before any consonant, except *b* or *w*, it has the nasal semivowel sound approximating *um*. Before *a* or *e*, the *m* becomes *mw*, and before *o* it frequently loses the *u* altogether, becoming a simple *m*.

n frequently has a nasal semivowel sound, and always when just preceding *ch*, *f*, *h*, *m*, *n*, or *s*.

ny has the sound of the Spanish *ñ*, or the English *ni* in minion.

ng' has a sound very similar to that of the *ng* ending of many English words. If one could divide longing *lo-nging* without changing the pronunciation, we would have the proper sound, which is never final, as all Swahili syllables must end in a vowel. The sound is also sometimes indicated by *gn*.

sh has the English sound and is usually treated as identical with s.

The *w* can be placed after any other consonants, simple or compound, except *f* and *v*; *y* can follow *f*, *n*, and *v*; *n* can precede *d*, *g*, *j*, *y*, and *z*; *m* can be placed before *b* and, perhaps, *ch* and *v*, in which cases it represents an adjectival prefix.

Used thus, *n* before *b* becomes *m;* before *l* or *r* it changes these to *d;* before *w* it becomes *m*, and the *w* becomes *b*, making *mb* instead of *nw*. Before *k*, *p*, and *t*, the *n* is dropped, and they become *k'*, *p'*, and *t';* before *ch*, *f*, *h*, *m*, *n*, and *s* it is merely dropped.

Cardinal numbers

mosi	one	kumi na tano	fifteen
pili	two	kumi na sita	sixteen
tatu	three	kumi na saba	seventeen
'nne	four	kumi na nane	eighteen
tano	five	kumi na kenda	nineteen
sita	six	makumi mawili	twenty
saba	seven	makumi matatu	thirty
nane	eight	makumi manne	forty
kenda	nine	makumi matano	fifty
kumi	ten	makumi sita	sixty
kumi na moja	eleven	makumi saba	seventy
kumi na mbili	twelve	makumi manane	eighty
kumi na tatu	thirteen	makumi kenda	ninety
kumi na 'nne	fourteen	mia (Arabic)	hundred

The ordinal numbers are expressed by the use of the variable particle -*a: mtu wa tatu*, the third man; *nyumba ya 'nne*, the fourth house; *kiti cha tano*, the fifth chair.

Months

There are two years in use in Zanzibar, the most common being the Arabic of 12 lunar months, each of which begins at the first sight of the new moon.

Arabic	Swahili	
Ramathan	Ramathani	First month
Shaowal	Mfunguo a mosi	Second month
Th'il ka'ada	Mfunguo a pili	Third month
Th'il hajja	Mfunguo a tatu	Fourth month
Moharram	Mfunguo a 'nne	Fifth month
Safr	Mfunguo a tano	Sixth month
Rabia al aowal	Mfunguo a sita	Seventh month
Rabia al akhr	Mfunguo a saba	Eighth month
Jemad al aowal	Mfunguo a nane	Ninth month
Jemad al akhr	Mfunguo a kenda	Tenth month
Rajab	Rajabu	Eleventh month
Shaaban	Shaabani	Twelfth month

The other year is the Nautical and Agricultural Year, which is roughly a solar year of 365 days. It is reckoned from *Siku a mwaka*, which occurs about the end of August. The last day of the year is known as *Kigunzi*, and the days are reckoned by decades instead of weeks.

Days

Juma a pili	Sunday	Alhamisi	Thursday
Juma a tatu	Monday	Juma	Friday
Juma a 'nne	Tuesday	Juma a mosi	Saturday
Juma a tano	Wednesday		

Seasons

demani	spring	masika	autumn
musimi	summer	kipupwe	winter

Time

saa	hour	mwezi	month
siku	day	mwaka	year
jumaa	week		

TEBELE

a	*a* in father	ñg	*ng* in finger
b	*b* in bone	o	*o* in no
c	Click [1]	p	*p* in pat
d	*d* in dale	q	Click [3]
e	*e* in fête	s	*s*' in sat
f	*f* in fat	t	*t* in tat
g	*g* in get; always hard	u	*oo* in fool
h	*h*, aspirate or guttural	v	*v* in vat
i	*i* in machine	w	*w* in was
j	*j* in join	x	Click [4]
k	*k* in kill	y	*y* in yet
l	*l* in lot [2]	z	*z* in zone
m	*m* in may	hl	*l*, aspirated
n	*n* in nail	dhl	*d* before aspirated *l*
ñ	*ng* in king	tj	*ch* in church

[1] Produced by pressing end of tongue against root of front upper teeth and forcibly withdrawing it.
[2] Also used in place of *r*-sound of other languages.
[3] Produced by pressing end of tongue against arch of palate and forcibly withdrawing it.
[4] Like sound of driver when urging on his horses; produced by pressing end of tongue against side teeth and suddenly withdrawing it.

The Tebele language, a variation of the Zulu, is one of those used by the Zambesi people.

NOTES

Each letter has one sound only, and every letter in a word is sounded. The stress is always on the penultimate syllable.

It is often impossible to distinguish between the sounds of *p* and *b*, *t* and *d*, *k* and *g*, *f* and *v*, *pf* and *bv*, *s* and *z*.

The article is represented by one of the vowels *a*, *i*, or *u* placed immediately before the prefix.

Numerals

nye	one	tantatu	six
bili	two	nonye	seven
tatu	three	. . . ficamnembili	eight
ne	four	ficamnomunye	nine
hlanu	five	tjumi	ten

Months (moons)

ugwindhla (autumn)	isilimo (spring)
Uhlolanja	Incwabakazi
Umpimbito	Umpandula
Umabasa	Umfumfu
ubusiga (winter)	ihlobo (summer)
Inkwekwezi	Ulwezi
Uhlañula	Indidazani [1]
Intulikazi	Uzibandhela
	Umpalazana

[1] Introduced every third year to rectify the calendar.

TEMNE

ā	*a* in father	ō̠	*a* in all
a	*a* in Mann (German)	o̠	*o* in not
ḁ	Almost *u* in but [1]	p	*p*
b	*b*	r	*r*
d	*d*	s	*s*
ē	*a* in way	š	*sh* in show
ē̠	*ea* in near	t	*t*
e	*a* in fat	tš	*ch* in church
f	*f*	ū	*u* in rule
g	*g* in gold, always	u	*oo* in foot
gb	Compound sound	w	*w* in we
h	*h* in horse	y	*y* in year
ī	*ee* in see		
i	*i* in sin		DIPHTHONGS
k	*k*		
l	*l*	ai	*i* in mine
m	*m*	au	*ou* in house
n	*n*	ei	*ey* in eye
ṅ	*ng* in singing	oi	*oi* in coin, nearly
ō	*o* in home	o̠i	*oi* in join
o	*o* in von (German)	ui	*ui* in congruity
		ḁi	([1])

---

[1] This is the only imperfect vowel sound in the language and is a short, deep, pectoral sound often used instead of the vowel sound *a*; when used as a diphthong ḁi both letters are given their proper sound, though each is contracted so as to form a short diphthong.

The Temnes live on the south side of the Sierra Leone River in about 11° to 13° west longitude and from 8° to 9° north latitude.

NOTES

Every vowel not marked long is short.

If two adjacent vowels are to be sounded separately, the dieresis is used: *a-rëï*, a day.

If *r* follows *t*, it is pronounced rather faint, as in true.

No word can begin with a vowel, except some prefixes and interjections.

Accentuation is usually placed on the first syllable of a word, whether it be a noun, adjective, verb, or any other part of speech. However, there are some dissyllables, especially adverbs and a few verbs with nouns and adjectives derived from them, that have the stress on the last syllable. There are also a number of compound words that have two accents, the second being generally the stronger and is marked with a double accent.

Euphony is so essential in the Temne language that changes must be made both in the vowels and consonants under certain conditions. These are made partly by elision of vowels or consonants, or an assimilation of both; partly by contraction, or by a change or an assimilation of consonants or vowels, or by the insertion of a consonant.

Cardinal numbers

There are distinct forms for the first five, the tenth, twentieth, hundredth, and thousandth numbers, but all others are compositions of these, and all take prefixes.

p'in	one	tr'ọfatr	ten
pạ-rạn	two	tr'ọfatr p'in [2]	eleven
pạ-sas	three	kạ-gbā (a score)	twenty
p'ānle, p'ānle	four	kạ-gbā p'in [3]	twenty-one
tr'amat	five	k'eme k'in	hundred
tr'amat ro k'in [1]	six		

Ordinal numbers

The word *trọtrọkọ* is used to express first and *trandọ* for second. All other ordinals are expressed by the numeral adjectives in connection with the relative pronoun and verb, *beka*, "amount to make", which is placed before the numeral.

Months

Pọlpọl, Wolwol	January	Aṅ'of a-bana	July
Baṅkele	February	Pāya	August
Gbaproṅ	March	Gbọtkọ	September
Bafu	April	Mufạr, Šakōma	October
Yantomi, Yaṅtomi	May	Torọkanẹ	November
Wōfe	June	Tranantia	December

These months do not agree exactly with our months, as Tranantia comprises most of December and a part of January; Pọlpọl most of January and a part of February, etc. They are lunar months and, after a lapse of years, an additional month is added to keep the seasons of the year as nearly as practicable in accord with the months. There are two seasons, the wet and the dry.

Week

alahadi	Sunday	alamusa	Thursday
tẹnẹ	Monday	arēma	Friday
talata	Tuesday	šimiti	Saturday
araba	Wednesday		

These names are derived from the Arabic and mean simply "first", "second", etc. The Temnes have no word for week, but use the Fula *yontore* with the prefix *a*, as well as the Arabic *sobūa* (hebdomas).

[1] Literally 5+1=6.
[2] Literally 10+1=11.
[3] Literally 20+1=21.

UMBUNDU

a	*a* in father	m	*m*
b	*mb*, almost	n	*n*
d	*nd*, almost	ñ	*ng* in singer
c	*chi* sound in change	o	*o* in note
e	*e* in fête	p	*p*
f	*f*	r	*r*
g	*ng*, almost	s	*s*
h	*h*	t	*t*
i	*ee* in feet	u	*oo* in boot
j	*nj*, almost [1]	v	*v*, soft
k	*k*	w	*w*, soft; semivowel
l	*l*, soft; or soft *r*	y	*y*; semivowel

[1] *nj* equals the *ndi* sound before a closed vowel.

This is the language of the people of Bailundu and Bihe, as well as other countries in west Central Africa.

NOTES

There are no diphthongs, but several combinations of vowel sounds produce a modified sound resembling a diphthong: *ae* and *ai* with a sound closely resembling the English *i* in shine, *au* like the broad Scotch *o*, and *oi* like the Portuguese *oi*.

All vowels may be nasalized, but *a*, *e*, and *i* most often take the nasal sound, which, however, does not affect the sound of the vowel.

Every syllable begins with either a consonant or a consonant and a semivowel, and ends with a vowel.

There is no article, the only trace being the *o* of the substantives.

Words are usually polysyllabic, and the stress is usually on the penultimate syllable unless that contains a semivowel, when it goes on the antepenult. If, however, the word ends in a combination of vowels, *ai*, *ae*, etc., the stress will be on the last syllable.

Numerals

mosi	one	akwiavali	twenty
vali	two	akwiatatu	thirty
tatu	three	akwiakwana	forty
kwana	four	akwiatanu	fifty
tanu	five	akwiepandu	sixty
epandu	six	akwiepanduvali	seventy
epanduvali	seven	akwiecinana	eighty
ecinana	eight	akwiecia	ninety
ecia	nine	ocita	hundred
ekwi	ten	ovita vivali	two hundred
ekwi la tanu	fifteen	ohukæ	thousand

Combinations of numerals are easy: *akwiavali la tanu* (two tens and five, 25); *ovita vivali lekwi* (hundreds three and tens five and five, 355).

The cardinal numbers do not differ from the ordinals in form; usage determines which is meant: *eteke litatu*, the third day, but *olonke vitatu*, three days, the cardinal taking the plural.

WOLOF

a	*a* in man; also in ark	k̄	Strongly guttural *k*
b	*b*	l	*l*
d	*d*	m	*m*
e	*e* in men; also *ea* in great	n	*n*
f	*f*	o	*o* in not; also in hope
g	*g*, always hard	p	*p*
h	*h*	r	*r*
h̄	Strongly guttural *h*	s	*s*
i	*i* in fit; also *ie* in field[1]	t	*t*
ī	*y* in yet	u	*u* in but
j	*j*	ū	*w* in wood
k	*k*	v	*v*

[1] *ai* is used for the English sound of *i* in idle, and *iu* for that of *u* in duty.

Wolof is one of the old languages of the tribes inhabiting Gambia in British West Africa.

Each letter in a word is sounded and each of the consonants represents but one sound, not the same letter for both hard and soft sounds.

Numerals

ben	one	fūk a nīar	twelve
nī-ar	two	fun-ūē-er	twenty
nī-at	three	nīar-fūk	
nī-an-it	four	nīar fūk a ben	twenty-one
jiū-rum	five	nīat fūk	thirty
jiū-rum-rum-ben	six	nī-an-et fūk	forty
jiū-rum-nī-ar	seven	jiū-rum fūk	fifty
jiū-rum-nī-at	eight	tē-mēr	hundred
jiū-rum-nī-an-it	nine	nī-ar tē-mēr	two hundred
fūk	ten	jiū-ni	thousand
fūk a ben	eleven		

Seasons

tshō-run	spring	nor	autumn
lō-li	summer		

Time

fun, bis	day	hut	year
ūē-er	month		

YAO

a	*a* in father; both long and short	n	*n;* before *ch* is *nj*
b	*b*[1]	ng'	*ng* in singing
ch	As in church [2]	ny	*ni* in minion
d	*d*	o	*aw* in saw; never *o* in only
e	*e* in get, almost	p	*p;* never aspirate [1]
f	([3])	s	*s* in sun; some dialects *s* in rise
g	*g* in gate; always hard [4]	t	*t* [9]
i	*ee* in sheep	u	*oo* in moon; never *u* in cube
j	*dy* sound [5]	w	([9]) ([10])
k	*k*, never aspirate [6]	ŵ	([11])
l	([7])	y	As in yet; consonantal
m	*m* [8]		

---

[1] When *n* is prefixed to *b, p,* or *w,* the two become *mb,* as *ambutile* for *anputile, kumbona* for *kumwona.*
[2] Preceded by *n, ch* becomes *nj.*
[3] The *f* occurs in foreign words only; in the Yao it is displaced by *p.*
[4] Before *e* and *i, g* becomes *j.*
[5] The *n* before *j* becomes *ny;* before *ch, nj.*
[6] Followed by *e* or *i, k* becomes *ch;* the combination of *n* with *k* forms *ng.*
[7] The initial *l* sound is produced by placing the tip of the tongue against the teeth ridge; when medial, the entire tongue comes into action. Between vowels, *l* is often dropped, *jegongo* for *ja ligongo.* After *n,* the *l* becomes *d,* or is dropped, *andinde* or *aninde* for *anlinde.*
[8] Before *b* the *m* is usually a modified *n; mb* may represent *np, nw,* or *mw; n* is always dropped before *m.*
[9] The *t* with *n* prefixed becomes *nd.*
[10] The *w* has an open vocalic sound made by keeping the lips well apart; prefixed to *n, w* becomes *mb* or *mbw.*
[11] To produce this sound arrange the lips for *b* (the sound merely, not the name of the letter), then open the lips slightly, keep the teeth well separated, and try to say "*w*". It is a very important letter, many words being differentiated by its use: *kuwala* (to wear) and *kuŵala* (to shine).

The Yao people inhabit the high tableland between Lake Nyassa and the coast, and their territory extends from the sources of the Rovuma River in the north to the Lujenda River in the south. They are an agricultural people, having little livestock. A few additions to their vocabulary have come from the Swahili on the coast, to which this language appears to be related. The excessive number of euphonic changes is at first a source of difficulty in acquiring the language. There are no harsh combinations of consonants, and the result of all of these changes is to give a peculiar softness to the speech, comparable to the Italian as contrasted with other European languages.

NOTES

The *ch, ng',* and *ny* are compound consonants.

The grammatical structure of the language, as in all those of the Bantu family, depends on the principle of what has been called "concord". The *nl* becomes *nd; nt, nd; nk, ng; nj, ny; nch, nj;* and *nw* before *e* or *i,* and sometimes before *a,* becomes *mbw; nw* before *o* or *u,* and sometimes before *a,* becomes *mb; nu, mb; np, mb; mu* sometimes *mbu* or *mbw; mw, mb* or *mbw. Ai* becomes *e; au, o; i* before another vowel, *y;* and *u* before another vowel, *w.* The *n* is dropped before *s, i, u, m,* or *n; Saso* for *nsaso, iiche* for *niiche,* etc. The *j* is often dropped after *ku,* the *u* becoming *w; kujaula* becoming *kwaula.*

All parts of speech consist of a root to which are added various prefixes and suffixes, the former being most important.

The accent is usually on the penultimate syllable, more rarely on the antepenultimate, but never on the final syllable.

There are no diphthongs.

Some words that are spelled alike have different meanings, dependent on whether the vowels are long or short. Also many identical words differ in meaning according to the inflection of the voice.   Taking the acute sign as indicating the rising and the grave the falling inflection, we have, for example, *nganga* (beer) and *ngangá* (a guineafowl).

Notation consists of the addition of fives, and numeration does not extend beyond 100.

Cardinal numbers

-mo	one	likumi na msanu ni-tatu	eighteen
-wili	two		
-tatu	three	likumi na msanu in mcheche	nineteen
mcheche	four		
msanu	five	makumi gawili	twenty
msanu na	six	makumi gawili ni-mo	twenty-one
msanu kwisa-wili	seven	makumi gutatu	thirty
msanu kwisa-tatu	eight	makumi mcheche	forty
msanu kwisa mcheche	nine	makumi msanu	fifty
likumi	ten	makumi msanu ni limo	sixty
likumi na-mo	eleven	makumi msanu ni ga-wili	seventy
likumi na-wili	twelve		
likumi na-tatu	thirteen	makumi msanu ni ga-tatu	eighty
likumi na mcheche	fourteen		
likumi na msanu	fifteen	makumi msanu ni mcheche	ninety
likumi na msanu ni-imo	sixteen		
		makumi likumi	hundred
likumi na msanu ni-wili	seventeen		

Ordinal numbers are expressed by the use of the preposition *-a* (of) with the plural of the object indicated, and sometimes also by substituting the adverbial numeral for the plural.   Examples: *Lyuwa lya gawili* or *lyuwa lya kawili*, the second day.   First is expressed by the verb *kutanda*, to begin.   The adverbial numerals once, twice, etc., are expressed by prefixing *ka*, as *kamo*, once; *kawili*, twice; *katatu*, thrice; *kacheche*, four times; *kasanu*, five times, etc.

YORUBA

a	*a* in bath	n	*n*
ai	*i* in mile	o	*o* in bone
au	*ou* in round, nearly	ọ	*ao* in water
b	(¹)	oi	*oi* in voice, nearly; *o* in long
c	*c*	p	*p*
d	*d*	q	*q*
e	*a* in babe	r	*r*
ẹ	*e* short in let	s	*s*
f	*f*	ṣ	*sh* in shop
g	*g* in go; always hard	t	*t*
h	*h*, aspirate; never mute	u	*oo* in boot
i	*e* in be	v	*v*
j	*j* in jam; always soft	w	*w*
k	*k*	x	*x*
l	*l*	y	*y*
m	*m*	z	*z*

¹ The *p* and *gb* sounds are unusual and can be learned only by ear.

Of the accents, none is used to mark stress, the tilde usually indicating a contraction, as *dābobo* for *da-aba-bo*. The acute and grave simply indicate the rise and fall of the voice.

Cardinal numbers

òkan, eni	one	ẹrindilógun, }	sixteen
èji, méjì	two	merindilógun }	
ẹ̀ta, mẹ́ta	three	metadilógun	seventeen
ẹ̄rin, mẹrin	four	ējidilógun	eighteen
àrún, márūn	five	ōkan-di logun	nineteen
ẹ̀fà, mẹ́fà	six	ogún, okŏ	twenty
méje	seven	ọ́gbòn	thirty
ẹ́jọ	eight	ogójì	forty
ẹ̀san, mẹsan	nine	ādọ́ta	fifty
ẹ̄wa, mẹ́wa	ten	ọgọ́ta	sixty
ōkanlā	eleven	ādọ́rin	seventy
ejìlā, méjìlā	twelve	ọgọ́rin	eighty
ẹtalā, mẹtalā	thirteen	ādọrūn	ninety
mẹrinlā	fourteen	ọgọ́rūn	hundred
ẹ̄dógun, mẹ̄dógun	fifteen		

Ordinals

ekini, nisājú	first	ẹkẹ́fa	sixth
ekéjì	second	ẹkeje	seventh
ẹketa, kẹta	third	ẹkejọ	eighth
ẹkẹrin	fourth	ẹkẹsan	ninth
ẹkarun	fifth	ẹkẹ́wa, kẹ́wa	tenth

Months

oṣù kiní ọdún	January	oṣù keje ọdún	July
oṣù	February	nlánlà, titóbi	August
oṣù ẹketa ọdún	March	oṣù ksẹan ọdún	September
oṣù kẹrin ọdún	April	oṣù kẹwā ọdún	October
oṣù kárūn ọdún	May	oṣù kọkànlā ọdun	November
oṣù kẹ́fà ọdún	June	oṣù kéjìlā ọdún	December

Days

ojǫ́ kini ǫsè̩ ti i̩s̩e ojǫ-isimi }	Sunday	ojǫ́ ke̩rin ǫse̩	Wednesday
		ijǫ́ karun ǫse̩	Thursday
ojǫ́ kegi lò̩s̩e	Monday	ijǫ́ ke̩fa lǫ́sè	Friday
ijǫ́ ke̩ta ǫse̩	Tuesday	ijǫ́ ikèhin ǫse̩	Saturday

Seasons

fifò	spring	akókò ikórè	autumn
igbà è̩run	summer	igba otutù	winter

Time

wákàti	hour	o̩s̩ù	month
ojǫ́	day	ǫdúṅ	year
o̩s̩e kan	week		

ZULU-KAFIR

a	*a* in father	n	*n*
b	*b*	o	*o* in pole
c	(¹); a click	p	*p*
d	*d*	q	A click
e	*e* in there	r	(²)
f	*f*	s	*s*
g	*g*, hard as in go	t	*t*
h	*h*	u	*u* in rule
i	*i* in ravine	v	*v*
j	*j*	w	*w*
k	*k*	x	A click
l	*l*	y	*y*
m	*m*	z	*z*

¹ The English sounds of *c* are represented by *k* and *s*, that of *q* by *kw*, while that of *x* is unnecessary since the *ks* sound does not occur.
² The English sound of *r* is also absent, the natives usually giving it the sound of *l;* it is also used for the guttural, like the strong German *ch* in auch.

The Zulu-Kafir is really the dialect of a small tribe along the southeast coast of Africa, though other variations of this language are spoken by different tribes within and far beyond the borders of Cape Colony. Most of these are commonly called Zulus because they were formerly under Zulu rule and still use that dialect. There are, however, large bodies of natives who speak dialects decidedly different, though the grammar of the Zulu is essentially the same for all.

NOTES

In compound syllables the vowel sounds, though similar to the above, are necessarily closer and shorter.

There are no diphthongs, but the *au* sound, when uttered rapidly, closely approximates the English sound of *ou*.

A slight aspiration is heard in many words after *b*, *g*, *d*, *k*, *p*, and *t*, which accounts for some roots, which appear identical, having a different meaning, which the native would indicate by a difference in enunciation.

Distinguish carefully between the sounds of *hl* and *dhl*, since there are some words, essentially different in meaning, which differ in sound only because of the insertion of the *d*. Compare the English *thigh* and *thy*, *thousand* and *thou*.

No consonant, except *m* and *n*, can end a syllable, and these frequently express initial nasal sounds, when it might be supposed that they were final: *ha-mban*, *a-ba-ntu*, etc.

The accent usually falls on the penultimate syllable.

Numerals

The natives count with their fingers, beginning with the little finger of the left hand; when the number 10 is reached, the hands are clapped together and the process proceeds as before.

Cardinal numbers

nye	one	amashumi'mabili	twenty-one
bili	two	nanye *or* ananye	
tatu	three	amashumi'matatu	thirty
ne	four	amashumi ay'isi-	sixty
hlanu	five	tupa	
isitupa, mkota	six	amashumi ashiyan-	eighty
isikombisa	seven	galombili	
shiyangalombili	eight	ikulu	hundred
shiyagalolunye	nine	ikulu nanye, *or* li-	hundred and
ishumi	ten	nanye	one
ishumi-nanye } ishumi-linanye}	eleven	amakulu'mabili	two hundred
		inkulungwane	thousand
ishumi-nambili } ishumi-linambili}	twelve	isigidi	hundred thou- sand
amashumi'mabili	twenty		

Ordinal numbers

Under "tenth" these are expressed by prefixing *isi* to the roots of the cardinals (*tatu* three, *isitatu* third; *isitupa* six, *isiisitupa* sixth) which thus become nouns and are placed after the nouns to which they refer. The word *ukugala* is, however, also used for *nye* (first). For "tenth" and upward the simple cardinal is placed after the noun to which it refers. Numeral adverbs for "once", "twice", etc., are formed by prefixing *ka* to the cardinals.

Months

Umasingana	January	Umaxuba ⎫	July
Ungcela	February	Umlulikazi ⎬	
Undasa	March	Uncwaba	August
Umbasa	April	Umpandu	September
Unhlaba	May	Umfumfu	October
Umhlungulu	June	Ulwesi	November
		Uzibandhlela	December

Days

Isonto	Sunday	Ngolwesine	Thursday
Umsombuluko	Monday	Ngolwesihlanu	Friday
Ngolwesibili	Tuesday	Umgqibelo	Saturday
Ngolwesitatu	Wednesday		

Seasons

isilimela	spring	ikwindhla	autumn
ihlobo	summer	ubusika	winter

Time

iroa, ihora	hour	inyanga	month
usuku	day	umnyaka	year
isonto	week		

○